D1384437

307.
7609
NIG

Nightingale, Carl
Husemolle... NEW BOOK SHELF

Earthopolis.

Guelph Public Library

33281930113086

307.
7609
NIG

Nightingale, Carl
Husemoller.

Earthopolis.

Guelph Public Library

33281930113086

$30.00

NEW BOOK SHELF

DATE	BORROWER'S NAME	

MAR -- 2023

BAKER & TAYLOR

EARTHOPOLIS

This is a biography of Earthopolis, the only Urban Planet we know of. It is a history of how cities gave humans immense power over Earth, for good and for ill. Carl Nightingale takes readers on a sweeping six-continent, six-millennium tour of the world's cities, culminating in the last 250 years, when we vastly accelerated our planetary realms of action, habitat, and impact, courting dangerous new consequences and opening prospects for new hope. In *Earthopolis* we peek into our cities' homes, neighborhoods, streets, shops, eating houses, squares, marketplaces, religious sites, schools, universities, offices, monuments, docklands, and airports to discover connections between small spaces and the largest things we have built. The book exposes the Urban Planet's deep inequalities of power, wealth, access to knowledge, class, race, gender, sexuality, religion, and nation. It asks us to draw on the most just and democratic moments of Earthopolis's past to rescue its future.

Carl Nightingale has taught urban history and world history for twenty-five years as a Professor at the University at Buffalo and the University of Massachusetts. He is Coordinator of the Global Urban History Project, a network of over 500 scholars working in this new hybrid field. His book *Segregation: A Global History of Divided Cities* (2012) was co-winner of the Jerry Bentley Prize from the World History Association.

EARTHOPOLIS

A Biography of Our Urban Planet

Carl H. Nightingale

CAMBRIDGE
UNIVERSITY PRESS

University Printing House, Cambridge CB2 8BS, United Kingdom

One Liberty Plaza, 20th Floor, New York, NY 10006, USA

477 Williamstown Road, Port Melbourne, VIC 3207, Australia

314–321, 3rd Floor, Plot 3, Splendor Forum, Jasola District Centre,
New Delhi – 110025, India

103 Penang Road, #05–06/07, Visioncrest Commercial, Singapore 238467

Cambridge University Press is part of the University of Cambridge.

It furthers the University's mission by disseminating knowledge in the pursuit of
education, learning, and research at the highest international levels of excellence.

www.cambridge.org
Information on this title: www.cambridge.org/9781108424523
DOI: 10.1017/9781108339353

© Carl H. Nightingale 2022

This publication is in copyright. Subject to statutory exception
and to the provisions of relevant collective licensing agreements,
no reproduction of any part may take place without the written
permission of Cambridge University Press.

First published 2022

Printed in the United Kingdom by TJ Books Limited, Padstow Cornwall

A catalogue record for this publication is available from the British Library.

ISBN 978-1-108-42452-3 Hardback

Cambridge University Press has no responsibility for the persistence or accuracy of
URLs for external or third-party internet websites referred to in this publication
and does not guarantee that any content on such websites is, or will remain,
accurate or appropriate.

To my parents. For opening my first books and unfolding my first maps. For handing me a metro ticket and saying – "Let us know what you learn!"

To all my dear colleagues at the Global Urban History Project. For gathering at the crossroads where cities meet their worlds. For celebrating the directions our stories can travel from there.

To all the courageous activists at PUSH Buffalo. For taking back the streets. For laying foundations of righteous, life-loving cities. For all the blessings you offer our Urban Planetary citizens to come.

Contents

Figures

Maps

Our Urban Planet in Space and Time

T HIS BOOK IS A BIOGRAPHY OF EARTHOPOLIS, THE ONLY Urban Planet we know of. It is a 6,000-year tale of many cities and the immense power they allowed humans as a species to wield over other humans and over large stretches of our host planet Earth. Starting with the birth of cities in many separate places at many different times, the book shows how we built urban environments to harvest increasing amounts of energy from the Sun and Earth and to transform it into multiple forms of amplified human power. The mix of energy and power that we compounded in cities grew and contracted in space over millennia – playing a central role in many of the "greatest of times" and the "worst of times" in human history. Today, as the power centers of a truly planetary Urban Planet, cities place our own unequal communities in precarious command of Earth's fertile lithosphere, its watery hydrosphere, its Sun-moderating atmosphere, and the entirety of its profuse halo of life. This biography of Earthopolis looks backward – and also forward – from our Urban Planet's most important crossroads in space and time.[1]

An Urban Planet is *urban* because only in cities can we harvest enough geo-solar energy to gather together as large, compact, proximate, diverse, specialized, anonymous, multiply fractious, and thus especially potent human political communities. In such urban built spaces and such urban communities, people can establish the political movements and institutions, gather the wealth, and devise the new ideas and technologies that undergird our increasingly pervasive influence on Earth. To explore the sources of this amplified human power, we must visit the relatively compact spaces occupied by our cities and the many diverse smaller spaces that make them up. In part, that means taking a six-continent, six-millennium tour of the greatest cities in history and all the urban power centers they housed: magnificent palaces, temples, fort-resses, parliament buildings, skyscrapers, and other monuments. We will find other forms of amplified human power in medium-sized and smaller cities and along ship-docks, in harbors, stadiums, fair grounds, rail stations, airports, power plants, and the like. Schools, universities, hospitals, clinics, libraries, and museums are all on the tour of power-augmenting spaces, as are ceremonial and performance venues, radio and TV transmitters, internet server barns, and "virtual" spaces. Much of our story takes place along thronging avenues and giant squares, but we will also tuck into smaller side streets, marketplaces, bazaars, and *souqs*, into enticing shops, eateries, and watering holes at the end of sinuous alleys. Finally, we need to tarry in the most intimate spaces of human power, the homes where we eat, bathe, make love, and go to sleep each night, readying ourselves for action once again the next morning. It is there that – one by one – we cultivate the dreams, and the Earth-altering capabilities, of each member of our generations to come.

Earth-altering indeed: an Urban Planet is also *planetary*. Building large and compact places such as cities requires us to build many more smaller and spread-out places too: villages, towns, farms, woodlots, mines, oil fields, and all of the communications and transport infrastructure that connects all of our habitats. Together, these dispersed built things allow us to gather natural energy and funnel it to cities for transformation into their especially potent forms of human power. As we built more cities, their sunshine-gathering "hinterlands" and their connective tissues grew and merged together to form what I call "urban worlds," made up of larger regions' worth of cities and smaller habitats. Over thousands of years, we used our cities to merge these regional urban worlds to create our Urban Planet. Because cities were born in many different regions separated by long distances, because each urban world contains many forms of human habitat, and because cities so often allow a small few of us to seize most of the power they generate at great cost to many more of us,

Earthopolis remains foundationally plural: multifariously diverse and profoundly unequal. Still, whether we wielded urban power as the repressive few or as the irrepressible many, all of us also built something singular – one deeply interconnected habitat of one single species on *our* single Urban Planet: Earthopolis.

States of plurality and singularity coexist on Earthopolis because an Urban Planet consists of four types of space made possible by city-amplified human power – spaces that connect concentrated human places with dispersed ones and that connect separate urban worlds with each other. I call these four large, eventually planetary spaces the realm of human action, the realm of human habitat, the realm of human impact, and the realm of human consequence. As people on all points of the compass – each in their own ways – used cities to build these realms, our actions, habitats, impacts, and consequences expanded across space, overlapped, contracted, and grew some more. As these realms grew to truly planetary dimensions at different times, they brought Earthopolis into being.[2]

The *realm of human action* consists of the intersecting geographical reach of our political movements, states, empires, commercial circuits, and more recently our nation states, capitalist corporations, and multilateral institutions – along with all of their administrative capacity, their wealth, their self-justificatory ideologies, and their violence. It also includes the space occupied by our systems for producing food, fuel, raw materials, and both artisanal and industrial goods; our practices of exploiting labor and land; our acts of reproduction and our waves of migration; our global religious and knowledge-creating communities; and our mass media and online spaces. Apart from our species' earliest experiments with fire and stone, our first global migrations, and our first agricultural regions, none of these larger realms of human action, nor their especially vast scope today, could have existed without cities. All of them, in turn, have made the growth and multiplication of cities possible. For good reason, we typically date the end of "prehistory" and the birth of "world history" to the birth of our first cities. So many of the most important chapters of human history involved multifarious human actions only possible in cities: often audacious, often supremely reckless and horrifically violent, often deeply hopeful and regenerative. As we will see, the spaces occupied by human action expanded and contracted over the first five and a half millennia of global urban history. The realm of action became a truly interconnected, planet-encompassing phenomenon only after 1500, when human imperial, commercial, and cultural activities connected most of the world's continents for the first time, thanks to the winds and currents of the connected World Ocean, signaling the birth of a truly planetary Urban Planet.

The second realm of Earthopolis, the *realm of human habitat*, grew in a similar way but on a different timeline. Before there were cities, our built habitat consisted of temporary camps dispersed across six continents and a few small regions of more permanent farming villages, some of which grew quite large. After some of these village-rich regions gave birth to the first cities, the influence of our urban-amplified actions began to radiate outward, affecting the rhythms of life in smaller and more dispersed places, and even determining the number of new camps, villages, and farms we built on Earth – as well as the number of new cities. Cities thus took a central role in generating the human habitat more generally, even though villages retained some autonomy, looked very different, harbored very different rhythms of life, defined themselves as non-urban, and often asserted power of their own over cities, sometimes in rural–urban conflicts that continue to this day. Nonetheless, the built habitats of increasing number of villages – along with the remaining smaller temporary camps and the bigger settlements we call by the ambiguous word "towns" – increasingly reflected their symbiotic and even existential connection to cities. Thus, even though the majority of humankind lived in villages for almost all of this story – only in the twenty-first century did we become a truly majority urban species – and even though many inhabitants of smaller places never visited a city or even knew of cities' existence, inhabitants of smaller settlements intermittently folded themselves into a realm of human habitat that was urban-dominated and that grew to encompass Earth as a whole. When that happened, it was also because the infrastructures we built between human settlements of all sizes had grown too. One good birthdate for the truly planetary realm of human habitat is 1900, when we laid telegraph cables across the Pacific Ocean, connecting the many diverse human-built and human-altered components of our habitat into a single contiguous whole.[3]

Today scholars sometimes call our human home on Earth the "anthrome." I prefer to designate the realm of our habitat as one of four constitutive spaces of our Urban Planet, because doing so clarifies the essential and foundational role that cities played in its growth, as well as the essential role that the bigger human-built realm of habitat plays in the growth of cities. Only a few small settlements of so-called "uncontacted people" now remain outside of this realm – if barely. Other than those, today's realm of human habitat includes all of our camps, villages, towns, cities, "megacities," "urban regions," and urban peripheries, including all of their explosively accelerating suburbs, and all of the self-built cities where a billion or more urban poor people live today. It also includes far more extensive spaces like farms, plowed fields, pastures, irrigation systems with their dams and canals, timberland clear-cuts, mines, and oil and gas fields, and all of the hard stuff that helps to connect the whole thing: pavements, rammed-earth tracks, rails, wires, cables, pipes, ship channels, sea-lanes, and jet-contrails. It includes the "soft" stuff too, notably the airwaves and the internet – other "spaces" separate from cities that are utterly dependent on cities and that make cities possible. Our billions of vehicles are also part of this realm. Each is a specialized human habitat of its own, designed precisely so that we can inhabit such a large Urban Planetary home. Long ago, ships allowed some of us to inhabit the seas and oceans for substantial periods; now we build our own islands, and some planners envision cities that will float out to sea, much like cruise ships, themselves often dubbed "floating cities." Our habitat also reaches skyward and into outer space, not only in hyper-tall buildings, but in the flight of planes, missiles, rockets, satellites, space stations, and dozens of extra-planetary probes and rovers. Back on Earth, Earthopolis's realm of human habitat now covers over half of our host planet's land surface. The cement, stone, brick, wood, steel, glass, and asphalt of our Earthly home now weighs more than the rest of the biosphere – more than all the world's living trees, plants, and animals – combined.[4]

The third province of Earthopolis, *the realm of human impact*, is the oldest of the truly planetary realms created by city-enhanced power, and it remains the most voluminous today. As we grew our cities, as we acted on larger scales, as we built an Earth-encrusting habitat, as we drew ever more heavily on energy from the Earth and Sun, and above all as we spread larger amounts of waste into ever-larger spaces beyond our own habitat, the Urban Planet began to annex, alter, interpenetrate, and often destroy spaces beyond, including the habitats of countless other species. Today, the realm of our impact reaches all across and deep down into Earth's solid tectonic plates. It reaches all of its surface water – liquid and frozen – and much of its groundwater. And, it reaches all of its gaseous atmosphere. In all of these spaces, our species affects the life of all other resident species. We know this combined realm of human impact best when we contemplate the size of our teetering urban landfills, the stench of our polluted waterways, the choking air pollution in far too many cities, and the spread of micro-plastics throughout the oceans, the continents, the air we breathe, and the bodies of many living creatures. Above all, we perceive it in the overheating of Earth's remarkable Sun-regulating, life-giving atmosphere – the result above all of our heavy use of hydrocarbon fuels. In the realm of human impact, our Urban Planet has thus fulfilled the boastful mission of the "Tower of Babel," the mighty ziggurat in the ancient city of Babylon. All of us now inhabit the "House of the Frontier of Heaven and Earth."[5]

That brings us to the fourth realm of Earthopolis, the realm of human consequence. As we annexed more of Heaven and Earth to our realms of action, habitat, and impact, we typically increased our numbers – recently at an accelerated rate that reflects a rapid jump in life expectancy. Yet we also paid stiffer costs, transforming large spaces that otherwise generate Earthly life, including human life, into zones of death. Over the millennia, this realm of consequence expanded and contracted in mighty wrathful surges, leaving behind scars with long-term effects on Earthopolis's other three realms. At those times, the otherwise expanding reach of human power went into reverse, causing some urban worlds to contract for a half-millennium or more.

Some of this city-enhanced realm of death is entirely of our own making, for the power we wield in our urban political communities is a volatile substance, capable of transformation into tyranny, war, slavery, and many other life-shortening forms of exploitation and inequality. The realm of consequence could also expand because of human experiments with geo-solar energy that have gone awry. Cities came into being about halfway into an 11,700-year period that scientists call the "Holocene Epoch" during which geophysical forces like the shape of Earth's orbit around the Sun and the tilt and wobble of our planet's axis produced relatively stable climatic conditions. Humans could harvest larger amounts of natural energy by farming and raising animals, allowing us to build the first cities. Nonetheless, geo-solar energy continued to surge and wane unpredictably, and our techniques for harvesting it could fail as often as they worked. As spaces that are both concentrated and dispersed, our city-expanded realms of human action, habitat, and impact are also ideally designed to encourage vast blooms of disease-creating microbiota. Their death-dealing life-energy could flare into pandemics, as we know from our baleful experience with Covid-19, the latest of many similar instances over the millennia. Meanwhile, by altering or destroying other species' habitats like forests, rivers, wetlands, estuaries, tundra, glaciers, and above all the oceans, humans who inhabited urban worlds toyed dangerously with Sun's relationship to Earth, sometimes forcing new large deathly surges of the realm of consequence. Today, our Urban Planet's wastes have become the crucial factor. By burning so much hydrocarbon and by dumping accelerated quantities of chemicals and greenhouse gases across the lithosphere, hydrosphere, and atmosphere, we have destabilized the Holocenic relationship between Sun and Earth. Many scientists who monitor such matters argue that a new epoch, named after us, has dawned in Earth-time: the Anthropocene. If so, cities are the cockpits of this new Epoch – and Earthopolis is at once the Anthropocene's avatar in time and its spatial manifestation today. In this Epoch, among other things, our heating of the atmosphere and the rise in ocean levels has caused "natural" and "human" disasters to blur while becoming more frequent and intense. Our Urban Planet's throbbing realm of consequence thus threatens to engulf greater swaths of Earth's remarkable halo of life than any geophysical force has in perhaps hundreds of thousands of years.[6]

Just as Earthopolis takes up enormous amounts of space, so its life story spans vast amounts of time. As a plural singularity, our Urban Planet's life is polyrhythmic, operating on different time scales at once. The birthdates of each of Earthopolis's oldest distinct urban worlds are scattered across the first 5,500 of the 6,000 years, the ancestral phase of its biography. Each of its four defining realms grew and retreated across Earth at their own tempo, achieving planetary dimensions at different times. Changes in the ways we harvested geo-solar energy operated on relatively long arcs of time. Changes in our use of human power were mostly shorter and choppier, if no less momentous. A biography of our Urban Planet allows us to inventory the many topsy-turvy increments of human time when, in specific places, we gained, lost, regained, then gradually accumulated the city-enabled human power that may mark a new Epoch in the far longer, four-and-a-half-billion-year life story of Earthopolis's host planet, Earth.

One useful way to define cities, in fact, is as spaces that allow us to bend time. A good measure of human power is the length of time over which we are capable of sustaining any action while minimizing the effects of competing actions: historians call such patterns of time "continuity." Conversely, another measure of human power is the capacity to suddenly "disrupt" actions otherwise sustained by continuous exertions of human power, and in so doing increase the velocity of change. Cities – and above all the particular forms of political community that they contained – allowed us to do both: to string out time and to break it. But there is more. Because urban political communities contain so many potentially conflicting factions, the ongoing outcomes of their struggles have always been especially difficult to predict at any given time. Therefore, cities also allow us to create times in which almost anything could happen next, when the actual outcome was so unexpected as to be nearly inexplicable. Historians call such times moments of "contingency."

In all of these ways, cities became essential to explain change. Their spatial design allowed various historical actors to put continuities, disruptions, and contingencies in motion, and as such they were a force of change in their own right. However, cities never explain any change fully on their own. While historians correctly credit them for bringing much of world history into being, cities did so only as *essential* and never *sufficient* causes of history. Full explanations for change also require us to examine how different segments of Urban Planetary political communities were able to amass the city-enhanced power they did to sustain, disrupt, or stir unpredictability within the flows of time when they did. Also, even more importantly: cities are tools we used – over time – to create larger-scale action, habitat construction, impact, and consequence, but they are also the ongoing and repeatedly updated *creation of* those larger-scale changes. As important as cause is to effect in history, so is the simultaneous transformation of effect into new cause. Cities are very effective places to build such "circular," "spiraling," "synergetic," or "self-perpetuating" patterns of time too, forms of continuity that historians sometimes call "processes." In general, we imagine processes of change to lie beyond the power of even their most powerful proponents to stop. Yet to know our Urban Planet well we should avoid overuse of the word "process." While cities can favor a momentum, they never put history on autopilot – "mechanizing" time or divorcing change from the effects of real human beings' collective, purposeful, and typically conflicting exertions of power that cities are so good at amplifying. In a world history that takes place in cities, all historical processes, even the most compellingly self-propulsive, are always subject to the same countervailing contingencies and disruptions that face all continuities in time.

To account for the vast diversities of spaces and times that make up the life of Earthopolis, I have divided this biography into three parts and twenty-five chapters. The three parts concern the slower rhythms by which city-dwelling humans transformed our means of gathering geo-solar energy and funneling it into cities. Accordingly, they are entitled "Cities of the Rivers," "Cities of the World Ocean," and "Cities of Hydrocarbon." The twenty-five chapters focus on the generally shorter changes in human action, habitat, impact, and consequence. Here, the focus is on the specific forms of power that cities, city-generated spaces, and urban political communities allowed us to create – movements, states, empires, wealth-gathering enterprises, and cultural institutions. In the chapters, the balance between continuity, disruption, contingency, and process is less easy to predict, and the story more often involves unexpected plot twists. Each of these chapters is organized around switches of cause and effect, demonstrating how cities played crucial roles in large-scale historical transformations that in turn transformed cities themselves, often with profound knock-on effects throughout the four larger realms that eventually coalesced as Earthopolis.

Part I, "Cities of the Rivers" covers what historians typically call the "Pre-Modern" period from about 4000 BCE to 1500 CE, when cities were first born, largely in river valleys – fueled by a combination of solar evaporation, planetary gravity, photosynthesis, and warm, wet, fertile soils. To guide us through Part I, I chose the Mesopotamian goddess Inanna, who, her mythmakers tell us, commanded a riverboat up the Euphrates River to deliver the first elements of city-ness to a place called Uruk. We built thousands of cities during these first five and half millennia of global urban history, including the first million-plus imperial capitals, many provincial, colonial, and mercantile cities, and the first seaports. Our realms of action and habitat expanded too. Our realm of action brought together many of the originally separated urban birth-worlds, creating composite urban worlds in parts of the Americas on the one hand, and – in separate developments during several long periods – across much of the Afro-Eurasian supercontinent. Roads, canals, ports, and new vehicles were essential to these new connections. Long before that, possibly by the first millennium CE if not before, the city-driven realm of human impact may have reached global dimensions, thanks to emissions from ancient industry and agriculture. For the time being, though, the largest-scale city-enabled destructive consequences we faced – our own wars, the first multi-continental pandemics, and floods and famines aggravated by deforestation – remained bounded by our realms of our action and habitat. Our population on Earth typically recovered afterward, growing to over 400 million by 1500 CE.

Part II, "Cities of the World Ocean" covers the so-called "early-modern" period, from about 1500 to 1780. Here we turn to a familiar guide, Christopher Columbus, but in an unfamiliar moment of sheer panic when his flagship the *Santa Maria* cracked open on a Caribbean coral reef. The incident inspired a strange Vision of Two Cities that revived his warlike, acquisitive, enslaver's spirit. During the years that followed, humans used the power of World Ocean currents and winds to build more million-plus imperial capitals and large administrative centers than ever before, the first global financial capitals, and hundreds of new cities – notably fortified colonial ports – on the ocean shores and up the rivers of six continents. The truly planetary realm of human action that came into being during this time was driven by imperial thefts of land, globalized forms of capitalism and slavery, "world" religions, secular knowledges of Earth as a whole, and a global consumer culture. Our realm of impact also extended deep into the World Ocean itself for the first time, and the realm of consequences swelled, including the first truly global pandemic, largely at the expense of the inhabitants of the Americas, and waves of species extinctions. Still, the human population more than doubled overall in response to our cities' growing harvests of natural energy, to about 900 million by 1780.

Part III, "Cities of Hydrocarbon" covers the "modern" period, from 1780 to the present, when our use of a much more potent – and far more wasteful – source of geo-solar energy, fossil fuels, increased all four realms of Earthopolis to planetary dimensions. The driver of a three-wheeled auto-rickshaw in the city of Delhi will guide us through this, the shortest yet the most tumultuous and therefore the longest section of Earthopolis's biography. It covers a period of radical acceleration in the number and size of cities, at first in Europe, the Americas, and Japan, and then – after a period of self-inflicted mass destruction during two world wars – the Greatest Acceleration of all, encompassing the world as a whole and especially the Urban Planet's poorest regions and China. Our largest cities quickly broke the million and two-million barriers, then detonated past ten, twenty, and even thirty million. The centers of our cities grew denser, the peripheries of cities expanded rapidly; cities exploded into urban regions; and cities and their suburbs merged with countrysides in large densely built semi-urban "*desakotas*" that covered vast areas. Infrastructures between and beyond cities encased Earth for the first time by 1900 and have grown more densely, if unequally, since then, creating physical and now virtual spaces that routinize human capacity for planetary action. Our population grew eightfold in a short 250 years, to nearly 8 billion. The realm of our impact, however, has sowed danger to every corner of Earth's biosphere. As a result, the realm of human consequence threatens to engulf Earthopolis as a whole; the future of our large, long, city-enabled reign over space and time is at stake.

The twenty-five chapters of this book are divided into overlapping series that explore different forms of amplified human power in cities. Most important, I believe, are urban political communities' creation of states (Chapters 1–5, 7, 8, 11, 12, 15–22, and 25). Early on, some cities managed to govern themselves for long periods without institutions that scholars recognize as states. Still, all had to handle intense contests over forms of power concentrated in cities, including natural energy, human numbers,

wealth, weapons, and competing ideologies. One of the saddest continuities in the biography of Earthopolis is the use of cities to accumulate most
of these forms of power in the service of authoritarian state rule, a reality
we still live with today. Yet cities also gave their inhabitants the power to
disrupt continuities of authoritarian power. At those moments, urban
political communities took the lead (often with help from rural allies) in
shifting governing power into the hands of the governed – sometimes
creating versions of what the ancient Athenians first called *demokratia* or
"People Power." In the late 1700s CE, a wave of people's revolutions arose
amidst increasing numbers of unpredictable conflicts in cities and built
hinterlands, now dispersed across large parts of Earth. The revolutionary
plot twisted in many ways after that, but, over time, revolutions led to
growing number of states based on the Power of their People. In the
meantime, we also discovered how useful cities could be as sites for non-
violent resistance to state power of all kinds, a form of political practice
championed by Mahatma Gandhi in South Africa and India. No matter
their particular relationship to their political community, states that draw
on city-enhanced human power are critical to understanding how we have
been able to act, build, and impose our impact on a planetary scale, and, in
so doing, how we also face the consequences.

One of these larger-scale extensions of human power came through
empire (Chapters 2, 7, 13, 17–21, 24, and 25). I define empire as practices
meant to extend state power beyond its original sustaining city and hinterland to rule other city–hinterland spaces, to rule entire urban worlds, and
often to rule spaces that previously lay beyond the influence of cities.
Empires came into being through violent conquest as well as enticements
mixed with threats of conquest. However, empires last only if the imperial
state is able to tax its enlarged territory and to feed and equip a military
force that undergirds its power to tax. Only in cities, and only by arranging
cities into administrative hierarchies, can we perform these tasks of imperial
administration over the long term – that is, create continuities of empire.
Conversely, people can only disrupt imperial continuity by means of political acts within cities or by attacks on cities from more dispersed places.

As urban communities enabled states to accumulate wealth as tax,
states encouraged the practices of small numbers of wealthy investors and
profit-makers to accumulate large pools of wealth of their own

(Chapters 3, 4, 8, 10, 14, and 22–25). To enable such actions, states allowed these wealth accumulators to keep the profits they amassed (after taxes) and helped them build wealth-grabbing institutions partly independent of states. States also accepted metal currency for tax payments, and, in so doing, cities made money itself possible. Scholars disagree vehemently whether to use the word "capitalism" for all money-making practices that fit the description of "state-enabled non-state investments in city-empowered wealth-amassing activities and institutions." However, historians do agree that cities allowed their richest profit-makers – merchants, estate and plantation owners, industrialists, corporations, and financiers – to amass very large sums of capital and to do so largely at the expense of others. These wealth-amassers exploited the laborers they hired, the enslaved people they owned, the primarily female caregivers who prepared all workers for work, and the smaller-scale moneymaking inhabitants of urban worlds, such as artisans, shop-keepers, and independent farmers. Thus, as cities and states created money and great wealth, they typically sustained another grim form of continuity: great poverty among the majority population of urban worlds, especially among women and among people whom states colonized, enslaved, or cast out. Cities and states, meanwhile, also allowed the richest profit makers to conduct their activities on very large geographical scales and over long periods of time. After about 1600 CE, they created something that all scholars call global capitalism, thus awakening one of history's most important city-accelerating forces. Yet in this way too, cities and states have been unpredictable, for cities are also the place where we have coordinated our best efforts to disrupt global capitalism and slavery – or tame their inequalities – most effectively by means of large protest movements and sometimes with help from states.

The political communities of our compact and dispersed urban worlds also decisively shaped the history of human culture (Chapters 5, 9, 15, 17, 18, 23, and 25). City dwellers – whose proximity allowed the sustained multi-directional conversations needed for knowledge making – together with wealthy states and their other wealth-amassing institutions encouraged the creation of knowledge, ideas, spiritual beliefs and practices, technological innovation, artistic expression, the design of material objects, and the desire for them. City-governing states also developed the first systems of writing – originally to make taxation, money, credit, and investment possible, but immediately spreading new ideas too. For accomplishments such as these, the early urban worlds are often celebrated as "civilizations." I find that word too self-congratulatory to suit the injustices so often involved in acts of knowledge making, notably because authoritarian states or wealthy elites used knowledge, writing, censorship, and monumental urban spaces to create propanganda to justify violence, inequality, and destruction. That said, even the most authoritarian states failed to control their urban political communities' highly energized interchanges of ideas. While cities could help states restrict access to knowledge, they also made it possible for popular movements and states to spread learning and technological know-how. Cities and city-powered states were essential for small-scale intellectual movements to grow into global religious and secular cultural communities. Cities alone could foster ideas capable of disrupting the power of states, empires, and other wealth-amassing institutions – as well as the class, gender, and racial inequalities they produced – often with revolutionary implications.

Energy from Sun and Earth, and human power – amplified in cities. Take these explosive life forces, compound them, and let them loose across lots of space and time. The mighty clamor you hear is the biography of Earthopolis, the only Urban Planet we know of. Be forewarned: this long, large story of creation and life is also long on large-scale destruction and death. It belies naïve celebration of cities – that we should blithely ennoble them as "Humankind's Greatest Invention" or "Cradles of Civilization," or claim extravagantly that they have always made us "Richer, Smarter, Greener, Healthier, and Happier." Yet this biography also rejects all ill-meaning forms of anti-urbanism. Cities are amplifiers of human power, for ill and, often, for good. At their best, they have helped us learn more about the relationship of Earthopolis, Sun, and Earth. They have helped us make our powerful political communities fairer and more accountable, and helped us better understand our cosmic vulnerability. Cities have helped us transform the primary means by which we harvest geo-solar energy in the past, and they could do that once again, as they now must. In all of these ways, we will need to get our cities right if we are to make our Urban Planet much more just, welcoming, knowledgeable, and capable of sustaining all forms of life in the 6,000 years to come.[7]

Before and Beyond: Big Things in Tiny Places

THE FANTASTIC FABLES OF THE FOUNTAIN OF JERICHO

Water from an underground spring gushes from a tiled fountain just outside the present-day city of Jericho. Letters painted on the tiles proclaim the spot "The Oldest City of the World." Off to the left, the inscription continues in smaller letters: "The site witnessed the birth of agriculture, animal husbandry, architecture with the first mud bricks, and religion with ancestor worship. For all these reasons this site [is] known as the oldest city in the world."[1]

There you have it, and from the "source" no less! If you detect a bit of hype in these words, you are not wrong. Local merchants painted the enthusiastic text on the tiles as part of a marketing campaign to entice tourists into town from the more glamorous beaches of the nearby Dead Sea. Who could blame them? Jericho today is a small, beleaguered Palestinian-run enclave deep in the Israeli-occupied West Bank – it could certainly use an influx of cash from the rest of the world. Also, the ruins of ancient Jericho are well worth the trip. They go back an astounding 12,000 years, to a time when a few hundred people built a small village next to the same spring that feeds the fountain. Two thousand years after that, people living on the identical site surrounded their houses with a wall and erected a twelve-meter-tall tower in the middle. That is the place the fountain calls the "Oldest City of The World." (It should not be confused with yet another version of Jericho, on the same site many thousand years later, about 1550 BCE, whose walls, the Bible tells us, came tumbling down to the sound of Joshua's trumpets.)[2]

Why fault the babbling fountain for its giddy enthusiasm? It turns out that the equation "big human accomplishments = Jericho = city" does not work out – and it is very important for a book about the role of cities in planetary history to clarify why. First, as we shall see, there is no evidence that the inhabitants of Jericho were the first inventors of any of the things the fountain claims for the site. Secondly, though Jericho's tower and walls suggest a kind of smaller "scale model" of the cities to come, life there differed in substance from later cities. Jericho had few inhabitants; all probably spoke the same language and followed similar customs. Most of its people farmed and raised animals, and there is little evidence of much specialization of activity. Jericho was probably run by a clan or kin group or two; it never gave birth to political institutions that could govern many diverse and highly disputatious networks of people who were unrelated or did not know each other. Also, ancient Jericho never created other Jerichos: no Jericho-dominated world of similar settlements arose in the region, as they did in most of the later urban worlds created by larger cities. Yet the last reason to be skeptical of the "First City" claim goes deepest into the fountain's evidence for city-ness. Big actions such as the invention of "agriculture, animal husbandry, architecture ... and religion" all first came into being at a time when all of us lived in settlements that were even smaller than Jericho: tiny temporary camps and small permanent villages. Only a few of these took on a smattering of features that we later attributed to cities, like Jericho's wall and tower.

All of that said, before we examine the very real, exponential boosts in human power that we gained from building cities, all biographers of Earthopolis must recognize the value in the fountain's fanciful fables. Cities could not have come into being in so many parts of the Earth unless we took some very big actions from much smaller places long *before* any urban birthday, in places often located far *beyond* the birthplaces of cities. These places included our much older, far tinier camps, our small villages, and our growing, slightly larger, ambiguous, perhaps town-like, habitats such as Jericho itself. These smaller settlements from before the age of cities also later coexisted for millennia alongside cities, many of them still located far beyond the influence of cities. That independent existence also helps us define the outer boundaries of urban influence as cities expanded, creating the first regional urban birth-worlds that would later merge into a truly planetary Urban Planet. Indeed, the act of expanding urban influence consisted heavily in drawing new, sometimes enormous, regions of relatively independent camps, villages, and small towns into cities' orbits. By

0.1. The Floating Village of the Uros People on Lake Titicaca, with the City of Puno, Peru in the Background

Long before cities, small, dispersed, and highly adaptable settlements allowed us to live in varied conditions almost all over the world – even on an island made of reeds that grew its own food in a lake high in the mountains tens of thousands of kilometers from the birthplace of our species in Africa. For millennia, many camps and villages also operated beyond the realm of urban influence. Virtually none do today. Factory-made boats and solar panels, signs welcoming overseas tourists, and the sprawling city in the background amply testify to the vast reach of Earthopolis, the only Urban Planet we know of.
iStock/Getty Images.

transforming these smaller, older types of places into city-serving (and city-served) settlements, by bringing them into existential negotiations or conflicts with cities, by multiplying the number of smaller settlements, or by growing them into new cities, urban birth regions annexed realms that dated from before, that existed beyond, and that continued to give their own independent character to new realms of otherwise city-dominated worlds. That is the most important lesson of the Fable of the Fountain of Jericho: settlements from before and beyond Earthopolis are just as important as the real "Oldest Cities of the World" to the biography of our Urban Planet.

CAMPING ACROSS THE CONTINENTS

For most of our time on Earth, from about 300,000 to about 12,000 years ago, we conducted all our largest-scale business from very small campsites that were there one day and gone the next, clusters of simple, disposable shelters made of branches, leaves, grass thatch, animal skin, antlers, bones, mammoth tusks (in Siberia), or compacted snow (in the Arctic).

Human survival over those thousands of centuries was our biggest accomplishment. Miles-thick ice sheets and severe weather enveloped large swaths of the planet for much of that time, yet our rudimentary huts, tents, windbreaks, caves, tipis, wigwams, yurts, hogans, longhouses, birch-bark cabins, sod houses, bone houses, and igloos helped us maintain our body heat through countless cold spells. In one particularly bad period about 75,000 years ago, Sumatra's Toba volcano erupted spectacularly. Some scientists believe its dark plume of gas and ash shut out the sun for a decade or more everywhere on Earth; yet somehow, about 10,000 of us managed to huddle together in the simplest of shelters against years of deeply frigid cold, perhaps even hibernating, but somehow surviving our worst ordeal and continuing the human story.[3]

During periods of more favorable weather, these campsites made it possible for us to do something very large indeed: we moved across Earth, outward from our warm base in Africa, first into Asia and Europe, and later across then narrow patches of water to Australia. Boats – temporary shelters that float – allowed some of us to head out from there across larger parts of the South Pacific Ocean, inhabiting islands as remote as Easter Island. By about 15,000 years ago, when we reached North and South America under circumstances scholars still do not understand, we became a global species, adapting our shelters to vastly different climates along the way. As the archaeologist Jerry D. Moore put it, temporary shelters were "the essential tool of … human adaptation" that made the collective project of human migration and habitation possible on a planetary scale.[4]

Moore is right, to a point: humanity needs shelter to survive, let alone to move and to adapt. Yet we do not survive on shelter alone. That was certainly the case in prehistoric times: it is more accurate to say that we used our shelters to help us accomplish other big things equally important to our survival. To gather basic fuel for our bodies, we ventured outdoors to forage – to draw water, hunt, fish, and harvest shellfish and plant-based foods in each of the new environments we colonized, and we came back to our huts and camps to cook collective meals. We tamed fire by inventing hearths, so fundamental to preservation of body heat and cooking in our homes to this day. We invented better stone tools to kill animals and process our food, and with tools came the first temporary tool-making workshops, the deepest ancestors of craft shops and factories. We made decorative objects for our homes and painted beautiful scenes on rock walls. We used all of these technologies fashioned from the non-human world to develop our own growing intelligence, our spoken language, and our capacity to plan and act together despite inevitable conflicts. In the process, we invented a wide variety of adaptable social institutions that could at times encompass multiple camps, families, bands, and large kin groups. As such, our camp dwellings allowed us to generate many ideas for governing increased numbers of people in one spot while also managing our unpredictable environment. These ideas diversified further in villages, then in towns and cities.[5]

The fact that our prehistoric campsites varied and were built for diverse purposes and environments (unlike beehives, termite mounds, or swallows' nests for example) is alone reason to debunk the Jericho fountain's wild claim that the inhabitants of Jericho "invented" architecture – interesting as its very old mud brick houses certainly are. Surely, it would be churlish to deny our much earlier foraging selves the credit for thoughtful and effective building design. That is not all, though. Camp dwellers also engaged in a version of long-distance trade, passing rare materials like amber, obsidian, and precious stones from camp to camp over thousands of miles from their point of origin. (Note, however, that in this system the camp where these items originated could not control the final destination of traded objects, as urban merchants could do much later.) Organized religion, too, far preceded Jericho – again contrary to the fountain's babble. Foraging campsite dwellers venerated the dead and the forces of nature. The most permanent structures foragers built, in fact, were burial mounds and shrines, which took big teams of people, somehow taking long breaks from foraging, to build. Stand-alone, temple-like structures such as the magnificent amphitheater of Göbekli Tepe in Anatolia (today's Turkey), from 10,000 BCE, surrounded by enormous, beautifully carved stone pillars, suggest that complex, highly organized cults of natural phenomena predated agricultural settlements like Jericho by 1,000 years or more (Göbekli Tepe also predated the vaguely similar site at Stonehenge by 5,000 years). Camp-dwelling people spread spiritual ideas as they moved, and thus our built habitats helped religion become a large-scale historical phenomenon in its own right, if typically limited to substantial regions.[6]

Most importantly, by building a strong connection between people, purpose, practice, power, and place, our camp-dwelling ancestors created the existential hinge in our relationship with the unbuilt world. This empowered relationship between people and place – in seminal forms that overlapped with cities' far more powerful political communities – allowed us to take what we needed from the natural world and to survive its often terrifying, mortal blows. It allowed us to expand our own built environment, and from there the range of our actions and their impact across ever larger stretches of our planet's surface.

Are these accomplishments big? Absolutely – enormous even: of fundamental importance to human existence up to our own day, including to the Urban Planet we built many millennia later. Clearly, cities do not have a monopoly on the biggest things that we have done. Were foraging campsites therefore *good*, that is, worth celebrating as the fountain suggests? That is much harder to say. As we built and rebuilt our little campsites, we also began building our capacity to impact Earth on a global scale – maybe even forever. Large-scale action gave way to large-scale impact, and sometimes we began paying the consequences too; at that point the morality of our "accomplishments" became far murkier. For example, when our particular branch of humanity, *Homo sapiens*, moved to Asia and Europe, we met up with other subspecies of humans that had left Africa before us. Though we were equipped with largely similar buildings, we had more brainpower, larger numbers, and possibly stronger social institutions – or at least ones more capable of collective violence. Over time, we wiped those other humans out, most notably the Eurasian Neanderthals and Denisovans – though only after many centuries of cohabitation and interbreeding. Meanwhile, large animals in Africa and Asia adapted to our hunting practices as we got better at hunting them; they learned to survive by fleeing us, and as a result animals like giraffes and rhinoceroses still exist today on Earth. However, by the time we used our ingenuity and our built environments to move to the Americas, we had become far better hunters. There we found huge beasts that did not fear us enough for their own good. Delicious, meaty American animals like giant bears, saber-toothed cats, mammoths, huge horses, and other herd animals disappeared as species after we arrived, maybe in part also because of spells of colder temperatures that were not our fault. Finally, as hunters, we also often set fire to huge meadows and forests to scare animals into our traps, and we altered rivers to capture fish. There, though, our impact was, for the time being, less marked and more fleeting, the consequences not as severe or widespread.[7]

With humans living in camps, the habitats of other animals and plants, not to mention the atmosphere as a whole, continued to change, far more in tune with forces like the variable strength of the Sun's rays, the tilt, wobble, and changing orbit of Earth, and the amount of volcanic or meteoric material in the atmosphere. In campsites, our own harnessing of purpose to practice, power, and self-built places may have helped us colonize the planet, but our impact was still a comparatively weak force as far as the planet and its other life forms were concerned.

IT TOOK MANY VILLAGES ...

That balance of life force slowly bent a little bit when, still as camp-dwelling foragers, we embarked on the slow invention of the somewhat larger, longer-lasting, unmovable, and less-disposable settlements we recognize today as villages – and eventually expanded them into towns. It was there that, in what were still mostly very tiny places, we did something else of global importance: we invented farming and animal taming.

Villages, agriculture, and pastoralism all became quasi-global phenomena beginning in about 10,000 BCE, as the dramatic climate gyrations of the Ice Ages slowly subsided into the Holocene's more muted rhythms of warming and cooling. The "Neolithic Revolution" that began then is probably too dramatic a name for events that stretched over many ensuing millennia, but the transformation was profound nonetheless. By 9,000 years later, only a small minority of us remained foragers. Though some pastoralists continued to live in dispersed temporary camps, village-based farming remained the majority form of human existence until our own twenty-first century, when, demographers tell us, we became a species whose majority lived in cities.

The spread of villagers was unlike the diffusion of campsite-dwellers, which started on one continent, Africa, and spread to the rest of the world. Instead, villages arose in separate clusters, spontaneously and largely independently from one another in at least seven different regions and times: the Fertile Crescent of Southwest Asia after 10,500 BCE; China after 7000 BCE; New Guinea after 4500 BCE; the West African Sahel, Peru, and Mesoamerica after 3000 BCE; and the Eastern Woodlands of North America after 2000 BCE. Over that time, village life spread outward at different rates from each of these regional nuclei. It arrived in the Nile and Indus valleys from the Fertile Crescent very early on and spread to Europe and North Africa after 4000 BCE, and India and Southeast Asia after about 3000 BCE. It spread across the entirety of North America east of the Mississippi by 1000 BCE and into what is now the US Southwest; and it arrived in Japan after 900 BCE.[8]

Nowhere was this Neolithic phenomenon sudden. The path to agriculture was long and multi-directional, passing back and forth between early adventures in gathering wild grain, experiments in cultivating stands of wild grasses or sowing particularly promising seeds, and windfalls from accidental or semi-deliberate botanical crosses. As farmers, we sometimes also transformed wild animal species into tamed livestock or poultry on the side. There were also larger-scale herders who eschewed plant-growing and focused solely on breeding and raising animals.

The habitats we built during the Neolithic reflected these diverse mixes of new practices and helped make them possible. From about 13,000 BCE, the Natufian people – named after the Wadi an-Natuf, in the uplands of what is today Israel – could forage for their region's wild grains, lentil-like legumes, and nuts, and kill migrating herd animals without needing to migrate like most nomadic foragers. In this very fertile spot in the Fertile Crescent, the Natufians built the world's earliest villages designed to last. They dug a round or an oval pit for each house, reinforced the sides with stones, added stone hearths, sometimes laid down paving stones for floors, and usually planted wooden posts in the foundations to support strong roof joists covered with brush. Then, when climate changes spread their various food sources more widely apart, the Natufians reverted to a "semi-sedentary" existence, visiting their hard, unmovable houses only in certain seasons. Then they began rebuilding permanent settlements after about 10,500 BCE, when a drying trend disturbed their upland economy, forcing a group of Natufians to move out of the hills into lower, wetter, flatter grasslands and specialize in wild grain cultivation. At these new sites, archaeologists have discovered the ruins of villages containing remnants of the first visibly domesticated grains of emmer wheat and barley, as well as stone storage facilities and larger numbers of heavy instruments for pounding grain. They also found the bones of domestic animals, identifiable from their smaller size. One of these sites, consisting of seventy or so beehive-shaped houses made of a relatively recent heavy, unmovable material – mud brick – is buried at the very bottom of the large pile of architectural remnants that we know as ancient Jericho.[9]

The variety and change in the Natufians' built habitats represent only a tiny sample of stories of many kinds of subsequent village-like places whose remains are scattered across the seven nascent agricultural regions and the nine millennia that it took farming and herding to go global. On the least settled end of the spectrum were people who went into herding animals on a large scale. Following the sweetening of the grasses their animals craved, pastoralists developed a nomadic existence still largely supported by tented camps, though some of their stone water-collecting structures stayed in place for many years at a time.

On the other end of the scale of sedentism, the houses of career agriculturalists could grow into large extended family compounds inter-mixed with stables aimed to mobilize the larger human and animal workforces that farming life required. Some of these farming settlements could get large and elaborate, such as Peruvian villages equipped with special ceremonial platforms, European villages built in the shadows of massive burial mounds, and the fortified cliff-side or mesa-top villages of the Anasazi in the western deserts of North America. In Jericho, long before that but 2,000 years after Natufians first settled the site, farmers took time from their work to build a massive retaining wall against seasonal floods, and a tower, possibly so that its inhabitants could observe, from on high and in awe, the bounty and the mortal threats of the surrounding natural landscape. In so doing, they expanded the conception of a village somewhat, transforming into something hard to characterize, perhaps a kind of town. Çatalhöyük, another large place built by farmer-herders two millennia later in Anatolia, had about 6,000 inhabitants, crammed into about 1,000 nearly identical houses that shared walls with their neighbors. Instead of streets, people climbed ladders to doors in the ceilings and then out onto the rooftops. In contrast to much smaller, much older Jericho, there were no surrounding walls or monuments. Later, the village settlements of the Ubaid culture grew, diminished, and grew again over thousands of years throughout Mesopotamia, another part of the Fertile Crescent. Some of these became town-like too, then disappeared. Around 4000 BCE – or maybe centuries before – two adjacent Ubaid settlements grew into each other, spawned a few larger buildings, then formed something altogether different: the early city of Uruk.

For Jane Jacobs, one of the greatest urban theorists, especially large early agricultural settlements present an enticing prospect. Jacobs speculated that places like Çatalhöyük, packed with people living close together and in contact with interesting nomads who may have pioneered early trade routes, could have developed something she liked to see in cities – a kind of synergistic mixture of teamwork, creative brainstorming, and pooling of resources that spontaneously generates new opportunities for the surrounding society as a whole. Big things, in other words, that were also "good" things. What if this "energized crowding," as other scholars have called it, existed at Çatalhöyük or even at Jericho? What if these places were therefore in fact the first true cities? Could we expect, then, that such underappreciated "cities" were also the true creators of agriculture, one of the most consequential things humans have done for the benefit of humanity? By extension, could we do what Jacobs and many other urban theorists clearly wanted to do: celebrate cities as the greatest things we have ever invented?[10]

As you may detect, the inscription on the fountain at Jericho and its claim to be the first of all cities is redolent of these giddy, city-celebrating speculations. There are many problems with the line of thinking, as others have discussed in some detail. The circularity of the argument – that energized crowding can occur only in cities, that agriculture must have been created through energized crowding, and thus that largish settlements from the early years of the Neolithic revolution must have been both cities and the cradles of agriculture – is only one of the problems. The archaeological evidence is another. Putting aside the unanswerable question of how big a settlement has to be, in absolute or relative terms, to qualify as a city (see Chapter 1), the size of Neolithic settlements rarely corresponded to the location of crucial innovations of the early era of plant and animal domestication. Was Jericho the birthplace of agriculture? Not exactly. Other Natufian sites to the north and south have somewhat older evidence of farming than Jericho. How about mud-brick architecture or monuments? No. It turns out that non-agricultural foragers who did not grow grain could build mud-brick walls and even monumental buildings, such as at Tel-Qaramel in northwestern Syria, where archaeologists found plenty of mud bricks that were 2,000 years older than Jericho's. On top of that, Tel-Qaramel had not just one, but five stone towers.[11]

Meanwhile, as both Jericho and Çatalhöyük came and went, other important innovations occurred elsewhere. It was in far smaller places that we replaced mud brick (dried in the sun) with far more durable fired brick, where we created rectangular houses that used land more efficiently, where we engaged in the earliest experiments in individual land ownership, where we invented pottery, glazing techniques, and from there moved to metallurgy, copper smelting, and precious stone setting. In little places, far away from Jericho and Çatalhöyük, we domesticated species such as cows and pigs, learned to milk animals, shear wool, and weave cloth. In similarly small places, we first harnessed animals to carry heavy loads, to thresh grain, and to pull carts and plows, thus vastly increasing the labor-power available for farming. Horses were probably first domesticated in tiny camps of nomads on the great steppes of Central Asia. In small villages, we also learned to increase crop yields by digging irrigation ditches, mucking manure onto our fields, and rotating our plantings to leave some fields fallow.[12]

Gender roles changed too in these small places, and not for the better, especially in agricultural societies that adopted plows, which men tended to dominate, allowing men the power to reassign women from their traditional place in the fields to a new segregated and more confined place in the home. (In places where there were no plows, such as West Africa, women retained considerable power in the fields and, later, in villages and cities.) Our clans and kin groups sometimes specialized in the new crafts we invented or became at least part-time traders, bringing new ideas and goods to villages further afield. A few got richer than others, as our village architecture attests: some of our houses and house–stable compounds grew much bigger and more opulent than those of our neighbors. In China's celebrated Banpo Village, a rectangular "great house" stood out in the midst of small round huts; later villages had many of these bigger places, often "ritual houses" that some anthropologists see as the sites of future temples. Like at its monument-festooned Peruvian contemporaries and be-towered Jericho, a kind of city-like, or at least town-like, "nucleation" was occurring – villagers were building central places for activities that were more important to the community as a whole than what went on in the rest of town. A small degree of spatial segregation became detectable too, by wealth, occupation, or even gender – the great houses of Banpo Village may have been designed as communal spaces for men whose wives were (as was often the case) pregnant. Meanwhile, the villages that were essential to our ability to make all of this momentous change grew in size too, then shrank then grew again. Sometimes they formed agricultural "mega-sites" larger than Çatalhöyük, like the remarkable ring-shaped settlements of Trypillia culture in Ukraine. While their thousands of houses may not all date from the same time, they suggest that, as farmers, we could imagine settlements on quite large scales.[13]

Was the "Neolithic revolution" a good thing, as the fountain at Jericho seems to imply? Evidence of the negative consequences of agricultural life has been mounting. For one thing, some anthropologists have pointed to those prominent "ritual houses" as prehistoric drivers of the economic and social inequalities that would later become yawning gaps in cities. Many villagers practiced slavery, and, in some places, hereditary forms of property ownership that cemented inequalities over the generations. Early warrior chiefs and even kings could bring multiple farming settlements under their power. Though both prehistoric and later urban political institutions could also take more egalitarian forms too, temples that emerged from sacred village spaces sometimes served as the nuclei for later urban states and empires. Demographers are also unanimous on the point that, already in Neolithic times, farming increased the number of people on Earth long before and beyond the first worlds of cities came into being. Overall, higher birth rates, caused by more time for sex and more need for labor, outweighed death rates, high as they were too. Indeed, as villagers, we almost certainly became less healthy. Our grain-based diets were less nutritious than those of foragers were. In villages, we lived in close proximity for long periods with each other and our animals, we relied on grain bins that attracted rodent and insect vermin, and we generated larger piles of waste (less of a factor in movable camps). Thus, as we domesticated plants and animals, we very literally domesticated new microbes and viruses too. The human bones and teeth that archaeologists unearth from Neolithic village gravesites show signs of new sicknesses and miseries. On average, early farmers' skeletons are several inches shorter than those of their foraging ancestors were. Village-dwelling children died in prodigious numbers, though those that survived did help us develop partial immunities to new diseases. All of this occurred in the context of a new geographical rupture between what we later called the Old World and the New, when rising seawater inundated the Bering Strait between the world's two supercontinents. Inhabitants of the Afro-Eurasian "Old World" had larger-scale contact with farm animals and thus more diseases and more immunity than did the peoples of the "New" Americas, where llamas and their relatives were the only large animals left to domesticate. That continental inequality in immunity would have devastating effects for Native Americans after the two worlds returned to sustained contact after 1492 CE.[14]

How did the growth of our built habitat and the scope of our farming and herding practices affect our relationship to the non-built environment? As the realm of our impact on Earth increased, the realm of consequence probably expanded too. Disease may not be the only way that Sun and Earth grew harder on village-dwelling humans. Since villagers were more invested, and in larger numbers, in specific fixed human-built and altered habitats, natural calamities in those spots could cause larger scales of human suffering. Did increased meadow burning, forest clearing, river damming, channel building, rice paddy flooding, and even the larger numbers of human bodies, gas-belching ruminant animals, and fire-heated buildings of Neolithic times alter the planet on the scale of the biosphere as a whole? The jury is still out. It is possible, according to some research, that the warming effects of the increased amounts of carbon dioxide and methane (particularly from rice growing) we let loose over the course of the Neolithic revolution may have tempered what otherwise might have been periods of severer Sun- and Earth-induced cooling. If so, that mild warming effect may have helped stimulate – and was also likely intensified by – another global transformation: the invention of the first cities.[15]

Where did that happen? Most scholars discount the fable of the bubbly fountain at Jericho, as impressive as the settlement's tower may be, and despite its early town wall. Most of the experts who study Çatalhöyük also call it a town – though that vague word does not add much to what we know about it. Wherever the Neolithic revolution spread, countless other smaller, medium-sized, and somewhat larger human habitats came into being, grew in size and density, at times sprouted largish buildings of different shapes and sizes, then receded, some destined to grow again. We have barely scratched the surface of the thousands of ruins they left behind, not to mention the many more that may lie underneath seas that have risen since the time they were built. Amidst all of those ruins, though, archaeologists repeatedly return to one region to find the earliest cities: Mesopotamia.

There, the Ubaid people engaged in a series of specific and interconnected acts of settlement design, building, and habitation that took inspiration from larger growing villages and towns, but that created something altogether new. No one undertook these acts in order to build what they knew beforehand deserved the name "city" – in fact, no word ever came into being for such a thing in any Mesopotamian language. Growing numbers of people gathered in larger settlements because, in their particular environmental context, they envisioned new, even escalating, advantages to doing so. Among these was increased human power: power that could be wielded *with* others and, too often, *over* others; power to increase harvests of natural energy from the surrounding environment for human use; and new power to moderate the impact of unpredictable shifts in natural energy governed by the Sun and Earth. Unlike at Jericho and Çatalhöyük, that power could also allow them to replicate their larger settlements – creating larger, region-wide, urban birth-worlds devoted to sustaining the multiplying cities they contained. Eventually, it meant merging these birth-worlds into a much bigger habitat whose realm of action, built structures, impact, and consequences encircled planet Earth as a whole.

PART ONE

CITIES OF THE RIVERS

I.1. A Riverboat Captain Delivers the Temple to Uruk
Bpk/Vorderasiatisches Museum, SMB/Olaf M. Teβmer.

According to one Mesopotamian myth, we sowed the first seeds of the Urban Planet on a night when Enki, the God of the Rivers, got drunk with his daughter. The place was Enki's temple at a place called Eridu, where the mighty Euphrates River pours into the Persian Gulf. Eridu lay in the midst of a fertile region where local mortals could harvest a diverse banquet of foodstuffs – from the river itself, and from nearby fields, pastures, hills, orchards, marshes, inlets, and lagoons. The people of the region lived in largish settlements like Eridu itself, but these were not yet cities – you could tell, because their inhabitants did not have the power to do any of the things that cities made possible. So, Enki's daughter Inanna, the fearsome goddess of power, war, and sex – a chaotic force of creation and destruction – took advantage of her watery father's drunkenness. She loaded all things that make up city life, called the Holy *Mē* in the local Sumerian language, into the hold of the "Boat of Heaven" to deliver them to humankind. Before her snoring father the River God knew it, Inanna had reached the next port up the Euphrates, then the next.

Awaking in a hung-over rage, Enki conjured up horrific beasts, each one worse than the previous one, to stop Inanna's delivery. Yet Inanna outwitted him at each turn. To hasten the final segment of her voyage, she called on the rivers to rise and flood the streets of a large place called Uruk. There she moored the Boat of Heaven at the splendid "Lapis Lazuli Quay" and unloaded the Holy *Mē*. One by one, Inanna gave the people of Uruk the basic ingredients of city life: urban social turbulence, statecraft, and empire; urban economics, commerce, and wealth; urban culture, writing, and knowledge; and, for good measure, all the great promises of urban life and all its great calamities.[1]

The story of Inanna is a myth, of course. Propaganda even. Since later Mesopotamian kings wrote it down to glorify their harsh rule, we should be wary of retelling it. Yet, in another way, just like the Fable of Jericho, it is a perfect allegory of the end of prehistory, and of the first five and a half millennia of urban and global history: the era of the Cities of the Rivers. Most of the first cities did in fact almost literally materialize from a few of the world's rivers. The emergence of cities in those river valleys was truly unlikely, subject to monstrous forces of destruction, conjured by godlike forces such as Enki's rivers, the Sun, and the Earth. We can easily liken the storms, floods, droughts, fires, earthquakes, and city-amplified epidemics in places like Uruk to Enki's many-faced monsters. Cities not only expanded our ability to build, but also gave us the power to destroy other cities. People who lived in villages and nomadic camps stole some of this power too. They remained a weaker force as the age of cities began, but a significant one. Some camp and village dwellers had horses, others small war-boats. Both could overrun the greatest city walls. With creation came destruction – and then more creation. Exactly as chaotic Inanna herself would have wanted.

Let us then board the Boat of Heaven and travel once again with the fierce rebel goddess, retracing her dangerous route up the Euphrates River from Eridu to Uruk and beyond, to see how it was that cities allowed us to do many new big things, both wondrous and terrible.

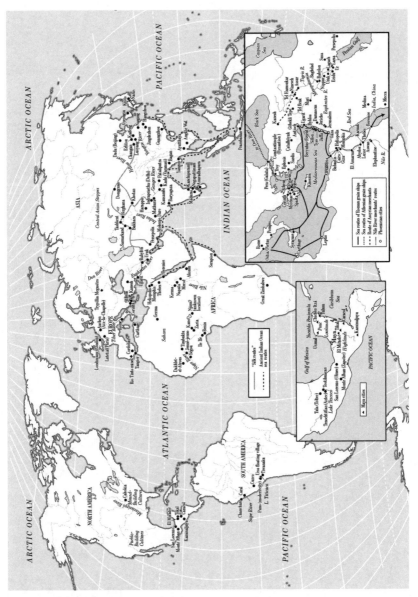

Map I.1. Cities of the Rivers
Map created by Joe LeMonnier, https://mapartist.com.

CHAPTER 1

Making Politics from Sunshine, Earth, and Water

THE GODDESS AND THE CONUNDRUM

Inanna's dash up the Euphrates was a reckless affair – among the mightiest of riverboat gambles. Yet, there was method to her madness, or so her worshippers later insisted. From the monstrous fracas of urban birth, a new, becalmed human order would arise, governed by the goddess herself. At Uruk, each of the hastily delivered Holy *Mē* would find their place.

We know this much primmer sequel to the chaotic "Boat of Heaven" story thanks to the Warka Vase, a supremely elegant object sculpted from a meter-tall column of alabaster, discovered by archaeologists in 1934 amidst the ruins of Inanna's temple in downtown Uruk. (Warka is the Arabic name for Uruk and the name of a contemporary Iraqi village near the ruins.) The artisan who carved the vase – at some point between 3200 and 3000 BCE – depicted the goddess's plan for her city in three friezes that ornament the object's outer surface. Inanna dominates the topmost of these friezes, standing at the very city center, in front of symbols indicating three built structures: her temple, a storehouse, and a gate. Celebratory pennants fly in the wind. Three figures, possibly priests and priestesses, but maybe also including a secular ruler, offer adoration, fealty, and gifts of grain and animals; the goddess's assistants spirit these last items into her storehouse for safekeeping. In the two friezes below that, the artist delved into things that make the city possible. In the middle, the goddess's devoted subjects, all depicted as men, walk toward her, zealously raising bowls of hard-won food to their goddess. They are completely naked, their collective public purpose stripped of any sign of crass individual interest. The third frieze at the bottom of the vase reveals the source of the gifts – the energy system of

1.1. The Warka Vase
In this depiction of Uruk from the 3000s BCE, the Euphrates River supports a fanciful city whose political community is completely aligned with its ruling institutions. A goddess oversees a state that ensures the city's power and order. In reality, the source of amplified human power in cities was geo-solar energy harvested in hinterlands and funneled into large, dense communities with a diversity of specialized and intensely competing interests. Governance of cities did require especially complex and potent institutions, but whether or not these took the form of states, they always faced political resistance – itself another source of urban-amplified human power.
Universal History Archive/Getty Images.

Uruk. Flocks of sheep gambol in the pastures, date palms bend heavily with fruit in the orchards, and copious stalks of barley and wheat sway in the fields to the same breezes as the pennants above. Then, at the very bottom of the bottommost frieze, the artist carved a solid wavy line that visually frames everything above it: the mighty, flowing, life-giving Euphrates River.

As serious biographers of Earthopolis we know better than to rely on evidence like ancient myths or alluring objects like the Warka Vase. Both smell strongly of propaganda, possibly served up by Inanna's priests or maybe a king eager to justify rule by armed force. To learn the hard facts – when and where the first cities were born, what life was like there, and why cities came into being – we need to turn to the authority of today's archaeologists. They are the professionals in the room: they make a commitment to spend their whole careers thinking about ancient urban birth-sites, often spending long hours on their knees painstakingly unearthing stuff far less glamorous than the Warka Vase from messy ruins. They poke trowels, brushes, and noses deep into layers upon layers of dirt, marveling over ancient brick and stone, eagerly scouting out pottery shards, bones, teeth, shells, wooden beams, charcoal fragments, plant remains, and pollen. Those tiny fragments of organic matter allow them, among other things, to date archaeological sites, which is crucial to establishing when inanimate brick, and therefore cities, came into being. More recently some archaeologists have also turned their craft upside down, taking to the air in planes far above their sites, snapping pictures with so-called "light detecting and ranging" (LiDAR) cameras that can detect the presence of old building foundations otherwise hopelessly entangled underneath rainforests of places like Central America or Cambodia. Whether by zooming in or out, the conclusions they draw from all the ruins are subject to debate among colleagues at big conventions, and must be peer reviewed before appearing in specialized journals. There are plenty of disputes – notorious scholarly rivalries even – and the dating methods (note the two-*century* estimate for the origin of the Warka Vase) are imperfect. Yet, in the end it is they who, as one of them put it, "recognize cities through the veil of dust and the sting of sweat in the eyes," producing the closest thing we have to the true truth about the babyhood of cities.[1]

One elementary lesson they teach us is that evidence from one city, say Uruk, is inadequate to make assumptions about cities in general. No one doubts that Uruk was one of the earliest cities, and, in the late 3000s BCE, it was the largest of many others in the southern Mesopotamian region of Sumer: 50,000 people lived there, in an area twice the size of twenty-first-century London's financial district – "the City." Its influence on other cities in that region was important, also without doubt. However, very different cities were arising far away at the same time or even before – in northern Mesopotamia 500 kilometers away from Uruk; along the Nile in Egypt; possibly independently in Nubia and Kush upriver; and in what is now southwestern Iran. By 2500 BCE, cities had cropped up even farther away, in the Indus Valley of today's Pakistan, where people did know about Mesopotamia yet built cities very differently; and in places where people had no idea that Mesopotamia existed: northern Peru and the Yellow (Huang Ho) River Valley of China. China would become world history's single most prolific city-building region, especially after new cities arose in the Yangtze (Chang Jiang) River Valley and beyond. Uruk remained a very large and influential center of Sumerian culture throughout the 2000s and 1000s CE, but its political power in the region waned as larger cities spread throughout Southwest Asia, North Africa, Greece, Italy, and the Mediterranean. After 1400 BCE, the Olmec people grew a brand new crop of cities in the river plains of Mexico's Gulf Coast, and the Zapotec people to the south built the fortress of Monte Alban high above the Atoyac River near today's Oaxaca. Both helped influence a huge proliferation of cities some centuries later in the Mayan mountains and the Yucatán Peninsula. In South America, cities also spread along the Pacific coast and, later, jumped high into the Andes near Lake Titicaca. Much later, these places inspired the builders of Cuzco and other cities of the pan-Andean Inka Empire. Mesoamerican cities resemble Andean ones in some ways. Though South–North influence remains unproven, early Mesoamerican cities clearly inspired later giants in Central Mexico like Teotihuacan (150 BCE to 550 CE), the Toltec capital of Tula (650–1150 CE), and the Aztec capital Tenochtitlan (1300–1521 CE).

Meanwhile, long before that, after about 500 BCE, another explosion of city-building activity occurred in the Ganges Valley of India that may reflect what were by that point long-submerged traditions from the Indus Valley; after that date, cities spread southward across India. The city of Aksum in the Horn of Africa dates from around 200 CE; its progeny includes centuries' worth of Ethiopian dynastic capitals. Same with the port cities on the Swahili Coast of East Africa: these are commonly thought to have emerged after 800 CE but evidence of earlier ports exists along the coast, and the Romans wrote of a port at Serapion near today's Mogadishu, Somalia. Across the then less-dry Sahara Desert, dozens of large towns arose from as early as 1900 BCE on, culminating in places like Dakhlet-el-Atrous (in today's Mauritania) and Garma (in today's Libya). After 400 CE in the Niger River's immense "Inland Delta" floodplain, numerous villages and towns partially merged to form the archipelago-shaped river cities of Jenné-jenno and Dia. Meanwhile, other, possibly autonomous, urban birth-worlds arose well into the Common Era: at Cahokia and elsewhere in North America's Mississippi River Valley from about 600–1200 CE; at Kano, Njimi, Ile-Ife, and Benin in three separate regions of today's Nigeria and Chad between 900 and 1200 CE; at Great

Zimbabwe and smaller nearby sites in Southern Africa from 1000–1500 CE; and in the South Pacific, at the large center of Nan Madol, the capital of the Sandeleur dynasty on the island of Pohnpei from 1200 to 1600 CE.[2]

After 1500, in a relative blink of global urban historical time, all of these birth-worlds came into contact with each other, each contributing in its own way to the contiguous realms of action, habitat, impact, and consequence we know today. However, we cannot forget the basic geography unearthed by urban archaeology: the component parts of Earthopolis had many birthdays and birthplaces. Thus, any single overlapping and interconnected Urban Planet we built much later on was, from birth, foundationally a plural phenomenon. Created by many hands, it was destined to remain forever multifarious and diverse, encompassing the breathtaking range of people, buildings, city designs, and city life that we know to this day.

Still, we cannot avoid an old conundrum. If no one city can ever represent city-ness everywhere else, how do archaeologists know when they have discovered a city at all – a new, certifiable "urban" birthplace and birthday? Is there, after all, something cities all share, everywhere and always? Maddeningly, despite a huge amount of "sweat," eye-stinging "dust," and much spilled scholarly ink, no archaeologist, no urban theorist, and no global urban historian has answered that basic question to anyone's full satisfaction.

A leap of faith is called for here, and I think we could do worse than give Inanna's reckless riverboat gamble a second roll. In the midst of spinning their lies, the goddess's mythmakers and vase-makers put their finger on five answers to the urban conundrum that also resonate well with hard evidence from archaeology. First, there is a dangerous yet life-giving source of water, courtesy of the Sun and Earth. Second, there are many, diverse, new types of people. Contrary to the central frieze of the Warka Vase but more aligned with the myth of the Holy *Mē*, these people have in fact many new interests, many new reasons for conflict, and, because they do not know one another, they have heightened needs for coordination, negotiated or imposed. Third, there are many new types of buildings and spaces, many of them larger than ever before – temples, storehouses, and gates for example – rising above other buildings assembled in settlements larger than any before. Fourth, there is some kind of governing institution, often definable as a state, not always. Fifth, most importantly, there is a new human drama made up of the power of all four elements: the river's capriciously delivered gifts, the settlement's unpredictable political community, the hodgepodge of built structures, and any (inevitably contested) efforts to capture the entire explosive mix within governing institutions designed to widen the scope of city dwellers' actions, their settlements, their impacts, and all the consequences.

Put these five ingredients into a single crucible of human making, boil it down, and behold the Goddess's Hypothesis of cityhood: cities are perilous yet miraculous places where we transubstantiate the power of Sunshine, Earth, and water into potent new forms of human politics – and, from there, into new measures of human power.

THROUGH THE VALLEYS OF THE SUNLIGHT OF URBAN BIRTH

Does this definition of "a city" solve all our problems? No, as we will see. Yet it is as good a starting bet as any – well worth playing out in Uruk and all the other chancy urban birthplaces of the world. As you may have detected, Inanna's proposal revolves around an argument in which cause and effect switch back and forth. Geo-solar energy creates cities, which enables new political dramas and possibly states, which together sort out how city dwellers handle more geo-solar energy. Theoretically, we could begin anywhere. I say, start with the Sunshine.

Sunshine, in the earliest history of cities, means rivers – uniquely user-friendly liquid manifestations of solar energy on Earth that also contain useful suspended solids. The Sun evaporates massive amounts of seawater, dumps it as rain and snow on the mountains, and from there, as freshwater, it follows Earth's gravity and its undulating planetary terrain down into valleys, dragging nutritious Earthly minerals with it into concentrated, elongated, wet, and fertile places. There, people can tap new bursts of Sunshine in the form of photosynthesis, bringing into being plants and animals that are useful for food and fuel. Add drinkable riverwater to the mix, and it is easy to see that the basic sources of human bodily power pile up most densely in river valleys. The more efficient the valley, the more resources, the greater diversity of resources, the more potently the Valley of Sunlight powers human bodies to do the work of producing resources, the more humans reproduce, the likelier they are to move and congregate in larger numbers in one spot, the more explosive the power of their concentrated, restive numbers becomes.

Since river valleys helped create thousands of villages and even town-like settlements in many places for many years before there were any cities, we need to know what made villages in any one river valley likely to swell into towns and then, quite suddenly, into even larger places. In the earliest urban birth-worlds, we also need to know why that happened so early, and, conversely, why there was such a delay, given that those regions were apparently primed to give birth to cities for millennia before they actually did. It turns out that Sun, Earth, and rivers help explain not only *why* cities came into being, but maybe also *where* they did and *when* they did – a rare perfect trifecta of causal thrust, the kind of holy explanatory grail that makes historians happy to be alive.

One thing that apparently matters a lot is the particular *shape* of the river valleys that gave birth to most of the very earliest cities in their regions. The Euphrates, Tigris, Nile, and the smaller Peruvian rivers such as the Supe, near Caral, flowed through especially narrow valleys. Deserts or relatively unfertile plains or mountains closely flanked what were otherwise bountiful but very thin ribbons of river-washed land. Villages clustered even more densely in such tight places, concentrating human numbers and labor power far more than in areas with wider fertile zones. Additionally, in Sumer, and possibly in Egypt and Peru, would-be city builders could also draw on the especially abundant natural smorgasbords available in places where freshwater ecologies lay close to the brackish water of rivers' estuaries. The availability of grain, lentil-like pulses, fruits, and plant foods of all kinds near sources for a variety of proteins from meat, fish, and shellfish meant that temporary shortages in one food source could be compensated for with an abundance of others. (Note that the extent to which the city of Caral relied on such an estuarine diversity of resources is a matter of ferocious dispute between archaeologists.) The buffets available in those places account not only for the larger numbers of villages that came into being there, but also for the presence of various early specialists in the food-creation business – grain farmers, vegetable gardeners, orchard keepers, bee-keepers, herders, fisher-people, and shellfish collectors, as well as other foragers, and perhaps a few people in the food packaging (pottery) and transport business. All of these foreshadow urban "specialization," an enormous force we will encounter very soon. No wonder, then, that in another myth about Inanna, the goddess's father Enki, himself the god of water, founded Eridu at the *abzu*, possibly a place where the river and sea met. Subsequent Mesopotamian temples contained a receptacle of water, also called the *abzu*, which commemorated the holy place from which their cities arose.[3]

Rivers in narrow valleys may also explain the timing of the first cities that arose on their banks. Ironically, the birth schedule of cities may have been set not by rivers' prodigious power to stimulate life, but by their immense power to destroy it. Rivers, after all, are governed by the Sun, and the Sun can take away as easily as it provides, by causing rivers to flow too low, thus creating crop-killing droughts, or too high, causing appalling floods. Climate scientists believe that beginning in the late 3000s BCE, the Sun's power went through a cyclical downturn, resulting in increasingly turbulent climatic conditions throughout the world's relatively temperate longitudes, where all of the oldest city-birthing river valleys are located. During the ensuing droughts and floods, villagers in wider fertile zones, such as those of the Indus and the Yellow River had more space in which to rebuild their settlements away from rivers. Perhaps that dispersal partly explains the somewhat delayed birthdate of cities there – despite the many villages and larger settlements that had waxed and waned in those regions for thousands of years before. By contrast, in Mesopotamia and other narrower fertile zones, droughts or especially destructive floods may have created enormous crowds of village-fleeing refugees with comparatively few places to go. Any fortunate settlement spared by these river-created crises might fill fast with desperate refugees seeking safe homes and food. In the mid-3000s BCE, the settlement of Uruk, which is situated on comparatively high ground, appears to have grown much faster than any other location in the region, suggesting that some calamity elsewhere in the valley may have been responsible. We could read the story about the monsters that Enki sent after Inanna – and her desperate call for "high water" to "sweep over the streets" of Uruk so she could reach the Quay ahead of her pursuers – as a story about floods that destroyed other villages in the region, but allowed Uruk to come into being as a refugee-filled city (though scholars think droughts were a more common reason for Mesopotamians to flee villages during this time). Later, a similar solar retreat may help explain city-building along the smaller rivers of the Olmec and Zapotec home-lands in Mexico, and in the Niger Valley of West Africa.[4]

For now, theories like this will have await confirmation from many years of archaeological research to come. It is important to note in the meantime that evidence from other urban birthplaces has brought the universality of the river theory of city birth into at least partial question. In turns out that, in Northern Mesopotamia, Uruk has two rivals for the title of first-ever city. One of these, Tel Brak, relied on a tributary of the Euphrates for its geo-solar energy and water. However, its near neighbor Tel Hamoukar sustained at least several thousand people – an overgrown town at very least, this one with a wall – long before 4000 BCE, not on river water but on rainfall and wells tunneled into deposits of groundwater. Did people at Hamoukar rely on the example of river-founded settle-ments at Uruk to build a city that they could not otherwise have imagined outside a river valley? Hamoukar contains some very early Uruk-like neighborhoods that may indicate such a vector of Urukian influence and thus reconfirm the river hypothesis. Alternatively, it may be possible that these two cities represent two separate routes from a common Ubaid village-and-town background to cityhood, somewhat weakening the "Cities of the Rivers" theory – despite the obvious role of rivers in so many of Earth's other earliest urban birth-worlds.[5]

No matter how archaeologists settle the matter of Tel Hamoukar, the earliest river-created cities do seem to have made it possible for people to imagine building later cities that relied on non-riverine water-born vectors of geo-solar energy. The cities of the Maya drew heavily on earlier river-birthed Olmec models, but the Maya built dozens of their famous pyra-mid-crowned cities far from rivers, by gathering water in paved reservoirs or underground cisterns. In other regions of the Mayan urban world, enormous swaths of modified wetland agriculture far from rivers have come into view, thanks to LiDAR technology. Rainforests powered large settlements and cities elsewhere too, including in the Amazon, in African capitals like Ile-Ife and Benin, and in Asian centers like Anuradhapura,

Bagan, and Angkor Wat. Lakes provided the primary source of liquid geo-solar energy for Tiwanaku, on Lake Titicaca in the high Andes, and Aztec Tenochtitlan, built on an island in Central Mexico's Lake Texcoco. In the Sahara, oases functioned almost like rivers, providing irrigation for large fortified places that some historians urge us to think of as cities.[6]

Long before that, of course, we began also building cities next to the sea, sometimes in areas with minimal fertile hinterlands. Here, we needed to refit riverboats for sea voyages – at first along the coasts, then sometimes venturing out of sight of land and relying on stars and the flight of seabirds to head in the right direction. At that point, we effectively availed ourselves of new vectors of solar energy – those that created sea-born winds and currents; and sometimes we additionally drew on the power of the Moon, in the form of tides that allowed our boats to enter and leave seaports. Bronze Age port cities of the Eastern Mediterranean, the Red Sea, the Persian Gulf, and the Indian Ocean were among the earliest of these sea-birthed cities. Some of these cities imported grain for their populations via the sea from distant ports that lay at the mouths of more fertile river valleys. The Greek city of Athens, for example, housed far more people than its modest nearby farmlands could support, thanks to the mariners who hauled grain to the city's port of Piraeus from the Don River, 1,000 kilometers away on the far shores of the Black Sea (distant Sicily was another source). Rome grew to the first million-plus city in world history because of massive seagoing ships that supplemented the grain harvest along the smallish Tiber Valley from many distant seaports situated at the mouths of other river valleys. Mostly Rome's grain-ships loaded up at the port of Alexandria – the era's other candidate for earliest million-plus city status – at the mouth of the especially narrow, fertile, city-rich River Nile.[7]

PROXIMITY POWER

As important as Sunshine, Earth, and rivers are to explaining both the birthplaces and the birthdates of cities, they only go so far. Harvesting geo-solar energy as food and fuel – no matter how user-friendly a city's delivery vehicle may be, no matter how strong the Sun's rays are at any place and time – is always an arduous business for humans. Billions of people have spent most of the hours of their lives working just to produce enough food, and to gather enough fuel and water to slake their own needs, let alone those of their small children and older relatives who can no longer work. Why should very large numbers of such overworked village or camp dwellers bother to expend even more of that hard-earned energy on building a city, especially since doing so also means they have to find time (and expend food) to lug heavy building materials across long distances? To answer that question, we need to turn from the vagaries of Sunshine and rivers to the vagaries of human affairs. What was it about cities that made them attractive enough to build – not only to the people who inhabited them but also to those who had to supply them?

One answer that combines urban space with economic force starts with the power of proximity. We have an incentive, this theory runs, to invest resources in creating places packed with people and buildings because those spaces of human proximity have far greater potential than smaller dispersed places to pay off in exponentially increased output. By virtue of their own demographic and spatial structure, cities mint more wealth than is required to build them. Therefore, the theory of proximity power goes, we build cities.

How does proximity power work? Start with the economic downside of cities: the more people and buildings we put together on one spot, the less able that spot is to produce enough food and fuel for the people crowded there. Worse, the larger a city gets, the less likely it can feed (and heat) itself from the land it occupies. Yet, the downsides of proximate living come with much bigger potential upsides. If city dwellers succeed in importing investments of necessities from dispersed places beyond their boundaries that are better designed for agriculture and fuel harvesting, people gathered in a city immediately gain far more time to do other things. That is the cue for Inanna to begin disembarking some of the most crucial of her deliveries onto the Lapis Lazuli Quay. New sorts of people come into being in cities, entering onto the stage of world history in especially large numbers for the first time: the large variety of food producers we already met are supplemented by artisans, market stall owners, and shopkeepers in far greater variety and numbers, and also merchants and moneychangers, the first financiers. The great urban theorist Jane Jacobs identified this first benefit of proximity power as "creating new forms of work" – usually abbreviated as "specialization" – a crucial aspect of most definitions of cities scholars have proposed over the years, and a main source of urban-amplified human power.[8]

There is more. Economists tell us that by decreasing the distance between increasing numbers of people, cities reduce the price, in transport costs, for human interaction more generally. Thus, human relationships in cities become not only more diverse, but also far more voluminous, and they recur more often and more predictably. These proliferating human encounters generate large, lasting networks of people willing to pool resources and offer each other mutual inspiration within and across lines of specialty. Thus, proximity can result in more innovative ideas, practices, and things. If some of those technologies increase the food- and fuel-generating capacity of dispersed surrounding areas, cities can acquire larger deliveries of food, and more country people can free themselves from the fields to move city-ward. Others may gravitate to urban opportunities in still newer lines of "new work" associated with new techniques. As more people arrive in the city from dispersed cultural communities, a city's diversity brings contrasting viewpoints into close range – that is, as long as invidious forms of urban spatial segregation do not intervene, as they often did. At its best, such diversity keeps routine interactions from getting stale and inspires still newer things. Urban diversity also creates large enough niches of people who may be willing to try new ideas or buy new things before everyone else does, thus generating pools of "start-up" financial support for specialized inventors and other pioneers of technological change.[9]

In all of these ways, economists conclude, urban proximity power creates "energized crowds" that increase the city's output far beyond any required initial investments, such as in building materials. "Energized crowds" require new types of spaces – shops, streets, delivery vehicles, marketplaces, and banks just to begin with. By squeezing such structures into already-crowded spaces, city dwellers increased the value of land, another avenue of opportunity and wealth. As that happens, proximity power breeds more output, more proximity, more city, and more economic output. To use another common economic definition of "the urban," cities become spaces of synergy: objects that are also verbs – even compound verbs – places of "busy-ness," where "all the [mutually reinforcing] action is."

It is easy to see why theories of proximity power could inspire a rather elated celebration of cities. For Jane Jacobs it meant extolling the small shops and the jumbled-up, multi-use buildings of her neighborhood in 1960s New York City, and attacking the god-like efforts of her nemesis, the city planner Robert Moses, to destroy such places and replace them with highways and uniform apartment towers (Chapters 19 and 25). On the other end of global urban history, it also led Jacobs to declare that Çatalhöyük and even Jericho must have been cities, and because of their built-in crowd-energized genius, must have invented the first agriculture (see the Prologue). While archaeologists never found evidence to support Jacobs on that point, they too embraced proximity power. As far as they can tell from limited data on ancient cities, the theory works across the millennia and across the world (that is, if all other things with the Sun, Earth, and rivers, not to mention with war-making states, remain equal). Still other scholars refer to proximity power when they celebrate cities as cradles of capitalism. Conversely, for critics of capitalism, proximity power supports a theory that cities come into being because cities allow capitalists or other elites to accumulate most of the city-created wealth in their own hands. From that comes the theory that capitalists (or some ancient version of them) have always driven most, if not all, of the "urbanization" that underlies today's Earthopolis.[10]

Just as with the theory of rivers, the theory of proximity power has limits. The problem is not that urban theorists and economists are wrong to connect cities with great pools of wealth, or that people do not build cities in order to accumulate wealth, or that capitalist practices were not deeply implicated in the growth (and inequality) of cities. Multiple chapters later in this book will explore Earthopolis's complex relationship to wealth and capitalism – and also why that relationship creates so much poverty.

The problem with any theory of proximity power focused solely on economic "outputs" is that it does not account for a much larger range of things people can do, or the forms of power they can accumulate, when they crowd together. Thus, these theories miss other essential reasons for people's desire to build cities. How does anyone get the power to determine that the economic benefits of city-building are desirable enough to demand that camp- and village-dwellers do the extra work required for the initial investment? As wealth from proximity power starts to accumulate, who decides which members of the "energized crowd," or for that matter which inhabitants of outlying farms or camps, get what share of the wealth a city creates? Who decides who does what work, "new" or otherwise, in the urban economic order, and for what pay in return? How do the few people who benefit the most from energized crowding prevent the majority of people who benefit far less from forming large "energized crowds" of their own (today we call them strikes, protest movements, or even revolutions) – and seizing the wealth for themselves? And what about the other predictable result of jumbling many people together, the fact that most people we see when we walk around a city are strangers – not from our family or kin, from a different clan or cultural group, possibly even different in physical appearance? Such "anonymity," after all is another classic way to distinguish a city from a town, village, or camp: the theorist Richard Sennett defined cities as "milieus of strangers." Yet, who guarantees that we will embrace the energizing potential of such primal urban anonymity, and who prevents the use of unfamiliarity as an excuse for fiercely "energized," even bloody, economy-destroying conflict?[11]

HOW EARTH GOT ITS *POLIS*

These questions point out big gaps in our answers to the urban conundrum that wealth accumulation alone cannot fill. Luckily, the Goddess's Hypothesis about sunshine and politics plugs these gaps copiously. In general, *politics* is the answer to all shortcomings of economics, and in the matter of city birth, this is maximally so. When we increased the size of our habitats we not only grew the power of our proximate numbers and overall wealth, we also increased the potential influence of persuasive ideas, charismatic personalities, and large politicized networks or alliances that could become the nuclei of social movements and governing institutions. Too often we could also increase the power of violence, notably that delivered by proximate humans wielding weapons. With all of that power, city dwellers could also secure greater energy harvests from settlements outside the city while cushioning themselves against bad times, such as when Earth, Sun, and mighty rivers refused to deliver energy required for human power. Early city-builders left much evidence that acquiring at least some of these forms of influence was a crucial incentive for the otherwise arduous business of city-building. The myth of Inanna's riverboat and the Warka Vase are good examples of this evidence, but archaeological ruins from many cities and their hinterlands amply support the same point: people who built cities did so to amplify their power – in many different ways – on Earth.

How did early city dwellers exercise this power? In far more ways than archaeologists – seduced by the monumental ruins of authoritarian states and empires – originally thought. Early urban governing institutions were as varied as the cities they served and as diverse as the pre-city governing traditions their inhabitants brought into cities. Governance also changed over time, likely amidst complex conflicts. The evidence is sparse, but there is enough to suggest that, in addition to enabling centuries of autocratic rule, cities often allowed us to share urban power more equitably, to use it against tyranny or in tyranny's shadow, and sometimes to wield it without assistance from a state at all.

At Uruk, the massive ruins of two temples at the center of the city, the city's immense surrounding walls, and extensive irrigation systems in the countryside indicate that the city likely came under the rule of religious or secular elites for at least some periods during the latter half of the 3000s BCE. No matter how authoritarian this "city-state" became, Uruk's governing institutions almost certainly had a complicated backstory that twisted and turned in tune with the elusive rhythms by which the city amplified the power of human knowledge through its temples. In the riverboat myth, the first characters to disembark at the Lapis Lazuli Quay were a dozen types of specialized priests and priestesses bearing new holy shrines for the city – along with "godship" itself. This is a plausible beginning to the story, for early cities and temples very often made each other. Long before cities, people built large gathering places where they could seek the support of the gods to help negotiate cosmic uncertainties. The fact that early cities so often sprang up around shrines and temples suggests that such large gatherings of devotees mattered to the business of expanding and concentrating our settlements. In Uruk, such buildings included Inanna's Temple in the monumental Eanna District, and the White Temple, the predecessor of all Mesopotamian ziggurats. By the late 3000s, these buildings dwarfed all others. The word ziggurat means "to build high" – to create monumental structures that took city dwellers' breath away. In Egypt, similar structures included the temple of the Sun-God Ra in Heliopolis (Sun City). In the Americas, it was the first pyramid–plaza complexes at Caral. In China, it was the square temple at China's Erlitou. Such temples often demarcated the first urban "downtowns," a sign urban theorists call "nucleation": the creation of smaller, denser, central districts that were more important to the city as a whole than other districts were. The various designs of temples – ziggurat, pyramid-and-plaza, or square-walled temple precinct – could set the tone for traditions of city planning in their regions that lasted for millennia. Because such acts of city-building and temple-building required enormous powers of coordination, the assumption, quite right in many cases, is that some kind of governing authority found ways to seize much of the power that accumulated in a city into its own hands.[12]

Still, all great temples began as small places, and they could grow and diminish in size over time. In Uruk the twin temples likely grew on the site of two neighboring Ubaid villages that swelled into each other. At first, Uruk's temples were about the same size as a typical house, but over the course of the 3000s BCE, they grew on average fifteen times larger or more. How then did these places accumulate power? Inanna tells us that the "art of power" she delivered at Uruk consisted of a grab bag of various "arts of speech" – including words that were "forthright," "slanderous," and "adorning" all at once. Was she saying that her priests engaged in propaganda – lies of state designed to dupe the people while priests hoarded the city's power? Priests did very likely organize great processions like the one on the Warka Vase: powerful human rivers flowing in awe upwards to the high temple through wide surrounding open spaces, festooned with fluttering pennants. Did such collective acts of devotion literally undress these worshippers of any conflicting self-interest and reengineer them as loyal subjects of cult rule?[13]

That story, like the vase, is probably too smooth by far. The fact is: building a city did indeed involve an existential gamble for all city dwellers – and for many surrounding villagers and foragers too. It was possible for large communities of people to share both hope and apprehension about the wisdom of founding a city – including city dwellers heightened dependence on distant farmers and an uncertainly flowing river – for all the basics of life. The cult of Inanna thus may in fact have allowed many larger urban interests to converge somewhat. Various groups in the city and beyond may well have organized themselves along lines of mutual obligation to help build the temple, feed the priests, and selflessly engage in big processions that also added to the city's religious prestige beyond its walls.

Coerced or voluntary, goddess worship could set other forces in motion among diverse people that actually did enhance the efficiency of the city's surrounding solar-energy harvesting grid. At Uruk, temple minders may have negotiated with villagers at greater and greater distances away from the city – or forced them – to engage in new experiments in agriculture. They may have called upon old voluntary labor sharing systems in villages – or they may have cajoled, hired, or enslaved laborers, some of them possibly desperate refugees – to dig irrigation ditches that diverted water from the Euphrates to the fields. Whether under the supervision of prominent villagers or officials deputized by the temple, thousands of people set to work increasing the size of fields, then reshaped them as long, slightly sloped rectangles. That way, water could flow from the ditches dug along the highest edge of the field to crops lower down. Such fields could also be turned with efficient ox-pulled plows, because the ox teams had to make fewer awkward U-turns in order to turn far more soil – thus offsetting the fact that such teams also required more grain to operate. Whether by convincing economic argument or by compulsion, wheat output exploded in fields like this near Uruk – at least during the good seasons depicted on the Warka Vase. More people could leave the villages to join Uruk's diverse, specialized artisan class. Soon new bronze-smiths forged harder plowshares, and leatherworkers used the skins of deceased oxen to strengthen the harnesses for plow-teams made of living ones. Agricultural labor further diversified itself along with other earlier food-producing professions. Orchardists expanded plantations of date palms for Uruk's dessert plates. Ranchers raised more oxen. Shepherds watched over larger flocks of sheep, whether owned by the temple or not, growing more wool to clothe more people in the city, thanks to the city's many spinners and weavers, typically women.[14]

Whether exaggerated through propaganda or actually experienced as wide-spread improvement in life, the temple could take credit for prosperity and diminished vulnerability to flood and drought. New institutions could come into being with still more attributes of a city-state, including the power to induce very large populations to pay taxes – another activity the Warka Vase so elegantly depicts as a religious or civic duty. The fact that religious leaders typically built granaries next to temples and hired assistants to run them is another signal that cities – defined by accretions of designed, built, and inhabited space – could help incubate states, defined by the capture of various increments of human power in institutional forms. Again, an ethic of mutuality could co-exist in fluctuating balance with compulsion. Large centralized granaries could dispense food as payment to a growing class of laborers, some living in the city, many living elsewhere in the hinterland. Freed from farm-work, they could devote their time and bodily energy as stone quarriers, clay-pit-diggers, and suppliers of wood needed to feed the massive kilns that made especially hard wood-fired bricks. Others became construction workers – once again possibly induced by mutual obligations or by coercion and enslavement – to pile millions of those bricks on top of each other and mortar them into urban structures, including Uruk's soon massive surrounding walls. Villages and the temple's farms also fed skilled city-dwelling craftspeople capable of fashioning astonishing adornments, such as the beautiful cone mosaics of the Temple of Inanna; later these artisans learned how to inlay gems like lapis lazuli. Those material adornments reinforced the "adorned speech" of the priests, adding material propaganda value or a genuinely shared sense of pride in the breath-taking temples themselves and the high regard or envy they inspired from other cities in the region.[15]

From there, other forms of urban power could accumulate in states, either supporting increasingly authoritarian forms of rule or, say, encouraging rotating councils of priests who consulted with representatives from various urban and rural communities. Either way, to monitor tax receipts and labor obligations, urban authorities built the first clerk's offices and record-filing rooms – another pair of urban inventions requiring larger, settlement-nucleating built structures. Those office buildings, the home of the earliest state bureaucracies, in turn gave shelter to still another, even more Earth-shattering form of urban knowledge-power – one that some scholars attribute to Uruk's Temple of Inanna itself in about 3200 BCE – the power of the written word. Writing, in one telling of the story, allowed scribes hired by the temple elites to strip anonymous, naked citizens even further down, re-inscribing their human worth as so many ledger entries on clay tablets that detailed tax payments received and debts owed by every one of the city's inhabitants. Or, such records could also help guarantee the efficient and more equitable distribution of grain doles, thus rewarding the lowliest builders of the city for the power that ultimately derived from their labors.[16]

Lastly, of course, temple bureaucracies could translate command of Sun, Earth, river, and food stored in the granaries directly into state violence, by relieving more farm workers of their backbreaking obligations and instead putting weapons – also made by local urban artisans with help from specialized ore-miners in the hinterlands – into their hands. The symbolic gatehouse that loomed behind Inanna on the Warka Vase hinted at the type of built spaces that would be required: city walls designed to deter armies from enemy cities, made of many bricks fashioned by many farmers turned into bricklayers. Not all early cities had defensive walls, but at Uruk they were linked with a charismatic god-king, Gilgamesh. Whether or not he ever existed, the city walls surely helped Uruk spread its massive influence across Sumer, into Iran, and throughout Mesopotamia (Chapter 2).[17]

According to the story of the Holy *Mē*, the "noble enduring crown," the "throne of kingship," the "noble scepter," and numerous sorts of weapons disembarked from Inanna's riverboat alongside the first city-building priests and priestesses. Yet at Uruk, we only have ambiguous evidence that a priestly caste declared themselves kings – or, as elsewhere, ceded the city-state's power to armed groups or cavalries that originated from outside the city. Conversely, some written evidence, plus the relatively open structure of the city's earlier temples, do hint toward periods when more cooperative or consultative forms of power sharing might have risen to the fore. That said, urban "order" such as that depicted on

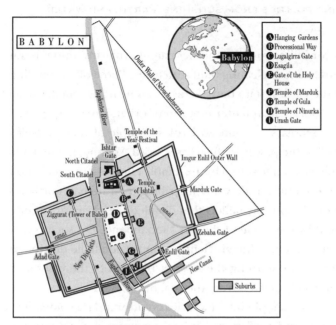

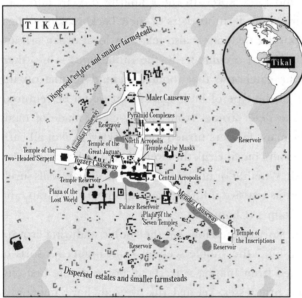

Map 1.1. A Tale of Four Urban Polities

Early cities mirrored their diverse governing institutions. Babylon's authoritarian state invested energy from the Tigris River into enormous temples, palaces, processional avenues, triple city walls, and the fearsome Ishtar gate. In the Maya city of Tikal, the authorities marked their power with high temples, platforms, and ceremonial causeways, but rulers did not monopolize collection of rainwater. A contested state is reflected in the city's lack of walls as well as a diverse built fabric punctuated by reservoirs that spread far into the surrounding rainforest. The layout of ancient Athens pivots upon the "democratic" meeting places of the Agora, the *boule* or city council, and the Pnyx Hill. But dependence on grain delivered by ship from far-off river valleys led to empire and authoritarian rule, exemplified by the Parthenon complex on

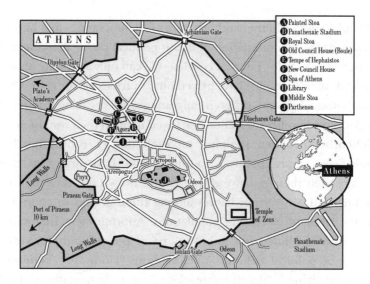

Map key for Athens:
- Ⓐ Painted Stoa
- Ⓑ Panathenaic Stadium
- Ⓒ Royal Stoa
- Ⓓ Old Council House (Boule)
- Ⓔ Tempe of Hephaistos
- Ⓕ New Council House
- Ⓖ Spa of Athens
- Ⓗ Library
- Ⓘ Middle Stoa
- Ⓙ Parthenon

ATHENS

Achamian Gate
Dipylon Gate
Plato's Academy
Agora
Diochares Gate
Acropolis
Areopogus
Pnyx
Odeon
Long Walls
Piraean Gate
Port of Piraeus
10 km
Long Walls
Ionian Gate
Odeon
Temple of Zeus
Panathenaic Stadium
Athens

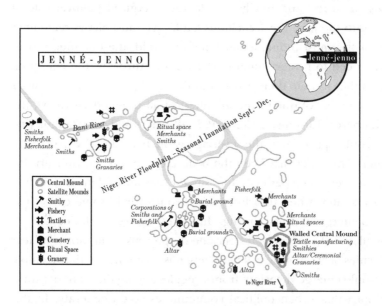

JENNÉ-JENNO

Jenné-jenno

Bani River
Smiths
Fisherfolk
Merchants
Smiths
Smiths
Granaries
Ritual space
Merchants
Smiths
Niger River Floodplain—Seasonal Inundation Sept.—Dec.

Map key for Jenné-jenno:
- Central Mound
- Satellite Mounds
- Smithy
- Fishery
- Textiles
- Merchant
- Cemetery
- Ritual Space
- Granary

Corporations of Smiths and Fisherfolk
Merchants
Burial ground
Fisherfolk
Merchants
Merchants
Ritual spaces
Burial grounds
Altar
Walled Central Mound
Textile manufacturing
Smithies
Altar/Ceremonial
Granaries
Altar
to Niger River
Smiths

Map 1.1. (cont) the *Acropolis* and by the city walls that ran between the city and the harbor ten kilometers away. At West Africa's Jenné-jenno, various artisan, merchant, and religious groups built a "clustered urban complex" consisting of seventy mounds punctuating the flood plain of the Niger River. There is a diverse center, but archaeologists who study the city doubt whether the word "state" is even the right word for the "heterarchical" governing institutions that built the city. Sources: Babylon: Richard Overy, *The Complete History of the World*, 9th ed. (London: Times Books, 2015) p. 80; Tikal: William Grey, *Tikal: Handbook of Ancient Maya Ruins* (Philadelphia, PA: University Museum, University of Pennsylvania, 1967); Jenné-jenno: Roderick McIntosh, *The Ancient Middle Niger* (Cambridge: Cambridge University Press), p. 187, adapted with permission of the author.
Maps created by Joe LeMonnier, https://mapartist.com.

the Warka Vase – whether authoritarian or "democratic" – may have been less important a manifestation of urban political power than was a city's aroused tendency for political conflict. We can only speculate about the terrific dramas that must have played out as various village councils, new urban artisanal groups, different migrant groups speaking different languages, or even religious factions gathered to build their own homes and neighborhoods, often stepping on each other's concentrated turf. Surely, even more political conflict would have arisen as temple minders used their putative divine connections (and their impressive buildings) to win various battles among these groups to control land and the labor of increasing populations. Appropriately, Inanna's gifts to city-hood included not only the "art of power" and weapons, but a range of political behavior ranging from "kindness," "counseling," "judgment-giving," "deceit," "treachery," and "lamentations" to "the kindling of strife," and finally, to add the energized political role of farmers into the mix, the "rebellious land." We must always remember that even the most monumental building could attest as much to its builders' need to protect themselves from overthrow by the energized crowds of the city as to their real accumulation of power. Many centuries later a counselor of one of the mightiest of all pre-modern rulers, the Tang Emperor Taizong of China (626–49 CE) used a metaphor that Inanna could appreciate: "the sovereign is the boat, and the people are the water. The water may keep the boat afloat, but it can overturn it." That advice remained perfectly apposite for "absolutist" kings more than 1,000 years later, when they lost their thrones (or in some cases their heads) to energized urban throngs during the age of revolution.[18]

Not all ancient urban states became despotisms at all, nor is it clear that all cities birthed "states" at all. There was no guarantee that a temple clique would emerge victorious from struggles among the many networks and groups that urban political communities could generate. In this regard, the enormous Central Mexican city of Teotihuacan has received much attention, since there is evidence that at some point around 300 CE, its people burned down the city's massive pyramidal temple and reinvested the region's wealth into neighborhoods for commoners. As archaeologists there continue to assess that evidence, others ask us to look beyond places like Mesopotamia, China, or the Inka and Aztec empires where cities served authoritarian states most faithfully. If we look past the big monuments, or if we dig more evidence from cities without temples or royal palaces, these scholars ask us to imagine that a more fluid and accountable form of polity – they call it "heterarchy" – was an even more widespread generator of urban birth than hierarchy. In the Indus and Ganges Valleys, and in West Africa, Greece, and Italy, inequalities of power were less sharp, or at least far more contested for significant periods of time.[19]

For example, the builders of Mohenjo Daro, the largest of the Indus Valley cities, did exercise enough central control to lay out the city streets on meticulous right angles, and they developed some of the most sophisticated of ancient drinking-water, sewage, and storm-water management systems, all excellent means of blunting such divine punishments as floods, storms, and disease. A hierarchy is also amply detectable in the difference between small and large houses, and between most of the city's neighborhoods and a raised "High Town." Yet no arrogant temple complex came into being at Mohenjo Daro, as at Uruk. Harappa, the second-largest city in the ancient Indus region, contains even less evidence of authoritarian rule. Elites and other groups seem to have built some kind of coordinating institutions – tense and conflict-filled no doubt – to run these cities. Similarly, the first cities in the Ganges River were surrounded by huge walls, but archaeologists have discounted the idea that authoritarian warlords were responsible for them. Rather, they may have come into being as communal, neighborhood-organized efforts of flood control (like Jericho's much earlier, far smaller, walls), and only later morphed into machines of war.[20]

The phrase "heterarchy" comes to us from archaeologists working in West Africa. In the Inland Delta of the Niger River, inhabitants of ancient Jenné-jenno walled a large central urban space, but most of the city was built on seventy or so separate settlements spread irregularly along some thirteen kilometers of the Bani River. When the Bani and the Niger flooded most of the region from September to November each year, Jenné-jenno became an archipelago of urban islands. Members of all occupational groups, including religious and commercial specialists, seem to have maintained facilities in the largest central island of the archipelago, perhaps indicating a council of some sort, but there was no monumental temple or palace at Jenné-jenno. Each of the outlying islands was an exclusive space for one or at most three of the city's groups, suggesting that even lowly fisher-folk and smiths sustained an independent political (and religious) base within the politics of the archipelago as a whole. Jenné-jeno was "self-organized"; no state directed its construction.[21]

Much more precise evidence of the unpredictability of urban polities survives from the cities of Athens and Rome, whose inhabitants famously deposed authoritarian rulers – at least for a time – creating what Athenians called *demokratia* ("People Power") and the Romans a *res publica* ("matters of the people"). Monumental buildings like those on Athens's Parthenon, situated on the "High City" (Acropolis), and Rome's Temple of Jupiter on the Capitoline Hill correctly suggest that the rule of priests and tyrants repeatedly punctuated popular rule, eventually abolishing *demokratia* altogether. However, the cities also contained spaces designed for collective decision-making by peoples' elected representatives such as Athens's famous Agora, its town council (the *Boule*, housed in the *Bouleuterion*), and the Pnyx, a Parliament that met in a natural amphitheater built into a hillside overlooking the city – with a fine view of any despotic dealings on the Acropolis. Rome's forum contained a *rostrum* that faction leaders could use to entice new members. The city's wealthiest residents could represent their competing interests in a Senate building. Elected "tribunes" supposedly represented the "*populus Romanum*" as a whole, and all members of that *populus* could technically seek impartial justice in magnificent law courts that surrounded the forum. These cities gave the English language many of its political terms. Sadly, "democracy" and "republic" are not the only ones. Both cities' political communities also provided fertile grounds for characters that left us with words like "oligarch," "despot," "dictator," "tyrant," "emperor," "authoritarian," "absolutist," "totalitarian," "charismatic," and even the Latin–Greek hybrid "populist demagogue." Such words contain many early lessons on the power of urban political life and its volatile consequences, but also lessons on the sheer fragility of democracy from its own urban infancy on.[22]

POWER AND THE CITY

So, now we know how Earth got its *polis*. It came from the Sun, from Earth's own planetary dynamics, and from spaces that humans designed, built, and inhabited to use natural energy to amplify our own power. By design, those power-building spaces were at once more extensive (in order to harvest more energy) and more compact (to build more power). All were larger, more populous, and more numerous. The compact spaces grew nuclei, divided themselves internally, and distinguished themselves from the more dispersed places by some kind of boundary – often with hard walls, later increasingly by transition zones that were more diffuse. The people living inside the compact spaces were more specialized, more diverse, and more likely to be strangers to one another. They interacted more, cooperated and clashed in increasingly complex ways, and thus transformed their numbers and proximity into institutions, wealth, knowledge, weapons, and technologies that amplified human power over other humans, over the extended parts of our own habitat, and ultimately over the Sun, Earth, and water that made cities possible in the first place. That augmented human power is the sign that our compact, growing, differentiated, diverse, specialized, anonymous, and complex spaces were becoming a city. [23]

How much power, and how many power-generating acts of building and habitation, mark the exact moment when one of our compact settlements became a "true city"? The answer to this "quantity question" has remained elusive to urban theorists ... and how could it be otherwise? Like other phenomena – including "states" – whose basic ingredients are difficult to measure and whose mutual combustion takes the form of an accumulating complexity of interactions, cities and the power they unleash defy any effort to mark a tipping point, even as they become unmistakably *urban* along the way. Once various human acts of city making allow us to exercise power through movements, institutions, wealth, weapons, technologies, and knowledge, the direction of our politics no longer depends on the spatial design or the social dynamics of the city alone. Each of these city-enabled conduits of human power can lead us along nearly infinite possible pathways of their own, affecting each other and bending time and space in ways too many to predict. Among the spaces we transform while exerting these forms of power, moreover, are the very cities (and the larger urban worlds) that amplified our power in the first place. For these reasons, urban history, like human history more generally, is foundationally multi-causal. It also switches cause and effect continuously and it defies any explanation that isolates or privileges the transformative force of any one political outcome of city making over any other. (Note: this caution also applies to understandably tempting contemporary explanations based on the paramount power of global capitalism).[24]

For a truly useful urban theory, I prefer the story of Inanna on the bucking riverboat to the story of Inanna perched serenely on the top tier of the Warka Vase. True: cities *can* help us create states, wealth-amassing systems, and mythic-goddess-revering ideologies. They can help us seize solar energy from the remarkable Euphrates Valleys of the Earth and transfer it into grand upward flowing processions of naked supplicants toward the ziggurat. Cities can help sustain self-aggrandizing, long-lasting "systems" and "orders" – whether "urban" ones, "imperial" ones, "world" ones, "geopolitical" ones or even "global capitalist" ones. In the same way, cities can also create other cities, lending plausibility to the idea that, in the absence of a defining threshold or outcome, cities are best defined as a "process" of urbanization – or even of "planetary urbanization." After all, the Urban Planet we live on today is testament to the fact that cities have allowed us to create far more city overall than they have destroyed. But none of such "processes" are set in stone. As Inanna warned us at the Lapis Lazuli Quay, cities come into being through both creation and destruction, and they can come to a catastrophic end in the exact same way. Ask the millions of people who lost their entire urban world, after centuries of assuming that Rome, or Changan, or Tikal, or Angkor Wat would last forever. Ask ourselves today – we who stand to lose much of our Urban Planet in what could be an eye-blink of global urban history. Unidirectional "processes" are just as inadequate as uni-causal explanations in telling the whole life-story of Earthopolis. They strip the clothes off too many human experiences, suck the blood from too many epic stories of conflict, flatten too many heart-stopping, plot-twisting moments of contingency, and ignore too many showdown moments of disruption that cities have helped us lace into the 6,000-year biography of our Urban Planet. As biographers of Earthopolis, our job is to tell its life story, not in smooth celebratory alabaster, but in a way that accounts for all of its surviving glories, all of its ordinary moments, and all of the many-*many*-jagged ruins of cities we have left behind. Cities are just plain *messy* things, by their own truest self-definition and by the vagaries of the very power they allow us to wield, and we need to understand them as such. Only as such can we pay adequate reverence to the existential chanciness of Inanna's river-boat gamble.

"Politics." Before moving on with the mess that is the biography of Earthopolis, let us pause for moment at the mess-creating nub of the matter. To the ancient Greeks, the word *polis* meant a self-governing "city state." Already in ancient times, though, as *polis* gave birth to *politics*, it took on the broader job of denoting the actions of any political community – including but not limited to any state or governing institutions that the community established, and including all contested claims that community placed on itself and any of its institutions. Still, as *politics* evolved it never lost its connection to *polis*, the city, correctly conveying the sense that human power and contest took different dimensions in cities than elsewhere. It is in that expansive yet still city-linked sense of politics that I add the suffix *polis* to the proper name "Earth" to generate a name for the only Urban Planet we know of: Earthopolis.

Indeed, as foundationally "political animals" – as the places that aroused humans' most powerful forms of political animality – cities did not hoard all of their pent-up power inside city walls alone, nor within a single larger space encompassed by a city and its hinterland. Cities, as their earliest builders well knew, could also empower humans to take complex, compound actions on far larger scales than those required to build cities themselves. With city-power, we also could build far larger and more dispersed habitats than were strictly required to supply cities. We could therefore leave behind far larger impacts on spaces beyond our own. And, we could face far larger consequences. The best and earliest evidence we have of this urban-enhanced political "output" comes from the ruins of some of the earliest cities. Relatively few of these cities were "city states" whose human power only allowed them to govern themselves. Most of the power we generated in cities was designed to serve a much more ferocious political animal, one whose name comes to us from the war-hungry inhabitants of the city of Rome: the *imperium*. In the most supercharged of our newborn crucibles of cityhood and political energy, we mixed still more Sunshine with still more politics and got empire.

CHAPTER 2

Igniting Empire

CITIES AND EMPIRES: SOME BASIC RULES

Of all large-scale actions that cities have allowed humans to perform, arguably the most consequential for the biography of Earthopolis were acts of imperial conquest and administration. To generate enough power for empire, city dwellers needed to transform enough natural energy from their river valleys (or other water sources) and from their large, energized polities to create armies (or navies, later airforces and other military instruments) capable of forcing other cities and their hinterlands to accept the conqueror's rule.

Not all urban political communities accumulated enough power in their governing institutions to become empires. The largest, longest lasting empires were born in river-powered cities, but not all river cities produced large empires. Authoritarian military dynasties, starting with those that rose to power in Mesopotamian city-states, possessed a built-in "momentum toward empire." Yet that formula was not universal either, for "democratic" Athens developed a fierce imperial streak, as, of course, did "republican" Rome, where imperialism led to tyranny, not the other way around. It is also very important to distinguish between imperial conquest and administration. Some of the largest acts of imperial conquest did not require cities at all: inhabitants of small nomadic camps in the Asian steppes and mountains could come together in large clan gatherings, and use the power of their herd animals – horses above all – to storm dozens or even hundreds of cities, including some of the largest in the world. So could the inhabitants of hardscrabble coastal villages along the Mediterranean, in Scandinavia, or along the East Asian coast. They could build swift attack boats that could destroy and loot cities at will, either from the sea or far up river valleys. For these nomadic raiders and "sea peoples," however, imperial administration was another thing. Actually sustaining an empire for long periods required a state powerful enough to maintain a standing army using bureaucracies capable of collecting a steady volume of taxes from the hinterlands. Such bureaucracies required large office buildings and storehouses, forcing conquerors who wanted their imperial rule to last – that is, to found a dynasty – to live in cities. More precisely, they needed to establish an imperial capital city whose bureaucrats could extend administrative rule across the extensive realms that also defined an empire. Much later, many of these same rules about cities and administration applied to "nation states."[1]

The reverse is also true. Empires transformed cities – as well as their hinterlands and their larger surrounding urban birth-worlds. To run an empire required many acts of urban redesign, construction, destruction, rebuilding, and habitation. Capitals typically grew dramatically in size and became home to higher concentrations of the empire's population. Capitals were also home to many more specialized, diverse, and energized people, activities, and buildings. Their monuments to imperial power – palaces, temples, and public squares for the dissemination of imperial propaganda – were larger, so these cities were more sharply nucleated and often segregated. Imperial cities typically required better, harder outer boundaries as well, for city walls served both as offensive weapons of imperial shock and awe and as defensive weapons that kept conquered cities or peoples from taking imperial counteractions of their own. Indeed, the growth and replication of cities – urbanization – was also essential to empire. No empire could function without a burgeoning archipelago of provincial capitals, local administrative posts, further-flung colonial cities, and city-like military camps and naval bases. Empire building required dispersing such city-building projects, subordinating them with structures devoted to the empire's armed or administrative power or flattering their inhabitants with capital-like improvements, in either way aligning subordinate polities with the dictates of the imperial capital. Extensions of the built environment beyond cities were just as important as increasing concentration. To project imperial power over long distances required enormously labor-intensive projects involved in the construction of transport and communication infrastructure, notably roads and canals. To protect vital agricultural hinterlands – which had to be extended as well – projects of wall building were also sometimes necessary in places distant from cities, often stretching along the entirety of an empire's borders.

As empires depended upon cities and transformed them, they also transformed the geography of the earliest urban birth-worlds. In many cases, emperors created polities that stretched across previously separate worlds, also amplifying urban economic and cultural activities that crossed the boundaries in between – as well as their impact beyond. The Persian Empire and the empire of Alexander the Great, for example, successfully joined the urban worlds of Persia with those of the Indus Valley, Mesopotamia, Egypt, and the Eastern Mediterranean. Rome merged many of these same ancient urban birth-worlds with somewhat younger ones in North Africa and Europe, reaching as far as Great Britain. Under the force of Chinese dynasties ruling from the capital city Changan, the urban birth-world of the Yellow River Valley colonized new urban zones along the Yangtze and Pearl Rivers, and in Central Asia and other parts of East and Southeast Asia. Urban birth-zones in South Asia expanded similarly, as did those in the Inka-ruled Andes, in Toltec and Aztec Mesoamerica, and in parts of East and West Africa at later dates.

It is true that pre-modern empires, even those built on copious geo-solar energy harvested in Cities of Rivers, never created a contiguous, truly planetary, Urban Planet during pre-modern times. The birth of a global Earthopolis would have to wait until the discovery of the connected World Ocean during the 1400s and 1500s CE. However, in the much-expanded urban worlds that pre-modern empires did create, large-scale commercial and cultural activities and large-scale environmental impacts often outlived the rise and fall of empires themselves, even the collapse of their largest capitals. Empires were so important to the creation of an Urban Planet precisely because they augmented the realms of human action, habitat, and impact – and thus the realm of consequence – beyond the realm of imperial power itself.

THE SPARKS OF *IMPERIUM*

Striking the first sparks of *Imperium* was a feat typically reserved for people who gained the most power in urban polities, whether strictly hierarchical or not. It should be no surprise that the city states of Mesopotamia were the first to contemplate the prospect. As powerful temples emerged from long dramas of Sumerian urban politics, they probably fell short of widespread territorial conquest and administration, but as early as 3500 BCE they were apparently able to combine their power over the grain storage warehouse with their control of the temple spectacle to extend their political, economic, and cultural influence into today's Iran and throughout Mesopotamia. They created this "Uruk World System," as one archaeologist called it, by setting in motion at least two large-scale urban industries: wool cloth and cheap, disposable, bevel-edged clay pots that they likely used to ration shares of barley to their populace. They persuaded local riverboat owners and pack-animal drovers to become what we know as merchants, trading Sumerian cloth for high-end building materials and adornments unavailable locally. These included cedar and other exotic lumber from places like today's Lebanon, stone from the mountains, and gemstones like lapis lazuli – the priests' favorite – available only from mines 2,000 kilometers away in what is today northern Afghanistan. Uruk's distinctive material culture spread widely. Massive piles of Uruk-style potsherds, the ancient equivalent of today's unrecycled single-use plastic waste dumps, have been unearthed from the 3000s BCE-level of city ruins across Mesopotamia. Archaeologists have found whole neighborhoods of Uruk-style houses in the midst of contrasting architectural settings at Tel Brak and Hamoukar 500 kilometers to the north of Uruk, suggesting colonial outposts. A few smaller, isolated Uruk-like settlements in central Mesopotamia might be waystations along regular north–south transport routes – early pieces of the larger, extra-urban, built infrastructure required for bureaucrats and merchants to remain in contact with each other at a time when humans, pack animals, and riverboats were the main form of long-distance communication and transport. Meanwhile, the temples of Uruk grew, as Sumer's states poured agricultural surplus and export revenues into new monumental building projects on the ruins of older ones deemed insufficiently glorious. The builders of these powerhouses gilded them with ever more lavish displays of imported wood, stone, ceramic mosaic, and gems, raising them ever higher toward the very heavens, and striking renewed awe among the god-fearing across the region – for the ziggurats were indeed visible from far away across the flat plains of Sumer.[2]

How much did Uruk's influence also rest on armed imperial conquest? We may never know for sure. Someone's army destroyed the walls of Hamoukar in a hail of clay bullets, launched from slings, as early as 3500 BCE, but we do not know whose bullets they were. Whatever the case, by stimulating large-scale movements of people and things throughout the region, Sumer's priests and its energized merchants and artisans developed the technical, the institutional, and even the built infrastructure needed for a succession of urban-based conquering empires in the region during the 2000s BCE. Copper from today's Turkey and tin from other distant locations both made their way to the humming specialized craft-shops in Mesopotamian cities. There, unknown metallurgists, possibly working in the forges of Uruk itself, ushered in the Bronze Age, named after the hard, moldable metal alloy that could be fashioned into more lethal weapons than earlier Stone Age cities had been able to produce. Other Bronze Age artisan-shops tinkered with the clunky ox carts of the time, experimenting with lighter wheels, eventually perfecting the lightweight, two-spoke-wheeled war chariot. Horses also made their way to the region around 2000 BCE from the nomadic camps of the Asian Steppes, by way of urban-anchored transport routes, to enlarged stable complexes in the cities and surrounding breeding estates.[3]

Once harnessed together, horses and bronze chariots – the most deadly of ancient machines of war – required new institutions that could use them effectively. Urban administrators turned their energized polities from organizing religious processions toward the project of organizing massive armies and cavalries, and warrior kings emerged, probably from armed communities (possibly descended from nomads) that rivaled the priesthood, to lead them. New multitudes had to leave the farms to become soldiers, and farms had to become more productive to feed them, stimulating new bronze-based plowing and threshing technologies and larger-scale irrigation works. The more extensive conquests that armies made possible also increased the size of armies themselves, as their generals captured more recruits and enslaved more people. Cities too could grow when engorged by war-refugees and forced exiles, their makeshift houses spilling beyond their walls – the first peripheral shanty-towns. Kings, ascending to power as priests themselves or rivals to them, used armies to seize the temples, turning them into accessory institutions whose mission now included the ritual anointment of kings themselves into semi-divine figures, as outright gods-on-Earth, and as mythic founders of cities.[4]

Over the course of the 2000s BCE, palaces, the god-kings' new homes, overshadowed the priests' temples, the granaries, and the clerks' offices atop the ziggurats in Mesopotamia. Palaces also crowned imperial monumental complexes of many styles in each of the world's most authoritarian urban archipelagos. Archaeologists do not know what the capital city of world history's first certain conquering emperor, Sargon the Great of Akkad (2334–2284 BCE), looked like, or even where it was. Yet his distant successor as conqueror of all Mesopotamia, Sennacherib (705–681 BCE) took the region's ensuing tradition of imperial architectural hubris to new heights. His "Palace Without Rival" at Nineveh combined inaccessibility – it was tucked behind a series of walls – with unmissable visibility, high atop the city's steep Kuyunjik Hill. Sennacherib drove a wide Royal Road from the city gates to the base of the palace gates to guarantee that his home received maximum admiration. He even decreed harsh penalties for anyone who extended their own ordinary building into his road: any such miscreant was to be "impaled upon a stake upon his own house." In acts like these, ancient emperors set the tone for cities', and empires', long complicity with authoritarian power.[5]

Even larger labor forces, enslaved and not, were required to build another key characteristic of imperial cities: their massive defensive walls, gates, and bastions. Whether or not Uruk ever became a conquering imperial capital in its own right, its walls were enormous by 3000 BCE. Ten kilometers in circumference, punctuated by 900 rounded bastions, the walls consisted of 100 million fire-baked bricks. Admirers called these walls a "cloudbank resting on the ground." Much later, at Nineveh, Sennacherib out-built Uruk, boasting that "the wall and the outer wall" of his capital rose "mountain high," thus well deserving of their names "The Wall Whose Splendor Overwhelms the Enemy" and "The Wall That

Terrifies Evil." Emperor Nebuchadrezzar II (605–562 BCE) of Babylon built the city 's three-part wall system (Map 1.1). The walls were fifteen meters in height, sixty kilometers long, and so thick that war chariots could scurry around on top of them, sowing fright among would-be besiegers. Foreshadowing the hydrocarbon age of cities, the walls of Babylon were mortared together with bitumen, possibly mined from an outcrop of what we now call the Kirkuk Oilfields of Iraq. Anyone who wanted to enter Babylon did so through the magnificent Ishtar Gate, with its millions of shiny blue-glazed bricks sculpted into fierce-looking drag-ons, bulls, and lions, a fine tribute to the goddess of war (Ishtar was Inanna's name in Babylonian). Once inside, a visitor's first sight was the ninety-meter-high, seven-tiered ziggurat, today best known as the "Tower of Babel" – "The House of the Frontier of Heaven and Earth."[6]

CHANGAN AND ROME

In China, similar dynamics over thousands of years helped develop the "Imperial City" or "Forbidden City" palace complexes of Chinese cap-itals, with their massive square outer walls. In 192 BCE, the Han Emperor Hui-di crowed that he had press-ganged over 320,000 slaves and laborers from as far away as 350 kilometers over the course of three years to ram together the twenty-five-kilometer earthen defensive walls around his capital at Changan. The course of the Bi River (a tributary of the Yellow River) forced Hui to remove a diagonal slice from the top of the trad-itional square plan, but he was quick to explain that the city's lopsided shape made it nothing less than an earthly mirror of the Big Dipper, the peak of the heavens. Naturally enough, Hui's palace occupied the pos-ition of the North Star.[7]

Changan and Rome, its contemporary on the other end of the Old World supercontinent, became the ancient world's imperial capitals *par excellence*. The two gloriously appointed imperial cities exemplify the importance of monumental architecture in forging empires. Hui's imperial residences, the "Endless Palace" (Weiyang) and "Palace of Perpetual Happiness" (Changle) conveyed imperial power in sheer size and impregnability (the Endless Palace may have been the largest ever built). The importance of outer walls to the conception of cities in China was such that the Chinese character most commonly used for wall (*cheng*) also came to mean city. Accordingly, the walls around Changan and subsequent Chinese capitals were far thicker than any built anywhere else, a fact that would have momentous importance in the history of warfare many centuries later (Chapter 7). Each gatehouse within the walls was a massive castle in its own right.[8]

As for Imperial Rome, it gave English-speakers not only the word empire (*imperium*), but virtually all the vocabulary Westerners possess about capital cities and monumental architecture, not to mention the word *city* itself (from the Latin *civitas*), and *urban* (from *urbs*). The word *capital* comes from the most important of Rome's seven hills, the Capitoline – crowned with temples (*templa*) dedicated to none other than Jupiter and Juno, the king and queen of the gods themselves. The nearby Palatine Hill is the source of our word for *palace*, reflecting the fact that Rome's emperors built a half-dozen of their increasingly sprawling personal residences on its summit. Between those two hills lay the famous *forum Romanum*, another political word that comes from the Eternal City. Under the Roman Republic (*res publica*), the forum became a symbol of deliberation and democracy, as we know, and the site of a *Senatus* and law courts. After Caesar Augustus overthrew the republic to become Rome's first *imperator*, he and his successors coopted the populist symbolism of the forum for dictatorial aims. Each emperor sought to out-forum each other, first adding monuments and ornaments to the original, then building new *fora* surrounded by imposing government buildings and temples throughout the city center named after themselves and dedicated to their own god-like glory. There they celebrated their imperial conquests on elaborately engraved columns, obelisks, and arches of triumph – named after the gaudy parades (*triumphi*) they organized through the streets of the capital, culminating amidst the throngs that jammed the forum dedicated to their own self-celebration. The *fasces*, an axe whose handle was reinforced by a bundle of bound sticks, figured prominently in this statuary; it symbolized the power of the *populus* of Rome as citizens, again, from *civitas*, a word that fused the political and the urban much like the Greek word *polis*. All of these words later served as roots for modern terms describing various forms of imperialist state institutions.[9]

2.1. Imperial Rome, *c.* 330 CE
The million-plus residents of ancient Rome lived off farms along the Tiber River (upper left) and grain from the Nile. Early kings built the temples of Jupiter and Juno on the Capitoline Hill (upper center). During 500 years of republican rule, public life centered on the forum, with its Senate, courts, and public rostrum. Emperors later built palaces on the Palatine Hill (center left) and "forums" devoted to their own glory (upper right). The Colosseum (foreground) and the Circus Maximus (far left) entertained the city's masses with blood sports and athletics, while aqueducts signaled the benevolence of imperial rule.
Author's photograph of "Plastico di Roma imperiale" at the Museum of Roman Civilization, Rome, Italy.

Capital cities' large buildings and open spaces were not only essential because their splendor glorified the regime. Palaces needed to be large for practical reasons too, above all to house ancient emperors' typically enormous families. These comprised the emperor's many wives, concubines, children, and other relatives, but also thousands of servants and entire detachments of armed palace guards. Women in the Chinese imperial household lived in separate palaces of their own watched over by eunuch guards who underwent castration at an early age to render them trustworthy enough for this purpose. A perhaps more familiar version of this practice came from much later, at the court of the Ottoman Empire in Istanbul, where the women's palaces were called the *harim* ("harem"). This segregated arrangement was meant to subordinate women to men in state affairs and control empresses' and queens' sexuality in order to guarantee truly royal male heirs. However, women used their sexual access to the emperor, or their control over their sons, or loyal armed slaves and eunuchs to extend their influence beyond the gender boundaries of the palace. All of the great ancient empires came under empresses' or queens' full or partial rule at one time or another, especially when royal heirs died, succeeded at too young an age, or were otherwise not up to the task of governing. Palaces also allowed rulers to force prominent aristocratic households to live in the imperial palace itself or in their own palaces in the capital, the better to keep these potential rivals in sight and prevent them from building their own imperial counter-capital back home. Each of these captive families required large retinues, as did a multitude of other high ceremonial officials and priests. Beyond the palace, countless bureaucrats in charge of all branches of the state – taxation, welfare, religious ritual, and the all-consuming business of warfare – all needed offices in which to work, keep their records, and communicate to lower officials throughout the realm (see Map 2.1 inset). Because capital cities were so large, they also required large municipal governments and even small armies of their own, and thus still other large and imposing buildings. Like all cities, capitals made it possible for imperial government to function simply because the state offices in such cities were located close to one another, thus minimizing the effort and expense of the many transactions between them.

For all these reasons, capital cities were always far larger than the rest of the cities in the same empire. Indeed, all of the largest cities in pre-modern world history were imperial capitals. Though urban population figures from this early remain highly speculative, our best estimates tell us that the capital cities of Bronze Age Mesopotamian and Egyptian empires were the first to top 100,000 inhabitants (Babylon may have had twice that under Nebuchadrezzar II), and Chinese capitals reached the 100,000 mark early in the Iron Age. Rome – possibly preceded by its rival, the Greek Pharaoh Cleopatra's capital at Alexandria, Egypt – topped a million during the imperial era, possibly closer to two million. After the conquest of Egypt, Rome's closest contemporary competitors for world's largest city included Han Changan, with somewhere between 250,000 and 400,000, and the Maurya and Gupta imperial capital at Pataliputra (Patna) in the Ganges Valley, which also may have been home to as many as 400,000 people. By 500 CE, Constantinople, the capital of Rome's eastern successor, the Byzantine Empire, had grown to over a half-million; its later rival, the massive circular capital of the Abbasid Islamic Caliphate (750–1258 CE) at Baghdad, likely passed the million mark after about 900 CE. From 600 to 1800 CE, though, the Chinese Sui, Tang, Sung, Yuan, and Ming dynasties repeatedly "out-capitaled" the rest of the world – perhaps only matched for short periods by Seorabeol (Gyeongju), capital of the Silla Empire in Korea, and Kyoto, Japan. The Sui and Tang (589–907 CE) rebuilt Changan as a massive square imperial headquarters several miles from the ruins of the Han city, where it easily passed the million mark (Map. 2.1). The remarkable Song dynasty (960–1279) built another million-plus capital at Kaifeng where they ruled until 1127, when the upstart Jurchen, a people from the Manchurian forests, built up a rival state that destroyed that city – with enormous implications, as we shall see. In retreat southward, the Song proceeded to build yet another million-plus capital at Hangzhou, where they ruled for the next 150 years. Their successors, the Mongol Yüan dynasty (1279–1368) developed the city of Dadu (later Beijing) into a gigantic square imperial capital. The Yüan's successors, the Ming (1368–1644), first ruled from Nanjing (Jinling) – yet another million-plus city – then moved to Beijing, which also quickly passed the million mark again and remained among the largest cities in the world until the present day.[10]

FURNITURE OF ADMINISTRATION

As dominant a role as capitals played in global urban history, they also confirm another reality about empires, namely that they depended on the building, rebuilding, and control of dozens if not hundreds of other cities, usually smaller than the capital but often quite large nonetheless. Domination of other cities was, after all, the first goal of ancient imperial conquerors – for each provided the crucial point of leverage over their surrounding taxable countrysides. Armed siege, or the threat of it, was sometimes necessary to acquire these desirable urban imperial assets, especially if they happened to be capitals of rival empires. Just as effective, though, were offers of protection and some autonomy – or, in Rome's case, partial "citizenship" – in exchange for tax revenues and the draft of soldiers. Despite, or perhaps because of, Rome's deserved reputation for military ruthlessness, its early expansion was far more the result of such supposedly peaceful "alliances," which gave subordinate cities yet another keyword, the title *municipium*, the ancient root of yet another modern urban keyword, "municipality." The Han and every other successive Chinese dynasty made similar arrangements with other would-be rival cities as they slowly and cannily reeled them into the overlordship of their court in the capital.

Both empires also sent loyal colonists and soldiers from the empire's heartland out to the frontiers to found new cities, often in places with little previous urban history. In Rome's case, this practice followed the example of the Phoenicians, Minoans, and Greeks, who founded colonial port towns throughout the Mediterranean, including Marseille, Cadiz, Cartagena, and Lisbon. The Romans absorbed all of these older places – sometimes by recolonization with Roman settlers, and sometimes, as in the case of Phoenician-founded Carthage (near present-day Tunis), by utterly destroying the city during the Punic Wars, then rebuilding it on Roman lines. In the case of the Han, expansion meant founding military outposts and merchant enclaves to the west of Changan along the so-called Silk Road, as well as in the then less-populated southern regions of China, including the Yangtze Valley.[11]

Both the Roman and the Chinese emperors went on to administer their empires through a vast hierarchy of such subordinate cities by reappointing them as provincial capitals. The governors they sent to these cities outfitted them with often only slightly less grandiose versions of the built accoutrements of the capital, including palaces, temples (even ersatz "Capitoline Hills" in some of Rome's provincial cities), theaters, markets, public baths, drainage and sewer systems, and aqueducts. The bureaucratic hierarchy of the Tang (618–907 CE) and Song (960–1279) dynasties required more cities and towns than any other empire of the time (Map 2.1). The very names of these cities reflect a very different understanding of cityhood than the Greeks' concept of *polis*, or independent "city state." Instead, Chinese cities were denoted by their place in an imperial hierarchy. Imperial capitals typically ended in the suffix *-jing* (Beijing, Nanjing) and provincial capitals with *-zhou* (Guangzhou, Suzhou). County prefectures were called *cheng* (the word-root that also means "walled area") and towns without administrative functions were called names ending in -*zhen* (as in Jingdezhen, the famous porcelain-manufacturing city).[12]

If capital cities made imperial rule possible by lessening distances between officials who needed to coordinate their efforts, emperors also required built environments that connected cities – and stretched beyond them – to accomplish the longer-distance tasks that ultimately confirmed the very measure of an empire. From the Assyrians on, ancient and pre-modern emperors focused almost as much energy on road building as on capital city-building. Like capitals, roads performed multiple functions; the words "communication" and "transport" only scratch the surface of their use as instruments to convey power. For imperial commands to travel from the palace to the provinces, their messengers needed roads, and from Sargon onward, emperors graded and compacted the earth into elongated hard surfaces so that these messengers could make their way across landscapes quickly without losing their footing or their sense of direction. The human and animal power involved in this rapid movement required securely built stations along the way, where messengers and horses taxed to their physical limits could eat, rest, and be replaced by the next horse and rider in communications relay systems. Mileposts, and landmarks that showed the way – effectively the first road signs – also oriented riders, allowing them to make the most of the daily energy they could store in their bodies. Often the emperor traveled these roads in person, usually in vast processions called circuits, meant to reestablish fealty from other city officials and gather taxes from them. Ten of the largest cities denominated as "zhou" were assigned a sub-capital function over the Tang emperor's ten power-reinforcing circuits (Map 2.1).

The largest empires had the longest roads. The Royal Road of Cyrus the Great of Persia, for example, stretched from his palace at Susa to his western boundary on the Aegean coast 2,600 kilometers away – also connecting the splendid cities in between that served as sub-capitals of administrative units known as satrapies. His subsequent successor Xerxes sought to extend that road into Greece (which he hoped to conquer) with an audacious pontoon bridge known as the Hellespont ("Greek Bridge") across the narrow gap we know as the Dardanelles Strait.

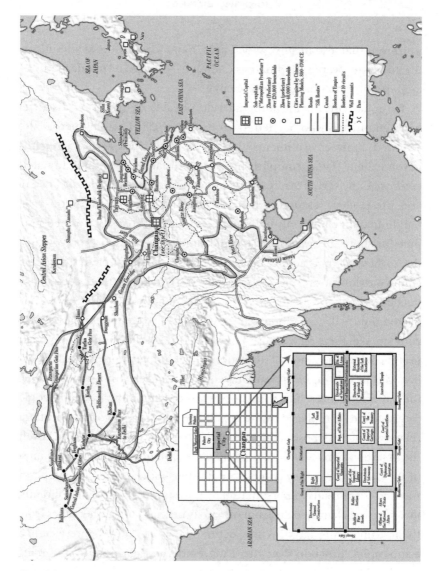

Map 2.1. The Urban Infrastructure of Empire: Tang China (618–907 CE)

For empires to last, capital cities with large buildings devoted to taxation, the military, and religious affairs were crucial, as in the "Imperial City" of the Tang capital Changan (inset). The Tang ruled over immense spaces by means of an administrative hierarchy of subservient cities. Making such a system work required roads and a Grand Canal, whose communication and transport functions extended dynastic rule. The Tang were less interested in the Great Wall against enemies from the steppes, preferring armed campaigns. But they strengthened colonial cities and forts along the "Silk Road" that carried their influence into Central Asia and beyond.

Sources: Information from Richard Overy, *The Complete History of the World*, 9th ed. (London: Times Books, 2015), pp. 138–39; Victor Cunrui Xiong, *Sui–Tang Chang'an: A Study in the Urban History of Medieval China* (Ann Arbor, MI: University of Michigan Center for Chinese Studies, 2000), Map 5.1 (unpaginated).

Map created by Joe LeMonnier, https://mapartist.com.

Though ancient city builders had long paved the streets lying within city limits, it was the Han and the Romans who first started the business we know so well today of paving the planet beyond city walls. The goal, of course, was to guarantee that atmospheric moisture would not turn royal roads into elongated bogs of impassable mud. That meant elaborate engineering, building, and constant rebuilding on very large scales – thousands of kilometers of ditches filled with crushed stone, overlaid with layers of other water-draining and stabilizing materials, sometimes held in place with curbstones, topped with paving stones or even the first asphalt, and arranged in a "crowning" pattern to encourage rainwater to run toward the roadside. Speaking of moisture, countless bridges and causeways were also required for river and swamp crossings. So important were roads to imperial power that emperors required local farmers to forgo long periods that they could otherwise devote to growing taxable food to maintain these channels of imperial authority.[13]

By the time of the Emperor Diocletian (284–305 CE), Rome had built 85,000 kilometers of road, variously paved. Contrary to the cliché, not all of those roads led to Rome: empires needed to connect provincial cities with each other almost as much as with the capital. The Han inherited an extensive road system from their predecessors, the Qin, and by 200 CE Han emperors had widened China's highways to nine lanes in some places and extended paved surfaces for a total of 40,000 kilometers. The Han also built relay stations, guard towers, and military bases between their colonial towns along thousands of kilometers of tracks into the grasslands and deserts beyond the boundaries of their empire, most notably along the famous Silk Road. Really a network of many variously maintained caravan tracks, the Silk Roads ran west from Changan through the 1,000-kilometer Gansu Corridor, in various directions around the fearsome Taklamakan Desert and up into some of the highest mountain passes in the world before connecting with east-bound routes from India, Southwest Asia, and Rome. As the Han emperors revealed when they sent imperial delegations on multiple-year-long westward treks in search of tribute from Central Asian cities, roads served to extend imperial conquest beyond its frontiers, not just to administer already conquered realms. Another immense built tool of Chinese imperial control was the Grand Canal, which was expanded greatly under the Sui and Tang dynasties and rebuilt many times after that. Building the canal required excavating 1,600 kilometers of ditch wide enough for several barges and lining many stretches with retaining walls. Builders also fashioned elaborate locks and harbor facilities, not to mention hundreds of bridges and the canal's parallel system of tow-roads. It served also to extend imperial power northward and southward from the Yellow River Valley throughout China. Eventually it made imperial rule from the city of Beijing, otherwise peripheral and situated in a relatively infertile hinterland, possible.[14]

HABITATS OF VIOLENCE

No empire, of course, ever came into being without military conquest – or at least the sufficiently fearsome threat of it. That brings up the role that military forces like ancient armies and navies played in the earliest kernels of the Urban Planet. Cities made standing armies possible: the particular forms of military force organized by urban empires (as opposed to nomads' tribe-based cavalries) relied heavily on the efficient organizational support made possible by the proximity of diverse actors that only a capital city could provide. Armies, in particular, also relied extensively on other multifunctional built environments such as roads and canals to move soldiers and their sustenance over long distances. Armies, like navies, are, in point of fact, quite city-like. They are large, dense, diverse, hierarchical, and nucleated; they act like energized crowds, and the shelters they build and rebuild are essential to their effectiveness. The big difference is that military forces lumber slowly across space, requiring more building and rebuilding each time they bivouac for the night. Yet, even in motion, they are utterly dependent on fixed cities and agricultural hinterlands; their effectiveness diminishes the farther they stretch their "supply lines" from the imperial capital. Armies also made new cities possible. Campaigning armies regularly built and destroyed massive camps as they conquered new ground, but longer-lasting camps meant to hold territory could sometimes serve as the nuclei for new cities, like the Chinese military outposts along the Silk Road, or the many cities in Great Britain whose names end in *-ceister* or *-chester* – all of them former Roman army camps (*castra*). Retired soldiers and sailors made excellent colonial settlers, and Roman generals often rewarded military service with lands in distant new towns (this practice also prevented rebellions by armed veterans back in the capital).[15]

All of that said, the main reason emperors created armies and navies was to conquer other cities, often with little concern about destroying built environments. Yet, that same fact is responsible for the creation of one of the most extensive features of cities, their surrounding walls. Walls, for their part, were designed to render opposing armies ineffective, but, as we shall see later (Chapter 7), they paradoxically also spurred armies and navies to increase the destructive capacity of their weapons – including a huge array of built instruments of siege-craft and, in Tang and Song China, the first suites of gunpowder weapons. Thus, over time, city walls actually increased military forces' effectiveness at delivering violence against other urban environments, as the Song emperor in Kaifeng discovered when his powerful gunpowder weapons fell into the hands of a conquering nomadic people who had captured urban weapons makers to enhance their power. In this way, cities' creation of armies left armies' positive or negative contribution to the size of the Urban Planet open to the strategic prowess, and often the mere whims, of the generals and emperors who commanded them.[16]

EMPIRES' OUTER LIMITS

From places like Changan and Kaifeng, Chinese dynasties unified gigantic stretches of East Asia under their power, at times reaching far into the Central Asian steppes and Southeast Asia. Rome's empire famously surrounded the entire Mediterranean, straddling all three of the Old World continents, including the original cradle of urban life in Mesopotamia. Both enabled even larger-scale economic and cultural activities. However, just as they demonstrated how extensive city-generated human activities could be, they also revealed the outer limits of the power of the urban polities of their time.

Self-destruction was one limiting dynamic of the growth of the built environment in ancient times. Dozens of Mesopotamian and Chinese capitals fell into ruins at various times thanks to armies conscripted, provisioned, and led from other would-be imperial capital cities. In 654 CE, then 4,000-year-old Uruk, which had long dwindled in size, was finally abandoned to the sand dunes after the armies of the first Islamic caliphate swept through the region. Tang Changan may have been a magnificent city of a million people at its peak, but in 881 CE a rebel general quite rapidly reduced it to "earth-heaps and wasteland," soon reclaimed by farmers. When Inanna delivered the power of "plundering of other cities" to the docks of Uruk, she recognized a grim paradox that lies at the heart of the ongoing life and repeated partial death of the emerging Urban Planet.[17]

As important a limitation on the urban world was the rivalry between cities and decidedly non-urban peoples, most notably nomadic camp dwellers or inhabitants of small villages beyond urban hinterlands. From the perspective of these people of the forest, of craggy inlets of the sea, and of the far steppes, cities may have indeed been generators of enviable imperial power. However, the fact that urban habitats packed so many people and so many important government activities in such small spaces, and the fact that cities depended existentially on resource-sucking city walls, on largely unprotected and highly flammable food sources in the surrounding countryside, and on slow-moving armies that exposed vacuums of imperial power the further they moved from the capital all made cities especially important – and vulnerable – targets. In this way, empire-creating cities, paradoxically, could also became empires' Achilles' heels. This was especially true when nomadic raiders, migrating villagers, unhappy peasant armies, or flotillas of "sea peoples" (often of mysterious or even mythical origin), eager to seize imperial wealth, appeared menacingly at the gates of even the most fearsome imperial capitals.

In most cases, the outer boundaries of empires were unmarked, simply the outer edges of agricultural hinterlands that fed the cities that had fallen under imperial control. As early as 1990 BCE, Shulgi, king of the Mesopotamian city of Ur and ruler of an empire that encompassed the whole region, attempted to change that situation with a harder boundary around his empire. To keep the nomadic Amorites from attacking Ur he forced thousands of laborers to erect a 250-kilometer wall between the Tigris and the Euphrates. It was a colossal show of power to be sure, and a dramatic expansion of the human built environment, but an equally spectacular admission of the fragility of the Mesopotamian urban world even at a point when it was several millennia old. In 1750 BCE, the Amorites outflanked Shulgi's long under-maintained wall and helped bring Ur and its empire down. Dozens of other groups of nomadic raiders plagued even the biggest, most fearsomely walled cities, and sometimes installed themselves in the palaces they ransacked, there to rule as urban kings or emperors themselves. Babylon's Hammurabi claimed descent from the same Amorites that toppled Ur, for example. Sea peoples from somewhere in the Eastern Mediterranean are widely believed to have brought that region's Bronze Age to an end, burning and pillaging many rich port cities in Egypt and Syria. Later even Sennacherib's terrifying Nineveh fell to an alliance of city-dwelling and camp-dwelling peoples.[18]

In the first few centuries of the Common Era, the Roman emperors revived Shulgi's folly on a much larger scale in the form of the 5,000-kilometer *limes*, a built border complex of earthen and stone walls and ditches, permanent army camps, and colonial settlements meant to keep various unconquerable forest, steppe, and desert peoples from threatening the Empire. Its best known segments consisted of Hadrian's wall in today's northern England, the *limes Germanicus* and other borders along the Rhine and Danube Rivers, the *limes Arabicus* against various peoples beyond the new Roman province of Mesopotamia, and the *fossatum Africanus* (African ditch) between the North African coast and nomadic peoples of the Sahara. Yet even as the *limes Germanicus* was under construction, Germanic peoples began crossing the border and living in Roman territory. They themselves had been pushed out of the forests by other forest dwellers further east, and Asian steppe dwellers even further beyond that. However, the Germans eventually built up enough power through guerrilla tactics and more conventional armed forces on imperial territory to invade Italy, then to sack Rome itself in 410 CE, bringing down the Western half of the Empire and forcing the emperors to rule from a new capital at Constantinople (Byzantion in Greek, today's Istanbul).

At that point, the West-European urban world was decimated: Roman buildings fell into ruins and many cities lost most of their population, in many cases reverting once again to small, crudely built settlements, amidst broken columns and statues, that did not recover in size for hundreds of years. Rome's own imperial fora became the site of farmhouses and flocks of sheep for hundreds of years. The small cities that remained became favorite targets of the seafaring Vikings during the ninth and tenth centuries CE. The Vikings' small Scandinavian villages, ruled by chiefs living in longhouses who gathered warriors from nearby by promising them urban loot, provided enough of a habitat to transform local forest products into innovative warships that put European cities at the mercy of repeated raids, arson, and plunder. Later, though, the Vikings established themselves as pioneer traders in cities throughout the North and Baltic Seas, the Mediterranean, and deep into the north Eurasian river systems, helping to found the state of Rus (Russia) and build capital cities like Kyiv and Moscow. In the meantime, power in early Medieval Europe generally shifted away from cities to dispersed rural aristocratic estates, each with smaller agricultural hinterlands and armies of retainers later known as knights. Would-be kings or "Holy Roman Emperors" only slowly reestablished power in capital cities, such as Charlemagne at Aachen (Aix-la-Chapelle) in the late 700s. They often spent much of their reigns shifting their courts and armies from one rival estate to another seeking allegiance from resident landholders – that is, when they were not launching campaigns against forest peoples to the north and east.[19]

Clearly, then, empires did not guarantee the continuous growth of the Urban Planet. The emperors of the Han dynasty, like Chinese dynasties before and after, were especially aware of the very high likelihood that all their work could be consigned, literally, to the historical dust-heap. The peoples of the grasslands and deserts far to the north of the Yellow River Valley were the most important threat faced by any ancient emperor – easily as worrisome as rebel generals, rival Chinese dynasties, or rebellions of peasants. During Han times, the steppe-dwelling Xiongnu largely lived in tents (some had urban or village experience), but it was their genius as herders and riders of horses that gave the Han nightmares. The famous Great Wall of China, all 21,000 kilometers of it, built across steep mountain ridges and across wide wastelands, had its roots in a previous dynasty, but the Han fortified its stone and earthen ramparts and towers, extending it for hundreds of kilometers to the west to guard the nearest approaches of the new Silk Road across Central Asia. Later dynasties pushed farmers out into the steppe to create further buffer zones, and some redirected water from the Yellow River into ponds and marshes, meant literally to bog nomadic cavalries down.[20]

These measures, like the Roman *limes* and Shulgi's wall, allowed cities and their sustaining agriculture-based states to survive and grow during certain periods, but they failed to resolve a more general conflict between Asia's tent-dwelling nomadic peoples and settled city-dwelling ones, which lingered into modern times. The Xiongnu mercilessly mowed the great Han capital Changan into its surrounding grassland in 311, and the forest-dwelling Jurchen did the same, with help from Chinese soldiers and technologies, to Song Kaifeng in 1126–27. The largest pre-modern empire of all arose in the steppe-lands of the nomads, when the great Central Asian chieftain Chinggis (Ghengis) Khan unified the nomadic Mongols, defeated the Jurchen, then fathered a dynasty whose horse-mounted "Hordes," now outfitted with Chinese gunpowder weapons, completely overran the then crumbling Great Wall, conquered China and Korea, and even invaded Japan. For good measure, his sons and grandsons headed west to destroy the "Golden Age" capitals of Islam's Abbasid Caliphate, the fabulous round city of Baghdad, then Damascus, then wiped out Moscow and Kyiv in Russia, burned Kraków, Poland to the ground, and stopped just short of besieging the small city of Vienna.

In the long history of the Urban Planet, the legacy of Chinggis Khan is paradoxical. On the one hand, he confirmed more than anyone else did that it does not always take cities to do something enormous, including the conquest by cavalry of most of the largest continent on Earth. Urban power centers may have heavily determined the life-courses of our earliest urban worlds, but so did largely unbuilt spaces where city-based imperial power simply could not reach. On the other hand, once again, it was beyond the Great Khan's own ruthless genius or that of his successors to do the actual work of administering an empire from horseback or a tent – even from the palatial tents that Mongol emperors forced their servants to pull for them on enormous wooden carts across the rolling steppe. Instead, Chinggis's son Ögedei, relying on Chinese advisors, built a fixed palace for himself and an enormous capital at Karakorum on the high steppe (many of its "buildings" were tents, to gratify Mongol princes' predilection for life on the move). Later, to engage in the business of taxing China and raising a loyal standing army from its subjects, Chinggis's grandson Kubilai Khan famously ordered a Chinese architect to build him a classic foursquare palace and walled capital city amidst the North Chinese grasslands at Shandu ("Xanadu"). When the water supply in that dry region became a problem, he moved a bit south to the city of Dadu, one of several capitals of the Liao, another forest-dwelling people that had experimented with city-based government. He renamed his new capital Khanbalik in his own honor. After the Ming dynasty overthrew the Mongols, they renamed the city again, as their "Northern Capital" – Beijing, moving there from Nanjing ("Southern Capital") – above all to keep their eye on future raiders from the steppes and forests.[21]

Essential as cities, and capitals in particular, were to imperial dynasties, they were also clearly fallible – intrinsically so, emblematic of urban polities' capacity to enable long historic continuities as well as moments of unpredictable contingency and disruptive calamity. Still, as instruments of empire, cities also gave us power to do things that were arguably more resilient and even larger in scale than empires themselves. Imperial cities played essential roles in expanding the scope of three other crucial arenas of human action: commerce and wealth accumulation; the transmission of knowledge; and even greater harvests of geo-solar energy, not only from rivers and other freshwater sources, but from the winds and currents of the saltwater seas as well. Each of these other human activities that took shape in swelling and contracting pre-modern urban worlds depended on imperialism, and all could court disastrous consequences. Yet all of them deserve exploration on their own, for all foreshadow the distant birth, after 1500 CE, of a truly planetary Earthopolis.

CHAPTER 3

Wealth for a Few, Poverty for Many I

THE GREAT URBAN WEALTH-GRAB

By igniting empires, cities also became the creators – and, in turn, to a great degree, the creations – of great treasure houses of wealth, typically owned by a small few. The wealth came from every part of the urban world itself and often far beyond, making escalating wealth-grabbing one of the largest-scale actions we took from cities. As with empires, the most hierarchical of urban states typically enabled the concentration of the most wealth in the fewest hands, especially when those states engaged in widespread imperial conquests that allowed wealth-gathering from the farthest away. The richest people in all of the Cities of the Rivers were the emperors themselves, the members of ever-larger imperial house-holds, the growing number of high officials needed to tax and regulate the economies, and the generals who stood by to make sure everyone played by the emperor's rules – if they didn't seize imperial power themselves.

In addition, the earliest urban states also encouraged a small group of wealthier people who did not work directly for the state to invest their wealth in profit-making enterprises of one kind or another. Some became landowning elites of various kinds, who controlled most of a city's surrounding farmland, sometimes passing the land down in their families; they often maintained homes both in cities and on the land. Others became merchants and financiers who borrowed and pooled capital from one another in order to buy rare luxury goods relatively cheaply and to get rich by selling them at a profit. Among merchants, the richest included a small group who accumulated wealth over longer distances than any other pre-modern city dwellers, even venturing beyond circuits plied by the most intrepid imperial tax-collectors. As all merchants knew, distance meant rarity, rarity meant luxury, and luxury meant claim to handsome profit back in the city. In that way, the mindsets and practices of early merchants came closest to those of people we call "capitalists" – even "global" capitalists – today.

Put all these rich people together and you get a tiny minority of city residents. Most people in the earliest birth-worlds of cities saw little if any wealth, except for the fact that they were the ones who produced most of that wealth's basic components. Farmers grew raw wealth in the form of food, bit by bit, from sunshine, water from the rivers, wetlands, oases, or rain-gathering receptacles, and hard labor in the fields. Thousands of enslaved people helped build the wealth of the earliest urban worlds on farms, in distant woodlots, and in mines, but also in virtually all activities inside city walls. Many other people drew some kind of living by making much smaller for-profit investments in cities' growing numbers of markets and shops. Their earnings varied from middling (artisans and shop-owners) to virtually nothing (caregivers and other hard laborers). Indeed, the earnings of most people who actually created wealth were tiny. Make no mistake: the majority of inhabitants of the Cities of the Rivers, even the wealthiest ones, lived in grinding poverty.

Unequal urban accumulations of wealth were most often the result of unequal hierarchies of state power. As city-states seized monopolies on taxation and violence, they gained enormous power over all economic life. One interpretation of Uruk, for example, holds that the priestly caste, for a time at least, directly employed almost all of the urban world's elite managers of farmland, all owners of urban land, elite merchants, artisans, shopkeepers, laborers, farmers, and the thousands of people that the state enslaved. Even if this is not strictly true, the temple did set in motion all of the unequal wealth-generating activities of urban Mesopotamia: large farms, giant work-crews who dug irrigation ditches and built monuments, artisan shops and state workhouses that made cloth and clay pots for export, and the warehouses and docks that allowed long-distance merchants to become active throughout the region.

Money itself also first came into being in the high temples of Uruk. Only an aborning state, by virtue of its capacity to channel geo-solar energy into enough power to tax its people, could also acquire the power to give value to pieces of metal by agreeing to accept them in lieu of grain (and earlier versions of currency) as payment for taxes. With the value of metal thus guaranteed, merchants could issue loans and borrow at interest. They negotiated with each other using denominations measured in weight of metal, then pressed their personal signature-seals into written clay-tablet contracts, themselves possible due to state administrative systems. Thanks to state certification of currency, finance and commerce could expand in scope, for even merchants from beyond the capital city's imperial territory were inclined to honor these contracts for purchase of goods.

Whether or not this "command economy" interpretation of Uruk is precisely accurate, most urban imperial states eventually gave landholders and merchants – and to a lesser extent artisans and shopkeepers – various degrees of leeway to manage their own wealth-accumulating affairs. That began with tolerance for the creation of pools of wealth owned by profit makers themselves. To be sure, state bureaucrats taxed these "private" pools of wealth, large and small. They also kept a close watch on all matters having to do with their cities' "energized" economic "crowds." After all, as we know, those crowds made up a volatile political as well as economic force. Still the authorities left plenty of room for competition, conflict, negotiation – and occasionally even outright resistance to the economic order.

If cities helped create opportunities for wealth, the reverse was true as well. City dwellers' economic interests – whether greed for great wealth at the top, or desire for a basic livelihood further down – were essential to city life, to cities' physical existence, and to the growth of the Urban Planet more generally. Modest incomes financed the building of a city's teeming shops and homes. Especially large accumulations of wealth financed the city's largest construction projects, and they enabled some especially wealthy urban actors to reach deep into hinterlands, and beyond. Eventually, long-distance commerce helped merge early city-worlds into regular, empire-supported circuits that reached beyond imperial boundaries or even between rival empires. Whether or not we call these larger activities "capitalism" – or call pre-modern city growth "capitalist urbanization" – there is no doubt that these activities depended absolutely on the state power that generated empires, and that moneymaking activities were essential to the expansion of urban birth-worlds into an Urban Planet.

Economic interest, however – including maximal greed – was inherently a political phenomenon. It could be satisfied only within a much bigger and more ambiguous universe of political motives, stratagems, power moves, conflicts, and alliances of convenience – each of which required a variety of mindsets, skills, and practices that the words "greed" and "interest" are insufficient to describe. In some cases, the city's poorest majorities, or middling sorts such as artisans, could forge their own places out of sight of the high palaces and temples of the rich to assert their own interests through varied political actions, including as guild members or as some version of what Romans called a "citizen," an urban resident with political rights. Wealthy landlords and merchants likewise continually struggled with state power, no matter how supportive. Sorting out all the ambiguity and contingency of interest and political exertion was the job of political communities within and outside the state that could exist only in cities. The outcomes there remained deeply unequal, but the dynamics at work were more unpredictable and more interesting than if they had been driven by the certainty of human material interest alone.

MAKING MONEY FROM SUNSHINE, HARD LABOR, AND SLAVERY

The wealth of ancient urban temple organizations, and later of kings and emperors, emerged from the same basic Sun- and Earth-given resources as states' political power: fresh water, food, people, human and animal labor, fuel, tools, plant- and mineral-based raw materials, land, buildings, and all the added frenetic energy closely packed cities could give to all of these. As we know, we did not need cities – or even town-like settlements that had a few city-like characteristics – to develop agriculture, or to control river water through irrigation, or to force people, enslaved or not, to labor in the fields. People living in small villages were capable of doing all of these things. However, the synergistic relationship between cities and their energy-collecting hinterlands – as well as the relationship between cities and empires – did allow us as a species, sometimes for centuries at a time, to dramatically increase the extent of human-altered farmland and pastureland, the number of villages, and the collection of geo-solar energy. Along with that came a growth in the numbers of farmers and herders who were more or less obliged to produce food. They, in turn, increased the amount of food humans could grow – both overall and per acre. That, in turn, increased the number of non-food-producing city-builders and city dwellers – as well as the village-dwelling majority – that farmers and herders could feed. It also increased the size of the human-built habitat more generally, the amount of wealth that could be produced by larger urban populations, and the wealth that could be accumulated by urban elites.[1]

Early states, using the power made possible by urban temples, palaces, and armies, took the lead in stimulating and controlling this wealth-generating countryside–city feedback loop. In China, for example, imperial officials worked with farmers to create the ancient world's most productive agricultural hinterlands. They built vast systems of dykes, weirs, and diversion channels to control the water and silt that poured down the Yellow River and its tributaries throughout the North China Plain. Later they built canals necessary for the arduous develop-ment of rice paddies in the even more flood-prone Yangtze Valley and up into the hillsides deeper into southern China. In some places, "night-soil" gatherers organized by the state collected human and animal excrement from urban streets and carted it to farms where farmers increased their yields by spreading the manure on their fields. Rice paddies, with their additional resident fish and ducks (which doubled as fertilizer spreaders and human meals), became the most productive suppliers of calories to urban dwellers of all. Some paddies could deliver two or three crops a year without requiring periods of fallow. China's agricultural policies (along with a temperate climate and the two rivers) help explain the especially high urbanization rates in China of between 10 and 15 percent, the enormous size of Chinese cities throughout the pre-modern period, and their immense re-acceleration in our own time.[2]

As states' territory expanded, they had to dispatch bigger teams of high officials to oversee more improvements to estates, to marshal more farm labor in the fields, and to gather more surpluses. As these officials gained power over their assigned districts, some took various degrees of hereditary ownership or "tax-farming" authority over large regions. Such on-site officials were the oldest ancestors of the rural aristocratic land-holders and provincial officials who dominated agricultural hinterlands of the world until our own time. Such rural elites could use their connections to state authorities, or build their own rival sources of wealth and power, forcing otherwise independent village farmers and herders to become peasants or serfs – that is, people more or less bound to lifetimes of toil in fields and pastures. Sometimes they assembled their own armies to rival those of the emperors.[3]

Between aid from the state and the depredations of aristocrats, did farmers and herders benefit from cities? Scholars disagree on this point, but even the most optimistic do not see much improvement for all but a few individual farming households overall, even over many millennia. Overwhelmingly, agriculturalists lived in poverty. Some farmers traded labor for the state in lieu of taxes, possibly increasing their income slightly. If they could not pay their taxes, they could get loans from governments or private moneylenders, but interest rates were high, and non-payment could lead to debt-slavery. Conversely, some kings periodically annulled farmers' debts by declaring years of "jubilee." In addition to supporting technical advances on farms, Chinese emperors notably strived to give farming families as much control over their land as possible to give them an incentive to increase yields – another reason Chinese cities grew so large. Even so, wealthy landlords – not to mention merciless rogue warlords and horse-riding steppe raiders – repeatedly reduced peasants to serfdom or starvation. Amidst all the hardships, small groups of peasants in some societies did manage to own plots of land. Of course, global urban history is also filled with stories of peasants who found ways to leave the fields for life in the city, or were forced to do so to build walls and monuments, or were called upon to replace city laborers during epidemics of urban disease. For such city-bound migrants, city life could bring improvements, for opportunities were sometimes available for them or their descendants in the urban world of artisans and shop-keepers. If not, they joined the masses of urban poor who survived off whatever dregs of the urban economy they could get their hands on, by selling their hard labor, by selling sex, by begging in the marketplace, or by hustling or stealing.[4]

In times of worst misery, farmers in the countryside sought more power over their economic lives by rebelling. The first 5,500 years of global urban history – Earthopolis's formative years – were replete with rural uprisings, many relying on farm tools as weapons to demand tax reductions, an end to forced labor, increased control over land, relief from famine, or even the delivery of parasitic landlords to divinely prophesied apocalypse. Recall that one of Inanna's foundational gifts to Uruk was "the rebellious land." Few of the hundreds of known pre-modern peasant revolts resulted in victories of any lasting sort. Some, such as those in China in 209–206 BCE, 17–27 CE, 611–19 CE, and 1351–68 CE actually succeeded in deposing reigning dynasties. In those instances, the collective strength of country peasants' many hundreds of thousands temporarily equaled that of the steppe nomads' cavalries as a threat to an urban-based empire. However, in all cases, peasant families had to return to the land to survive. Rulers who took power on the backs of peasant revolts quickly lost touch with the roots of their power, unfailingly resuming unequal systems of agricultural exploitation whose echoes resonate in our time.[5]

In worlds dominated by the Cities of the Rivers, the experiences of peasant farmers had many parallels with those of the smaller but still very large populations of enslaved people. While slavery in villages existed long before cities, all ancient urban birth-worlds saw a pronounced growth and diversification of the institution. As the number of enslaved people grew, so did the geographical scope of activities required to capture and enslave them. In the earliest cities, enslaved people occupied many more diverse spaces than peasants did: they lived throughout cities themselves as well as on farms or estates. In part, this was because the route to enslavement varied. Some were peasants enslaved to their creditors in the hinterland. Convicts from the city itself could end up enslaved. Many of the enslaved were captives of war from wherever imperial armies campaigned. In Mesopotamian cities, the word for slave denoted their origins "in the mountains," that is, among nomadic herding peoples that urban armies managed to capture. Emperors and pharaohs regularly forced the enemies they vanquished in other cities to relocate *en masse* to their own capital as at least semi-slaves – the Judean exiles forced to move from Jerusalem to Babylon were the most famous.

Merchants bought and sold slaves over long distances as servants to wealthy households just as they sold other luxury objects; the Phoenicians and Greeks did so across the Mediterranean world and into the Black Sea. The Romans extended slaving further, across their entire empire and beyond its frontiers. At least a quarter of the inhabitants of the city of Rome were enslaved, and the slave markets in Roman cities were vast gruesome spaces.[6]

As the property of their owners, enslaved people were liable to be bought and sold on a whim, and were deprived of all social rights. Every sort of harsh treatment of enslaved people was legal, including murder. At different times in most early cities, from Mesopotamia, Egypt, the Mediterranean, the Indus, China, Peru, to Mesoamerica, slaves could fully expect to be killed when their masters died in order to join them in their tombs – for continued service in the next world. Many others, including very young men and women, ended their lives as priests' sacrificial victims to gods, notably in the sacrifices high atop the temple-pyramids of the Aztec capital of Tenochtitlan, or in elaborate processions led by Inka priests from Cuzco to high Andean mountaintops.[7]

That said, urban enslavers employed their human property in many diverse capacities – from hard laborers and sex slaves on the more exploitative end of the spectrum, to household servants, artisans, soldiers, teachers, scribes, accountants, and, at the upper end, as castrated eunuchs who guarded courtly families or who led elite imperial bodyguards. Thus, a very small number of enslaved people could live quite well. Some acquired literacy, officiated at religious rituals, issued loans in their own right, and otherwise rose in rank within important mercantile or ruling households, the army, or the palace itself. Some urban slaves owned slaves of their own. Others bought their own freedom, acquired freedom as an act of generosity on their master's part, or became free as the result of royal jubilees ending debt servitude. A very small few rose to great prominence at court as concubines of the emperor, or as armed palace guards who kept the emperor's sexual rivals away from imperial wives and concubines. Others rose within the armed forces, as in the case of the eunuch Zheng He in Ming China in 1402 CE, to admiral of the premodern world's largest imperial navy.[8]

3.1. Fresco Depicting Enslaved Laborers Building a Wall in a Roman City
To build cities and to amass vast unequal pools of wealth, urban elites depended on the muscle, sweat, and agonizing labor of millions. From ancient times to the modern era, enslaved, captured, and forced laborers made up large proportions of the construction crews who lifted the billions of tons of materials required to construct the human habitat on Earth. In our own time, urban developers in many parts of the world continue to exploit the "informal" labor of the world's poorest and most vulnerable people, sometimes including the twenty million laborers who experience enslavement worldwide in the twenty-first century.
Hulton Archive/Getty Images.

Since enslaved people in cities held many different social positions, they also inhabited very different urban spaces, from closets, garrets, and backyard shacks to the exterior rooms of Roman noble homes, army barracks, the female quarters of the palace, and the imperial throne-rooms themselves. In general, they possessed less power to organize as a cohesive mass movement than village farmers did, and slave rebellions were rarer than peasant ones were. The two best-known slave uprisings in pre-modern times, the Spartacus rebellion of 73–71 BCE in Roman Italy and the Zanj uprising of African plantation slaves in Abbasid-ruled Mesopotamia in 869–883 CE, ended in brutal armed repression. When the enslaved gladiator Spartacus raised an army of rural slaves and threatened Rome itself, Roman generals defeated him, and then erected

6,000 crosses on the main roads leading into the capital, onto which they nailed all surviving Spartacists – a grim monument meant to deter any future slave rebellions. The Zanj rebels ruled the large lower-Euphrates city of Basrah for some time, but the Abbasid army killed at least several hundred thousand of them in a fourteen-year military campaign that finally suppressed the movement. Both rebellions gave nightmares to urban elites for years afterward. However, slave revolts had a more decisive impact much later, during the years before and during the revolutionary era of the 1700s and 1800s CE, than they did in ancient times.[9]

THE ENERGIES – *AND POLITICS* – OF SHOPS

As the first cities came into being, they radically enlarged the world's population of artisans, shopkeepers, and market stall owners. Among the Holy *Mē* in Inanna's Boat of Heaven was a full list of such city-energizers, from woodworkers, coppersmiths, scribes, smiths, leather-makers, fullers (wool processors), builders, reed workers, and prostitutes. These artisans embodied urban specialization itself, along with fellow shopkeepers who dealt in urban regions' especially diverse foodstuffs or who served prepared meals in early versions of taverns or restaurants, plus service providers like owners of small temples or itinerant schoolteachers. Their activities infused city streets with an economic and cultural buzz – and chaos – that many of us deem the very essence of city life to this day.[10]

This energy is hard to capture in a bottle, let alone a time capsule, but urban historians have discovered at least some evocative evidence for what ancient city shopping districts were like. Roman writers, notorious for complaining about the Eternal City's busy streets, accidentally do a good job of bringing the city's pulse back to life. "Rome was … just one big shop," griped the poet Martial in the second century CE. The "right to live is denied … in the mornings by the schoolteachers, during the day by the breadmakers, and during the day by the hammering of blacksmiths. On the one hand, there's the money changer jingling his stock of … coins on a dirty table [*banca*, the origin of the word bank]; on the other there's the Spanish goldbeater,

3.2. Artisan Shops and Merchants in Song Dynasty Kaifeng (*c.* 1100 CE)

A classic urban "energized crowd" pulses in this detail from a silk scroll depicting Kaifeng, the capital of the Song dynasty. Customers fill a giant restaurant (center). Owners of craft-shops, street-stalls, teashops, sex shops, and produce wagons vie with temple monks and beggars for cash, desires, and souls. Laborers carry goods in baskets suspended from shoulder poles. A thousand years before automobiles, traffic is intense: carts, draft animals, and a gentleman in a servant-carried sedan chair compete with pedestrians in the street. Merchants, possibly from Central Asia, join the throngs, their camels lugging "all the delights of the world" into Kaifeng.

Werner Forman/Universal Images Group/Getty Images.

striking the splintered stone with his shiny mallet. .... it seems as if all of Rome is at my bedside."[11]

More than 1,000 years later, in 1147 CE when the memoirist Meng Yinglao wrote about the commercial streets of Song-era Kaifeng, he was much more enthusiastic. These places he wrote, are

> thriving beyond measure ... The shops are filled with gold and jade art objects and curios, haberdasheries and draperies. ... The street inside the new Fengqiu Men gate is lined on either side with shops extending over ten *li* [five kilometers]. On the checkerboard of streets and lanes there are thousands of shops, large and small, with wine shops, teashops, and confectionaries scattered about. ... On the square next to the Hall of Buddhas, the Taoist priest Meng sells his special recipe honey-preserved fruits, Zhao Wenxiu displays writing brushes of his own handwork, and Pan Gu offers his special ink sticks. Along the corridor on either side, nuns standing behind stalls sell embroideries, stockings, collars, embroidery patterns, bridal headwear, hats, false hair-coils, silk threads, etc. in every color and shade. In the courtyard inside the second and third gates are tents and sheds and awning-covered stalls where traders sell rush cushions, bamboo mats, screens, curtains, basins, spittoons, saddles, bows, swords, fruits, salted meats, etc. ... Business goes on till the wee hours of the morning. The brilliant lights of the wineshops are dazzling; even more so are the beautifully dressed and painted prostitutes ... Even when it rains or snows heavily there are salted beans with ginger, fried entrails, fried liver, crabs, walnuts, pears, pomegranates, haw[thorn fruit]s, steamed rice cakes, and bean soup. Tea sellers arrive by the third watch to serve those who have been delayed past midnight ... Truly these booming markets have turned the [Kaifeng] night into day.[12]

Vehicles were intrinsic to the built environment of markets, for the artisanal and shopkeeping economy required delivery carts, pulled both by people and by animals, and thus epic traffic jams formed, as carts tried to part the throngs of walking customers and gangs of enslaved body-guards making way for the sedan chairs of the rich, carried by their enslaved colleagues. No one in history whined about urban traffic more eloquently than the Roman satirist Juvenal:

> Ponder this city, in which the crowd that flows without interruption through the broadest streets is crushed whenever anything stands in the way to hinder its course as it pours like a speedy river. ... The carts thundering by through the narrow twisting streets and the swearing of drivers caught in a traffic jam would even snatch away sleep from an emperor.[13]

In point of fact, the streets themselves, not to mention most of the built environment of the city, were themselves the creation of artisans – the builders, carpenters, stone masons, marble workers, tile-roof layers, and in some cases glaziers whose shops, carts, supply yards, and construction zones all added to the unexpected textures of the city. Juvenal had choice words for urban construction crews that might be familiar to city residents today:

> As it approaches, a huge fir log sways on a wagon and another huge cart hauls a whole pine tree. They nod back and forth threateningly way above the people. For if the axle that's lugging a heap of marble snaps and spills the whole overturned mountain on the masses, what would be left of the bodies?[14]

As Juvenal also complained, the typical buildings that artisanal builders constructed – speculative complexes such as Rome's five-story *insulae* – could turn a profit only if their outer walls intruded far into the street, or if their upper stories leaned far out overhead, so that landlords could jam as many rent-paying tenants into them as possible. That allowed even less space for pedestrians and carts, not to mention street stalls, in the streets in between – and hence aggravated the traffic. On top of that, indoor plumbing in Roman apartments was too expensive, so the contents of residents' chamber pots also regularly rained down on the heads of passersby (and into huge piles of already deposited horse excrement). The streets, far from being paved in gold, were covered with a smelly brown slime – pounded by the sandals of passersby – that added its own intensity to the urban experience.[15]

As these keyhole-glimpses into city streets of the distant past suggest, the concentration of diverse activities in small spaces provided a kind of spatial fuel for the hot crucibles of urban commerce and wealth making.

Today's theorists of "energized crowding" tend toward Meng Yinglao's enthusiastic view of small shops, that their sheer number and proximity allowed cities to "thrive beyond measure." In part, this was simply because shops supplying food and fuel allowed city residents to eat and warm their homes without spending most of their lives farming or woodcutting – activities unsuited to cities anyway. And, of course, larger numbers of customers allowed more people to make a living making and selling things. Skilled artisans benefited in other ways from close existence, since proximity increased the likelihood of mutual inspiration, high-level training, pressure to maintain high standards of work, formal agreements to ensure quality of goods, and cooperation on larger-scale projects. Cities gave artisans easy access to the labor power of apprentices, manual labors, and, too often, enslaved people. Concentration also meant cheap transport costs – despite those time- and money-sucking traffic jams. Lastly, urban marketplaces gave artisans and shopkeepers direct access to a large and varied public whose desires might be fickle, but whose diversity could supply artisanal innovators with enough niche customers to underwrite new techniques, products, and life-enhancing technologies. These, in turn, could create new economic opportunities, new forms of artisanal work, and new wealth.[16]

If cities provided their own form of power to artisans and shop-owners, they also engendered cutthroat competition and conflict. The energy of crowded streets created street politics. Urban "proximity power" could mean fierce contests over small spaces that promised big profits, and also plenty of cruelty and exploitation. Apprentices and journeymen, who typically lived under the roof of master artisans, often suffered egregiously, earned minimal wages, and often drifted into the city's vast numbers of poorer laborers, beggars, and slaves, and into criminal undergrounds. Urban artisan shops, like the craft-producing farmhouses on which many were modeled, often replicated the degree of patriarchal rule of the countryside. In cities that grew out of plow-based agricultural societies, men wielded most power over the more lucrative forms of craft-making and got most recognition for their skills, no matter how much they depended on women's craftwork in shops that typically doubled as homes in which women provided most of the care required for the next day's shop-work. Horticultural agriculture, which tended to give farming women more status, may explain why women who later moved to West African cities, for example, have long been more active as market merchants than men are. Meanwhile, in patriarchal Song-era Kaifeng, the nuns who sold embroidery and clothes no doubt benefited from independence from husbands. However, cloth-work, such as spinning and weaving, and beer brewing were nearly universally considered women's work in pre-modern cities. Women also wielded power over urban shops more generally as customers, since they did much of the purchasing of food and household items. Because they knew household budgets best, women often spearheaded the raucous crowds that gathered throughout global urban history to demand lower prices on bread.[17]

For all of that, the state was probably as important in igniting artisanal activity as "energized crowding" on its own. For artisans and shopkeepers themselves, the politics of urban space and wealth always involved wondering how much leeway the emperor (disturbed by market noise in his sleep or not) would allow to ordinary people to make their living by making and selling things. One "hierarchical" interpretation of Uruk holds that priests controlled much of the urban artisanal economy, forcing some of the more skilled artisans out of their homes, some into captivity in studios on the ziggurats to provide luxury items directly to the king. At Uruk, rulers may have augmented cloth production by forcing enslaved women to work in a building that one archaeologist describes as "half-factory, half-prison." Other early Mesopotamian artisans may have had to meet quotas for the palace before they sold anything to other commoners. Millers and bread bakers worked in tune with the temple's barley distribution system; during some periods they may have faced restrictions on selling wares from their own shops. Still, it is interesting that when it came time to praise the city of Uruk, the author of the earliest piece of human literature, *The Epic of Gilgamesh*, took time out from narrating the heroics of King Gilgamesh to call the city "the smithy of the gods." Indeed, it is likely that the city's metalsmiths were among the earliest experimenters with alloys such as bronze that were so important to the more efficient grain fields and the first imperial conquests, and thus to the state's monopoly of taxation and violence. Gunpowder was another likely urban artisanal invention, the work – much later – of Tang and Song-era Chinese artisanal apothecaries who often destroyed their own shops as they "improved" their explosive products. So were innovations in disposable pottery design and manufacturing, the arts of cloth weaving and dyeing – the horrific female slave system notwithstanding – and the design, construction, and decoration of monumental buildings.[18]

Kings and emperors' political calculations about artisans had to take into account, on the one hand, their potential to make immense technological breakthroughs and, on the other, the headaches involved in governing thousands of talented people, their unruly employees, and their often very unhappy poorer customers, all of them thronging urban streets that were chaotic enough on normal days. Artisans, of course, had to pay taxes to the king; they also faced price caps, regulations on treatment of apprentices, and confinement to particular areas of the city zoned as marketplaces. In cities the world over, practitioners of some particularly noxious-smelling or dangerous crafts, like metalsmithing, clothes dyeing, leather tanning, or lime-burning, were forced to do business outside the city and downwind to avoid troubling the noses of the more exalted city residents, not to mention putting the city as a whole at risk of fire. This was also true in High Medieval London, where smiths and lime-burners burned coal, offending the nose of the king. He sent them packing to districts far downwind. Even regimes most favorable to urban commerce, such as the Romans and Aztecs, experimented with restrictions on "the good order and control" of market behavior, to use the words of Spanish conquistador Diaz de Castillo upon his wide-eyed arrival in 1519 in the marketplaces of Aztec Tenochtitlan. These restrictions included the "fixed placement" of stalls, efforts to widen streets to make urban crowds and traffic more controllable, laws establishing one-way streets (such as those at Pompeii), and restrictions on hours of operation, which included general curfews. The Northern Song dynasty stands out among pre-modern regimes for its especially enthusiastic support of artisans and petty commerce. Few cities had markets that stayed open all night, like the one Meng Yinglao described in the dynasty's capital of Kaifeng – a buzzing city that truly never slept at all.[19]

In the midst of all that, artisans and shopkeepers also "ordered" urban spaces and institutions to their own advantage. It is possible that they could rely from the very earliest times on what one scholar called "corporate entities" which advocated for their interests – the distant forerunners, perhaps, of High Medieval Europe's powerful craft guilds. In less authoritarian places, like Jenné-jenno in the Niger Bend of Africa, artisans maintained their independence by isolating themselves in their own village-like neighborhoods separate from those of other organized artisanal groups. This was especially important for ironsmiths, whose fiery shops many cultures deemed open portals to the supernatural world. Special streets or neighborhoods devoted to individual crafts are well-known parts of cities in most regions of the world, even if they were never as exclusive as such street names as "Baker Street," "Butcher's Alley," and "Shoemaker Lane" suggest. However, when artisans were appointed overseers of craft market stalls in the sprawling Western Market of Tang-era Changan, or when they gathered in full-blown craft guilds, they could congregate in spaces outside the view of the emperor to gain a voice in otherwise overwhelmingly authoritarian societies – sometimes leveraging the power of rebellion or at least the threat of it. Some used their voice to affect crucial state policies like taxation, social welfare, and military recruitment, particularly at the municipal level, achieving an informal variety of political rights. In parts of High Medieval Europe, they acquired formalized political rights tied to urban residence, based on a revised version of Roman-era citizenship. These rights may have laid a foundation for the revival of democracy during revolutionary times much later.[20]

SHOPS BEYOND THE STREETS

Absent formal rights or democracy, artisans who cooperated with royal bureaucrats or richer merchants could also benefit from even further upscaled operations of wealth creation. These could include expensive cutting-edge technology and new expansions of the built environment. Waterwheels or windmills that could grind flour, operate bellows in foundries, spin silk, saw lumber, and even stamp ore all date from Roman and Han times. For the most part, the site of these large contraptions depended on sources of flowing water, so many were located outside town – along with sometimes imposing edifices that sheltered the various machines that the mill wheels were designed to power. In some cases, special aqueducts brought the waterpower directly into the city, as in the case of the grain mills on Rome's Janiculum Hill around 200 CE, which were installed around the time that the imperial dole officers decided to give the poor their rations in baked bread instead of grain.[21]

All crafts required complex supply systems for acquiring raw materials, and hence they required built, even urbanized, hinterlands of their own. Bakers, butchers, fishmongers, restaurant owners, and wool cloth manufacturers all relied directly on cities' plant- and animal-producing hinterlands, along with the boats, docks, warehouses, and roads needed for transport of the bulky raw materials they processed in their shops. Potters, glassmakers, and builders needed distant clay-pits, sandpits, and quarries for basic materials that could originate even beyond cities' farm belts. Anyone who relied on fire to produce craft goods needed prodigious amounts of wood, charcoal, or more rarely coal itself. Potters, glassblowers, lime-burners, and metalsmiths were the biggest customers of the foresters and char-kiln operators who moved between distant forest camps and the fuel-yards of the city itself.[22]

Sometimes the artisanal city itself moved to the source of raw materials and fuel. To ensure a huge supply of porcelain jars, plates, cups, and other items, the Han emperors built Xinping, an entire city devoted to the perfection of porcelain. It was located near deposits of the finest clay, near forests filled with firewood, and along the Yangtze River in world history's greatest food-producing hinterland. The Song dynasty later expanded this city dramatically and renamed it Jingdezhen. The city and villages nearby were home to thousands of artisans, including specialists in each stage of production, long foreshadowing twentieth-century assembly lines.

Pre-modern metalsmiths relied on the most distant of all sources of raw materials, mines that could lie hundreds or even thousands of kilometers away. In the Rio Tinto copper and silver mines in Roman Spain (which are still in operation today), or in the dozens of shifting iron mining operations in the quickly disappearing forests north of the Yellow River in Song China, the process of extraction, ore crushing, and high-temperature smelting could bring giant, city-like camps into being. Thousands of workers and artisans crowded these places, amidst water wheels, mine-draining machines, and thundering stamping equipment, not to mention the vast and teeming subterranean shafts and galleries that made up the "streets" of mine-cities themselves. To operate, these underworld metropolises needed their own food and fuel hinterlands, including complex systems of water diversion and extensive wood-harvesting operations.[23]

As forests disappeared in the immediate vicinity of Song-era Chinese iron mines, they brought into being a second set of mining camps that were devoted to extracting a new form of fuel – coal, which many residents of the capital Kaifeng used to heat their homes several centuries before smiths first used it in London. As my multiplying references to Song China suggest, historians associate the dynasty with the closest that any pre-modern society came to a real industrial revolution. If the Jurchen had not flattened Kaifeng in 1126–27 – followed by the Mongols' capture of the new Song capital Hangzhou 150 years later – the pre-modern world's urban artisanal economies may have given birth to Cities of Hydrocarbon far earlier than they actually did.[24]

CHAPTER 4

Wealth for a Few, Poverty for Many II

"THE RARITIES OF THE WORLD": MERCANTILE CAPITAL

"Available here," Meng Yuanlao wrote of the street markets of twelfth-century Kaifeng, "are all the rarities of the world." His insight is crucial to us as we explore how large-scale actions of unequal wealth making in cities slowly merged separate urban birth-worlds into a truly planetary Urban Planet. As Meng implies, artisanal activity, the smallest form of urban wealth-creation, was itself an *intrinsic part* of the most extensive. Artisans and shopkeepers may have created so much of what we know as city life, but they could do so only because the practice of their craft depended in many ways on the larger-scale practices of another group of essential urban actors: merchants who specialized in acquiring "rarities" from "all" of the world and bringing them to market in churning places like Kaifeng.[1]

The "world" trade of ancient urban merchants was unlike the practices of gift giving between village chiefs that had moved prestige goods haphazardly over long distances in pre-urban times. To meet the needs of cities, long-distance commerce had to be much larger in volume. Merchants needed to gauge demand for goods in their destination city beforehand, and determine the exact source accordingly. Such point-to-point delivery needed to follow a reasonably predictable schedule.

These practices required spaces that are just as foundational to cities as shops and marketplaces. Locally based merchants required stout houses with office and conference rooms and large warehouses. Merchants hailing from afar needed local accommodation, typically located in special commercial districts. Overland merchants needed large stables for transport animals. Extensive road networks were just as essential to such merchants as they were to emperors and their generals. So were waypoints, roadside inns, and caravanserais for nighttime stopovers (again equipped with stalls and forage for animals). Where possible, merchants needed the state to provide armed watchtowers and even walls along roads to keep bandits and nomadic raiders away from commercial caravans with their huge loads of money and luxuries. Merchants who relied on the winds and currents of the sea needed specially designed port cities typically located in natural harbors further outfitted with wharfs, boatyards, and dredged channels where there were sandbars, lighthouses, and massive stone or concrete breakwaters to calm the waves and allow ships to rest safely in stormy weather. There were also the ships themselves. We think of them as vehicles, but they were also special built environments in their own right – concentrated, socially complex, and designed precisely to extend the reach of activities in one city to another – across wide stretches of water, over long travel times, amidst raging storms, and in spite of attacks by "sea peoples" or pirates along the way. Massed together in harbors, ships created their own floating neighborhoods; very often ships' masts were the most prominent features of pre-modern cities' skylines, as impressive as the temples and palaces of local rulers.[2]

"World" commerce brought far more wealth into far fewer hands than did shops and marketplaces. The larger scope of merchants' activity, the larger built environments they required, and the larger forces of protection they needed to do their work all meant that they depended even more heavily than artisans and shopkeepers did on power within the hierarchies of urban states. The most important state support for mercantile activity was the invention of money itself. Money is a classic creation of city-based states, and it plays a big role in cities' capacity to amplify the scope of human action. To ease the delivery of distantly sourced "rarities" to palaces and temples, state officials accepted silver or other metals from merchants as tax payments in lieu of bulky shipments of grain. Thus sanctioned by the state, metal currency gave merchants an easily transportable and easily lendable marker of reasonably stable value that allowed them to purchase shipments of luxuries far away and then sell their wares at a profit, sometimes in larger amounts of the same metal. Later, the Greeks invented coins with local rulers' faces stamped on them to verify that the metal contained in the coin met state standards for purity and weight. The goal there was to prevent florid disputes among merchants about the measurement of raw pieces of silver and gold. (Because counterfeiting was relatively simple, coins provided only a partial solution). The word *money* is another urban vocabulary term that we owe to the city of Rome – from the mint building located in the Temple of Juno Moneta on the Capitoline Hill. The Romans gave Jupiter's wife Juno the epithet "Moneta" because flocks of her sacred geese once warned (*monere*) the city that a barbarian army was descending on the city walls to seize its treasure. Later, money even took the name of the empire's monumental hill itself: Capital, homage to money's original form as state loans. In turn, government mints and artisanal money-weighing, money-changing, and money-lending shops made up the first built structures of what we later called urban financial districts.[3]

If cities expanded long-distance commerce, commerce helped expand early urban worlds. By the time that Meng wrote in the 1100s CE, the "world" of long-distance trade between cities had indeed grown to enormous proportions. Not the *whole* world, strictly speaking – not yet – but certainly a very large space that at least intermittently extended from one farthest end of Eurasia to the other, and that included much of Africa as well, and much of the Indian Ocean shore. Overland trade extended urban influences into areas previously only suited to nomadic life. Urban merchants drew on camel or horse herders for means of transport, and nomads themselves went into business as traders and even city builders; rich cities like Central Asia's Samarkand, Petra in Arabia, and the Sahara oasis towns grew largely on commercial wealth in distant steppes or otherwise inhospitable deserts. Trade circuits in the Americas were smaller, though still impressive considering the lack of cart-pulling animals and large seagoing ships. One of these circuits encompassed the entire Andes mountain chain via the Inka road system. Mesoamericans traded with the Pueblo peoples 2,000 kilometers to the north.

Seas and oceans also opened to urban influence early on, as ship owners extended cities' river-channeled harvests of geo-solar energy to include that delivered through the winds and currents over open water like that of the Mediterranean Sea, the Indian Ocean, and the China Seas. By investing in large ships and expensive cargos, shipowners brought enormous wealth back to their seaport cities, yet they also incurred enormous risks, as attested by thousands of rich shipwrecks from this period. For that reason, most pre-modern sea-going merchant ship captains were loath to travel far beyond sight of land, thus also drawing an outer limit on urban influence over the sea that was not broken until the mid-1400s. Long before that, as if openly defying such limits on the waterier realms of urban worlds, traders from a few smaller-scale boat-building settlements plunged far further into the oceans than city-based merchants. In the 900s CE, the Vikings famously traded foodstuffs and plundered luxuries across the North Atlantic, including with tiny short-lived settlements in Greenland and Labrador. By that point, Polynesian traders were hauling goods on seagoing canoes – steering according to the position of the stars and the flight of seabirds – soon amassing enough wealth to fund large dynastic island capitals, whose realms spread across thousands of kilometers of the South Pacific.[4]

MERCHANTS AND MONEY IN THE *BIT KĀRUM*

From the ruins of Uruk and other Mesopotamian sites, we know some of the origins of the Old World's urban-enabled, supercontinental and ocean-spanning circuits of mercantile activity. Temple officials in places like Uruk worked with herders and boat-makers to pile woolen cloth and perhaps other local goods, including any food needed for the journey, onto pack animals or large-bottomed rivercraft. Thus blessed by the temple, they transported their wares across wide-open country-side, or upriver, or across parts of what we know as the Persian Gulf, to wherever they could exchange their cargo for tin and copper to make bronze. They also traded for building stones and especially impressive cuts of rare timber, as well as Mesopotamian elites' beloved lapis lazuli and other gems for temple decorations and prestige objects. Finally, increasingly, merchants acquired the ultimate "rarities" of the day, gold and especially silver, the basis for more palace ornaments as well as for money itself.[5]

The myth of Inanna mentions that the goddess, upon arrival in Uruk, unloaded her gifts of urban *Mē* at a *kārum*, that is, a wharf or quay, called the Lapis Lazuli Quay in honor of the city's most distantly sourced rarity. In the languages of Mesopotamia, the term *kārum* also meant "merchant." Archaeologists have not yet discovered this actual site at Uruk, but Inanna's trip from Eridu to Uruk involved stops at several other riverside *tamkārum* along the way. At Uruk, other documents suggest the *kārum* may have consisted of a separate mercantile neighborhood. Jump far ahead, to the 1800s BCE, and the impact of long-distance trade on the built environment was much more extensive. Far to the north, in the silver-mining districts of Anatolia, lie the ruins of the city of Kanesh, high on a hill. Outside the walls and a bit down the hill are the remains of a full-fledged overland mercantile district, the whole thing called "The Wharf" – *Kārum*. The district itself had two parts, one for the houses of local Anatolian merchants, and another for those of their colleagues from Assur, the great Mesopotamian imperial capital 800 kilometers to the south. Each merchant house (known as a *bit kārum*) contained spaces devoted entirely to striking the intricate deals required to trade tin and wool from Assur for Kanesh's silver, as well as various deals involving the regional traffic in copper.[6]

None of this large-scale profit-making activity, the earliest ancestor of capitalism, could occur without the comparatively tiny domestic spaces in these houses. "Conference rooms" in the *bit kārum* allowed merchants to size up potential partners and negotiate agreements, first relating prices of goods in weight of silver, then concerning the proper weighing stones and scales to use to measure the silver rods and ingots that served as international currency, then the terms of loans – interest rates, repayment schedules, and consequences of non-payment. These matters were very serious – not something to haggle out in the market square or on the high road, but requiring a formal, sheltered setting where all parties could look deep into each other's souls for signs of trustworthiness. For people who would soon part ways over long distances and long periods owing enormous sums of money or goods to each other, the incentive to cheat was large. Yet no one made any money without establishing some degree of trust. Clay contracts for these transactions contain not only the seals of the main parties to a deal but also those of a large number of witnesses, meant to hold a good section of the *kārum*'s residents to account. The consequences of breaking some of these ancient business deals were dire: unpaid creditors were sometimes empowered to sell a debtor's own wife or daughter into slavery. Merchant houses also needed to include sealed back rooms in which to file signed contract tablets in case of disputes, and to store valuable merchandise while it awaited shipment. Their practice was to plaster the doors of these vaults shut with clay that they then rolled with a cylindrical seal, imprinting it with a pattern unique to the merchant and guarding against tampering by rivals.[7]

The exterior facades of the *bit kārum* could also signal their owners' growing wealth in relationship to that of kings. For example, at Ugarit, a busy Bronze Age seaport on the Mediterranean coast of Syria, archaeologists tell us that the richest merchants built their houses in similar styles to that of the royal palace, sometimes in the same neighborhood. The architecture of these houses not only signaled class pretensions but also reaffirmed their owners' trustworthiness, much like the stolid bank buildings of the twentieth century, with the space above their Roman-era inspired columns engraved with that keyword "Trust." So important were the architectural descendants of the *bit kārum* – merchant houses – to long-distance trade that merchant companies called their firms "Houses" well into the twentieth century.[8]

THE POLITICS OF MERCHANT CAPITALISM

As the kings of Ugarit knew well, and as kings and emperors throughout the pre-modern era were just as aware, merchants commanded considerable power over the wealth-producing capacity of cities. Merchants' fancy houses reminded every king of two uncomfortable facts. One, that merchants' wealth and power could rival that of kings. And two, that kings' power, insofar as it rested on the capacity to hoard and display rare expensive things, rested on merchants' capacity to exercise their economic power and supply kings with foreign luxuries and raw materials for locally made ones.[9]

In some places, like Byblos, Tyre, Sidon, and Berytus (Beirut), the port capitals of the famous Phoenician merchants that sprouted up a few hundred years after mysterious sea peoples supposedly burned Bronze-Age ports like Ugarit to the ground, cities were ruled by merchants themselves. The Phoenicians, who may have descended from Ugarit's destroyers, constructed dozens of other port towns throughout the Mediterranean similarly dominated by wealthy merchants. From their North African settlement at Carthage, they reached Spain, Portugal, Morocco, Northwest Europe, and the Red Sea, and may have even circumnavigated Africa. They founded the great cities of Leptis Magna, Palermo, Ibiza, Cadiz, Cartagena, Tangier, and Lisbon, among many others. Minoan merchants based in the palace cities of Crete, and Mycenaeans and Greeks from other Aegean ports and islands imitated the Phoenicians by establishing their own Mediterranean archipelagos of trade cities: Syracuse on Sicily and Marseille among them. Their counterparts in the Silk Road trade of Central Asia held controlling sway over the fabled merchant cities like Bukhara and Samarkand. So did later African and Asian merchants in Indian Ocean port cities like Mogadishu, Mombasa, Kilwa, and Sofala along the East Coast of Africa, and at Calicut, Malacca, Guangzhou, and Hangzhou further east. During Europe's High Middle Ages, similar merchant-run polities grew at Genoa and Venice in the Mediterranean and in the Northern European sea and river ports run by the Haneseatic League of merchants, stretching from Cologne, Hamburg, Lübeck, and London as far as Novgorod in Russia.[10]

In many of these places, merchants also become important landowners within the city, thus controlling yet another key form of urban power and wealth. On clay tablets from early merchant archives in Ugarit, archaeologists discovered a royal grant of prime royal orchard land to a prominent merchant. Under the deal, the merchant agreed to re-invest proceeds from the dates and olives grown on this land in new ships and crews so that he could supply the king with luxuries from elsewhere in the Mediterranean. This points to another way in which the city itself could power up long-distance mercantile activity and create enormous amounts of wealth, literally from the ground up. Because urban real estate was so essential to all other urban wealth-creating activities, it was very valuable in its own right. In cities where state authorities allowed it – Babylon and Rome among them – the purchase and sale of urban land was another foundationally urban practice of wealth accumulation that looks a lot like today's capitalism.[11]

For the most part, though, kings kept control over local and foreign merchants by an ingenious strategy involving power built directly into allocations of land, and thus the spatial layout, of their city. As the Anatolian kings who established the *Kārum* of Kanesh demonstrated early on (perhaps imitating earlier rulers such as those of Uruk), it was possible for kings to benefit from merchant power while avoiding succumbing to it simply by enclosing foreign merchants in a separate urban district. The exact policy could vary. Either there was a wall around the district or not; the place could be put at a distance from the city or not; there could be a curfew or not; the merchants could hold the key to the district's gates or the king's representative could keep it themselves, thus potentially turning the merchant district into a nighttime prison. Other built facilities, such as customs bureaus and commercial courts, were also often located in these enclaves, keeping merchants up to date with tariff payments to the king, and resolving frequent disputes between merchants before they got out of hand and created social unrest. In all cases, kings knew that merchants often irritated the city's artisans and other ordinary people. As creditors, merchants could attract resentment for forceful insistence on repayment or for charging too much interest: at worst, merchants were open to the charge that they lived languidly off the sucked blood of others. Because of this, during politically precarious times, kings could single out merchants as scapegoats for the king's own failings. The fact that foreign merchants dressed, spoke, acted, and worshipped in strange ways could add fire to these attacks. On the other hand, if anti-foreign sentiment should arise spontaneously, walls around the merchant district could serve to deter urban mobs, protecting their inhabitants, and more importantly, the goods the king wished to acquire from them.[12]

The historian Philip Curtin called urban merchant quarters "one of the most widespread of human institutions over a very long run of time . . . [from] the invention of agriculture [to] . . . the industrial age." Examples range from the *jundi* for long-distance merchants and officials in Han Changan; the special stalls allocated to Central Asian Silk Road merchants in the rebuilt version of Changan during the Tang-era; the cosmopolitan *fanfang* at the Southern Chinese port of Guangzhou, which harbored merchants from as far away as the

Swahili coast; the massive caravanserais outside of Samarkand and other Silk Road cities that were equipped to handle giant numbers of horses and camels as well as weary merchants; the Genoese district of Pera (or Galata) across the Golden Horn from Constantinople (Figure 4.1); the *fondacci* of Italian merchants throughout the Mediterranean; and the *Sabon Gari* or *zongos* for trans-Sahara merchants in the Sahelian capitals of West Africa. The "ghettos" for Jews that Venice and soon other European cities established after 1500 CE fit some of the same model, of separate quarters designed for people that local rulers found useful to the state's finances and other social needs. In their case, Christians' deep hatred of Jews added to campaigns that scapegoated ghetto residents as reviled foreign merchants and creditors.[13]

THE BUILT HABITAT OF LONG-DISTANCE COMMERCE

To benefit from long-distance trade, leaders of urban states and merchants had to cooperate as well as rival each other. In the process, they built structures in and between cities needed to establish regular activity linking such disparate and largely disconnected urban worlds on either end of large continents. Such expensive things required royal investments, especially in roads, paved or otherwise. We have already encountered the Han and Song efforts to fortify the mostly unpaved Silk Road that linked Asia with Europe and Africa. Merchants traveling back and forth along this perilous route could rely upon a string of series of garrison-and-market cities such as Dongguan, Turfan, and Khotan – places that were home to friendly settlers, with a small troupe of soldiers, and staffed with Chinese officials. Multiple smaller isolated forts and towers lay between these destinations, and there were even enormous gates at the top of mountain passes. Most expensive was the 1,000-kilometer stretch of the Great Wall that paralleled the route through the narrow Gansu Corridor, where merchant caravans, like imperial armies, were especially vulnerable to nomadic raiders. Once in Central Asia, merchants relied on caravanserais, stables, and warehouses built by mercantile authorities there. That said, most long-distance Tang-era Chinese merchants by far lived and worked on the 20,000 kilometers of

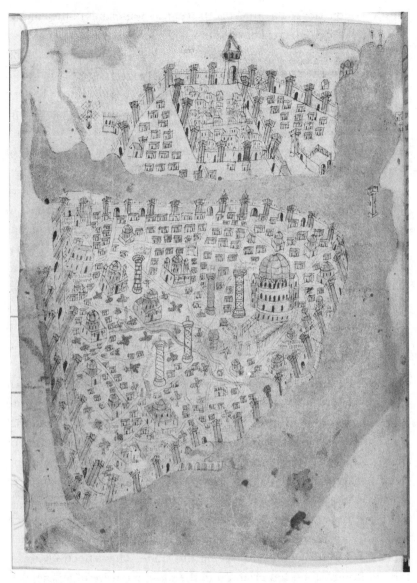

4.1. The City of Constantinople and the Merchant Quarter of Pera
Few seaports are as hallowed as the "Golden Horn" of Constantinople. Greek merchants founded the city as Byzantion in the 800s BCE. After 1100 CE, merchants from Italian cities like Genoa and Venice coveted the docks of the Golden Horn. Fearing them, the Byzantine emperors forced Genoese and Jewish merchants to live separately across the harbor at Pera (Galata). The Genoese defied imperial orders, and fortified Pera, increasing their influence. Later, in Venice, the ruling merchant council confined Jews in a neighborhood called the ghetto, scapegoating them for the city's problems. These districts exemplify the complex politics of mercantile capitalism in its earliest millennia. DEA PICTURE LIBRARY/De Agostini/Getty Images.

mostly paved roads that connected the central homelands of the empire, and along the various versions of the 1,600-kilometer Grand Canal.[14]

The Romans famously made similarly expensive investments in built infrastructure for intercontinental trade. Thanks to roads that led from the Mediterranean ports eastward, Central Asian and Middle Eastern traders connected to China brought the craft of silk making to Rome. Chinese-made silk has been discovered in Roman-era ruins in Britain, and Roman coins appear in former coastal cities all along the coasts of the Bay of Bengal, Vietnam, and southern China itself – even if few individuals made it all the way from Changan to the Eternal City before the 1200s CE. Another very long trade route reached across the Sahara to Nubia (in today's Sudan) from the south of Egypt. There the Romans built a string of fortifications and oasis towns to acquire gold, ivory, animals, and slaves. Goods from India also arrived in large quantities at markets in Rome, thanks to merchants associated with cities like Axum in the Horn of Africa, who transported goods by ship between dozens of port cities along the Red Sea, the Persian Gulf, the Arabian Gulf, and even the Bay of Bengal. To travel between India and Rome, Asian and Roman merchants offloaded their Indian Ocean goods at small Red Sea ports like Berenike for transportation by pack mules across the Eastern Egyptian desert to the upper Nile. There dockworkers transferred the loads onto riverboats for the trip to the much larger port of Alexandria, where they were again transferred to seagoing ships for the last leg of their trip across the Mediterranean. Alexandria was also the loading point for heavy shipments of Rome-bound Egyptian wheat, essential to Rome's explosive growth as well as its system of free grain and bread for its restive poor. Companies of ship-owning Roman merchants, which some scholars liken to modern capitalist corporations, bid against each other for the privilege of overseeing this trade. They effectively transformed Rome's food hinterland into the most extensive of any ancient city – rivaled only, much later, by Kaifeng's reach into the Yangtze Valley rice-lands and beyond. Many of Rome's enormous enslaved population also arrived on ships from ports along these various sea routes.[15]

Rome's contribution to this early supercontinental mercantile capitalist economy would not be possible without the city's own twin harbor facilities on the Mediterranean coast: Ostia and Portus Augusti, the port of the Augustan emperors. Portus was a massive undertaking of engineering and construction conducted at imperial expense. Emperors Claudius and Trajan who financed it were so proud of the results they gave their own names to its dredged basins, canals, docks, and cavernous warehouses, which could handle shipments from dozens of the largest ships of the day. Three kilometers of breakwaters surrounded the main Port of Claudius to shield ships docked within from high waves. The Roman historian Pliny the Elder extoled the new durable material artisans used when building the Portus breakwaters. Roman cement, he noted, "becomes a single stone mass" when "it comes into contact with the waves of the sea and is submerged." In 2006, mineralogists confirmed Pliny's observation: the volcanic ash used in the jetties, when mixed with lime and salt water, created a crystalline structure far more durable than the concrete of our own day, which tends to dissolve over time, especially in contact with sea salt. That said, the most impressive example of marine architecture in the ancient world was at Rome's rival city, the pharaoh Cleopatra's capital at Alexandria, Egypt. There, her ancestors had built a 1,200-meter-long breakwater connecting the city's docks with the famous three-tiered Pharos lighthouse. At 100 meters tall, Pharos was the closest the ancient world came to a true urban skyscraper – or a "world trade center."[16]

None of the world's trade routes would have been possible without their biggest, beating urban economic hearts – the imperial capitals of the day. Not only Rome or Changan, whose centrality to the Silk Road we know well, but also massive capitals like the Indian Maurya and Gupta dynasties' capital of Pataliputra on the Ganges. Archaeologists know far less about Pataliputra than Rome, but its 400,000 inhabitants and its enormously wealthy palace court surely helped drive demand for mercantile activity in large parts of the Indian Ocean. After the fall of Rome, the multiple "nodes" of the supercontinental economy shifted in relative importance, even as trade – and, critically, maintenance of the built infrastructure – along the main routes ebbed and flowed. As Rome declined, silt from the Tiber clogged Ostia and Portus. Byzantium (Constantinople) took over as the center of the Mediterranean trade. Baghdad and Damascus powered mercantile activity in the Middle East; Kanchipuram, Delhi, Angkor Wat, Pagan (see Figure 5.1 in the next chapter), and Ayutthaya in South and Southeast Asia; and Kaifeng, then Hangzhou, Guangzhou, and Kyoto in East Asia. The Mongols destroyed many of those capital cities, rudely disrupting supercontinental trade for a time. Still, the "Mongol Peace" that followed later actually helped reopen the Silk Road, and added new branches further north, for the regimes at Karakorum and other Mongol capitals provided better protection for merchants in the dangerous Central Asia stretches than the Chinese emperors could ever manage. It was only under the Mongols' watch that fabled North African and European travelers and merchants such as Ibn Battuta of Tangier and the Polo Brothers of Venice first made their way across the entire supercontinent.[17]

Long-distance trade in the Americas was also driven by multiple urban centers during the first millennium and a half CE, being promoted by authorities in marketplaces and merchant quarters of cities like Teotihuacan, Tula, and Tenochtitlan in Central Mexico, and Tiwanaku and Cuzco in the Andes. The Inka built perhaps the most impressive of all paved pre-modern road systems. Their stone paths and staircases up and down the Andes and across some of the highest passes in the world allowed llama caravans and human-carried trade to connect urban marketplaces (and imperial administrative centers) thousands of kilometers apart.[18]

Yet, on the eve of Christopher Columbus's voyages across the Atlantic, the center of the world's economic gravity shifted decisively, for a brief time anyway, far to the East, along the coasts of the China Seas and Indian Ocean. The largest shipbuilding facilities built before modern times were located on China's Yangtze River in Nanjing, the first capital of the Ming dynasty. There, Emperors Hong Wu and Yongle financed five separate complexes, dominated by the thirteen massive dry docks of the Longjiang shipyard. More than 20,000 specialized artisans worked there, making these yards probably the most extensive pre-modern urban industrial area. There they built the flagships of the famous Ming Treasure Fleet, commanded by the eunuch admiral Zheng He from 1402 to 1433 CE. The fleet itself was the largest to sail the seas before World War I; it consisted of the largest ships built before the invention of modern steel-clad battleships. At 400-plus meters each, a dozen or more of these super-junks sailed together in seven voyages into the Indian Ocean, surrounded by hundreds of smaller support vessels. The fleet was essentially a floating capital city, complete with its own ocean-going hinterland, for some of the ships were equipped with vegetable gardens, livestock paddocks, and fish tanks. It embodied as much monumental power as any Chinese Forbidden City: from afar, its high bamboo sails seemed like approaching storm clouds. As the fleet entered ports in Southeast Asia, India, Arabia, and East Africa, local rulers and merchant communities hastened to make deals with the admiral for shipments of expensive tributes to the Ming emperor. Tons of luxury goods, including an entire menagerie of African animals, made their way back to China, much of it ending up in the real Forbidden City in Beijing, which Yongle constructed in 1417 as his dynasty's permanent capital. The city's teeming marketplaces, filled to the brim with the "rarities of the world," would soon help to attract a million or more inhabitants to the great Ming capital. Thus, Yongle and Zheng He added new layers to a supercontinental realm of human action, built upon large capital cities, roads, canals, forts, caravan cities, and seaports. In the meantime, city-based circuits of ideas and knowledge followed in these elongating paths of empire and commerce, creating yet another layer of built environment essential for the approaching birth of Earthopolis.[19]

CHAPTER 5

How Knowledge Became Power

CIVILIZATION, PROPAGANDA, AND THEIR DISCONTENTS

Of all the human accomplishments for which cities have taken credit, the one with the most grandiose name is "civilization." The word comes from the same Latin root as *city*. Even someone as excited about cities – and as ambivalent about "civilizations" – as the great urban historian Lewis Mumford defined cities both as a "manifestation" of civilization and a "structure specifically equipped to store and transmit [its] goods." The idea that cities were both creations and creators of civilization is not new; it goes back to the foundation myth of Inanna's delivery of cities, alongside civilization, to Uruk. In addition to the arts of power, wealth, craft, and trade, the Holy *Mē* included "cultivated behavior," knowledge, "careful speech," music, "the perceptive ear, the power of attention," writing, law, cutting-edge sexual experimentation, and "the rejoicing of the heart."[1]

Though the myth of Inanna acknowledges the deep flaws of urban societies, other Mesopotamian texts consistently celebrate the *Mē*-blessed lives of city dwellers in contrast to the benighted existence of those who live in rural areas and the wilderness. In these texts, nomadic tribespeople most often played the role of the extreme "other." Whereas city dwellers have fine houses, clothes, food, and rituals, the nomad is "dressed in sheep skins; / He lives in tents in wind and rain; He doesn't offer sacrifices ... / He eats raw meat, lives his life without a home, and when he dies, he is not buried according to proper rituals." The premodern world produced many similar sentiments contrasting urban civilization with nomadic roughness. Chinese commentators lauded what they held to be their supreme form of culture based on farming, "palaces and houses to live in and capitals to rule from," contrasting it with the pastoralist peoples of the north who "lead a migratory life in all seasons, carts and horses are their home." The Greeks' idea of *polis* not only elided the city and the state, it equated cities with high rhetoric, rationality, organized debate, good law-making, and proper religious shrines – in contrast to the camps of the *barbaroi* – literally the people of coarse speech who live far from cities according to the harsh law of clan, blood, and war. The Romans too saw their civilization as literally inhabiting the *civitas*, even when some commentators (like the historian Tacitus) despaired that city life had softened the Romans' traditional prowess in war, to the advantage of grittier, forest-dwelling Germanic barbarians. These ambivalent attitudes about cities and civilization also have long legacies. It is easy, for example, to see how ideas like Tacitus's were later used to support more dangerous ideas associated with "race." His critique of cities awash in pleasure-seeking, when mixed over time with biblical images like those of Sodom and Gomorrah and hellish urban imagery in other cultures, also spawned anti-urban thought based on the idea that cities actually undermined morality and civilization – or, in the nineteenth century, that cities despoiled the environment. Still, the more triumphant idea that cities are the vessel of all that is good about civilization resonates to our own day among the most enthusiastic boosters of city life. Among their sentiments is the idea that "energized crowding" in cities creates not only wealth but heightened intellectual innovation.[2]

I prefer to avoid the casually city-congratulating (and later casually racist) overtones of the word "civilization," and return to the far messier cargo that Inanna discharged on the wharves of Uruk. To recycle Mumford's words, ancient cities may have "stored and transmitted" knowledge, learning, and the other best parts of city life but they did so almost as unequally as they did power and wealth. Moreover, the powerful city dwellers who designed much of urban culture, including the built environment of cities, did so precisely to exalt inequality and their own violence. For the less fortunate city dwellers, the Holy *Mē*, as Inanna's mythic bill of goods frankly attests, also included "lamentation," "consternation," "dismay," and "strife" – all in plenteous quantities, throughout the millennia, and well into our own day.[3]

Dwell for a moment on Mumford's words "stored" and "transmitted." Long before the hard-drive and the digital Cloud, let alone the telegraph, radio, television, or internet, cities themselves were indeed at once the most important *storehouses* of powerful knowledge and the most important *medium* of mass communication. Built space was essential to establishing any idea of "truth" – whether official or deeply subversive. Authoritarian rulers knew this fact well. Temples, palaces, gates, and walls, preferably munificent and set up on high where all could see, cleanly combined both the medium and the message of authoritarian rule: believe and obey – or be crushed. Sometimes god-kings cultivated their power through distance and mystery, like Sennacherib in his palace high above Nineveh or the Ming emperors' Forbidden Palace in Beijing. Others took their cues from practices going back to Uruk, supplementing the magnificence of built structures with sensational public processions. All authoritarians displayed their power in spaces such as squares and marketplaces that exemplify cities' characteristic power to gather great crowds of people. The stone steles engraved with Hammurabi's comparatively enlightened law codes, like the more horrific laws of some earlier Mesopotamian rulers, likely stood in such gathering places; by contrast, so did wooden tablets displaying Solon's rules for democracy in the Athenian Agora. The intimidating carved bulls, lions, and dragons that greeted ordinary commuters, foreign merchants, or ambassadors at Babylon's Ishtar Gate delivered a less subtle public message of imperial power to all. In Rome, as we know, the first emperors took command of the forum, organizing triumphal parades through city streets in honor of their conquests. Then they built their own imperial fora with triumphal arches and tall columns inscribed with boastful words or heroic scenes meant to shower large captive audiences of market goers and passersby with imperial propaganda. Theaters and the first athletic stadiums also played a role. For unruly Roman citizens who needed still more convincing, Vespasian added the great Colosseum (Figure 2.1), a vast gathering space where recipients of free imperial bread could also get free gladiatorial circuses – and sometimes even a glimpse of the emperor himself, majestically dispensing commands of life and death.[4]

The public display of a state's power to murder was among the most chilling – and, sadly, to many of its subjects, most compelling – ways for political authorities to use urban space for propaganda purposes.

Beheading, disembowelment, burning at the stake, drawing and quartering, and hanging in crowded city squares and marketplaces were sanctioned at different times by all states and religious traditions of the pre-modern era; they persist in some cities today. These spectacles allowed states and spiritual authorities to show their intolerance of crime or dissent, yet they could also deliberately whip up vigilante justice against foreigners, women, religious minorities, or, in the case of the Spanish Inquisition, people its reigning priests deemed "heretics."[5]

The practice of public human sacrifice overlapped that of execution, as criminals or dissenters sometimes served as victims. The purpose of sacrifice was to legitimatize the state's monopoly on violence by dramatizing its appeasement of the gods in the most awe-inspiring way possible. Often that meant selecting "purer" victims, including children, for state murder, and ritually deifying (and drugging) them to ease compliance. It is important to note that human sacrifice, one of several other markers of intensifying Neolithic-era inequalities, predates cities. Also, while evidence of such sacrifices exists in virtually all pre-modern urban worlds, scholars interpret it many ways, and it is possible that some urban states actually dampened a practice that was more widespread in village societies. However, there is little disagreement that the most spectacular combination of human sacrifice and urban architecture occurred at the top of pyramids devoted to the Sun and Rain gods in the Aztec capital of Tenochtitlan. High above large plazas where crowds could gather, the emperor's priests sought to guarantee better harvests by laying the living bodies of sacrificial victims – who might be young female slaves or high-status youths groomed for this service to the state – on their backs on concave altars that opened their chests upward. With a single swipe of an obsidian blade, the officiant would crack open the victim's ribcage, scoop out their still beating heart and raise it to the gods, then toss the lifeless bodies down the pyramid steps. Other temple minders would later recover the bodies, sever their heads and display the skulls on racks. In these ways, urban spaces could transform imperial "knowledge" into molten authoritarian power.[6]

CITIES' AXIAL AGE

That said, cities – like "truth," culture, religion, and "civilization" – are capable of mystifying shifts in shape. If cities could be obedient messengers of overweening imperial propaganda, the broader, extra-state, realms of their energized polities also proved useful for those who wanted humans to think beyond official truth, often beyond the spaces that delivered state propaganda. How do we know whether an emperor was faithfully following the Mandate of Heaven as he claimed? Is there a good that is greater than that of the emperor's word? How do we find out? Once we do discover better truths, how should we slip them past the censors and propagate them throughout the Empire, and beyond?

Writing in the 1940s of our own era, the philosopher Karl Jaspers noticed an astonishing historical coincidence. Beginning about 1000 BCE, and accelerating over the next 500 years, all cultures of the Old World nearly simultaneously developed new perspectives on matters of the divine, the good, and the nature of power that, in some way or another, transcended state propaganda. Local cults that had little state support at first grew into large region-spanning embryos of "world religions." Schools of secular philosophy won converts over long distances. A supercontinental "Axial Age," Jaspers argued, had come into being.[7]

Why did this happen? Historians still debate whether anything so large really deserves a single name, let alone an overarching explanation. By the first millennium BCE, neither imperial rule nor long-distance commerce – even that along the Silk Road – had yet connected East Asia and the Middle East or Mediterranean consistently enough for intellectual inspiration to reach across all three of the Old World continents. Without answering those questions in full, we do need to note that cities played a consistent role in this prolonged moment of knowledge innovation everywhere in Afro-Eurasia. So did the hard "bones" of their expanding urban worlds – the built infrastructures of transport, communication, and imperial power that connected cities and reached beyond.

From the beginning, ancient cities' feverish temple–palace bureaucracies, and the diverse groups of people who maintained special shrines or street-schools in the city's neighborhoods and marketplaces, provided a fertile ground for especially talented theologians, priestesses otherwise held apart from male-dominated ziggurats, auspice-readers, soothsayers, astrologists, prophets, griots, scribes, saints, sages, scholars, philosophers, teachers, apothecaries, and even the first scientists. Written texts were their most powerful medium for storing and spreading knowledge. Emperors, of course, used texts too – writing was the invention of palace tax collectors after all, and the palaces contained huge storerooms filled with knowledge about the behavior of royal subjects. Still, it was hard to keep urban literacy caged on top of the ziggurat for long. Unlike the construction of monuments for propaganda purposes, it was relatively cheap to write and exchange texts between literate individuals. Financial outlays were limited to purchase of clay tablets, Egyptian papyrus scrolls, Mediterranean parchments and vellums, or Chinese bone, bamboo strips, silks, and, much later, paper – yet another invention of urban artisans of the Song dynasty that later spread across the Afro-Eurasian world. In the Americas, the Maya used pottery, bark, and skins for their own version of an Axial Age, which occurred much later, after 600 CE. These media were relatively light and compact, allowing people who traveled long distances for a living to transmit unofficial knowledge from city to city, teacher to follower, and generation to generation. Well-beloved urban clerics and teachers could spread their innovative ideas and conversations by ordering deputies bearing doctrinal documents to venture into the same networks of roads, waystations, forts, wharves, and ships that emperors built to wield power and that merchants used to make money. Along the way, such conveyors of Axial thought could build structures more suited to the specialized business of storing and spreading knowledge. Indeed, the transmission of propaganda-transcending knowledge could also attract elite and even imperial sponsorship. No doubt, some of the new knowledge about benevolent rule rubbed off on rulers themselves. More often, such patronage of transcendent knowledge paid dividends in subtler and more persuasive forms of imperial propaganda. Either way, emperors found it useful to invest in expansions of their cities' stock of schools, universities, libraries, monasteries, and places of worship that were either independent of royal propaganda machines or more easily surveilled by them, all the while using these built spaces as symbols of a supposedly more humane version of royal power.[8]

Upon this built infrastructure, intellectual systems founded in the minds of individual scholars or leaders became the nuclei of world-altering knowledge systems and religions such as Confucianism, Hinduism, Buddhism, Zoroastrianism, Judaism, and Hellenistic philosophy. The founders of these Axial Age modes of knowledge, and their hundreds of millions of followers, laid down yet another vast foundational layer of what soon became a truly planetary urban knowledge-storing and knowledge-moving machine that included places of worship, schools, monasteries, and libraries in cities and along the roads, rivers, and seaports that connected them. Later, Judaism helped inspire two monotheistic rivals, Christianity and Islam, which built even more extensive spiritual and intellectual habitats upon the skeletal system of the ancient world's imperial and mercantile infrastructures. During the years 900 to 1350 CE or so, systems of thought first born in the Axial Age contributed to further bursts of world-connecting innovation that historians denote as the "Golden Ages" of Song China and Abassid Islam, and, later, the "High" Middle Ages of the Christian world. By that point, Islam in particular had cemented the now bi-millennial legacy of the Axial Age by creating networks of mosques that reached from the western end to the eastern end of the Old World supercontinent. In this, the vastest of all pre-modern knowledge communities, *muezzin* perched high in minarets of thousands of mosques in hundreds of cities called tens of millions of otherwise very diverse followers to prayer five times a day. All bowed in one direction: toward the Holy City of Mecca.[9]

LAUNCHING "WORLD RELIGIONS" IN ASIA

As the great Chinese scholar Confucius (*c.* 553–479 BCE) learned to his own dismay, being able to articulate a philosophy of the good state, based on virtues such as self-improvement, the harmonious interplay of the classes, pious deference between generations, and wise imperial interpretations of the Mandate of Heaven, did not mean that emperors would actually practice what the great thinkers of their age taught and wrote. During his entire life, which coincided with a period when imperial control broke down and regional leaders fought for supremacy, he found little interest in his ideas even as he traveled between warring rival capital cities in search of court sponsorship. When, long after his death, the Han dynasty officially adopted his doctrines, they did so with official twists that allowed far more latitude for arbitrary and militaristic rule than Confucius would have deemed truly wise. However, Confucius's teachings did meanwhile become foundational texts of Chinese civilization, and studying them became a crucial test for young aristocrats and even for less privileged commoners who wanted to make a career of service to the Empire.[10]

The Han established an Empire-wide system of schools to identify promising students and prepare them for potential imperial service. For those who did well, the next step was to attend higher academies and pass ferocious tests of memorization in examination halls. In Han Changan, the Imperial University, the first of its type in world history, trained the empire's very highest officials and may have had tens of thousands of students as early as 100 CE, including some from quite modest backgrounds. Emperors of the Tang, Song, Yuan, and Ming dynasties later revived and extended these institutions after various periods of imperial collapse.[11]

If cities helped spread Confucian influence, the reverse was true too. *The Artificer's Record*, a section of one of the texts students learned in Chinese academies, has the honor of being the world's oldest textbook on urban planning. First written and revised by students of Confucian thought during the 300s BCE, it elaborated longstanding practices of Chinese emperors and their diviners. It established that the capital city of any virtuous dynasty with hope of longevity ought to take the form of a square, further subdivided into nine smaller squares in a three-by-three grid, with all sides facing the four cardinal directions. The ideal placement for the palace was in the central or north-central position of the grid, where it could best channel heavenly power into the earthly city itself – and beyond that to the Celestial Empire as a whole. The difficult sites of some Chinese capitals – like Han Changan itself, as we have seen – meant that planners sometimes honored these principles only in their imaginations. However, Chinese Axial Age urban thought continued to strongly influence the design of the Sui and Tang dynasties' relocated and rebuilt capital at Changan, the Song dynasty's Kaifeng, and the Yüan and Ming capital at Dadu/Beijing as well as cities throughout the

Chinese south. The influence of *The Artificer's Record* reached to resplendent cities like Nara and Kyoto, Japan; Gyeongju (Kyongju) in Korea – known for a time as the "miniature Changan"; and Hanoi in the area today known as Vietnam, not to mention the Mongol capitals at Karakorum, Shandu, and Dadu or Beijing.[12]

By that point, Axial Age knowledge had spawned even more widely diffused nuclei of future world religions elsewhere in Asia, along with their own traditions of urban form and knowledge-power. Hindu Brahmins and other holy people specialized in building elaborate temples and organizing mass pilgrimages to holy sites, some involving cities that otherwise housed relatively little secular power. Kashi – today's city of Varanasi or Benares – was arguably the holiest of all and certainly one of the oldest. In the imagination of pious Hindu pilgrims, the city's chaotic-seeming labyrinth actually contains an ordered, spiral-shape *yatra*, or spiritual pathway that leads from the city's outskirts toward the center. This spatial experience of increasingly purified connection to the divine culminates in a plunge into the holy waters of the Ganges River. As pilgrims coil along this holy path toward the river, they pause to pray at shrines and potent phallic *lingams* placed at crossings. In the built practice of Hindu devotion, countless smaller shrines can be found in homes and courtyards throughout India. On the other geographical extreme, the mass annual pilgrimages to dozens of Hindu holy cities must count as the largest-scale and oldest regularly scheduled circuits of human movement devoted to any religion, only later rivaled by Islam's *hajj* to Mecca. By contrast with these city-connecting activities, the Hindu caste system segregated the neighborhoods of South Asian cities probably more systematically than any other pre-modern urban world – on the grimmer theory that the higher capacity for ritual purity possessed by upper castes could be threatened by encounters in urban spaces with the "pollution" of lower castes – and especially of "untouchable" out-castes.[13]

The teachings of Siddhartha Gautama, the Buddha, perhaps best illustrate the relationship between cities and the transformation of a small cult into a continental, and later global, knowledge-power phenomenon. His teachings were legendarily conceived during a period after the Buddha forsook the palace of his birth and devoted himself to an ascetic life deep in the jungles of the Ganges Plains. Yet the wisdom he produced there subsequently spread from Varanasi, where the Buddha emerged from the forest to assemble his first group of acolytes, into a highly energized world of spiritual ferment in the rival capital cities of kingdoms in the region. South Asia's powerful Buddhist rulers included the Mauryan Emperor Ashoka the Great, who conquered smaller Buddhist dynasties and made Buddhism his state religion. He, like those he conquered, funded the construction of Buddhism's classic monumental structures: temples containing enormous statues of the Buddha himself, pagodas, stupas, and above all separate monasteries and nunneries. These traditions and structures later diffused outward, thanks to traveling male monks and merchants but also influential groups of nuns, making their way from India to Southeast Asia and to China, Tibet, Korea, and Japan. Interspersed among the waystations and guard towers of the Silk Road, for example, were dozens of remote Buddhist monasteries, nunneries and libraries, most notably that of the "library temple" in the Thousand Buddha Caves near the garrison city of Dongguan. Chinese emperors allowed Buddhist monks to take over hilly territories that were less conducive to grain growing. There, devotees of the Buddha logged the surrounding forests to build magnificent mountaintop monasteries or convents, surrounded by substantial settlements that allowed them to accrue vast wealth, including many enslaved laborers. In contrast to this dispersed spiritual infrastructure, Buddhists also implanted themselves in the concentrated urban hearts of dynastic China. Tang-era Changan, for example, was home to as many as 300 Buddha Halls (or *fotang*), including several temples in the palace complex, and hundreds of street-corner shrines – that is, until an emperor issued edicts persecuting Buddhists. Elsewhere in Asia, Buddhist kings built enormous monuments, such as the 10,000 pagodas of the Burmese capital of Pagan (Figure 5.1) and the Shwedagon or Golden Temple in today's Yangon (Rangoon). Buddhist kings also took over what was originally the palace of a Hindu dynasty at Angkor Wat in today's Cambodia, and transformed it into the largest religious structure in the world, its tall "lotus-flower" towers rising serenely above a vast city of as many as 400,000 people. Visitors to today's Kyoto, Japan, another early center of Buddhist thought, can get perhaps the best sense of the feel of a pre-modern Buddhist city – with its spectacular ring of vermillion pagodas and golden temples, its thousands of alleyway shrines, and, on

5.1. The Pagodas of Bagan
Few states celebrated their basis in an Axial Age spiritual tradition more fervently than the mighty Bagan (Pagan) Empire in today's Myanmar (*c.* 800–1257 CE). Its capital on the Irrawaddy River was home to as many as 200,000 people, with 10,000 pagoda-shaped Buddhist temples spread throughout the surrounding plains. Yet Bagan is only one point in a Buddhist urban world that reached from India to cities like Yangon (Rangoon) and Angkor Wat, and via dispersed monasteries along the Silk Road to the capitals of Mongolia, China, and Japan. Cities were critical to the transformation of local cults into what much later, became "world religions."
MLADEN ANTONOV/AFP/Getty Images.

festival days, its processions of magnificent lantern-filled floats, tugged through the streets by devotees from each one of the city's neighborhoods.[14]

JERUSALEM, ROME, AND MECCA: THREE CITIES
OF THE ONE GOD

The great South and East Asian traditions of city-building and knowledge dispersion reached enormous scope, but in pre-modern times, they made only little headway west of today's Afghanistan. Nineveh, Babylon, and the Persian capital of Persepolis all served as great independent centers of Axial Age scholarship and lawgiving. Mesopotamian emperors like Ashurbanipal and Nebuchadrezzar built early versions of libraries that contained what were by then millennia-old tablets from as far back as Uruk. In Persia, some inspiration from Hindu practices arrived from the East; the Persian prophet Zoroaster may have incorporated these into his own system of worship focused on the supreme god Ahura Masta (the Buddha may have picked up some Zoroastrian concepts that did travel the other way). To create spaces of sufficient ritual purity, Zoroastrian priests built dozens of fire temples across the Persian Empire, including high on a hill in Emperor Cyrus the Great's enormous capital at Persepolis. These survived the Muslim conquest 1,000 years later, and remain an important feature of today's Iranian cities; dozens of fire temples also operate in today's Mumbai, where "Parsi" (Persian Zoroastrian) families became prominent overseas merchants in the eighteenth and nineteenth centuries CE.[15]

Thanks in part to Zoroastrian influences, Babylon's highly charged mixture of cultures – later associated with its ziggurat, the "Tower of Babel" – also may have helped give birth to the Axial Age's ultimately widest-circulating impulse, the idea of a single God. If so, the invention of monotheism was also inseparable from Jerusalem, the holy city with the most tumultuous history of all. In 586 BCE, Nebuchadrezzar of Babylon conquered Jerusalem. He destroyed the temple that the great lawgiving King Solomon had built on the city's Mount Moriah, the so-called "Temple Mount," and then dragged Jerusalem's inhabitants into exile in Babylon. Zoroaster's inclination toward monotheism had reached Babylon by that point, and it may have inspired exiled Jewish prophets like Ezekiel, Jeremiah, and Isaiah to refine the Judeans' worship of a single, undivided god, Yahweh – in their case as a force to rally a movement for anti-imperial liberation. The Torah, the scriptural basis for his veneration, was probably composed in centers of Jewish learning in several cities of Axial Age Babylonia. Once Babylon had fallen to the armies of the Persian Emperor Cyrus the Great in 559 BCE, the new ruler allowed Jews to return to Jerusalem, where Jewish kings proceeded to build a Second Temple to Yahweh. Much later, in the first century CE, King Herod rebuilt the Second Temple even more magnificently, constructing a massive retaining wall to expand the building's footprint atop Mount Moriah. Today, we know the remaining portions of Herod's retaining wall as the Wailing Wall, the holiest site in Judaism (Figure 5.2).[16]

5.2. Jerusalem's Old City from the Air
Through Jerusalem's Jaffa Gate (1538 CE, foreground) we can travel back throughout the history of monotheism. At the al-Aksa Mosque and the golden Dome of the Rock (692 CE, upper right), Allah taught Mohammad to pray toward Mecca. The Church of the Holy Sepulchre (300s CE, center) contains the site of Jesus Christ's crucifixion and the tomb from which, Christian doctrine holds, he rose as humanity's savior. The Wailing Wall, part of the Second Temple (516 BCE, beneath the trees between the two mosques) is Judaism's holiest site. These spaces remain as deeply contested as they are hallowed, further attesting to cities' history as creators and creations of world-spanning religious traditions.
Maremagnum/Corbis Documentary/Getty Images.

In the interval, the Macedonian King Alexander the Great, and later Roman generals, swept across the earliest urban birth-worlds, spreading the so-called Hellenistic civilization with them. Much of that culture had emerged in the 400s and 300s BCE within the highly charged democratic and religious politics of the city of Athens. Along the *stoas* (columned porches) that surrounded the city's Agora (Map 1.1(C)), several open-air schools of philosophy operated, most famously that of Socrates, which his student Plato formalized into an Academy that trained Plato's star student, Aristotle. Such schools were at once the exemplar of democratic citizenship in the *polis* and the target of the suspicious cabal of Athenians who, in a moment of political upheaval, put Socrates to death. Dramatists like Euripides and Sophocles brought questions about the relationship between gods, states, and humans to huge theaters in the city, and elsewhere in Greece. A hundred and fifty years later, Alexander appropriated the prestigious mantle of Greek scholarship and art as he led his rampaging armies across the crumbling Persian Empire and beyond. He and his successors built numerous libraries in the many cities he founded with the name "Alexandria," none more ambitious that the Great Library of the Greek Ptolemaic Pharaohs in the largest of all Alexandrias, the one in Egypt. In Jerusalem, Jewish scholars absorbed many of these Greek influences. Yet, Jerusalem fell once again, this time to a siege by the Roman General Pompey in 63 BCE. At that point, Jewish monotheism encountered the sharp hostility of the city's newest conquerors.[17]

Rome was ordinarily quite tolerant of the gods of its conquered peoples, even outmatching Babylon in cultural diversity. The Eternal City contained temples to the entire Greek pantheon – including, after 128 CE, the great cement-domed "Pantheon" itself. The Egyptian goddess Isis had several temples in Rome. There were many sites devoted to bloody rituals demanded by the Persian bull-god Mithras. Roman polytheism also mixed freely with Greek secular thought. Prominent Roman thinkers like Lucretius, Cicero, and Seneca spent much of their careers in Rome elaborating the work of Aristotle and Plato, not always in ways that were flattering to emperors. Insistence on a single god, however, fit especially poorly into the multifarious spiritual universe of Rome, especially one in which emperors themselves aspired to join the pantheon's ranks. Though many Jews lived in Rome, the empire often persecuted them brutally, crucifying many. One of the victims was the Jerusalem artisan turned would-be Jewish Messiah who called himself Jesus Christ. His crucifixion atop a rocky outcrop called Golgotha, then located just outside Jerusalem's walls, inspired his followers to spread his teachings throughout the port cities of the Greek and Roman world – notably through the "Epistles" of the Jewish convert Paul to Christians in Athens, Corinth, Ephesus, and Rome itself. Meanwhile, in Jerusalem, the Jews rebelled rather than accept the installation of a statue of a Roman emperor on Herod's Temple Mount, and the Roman Emperor Titus destroyed the Temple in 70 CE. Titus then commemorated his achievement by building a fabulous triumphal arch in the Roman forum (his father Vespasian had previously looted the Temple for cash to build the Roman Colosseum). Soon the Romans expelled Jews from Jerusalem and ordered them never to return.[18]

Amidst ongoing Roman persecution, Jewish and Christian thinkers and martyrs, including many devout women, continued to develop their faiths clandestinely in Antioch, Edessa, and various other cities of the Roman and Persian Empires, using small urban meeting places they called synagogues and churches. Christian doctrines spread to Ethiopian capitals, Indian Ocean seaports, Central Asian cities, and as far as Tang Changan. In 330 CE the Roman Emperor Constantine reversed three centuries of anti-Christian policy and declared Christ's teachings to be the official religion of the Empire, thus bringing to fruition Jesus's own desire to govern his church from a "rock" in the Eternal City itself. The Christian popes dedicated a new basilica in Rome to their predecessor, Christ's principal apostle St. Peter (*Petrus*, the rock), which remained the capital of Roman Catholicism beyond the fall of the Empire and until our own time. The remaining Eastern or Byzantine Empire established a rival center of Christian faith in Constantinople, at the Emperor Justinian's magnificent multi-domed basilica, the Haghia Sophia – Holy Wisdom. In Jerusalem, Constantine began construction of the Church of the Holy Sepulchre, encompassing the rock of Golgotha where Jesus was crucified and the tomb (sepulchre) where, the Gospels affirm, he rose from the dead three days later, founding the Christian faith.[19]

As Western cities declined, Roman Christian churches and soon monasteries proliferated, despite the fact that Germans, Vikings, and later Arab armies burned thousands of them as soon as they were built. The cross-topped spires or clanging bell towers of Christian churches and cathedrals have since become a proud symbol of town-hood and city-ness across large stretches of the world. Monasteries and convents, whose origins go back to Middle Eastern establishments in the 200s CE, also began proliferating in rural areas of Europe during the early Middle Ages, taking similar form to the aristocratic estates that surrounded them, and ruled by abbots or abbesses with as much power as great lords. Monks and nuns laboriously copied and shared holy texts. As in Buddhist Asia, some of these Christian monastic centers of learning became the nuclei of new towns and cities.[20]

After Rome's fall, however, the center of gravity in global urban knowledge-power production shifted east to Byzantium and, even more consequentially, to the cities of the Arabian Peninsula. There the

Prophet Mohammad brought into being the youngest of the three great monotheistic faiths, based on the Quran – a text that his single god, Allah, dictated to him on a mountaintop near the caravan city of Mecca. Islam shared Abrahamic roots with Judaism and Christianity, and Muslims likewise revered the Temple Mount in Jerusalem, since, as the Quran maintains, Allah took Mohammad there on his final journey to Paradise. It was in Jerusalem that Allah taught his prophet how to kneel in prayer in the direction of Mecca five times a day. Shortly afterward Mohammad's successors, the caliphs, conquered Jerusalem. They built the resplendent Dome of the Rock above the foundation of Herod's Second Temple on Mount Moriah, where it remains to this day. Nonetheless, Mecca and nearby Medina (where Mohammad began Islam's inaugural *hajj*) remain the two most sacred cities in Islam.[21]

As Mohammad's successors the caliphs spread Islam by the sword and by the word, they followed the prophet's commandment to encourage learning and thought wherever they went. Even the most splendid mosques were open to all Muslims, and the caliphs' magnificent palaces included large public halls where officials, and even the Caliph himself, held audiences to hear ordinary people's struggles and resolve disputes. Systems of gender segregation, which kept many women secluded in interior apartments of their homes or screened off sections of mosques, meant that direct access to power was largely limited to men. Quranic learning was also widely available to men at mosques and schools (*madrassas*) in towns and cities across the Islamic world. The caliphs also invested heavily in higher education. In his great circular capital at Baghdad, the Abbasid Caliph Harun al Rashid built a House of Wisdom, whose libraries stored religious texts from many faiths as well as Arabic translations of Aristotle and Plato. Muslim imams built important mosques, libraries, and universities even at the far ends of the Islamic world, such as Timbuktu in West Africa, Cordoba, Spain, in cities along the Silk Road deep into western China, and in port cities throughout South and East Asia, including Guangzhou. Among other things, librarians and scholars in places like these debated Axial Age philosophical texts from Greece and Rome, preserving their existence during a period when Christian centers of learning went into comparative eclipse. During the "Golden Age" of Islam, despite a widening split between rival Shia and Sunni sects and despite differences in practice that reflected its great geographical reach, Muhammad's teachings underpinned a community of worshippers numbering in the tens of millions stretching from one end of Afro-Eurasia to the other. All Muslims hoped for the chance to fulfill one of their faith's sacred obligations, to make a pilgrimage – the *hajj* – to Mecca at least once in their lifetimes. This foundational requirement was imaginable only because Islam also consisted of an immense urban world of its own making, a dispersed archipelago of mosques and schools in hundreds of cities all connected by a multi-continental infrastructure of overland and seaborne travel. Indeed, the multifarious *dar al-Islam* perhaps did more to prefigure the Urban Planet to come than any other Axial Age assemblage of built structures.[22]

As a "Golden Age" of learning peaked in the Islamic world, the Roman Pope Urban II issued a call to priests and monks across Christendom to raise armies for a crusade against the Muslim rulers of the biblical Holy Land. Once again, the city of Jerusalem became a flashpoint of battles over Axial Age faith. When Christians took the holy city in 1099 CE, they put hundreds of Muslims to the sword. The Dome of the Rock survived, though, and eighty-eight years later, the Egyptian Sultan Saladin the Great showed far more mercy when he retook Jerusalem. He reopened the city to all faiths, though he assigned each to a separate neighborhood – the origins of the Jewish, Christian, Muslim, and Armenian Quarters that pilgrims and tourists visit in Jerusalem's Old City today. Muslim rulers' tolerance toward Jews also contrasted sharply with their intense persecution across Europe, where raging urban mobs killed many, and where kings expelled them from cities and entire kingdoms. This presaged their confinement to "ghettos" in places like Venice, Rome, Amsterdam, Vienna, and Frankfurt after 1500 – spaces meant to stigmatize, not to glorify, a tradition of learning, but where Jewish scholarship flourished nonetheless.[23]

Meanwhile, ironically, as battles between Crusaders and Muslims continued during the ensuing century and a half, the Axial Age texts stored in Islamic libraries became increasingly available to clerics and scholars in now rapidly growing cities of "High Middle Ages" Western Europe, many of them built on the sites of long-obliterated Roman colonial cities. Increasingly confident Christian kings – as well as powerful rival aristocrats who preferred urban life to their rich estates – built brand-new crenelated city walls around these cities, and erected magnificent castles topped with pepper-pot towers that vied uneasily for prominence on the urban skyline with the soaring spires of Roman bishops' increasingly ornate Gothic-style cathedrals. As European scholars revived their efforts to expand knowledge in these environments, many of them formed guilds similar to those of other artisans, which included their students. The students in some cities, like Bologna and Paris, became a strong enough economic and political force to demand royal and clerical sponsorship for new centers of learning that were at least partly independent of both the church and the castle. In this way, Europe too acquired its first urban universities.[24]

"CIVILIZATION" AT THE LIMITS

From about 900 to 1400 CE, Axial Age knowledge traditions approached their two thousandth birthdays amidst "Golden" and "High" Ages of various pre-modern knowledge communities, centered in the dynastic capitals of China; Baghdad and other caliphal capitals like Damascus and Cairo; holy cities like Varanasi, Angkor, Kyoto, Mecca, Jerusalem, and Rome; Eastern Christian Constantinople; and Gothic Europe's university towns and monasteries. How many people, then, were touched in pre-modern times by the transcendent power of urban-amplified learning and knowledge? The evidence remains hard to assess.

First, ongoing warfare conducted by authoritarian rulers, both secular and spiritual, repeatedly interrupted intellectuals' efforts anywhere in the world to convert transcendent knowledge into power. Nineveh, Babylon, and Persepolis barely survived the early Axial Age itself. Alexandria's great Library fell long before the Golden Ages, thanks to neglect under Roman rule (Julius Caesar seems to have burned at least part of it to the ground by accident). When invaders laid Rome and Changan to waste, both cities lost untold storehouses of knowledge, including in Changan's case the world's first university. The same happened after brutal conquests of Baghdad, Kaifeng, and Hangzhou by Mongol raiders, and after Viking raids on beleaguered Christian cathedral towns before the High Middle Ages. Even at times when emperors most generously patronized scholars, they also practiced severe censorship, enforced by their own city-enabled systems of state violence. As with the persecution of the European Jews, cities may have stimulated countless impulses of creative thought, but they also unleashed forces that occluded the imagination in ways we can never measure.[25]

Second, evidence for an exact count of fully literate people – those proficient in reading and writing, whatever that means exactly – is lacking. Scholars of pre-modern literacy divide into very pessimistic and only slightly more optimistic schools of thought on the matter. By the most optimistic estimates, only about one in five people who lived during the five millennia between the invention of writing in Inanna's temple (3200 BCE) and the rise of empirical scientific thought (after 1500 CE) acquired even the most basic proficiency in reading and writing. Those rates were far lower among women, and slightly higher in the capitals of the Song and Abbasid dynasties and in European university towns. Advanced learning and a life of the mind was a luxury for the tiniest of minorities. Still, there is agreement among today's researchers that cities provided pre-modern people, including many women, with much better opportunities than villages did to acquire some shreds of power through literacy – if not in formal educational establishments, then at least as a byproduct of work in marketplaces, artisan shops, and merchant houses, or from participation in more sophisticated urban religious spaces. Emperors' written inscriptions on monuments meant for popular consumption and profuse evidence of graffiti on Roman walls suggest that many otherwise unschooled people at least possessed some literacy skills.

Meanwhile, religious thought and practice – leavened with philosophical insight or not – provided opportunities for hundreds of millions of people to experience awe and perhaps some comfort amidst what remained a harsh and deeply unequal world. If so, their imaginations often turned to the next subject we must cover, the wrath of forces emanating from the Sun and Earth. Most of the victims of this wrath could only begin to understand it as the displeasure of the gods. There was no misunderstanding the consequences, however: humans as a species had to contend with limits on our endeavors, city-assisted and city-enlightened or not.[26]

CHAPTER 6

The Realm of Consequence

INANNA'S WAGER, 5,500 YEARS ON

We have reached the year 1500 CE, a good time to survey how far we have come. We are five and a half millennia into our journey, a full nine-tenths of the way through the biography of our Urban Planet, yet we have merely covered the formative years: the pre-life of Earthopolis, the years preceding its birth as a truly planetary Urban Planet. That birth was about to happen, for after 1500 a new surge of growth began. This surge, unlike dozens of earlier periods of growth in many places and times, merged all of the original birth-worlds into a contiguous urban world both plural and singular. We would build hundreds of new cities, augmenting our own power by stealing immense new draughts of energy from Sun and Earth, not just from rivers any more, but also, for the first time ever, from the entirety of the world's connected oceans.

Before going on, though, there is an important matter to clear up. What should we think of all of these "surges"? If cities are such potent crucibles of natural energy and human power, why did Earthopolis's formative years follow such a lurching, wave-like motion, not a sleek, continuous upward line of growth? What happened between surges? Could the miracle of urban amplification go into reverse? How can we fully know what caused the four realms of the Urban Planet to take truly planetary dimensions if we do not also know how they could lose power or energy or both at once – and then shrink?

Once again, Inanna warned us, long ago. The creation of cities was a wager for the ages. The coin that the goddess flipped at the Lapis Lazuli Quay was rigged in her own paradoxical likeness: creation on one side, destruction on the other. Remember: cities can help us warp time into long continuous trends of creation and expansion, but natural energy and human power can also disrupt such continuities in time, sometimes in the form of mass destruction. Many of the world's holy people echoed Inanna's admonition. At all West African crossroads, urban and otherwise, lurks Eshu, the guardian of the underworld and the gods' abode, truth-teller and liar, creator and flouter of rules, and the ultimate holder of our fate. In holy Varanasi, Hindu pilgrims must handle similar uncertainty, pouring milk over the erect phallus of Shiva at each intersection along the Holy *Yatra* to quiet the god's restless powers of destruction. Similar street corner erections, called *herms*, in ancient Athens reminded citizens that their destinies lay in the hands of the genial grifter Hermes. All of the gods of fecundity – Chinese farmers' many nature gods, the Egyptian Sun God, the Greco-Roman Demeter (Ceres) – had their tragic sides. Our cities are nothing if not "Promethean," yet the gods punished Prometheus for stealing the fire; they chained him to a rock and commanded the buzzards to peck his liver out once every day. Even the One God of the monotheists had two faces: the loving shepherd and the angry destroyer of his flock. So did, in a way, the far more peaceful Buddha, whose path to Enlightenment required long and deep contemplation of *Dukha*, the cycle of human suffering. The Sun Gods of the Americas – Virachocha of the Inka and Huitzilopochtli of the Aztecs – promised long life and prosperity, but, as we know, only at the greatest of all prices: we had to march possibly hundreds of sacrificial victims, especially ones in the prime of life, to the top of the pyramid. When the priests of the Sun God raised these victims' severed hearts skyward, still coughing blood, they laid their existential bets without a second thought: only public killings at the heart of the city could guarantee more life in a wider world of cities.

Since then, we have learned other ways to comprehend the uncertainties of the urban coin flip. Both of the sources of cities' very existence – natural energy from Sun and Earth and human power from cities' energized political communities – were mighty forces, but they also explain urban unpredictability. As we built cities and their surrounding urban worlds, our realms of action and habitat had growing impacts – on our own habitats as well as on the habitats of other species. That in turn increased the likelihood of destructive consequences, some of which took on a gigantic geographic scope of their own. For one thing, as we already know, cities increased our political communities' capacity for "intraspecies" self-destruction through war, inequalities of all kinds, including slavery, and severe limits on the well-being of the majority of the enlarged human populations that cities made possible. We also put more people in the path of "exogenous" disasters – those due to destructive pulses and withdrawals of energy from Sun and Earth. These moderated during the 11 previous millennia of the Holocene Epoch, but they could still rage far beyond what we could control even as city dwellers. In addition, though, our impact on the habitats of other species, before 1500 most notably on disease-causing microorganisms and forest trees, also had consequences. Those "interspecies" impacts could add "endogenous" – that is, human-generated – force to exogenous disasters. At those moments, cities suffered the ultimate consequences of the same twinned forces that brought them into being, by becoming crucibles for human-amplified, life-destroying bursts of geo-solar energy.

Either way, Inanna did not lie. The realm of consequence, a surging and retreating space that encompasses both the life that our cities created and the life it destroyed, perhaps defines the boundaries of our emerging Urban Planet in a more culminant fashion than its other three realms. As exogenous and endogenous cycles of hot and cold, fecundity and desolation, war and peace crisscrossed each other in time and on Earth, they help account for both the surges in the size of our early urban worlds and the gaps between the surges. This explains why pre-modern cities were only slightly less likely to fall to the Earth as they were to rise. Sometimes all the most powerful imperial states, all the biggest pools of wealth, all the newest technologies, all the largest religious ceremonies, and all of our own potent exertions of human power could not put them back together again.

The Urban Planet's formative years – the pre-life of Earthopolis – left deep scars on its later life. New, immense acts of urban creation would follow after 1500 CE, yet the forces of destruction also gained strength. Perhaps that consequence is as predictable as things got on Earthopolis. As we gave birth to the first truly planetary Urban Planet we know of, its dark flipside grew quickly too, as we know all too well today.

GODS OF LIFE AND WRATH

Cities, concentrated habitats that relied on extended human created energy-collecting hinterlands, worked only in relationship to their own much larger, astronomical, hinterland – the one that reached 150 million kilometers into space toward explosive nuclear fission reactions in the heart of the Sun. The pessimistic economist Thomas Malthus was wrong that the amount of energy the Sun delivered to humans on Earth was finite and fixed for all time, capable of sustaining only so many of us and no more. Climate scientists now know that, even in the relatively peaceful Holocene, the Earth's relationship to its star changed continuously, including many times during the 6,000-year life span of Earthopolis. Sometimes our stellar furnace grew far hotter for centuries at a time, or colder. The Earth's orbit or axis wobbled according to its own rhythms, at times stretching toward or away from its heat source. The planetary atmosphere's blanket of gases changed in composition, letting too much sunshine in or reflecting too much out in unpredictable patterns that Earth's own volcanoes disrupted dramatically by unfurling umbrellas of ash that blocked the Sun's rays. Humans had some say in the matter too. Even in the pre-modern era, as we know (Chapter 3), our riverine and other aqueous energy collectors could steal extra stellar fire or moderate its excesses if we expanded the acreage of cropland, pasture, or woodlot, or if we improved our technologies and farming practices to increase the amount of food or fuel that each acre produced. The era's few coalmines could provide supplemental bits of solar power in fossilized form.

However, in another way, Malthus was right, for waxing and waning bursts of geo-solar energy often overwhelmed even the amplified human power they allowed us to generate in cities. At moments of energy excess or shortage, our geo-solar collectors could fail catastrophically. In Cities of the Rivers, too-high or too-low water levels were the most obvious sign that things were dangerously amiss. Floods or storms could melt our ramparts back into mud or wreckages of stone. Masses of river silt, salt, debris, or hot sand from advancing deserts could bury our highest ziggurats. Droughts could dry ditches and reservoirs, bringing famines that left cadavers bloating in the streets. Fires could incinerate the forests and rage through urban tinderboxes. Volcanoes could bury us in lava and ash or cause killing winters. Earth itself could quake, and tsunamis could suck all of us – cities and all – back into the seas where life first emerged. Amidst such events, exogenous forces could make endogenous disasters like wars more common. They could intensify cities' incubation of disease. They fell heaviest on the most vulnerable majorities, including farmers, the poor, and enslaved people. And, by their very design, cities could amplify the death toll, by putting more people in the path of disaster. Whatever their shape, exogenous geo-solar disasters visited cities hundreds if not thousands of times over the first five and half millennia of global urban history.

The climate historian John L. Brooke has made the most thorough historical investigation yet of the role of Sun and Earth in human history, assessing their capacity both for nurture and for death. Carefully dating the Holocene's relatively moderate climate swings, he added credence to the heavily debated idea that, during the 3000s BCE, the Sun's waning rays caused cooler and more unstable weather in temperate zones, leading to cataclysmic droughts and floods that may have played a part in concentrating climate refugees in places spared from the calamities, possibly including Uruk. More often, though, cities grew when the weather got better, during the Holocene's centuries-long "Goldilocks" periods that Brooke calls "Climate Optimums," when the amount of solar energy combined with Earth's tilt toward the Sun, the composition of our planet's atmospheric gases, and quieted volcanoes gave us not-too-hot, not-too-cold weather that was easiest for our own energy collectors to manage. The Bronze Age consisted of several of these moments; the Iron Age and the Axial Age (after 1000 BCE) likely began during others. Our numbers on Earth typically grew during these periods of Climate Optimum, roughly doubling during the Bronze Age and doubling once again after we started using iron. After 200 BCE, when empires based in Rome and Changan bookended the Afro-Eurasian supercontinent, they benefited from another period of Climate Optimum, and the human population rose to a quarter billion by 300 CE. An even longer Climate Optimum undergirded the successive Golden and High Ages in Afro-Eurasia from 900 to 1350 CE, when the world's population rose even higher, to some 400 million. At point, the tri-continental *dar al-Islam*, then the "Mongol peace" that followed the conquest, and then Ming admiral

Zheng He's Treasure Ships made it possible for armed forces, merchants in caravans or on ships, and pilgrims to move across and between the diverse Afro-Eurasian urban worlds that nonetheless intersected with each other enough for some contemporaries to imagine them as parts of an increasingly singular, supercontinental whole. From 1271 to 1292, the Polo Brothers of Venice, and from 1325 to 1347, the far greater traveler Ibn Battuta of Tangier proved that it was possible to wander from one end of the "Old World" to the other, and write back home about hundreds of splendidly powerful, rich, and learned cities – strung along roads and sea-routes stretching from Timbuktu to "Xanadu."[1]

Conversely, periods of urban growth went into sharp reverse during cycles of less optimal exogenous conditions, typically affecting some regions more than others. Periods of calamity likely aggravated to some degree by climate change include the following: (1) Three multi-century slowdowns in growth in Bronze Age Mesopotamian and Egyptian city-building – in 2200–2000, 1650–1500, and 1200–1000 BCE; the last of which was accompanied by nearly two centuries of droughts in the Middle East and horrific floods in China. (2) The collapse of the Indus Valley cities around 1900 BCE. (3) The Warring States Period in China (475–221 BCE), when the smaller rival cities of Confucius's time devolved into especially brutal conflict in the years after his death. (4) The fall of the Han dynasty and the subsequent sacking of Changan after 220 CE. (5) The westward movements of Asian nomadic peoples, who pushed Germanic groups into Roman territory, setting in motion a series of sackings of Rome that soon collapsed the Western half of the Empire and drastically depopulated the "Eternal City" itself as well as all other cities in the region. (6) The collapse of the spectacular Mesoamerican city of Teotihuacan in the 500s CE. (7) The decline and abandonment of Mayan cities from 800–900 CE, likely during a series of severe droughts that drained their cisterns and reservoirs. (8) The collapse of the great Southeast Asian capital of Angkor Wat in the 1400s CE, also likely due to drought – and the siltation of its canal system caused by over-logging of forests for use in the city's palaces. Finally (9), after 1350 or so, the "Climate Optimum" of the Golden and High Ages of Afro-Eurasia waned. Atmospheric temperatures began to cool across the northern hemisphere, foreshadowing the Holocene's most turbulent period, the "Little Ice Age" of the 1600s. However, even before

1300 the descent from the Optimum contributed to widespread famine and the Black Death of bubonic plague, the most destructive pandemic in history, responsible for the deaths of between seventy and 200 million people. Though plague continued to ravage cities long after, an easing of lower temperatures during the 1400s allowed the world's biggest urban worlds to grow once again – as attested by giant cities in Ming China, the Muslim empires of South and Southwest Asia, the Renaissance kingdoms of Europe, the Russian Empire, West Africa's Songhay Empire, and the Inka and Aztec empires in the Americas (Chapter 7). By 1500, humanity had once again broken the 400 million mark, even as the discovery of the interlinked World Ocean ultimately ensured greater population surges to come.[2]

MICROBES AND HUMANS: AN URBAN DEATH DANCE

As the size of our slowly merging urban worlds ebbed and flowed within changing outer limits set by the Sun and Earth, our own actions in cities, soil-lands, rivers, forests, and the atmosphere altered and sometimes intensified the destructive impact of otherwise exogenous currents of geo-solar energy. While our own "endogenous" actions were responsible for these deathly expansions in the realms of impact and consequence, our Axial Age religious traditions and science only foggily illuminated our own role in letting them loose. This limited knowledge left us with only a few ideas about what we could do to stop them.

Most striking was the ways cities altered our relationship to our own most dangerous biological rivals on Earth, disease-causing viruses and bacteria. Our species's predilection for concentrated and dispersed habitats precisely matched these tiny enemies' own tastes in a home. While cities gave us indubitable power to expand our numbers (in surges) from 4000 BCE to 1500 CE, our enhanced capacity to set off epidemics of infectious disease must rank high on our long list of large-scale disruptive consequences to city life.

True, the human experience with such scourges far predated the urban age. Malaria, the biggest killer of all, was a disease of the Neolithic revolution. Farmers disturbed forests, thus creating sodden spaces in and around plowed fields that could breed mosquitoes and the devastating plasmodia that they injected into human bodies. Domestication of herd animals also opened people up to a wide array of pathogens like influenza, whooping cough, tuberculosis, chicken pox, measles, and other animal "poxes."[3] That said, during the first five millennia of their existence, cities made disease much worse and spread it to more people in more places, including back into the villages. As we know too well from the Covid-19 pandemic of 2020, pathogens pass between people (and between animals and people) in dense urban human habitats far more effectively than in villages, and they mutate more rapidly. The powerful feedback loop that cities set in motion between dense spaces and larger, more diffused human-altered hinterlands and between previously distinct urban worlds often caused us to literally "domesticate" new disease-causing microbiota, and spread misery of all kinds over large distances. In their larger-scale movements, urban-based merchant ship crews, caravan drivers, and imperial armies all helped (without knowing it for the most part) to replicate one city's underworldly microbiological visitation in many other cities. In grim times like this, to use Brooke's words, "the city became a glittering palace of death." Or, to use the even grimmer phrase coined by the pioneering historian of disease William McNeill, "urban population wastage" was an ongoing reality, forcing agricultural villages "not only to produce more food than they themselves consumed in order to feed urban dwellers, but also to produce a surplus of children whose migration into town was needed to sustain urban numbers." Cities thus depended on hyper-charged ideals of fertility in their own cultures and those of their surrounding villages (as the goddess of sex, Inanna was only one among many who played a role in propagating these ideals), as well as at least some tolerance among city dwellers for the in-migration of often strange-seeming forest, steppe, desert, and mountain folk.[4]

It is also true that cities could act as a moderating force on the diseases they whipped up. The earliest public health measures were one such counterforce. In an age when people possessed no knowledge of the link between microscopic organisms and disease, our best explanations in ancient times focused on divine rage, and the so-called miasma theory: that sickness came from the stench of urban air, water, and waste. Though these theories limited our success in stopping disease, some religious traditions did encourage artisanal nursing practices that could forestall the worst. Public health measures such as isolation of the sick are inscribed in ancient texts, including the Bible, and "social distancing" measures were built into such greeting behavior as bowing in Asia and were applied, far more invidiously, in the segregation of "clean" and "unclean" castes in India. Variolation, the deliberate injection of infected material into bodies to forestall deadlier forms of disease, was practiced in many pre-modern cities, if never in large-scale public health campaigns. Efforts to clear cities of foul-smelling water and air through widened streets, and early sewer systems such as those at Mohenjo Daro and many Chinese and Roman cities helped. So did the first quarantine measures, which were enacted during the Black Plague years at Ragusa (Dubrovnik) and Venice. These forced arriving ships' crews to wait forty (*quaranta*) days on board before disembarking.[5]

Meanwhile, cities also translated their density, diversity, and churning populations into a capacity to increase immunity to the worst diseases. This was especially true for the diseases people originally acquired from animals but that could be passed directly from human to human by spitting, coughing, or sneezing at close quarters. After killing many city dwellers, such zoonotic diseases, including measles and chicken pox, survived in cities for two reasons. First, cities provided enough human hosts that some acquired immunity, thus allowing the disease to live on in milder forms that did not kill off all the city's inhabitants or the pathogen itself. Secondly, cities encouraged a constant new supply of non-immune human hosts – in the form of large numbers of newly born children and newly arrived migrants. The more virulent forms of the disease lived on by killing these new hosts, but, overall, the minority of urban children who survived these diseases acquired immunity in adulthood. Thirdly, by living close to animals that suffered from poxes that only mildly affected humans, some urban residents were effectively inoculated against deadlier versions that could arise – which was important to the difference between Old World and New World immunity to smallpox. No matter the route to immunity, large populations of urban dwellers could pass their defenses outward to at least parts of cities' own hinterlands.[6]

Until the revolution in microbiological science of the nineteenth century, cities' defenses against disease were repeatedly outflanked by

6.1. Praying to the Goddess of Smallpox for Protection from Disease
The port city of Negapattinam, like others across the world, was prone to pandemics transmitted from one urban world to the next on ships. Known since ancient times as a key transit point of goods from China to Rome, it also became a center for the worship of many Hindu gods, including Mariatele, the goddess of smallpox. To gain her favor, some worshippers pierced their skin with sharp instruments. In this image dating from an epidemic of the eighteenth century, a man is hoisted high above the temple square in supplication, suspended by hooks gouged into his lower back.
Universal Images Group/Getty Images.

their built-in proclivity to arouse new scourges and spread them. The danger grew as urban worlds grew and merged. Since humans in premodern cities acquired immunity region by region, activities that reached between regions – imperial conquest, trade, religious proselytization, and pilgrimages – could all bring unfamiliar maladies to untouched cities and entire urban regions. Smallpox, a disease of Central Asian herd animals, was absent in the classical Roman and Chinese empires. However, as both empires encouraged trade across the Old World during the 200s and 300s CE, bursts of smallpox (or something a lot like it) began spreading to either end of the supercontinent from an as-yet-undetermined source, possibly located in Africa, India, or the Tibetan plateau. In the Mediterranean and in the Yellow River valleys this scourge killed untold millions, and it may help explain the growing weakness of both empires in the face of threats from forest and steppe peoples after 200 CE. During those years, Rome's renewed imperial reach eastward came at the cost of several empire-wide pandemics, possibly originating in India.

As Rome itself fell to Germanic invaders, the first pandemic of plague spread throughout Roman cities in 541–49 and lingered for several centuries, by which point the disease aggravated the depopulation of Western Europe. Later, the Mongol conquest opened new supercontinental transmission pathways for *Yersinia pestis*, the plague bacterium. While the exact routes remain unclear, one recent historian argues that grain carts meant to feed horsemen besieging Baghdad in 1258 unwittingly delivered the rats that carried the fleas that carried the virus from remote wild rodent habitats into the heartland of the Islamic urban world. From this new "reservoir" other outbreaks followed, most famously during another Mongol siege of the Genoese colonial city Kaffa in Crimea (1345). Facing an outbreak in their own ranks, Mongol generals catapulted bodies of their dead warriors into the city. Whether because of that early act of biological warfare, or because plague rats simply scurried across the siege lines, Genoese ships from Kaffa soon brought the disease to Messina, Tunis, and port towns throughout the Mediterranean. The quarantines at Ragusa and Venice may have delayed the viral storm there, and thousands who could fled the cities. But the virus soon completely upended urban life across Europe, North Africa, and as far away as Moscow, dealing horrific death to half or more of many cities' inhabitants. The cooling climate made this most deadly of all pandemics worse, but throughout the first five and a half millennia of urban history, epidemics likely played as big a role as exogenous disasters and endogenous warfare in explaining episodes of mass urban collapse.[7]

FIELDS, FORESTS, AND THEIR DISCONTENTS

Other human-created destructive consequences arose from our single most impactful acts of habitat building in pre-modern times – the redesign of field and forest hinterlands aimed to increase our geo-solar energy harvests to support cities. The consequences of these acts and impacts could take some time to gather strength. However, once we let loose the Pandora's box of soil degradation and erosion, river silting, deforestation, wood-fire pollution, and even the first substantial emissions of greenhouse gases, we likely stirred up still other unpredictable forces of geo-solar energy. When that happened, the boundaries between exogenous and endogenous disasters began to blur. Human impact on the geo-solar climatological system increased, igniting new surges in the realm of its destructive consequences.

As we know from the earliest cities like Uruk, urban institutions and cities' energized artisanal inventors gave us technological advances, like irrigation and metal plows, that expanded our harvests of solar energy for city use, even at times when climatic conditions were less than "optimal." These actions could also involve more felling of forest trees, which cities needed in any case for firewood, charcoal, and building material. Even from the earliest times, cities thus gave us the power – and increased our existential need – to test the changing elasticity of "Malthusian" limits set by the Sun and Earth.

Mesopotamian cities came into being and grew over time precisely because they served as the site of state institutions capable of extensive alterations to croplands in the Euphrates and Tigris flood plains. And yet, the nutrient-rich silt that the rivers washed from the mountains into the Mesopotamian flood plains also contained traces of infertile salt. Rivers typically flush river-salt into the sea, producing the concentrated saltiness of seawater. But when state authorities in the region diverted river water into thousands of miles of irrigation ditches, the flow of water slowed, weakening the flushing process and increasing evaporation, thus raising the concentration of salt in the fields and increasing the likelihood that it would leach into the soil. To make matters worse, the structure of Mesopotamian soils did not allow river salt to titrate downward into the earth as efficiently as other soils did. Projects of city energizing thus also set in motion drip-by-drip processes of choking Mesopotamia in brine. Though scholars continue to debate the importance of soil salinization in the region, it remains the leading theory explaining why, after three long millennia – and after the *coup de grâce* of Persia's conquest of Babylon in

539 BCE – Mesopotamia lost its capacity to generate fearsome world-conquering capital cities for over 1,000 years. Only when Harun al-Rashid and the Abbasid caliphs were able to deploy a wide range of new hydraulic technologies and hundreds of thousands of African slaves (not to mention gather the large armies they needed to subdue the Zanj rebellion) did they restore the lower Tigris and Euphrates to agricultural production on a scale needed to feed a million people in the caliphs' then-brand-new capital Baghdad, and extend Islamic power over large parts of three continents.[8]

In China and Rome, and later during the Golden Ages of the Tang, Song, and Yüan dynasties and the High Middle Ages in Europe, increased agricultural activity relied on various new technologies and practices (Chapter 3). Yet it also came at huge expense to forests. "Day by day," wrote the Roman poet-philosopher Lucretius in 50 BCE, "they would constrain the woods to reside more and more up in the mountains." He was describing enslaved axe-wielders chopping down trees on the edge of an Italian estate, enlarging their owners' agricultural land. Even on the edge of the wilderness, these tree-choppers were doing essential urban work, feeding, fueling, and building bigger cities such as Rome.[9]

Like disease, human deforestation existed well before the urban age. Foragers burned woodland to scare animals into their ambushes, and villagers cleared many more acres for farming, house building, and home heating. Yet in Rome, Changan, Teotihuacan, Jenné-jenno or any pre-modern city, wood in far greater quantities was foundational to the very existence of the built habitat and to life in it. Homes in cities with chilly winters could require huge log piles or whole storerooms of charcoal to keep braziers lit throughout the day and night. In all climates, metalworkers, potters, cloth dyers, tanners, and tavern cooks all burned huge quantities of wood to keep the urban artisanal economy humming. Many cities were of course literally built of wood itself, including most of the houses and shops in million-strong Tang-era Changan, Song Kaifeng, and Japan's Kyoto. Yet cities built of brick also required massive wood or charcoal furnaces to produce their basic building blocks, in addition to any of their buildings' ceramic floor tiles and clay roof tiles. The famous Roman cement that held the city's bricks together – and that held the waves at bay at Portus Augusti – required blazing hot charcoal furnaces, because lime, one of its key ingredients, had to be baked at high temperatures. Monumental architecture needed to look impressive inside as well as outside, and for much of the first 5,000 years of city-building, the only structural elements available to hold the ceilings of palatial interior halls, atriums, or temple sanctuaries aloft were long, straight, thick wood joists harvested from especially old trees. (Rome's Pantheon was a rare early experiment with structural cement.) Ships that provisioned cities required similarly large and straight logs for masts and keels. Emperors, merchants, and shipbuilders often tried to conserve stands of old trees for these purposes. However, even by Roman times, the ancient cedars of Lebanon had suffered severe depletion because of the use of ancient trees in buildings that graced hundreds of earlier imperial capitals, not to mention in Phoenician ships. By the end of the Roman period, shipbuilders at Portus Augusti were sourcing large timbers from as far away as the Black Sea. Meanwhile, Roman generals on campaign along the *limes* of central Europe felled countless trees for the wooden palisades around the *castra* (camps) of their armies. Back in Rome, in the middle of a special new forum, Emperor Trajan erected a triumphal marble column in honor of his conquest of barbarian Dacia. The artisans who carved intricate images of his exploits on the shaft of the column gave ample space to the heroic lumberjacks who had made the empire's conquests possible. Once the army had moved on, legionnaires typically burned the *castra* to the ground to keep it out of enemy hands – yet another way forests were sacrificed to the expansion of early urban worlds.[10]

The mining and smelting of metal in pre-modern times also consumed massive areas of forest; in northern China, miners regularly ran out of nearby firewood needed for smelting and were forced to abandon mines still rich with ore. Wood- and charcoal-smelted iron also made up a growing part of pre-modern buildings, at first only for nails and other hardware, but some of world history's first metal girders helped lift the roofs of palaces at Kaifeng.[11]

Cities' biggest assault on forests, not surprisingly, came from the expansion of farms. Most new cropland and pasture came into being on land that was once forest. In some places, wetlands, moors, fens, bogs, swamps, and, in Holland, even saltmarshes met some of the same fate as forests. Often, the potential wooden fuel or building materials from cleared forests never made it to urban markets, because farmers found it far more effective to burn the wilderness into submission than to harvest its heavy products and painstakingly transport them to market; in this way, burned trees resemble the wasteful gas flares of today's oil fields and refineries. Conveniently, ash from burned trees and other vegetation pre-fertilized the new farmland, and agricultural products often promised more profits than wood over a longer period.[12]

Historians are only now examining available evidence to reveal the exact dimensions of the impact that pre-modern cities, towns, villages, fields, and pastures had on forests and other wildernesses. The environmental historian Michael Williams has provided one early estimate for High Medieval Western and Central Europe. There, forests covered four-fifths of the territory after the fall of Rome, but only two-fifths by 1300. The figures for China are likely more drastic than that. The once thickly forested North China Plain was nearly all given over to loess agriculture as early as Han times. As much or more Chinese forestland fell to the axe and fire during the Tang- and Song-era settlement of the south. Forest-dwelling "primary species" of animals like tigers and elephants, once plentiful in China, nearly disappeared over the course of the pre-modern era. Yet, as dramatic as these extensions of our realm of impact certainly were, we must remember that this was just a minute beginning. By 1500, recall, neither cities nor their broader rural human-built and human-altered penumbra had reached the vast temperate forests of North America, Siberia, Australia, or most of Earth's tropical rainforests, except in the Mayan Yucatán, and the forests around Angkor Wat in Southeast Asia.[13]

FURIES OF SILT, SMOKE, MUD, AND GAS

Either way, the realm of consequence expanded alongside these impacts. Forests amply punished city dwellers for the sacrifice of trees. Four words summarize the furies of the lost forests: silt, smoke, mud, and greenhouse gas. First let's consider silt. Most early cities sat on top of river silt, but, as Mesopotamians discovered, playing in the dirt was a perilous business, and salty irrigation channels were only the beginning. Plowing land and cutting trees in large numbers loosened soil on fields and, most consequentially, on the steepest slopes of mountain forests, allowing silt to run more copiously into the rivers. Once silt had accumulated on river bottoms, spring floodwaters rose higher than they would otherwise, often meaning that the great rivers that gave life to cities flooded more, rose permanently, or spilled into new courses. Rome came into being despite the repeated floods of the Tiber because the successors of Romulus and Remus chose to build their dwellings on top of its famous seven hills; when the Romans mounded earth between the hills to create the city-connecting forum, the Tiber often flooded it still. (The runoff was tunneled into the city's sewer, the Cloaca Maxima, essentially a masonry-covered stream that led back to the river.) Yet Rome's demand for firewood and charcoal aggravated the flooding even as the city expanded into lower-lying areas. While periodic floods played only a small part in the city's fall, the silt they brought down from the Apennines did gradually move the Tiber's mouth out to sea. By the 500s CE, the great imperial boat basins of Portus Augusti had clogged up. Today, the site of the greatest port of the ancient world lies seven kilometers inland.[14]

The Han, Tang, and Song emperors had a much harder time with the unruly Yellow River, whose waters grew yellower by the year as the agriculture on the western loess plateau released more of that fine-grained material into the water. During the rainy season, the river flushed loosened loess across the North China Plain, amply feeding the single largest regional concentration of humanity on Earth. Yet, when the rains stopped for six months of every year, the yellow silt settled to the river bottom, raising water levels accordingly. To keep farms, towns, and whole cities from inundation, imperial dynasties who wanted to remain in power needed to build massive dykes on both sides of the entire 2,000-kilometer river valley, the equivalent of another "Great Wall of China." Enslaved laborers and peasants had to rebuild big segments of these retaining walls every year, a task that grew more arduous when the river's silt also blocked up the Grand Canal (Figure 6.2).

In 1128, the Song governor of Kaifeng tried to use this fundamental weakness in his capital city's own favor: he opened dykes north of the city to drown the Jurchen cavalries who were besieging his capital's walls.

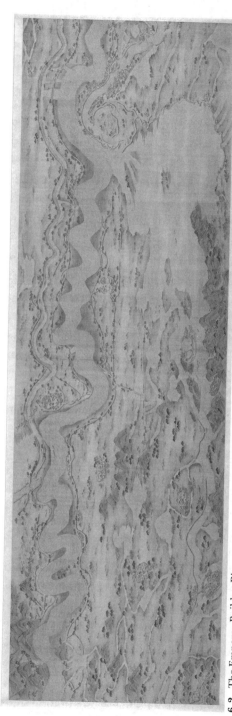

6.2. The Emperor Builds a River

Rivers made cities possible, but building cities could mean rebuilding rivers. The yellowish silts of the Yellow (Huang Ho) River of China replenished the soils that fed some of China's greatest capitals, but silt also made the river flood-prone. Governing the river was essential to the great imperial dynasties. Emperors forced farmers to leave fields and build hundreds of kilometers of dykes, as pictured in this 1790 map from the Qing dynasty; a good indication of the extent of the river building and rebuilding that was required over four millennia to grow the world's largest concentration of cities. Heritage Images/Hulton Archive/Getty Images.

Seventy years later, the series of floods and silt deposits he helped to unleash caused the massive river to radically shift its course. Instead of a sharp turn to the north just downriver from Kaifeng, the river found an opening to the south. In a single anthropogenic stroke – conducted in the name of the survival of a city no less – the delta of the Yellow River moved from a point north of the huge Shantung Peninsula to a point 700 kilometers south of it. Loess poured into the new channel, emptying into a completely different portion of the East China Sea that quickly required a new name: the Yellow Sea. From there, ocean currents carried the silt further south to the region of Hangzhou, where new acres of farmland emerged from the sea, helping to spur already extensive rice cultivation in China's other mighty river valley, the Yangtze. Meanwhile, even further south, rice paddy development in Southern China caused silt to build up in the bay of the great port city of Guangzhou. By 1700, that port city no longer lay on the ocean where it was first built, but far inland, on the new Pearl River Delta, a silty platform for one of the twenty-first century's greatest regional concentrations of urban humanity. Rivers may have created cities, but cities now also helped create rivers (indeed, the mouth of the Yellow River has since shifted numerous times from the north to the south of the Shangdong Peninsula).[15]

That brings us to smoke. Sustaining urban history over its first 5,000 years required prodigious amounts of wood and charcoal burning, another vast tax on the forests. Where did all the smoke go? Much of it directly into the lungs of city dwellers, of course, and of rural forest burners and charcoal makers. There, it no doubt aggravated the respiratory symptoms that both city dwellers and farmworkers suffered during epidemics of infectious disease. Much of the rest of the smoke rose into the planet's atmosphere as particulates and ambient carbon. In our own time, climate scientists studying ice cores from the glaciers in Greenland found lead-saturated carbon grime in layers that date to Roman times. Lead isotopes present in these deposits link them directly to the massive wood and charcoal fires needed to smelt silver at the Empire's Rio Tinto mines. As these traces of Old World smoke in the extreme reaches of the New World suggest, the Romans had already begun the process of filling the atmosphere as whole with human-generated toxic wastes. The massive coal fires in Chinese copper mines and in Kaifeng's tens of thousands of fireplaces made their own substantial contribution to this ancient grime captured in the Arctic. By spreading air pollution over such distances, pre-modern urban worlds they extended the realm of human impact deep into the planetary atmosphere, far beyond the boundaries of our pre-modern realms of action and habitat.[16]

More important, possibly, for the consequences of these impacts are the questions of mud and gas. For all of the wood and other plant material people burned to bring the first cities into being, and for all the carbon dioxide that plowed fields let loose into the atmosphere, ancient city dwellers still did not achieve the hell-raising power we possess today to alter the atmosphere's prevailing temperature in drastic enough ways to imperil the entire human experiment. In pre-modern times, despite building a planet-wide realm of human impact, our realm of consequence remained far smaller; "exogenous" astrophysical and tectonic events such as volcanic eruptions still explained almost all variations in climatic temperature. Still, some researchers do believe that ancient cities' mania for deforestation may have given us slightly more capacity to alter the atmosphere's temperature than we had when we lived in camps and villages alone. If so, this was probably not because our diminished forests could absorb less carbon dioxide – one of our many problems today. On its own, ancient increases in emission of this greenhouse gas might have helped warm the atmosphere, but the effect was probably offset by the lighter surface color ("albedo") of larger crop fields that replaced the darker forests, cooling the atmosphere by reflecting solar heat back out into space. Also, aerosols dispersed by wood burning and metal smelting, such as during Rome's peak, may have blocked solar energy somewhat, in the same way as volcanic ash, adding an anthropogenic cooling effect to the many other forces affecting atmospheric temperature.[17]

More important was the effort to feed rice to the vastly increasing number of cities, towns, and villages in southern China. Chinese rice growers, like other farmers, chopped or burned countless trees to make room for new rice paddies as China's built environment expanded westward up the Yangtze as far as the western Szechuan basin and southward into the watersheds of the newly forming Pearl River Delta. Constructing these water-flooded rice factories, many of them involving lagoons that climbed stepwise up the sides of hills and mountains, required the most advanced irrigation and hydraulic engineering technology of the time. In addition to one of the era's largest episodes of deforestation, rice growing also involved millions of peasants turning untold millions of tons of wet, gassy muck each season to prepare the paddies for what could be centuries of hyper-productive crop growing. If preliminary findings are correct, the release of methane from this muddy human enterprise played a role in moderating the atmosphere's cooling during moments of otherwise adverse changes in the relation of Earth and Sun.[18]

Before 1500, these methane releases, along with atmospheric plumes of wood-smoke, hold the title of the single largest thing we did to the relationship of Earth and Sun in the name of nurturing cities – arguably the most significant gateway we opened into the Anthropocene Epoch during pre-modern times. Within a few years, thanks to sailing ships that we launched into the currents and winds of the newly discovered World Ocean, humanity's urban-amplified realm of action and habitat would start to catch up in geographical size with our planetary realm of impact. Yet at each moment of Oceanic expansion, we would continually replay Inanna's original gamble on the roiling Euphrates River: that our surging actions, habitats, and impacts could somehow continue to outpace the surging scope of their most disastrous consequences. In the matter of realms of impact and consequence, Cities of the Ocean increased the stakes of that urban gamble – while widening the space on Earth that we put at risk.

PART TWO

CITIES OF THE WORLD OCEAN

Construccion de la Fortaleza de la Navidad.

II.1. Building "Christmas City"
De Agnostini/Getty Images.

Dawn rose on Christmas morning, 1492, to find Christopher Columbus drowning in tears of grief. Yet as the day passed, an exalted vision came to him – of two resplendent cities on two sides of an Ocean. By evening, he was euphoric. On the next day, the Admiral of the Ocean Seas celebrated with abandon, shooting off guns and a cannon on a Caribbean beach.

Why such roiling waves of emotion? On the night before Christmas, when Columbus's beloved flagship *Santa María* lay calmly at rest in a bay

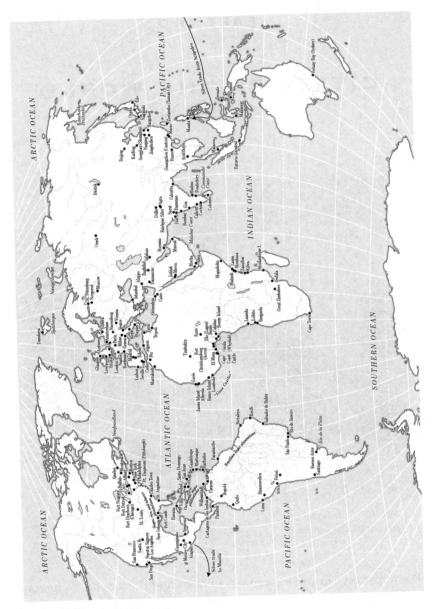

Map II.1. Cities of the World Ocean
Map created by Joe LeMonnier, https://mapartist.com.

along the north coast of what is now Haiti, the ship's keel caught a submerged coral reef. The reef would not let go; the surf pushed and pulled; and by morning the hull had split wide open. The most famous ship in world history, dedicated to none other than the Mother of God, was lost. As the day dawned, a despondent Columbus turned to gracious local Taíno villagers to rescue the ship's cargo, which they secured in two houses on shore.

Then suddenly, Columbus beheld his luminous vision. The disaster, he later wrote, "was really a piece of good fortune." "The Lord," on his own birthday, "had caused the ship to stop here [so] that a settlement might be formed." Regaining his masterly demeanor, Columbus ordered the ship timbers moved to the shore opposite the village, to build a "tower and a fort." Villa Navidad – "Christmas City" – built on Taíno land and populated by Spanish settlers (the now-former crew of the *Santa María*) would give great glory to King Ferdinand and Queen Isabella in far-off Spain. From its harbor, Columbus would ship vast streams of riches, especially gold, back across the Atlantic. Spanish friars would travel back to Christmas City to convert the Taíno to Christianity.

Amidst visions of glory, gold, and god, Columbus envisioned a second, even more luminous city: Jerusalem! With a fort securing the riches of the Americas, Spain could afford to attack the Muslim infidel and retake the Holy Land for Christendom. Columbus's celebratory mood was now as boundless as the ocean. The next day, he treated the Taíno village chief to a demonstration of a "Lombard," a new-model long-bore cannon that the Spaniards had nicknamed the "wallbreaker," whose boom caused the villagers "to fall to the ground."[1]

Columbus was certain: this very moment "originated so many things." He is not wrong. Fourteen ninety-two is truly one of the most important – and most infamous – dates in world history. Yet what was so significant and new? In the long life of the Urban Planet, Villa Navidad was barely a blip. Before the year was out, the Taíno had burned the ramshackle "fort" to the ground, leaving no settler alive. The next Christian reconquest of Jerusalem did not occur until December 1917. City walls and towers, for their part, were hardly a new trend; they went back to Uruk – and even Jericho. Sailing ships were ancient too. Overseas colonial towns went back at least to the Phoenicians. True, Columbus's wall-breaking cannon was the newest model, but the gunpowder that made it go boom went back to the ninth century, the invention of Tang-era alchemists in Changan.

No: the crucial thing was the World Ocean. Columbus was as dimly aware of its full, brimming extent as he was wrong about having reached the "Indies." It took until 1517 for mariners sailing with Ferdinand Magellan to transform Columbus's single-ocean feat into solid proof that the Atlantic connected via the Pacific to the Indian Ocean and back around again. All it took was to design a watertight, floating built environment with strong masts and sails in an urban shipyard, then to fit it with cannons and black powder from local artisan shops. From armed ships, people in one city could build hundreds of new cities, not only on the shores of the "New" supercontinent, but everywhere that Ocean waves lapped the edges of Earth's urban worlds.

For the realms of human action and human habitat, the World Ocean dramatically escalated the possibilities of scale. New cities on all ocean shores made empires, commerce, theft of land and labor, migration, and the spread of religious and consumer cultures into global projects. A habitat that spanned the Oceans, an aborning Urban Planet, demanded a new mix of human settlements: plenty of great capitals and provincial cities to be sure, but also dozens of forts built in harbors from ships, under covering fire from their cannons – places like "Christmas City" that actually lasted. These would become far more important and numerous than ever before, as would the new colonial port cities that rose up under the forts' protection. New urban hinterlands followed in these cities' ocean-spanning wakes and stretched deep into all continents: food-growing farms, mines, cash-crop-growing plantations, forest trading posts, and marine processing plants on far shores meant to slake awakened consumer desires thousands of watery kilometers away. The World Ocean also offered its own source of sheer energy, a gamut of winds and currents powered by the Sun and the spin of the Earth that amplified transport, communication, and extensions of political power – like a prodigious royal road that gave out fuel for free. Filled with finned foodstuffs useful to nourish crews and landlubbers alike, the World Ocean acted as a giant new urban hinterland in its own right, radically amplifying our sources of human protein. Like an enormous mine, it also provided a new fuel for fire, notably in the form of whale oil for millions of lamps in homes and buildings.

All of these things allowed us to push at the outer limits on our population set by Sun and Earth. The 400 million of us on Earth in 1492 more than doubled by 1800, despite the cruel "Little Ice Age" crises of the 1600s. In exchange for its services, the World Ocean also became a vast new realm of human-led planetary impact and destruction. The realm of consequence thus also flared to global dimensions, starting with diseases that Columbus brought from the Old World to the New, ravaging the Taíno village where he landed and the great cities of the Americas beyond.

By forging new crucibles of human power along all shores of the World Ocean, we annexed and ravaged greater swaths of our host planet, soon encouraging even more decisive and dangerous experiments with hydrocarbon energy. An enormous "hinge" creaked open within the long biography of Earthopolis, separating its pre-modern pre-life and the truly planetary urban accelerations that define modernity as we know it. From our vantage point, it seems clear that "early modern" Cities of the World Ocean also began opening new temporal gateways within the far longer biography of Earth itself. Uncertainly at first, then far more quickly, Earthopolis orbited its way through this quickening gauntlet into a new Epoch – when human power, compounded above all in cities, mattered as much to the life of Earth as its own energies and those of its Sun.[2]

CHAPTER 7

Bastions, Battleships, and Gunpowder Cities

A GLOBAL URBAN ARMS RACE

Building a walled city, from a ship, on a far ocean harbor, under cover of cannon fire. Christopher Columbus was neither the first nor the last to attempt this. Over the course of the century preceding 1492, as the Black Death receded from the great capitals of Afro-Eurasia, and as military power accumulated in Tenochtitlan and Cuzco in the Americas, new city-created and city-creating empires arose in all of the world's oldest and largest urban birth regions. All recycled the old rules about cities and empires. An especially high capacity for state violence harvested from Sun and Earth in one city allowed its masters to force other cities and their hinterlands into alignment with a central authority, enshrined in palaces, temples, and offices in the newly anointed imperial capital and delivered over long distances by roads and canals, and (in a growing number of cases) across windswept currents of saltwater. Not all of these imperial states possessed cannons, gunpowder, or even city walls, but as the 5,500th birthday of cities came and went, all of them contended with ships carrying these instruments of violence to or from their oceanic shores. Thus, each of the new empires, in its own way and from its own direction, contributed to two new facts of global urban history. First, the winds and currents of the World Ocean had become a potential delivery device for city-energized imperial military might everywhere. Second, walled cities on ocean shores designed by imperial states to deploy gunpowder violence were becoming the skeletal system of the first truly planetary Urban Planet we know of. That Urban Planet remained foundationally plural and permanently diverse in its component urban worlds, yet these worlds also interacted more than ever before, becoming something almost as singular as it was plural: one vast realm of city-amplified political contest that richly deserves both the planetary and the political syllables in the name Earthopolis.

When was Earthopolis born? There is no single birthdate, for an Urban Planet is made of many ingredients, each with their own relationship to time. Christmas Day 1492, when the employee of an Old World king used the Atlantic Ocean to found a fortress city in the Americas is one birthdate, but that one is far too pat for such a complex matter. We could also push it forward to 1517, when Ferdinand Magellan, another mariner in Spanish royal employ, proved that the Oceans were all connected; or to 1571, when the first regular trans-Pacific shipping service, also a Spanish enterprise, began. If so expansion was not guaranteed, for Sun and Earth pushed back sharply in the 1600s Little Ice Age, when a hundred million or more died worldwide in hoary cold snaps, famines, pandemics, floods, droughts, urban fires, and climate-intensified wars. Conversely, we could date Earthopolis's "early modern" birth backward in time to the Tang dynasty of China, whose artisans first experimented with gunpowder in the 800s CE; or to the Song, who first experienced gunpowder's explosive power in relationship to the walls of their capital city in the 1100s CE. Centuries before 1492, those deadly inventions were responsible for an escalating, supercontinental arms race between the various empires of Afro-Eurasia. As increasing numbers of direct empire-on-empire confrontations occurred, often for the first time, the diverse designs of guns, ships, and city walls in each region began to matter more to the course of global urban history as a whole than ever before. Meanwhile, the macro-spatial relationships between the Oceans and the supercontinent's imperial territories began to matter more to the outcome of these conflicts.

The upshot was this: as states based in Cities of the Rivers gradually built more Cities of the World Oceans, smaller upstart kingdoms in one region – Europe – faced far greater political and economic incentives to develop the cannons, ships, and city walls required to take the imperial lead on the now increasingly Ocean-defined geopolitical stage. This fact was ironic, for, since the fall of Rome, European cities and states had been small and relatively powerless by world standards, even after the High Middle Ages and the Black Plague was followed by a "Renaissance" of urban wealth and learning. Columbus by no means "won" this

Ocean-fueled arms race in 1492. The real European victory, if that is what it was, would wait until the Age of Hydrocarbon. In the meantime, a broad "parity" in Old World imperial power persisted. That said, shipborne Europeans did become uniquely ubiquitous participants in many of the many political dramas that took place across the new Urban Planet, and in *all* of the new Cities of the Oceans. Europeans also took exclusive advantage of the technological and microbiological differences between the heretofore long-separated "Old" and "New" Worlds that led to the Spanish conquests of the Aztec and Inka Empires. Unprecedented transoceanic thefts of sovereignty, which Europeans gradually extended, despite ongoing resistance by Native peoples, via more cannon-toting walled cities on seashores to the Americas as a whole, became an essential political tool for unprecedented Ocean-, city-, and gunpowder-powered thefts of land, labor, and natural resources (Chapter 8). Only much later did that wealth, increasingly coordinated from European imperial capitals by Ocean-going capitalists, help tip the Old World imperial balance to Europe's – and then specifically to Britain's – favor.

THE STATE OF THE GREAT IMPERIAL CAPITALS

Long before that happened, in Mesoamerica and the Andes, cities' millennia-old commitment to authoritarian hierarchy lived on lavishly, as the Europeans who supposedly "discovered" the continent found to their amazement, followed by grudging respect. The Aztec and Inka empires had ruled for several centuries over the Americas' two oldest urban birth-regions – from two enormous capitals, Tenochtitlan and Cuzco. No moment better captured the irony of Europe's suddenly enlarged role in global urban affairs than when Spanish conquistadors got their first breathless view of Aztec Tenochtitlan from a nearby mountain pass. Laid out in its splendor on an island in the middle of Lake Texcoco, the vast capital was spiked with an enormous pair of pyramid-shaped temples devoted to the Aztec gods of the Sun and Rain. Radiating causeways led to dozens of other large lakeshore cities. Sumptuous gardens made of decomposing grass rafts floated across the shallow lake, providing a vast diversity of foodstuffs to the city's residents. A stupendous backdrop of jagged volcanic cones framed the whole picture.

For Hernán Cortés and his Spanish soldiers, nothing in Europe remotely compared to what they saw, unless it was an idealized image of Rome or Constantinople, cities few of them had ever visited.[1]

Back in Europe, cities were in fact mostly far dowdier than Tenochtitlan. After 1500, most had rebounded from the disastrous population losses of the Black Plague years, and some even grew faster than they had in the "High" Middle Ages. The power of European kings was growing, as reflected in the castles, cathedrals, and crenelated walls of capitals like Ferdinand and Isabella's Toledo (soon supplanted by Madrid) and other capitals like Lisbon, London, Paris, and papal Rome. Powerful, self-governing Italian cities like Genoa, Venice, and Florence had rebounded spectacularly from the Black Death to become centers of "Renaissance" learning replete with architectural jewels. Far to the east, in Moscow, a dynasty of Slavic grand dukes hired Italian architects to refurbish their modest castle. Ensconced in this new and fearsome "Kremlin," they took the title Tsar (Caesar), rulers of what soon became a supercontinental empire called Russia. Much later, in 1631, the dashing "Sun King" Louis XIV signaled the apogee of "absolute" royal rule by transforming a hunting lodge at Versailles in the Paris outskirts into a palace of such magnetic draw that French nobles would spend big parts of their lives there, vying for the king's favor rather than plotting his overthrow. Prussian and Austrian kings soon imitated him at Sanssouci near Berlin and at Schönbrunn in the suburbs of Vienna. The Russian Tsar Peter the Great was so attracted to European absolutism that he left medieval Moscow behind, to fashion an entirely new Western-style capital at St. Petersburg (dedicated in 1712) on the Baltic Sea, designed to connect his Eurasian empire more firmly to Paris and London, where he grew up as a prince. He ensconced himself in a fleet of in-town and out-of-town palaces in St. Petersburg that looked a lot like his childhood homes in the West.[2]

Similar transformations were spreading around the Islamic world. Jump back in time to the Niger Bend of Africa around 1492, where the Muslim Songhay Empire, heir to the storied empires of Ghana and Mali, grew to its greatest extent. Its rulers stretched the walls of the ancient imperial capital of Gao, the great mercantile town of Jenné (on one part of the site of ancient Jenné-jenno), and the center of Islamic learning at

Timbuktu. On the north side of the Sahara, the capital of the Islamic Caliphate had meanwhile moved from Golden Age Baghdad (after the Mongol conquest in 1258) to Cairo and from there to Istanbul, the capital of the Ottoman Turks. The Muslim Ottomans captured the ancient city previously known as Constantinople from the Byzantines in 1453 as part of the creation of their own new multi-continental empire, and festooned the city's skyline with domes and minarets of dozens of mosques, crowned by the Ottomans' sprawling Topkapı Palace. Cairo and Damascus (another former capital of the caliphs), remained very large cities, allowing Egyptian and Arab rulers to maintain some autonomy from Istanbul. Yet the Sunni Muslim Ottomans' most hated rivals ruled from Shiite Persia. There, the Safavid dynasty built its capital at Isfahan, with its radiant blue-domed mosque, the lavish al-Qapu Palace, and the largest city square on Earth, named "Image of the World" (*Naqsh-e Jahan*). Meanwhile another Islamic dynasty, the Mughals – descended from a line of Mongol emperors as their name suggests – ruled North India from Fatehpur Sikri, a resplendent confection of red sandstone palaces and mosques set off by walls and a fifty-meter-tall gatehouse. Inside, Mughal princes amused themselves on the outdoor Pachisi Court, playing what we know as the board game "Parcheesi" – in their case, using live slave girls as the pawns. A faulty water-supply system apparently caused the Mughal *badshahs* to shift their capital to nearby Agra, famous for the Taj Mahal, an achingly beautiful mausoleum for Shah Jahan's favorite wife that was constructed by 20,000 of India's finest artisans. In 1648, Jahan moved his capital again, to Delhi, the site of a half-dozen earlier Indian imperial capitals. There, he ordered the construction of a massive walled city named Shahjahanabad, crowned by the commanding Red Fort.[3]

The largest city in the world, however, was still located in East Asia. In China in 1368, the Ming dynasty overthrew its Mongol overlords from its own capital in Nanjing ("Southern Capital"). Then, in 1417, to remain alert to future threats from the steppes, the Yongle Emperor rebuilt the Mongol capital at Dadu, renaming it Beijing ("Northern Capital"). One million laborers, conscripted from as far away as today's Vietnam, dug up tons of local soil and compressed it between wooden frames to build the city's eleven-meter-high square walls. In the propitious north-central quadrant of the city, some 100,000 workers and artisans fashioned a three-quarter-square kilometer "Purple Forbidden City" – named after the color for martial valor. Surrounded by several kilometers of walls of its own, the Forbidden City consisted of dozens of palaces for the imperial family, their powerful eunuch slaves, and the emperor's hundreds of courtesans. Imperial troops forced thousands of families to relocate from Chinese cities further south to populate the capital, which soon surpassed a million inhabitants, spilling beyond the walls into a giant area to the south, forcing Yongle's successors to enclose the new section of the city with another massive rectangular wall. Yongle widened and extended the Grand Canal so barges loaded with rice and other provisions from the south could reach Beijing and supplement harvests from its relatively poor hinterland. Recall that all of this occurred at the same time that Yongle was outfitting the largest fleet of ships in world history. His successors' abandonment of that naval project, which might have otherwise deterred Europeans' later incursions in Asia, in part reflected their decision to focus resources on the northern defenses – including that second wall around the southern suburbs of Beijing – and many new palaces in the Forbidden City. The Mongols did attack in 1449, and nearly made off with Beijing. Yongle's successors accordingly refocused their immense dynastic energies away from mega-ships to rebuilding thousands of kilometers of the Great Wall along the border of their empire to Beijing's north, creating the stupendous string of fortifications and towers tourists visit today.[4]

None of those expenditures spared the Ming from the fate of so many previous Chinese dynasties. In 1644, amidst devastating famines of the Little Ice Age, rulers of the Manchu people from the sparse farmlands of the northeast entered the Forbidden City at the head of an eight-part army of Manchu warriors, Mongol horsemen, and Chinese soldiers. Each of the eight regiments flew a banner of a different color and fringe. Assuming the dynastic name Qing, the conquerors divided the area around the Forbidden City into an "Inner City" for soldiers and generals from the eight banners, and forced all of that area's non-banner Chinese residents into the rectangle to the south, known as the Outer City or, later, the "Chinese City." Soon they built a system of internal walls, sentry posts, and over 1,000 street gates that divided both of these larger sections of town into dozens of smaller neighborhoods. To the sound of a massive drum high in its own tower, a force of 25,000 gendarmes and bannermen closed these gates at nightfall to maintain order. During the 1700s, when few cities in the world had anything resembling police forces, Qing Beijing's was by far the most formidable.[5]

Even so, a rival to Beijing's sheer grandeur and enormous population arose at the same time further to the east. In Japan, the Tokugawa shoguns who unified the country in the 1590s chose the sleepy seaside town of Edo as the site for their own fearsome dynastic castle. They surrounded it with a complex of thick walls of stone, wide moats, temples, gardens, and vast squares that, like earlier Japanese capitals, resembled those of China. In a manner similar to the later king of France Louis XIV, the shogun Ieyasu forced the country's 400 fractious *daimyō* (nobles) to leave their own castles in the countryside every other year to reside in a special district in Edo. For good measure, the *daimyō* were also obligated to install their wives and heirs in the city's mansions as permanent, genteel hostages of the shogun. Their decommissioned armies of samurai also lived in neighborhoods of their own near the castle. Commoners (known as *chōnin*) received still other separate neighborhoods, with artisans enjoying higher status over often-wealthier merchants. Thus began the rambling spread of another million-plus city that probably outgrew Beijing in the eighteenth century, and that would later become world history's largest city ever, under the name Tokyo ("Western Capital") after 1868.[6]

Many of the dynasties that built these capitals – including Istanbul, Isfahan, Delhi, and Qing Beijing – hailed from regions on the fringes of urban power, where a few fortified towns arose among farms and settlements of herders and foragers. The Ottoman Turks and the Mughals were direct ancestors of Central Asian nomadic peoples; the Safavids arose in small religious centers in the Iranian mountains; and the Qing were Jurchen, whose defeat of Song dynasty 500 years before we will reexamine shortly. Yet it fell to the Qing and the Russian Tsars, another dynasty descended from villagers and nomads, to fashion urban-administered armed forces that mixed gunpowder armaments with enough grasslands martial prowess to end Asian steppe peoples' millennia-long reign as the arch-nemeses of city-based empires. Regions like Manchuria itself, Mongolia, Xinjiang, the "Black Earth" districts of today's Ukraine, and the immense forests and taiga of Siberia all came under increasingly effective urban-administered rule during this time. In 1761, the Qing Emperor Qianlong conquered the Central Asian Mongol state of Dzungaria, the last steppe-based armed force capable of threatening Chinese cities. Soon Beijing's rule extended, as it does today, to subordinated colonial capitals in Xinjiang and Tibet. Moscow's eastward urbanizing reach was even more impressive in scope, involving an 8,000-kilometer string of riverside trading posts, portages, and bastion fortresses – many of which served as kernels for the cities that were connected two centuries later by the Trans-Siberian Railroad. Treaties between Russia and China in 1689 and 1727 established a 7,500-kilometer border between the two empires, putting an exclamation point on their massive territorial conquests. This was an enormous extension of city-based human power over the largest continent. Yet it still had its limits, as later would-be conquerors of Asia would learn when they failed to subdue peoples whose power emanated from Afghanistan's mountain redoubts, Arabia's desert oases, or rainforest base-camps in Vietnam.[7]

BASTIONS OF THE OCEANS

The longest strings of new empire-building cities from this period, though, came into being along the shores of the World Ocean at places where shipborne, cannon-toting Europeans like Christopher Columbus met up with Americans, Africans, Asians, Australians, and Polynesians – with varying degrees of connection to the largest empires in their region and with varying expansionist goals of their own. Europeans are often treated as the central protagonists in this drama of global city-building, and it is true that their presence on this soon-planetary urban stage was uniquely ubiquitous. However, the drama played out differently in different regions of the world, largely depending on the particular seashores on which the era's largest empires sought to impose their power though military technology updated to meet the deadliest standards of the day. In another paradoxical twist of historical fate, the particular ways by which gunpowder, cannons, battleships, and fortress designs circulated across continents and oceans help to explain why Europeans – who possessed some of the world's weakest trappings of traditional imperial power – played the pervasive role they did. Overall, the Native empires of the Americas – which did not possess iron weapons, armor, horses, gunpowder weapons, battleships, or any way of developing them – provided the least deadly response to European advances. Native American villagers and camp dwellers, kingdoms and city-states in Africa, and empires in Asia followed in order of increasingly lethal resistance. China and Japan were most successful in smacking Europeans back into the oceans whence they came. Most of the new European colonial cities in Africa and Asia arose only on coasts that lay on the outer edges of the territorial might of local continental empires. These particulars mattered: the violent birth of a connected Urban Planet derived from many separate world-connecting actions taken from many cities, as it still does in our own even more "globalized" era today.

There is a backstory to the uneven spread of the gunpowder revolution. Long before 1492, Chinese apothecaries in the teeming artisan shops of Tang Changan (618–907) and Song Kaifeng (960–1126) experimented with setting fire to mixtures of charcoal and nitrates to cause spectacular explosions, sometimes burning their craft-shops to the ground. Throughout their long centuries in power, the Tang and Song continued the old regional arms races against states founded by village- and steppe-dwelling peoples to the north. The enemies of the Song, as we know, were the Jurchen. Like their Qing descendants 500 years later, they blended regional traditions, such as breeding superior warhorses, with the latest Chinese urban, administrative, and military techniques. To keep these fearsome enemies from storming their cities, Chinese gunpowder specialists worked with other smiths and artisans to direct their invention's explosive power against the bodies of enemy soldiers and horses, at first via flame-throwing arrows and other projectiles. When the Jurchen besieged the Song capital of Kaifeng in 1126, Song soldiers stationed atop the city's massive walls catapulted state-of-the-art "thunderclap bombs" – bamboo and later iron balls stuffed with gunpowder that rained fire and porcelain shrapnel on the retreating Jurchen. In the meantime, though, the Jurchen had captured plenty of urban artisans willing to work against the Song. When the Jurchen returned the following year, they catapulted dozens of thunderclaps of their own over Kaifeng's walls, threatening the city's flammable fabric of elegant homes, shops, and streets. It was a grim demonstration that gunpowder could sow even more deadly mayhem when used *against* cities. The Song handed Kaifeng to the Jurchen, retreating to Hangzhou, a new capital they built far to the south.[8]

Warfare and arms races continued in East Asia over the next few centuries. Soon Chinese imperial armies and the Mongols – the latest, greatest threat from the Steppe – were firing flamethrowers, rockets, and the first bullet-slinging guns at each other. The Mongols used these same weapons, along with thousands of their best warhorses, to sow mayhem in cities across the Golden Age Islamic urban world and Russia, singing the fringes of urban Europe. Soon they returned to East Asia, mowed down the Jurchen, and fought the Hangzhou-based Song for sixty years, in the end subduing the dynasty's massive capital and ruling all of China themselves, as the Yüan dynasty, from 1271 to 1368.[9]

Amidst this supercontinental tumult, gunpowder – and guns themselves – arrived in the rest of Asia and Europe, and from there to many capitals in Africa (the Songhay emperors did not adopt gunpowder weapons, a mystery that historians have yet to unravel). In about 1375, French weapon-smiths in the city of Caen began forging especially large guns, aimed not so much to destroy people's bodies and homes as in China, but to launch large stones and iron balls against city walls. Europeans invented "wall-breaker" cannons – not the Chinese or the Mongols, who had much more experience with guns – because the city walls in Europe actually shattered and collapsed when cannonballs hit them. In China, as the military historian Tonio Andrade has shown, emperors built city walls that were far thicker than anyone else's in the world. The core of these walls, which made up most of their thickness, was made of rammed earth, and their brick or stone outer faces angled away as they rose upward from the ground. No one in China, including the Mongols, ever imagined that gunpowder-launched projectiles would have the force to breach such walls, for the combination of thickness, earthen core, and angled design would have easily absorbed and deflected the force of anything that hit them. In China, catapults, not cannons, were the best way to deliver gunpowder, as the Jurchen had demonstrated, by launching it *over* the walls.[10]

In Europe, meanwhile, city walls had made a spectacular comeback only a few centuries earlier, during the High Middle Ages. These were "curtain"-style walls – tall, visually fearsome stone structures that rose perpendicularly from the ground, with crenelated parapets along the top, punctuated regularly by imposing round or square towers designed to flank besiegers. Europeans thought of their walls as being massive, but few of them were even a third as thick as China's, and most were less than one-twentieth as thick. Even shot from long distances, cannonballs easily shattered these brittle, highly exposed targets. Cannons such as those from Caen, in fact, quickly rendered the entire grand tradition of medieval fortification obsolete. Soon the king of France was launching cannonballs at walled Italian cities, capturing one Renaissance gem after another to resolve his gripes with the Pope in Rome. Word got around fast. In 1453, the founder of the Ottoman Empire, Sultan Mehmet II the Conqueror, hired European cannon-smiths to help him lay siege to the sixth-century walls of Constantinople, which were indeed especially thick by regional standards. The Byzantine emperor possessed perfectly murderous cannons of his own, but Mehmet blew wide holes in the walls and, after executing a few other strokes of military genius, won the siege. Thus did Christian Constantinople become Muslim Istanbul.[11]

Once Europe's besieging armies possessed cannons, European fortress designers had no choice but to rethink their idea of a town wall from the ground up – both as a defensive measure and as an offensive weapon in its own right. Leadership came from the builders in Italian cities humiliated by the cannoneers of the king of France. Especially gifted Renaissance artisans named Michelangelo and Leonardo da Vinci helped with sketches for these new walls. The result was what the French called the *trace italienne*: low, thick, earthen walls faced with brick or stone and protected by a series of triangular bastions whose sharp points protruded from each corner in the wall.[12]

Angular bastions were the crucial innovation. They were wide enough on top, unlike medieval parapets, to accommodate wall-defending cannons, which needed space to recoil. More importantly, the bastions' angled points allowed the city's own cannoneers and gunners stationed on any one bastion to rake all of the ground between that bastion and its neighbors on each side. This eliminated the notorious "dead zones" that lay in front of round medieval towers and that made them vulnerable to enemy siege-towers and sappers – soldiers trained to dig tunnels under walls and blow them up with explosives. Finally, the new bastions' thick angled walls, like those in China, deadened and deflected the impact of enemy cannonballs.[13]

Such so-called "Renaissance" fortifications, and later, even fancier "Baroque" ones, became a nearly ubiquitous part of the urban geography of Europe between about 1500 and 1800. This period in European history is known for vast new strides in human culture and knowledge, as we shall see, but it also ranks among the bloodiest anywhere at any time. Europe's many increasingly powerful states fought each other for territory or, when succession to the throne of another country came into dispute, on behalf of their preferred candidate. Above all, they fought about religion. This period also encompasses the Reformation, when Protestant movements began questioning the authority of Catholic Rome, and the Counter-Reformation that the Pope called in order to obliterate Protestantism. In the 1600s, amidst Little Ice Age climate disasters, warfare grew even fiercer, killing tens of millions and spurring deathlier innovations in weaponry. Military engineers – notably Sébastien Le Prestre de Vauban, who worked for Louis XIV – refitted bastions with such lavishly named features as "ravelins and redoubts, bonnettes and lunettes, tenailles and tenaillons, counterguards and crownworks and hornworks and curvettes and fausses brayes and scarps and cordons and banquettes and counterscarps," to quote the military historian Charles Townshend. His breathless list is missing another crucial innovation, the "glacis," a large area of unobstructed downward-sloping ground surrounding a fortress whose goal was to force besiegers out in the open and put them in a gravitationally disadvantaged position while keeping their cannons far out of range of the city. Square-shaped forts with angled bastions at each corner worked well enough, but military engineers increasingly pressed their clients to spend more on pentagonal, hexagonal, or even octagonal fortresses to increase the effectiveness of the design. They also urged town planners to expand central squares as mustering points for a city's defenders, and straighten internal streets to enhance soldiers' ability to report to the bastions. Ancient Roman models derived from gridironed *castra* (army camps) and the architect Vitruvius's plans for ideal geometric cities all provided additional inspiration at a time when many had absorbed a mania for the bloodcurdling wisdom of ancient war-craft.[14]

Meanwhile, the invention of cannons also required a redesign of ships. Shipbuilders in Europe and throughout the Mediterranean had already developed especially maneuverable ships. Their many, differently shaped sails and their complex rigging systems allowed crews to catch the wind from many angles and even sail quite quickly against it. These technologies came in part from the designs of Muslim shipbuilders, but they also reflected the fact that the sea currents and wind patterns surrounding Europe were more complex than those in the Indian Ocean and China Seas, where the seasonally alternating monsoons allowed long trips with simpler rigging systems. Once Europeans had cannons, naval architects began redesigning their ships as mobile bastions for naval assaults against other ships – and against fixed bastions on coastlines. Over time, they found ways to place ever more terrifying rows of outward-pointing cannons onboard. They allowed extra room on deck for cannons to recoil and give sailors the space they needed to reload in ways that did not expose them to enemy fire or put them at risk of falling overboard. Ships' rigging systems, meanwhile, provided military advantages as well as navigational ones, for they allowed greater mobility in attacks.[15]

By the time of the discovery of the World Ocean, Europeans had thus taken a small lead in developing three crucial instruments of state violence. Working together, cannons, bastions, and battleships made up the essential toolkit for extending European power to distant shores. The Portuguese were quickest to take up this opportunity in their search for a defensible route south and eastward around Africa into the Indian Ocean. Columbus's voyage across the Atlantic represented a second thrust. As every schoolchild knows, he hoped to get to China faster by sailing westward. Villa Navidad was his first attempt to lay claim to that route for Spain. Within a few decades, cannon-snouted ships from Holland, Britain, and France followed in hot pursuit. The seashores of Africa, Asia, the Americas, and later Australia began collecting dozens of seaside fortresses. Many of these became kernels of the most significant cities in world history.

(A)

(B)

7.1. A Tale of Four Fortifications

City walls speak volumes about the early-modern era's World Ocean-borne arms race. In East Asia, gunpowder weapons could not breach especially thick walls like those of Osaka Castle (A). In Europe, city walls like Nuremberg's (B) shattered in contact with cannonballs, so new imperialist states built more cannons and thicker, geometric bastion fortifications, as in Lima, Spanish Peru (C). Gunpowder came to sub-Saharan Africa later, but rulers like the Obas of Benin (D) deterred outside imperialists with guns and an astounding 15,000 kilometers of earthen walls around their capital city and other towns. Only after 1800, using deadlier weapons made in factory cities, did Europeans end centuries of global military "parity."

(A) Keystone/Hulton Archive/Getty Images. (B) ullstein bild/Getty Images. (C) John Carter Brown Library. (D) Corbis Historical/Getty Images.

(C)

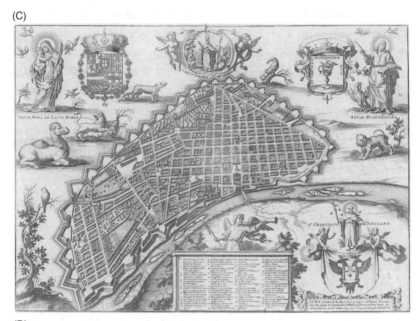

(D)

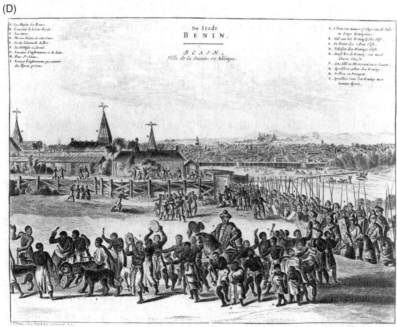

7.1. (cont.)

The Kingdom of Portugal pioneered this business well before 1492. The Kingdom came into being as a military alliance dedicated to the eradication of the Morocco-based Muslim Almohad Caliphate from the Atlantic shores of the Iberian Peninsula – a task Portugal accomplished in 1263. The Portuguese *Empire* emerged when the Kingdom extended this "Reconquista" along the shores of Morocco itself and beyond. The location of the new Portuguese capital at Lisbon – itself a former Muslim fortress city named Al-Ushbunna and an ancient Phoenician trading post named Alis Ubbo – on an Atlantic river-mouth made it ideally placed to outfit the nimble Mediterranean merchant ships known as caravels with cannons and send them on bombardment missions. The first overseas Portuguese forts were repurposed Moroccan ones along the West African coast. As part of a more general plan to diminish the power of Islam, Portuguese expeditions outflanked by sea the Moroccans' lucrative trans-Sahara caravans to the gold mines of the Songhay Empire in West Africa. In 1483, stevedores on the Lisbon docks loaded four larger supply ships with stone, brick, lime, and bronze cannons, followed by 500 soldiers and 100 stonemasons. The little fleet sailed to a spot in today's Ghana that the Portuguese called El Mina ("The Goldmine"), on a coast far from Songhay control. There the leader of the expedition, Diogo de Azambuja, paid off the ruler of a nearby village and built Europe's first overseas castle, still in the medieval style (gunpowder weapons were still absent in West Africa, and bastions were just coming into style in Europe). Significantly, they called this fort a "factory" (*feitoria*) after the Latin word *factor*, "doer," which had recently acquired the meaning of "commercial agent." Over the ensuing decades, royal factors stationed at El Mina traded with African gold merchants and sent substantial yearly shipments of the yellow metal back to Lisbon. Soon the *feitoria* took on a more reprehensible, and more lucrative, role as an on-loading facility for slaves destined for the sugar plantations run by Portuguese settlers in Brazil.[16]

Meanwhile, the Portuguese admirals Vasco da Gama (in 1497–1502) and Pedro Cabral (in 1500–1) launched cannon-equipped caravels and supply ships into the Atlantic and around Southern Africa into the vast ancient trading realm of the Indian Ocean. Da Gama loathed Muslim traders, and his cannon-wielding crews overwhelmed the generally unarmed merchant ships of the region, as well as various local authorities who ran the Ocean's port cities. However, because of Asia's long traditions of iron-founding, gunpowder weapon-making, shipbuilding, and fortress architecture, the state of military parity persisted between all of the Old World's largest gunpowder empires. Europeans' innovative weapons inspired imitations in Asia, prohibiting da Gama's successors from making substantial territorial conquests there. The Ottomans sent battleships with equally deadly weapons down the Red Sea against the Portuguese, minimizing European access to western Arabia. The Portuguese also came up against the Ming dynasty, the original "Gunpowder Empire," which had built a massive arsenal against the remaining Mongol states under the direction of the powerful Military Armory Bureau in Beijing. When Portuguese caravels arrived in the Pearl River off Guangzhou in 1521–22, Ming officials encountered European cannon-fire for the first time. They quickly built imitations of the Europeans' big guns and used them to scatter Portuguese caravels back into the South China Sea. Still, the Portuguese quickly found many seams on the far edges and in between the realms of Asia's great gunpowder powers. In 1510, for example, the Portuguese admiral Afonso da Albuquerque captured Goa, the most important pepper port on the Malabar Coast of India, a region largely outside the influence of the Mughal Empire. A year later, he seized the storied entrepôt of Malacca in the narrow waterways of Southeast Asia, by directing his slippery caravels to zig and zag around the city's own booming cannons, then landing troops who seized the city for the Portuguese king from other groups of merchants and local leaders, including a powerful community of Chinese merchants. Finally, in 1515 he snuck into Hormuz, a city which occupied a key choke point in the Persian Gulf but which lay on the fringes of both Ottoman and Safavid power. It was thus that a mighty fortress dedicated to Our Lady of the Conception arose at the very heart of the Muslim world.[17]

From these choice locations, other Portuguese conquistadors built an increasing chain of fortresses at the harbor-mouths of the most lucrative ports in the Ocean: at Moçambique Island (in the 1540s) and Mombasa (1593) on the East African coast; at Diu (in 1538, after a massive sea battle against the Ottomans that could have gone either way) and Daman

(1559), both on the coasts of the cotton-cloth producing region of Gujarat; at a half dozen other ports on the pepper coast; at Colombo on Ceylon (Sri Lanka, in 1517); and at the clove-growing island of Ternate (1522) in the Moluccas. At Goa, the Portuguese built a glamorous capital with a vice-regal palace, a cathedral, a grand inquisitor's office, and lavish establishments for noblemen and all of the monastic orders of a pious Catholic nation. Portuguese officials could now boast that they ran the "State of India" (*Estado da India*) from the "Rome of the East."[18]

From there the Portuguese realm expanded further: on the southern Chinese Coast, the Portuguese exploited the Ming navy's spotty control of the Pearl River Delta area, with its swarms of pirates. After a Portuguese admiral helped Ming officials police the area, they reluctantly awarded Portuguese traders a tiny finger of land called Macao in 1557. Later, when a few Portuguese caravels accidentally drifted onto the shores of Japan, their captains negotiated a concession with a still-independent local *daimyō* to run a port in Nagasaki Bay (1571). That gave the Portuguese access to Japanese silver, and soon led to the conversion of thousands of Japanese peasants to Christianity, including Nagasaki's *daimyō* himself. Back in the Atlantic, meanwhile, Pedro Cabral's claim to Brazil gave Portuguese ships stopping points on the long trip to the East – at Recife (1537), Salvador do Bahía (1549), and Rio de Janeiro (1565). The slave-raiding village of São Paulo, just inland from another Brazilian port, also dates from this time. By the 1560s, cannons mounted on bastions all along a 30,000-kilometer chain of ocean forts could transmit a decree issued by the king of Portugal in Lisbon: henceforth all local merchants must pay protection money in exchange for a *cartaz*, or passport, required for access to any of the many lucrative harbors the King controlled.[19]

Meanwhile, Christopher Columbus, and other explorers funded by the kings of Spain who sailed in his wake, blundered through the Caribbean trying to make something of islands that they still assumed lay in the "Indies" and thus not far from Portuguese forts in Asia. "Christmas City" failed, and so did a second nearby fort named Ysabel (after the Spanish queen), but in 1502, Columbus's brother Bartolomeo built the first permanent fortified nucleus of a European settler city in the

New World, the Ozama Fortress at Santo Domingo (the capital of today's Dominican Republic). From that base, Spanish conquistadors – soon alerted by the Magellan expedition that the Americas were in fact a "New World" very distant from Asia – launched more ships and cannons against the Mesoamerican mainland, and later, across Central America against the Peruvian coast. Simply by breathing out into the New World air they loosed a toxic cloud of Old World pathogens that soon caused massive outbreaks of smallpox, typhus, whooping cough, chicken pox, and measles among Native Americans, who possessed no large livestock to give them immunity. (Malaria arrived some time later from Africa in the guts of mosquito larvae that managed to ship themselves across the Atlantic, probably in a barrel of drinking water.) The Taíno, Arawak, and Carib natives of the Caribbean were the first to bear the brunt of this microbiological assault: up to 90 percent of the inhabitants of many islands died miserable deaths within a few decades of Columbus's arrival. On the far more populated American mainland, disease was even more devastating in terms of sheer numbers if not percentages, reducing the 20 to 30 million people of the Aztec realms, for example, to a little over a million during the course of the 1500s.[20]

Colonial city-building in the Americas followed a more lethal pattern than in Asia. When Hernán Cortés (in 1519–21) and Francisco Pizarro (in 1528–32) advanced on Tenochtitlan and Cuzco, their respective opponents, the Emperors Montezuma and Atahualpa, mixed diplomacy with deployments of tens of thousands of foot-soldiers equipped with cotton armor and bows and arrows. As they well knew, the conquistadors' tiny rag-tag armies could call on reserves from Santo Domingo or Seville, clad in iron, and armed with horses and cannons. The conquistadors allied with local rebels, like those of Tlaxcala, a city run by a governing council very different from Aztec – and Spanish – imperial rule. Disease ravaged Tenochtitlan, and, in 1521, Cortés seized the island capital after pummeling it with cannonballs from barges in Lake Texcoco. European soldiers who once marveled at Tenochtitlan now razed its great pyramids to the ground. The conquistadors reused the rubble for their own palaces and, later, a massive cathedral looming over Spanish Mexico City's new Plaza Mayor. Similar devastating events occurred in Cuzco ten years later, despite the spectacular stone walls of the Sacsayhuaman fortress, guarding a city that the Inka saw as the very center of the Sun's rule on Earth.[21]

To administer these large newly conquered realms, and to exploit the Mexican and Peruvian silver mines they found shortly after conquest, Spanish viceroys needed to build much more extensive networks of capitals and provincial cities beyond the shores than did the Portuguese in the East. They centered these networks on the new cities of Mexico City and Lima, Peru, which we will visit again several times in upcoming chapters. The most heavily fortified places in the Spanish Americas, though, were the ocean ports that launched the Spanish kings' famous annual fleet of treasure ships laden with American silver. As these fleets received increasing hostile attention from the battleships of Dutch, British, and French privateers, the region's urban fortification systems grew more serious. Makeshift wooden stockades (as at Villa Navidad and elsewhere), gave way to medieval castles (like the Ozama Fortress), square and pentagonal bastion forts such as at Veracruz, Acapulco, Havana, and the massive el Morro in San Juan, Puerto Rico, and a complete system of surrounding walls and bastions at Cartagena de Indias (on the Caribbean coast of today's Colombia). By 1688, Lima's surrounding walls included no less than thirty-four baroque bastions (Fig 7.1C).[22]

The lynchpin of the Spanish empire as a global force, however, lay on the far side of the Pacific Ocean at Manila, a growing trading post for Filipino, Muslim, Chinese, and Japanese merchants. The Spanish seized the place in 1571, razed it to the ground, and built it anew as a walled city with four angled bastions and a smattering of churches and municipal buildings. There, American silver – guarded as always by cannons, sharp-edged bastions, and regular visits from warships – gave Spain, and soon the West as a whole, much freer access than ever before to the luxuries produced in the craft-shops and industrial towns of Ming China (Chapter 8). Though Manila was not quite as splendid as contemporary Goa, it allowed Spain to draw even with Portugal in global imperial dominance. After the unification of Spain and Portugal in 1580, colonization of the Americas was secure, and Spanish fortress and city builders continued their work – in places like Saint Augustine, Florida (1565, the oldest city in what later became the USA), Buenos Aires (1536), Santiago de Chile (1541), Quito (1534), Bogotá (1538), Caracas (1567), Santa Fe (1607, another early US city, today located in New Mexico), and, much later, in the province of California, San Diego (1769), San Francisco (1776), and Nuestra Signora de Los Angeles (1781).[23]

URBAN OCEANS IN PLAY: THE INDIAN AND THE PACIFIC

The year 1571 marks a key moment in the life of Earthopolis, along with those of 1492 and 1517. It was then that Spanish Acapulco and Manila connected two long strings of World Ocean port cities into a global ring that could assure continuous shipborne imperial and commercial activity that circled Earth entirely. This explosive act of merging separate urban worlds was one of several crucial birthdays in the first truly planetary Urban Planet, for the Acapulco–Manila circuit allowed Iberian kings to rule the World Ocean throughout the remainder of the 1500s and beyond. Yet the Iberian kings also provided rival European imperialists and merchants with well-marked saltwater routes to Asia, Africa, the Americas, and soon Australasia and Polynesia as well. As American silver flowed into Europe, rival would-be empires gained the financial means to outfit their own ships with cannons and to build new fortresses across the oceans, or seize and reuse Iberian ones that were already there. Rulers in Holland, England, and France at first hired ruthless privateers to steal Spanish silver outright. After 1600, though, they chartered merchant companies with royally guaranteed monopoly power to colonize and exploit specific segments of the World Ocean shores themselves. In the Indian Ocean and the China Seas, the Dutch, British, and French East India Companies rode their investors' longing for profit along with national and Reformation-era religious fervor directly into the teeth of the Catholic Portuguese *Estado da India* and its hated *cartaz* system; soon they disrupted the Spanish Acapulco–Manila circuit as well. The charters of world history's first multinational corporations gave them the power to raise their own armies and navies, which soon outgunned Iberian caravels and warships in harbors and on the high seas, and besieged their colonial cities. Along the way, the new companies tested the ability of various Asian empires, coastal city-states, and urban merchant communities to respond militarily.

Dutch ships led the assault. Built in the East India Company's huge naval yard in Amsterdam while the city was leading a revolution against Spanish rule, these cannon-toting floating bastions soon blockaded Portuguese Goa in 1603 and 1643, and took Malacca and Colombo along the way. In the relatively poorly armed Southern Indian city-states of the Malabar and Coromandel Coasts, the Dutch acquired land by negotiation or force and built dozens of new forts and trading posts. Soon Dutch Company officials elbowed their way into East Asia. For some time Dutch East India Company merchants held on to a four-sided bastion fort at Zeelandia (today's Tainan City) on Taiwan, an island which up to that point was mostly inhabited by people living in small villages and camps. The Dutch hoped Zeelandia would help them rival Iberian-controlled Macao and Manila, but in 1661 the Ming general Koxinga fled invading Qing armies by sailing to Taiwan with a fleet of pirates that had grown up among the canny sea peoples of the Chinese coast. He besieged Zeelandia using European-style cannons, and a renegade German military engineer helped him build anti-bastion siege engines to blast his way into the fort. By claiming Taiwan as a refuge for the Ming, he provided ample evidence for the continued geopolitical parity between Asia and Europe. The Qing soon proved more powerful still. First, they undercut the power of Chinese pirates by forcing millions of people living within five then fifteen kilometers of the southeastern Chinese coast for 1,000 kilometers in every direction to leave their villages and boats behind. It was one of the largest-ever human-directed acts of mass depopulation of a human built environment. Meanwhile, the Qing built a navy from scratch, destroyed the remaining pirates, then killed Koxinga and seized Taiwan. Soon the Qing army, a conquering force that first arose in forest villages, began transforming Taiwan's own villages and camps into one of the most heavily urbanized parts of the world. The cities and the towns of the Chinese coast opposite soon filled back up too, this time without the piracy business, which mostly disappeared for a century. Following that, the Qing, like the Ming in the 1430s, once again, fatefully, allowed a giant but now unneeded Chinese navy to molder and disappear.[24]

The Dutch were marginally more successful in Japan than in Taiwan. Once the shogun Ieyasu had succeeded in subjugating his rival aristocratic *daimyō*, he faced a new threat from Spanish ships and a rebellion of Japanese Catholics that he blamed on the Portuguese at Nagasaki. The Protestant Dutch, deftly exporting Europe's religious wars (and their own war of independence against Spain) to East Asia, sank some Catholic Iberian ships and helped Ieyasu put down the rebellion. The shogun expelled the Iberian Catholics, crucified thousands of Japanese ones, and rewarded the Dutch East India Company with a monopoly over Europe's trade with Japan (Korean and Chinese merchants could visit as well). The Dutch had to agree to strict terms, however. The treaty confined the Company's ships to the small port of Hirado, and later to a heavily guarded island called Deshima in Nagasaki harbor. There the shogun's officials confiscated the sails from newly arriving Dutch boats each trading season until they were satisfied that the Company employees had paid a good price for their goods and bore no subversive intentions against Japan.[25]

Meanwhile, the Dutch succeeded in acquiring a much more promising outpost in Southeast Asia. In 1618, the Company's bellicose agent Jan Pieterszoon Coen shot his way into a small village on the island of Java called Jacatra. On its smoking ruins, he built a *Kasteel* with four sides and bastions on each corner. In the ensuing years, it survived dozens of cannonades from the British and the Muslim Mataram of Java. Amidst all the adversity, the city of Batavia grew up around the flanks of the *Kasteel*, becoming the base for Dutch dominance over the Spice Islands and East Asian trade until the twentieth century. Appropriately for a city named after the Latin word for "Holland," it was located on low-lying land at the mercy of ocean tides – and, thanks to Dutch engineers, it soon boasted of a canal system much like that of Amsterdam. Today we know it as Djakarta, after the original village on the site. Getting between Amsterdam and Jacatra/Batavia required a halfway point similar to what the Portuguese possessed in Brazil, where sailors could stop to refill their water pots and combat scurvy by ingesting vitamin C from fresh vegetables. In 1652, to acquire such a refreshment facility, the Dutch naval officer Jan van Riebeeck seized land from the cattle-herding Khoikhoi people near the Cape of Good Hope in Southern Africa and built yet another bastion fort, this one a pentagonal affair. It became the kernel of the city of Cape Town. Tourists can visit this fort, and the Company's nearby vegetable gardens, to this day.[26]

The British and the French arrived in the Indian Ocean not long after the Dutch, bringing their contrasting views on fortresses. The headquarters of the British East India Company was in London, an island city whose security relied less on fortifications than on the natural barrier of the English Channel. Its officials cherished the idealistic hope that they could focus on "trade over war" in Asia: part of their business plan was to out-earn the Dutch by spending less up front, for example, on fortifications. The French, whose growing power in Europe rested heavily on more than 100 border fort-cities designed by Louis XIV's fortifications genius Sébastien de Vauban, were much less shy about throwing up baroque combinations of bastions, ravelins, contrescarpes, glacis, and other frightening things wherever they went.[27]

In South Asia, both Britain and France came up hard against the Mughals of India, who sought to expand their power southward across the subcontinent. While principally a land-based empire with few concerns for what Europeans did on the coasts, the Mughals did administer a port at the city of Surat in the Bay of Cambay. There, Mughal officials relentlessly toyed with resident European merchants, who maintained offices and storerooms in un-walled "factories" (named after the Portuguese *feitoria* at El Mina). For the Surati officials, accommodating foreign merchants' lust for profit was a minor priority compared with shipping tens of thousands of pilgrims to Mecca each year, and they sometimes forced Europeans to give up that year's trading so they could ferry *hajjis* to Arabia instead.[28]

The British solved this intolerable situation by scouting out three Indian villages that lay either outside or on the fringes of Mughal control: Madraspattnam on the cotton-cloth producing Coromandel Coast; Bom Bahia ("Good Bay"), a small Portuguese island settlement near the pepper coast, and Dihi Kalikatta in silk-producing Bengal. Despite considerable internal resistance, Company headquarters in Leadenhall Street, London, released funds for two four-sided bastion forts at what became Madras (1640) and Bombay (1683). They also built a much ricketier affair called Fort William at Calcutta (1690), where the particularly powerful Mughal governor of Bengal was far warier of bastion-building foreigners.[29]

British governors on the spot welcomed the money for walls. All three of these new forts faced threats of all kinds. Mughal forces threatened in Bengal and tried to extend the empire southward toward Madras, and in Bombay rebel Maratha raiders were eager to use the city as a base for their effort to replace Mughal rule with a Hindu empire of their own. In all three places, the British faced threats from Portuguese, Dutch, and French battleships. Just forty kilometers south of Madras, the French built a spiky, star-shaped fortress *à la* Vauban at Pondichéry, next to which Governor Joseph-François Dupleix built a spectacular baroque palace *à la* Versailles. Soon he and his mercenaries were claiming large chunks of South India for France, fanning a series of intercontinental wars with Britain that affected fortress cities as far away as Europe, the Caribbean, and revolution-era North America. These wars did not cease until Napoleon's defeat at Waterloo in 1815. In one early episode in 1741, the French navy bombarded the relatively cheap British fortress at Madras into submission, and then razed it to the ground along with the entire surrounding town of Indian merchants. They replaced it with a nine-sided bastion fort and a 400-meter *glacis*, which the British soon regained under a treaty that marked a temporary lull in Anglo-French hostilities around the world. Still, it took until 1756 for the British to learn their lesson about the danger of inexpensively built forts – in a singularly humiliating moment known as the "Black Hole of Calcutta." That story belongs to a new chapter in the biography of the Urban Planet, when Europeans translated their own internal experience with war to decisively outgun other empires in Asia. At that point, they had also began to supplement the energy of the Ocean (and gunpowder) with solar energy stored deep underground: coal.[30]

URBAN OCEANS IN PLAY: THE ATLANTIC

When Europeans succeeded in reaching that point of World Oceanic dominance, it was also in part because of the power they had tapped since 1492 from the Americas – power that, in turn depended on Europe's especially pervasive monopoly over the Atlantic. Along most of the shores of the "New" World, Europeans faced no competition from other Old World gunpowder empires. Outside of the Aztecs and Inka, Native Americans resisted European presence for the most part from small agricultural villages and foraging camps, many of which fortified themselves behind wooden palisades to protect themselves from the new threat. There, Native peoples trained small bands of warriors and armed them with guns acquired from European merchants to conduct guerrilla raids and canoe attacks through the heavily forested coastal inlets and river valleys against European settlements. They succeeded in holding off small groups of isolated settlers over substantial periods. However, in the longer term all retreated in the face of disease, genocidal warfare, and increasing waves of white settlers. Unlike in Asia and most of Africa (the Cape of Good Hope excepted), European arrivals in the Americas intended to settle permanently. They uprooted and burned forests inhabited by coastal Native peoples in order to build European-style farms and soon plantations loosely based on European estates. We will soon follow the grim results of this conquest, as European mercantile companies delivered untold wealth back to Europe by reinvesting American silver into such "improvements" of seized American land, by capturing American Native and African labor, and by using these resources to slake Europeans' passion for sugar, tobacco, and other cash crops, eventually including cotton. In the meantime, just as Columbus had imagined at Christmas City in 1492, wooden, then stone bastion fortresses, supported by the usual warships and cannons, were essential to all European colonial operations in this intensifying oceanic gyre of imperial capitalism.[31]

European merchants who sailed along the Atlantic coast of Africa built the early-modern Bastion Planet's grimmest fortresses: the "slave castles." Long before European contact, the forests and savannahs inland from these coasts supported numerous large city-states. Some, like Benin (possibly founded as early as 800 CE in today's southwestern Nigeria) grew into kingdoms that controlled other towns and cities. The power of the *Obas* (kings) of Benin rested on an astounding 15,000 kilometers of earthworks, sometimes rising eighteen meters tall, that surrounded the capital and reached out to its tributary towns; this "Great Wall of Africa" counts among the largest structures ever built (Figure 7.1D). Nonetheless, these kings' control over other towns and villages ebbed and flowed, later allowing Europeans to make Faustian bargains with local chiefs on the coast to set aside land on harbors or beachfronts for dungeons and fortified warehouses, designed to assemble captive human cargos for shipment to the Americas. Like other fortified mercantile headquarters, the perimeter of slave castle complexes was reinforced by bastions and cannons aimed to keep locals and rival companies away. Yet from the moment the Dutch captured El Mina from the Portuguese in 1637, these structures became flashpoints in the global gunpowder arms race. Over the next 175 years, Europeans of many stripes, including merchants from smaller ports like Antwerp, Copenhagen, and Stockholm, fought bloodily over these sites, and they changed hands often. Some also fell under the control of new African kingdoms like Dahomey (based at Abeokuta in today's Republic of Benin) and Ashante (at Kumasi in today's Ghana), whose power came from trading enslaved Africans for European guns and cannons. Either way a grisly string of enslavement factories stretched from Cap Vert in the west, eastward along the shoreline of the Gulf of Guinea, including Gorée Island, Albreda, James Island, Lomboko, Bunce Island, Cape Coast Castle, Fort Christiansborg, Dahomey's slave port at Ouidah, Bonny, Calabar, and, in Portuguese Angola, Lobito and Luanda. The city of Lagos – West Africa's largest today – came into being as Eko, a coastal fortification of the Oba of Benin, but later transformed into a largely self-governing slave port with its own Oba in the 1760s.[32]

Unlike other trade "goods," enslaved Africans constituted a global geopolitical force in their own right, for, as their masters correctly feared, the enslaved were capable of mounting rebellions that could undercut the entire European colonial enterprise. The prisons and keeps that enclosed slaves on the African shore recognized the potential of their power, as did the design of slave ships themselves. The historian Markus Rediker has closely examined the evidence about the built environment of these most horrifying of vehicles. He notes special architectural design features, such as "barricadoes" around the highest decks meant to protect slave ships' captains and crews from slave mutinies. Captains aimed the cannons perched on these "floating bastions" not at other ships, but at the ships' own decks and the holds below, which teemed with human cargo. Slaver crews also ringed the ship with special nets that prevented the enslaved from jumping over board, thus denying their captors' the future profit they hoped to get by selling the living bodies of those they enslaved.[33]

The dozens of castles and forts along the Brazilian, Caribbean, and Gulf Coasts of the Americas, and peppered throughout the Caribbean islands played similar roles. In addition to consolidating the seizure of Native American lands, they served to suppress revolts of the enslaved, kept rival European pirates and battleships out of harbors, and in so doing allowed new commercial port cities to come into being under their protection. Willemstad on the Dutch island of Curaçao was born under the shelter of five nearby forts, allowing several others to come into being along the coast of Dutch Guyana. Bridgetown, Barbados was covered by nearby Fort St. Ann; Port Royal, the original nucleus of Kingston, Jamaica, by Fort Charles; the aptly named Brimstone Hill Fortress on St. Kitts allowed settlements to grow there. The French built Fort-de-France on Martinique and Fort de Rocher on Tortuga island, which provided a base for the French capture of Saint-Domingue – soon the region's richest sugar-producing colony – on the western end of Spanish Hispaniola. On the mainland of North America, in the equally promising French sugar-producing colony of Louisiane, the French built Nouvelle Orléans, yet another Vauban-inspired fortress town, this one with eight bastions.[34]

Nowhere on Earth, though, did European fortresses establish more enduring Urban Planetary power than on the East Coast of North America. The Spanish took the lead in this endeavor, with the city of Saint Augustine, Florida as early as 1565, and it was not until 1607 that the British followed up with a comparatively rickety triangular palisade at Jamestown, Virginia in 1607. Soon though, a vast string of British forts allowed London to secure the continent. In New England, coastal villages of colonists elbowed into spots between Native palisade villages, as relationships over trade and land grew testier, as European disease spread, and as colonists launched wars of conquest. Amidst genocidal conflict, the colonists built a string of hard places that stretched from Portsmouth, New Hampshire, to the five seventeenth-century forts that protected Massachusetts Bay and Boston Harbor, through citadels at Newport, Saybrook, and New Haven on the Long Island Sound. Yet another

British redoubt arose at the mouth of Chesapeake Bay, and still others in the Carolinas at Wilmington and on the Sea Islands. Along the way, British navies also forcibly acquired the Dutch Fort Amsterdam at the tip of Manhattan from the Dutch, the sprawling granite bastions above French Quebec City, the Louisbourg fortress that guarded the entry to the St. Lawrence River, and Fort Condé, the Vaubanesque war nest that glowered over Mobile Bay. The North American East Coast also contained the single early-modern urban settlement in the world that explicitly rejected any need for fortification, let alone cannons: Philadelphia, Pennsylvania, founded as a "Holy Experiment" in pacifism and supposedly "brotherly" urban "love" for Native peoples by the Quaker William Penn.[35]

The first goal of these transoceanic projections of British power was to seize coastal, then riverine land from Native peoples, a conflict that began as fortified Native villages proliferated along the coast and then slowly fell to the settlers. Later it involved a campaign by a massive shipborne army to prevent North American colonists from overthrowing British rule, which ended in 1781 after the American revolutionary army besieged Yorktown, a port the British hoped to develop as a fully fortified naval base (Chapter 11). Once independent, the USA acquired still further chains of forts that the British had seized from the French, these on the Great Lakes and rivers of the interior of North America: Fort Detroit (1701), Fort Niagara (1726), Fort Duquesne (today's Pittsburgh, founded in 1754), and St. Louis (1764), in addition to the renamed New Orleans. In 1801, the American army connected these two continent-spanning chains of soon-to-be cities by building Fort Dearborn on the southwest corner of Lake Michigan, a swampy spot the local Potawatomie people knew as "Chicagou," where the watersheds of the Lakes and the Mississippi mingled in ways that portended the growth of a massive city to come. With these acts of fortress accumulation, the USA joined other imperial powers in using built space to extend state violence over enormous territories. In its case those acts gave birth to the largest urban military-industrial complex ever, one destined to supplant the British Empire at the spear-point of Oceanic – and Hydrocarbon – hegemony during the twentieth century (Chapters 13, 14, 19, and 21).[36]

CHAPTER 8

Wealth from the Winds and Waves

OCEANS OF CAPITALISTS

Imperial glory was not the only prize at stake for the builders of the Cities of the Oceans. The main purpose of all the new forts was an immense new wealth grab – this one assisted by the welling waves and the bracing smack of wind against sail. Much as Columbus had anticipated at Christmas City, commercial seaports grew beneath cannons' snouts, infusing mercantile competition everywhere with the hostility of the new global arms race. Along the shores of the Atlantic, far dastardlier acts began. Over the next four centuries, Europeans stole the land, labor, and mineral resources of Native Americans on two continents, all the while enslaving millions of Africans, transporting them to the Americas and coercing them into hard labor. Put these city-enabled, blood-soaked, profit-making projects together and, for the first time, a whorl of wealth hoarding began to spin worldwide. "Capital," a new word for investments underwritten by state violence that were designed to swell private profits, began circulating globally in both name and kind as well, especially after 1600. Partly for that reason, historians are comfortable calling the post-Columbian wealth grab exactly what it soon became: the birth of "global capitalism." Like Earthopolis more generally, the Ocean- and city-driven capitalist money-spinning circuit made up a singular realm of interconnected action that was also foundationally plural. Following the lead of stretching empires, people from all of the world's cities, all of their associated hinterlands, and all stations of life played some role in its slow, painful birth.

Not least were those who labored under the most crushingly subordinated circumstances. Over the course of lives shortened by forced work, millions of enslaved people built many of the cities and plantations that set the machinery of moneyspinning in motion. Toiling under the lash on great plantations, they fed the capitalist gyre with its most profitable commodities – even as urban slave markets converted their very bodies into one of the era's supreme forms of capital. Under their ever-present threat of plantation uprising, enslaved people also made sure that the politics of pan-Oceanic capitalism spun uneasily on its skewed axis.

Meanwhile, ordinary "free" farmers and peasants everywhere repositioned themselves within the world's countrysides to feed the new cities. Global capitalism would not have come into being without them, and in particular, it depended on millions of European indentured laborers also treated as capital: displaced peasants, outcasts from the religious wars, and poor city dwellers who crossed the Atlantic to settle farms and towns in the Americas. There they transformed Native land into seaport hinterland, added their muscle and sweat to the labor of urban shops and docklands, and infused the wobbly politics of global capital with severe grievances of their own.

Merchants, of course, were crucial to the birth of global capital too, both as profit-seeking animals and as political ones. Traders came to the oceanic capitalist vortex from all ocean shores, took risks of many kinds, acted on many scales, and gained highly unequal rewards. Even as their lands receded, Native American villagers and camp dwellers traded valuable commodities from forests, creeks, and inlets to trading posts near European forts and ocean-side cities, often to their sustained advantage. City-dwelling long-haul Mesoamerican and Andean merchants participated too, long after conquest. Meanwhile, all along the coasts of Afro-Eurasia (and for centuries before Columbus), urban merchant communities had independently extended the reach of their activities farther outward into the winds and waves. Some of these trading communities took local authority into their own hands, founding independent city-states in unruly harbor towns, whose governance imperial courts sometimes willingly handed over to councils of merchants (in exchange for a tithe on the profits, of course). Other merchant communities had lived overseas for generations, far from imperial oversight, in millennia-old foreign enclaves that shared walls with many others. In the Indian

Ocean, they included African merchants from the cities of the Swahili Coast, Gujaratis, Parsis, Bengalis, Tamils, Arabs, Omanis, Armenians, and Jews. Further east, in the Straits of Malacca and the China Seas, Chinese, Hakka, Fujianese, Japanese, Javanese, Buginese, Makassarese, and many other merchants could be found in all ports of the region. In Europe meanwhile, the merchant republics of Genoa and Venice held sway in the Mediterranean and Black Seas. English, Dutch, German, Scandinavians, Slavs, Balts, and Russians plied the trade between the Hanseatic cities and republics of the North and Baltic Seas. Meanwhile, although trade along the west coast of Africa also went back centuries, merchants there only began playing roles in the Oceanic trade when Europeans started outfitting the coastline with factories designed for transshipments of gold and enslaved people.[1]

As multifarious as global capitalism was at birth, there is no question that European merchants became uniquely engaged with *all* of the other merchant communities of Afro-Eurasia; more crucially, they were the only Old Worlders involved in the especially vast plunder of the Americas.[2] The explanation for this conundrum does not lie in any unique form of expansionist genius, as Western racists later tried to argue, nor in white peoples' advanced proclivity for money-grubbing. Here, as in the question of Europe's new role in global politics, the region's geography and its continental position vis-à-vis the open Oceans mattered. Europe's spot at the meeting point of the Mediterranean Sea, the North Sea, and the Atlantic presented its sea-going money-seekers with what theorists of global capitalism call a "spatial problem" whose only "spatial fix" was the World Ocean itself, starting with the nearby Atlantic. Essential to that big fix were smaller spatial fixes: many new moneymaking cities – of multifarious design, all unprecedented, all along the Ocean shores and inland from there.[3]

Start with the problem. Before 1492, Old World commerce centered overwhelmingly on trade routes linking various parts of Asia and Africa, above all in the Indian Ocean and China Seas. Europe occupied a backwater. The craggy "peninsula of peninsulas" on the far northwest of Afro-Eurasia produced little that people in the rest of the supercontinent could not make on their own. The only way European elites could satisfy their desire for African or Asian "rarities" – gold, spices, silk, cotton cloth, porcelain, fragrances, and medicines – was to tax their own realms' agricultural and mineral base, convert that wealth into scarce metal money, and ship treasury-punishing chests of coins and bullion to the hated Muslim merchants who guarded the gates to West Africa and Asia. The political geography of the pre-Ocean world economy thus functioned to drain Europe of precious metals and to whet desperate greed for more. Both gained further propulsion from Christian Europe's furious sense of grievance against Islam.[4]

Indeed, the problem itself contained the fix. Just as European states' weak city walls translated into stronger gunpowder weapons, so their weak geo-economic position offered a few European cities a few tools that turned out to be essential to outflanking their rivals via the Oceans. Before Columbus, merchants in some European cities – notably Venice and Genoa in the Mediterranean and the Hanseatic cities in the northern seas – had grown rich (and politically independent) from their particular geographical position within the supercontinental backwater. Not only did they pocket profits by monopolizing commerce with Muslim traders, they also imported especially promising raw materials from shores accessible to them just to the east. The Genoese transplanted sugarcane from Southwest Asia to the Mediterranean and the Canary Islands. In the northeast, Hanseatic traders shipped stout ships' masts and pine pitch from the forests of the Baltic seacoast to their own shipyards; and Dutch fishing boat owners pioneered on-board processing of a particularly tasty recipe for salted North Sea herring, useful for feeding both long-distance sailors and growing numbers of urban land-lubbers alike. Meanwhile, in the Mediterranean, North, and Baltic Seas, unpredictable wind patterns and treacherous currents between these trading cities favored innovations in shipbuilding and sail rigging, just as the short distances between Europe's peninsulas and islands lowered the risks of experimentation and thus increased its frequency.

As we know, Europe's collection of medium-sized and small states fought each other continuously, more so than in other parts of the gunpowder universe. Thus, European kings regularly outspent their tax receipts from rural estates, and were forced to call on wealthy money-lending families in mercantile cities who alone could cover massive expenditures on weapons. In a few of those cities – Genoa, Venice,

Antwerp, and Amsterdam among them – banks accordingly developed innovative ways to finance both warfare and mercantile exploits. These urban banks, as we will see soon, were alone capable of priming the money pump that Portuguese and Spanish kings needed to fix Europe's backwater problem by sailing onto the World Ocean, building the cities required, and in so doing redefining which winds and waves in which water mattered most to the world of wealth as a whole.[5]

THE SILVER CIRCLE

To see how this worked, we need to return to craggy Europe before 1492. Note to start that neither the especially aching motives nor the increasingly sophisticated means of Ocean navigation were present in the urban-based polities of West Africa, which were similarly positioned to take to the Atlantic. Unlike Europeans, West Africans possessed some of the largest gold mines in the world, allowing them to satisfy their long-distance luxury needs via the seas of Saharan sand from Muslim caliphates whose religion many of the largest African kingdoms shared. These kingdoms thus possessed no backwater problem requiring an oceanic fix, and in any case, commerce along the relatively un-indented West African coastline, unlike Europe's, neither demanded nor encouraged maritime experiments with new ocean-going shipping technologies. Meanwhile, in 1400s Europe, wars intensified all of the region's means for Oceanic exploration, increasing all the motives involved – starting with a mounting hunger for precious metals to pay soldiers and buy weapons. That hunger was especially acute for the royal houses of Portugal and Spain, who strained their gold and silver holdings more severely than other European powers during conquests of Muslim-controlled areas on the Iberian Peninsula. Their rash decision to expel their kingdoms' Jewish inhabitants, who often helped kings with loans, did not help matters. The two Iberian powers also shared a prime southwestern geographical position on the continent that allowed them to take the lead in refining sailing technologies needed for the particular winds and currents of the circum-African and trans-Atlantic ocean waters. Both Portugal and Spain, finally, succeeded quickly in procuring new sources of shiny metals on the far ocean shores they explored, a fact that helps to explain the acceleration of their imperial and commercial advance over the course of the 1500s.

Portugal, as we know, acquired direct access to West African gold at El Mina well before 1492, allowing its kings to build more ships, forge more cannons, and build more fortresses and merchant *feitorias* along the circum-African route to Asia and its luxuries. More about them soon. The Spanish state's hesitant investment in Columbus's Atlantic adventures took longer to pay off. Columbus found some gold on Hispaniola and elsewhere, but the big game changer only came when Spanish conquistadors of the Aztec and Inka empires followed Native guides to silver mines in Mexico and Peru. In 1545, one conquistador's Native servant, a man named Gualpa, led his master to the single most productive silver lode in the world, high in the Andes at a mountain appropriately named Cerro Rico – the Mountain of Riches.[6]

The city of Potosí (located in today's Bolivia), which came into being at the base of this towering money-mine high in the Andes, was a crucial urban birthplace of global capitalism, an urban "fix" in its own right that soon, and rather uncannily, made Oceanic fixes possible both in the Atlantic and in the Pacific. At first, it served as a modest base for Native prospectors whose ingenious *guayra* furnaces, ideal for smelting the mountain's richest ores, lit up the town's evening skies from high on the slopes. The Spanish Royal Treasury, now relocated to the new Spanish capital of Madrid, began to swell almost immediately thanks to a 20 percent tax levied on these miners by Spanish officials in Potosí. When the purity of Cerro Rico's ore diminished below yields suitable for indigenous furnaces, Madrid was quick to react. In a few short years, the iron-fisted Spanish Viceroy Francisco Álvarez de Toledo transformed Potosí into a mining complex of unprecedented industrial scope. By the early 1600s, no fewer than 160,000 people (about the population of Paris at the same time) inhabited a ramshackle mess of houses, shops, factories, and government buildings in what had recently been a frost-bitten mountain wilderness.[7]

To build the money-mining city of his liking, Viceroy Toledo reintroduced an Inka-era labor tax called the *mita*. The new law empowered a small army of labor recruiters called *curacas* to order Indian village elders from the surrounding provinces to impress one-seventh of their male inhabitants aged fifteen to fifty and drag them off against their will – roped to mules if necessary – to a mustering ground outside Potosí. There, whip-wielding overseers sent the bulk of the *mitayo* workforce, with sputtering candles fastened to their wrists, into the gloom of Cerro Rico's mineshafts and galleries. Descending into the sinuous labyrinths by means of sixty-foot wooden ladders, they felt their way toward the clank of miners' crowbars, loaded their satchels with fifty kilograms of ore, and returned by the same route, often only to be rewarded at the surface with canings and whippings by overseers if quotas were not precisely met.[8]

On the outside, meanwhile, another pharaonic army of *mitayos* moved around big chunks of the surrounding Andes peaks to form a system of dams that retained rain and meltwater in eighteen separate lagoons in the upper valleys behind Cerro Rico. These lagoons fed a fifteen-kilometer millrace that rushed furiously into the city, spinning waterwheels at Potosí's 100 ore-stamping mills. Next to these thundering mills were the "patios," rectangular wooden basins containing a toxic sludge of now-pulverized ore-dust, water, salt, and mercury. Still other *mitayos* waded up to their knees in this soup, slowly amalgamating the mercury with silver in the ore. Mercury was essential to the project, but getting it to Potosí involved another set of mines located 1,000 kilometers away, in another high Andean valley, at a city called Huancavelica. Llama and mule trains brought dripping sheepskin bags of the highly volatile poisonous substance out of Huancavelica down to Pacific ports at Pisco and Chincha, near Lima. There the cargos were loaded on ships for the 900-kilometer ocean trip south to another port, at Arica (in today's Chile). From there, more mules and llamas hauled them 600 kilometers and 3,500 meters above sea level to Potosí, where their contents were dumped into the patios. Once silver from Cerro Rico and mercury from Huancavelica had bonded under the bare feet of *mitayos*, new teams of workers packed the amalgam into clay pots and placed it in furnaces where the mercury vaporized – much of it into the lungs of workers and into the thin air of the city. The whole operation, from mines to dusty stamping plants to poisonous patios and furnaces, operated at catastrophic cost to the health and life of all concerned.[9]

Out of Potosí's mineshafts – "two thousand doors where men enter into Hell" – Native Andeans literally dug their era's "global capital" out of the ground. From the 1540s to 1800, over 150,000 tons of silver ingots emerged from Spanish American silver mines – fully half of that from Potosí alone – into marketplaces around the world. The royal house of Spain itself managed the key profit-making core of this urban oceanic operation. The royal mint in Potosí stamped the ingots into pesos (also known as Spanish Dollars or "Pieces of Eight"), where they were loaded once again onto llamas and mules for transfer to Panama-bound ships at Arica. At the isthmus, mules and more ships moved pesos to fortified ports like Cartagena de Indias and Havana, where more silver arrived from Mexico's Guanajuato. Battleships then escorted creaking Treasure Ships past Caribbean pirate nests like Port Royal, Jamaica and Petit-Gonâve, French Saint-Domingue. Privateers there bore commissions from London and Paris to seize Spanish pieces-of-eight, whole ships, and even ports. Most American treasure arrived safely in Seville and thence to the royal counting houses in Madrid. However, the king of Spain used Potosí silver to buy cannons from enemy weapons makers in Northern Europe, enriching merchant companies there and priming the pump of banks, most notably in Spanish-controlled Amsterdam, that financed other rival European kings' bloody wars across the continent. Meanwhile, hundreds of tons of smuggled silver (some of it mined by Native Americans on their days off) made its way east to the Río de la Plata in today's Argentina, where it swelled the population of the small port city of Buenos Aires and sparked the growth of a giant Spanish hinterland of settler-owned wheat fields and cattle ranches. Most importantly of all, increasing amounts of Potosí's and Guanajuato's silver made its way to the Mexican Pacific port of Acapulco, where it was loaded onto galleons for the 10,000-kilometer trip to Manila in the Philippines. There it joined yet another substantial current of silver, this one mined by tribute laborers of Japanese *daimyō* and transported on Portuguese and other merchant ships to Macao. The destination of both of these streams of pale white metal was the same: China.[10]

If Potosí was a principal faucet of global mineral wealth, Beijing – and dozens of other massive, pulsing cities of Ming and later Qing China – were nearly insatiable money drains. Since the days when the Forbidden City shut down the great tribute-seeking sea voyages of the eunuch admiral Zheng He, the Ming dynasty had adopted what one of its historians calls a "defensive" pose toward the Chinese merchants who had fanned out in the admiral's wake. In places like Malacca, Bantam in Java, and the Philippines, these merchants established overseas Chinese enclaves, where they disregarded most of the emperor's orders from far-off Beijing. Because of the large volume of their trade, Chinese merchants preferred to deal in silver rather than large piles of copper, too-rare gold, or the now-debased paper currency that Chinese emperors had first invented 500 years earlier – once again during the Golden Age of the Song dynasty. The Ming emperors at first resisted merchants' preference for silver, but in 1580, they finally yielded. Zhang Juzheng, Senior Secretary to the Ming Wanli Emperor, had no knowledge of Viceroy Toledo's work in Potosí at the exact same time. However, when he issued the "Single Whip" law that consolidated all of China's taxes into a single payment – to be paid in silver – his decision probably did more to make the Spanish Empire (and its World Oceanic fix) a viable enterprise than any decision made in Madrid. Pause for a moment to note this situation: it was a Chinese official, not a European one, who acted as midwife to humanity's first truly global economy.[11]

At that time, China's artisan quarters and industrial cities produced many of the goods that consumers elsewhere wanted most – silks, porcelains, and, later, chests for the increasingly popular stimulant tea. (Pause once again to contemplate how the sixteenth century rhymes with the twenty-first.) Chinese merchants, still ignoring restrictions from Beijing, loaded these luxuries and leafy stimulants onto junks in small south-coast ports like Shuangyu, Liangang, and Yuegang where Ming officials were scarce, and peddled them past gauntlets of pirates throughout East and Southeast Asia. When European ships began lugging silver from the Americas into the region, they gave a large boost to Chinese industry and its largely illegal export trade. The boost continued even after the Japanese shogun expelled the Portuguese from Nagasaki, causing that rival stream of silver to decline. Other Asian merchant communities also wanted silver to purchase Chinese goods, so they too accepted pesos from Potosí for luxuries from other Asian ports – spices, pepper, Indian cotton cloth, gemstones, gold, rare woods, horses, dies, medicines, and incenses. Some of these items made their way to West Africa, to be traded for enslaved captives, and to

(A)

(B)

8.1. A Tale of Four Capitals of Oceanic Capital

Here we visit four corners of the early-modern capitalist Urban Planet. The world's currency came from silver mines like Potosí's Cerro Rico (A), thanks to Native American forced laborers who dug reservoirs (left) to power stamping mills and poisonous annealing ponds (right). On industrialized sugar plantations (B), enslaved African workers – a form of capital themselves – grew cane on land seized from Native Americans (left), crushed it in mills (upper right), and boiled the sap (center) to produce the most valuable commodity in the Atlantic trade. At Manila (C), silver ships and Ming dynasty tax officials made truly planetary ocean-borne commercial circuits possible. Europeans built segregated port cities to deal in Asian goods and spices; here the British navy has temporarily seized Manila's Spanish "Intramuros" district. At Amsterdam (D), merchants formed the first multinational corporations, headquartered in the harbor (bottom left). A stock exchange (above the Damrak Canal, center) anchored the first global financial center. Suburban real estate projects (left) added to growing mercantile wealth.

(A) Universal Images Group/Getty Images. (B) Christophel Fine Art/Universal Images Group/Getty Images. (C) Hulton Archive/Getty Images. (D) Archive Photos/Getty Images.

(C)

(D)

8.1. (cont.)

Europe, or back the other way in Manila–Acapulco galleons heading back to the increasingly lavish colonial cities of the Spanish Americas.[12]

CITIES OF STOLEN LAND AND LABOR

From Europe, imperialists re-invested American silver in projects to rebuild their New World coastal cities for another Ocean-sized enterprise: the plundering of the Atlantic world's land and labor. Once in control of these two other forms of capital, they could seize a third, the many other rich natural resources of the Americas. Native Americans, Africans, and Asians did not sit to the side as Europeans' triple theft of the world's "factors of capital production" unfolded: they fought back, with very different means and amidst different political dramas, even as many were forced into hard labor on stolen land. Amidst these dramas, colonial fortress towns all along the Ocean shores transformed into many more urban birthplaces of global capitalism – each of them tense and politically hyper-charged.

The many shapes these cities assumed, beyond their be-bastioned kernels, reflected the diversity of their roles in the new whorl of wealth plundering, the political conflicts involved in playing those roles, and the ways their colonial rulers thought about the composition of their typically very diverse populations. Were imperial forces able to capture the hinterlands of their colonial cities, or did their power only extend, as the British negotiated at Madras, the distance of a cannon shot from the fortress? Did the European inhabitants of the city consist primarily of colonial officials and merchants, in which case most planned to move on to the next posting or port within a few days or years – or were they permanent settlers, as in the Americas, whose goal was to raise new generations on new shores and frontiers? If the latter, what was the ratio of male to female settlers? What about the Native population who previously owned the land underneath the new colonial city – was it growing or declining? How about the size of forcibly introduced populations, most notably enslaved Africans? All of these questions about colonial cities mattered greatly to the urban design strategies imperialists adopted to translate armed force into actual seized capital. New political words emerged in the Cities of the Oceans, in the form of divisive Western concepts such as "blood," "nations," "peoples," "castes," "complexions," and "races." When officials used such categories to determine the conditions of labor or to block access to urban land – sometimes, but not always by means of what we later called "racial segregation" – the new words created new axes of economic inequality and urban design that helped European authorities hold onto imperial control and promote their projects of global plunder.[13]

The global wealth-grab of the early-modern era was most extensive in the Americas. There, Columbus's grandiose dream of seizing large continental hinterlands and Native labor forces from bases in colonial cities and run by permanent settlers turned out to be more plausible than in Africa or Asia. In the Caribbean, New Spain, and Peru, Madrid's *encomienda* system allowed conquistadors like Hernán Cortés to seize large Aztec administrative cities and to redirect traditional tribute and labor levies for their own personal gain on gigantic landholdings. The new Spanish aristocracy that thus arose could call upon Native workers, under conditions that resembled slavery, to flatten their ancestors' garden-like tropical agricultural landscape in order to raise cattle, sheep, goats, and new grains such as wheat introduced from Europe. As Native populations declined, the Spanish state ran an even more invasive Native labor allocation system called the *repartimiento*. Palatial *haciendas* (plantation houses) arose in Mexico as Spanish noblemen seized or fraudulently acquired plots of Native land and cobbled together enormous estates or *latifundias*. Add to that wealth all the money from the silver mines, and you have the economic recipe for some of the grandest of world history's colonial cities.[14]

As we know, Mexico City, the capital of New Spain – named after the Mexica, the Aztec imperial clan – arose upon the ruins of Emperor Montezuma's splendid capital Tenochtitlan. Cortés himself began the work, by claiming a large rectangular stretch of land to the southwest of the flattened temple to the Aztec Sun God, and laying out the city's Plaza Mayor. There, on the spot formerly occupied by the palace of Emperor Montezuma, Cortés forced Indian laborers from his *encomienda* to erect a new palace for himself, a move soon copied by other conquistadors, as well as aristocrats newly arrived from Spain, and the viceroy himself. Forced laborers soon added government buildings, including the headquarters of the labor bureaus and rapacious land courts, a church, monasteries, a university, and finally the largest cathedral in the

Americas, which presides over the Plaza Mayor – now known as the Zocaló – to this day.[15]

To protect this vast urban apparatus of state and church from potential rebellions by the city's poor – including the very laborers who built it – the Spaniards at first practiced a rigid form of "nation"-based urban segregation. They demarcated a *ciudad de españoles* at the city center, containing the plaza and all of the most important buildings, aligned on a larger rectangular grid of streets called the *traza* – which resembled the layout of Roman colonial towns. The colonial authorities relegated the Native American population, a majority at the city's founding, to neighborhoods that pre-existed the conquest at the four corners of the *traza*, renaming these *barrios de Indios*. Unlike in most Dutch, English, and French colonial cities in the Americas founded later, Spanish settlers in Mexico were overwhelmingly male and single. They routinely crossed Mexico City's "national" boundaries in search of partners for sex and sometimes marriage. As the Native population began to diminish amidst outbreaks of plague and smallpox, and the Spaniards imported increasing numbers of African slaves, the mixed population of the city grew and the "national" boundaries faded. Though the Spanish authorities made a few attempts to reestablish the line, the *traza*, like the city as a whole, became a largely *mestizo* (Euro-American) and *mulatto* (Euro-African) city, with richer (and usually lighter-skinned) people tending to live in the nicer apartments on the ground floor and poorer people on the upper floors – a bit like in ancient Rome's *insulae*. To forestall rebellions, authorities switched from "national" designations to a system of legally registered *castas*, which divided and conquered the poor into dozens of subcategories and doled out differential privileges based on groups' varying quantities of Spanish, Indian, and African "blood."[16]

Meanwhile, forced labor continued apace, most notably in service of the so-called *Desagüe* – or "de-watering" – of the lake that, in Aztec times, completely surrounded Tenochtitlan. The Spaniards had no use for the complex ecosystem of floating gardens in Lake Texcoco that the Aztecs had used to feed their island city. Rains regularly raised the lake levels, flooding the city, including the Plaza Mayor, which became a two-meter-deep rectangular lake itself for four years during one particularly bad spell. Under the *repartimiento*, the viceroy and his Dutch engineers put people from various low-status *castas* to work hauling earth and rock to form dykes that typically washed back into the lake at the next flood. One viceroy had the great idea of draining the lake via a tunnel through surrounding hills into a lower river valley beyond, a task that recalled the hellish mine-work of Potosí, only hotter and wetter. When the tunnel collapsed too, the state began digging an open-air drainage canal through the same hills, a task that took well into the nineteenth century. Only then did forced hard labor create enough dry land (albeit in the form of mudflats that dangerously amplify the region's earthquakes) for Mexico City to become the megacity of today.[17]

Enslaved Africans, meanwhile, began to arrive in Mexico and the rest of the Americas in larger numbers than European settlers. Europeans could not seize large pieces of land in Africa because of their own lack of immunity to malaria, but their theft of African labor was among the most extensive crimes in world history. Like other large-scale early-modern human endeavors, Atlantic slavery was both a creator and a creation of the emerging Urban Planet. African laborers, as one historian put it, "were responsible for the built environments of several continents," most notably those of the Americas, but also of coastal Africa itself and many places in Europe. Conversely, cities on all three of these continents – many of them home to substantial numbers of enslaved people themselves – were essential to the enormous project to extract wealth from the premier land- and labor-thieving institution of the day, the American slave plantation.[18]

To get there, enslaved Africans suffered through months of life in chains, in a succession of dank, dark, dirty, insalubrious, confined, crowded spaces – with armed guards stationed at narrow openings. We have already met the first stop in this journey, the slave prisons in colonial castles along the African coast, where many captives languished for a year or longer as part of European shipping companies' efforts to acquire wholesale volumes of human cargo. These dungeons' infamous "Doors of No Return" led directly to the infernally crowded below-decks of slave ships. The low ceilings and rough floors of these dark holds were typically hammered together by the ship's crew as their captain waited offshore for the castles to assemble large-enough human cargos. The chained, seasick, brutalized inmates who survived the often months-long "middle passage" – typically lying prone in a six-foot by sixteen-inch space between neighbors on each side, often washed by each others' urine and excrement and tormented by ship's rats – then faced further periods of imprisonment on the American side of the Atlantic. Sometimes they remained for months in the ship's slave-holds as captains negotiated higher prices in a succession of New World slave ports. For most who actually debarked, their first view of the Americas came from dingy, back-alley slave prisons in Bridgetown, Barbados, Charleston, South Carolina, and New York City, or larger slave yards such as those in Rio de Janeiro, Kingston, Jamaica, or Cartagena de Indias.[19]

Urban slave markets were the next circle of the infernal built environment that made the plantation system function. Sometimes slaves experienced their transformation from human cargo into retail object on ship, on the quay, or in town squares next to the harbor. Other cities built special structures to facilitate larger volumes of sales. These had holding cells, lurid viewing rooms, and auction halls. No matter where it occurred, the purchase of an enslaved person instantly transformed human beings into a slave owner's most important form of wealth, capital in human bodies that was essential to extracting further wealth from stolen plantation land. That wealth quickly rivaled the impact of silver on the world economy and on the shape of the Urban Planet.[20]

Most enslaved people – Africans or the slowly dwindling population of Native American slaves – lived on plantations in rural areas. Plantations were not cities by most measures. However, they were ideal nurseries for global capitalism in its infancy, for they took two forms of capital, stolen land and labor, and turned them into a third, some kind of cash crop – thus generating the crucial outcome, profit. In Brazil after 1570, governors doled out large grants of land taken from the indigenous Tupi, whose populations declined amidst disease and European slave raids, such as those launched from São Paulo. Planters and their overseers infamously worked their slaves to death in vast, steamy, snake-filled sugarcane fields, soon replacing their human labor force by importation from Africa rather than by natural increase in the Americas. They also used slave labor to build the industrial infrastructure needed for sugar processing on the plantation itself. That included cane-crushing mills driven by water wheels, blazing-hot sap-boiling houses, fuel-lots to feed the fires, and purging-houses where the sugar crystalized in cone-shaped ceramic containers. On top of that were crude residential quarters for slaves, a sprinkling of smaller settlements for tenants, overseers, smiths, and other artisans, and the planter's own great house, which dominated the landscape. Though small in comparison with cities, rural sugar-producing industrial complexes were among the most extensive forms of human-built environment in early-modern South America, the Caribbean, and Louisiana, and not only because the demand for sugar increased immensely during this time. Sugarcane also rapidly depleted soil quality and thus required constantly expanding areas of cleared land. Moreover, keeping the vats boiling required enormous supplies of firewood. Even when cane husks were added to the fire, sugar plantations depleted forests at a rapid rate far beyond the fields. Tropical sugar plantations also served as the models for the later, and perhaps better-known, cotton plantations of the United States South.[21]

Of course, nothing happened on plantations without constant interaction with coastal cities. Those cities depended on their own large numbers of enslaved residents, who, by extension, were essential to the smooth operation of the entire Atlantic wealth-making project. Though they made up only a minority of the American enslaved population as a whole, they could make up a majority or a large plurality of the inhabitants of these busy, tense seaport cities. Slave cities were themselves capitals of three forms of capital – the enslaved themselves, urban real estate, and merchant profit. Outside Mexico and Peru, most slave cities were built in regions with Native populations who had largely lived in villages and camps. European settlers bought or captured the land for their settlements from Natives early in these cities' history, and like in European cities, typically carved it into small plots, each of which came with a registered title of individual ownership, allowing owners the power to sell and buy portions of the city as they changed in value. Settlers who were not aristocrats could often afford some of these lots, a major transformation that loosened Old World inequalities in wealth somewhat. Those "white" settlers and their descendants benefited from the rapid appreciation in wealth that urban land in growing cities could provide. In addition, of course, urban slave owners did everything they could to amass returns on their investments in human capital, first by denying the enslaved any right to own land, secondly by employing their human property in domestic service and in their own businesses, and thirdly by hiring the enslaved out to the city's other commercial houses, artisan shops, and small industries.[22]

In doing the latter, enslavers' investment strategies directly contradicted their own sense of security and even the stability of their rule over urban space. Though hired-out enslaved workers in cities could not buy land, they had far more latitude than their plantation counterparts to move around, meet each other, build associations, invest in small hawking businesses, practice their religion, entertain themselves, and mingle with small populations of restive free Blacks and poorer white people. The state's big guns may have loomed menacingly from the fortress that brought the slave city into being, but that form of blunt official power could not stop rebellions from hatching in back alleys, unlicensed taverns, or unauthorized shantytowns. Because of these threats, enslavers in port cities of the Americas never considered developing separate (or what we now call "segregated") neighborhoods for whites and Blacks. To gather so many people forcibly deprived of freedom in one place, enslavers rightly feared, could be tantamount to mustering a rebel army against themselves, potentially creating an existential threat to Atlantic slavery as a whole. Instead, enslavers did whatever they could to keep the people they enslaved under their own supervision. Household segregation was one technique of control. The wealthiest enslavers built whole wings of their houses for their human property, usually behind the main house and hidden from street view. Those of more modest means confined the enslaved to closets and attics, or backyard shacks, kitchens, or washhouses. Some masters who could not afford segregation laid down a mattress in their own bedrooms for their personal attendants.[23]

When urban enslavers hired out enslaved people to others, these domestic surveillance systems gave way to slightly more freedom of movement and action in the streets – including, to enslavers' greatest consternation, at night. "How many of us," wrote one nervous enslaver in Charleston "retire on a night under the impression that all our servants are on the premises and will continue there till morning? And how often is it quite the reverse ... [and they] are quietly ensconced in some dark street of villainy?" For the enslaved who did not return each night, laws multiplied throughout the late 1600s and 1700s prohibiting more than two or three enslaved people from congregating, forcing them to carry lanterns, and mustering soldiers or other officers of the peace to enforce curfews. Atlantic port cities also possessed a soundscape meant to intimidate the enslaved: the drums of the detachments of soldiers, and the ringing bells or shouts that announced curfews. Authorities also repeatedly tore down the shacks of informal "Africa Towns" or "Little Ouidahs" that sprouted up beyond the eyes of the owners. In our own time, Rio de Janeiro has become infamous for destroying hillside shack-cities known as *favelas* inhabited by the city's poorest (and typically darkest-skinned) residents. These shack towns – and ruthless episodes of shack destruction – go back to the city's slave era.[24]

To increase their capital in enslaved people, enslavers also had to prevent less-fortunate Europeans – who made up a majority of the white population and had plenty of their own grievances – from joining with Africans in rebellion. To do this, colonial officials in slave cities supplemented their guns and laws with political–legal distinctions of "color," "complexion," and "mixtures of blood." In Brazil, where the European female population was low, and where European settlers deemed a large Eurafrican population a natural outcome of settlement, the authorities often gave part-African *mulattos* and some Blacks free status and privileged positions, such as employment as overseers or soldiers, to discourage them from developing solidarity with enslaved people. In British North America, where the European female settler population was by contrast relatively large, the authorities declared cross-color sex taboo and even illegal in some places. They reserved the new privileged category "white" for all people apparently born of two European parents, no matter how downtrodden, hoping that this privileged color title would convince all whites to identify with the owning class and prevent them from joining in the struggles of Blacks. Accordingly, "white" Anglo settlers were encouraged to think of all mixed people, no matter their color, as Black. In many places, officials also passed laws ensuring that children born to enslaved women, including children with white fathers, inherited their enslaved status from their mother. None of these divide-and-control measures prevented urban or plantation-based slave revolts. Whites joined many of them, such as in New York in 1741.

Such rebellions rocked the Atlantic world much more regularly than in pre-modern slave cities. Officials usually repressed unrest with an iron hand, but enslaved people's acts of resistance supplied momentum to the growing, Atlantic-wide movement to abolish slavery, and eventually to the great urban revolutions of the modern era (Chapters 10 and 11).[25]

CITIES OF SPICE AND SEGREGATION

Meanwhile, in colonial cities of the Indian Ocean and the East Asian seas, very different innovations in global wealth accumulation were taking place, each of them "fixes" to Oceanic commerce involving different forms of urban design. Here, rapid conquests of hinterlands and massive enslavement of the inhabitants was impossible because of the geopolitical and technological parity between Europe and the region's largest states. The long distances from Europe – as well as tropical disease in some places – made large "white" settler populations impossible. Most of the tiny groups of European officials and merchants who lived in East African or Asian colonial cities did so for short administrative or commercial sojourns. Real-estate speculation was much quieter among Europeans, who typically owned only tiny portions of the city, if they bothered investing in land there at all. There were virtually no European women in town, and the locally born Eurasian or Eurafrican population was typically larger than that of Europeans – whether Catholic Iberian or Northern Protestant. Overseas merchants from Africa or Asia also typically outnumbered European ones. The vast majority of these cities' inhabitants came from African or Asian villages and other cities nearby; these locals oversaw most of the business of providing the colonial city's homes with products from agricultural, artisanal, and commercial hinterlands that Europeans did not control. Such cities too were capitals of capital, but most of that capital derived from goods and money sold to Europeans by African and Asian merchants by means of loans from local financiers. Europeans built their own capital by borrowing money, buying these goods, selling them at high enough profits elsewhere in the Indian Ocean world, and finally using the proceeds to pay back the loans to African or Asian financiers. As far as Europeans were concerned, proximity to these local merchant-financiers was the main reason to found a city anywhere on the shores of the Indian Ocean or the China Seas.[26]

Wealth creation by means of transoceanic commerce in the eastern hemisphere had fewer moving parts than the slave trade and plantation system of the Atlantic world, and it more closely resembled economic activity from ancient times. Still, the enlarged geographical scale of this enterprise, and the fact that its main suppliers of capital and goods were technically subjects of very powerful emperors with gigantic armies, did present novel challenges. To meet them, European city builders invented a variation on the ancient *kārum* – an overseas merchant district that they attempted to rule themselves despite their lack of control over the surrounding urban hinterland. To impose this truncated form of urban-based overseas imperial power, they relied on the usual bastions, battleships when available, and a fortified royal or Company headquarters that doubled as a municipal government building. Such seats of government also had the power (under the imperfect supervision of the distant Company Court or central headquarters back in Europe) to conduct diplomacy or war with any local ruler who controlled the provisioning of the town or who considered local merchants and financiers their subjects. European merchants, of course, also surrounded these built nuclei of overseas mini-states with the bric-a-brac typical of a commercial town: merchant houses, offices, large expanses of warehouses – known in South Asia as *godowns* – and, of course, dozens of high-masted cargo ships in the harbor.[27]

Still, Europeans in these ocean-side colonial *kārums* faced another spatial-political dilemma. Where should they allow their local business partners to build their own facilities? Colonial officials were of course eager to encourage lucrative deals, but they also suspected wealthy Africans or Asians to be spies for local governments or co-conspirators with rival European states or companies. Like slave cities in the Atlantic, colonial cities in the East were very tense places, subject to attack or uprising at any time. As heads of would-be monopolies, European officials also suspected other merchants from Europe, not to mention their own employees, of making lucrative side deals that ate into royal or Company profits. The spatial solution for this push-me-pull-you drama, unlike the similar profit-versus-security dilemmas of Atlantic slave owners, was usually some kind of large-scale separation barrier between Europeans and all other inhabitants of the city. In the capitals of capital on shores of the Eastern oceans, segregation also tightened overall during the seventeenth and eighteenth centuries, unlike the falling barriers in increasingly intermixed Atlantic World cities like Mexico City.[28]

Where exactly the dividing line ran in these Eastern Ocean cities, whether it involved any built structure such as a wall, and which names authorities gave to the groups on either side all differed from place to place, depending on the evolving local chessboard of political forces. On the urging of Portuguese clerics, for example, the *Estado da India* passed an ordinance forbidding interactions between urban "Christians" and devotees of other religions in its Asian cities. Secular officials, however, enforced this law irregularly. A concentric line of walls ran around the fortified *feitoria* and the Christian district in Colombo, for example, but not in Goa itself, which had a reputation for mixed neighborhoods – though officials destroyed all mosques or temples in the area. At Macao, the Portuguese built a surrounding wall across the landward side of the peninsula occupied by their small city, but the Ming and later Qing authorities controlled its main Circle Gate, which was the only route by which provisions could enter town. The emperor, for his part, prohibited his Chinese subjects from entering Macao, and his local officials used the threat of a cut-off of supplies as a way to meddle in the Portuguese city's politics.[29]

At Manila, the Spanish were more serious about segregation. They built a massive four-bastioned wall around the large Spanish quarter, known as *Intramuros*, and passed legislation that imposed the death penalty for Chinese people who remained inside the walls after dark. Cannons on the walls pointed not only at the port to scare away pirates, but also onto the rooftops of neighboring Parian and Binondo, the city's two Chinese districts. At Batavia, the Dutch took a step further and created something close to an apartheid system, with a Chinese district in town surrounded by canals and guarded at its single exit point, as well as *kampungs* (Malay for "village") outside town for various groups of local people who were considered especially dangerous security threats. Dutch officials and soldiers oversaw a kind of pass system involving lead tokens to control the movement of Javanese residents in and out of the city. On the other hand, in places like Nagasaki, the Dutch had far less control, as we know. Local Tokugawa officials took the upper hand in segregation, somewhat like the king of Kanesh in the Assyrian *kārum*. They forced the Dutch to remain on the small island of Deshima, and, like the Ming authorities at Macao, imposed an elaborate regime of diplomatic protocols for interactions with Japanese customs officials and merchants.[30]

At the British East India Company's capital at Madras, officials imitated the Portuguese at Colombo and elsewhere by walling off what they originally called "the Christian Town" around Fort St. George and the houses of Company employees, in addition to those of allied Portuguese and Armenian merchants. An enormous "Gentue [Hindu] Town" grew up right outside the walls. Local merchants flocked there to peddle loans and sell cotton cloth produced in the villages in the surrounding region, ruled by a shifting array of local princes and Mughal generals. The Company merchants made money by reselling this cloth in Java and elsewhere in exchange for spices and Chinese luxury goods, then repaying loans they took out in Madras with profits amassed in Asia, Africa, or back in Europe. Asian merchants bought land in the Asian section of town and build huge mansions, temples, and, above all, acres of *godowns*. Europeans, however, fretted constantly that local princes, maverick generals of the Mughal Empire, or the hated Dutch and French might use this dense Asian built space as cover for an attack on the Christian Town. For several decades, the Company harangued their local business partners to pay for a second wall around what they soon called "*Black* Town" – importing what they saw as the demeaning color category "Black" from the Atlantic world to express their frustrations at the Indians' stubborn resistance to the tax. Finally, the hard-handed governor William Pitt imprisoned the company's richest "Black" clients and forced payment of the tax. Meanwhile "Christian Town" became "White Town," a name meant to threaten the independent-minded Portuguese and Armenians – who were Christians, but not clearly "white" – that any mischief on their part could get them expelled from the privileged district. Expelled they were in 1748, when the British regained Madras from the French and accused their Christian allies of engineering the city's betrayal to a mortal archrival. Madras's "White Town"/"Black Town" terminology became a common way to designate separate zones in future colonial cities, most notably in Bombay and Calcutta – even as "white" and "black" became foundational categories of the increasingly politicized concept of "race" in the 1760s.[31]

MONEY FROM THIN AIR ... AND HARD GROUND

As these stories only begin to suggest, the birth of global capitalism was a haphazard, multifarious, uncanny affair – in addition to being a bloody one. Theorists sometimes refer to it as a "process" (and its urban side as a "process of capitalist urbanization"), but terms like that smooth out all the pangs, fits, and starts that brought the early-modern world economy into being, suggesting somehow that once Columbus had landed at Christmas City, the rest followed as a matter of natural course. In fact, as we have seen, each Ocean city embroiled would-be capitalists in political dramas of characteristic capriciousness along the way. Even more unpredictable was the Ocean itself, one of the mightiest avatars of the power of Sun and Earth (and Moon), which not only magnified the volatility of natural power – the *Santa Maria* was only one of thousands of early-modern shipwrecks – but did so on a scale that merchants and even kings found confounding. The Ocean and its cities may have served as "spatial fixes" for Europe's backwater problem, but they presented spatial problems of their own – for anyone, anywhere, who wanted to use them to make money.

The biggest problem was upfront money – capital itself – and risk management, or insurance, which required yet another massive form of pooled capital. Making profit from merchant voyages of such great length and such great risk required very large ships with large crews (not to mention many cannons and cannoneers). Once full, their larger cargos had to run far longer oceanic obstacle courses before arriving safely in ports where their owners could actually claim profits. Losing the *Santa Maria* to a coral reef was heartbreaking enough, but the shipwreck of a fully loaded Portuguese pepper galleon, a silver-filled Spanish Treasure Ship, let alone an Atlantic slave ship represented an entirely different class of complete loss. Note that similar upfront and insurance problems beset owners of vast tracts of conquered land, notably those whose profitability required upfront purchases of hundreds of slaves.

In an age when a simple exchange of letters between Europe and Asia could easily take two years, the problem of governing Oceanic (or continental) space remained unfixable. Nor was it possible – in an age of geopolitical parity, when the capitals of superpower imperial dynasties remained by far the largest cities in the world – to dominate all aspects of wealth creation worldwide from any single "center." However, as time went on, capitalists experimented with different solutions to the upfront money and risk management problems. At each point, they sought their ultimate "fix" in cities – especially cities with large "energized crowds" of very rich people – proximate profit-makers who could mutually agree that they could, in the long run, hoard more wealth if they contributed part of their own stash to larger wealth-multiplying funds. Such acts of financial magic also required complex governing institutions and specialized urban spaces to house them. Merchant capitalists also benefited from the rising value of urban land, itself caused by the crowding of rich people (and laborers) into cities. As their search for an urban fix to oceanic problem evolved, capitalists began giving certain cities, and specifically their new financial districts, more power over capitalism on a global scale. As they did so, they also took a many-headed beast and gave it more of a center, giving its plurality a volatile form of singularity.

Banks, named after the *banci*, or benches (sometimes called "counters"), that moneychangers in the ancient and medieval Mediterranean laid out for their customers, were one such urban built institutional habitat. The city of Genoa, Italy had one, housed in the magnificent Palazzo San Giorgio on one of the city's central squares. The Palazzo had previously served as a prison (Marco Polo, from the rival city of Venice, spent some involuntary time there), but it was rehabilitated in 1402 for the purpose of storing and profitably redeploying the wealth of the city's mighty merchants, including that of Genoa's soon-to-be favorite son, Christopher Columbus. Like banks today, the merchant-director of the bank of St. George paid its contributors rental payments (interest) on their money in exchange for the liberty to loan, in exchange for a higher rate of interest, substantial portions of the bank's larger accumulated treasure to people with need for especially large sums of upfront money.[32]

The kings of Portugal and Spain were among the Bank of St. George's biggest customers. Earlier, the kings had rented large masses of other people's money from the bank (and others in Italy, Germany, and the Low Countries) to pay for weapons and soldiers during the *Reconquista*. When the Portuguese king decided to rival Genoa's own merchants in the business of importing spices, he founded the *Casa da India* in a palace in his own capital of Lisbon, which operated essentially as a "wholesale grocery company" (because it primarily sold spices) owned by the king. Its governing officials borrowed money from banks, including that of St. George, to build the ships and pay for trade goods and the crews necessary for the trips around Africa to get spices. In Lisbon, the *Casa de Armagens* (Weapons House), next door to the *Casa da India*, borrowed from the same sources to buy the cannons and the materials for battleships and fortresses needed to enforce the *cartaz* system and guarantee the king's grocery monopoly. A *Casa de Escravos*, also nearby, took out similar loans to buy enslaved laborers for Brazilian sugar plantations. Ferdinand and Isabella did much the same in Seville at the *Casa de Contratación* (The Contracting House – note the historical persistence of use of words for "house" to describe what were essentially the court's corporate headquarters). Royal officers there took out the loans necessary to build Potosí as an industrial concern, and oversaw the arrival of the treasure ships containing the 20 percent of all mined silver levied at American mints.[33]

All of this worked very well for a time. Kings could of course tax their largely agricultural subjects for money, but sending tax collectors from farm to farm or estate to estate was a time-consuming process, filled with graft – and bad crop years meant smaller royal coffers. Bank loans were a much surer way to raise money, and the profits from monopolies on spices, sugar, and silver could usually cover the interest and then some. The problem was that kings did not just engage in grocery buying or silver mining. They also needed to pay people to regularly inflict violence on their subjects, their *mitayos*, their enslaved plantation workers and other forced laborers, on Native people unwilling to give up their land, and above all on the pirates, armies, and navies of their religious and dynastic rivals. During the 1500s, the kings of Spain and Portugal spent far more on expensive instruments of state violence – think of the Great Armada that the Spaniards raised against Protestant Britain, for example, or the soldiers they sent to their deaths in the eighty-year war they waged against the Dutch – than they gained in profits from spices, sugar, or silver. By the 1580s, all of the *Casas* in Lisbon and Seville were bankrupt: literally, they could not pay back their loans to places like Genoa's Palace of St. George. Everyone knew this, including the Italian, Dutch, British, and French merchant bankers who put their own countries in danger of attack by lending the Iberian kings their upfront capital for cannons.[34]

The financial woes of Iberian kings helped inspire new urban institutions for funding large-scale violence and trade. Amsterdam, a Spanish-run city in Holland filled with wealthy Protestant grain, lumber, and herring merchants who played a strong hand in local government (much like the merchants of Genoa), also possessed banks that lent money to many warring European monarchs. The city was awash in "Pieces of Eight" and other silver coins mined in Potosí and Guanajuato, whose value in international banks was largely based on what Dutch merchants would exchange for them. Then Dutch merchants themselves sought to raise money for the fleet of battleships and long-haul vessels they needed to fund a lengthy war of independence from Spain, to wipe out the Iberian *Estado da India*, to take over the Atlantic slave trade, and even make a play on Brazilian sugarcane fields. To do this, they created a new financial institution. They called it the *Koopmansbeurs*, the "Merchant's Purse" – what the French call the Bourse, and what we call a stock exchange.[35]

Amsterdam got its name from a dam that its medieval inhabitants built across the mouth of the Amstel River. It was outfitted with a sluice gate meant to control water rushing in from the tides and outward from heavy rains in surrounding low-lying swamps and farmland that could overflow Amsterdam's famous network of canals. The mouth of the river was called the Damrak, or Dam's Reach, and was spanned at one end by a wide bridge. It was on this bridge, with the masts of countless ocean-going ships in view, that merchants began to buy and sell a brand new type of money – shares (or stock) in the Dutch East India Company. The idea was for the Company to forgo loans, with their interest payments, for the much larger sums of money that merchants could contribute to a collective pool owned by the shareholding merchants themselves in exchange for a guaranteed share of the profits equal in percentage to that of their stake in the pool of upfront capital. As we know, the merchant-friendly government of the rebel province of Holland, which met in Amsterdam, added into the deal that this Company could – and should – use violence against anyone who stood in the way of bringing profits back safely. Similar Dutch companies received charters in the years to come, such as a West India Company for sugar, an African Company for slaves, and a Greenland Company for whaling. Meanwhile, depending on what they heard about the prospects of these companies at any time, Dutch merchants could buy more company shares, thus increasing their value – or sell them off, if they felt they were in danger of losing value. To guard against disasters that beset this type of long-distance business – such as shipwrecks or piracy – representatives of yet another type of reserve pool of capital became prevalent in Amsterdam as well: we know them as insurance companies. Also, because the merchants of Amsterdam possessed the best information available on the current state of all matters mercantile in the world, the price they were willing to pay for stock and insurance, not to mention silver, spices, or sugar, was very valuable information outside of Amsterdam. Accordingly, Amsterdam merchants published these prices in what amounted to the first financial newspaper, which was eagerly purchased and read by any investor anywhere who could lay their hands on it. All of these institutions needed specialized "houses," some of them in the city's stepped gable merchant houses, some in larger purpose-built headquarters. Soon the *Koopmansbeurs* got its own building, with an open-air courtyard to remind traders of the atmosphere of the original open-air stock exchange. For the sake of convenience and easy exchange of information, it was good for these buildings to be located right next to each other. It was thus that the Damrak – a tiny neighborhood containing people and institutions that coordinated a vast amount of economic activity across the world – became history's first financial center, elevating Amsterdam to the summit of the worlds' many capitals of capital.[36]

By the late 1600s, though, it was London's turn to displace Amsterdam from atop the summit of global capitalism. London too had a stock exchange; like Amsterdam's it took its model from an earlier exchange in the Flemish city of Antwerp that dealt not in shares of companies but in bets on the rise and fall of prices of goods like wool, salt, paper, and coal. London's Royal Exchange, located downtown across from St. Paul's

Cathedral, forbade most traders from entering its precincts because they were too rowdy. A man named John Casting therefore organized a trading floor at another important new institution in the global economy – Jonathan's Coffee House (more about which in Chapter 9). Soon, shares of the British East India Company, issued from its headquarters in Leadenhall Street, did brisk business in the shop and in the nearby streets, an area Daniel Defoe called the "stock-jobbing globe." The rise of "the City," the name by which we know London's financial district today, began a few decades after that of Amsterdam's Damrak.[37]

The kings and queens of England had problems similar to the king of Spain, in that they wanted to fight wars, but could not raise enough money to fund them from taxes, bank loans, and even court-owned shares in the British East and West India Companies. Fending off the Spanish Armada, then a revolt by England's own Parliament, then a bloody civil war, and then wars against the Dutch and the French in many places in the world all quickly emptied the Royal Treasury and put the Crown in hock to British and continental bankers. After considerable debate, in 1694, London moneylenders and royal exchequers came up with the idea for an institution called the Bank of England. Its be-columned central headquarters soon arose near the exchanges and coffeehouses on Threadneedle Street. The solid design of this edifice was meant to reassure subjects of the Crown that it was a good thing for all English subjects that the king engage in the following bit of business. In the name of his own new Bank, he would license Britain's largest private banks to lend out money in larger amounts than ever before, not in coins, but in the form of paper "bank notes." These would bear the king's seal and a written guarantee that the Crown, based on its armed sovereign authority, would back up the bank loans, and, most importantly, that it would accept the notes as payment for taxes from its subjects.

The Bank of England amounted to a massive bet. The increased amount of money the government and its licensed banks created "out of thin air" would stimulate the economy so powerfully that, even after expenses for wars and other investments were taken into account, the wealth of Crown, country, and the world as a whole would grow continuously, as a result of private banks' wise investment choices. On some level, this was absurd: the king continued to spend too much on weapons, and the banks made some extremely poor decisions – as the bursting of the famous South Sea financial bubble in 1720 proved. The Bank of England was never intended as a tool to spread money more equitably to urban majorities of poorer laborers, let alone slaves or Native people. Yet on another level, it was a stroke of genius of a highly ambiguous kind. From Threadneedle Street, the Bank of England soon allowed people to use its "pounds sterling" (a name for its pieces of paper money that made them seem like real silver) to underwrite all of the activities in the Ocean cities that flew a British flag. In this way, fortified British colonial cities grew and multiplied further, along with cannons, armies, slave ships, spice ships, plantations, sugar ships, and the largest assembly of gunboats that the world had seen since that of the Ming admiral Zheng He. Investments in coalmines, textile mills, and new plantations that grew cotton would be next.[38]

As money poured in and out of London from all of the Oceans, it also sloshed into other large British slave ports like Bristol and Liverpool, mercantile ports like Glasgow, and – very significantly – coal ports like Newcastle upon Tyne. People began moving to all of these places, and moving money there. Most often, though, they came to London, crowding the City's cramped medieval space, and encouraging property owners to jam ever more people into houses that bowed far out over the streets. In 1665, amidst hardships from the climate downturn and civil war, that density helped incubate a horrific outbreak of plague that killed tens of thousands, and in 1666, one of the dozens of bakeries required to feed all these people caught fire, sparking a conflagration that turned two-thirds of the city into ash, including the Royal Stock Exchange. After these compounding disasters, wealthier people began seeking plots of land beyond the old walls. The king and other aristocrats who owned the land to the city's west parceled it out for profit, and developers created what we know as the "squares" of the West End – Leicester Square and Soho Square to name the most famous today – plots for houses surrounding a fenced park with trees. Covenants in the title deeds for these plots obliged owners to build expensive houses there with the goal of keeping tenements for "lackies and pages" out of the neighborhood. Plantation owners who tired of life in Barbados and Jamaica, and merchants from the East who had made mints in places like Madras and Calcutta poured their earnings into these plots, giving them a semblance of the life of grand aristocrats out on their rural estates while keeping them close to the action in the City. Similar extensions of European cities occurred as the Little Ice Age waned – in the new canal districts of Amsterdam (thousands of stout Scandinavian tree trunks had to be pounded forty feet into the city's marsh-muck to support the houses) and the northern and western districts of Paris. Edo, the capital of Tokugawa Japan, also burst its boundaries at this time – possibly in part due to capitalist expansion elsewhere, but mostly due to the galloping mercantile economy within the archipelago and a hot local real estate market generated by the shogun's orders that *daimyō* house their families in his capital.[39]

Before moving on, notice what has happened here: inhabitants of the richest capitals of capital had created what we can recognize as the first recognizable and truly global version of today's "Finance, Insurance, and Real Estate" (FIRE) industry. Once created, capitalists used this industry's speculative energy – derived from thin air, from the hard, lucrative land under the city itself, and from the proximity power of people in hundreds of new Cities of the Oceans, to take a role in the creation of the Urban Planet that rivaled and soon arguably eclipsed the big building projects of empires themselves. Thanks to the Cities of the Oceans, global capital had found its own global capitals. There, in its own multiplying many-ness and in its concentrated power, global capitalism became a permanent, and soon predominant, economic and political force in the expansion of Earthopolis as a whole.

CHAPTER 9

Consuming the Earth in Cities of Light ... and Delight

NEW DAWNS ON DARK OCEANS

The bloody birth of global empire and capitalism in Cities of the Oceans should serve as an enduring corrective to urban theorists who blithely celebrate cities for their "dynamism" or, even more extravagantly, for "civilization." Surely, Columbus's visit, with ship, fort, and cannons, to Villa Navidad was as portentous as Inanna's delivery of destruction-laced bursts of creative energy to Uruk. The reach of humanity's destructive impact spread further beyond that of our own habitat. We and other life forms paid the price in a surging realm of deathly consequence, aggravated in this case by disquieted cycles of geo-solar energy during the 1600s. Yet, by the 1750s, Earthopolis was just as surely a more knowledgeable, scientifically aware, and literate place than it was in its much less intermerged form before 1492. Much of the new knowledge about the world, furthermore, was captured in the same new Cities of the Oceans that did so much to extend state violence and profit-mongering plunder. Such knowledge, in turn, played its own large role in merging the many realms of city-driven action and habitat into a genuinely planetary Urban Planet.

Clerics and scholars used urban spaces of many kinds to extend traditions of learning inherited from the ancient Axial Age – and their many routes to earthly justice and salvation through divine revelations from the heavens – while modifying them in important ways. Some regional faiths, notably the rival Roman Catholic and Protestant forms of Christianity outpaced Islam and Buddhism to become the first truly global World Religions, present on all six inhabited continents. At the same time, in some cities – especially European and American university towns that were able more directly to assimilate currents of knowledge from around the world – travelers and scholars also opened many minds to a Second Axial Age, often celebrated as an "Age of Enlightenment." Its sources were located on Earth itself: in the stimulated minds of people discovering the world as a whole for the first time, in the new spaces, animals, plants, and minerals they learned about for the first time, and in observations, experiments, calculations, and "rational" interpretations that scholars and amateurs applied to what they found.

Meanwhile Cities of the World Ocean also transubstantiated the dross of conquest and greed into an increasingly glamorous world of things and urban pleasures. Oceanic wealth and knowledge helped craft shops (including a few larger artisanal complexes) and entertainment zones to expand the range of their offerings – as well as the size of their built presence in urban space. The numbers of consumers also grew, along with their desire for luxury "rarities," new foods and beverages, household goods, books and newspapers, and the arts, including staged performances in secular as well as spiritual genres. All of these things, materials, and art forms diversified the class, race, and gender identities that city dwellers themselves could perform at home or upon anonymous urban "stages" like streets and squares. They also brought into being vibrant and altogether new urban commercial and intellectual spaces: coffee shops, bookshops, print shops, popular theaters, and a wide range of dissident religious gathering places.

Religious authorities and the state sought to control the new strains of thought and space-building, just as they had sought to control artisan shops and marketplaces since the earliest cities. Yet these new "thinking spaces" widened and agitated the political communities of many cities, and more people – still too few, but increasingly vocal nonetheless – became far bolder critics of the dogma of state and religion. This boldness was overshadowed by the dark fact that some "enlightened" critics invented new forms of propaganda of their own, such as the idea of "race," which cast doubts on the fundamental equality of all humans, and which soon helped to justify even vaster acts of global conquest and plunder. Yet the idea that government should rest on the consent of the governed – People Power, or the power of the urban and even rural *polis* as a whole – also made greater strides, outpacing the "democratic" visions of many types from pre-modern times. In this way, Cities of Light and

Delight built upon wealth plundered by global imperialists and capitalists also became the revival grounds of mass movements for the more just, equal, less exploitative, and more accountable Urban Planet we need even more desperately today.

LIGHT FROM HEAVEN AND EARTH

Gunpowder-based imperial power and the discovery of the World Ocean were enormous boons to clerics from all the world's most extensive religious communities. Religious authorities piggybacked on the expanded patronage of kings and emperors to increase the institutional and spatial footprint of faith and worship, and to diffuse transcendent knowledge and power to more souls in ever farther-flung new realms. The Ming and Qing emperors of China and the Tokugawa shoguns of Japan continued long traditions of endowing beautiful Confucian and Daoist temples and Buddhist or Shinto shrines and monasteries, including many on the grounds of their own palaces and pleasure parks. Buddhist authorities crowned the expanding reach of their faith with some of its most distinctive monuments, such as the Dalai Lama's Potala Palace in Lhasa (1645) and the Wat Phra Keow temple complex in the new Thai capital of Bangkok (1767). In India, Sikhism, destined to emerge as a world religion in the twentieth century, gave the world the Golden Temple of Amritsar (1604, rebuilt in 1809) and an infrastructure of *gurudwaras* that spread throughout cities of the Punjab region where it was born – and beyond.[1]

In the Muslim world, we have already met the resplendent mosques of Safavid Isfahan and Ottoman Istanbul. The Ottomans also rebuilt the Holy Kaaba in Mecca to deal with rain damage and accommodate growing numbers of *hajjis*. Mount Moriah in Ottoman Jerusalem remained a Muslim shrine, but officials treated Christians and Jews in the city respectfully, if under their own separate authorities and in separate quarters of the newly rebuilt city walls; Jerusalem's long Ottoman period was the most peaceful in its troubled history. New, Byzantine-inspired domed mosques arose in cities across the Ottoman lands, from Algiers in North Africa to Sarajevo in the Balkans, Edirne and Smyrna in Turkey, Aleppo, Jaffa, and Gaza in the Levant, and the great Sulaiman Pasha

Mosque of Cairo. In India, the Muslim Mughals responded with the Jamma Masjid at Delhi (1656) and the Wazir Khan Mosque in Lahore among many others, while West African imams rebuilt the three great adobe mosques of Timbuktu and an early version of the more famous mosque at Jenné.[2]

The Christian world, meanwhile, was embroiled in the ferocious civil wars of the Reformation era, but its rival sects combined to spread Christianity's urban presence farther than that of any world religion. Renaissance Italian architects had already begun a stylistic revolution away from medieval gothic cathedrals toward domed, be-columned structures inspired by the basilicas and temples of ancient Rome. The results included masterpieces like the cathedral of Florence, and a new capital of the Papacy in Rome at St. Peter's Basilica, until recently the world's largest church. To outclass dourer Protestant rivals, bishops of the Catholic Counter-Reformation indulged in lavish spending on churches designed in a far more ornate variation on the Roman style called the baroque – the ecclesiastical answer to the "baroque" fortresses we have already met. Defying their own pious grumbling about the profligacy of the new secular consumer culture, clerics filled these places with lavish treasuries of gilded statuary and glittering decoration. Shimmering edifices of worship spread thus throughout the Catholic cities of Europe, notably in Vienna, Prague, Dresden, Paris, Madrid, Lisbon, and pontifical Rome. Imperialists and missionaries from some of these places then further spread the style to their overseas realms. Portugal's "Rome of the East," Goa, India, earned that title in part on account of the baroque Basilica of Bom Jesus and the church of St. Cajetan, but structures like these could be found everywhere from the remote mining towns of Brazil to the colonial capital at Salvador do Bahía and Macao in China. Spain erected a baroque cathedral in Mexico City, as we know, but also in dozens of its provincial capitals across New Spain, the Caribbean, Peru, and the Philippines. The Spanish missions, whose goal was to convert Native Americans to Catholicism, collectively formed yet another widespread built environment. The small clusters of church buildings, schools, and living quarters, designed in various versions of the "mission" style of architecture, spread into remote areas from California to Patagonia, often forming the nuclei of new towns and cities. The

French, meanwhile, ornamented Pondichéry, their capital in India, with a baroque cathedral that the British forces at Madras repeatedly targeted with cannon fire, necessitating several episodes of reconstruction. Meanwhile, starker (if still haughty) styles of church building characteristic of Protestantism sprouted up in the cities and small towns of Northern Europe, North America, the Caribbean, Southern Africa, the Indian coast, the Spice Islands, and soon Australia. "Higher church" Anglicans in Great Britain took more from the patterns of Roman Catholicism, as attested by the graceful dome and ornate interior of St. Paul's Cathedral in London. More standard-issue neo-classical and neo-gothic Anglican churches were often among the first buildings British colonists built whenever they founded a city anywhere, well into the twentieth century.[3]

As pervasive as formal temples and churches became during this time, practices associated with various forms of popular religion probably took up more urban space, and usually elsewhere. Often these less formal spiritual spaces lay out of ecclesiastical authorities' line of sight, but popular religion could just as easily explode into view in parades and processions in neighborhood streets or monumental squares. Gauging the extent of Christian conversion in the Americas, for example, requires visits to multitudes of "syncretic" spatial practices. Native shamans offered amulets and incense for ancestor worship on the steps of New Spain's colonial churches. African slaves and freed-people mixed African deity-worship with reverence for Catholic saints in improvised spaces across the city and on plantations. In the Hispanophone Afro-Caribbean, the similar syncretic mixture was known as *Santería,* and its places of worship were called *cabildos.* In French Saint-Domingue, Vodou priests ministered to their huge congregations in modest temples known as *peristils.* In Brazil devotees of Candomblé met in *casas* or in larger *terreiros* (yards). Many of these practices originated in West African port towns, but practices modified in the Americas sometimes returned to their continent of origin, diversifying rites in Ouidah, Lagos, and other African slave ports. A similar transatlantic dynamic occurred with dissenting groups of European Christians who settled in North America, such as the Puritans, Quakers, and Amish, who retreated to clandestine places of worship called "conventicles" or "meetinghouses" (for the plainspoken

Quakers) when they faced persecution, but still managed to sustain connections with practitioners back in Europe. Eventually some played crucial roles in the movement against slavery. In Asia, popular religion was an omnipresent part of the urban landscape, as we have seen. Household and neighborhood shrines and small temples defined the spiritual world of each of the many lower-caste *jati* of Hindu cities. In her research on Beijing during the Ming and Qing dynasties, historian Susan Naquin has documented the existence of hundreds of temples devoted to various popular deities that mixed in worship of natural phenomena and ancestors with elements of Buddhism, Daoism, and Confucianism. The streets of Kyoto and Edo teemed with Shinto and Buddhist shrines and, on holidays, massive processions.[4]

As places of worship consumed ever more space on Earth, so did places for more secular contemplation. Thanks to travel between ports of call on the World Ocean, intellectuals and scholars of all stripes were able to consume and assimilate more knowledge about far corners of the planet than ever before. New knowledge also traveled faster between capitals of the gunpowder empires, despite hostilities between them. In part, this was thanks to the proliferation of papermaking, printing, bookmaking, mapmaking, and, soon, the first newspapers. As printed knowledge accumulated, urban libraries continued to serve, as in ancient times, as storage sites and as places where scholars could assimilate large quantities of earlier work. Much of this knowledge, as before, took the form of commentary on divinely revealed wisdom, but an increasing number of scholars began to argue that, by applying human reason to observations from around the globe, mathematical calculation, and rigorous experiments, people could set out on another route toward new learning. This was no sudden "scientific revolution": the second Axial Age in secular thought opened slowly and tentatively, from interchanges between imperial courts, churches, monasteries, and urban university centers across the world – and it mixed spiritual knowledge with human discoveries on Earth. By the 1700s, some more avowedly secular scientists and philosophers had begun to hint, with great audacity, that their form of knowledge possessed a higher claim to "Enlightenment" and universality than that derived from the gods.[5]

Like many "early-modern" phenomena, the sharing of thought by means of printed paper actually went back far earlier, to the Song dynasty of China, whose urban artisans first experimented with papermaking, wood block publishing, and various forms of movable type. In part because the thousands of characters typical of East Asian languages made movable type expensive, it did not become a force of mass publication there; the imperial court in Korea even restricted the activities of typesetters to the palace alone. Nonetheless, inter-imperial intellectual exchanges flourished. The Yüan dynasty in Dadu (as the Mongol emperors called Beijing) drew heavily on the scientific and artisanal expertise of Central Asian, Persian, and Arabic artisan-scholars and spread movable-type technologies to Central Asia. Arab scholars, as we know, helped High Medieval Europeans rediscover the texts of the classical Mediterranean. In 1440, Johannes Gutenberg, a goldsmith from the German city of Mainz, first used metal movable type and a printing press to print the first books in the twenty-six-letter Roman alphabet, which proved especially amenable to the technology.[6]

After the discovery of the World Ocean and the European conquest of the Americas, interchanges within the Old World and across the Atlantic intensified, as printed books proliferated throughout Europe and then sailed with merchants and clerics to far-flung colonial cities. Europeans and other outside scholars found their way into Asian imperial courts. The Mughal Emperor Akbar was inspired to consult leaders of all the world's major religions at his palace in Agra for advice on how a Muslim sovereign could run a majority-Hindu empire. The Ming Wanli Emperor, the head of a dynasty that otherwise maintained a defensive posture towards outsiders, invited the Italian Jesuit missionary Matteo Ricci to the Forbidden City, where he and his successors influenced Confucian scholarship well into the Qing period, resulting in the publication, using movable type, of enormous encyclopedic works long before the European Enlightenment. Ricci also founded a church in Beijing, which was later rebuilt in baroque style as the Cathedral of the Immaculate Conception. As the Tokugawa shogun Hideyoshi rose to power in Japan, he made a side trip to Korea and kidnapped the court typesetters. Their expertise helped stimulate a book publishing industry in the cities of Osaka and Kyoto. After famously restricting foreign influences in their realm by expelling Portuguese Christians, the shoguns nonetheless kept in close touch with currents of global thought by means of Dutch and Chinese diplomats who brought scholars with them on court visits from Nagasaki to their new intellectual center in Edo.[7]

Knowledge of Earth and our planet's place in the universe famously expanded during this period of feverish intellectual exchange, especially as the increasingly wealthy university towns of Europe sucked in scientific knowledge from the Americas, Asia, Africa, and soon Australasia, along with simultaneous discoveries about people, plants, animals, and landscapes in the hinterlands of colonial cities on all continents. Earth began to appear much more as we know it today. Arab and Persian scholars had long been skeptical of traditional geo-centric models of the universe, but their Sun-centered model gained its most powerful advocates in Copernicus's Kraków, Galileo's Pisa, and Tycho Brahe and Johannes Kepler's Prague, culminating in Cambridge, England with Newton's theory of the role of gravitational pull in planetary motions. Cartographers printed increasingly accurate maps of the world, starting with top-secret charts of the approaches to strategic harbors compiled by ship pilots at the *Casa da India* of Lisbon and the *Casa de Contratación* in Seville. Another Arab invention, the globe, underwent a redesign in Europe to include the Americas for the first time. Thanks to the printing press, maps and globes became consumer items in their own right. One best-selling and oft-reprinted atlas of 1572, *Civitates Orbis Terrarum* (*Cities of the World*) – the work of a copper engraver from Cologne named Georg Braun – contained hundreds of detailed bird's-eye views of cities across Europe, with a smaller selection from other continents. Using new techniques for representing spatial depth on a two-dimensional page, it gave readers the chance to "fly over" important components of Earthopolis as it appeared when it first encircled Earth. Superb, locally produced, and widely circulated city maps of Istanbul, Beijing, and Edo, among other cities, date from the same era. Spectacular woodcuts of ordinary street scenes, another invention of the Song (Fig. 3.2), now proliferated, notably in East Asian cities. Dozens of travel writers supplemented these views with enticing descriptions of ports of call and spectacular capital cities, all of which sold well in bookshops.[8]

Once the mixtures of expansive spiritual and earthly knowledge filtered into the streets and shops, spaces where the vast majority of the new Urban Planet's residents lived, both forms of light fused and transformed. Cities were also places where the spark of new knowledge, the desire for new things, and the stimulation of staged and spontaneous social drama all fused. There the Ocean-spanning Cities of Light became Cities of Delight: birthplaces of a new planetary culture of consumption and performance.

CITIES OF DELIGHT

Throughout global urban history, cities have attracted both praise and damnation as places abounding in material things, pleasures, and amusements. As in ancient times, early-modern people went to the city, not the village, to buy objects or experiences that enhanced physical comfort, saved hard labor, sent them into transports of joy, heightened how they saw themselves as individuals, or invited them to cross tabooed lines in entertainment or sex. In the Cities of the Oceans and beyond, all of these delights grew far more diverse and more accessible to more people. The expansion of efficient ports and financial centers on all continents allowed new raw materials to come to urban markets at cheaper prices. Stall-keepers in marketplaces and shop-owners still needed to contend with state authorities and private associations such as guilds, but new products opened up new lines of business that loosened some of these restraints, especially in far-off colonial cities where the power of state and guild was weakest. Spiraling mercantile wealth also expanded discretionary income, and as local artisan shops made new things, the cities attracted more shoppers and larger crowds for mass entertainments, particularly in urban theaters. As cities created delights, delights attracted new people to live in town, stimulating the growth of the Urban Planet.[9]

In addition to regulating urban markets and shops, emperors, kings, and aristocrats had long used sumptuary laws to retain a monopoly on the finest of urban consumer goods, using them to adorn or enhance their palaces of course, but also to display on their own magnificent person as they paraded their bodies in the public spaces of the city. Their

(A)

(B)

9.1. Cities of Light and Delight: Edo and Paris in the 1700s

Oceans of new goods, pleasures, and ideas swept the streets of early modern cities. In Edo (A), shoppers and revelers thronged the gates of the Yoshiwara pleasure district, filled with teahouses, *kabuki* theaters, and sex markets. Lanterns and woodcut signboards prefigured the neon advertisements of today's Edo – Tokyo. In Paris's Palais Royal (B) – a large courtyard pleasure garden off- limits to the king's soldiers – entertainers perform free of censorship, booksellers sell banned books, and intellectuals debate dangerous ideas like "the rights of man." Men and women engage in a complex language of high fashion thanks to raw materials sourced from across the Urban Planet's spreading consumer hinterland. (A) Fine Art/Corbis Historical/Getty Images. (B) Bettmann/Getty Images.

monopoly on expensive delights began to fade, however, as new urban elites emerged out of ocean-going commerce, as they hired growing numbers of clerks on salary, as high-end artisans grew wealthier, and as growing numbers of modest government officials hobnobbed with the *nouveaux riches* in public places. Aristocrats, such as Japan's samurai class, sometimes went into debt to merchants, allowing an otherwise despised class of commoners some power over bluebloods. The streets became a stage for the pretensions of a new buying public that some historians deem the historical nucleus of the "middle class," a minority of city residents that was substantial enough in size, and so deeply associated with the hum of city life that the French simply called them "the town set" – the bourgeoisie.

Meanwhile, people with far more modest means could afford some version of consumer culture too. Despite a pattern of falling wages overall in the world during this period, economic historians argue that wages did edge up in some cities, most notably those with the most extensive pan-Oceanic ties, such as Madrid, Paris, Amsterdam, and especially London (Chapter 10). Cities in India and China that produced globally traded consumer goods may also have participated in this countertrend of rising wages. For the vast majority of people, even in these hotter job markets, pay was still extremely low by today's standards, and most was consumed by food, fuel, rent, and basic clothing – if it wasn't gobbled up entirely by those other scourges of global empire and capitalism, wartime inflation or cyclical recession. That did not stop merchant houses, shops, and entertainment venues from adapting their offerings to relieve this "mass audience" of any money they had left over. Moreover, during this period, urban delights filtered in greater streams outward from richer cities into towns, villages, isolated farmhouses, and even to nomadic or smaller-scale settlements in forests, deserts, and mountains. By allowing us to create new synergies between cities' pulsing smaller-scale activities, larger rural–urban dynamics, and the largest of transoceanic and trans-continental activities, the newly planetary Earthopolis allowed us to bring a near-global secular consumer culture into being. There the desires it inspired grew, and so did uneasiness among leaders of absolutist govern-ments, world religions, and even "Enlightened" schools of secular philosophy.[10]

Urban-based global consumer culture and the popularization of new Earthly knowledge grew alongside each other. Reports of new "curiosities" – strange plants, animals, and minerals from far ocean shores – usually arrived not long before the actual items themselves, followed by new products made from them. Plant-based provisions from the Americas did more to change the consumption habits and life expectancies of more people worldwide than anything else in this period. Potatoes, sweet potatoes, corn, beans of many kinds, squashes, tomatoes, and peanuts topped the list – so did baneful tobacco. All found ways to farms, marketplaces, cuisines, and urban eateries across Afro-Eurasia during the 100 years after Columbus, increasing the diversity of sources of nutrition and thus the health of city dwellers and villagers alike. Meanwhile, Old World foods – beef, pork, lamb, mutton, chicken, wheat, rice, rye, oats, bananas, citrus fruits, cherries, peaches, apricots, and grapes in addition to sugar – spread to the New World even faster, though these did little to erase the grim death-dealing impact of disease-bearing microorganisms on Native peoples. Sugar, an Old World crop that flourished in the New, circulated globally, offering a source of calories whose nutritional emptiness nonetheless crucially supplemented what the growing urban populations of Europe and Asia could extract from their increasingly burdened grain fields. The circulation of these crops was yet another phenomenon that the Urban Planet helped set in motion; in turn, the global dispersal of new nutrients helped explain the growth of the built human habitat and the more than doubling of the human population to some 900 million by 1800.[11]

As important as these foodstuffs were, three relatively non-nutritious dark brown drinks made from the seeds, fruits, and leaves of squat, tropical or semi-tropical trees arguably affected urban social life more thoroughly. Coffee, chocolate, and tea had previous lives as consumer commodities in distinct regions, but ocean commerce made them – and the specialty shops that sold them – into iconic fixtures of urban life everywhere during this period. The name of Mocha, a port city located on the southwestern corner of the Arabian Peninsula, is rightly famous in global coffee culture. In the 1500s, increasing numbers of Arabian and Turkish ship-owners stopped at Mocha for cargos of brown beans grown in a neighboring valley, which was one of the few in arid Arabia that trapped the errant rain clouds needed to irrigate coffee trees. The merchants resold their beans at high mark-up to brewers in cities like Cairo, Damascus, Aleppo, and above all Istanbul. There, in hundreds of special small shops, specialized artisans ground the beans into a tarry paste we still know as Turkish coffee, transforming the business of drinking a mouth-puckering product into a pleasant social experience and stoking the particularly "energized" form of consumer desire we know as caffeine addiction. In Istanbul, the city's 300 *hamams*, – its famous "Turkish bathhouses" – had long provided copious opportunities for "chitchat, gossip, and political grumbling"; coffee shops now vastly expanded that realm.[12]

In Europe, according to the foremost historian of London coffee-houses, a group of taste-leaders known as "virtuosi" – amateur enthusiasts of the new global knowledge – encouraged a dubiously condescending fascination for the customs of the East that today's scholars call "Orientalism." Their conceits included the bravery to cough down the bitter "hot black broth" of the Turks. Although the Venetians had imported the habit from Istanbul earlier, coffee shops began cramming the streets of London, Amsterdam, and Paris, possibly in the wake of a pioneering venture in the university town of Oxford (1650). Demand in Holland grew strong enough – and Ottoman customs agents at Mocha were inhospitable enough to European merchants – that the Dutch East India Company set up its own coffee plantations in Java, erasing the Mocha trade and giving the black drink another enduring geographical reference. Slave-tended coffee-bush plantations sprouted amidst the sugar lands of Brazil and throughout the Caribbean, even as they spread from Arabia to mountainous Ethiopia, filling out the global hinterland that supplies the world's urban coffee shops to this day. Meanwhile, chocolate, formerly an exclusive ritual drink that stiffened Aztec emperors' resolve before their bloodthirsty interviews with the Sun God, also appeared on the menus of urbane coffee shops, thanks to cacao plantations that grew up amidst the sugarcane fields of South America (West African cocoa plantations came later). Sugar consumption increased alongside that of coffee and chocolate, because Europeans needed more spoonsful of the sweet stuff to overcome the bitterness of coffee than did Istanbullus and Cairenes. Then, in 1711, ship captains of the British East India Company managed to get permission from Qing authorities to visit the ancient port of Guangzhou, which Europeans knew as Canton. There Company merchants skeptically purchased a few chests of dried leaves from yet another sort of caffeinated bush. Chinese tea-drinkers associated the beverage with the glorious court of the ancient Han dynasty, and highly refined ceremonies were devoted to its preparation. By the 1500s, almost everyone in East Asian cities could afford cups of tea, ladled less ceremoniously from steaming vats in stalls located on every street corner. For reasons that historians have not quite fathomed, British consumers took more avidly to this drink than other Europeans, and, over the course of the 1700s, many of London's coffeehouses were replaced by teahouses. By the end of that century, tea drinking had reached the remotest towns of Scotland's Outer Hebrides, and the habit had traveled beyond the bourgeoisie to become the stimulant of choice for Britain's new industrial working class. For its enslaved working class as well: archaeologists discovered fragments of teacups and teapots at the site of the slave cabins on George Washington's plantation at Mount Vernon, Virginia. Various tea drinking customs, most famously involving the addition of masala spices, mint, and thicker doses of sugar, also appeared in urban shops across South Asia and the Ottoman world.[13]

The importance of teahouses and coffeehouses went far beyond creating desire for "necessities that were previously unknown," though caffeine (and stimulation more generally) played a role in all of these versatile shops' many activities. Tobacco, a more dubious New World product, filled all spaces of the urban planet with exhaled smoke – and nicotine addicts – during this time too. In Beijing, the city's police forces were known to closely surveil the city's streets to thwart unauthorized assemblies of ordinary people, also generally discouraging public encounters between men and women. But teashops, wine shops, restaurants, and inns, along with bathhouses, provided places of all-day, and in some cases late-night, mixed-class and mixed-sex conviviality that were literally more screened off from the authorities. For some, the inner sanctums of temples provided an even more secure refuge. In Beijing, and in Edo's especially bubbly Edobashi merchant quarter, teahouses doubled as sites for storytelling and theatrical performances, sometimes only distinguishable in their size from Edo's enormously popular *kabuki* theaters. In Edo, teahouses were often run by women; many used the boiling vats, tables, and wait-staff as a front to sell sex behind layers of screens in the back of the shop. One woodprint of this *ukiyo*, or "floating world," as Japanese urbanites called their Cities of Delight, suggests the city even possessed "shopping-mall"-like spaces where teashops, theaters, brothels, and street amusements jumbled together with other shops.[14]

In London, the nearly 1,000 coffeehouses of the early 1700s were especially multifunctional. We have already learned how Jonathan's Coffee House served as the center of an informal stock exchange district. As in Istanbul, coffee shops also did duty as gossip mills, neighborhood councils, barbershops, bathhouses, gambling dens, social clubs, theaters, inns, brothels, and "penny universities" – "thinking spaces" for the digestion of current affairs, science, and exotic "curiosities" in general. In a few cases, they became rare public places exclusively devoted to all-female sociability. Financial information, newspapers, and books were available with coffee free of charge, and the reputation of urban cafés for caffeine-induced intellectual innovation dates from this time. The pioneering coffee drinker and Oxford "virtuoso" John Evelyn launched an early version of urban environmentalism with his critiques of London's growing coal pollution in the 1680s. In Paris, cafés became even more famous for philosophizing and politics, in particular, the Café Procope, where Enlightenment luminaries like Voltaire held forth, and where Diderot and d'Alembert reportedly conceived their famous *Encyclopédie*. Historians use the phrase "the republic of letters" to describe the intellectual ferment generated by ordinary Parisians during the 1700s in coffeehouses and in bookstores, as well as in the *salons* organized by society women in their aristocratic parlors. Sidewalks too became zones of light and delight, as Parisian cafés spilled outdoors. The quayside stalls of the city's famous *bouquinistes* along the Seine also date from this period.[15]

Popular theaters assembled even larger, probably more diverse crowds than coffeehouses, and as such, they troubled imperial officials even more – probably rightly so, given the subversive messages they were capable of conveying. One of the great coincidences of the late 1500s was the nearly simultaneous rise of Shakespearean theater in London and *kabuki* in Kyoto. The two traditions had very different origins. In London, theater worked its way from public readings and rhetorical displays in schools, universities, and the Inns of Court, a residence complex for aspiring lawyers, then moved from there into specially designed theater buildings (such as Shakespeare's Globe Theatre) built by artisanal entrepreneurs and writers. In Kyoto, groups of women performed the first *kabuki* in Kyoto's dry riverbeds, attracting big crowds there and then the attention of the emperor, before settling into special buildings in the city's shopping districts. In both cases, the combination of historical or romantic drama, stylized acting, costume, makeup, gender bending, and mockery of aristocratic pretension drew crowds unlike any other place in the human built environment. Tickets to theaters in both traditions were offered on a sliding scale, allowing diverse crowds to attend, even if poorer people had to make do with the least desirable seats. Kings, shoguns, and various municipal and religious authorities alike tried to put the lid on the ribald, socially upending energy that these places could generate – though the royals sometimes attended popular theaters themselves. Whatever the case, in both London and Edo, authorities forced women out of roles as actors, thus forcing men to play women's roles. In both cities, officials heavily restricted where theaters could be located, often closing them down entirely.[16]

Their efforts did nothing to stop the rise of the first genuine forms of urban mass culture – and with it, perhaps the seeds of something else new: mass political protest (Chapters 11 and 12). Traveling troupes of actors made sure to provide the same to surrounding towns and even villages. In London, and to varying degrees in Paris and Amsterdam, historians have given these various public spaces of consumer culture the credit for generating some of the democratic culture of the Enlightenment, and growing appeals to the "rights of man." In Britain, coffeehouses and theaters provided some of the venues for speakers who helped build the world's first cross-Ocean, cross-class, cross-gender, cross-race popular political movement, dedicated to the abolition of the slave trade. In foreshadowing the revolutions to come, these various tiny yet prolific and well-populated urban spaces – middle class and popular alike – had much in common with the back streets of informal African neighborhoods and the taverns of slave cities like New York where Black and white laborers and itinerant Creole sailors hatched rebellions against the plantation system. For some, the French revolution itself began in Paris's pre-eminent theater and shopping district, the Palais Royal, not a royal palace at all, but the planned brainchild of the liberal aristocratic Duke d'Orléans. On land that was off limits to royal soldiers on account of inherited privileges granted to his family, the duke assembled a tumultuous shopping-mall (one that might not have been out of place in far-off Edo) of theaters, performance spaces, coffee shops, and speakers' corners. In the Palais Royal, dangerous democratic ideas were allowed to flow free.[17]

Warm brown drinks and cheap theater seats may have stood out in the galaxy of urban delights, but the universe of urban consumer culture extended far beyond. Craftspeople outdid themselves as new materials and new customers demanded new feats of artisanship and specialization. Printed advertisement placards grew larger and gaudier in the streets, prefiguring the neon and digitized shopping strips of our day; newspapers also carried ads for shops and the latest ship cargos for the first time. The clothing business took to the streets more lavishly than before, both in the shops and on the bodies of shoppers. Tailors, dressmakers, kimono weavers, button makers, jewelry smiths in all media from glass to gold, fur dressers, makers of beaver-skin hats, shoemakers, pipe makers, umbrella makers, and leatherworkers tapped the discretionary funds of their clients – then as now drawing on styles worn by popular actors. In so doing, they threw sumptuary laws into the dustbin of history, allowing people with meager discretionary budgets to dress at least a bit like an aristocrat. Clothes, of course, offered a non-verbal language of status, masculinity, and femininity to their wearers and to the increasingly anonymous strangers they encountered in growing cities. In Mexico, artists who specialized in "*casta* paintings" (popular consumer items themselves) used the cut of people's clothes as much as the color of their skin to signify their subjects' position in New Spain's elaborate colonial pecking order.[18]

Sartorial languages of the day possessed rich, finely tuned vocabularies. One important early distinction was between the fancier "worsted" wool cloth and plainer "broadcloth." When the Black Plague killed off enormous numbers of villagers in Britain, former farms gave way to sheep grazing lands that were more extensive than in the rest of Europe. With more grass to graze on, British sheep grew more luxuriant hair that could be woven into longer threads and denser, smoother fabrics. Across the continent, more fashionable worsted wool outsold scratchier Italian and

Flemish wools, causing the woolens industries of Milan and Bruges to diminish during the late 1400s and allowing London, the main export point of the new cloth, to grow more rapidly. Later, the city became a great center of cotton fashion as well. Merchants from the British East India Company could choose from some eighty-five different types of cotton fabric when they sailed into Madras, Bombay, or Calcutta to sample the wares from the surrounding Indian textile villages. In those villages, members of the many castes employed in India's cloth making industry could weave, dye, and stamp cotton in innumerable textures and patterns. Customers in London, women foremost among them, were eager to buy cutting-edge Indian fabric styles for dresses, not to mention curtains and upholstery in the urban homes where they entertained. The trick for the Company's male merchants, when haggling with their counterparts in Asia, was to prophesy which way the mood would swing in the parlors, salons, and, above all, the shopping streets 10,000 kilometers away. Silks from China, Bengal, Persia, Turkey, and even Italy – anywhere orchardists could grow mulberry bushes and acquire the highly technical expertise involved in silk weaving – added to the possibilities. So did the soft, insulating skins and furs of dozens of North American or Siberian forest creatures. Deer, sable, mink, fox, raccoon, and beaver all made their way into dresses, coats, and hats that outdid wool in warming bodies against the cold of wintertime London, Moscow, or Beijing.[19]

Cotton, however, was much cheaper and more versatile and thus held greater promise as a mass consumer item. Slave merchants in African ports were just as willing as fashion designers in London or Paris to accept Indian muslins, calicoes, Madrasses, and chintzes as currency. Slavers also accepted other adornments, such as Venetian glass jewelry beads, and a long list of commodities from all Ocean shores including iron bars, the cowrie shells of the Maldive Islands, and guns made in the humming craft shops of Birmingham (Chapter 13). On plantations, enslaved laborers needed clothing, and because of that, plantation owners were important purchasers of cheaper cuts of cotton cloth. Lighter weaves of cotton, unlike the wool that Europe had tried to peddle to people in warmer climates, were in demand throughout the tropics, long before anyone imagined growing that fiber on slave plantations in North America. Instead, the Indian system of village-based cloth production gained competitors elsewhere, as peasant households in villages near European and East Asian cities redirected their family labor into a pre-factory version of the textile industry. In country cottages, women and children used previously idle time, including once relatively unproductive winter months, to spin cotton thread. In this way, they too earned cash to buy the raw basics of urban consumer culture, giving the world of things another source of demand. Japanese farmers near Osaka began growing cotton in the late 1600s, and cheap cotton cloth found a market among lower-ranked samurai and *chōnin* (commoners) of Edo. In China, the Yüan and Ming emperors had earlier expanded cotton growing by giving tax breaks and doling out expertise. The Yangtze Delta city of Songjian (part of which included a then-smaller village called Shanghai) became a center of textile production. Chinese peasant women spun thread in the sur-rounding villages and brought the warps and wefts they fashioned on farmhouse looms into town for processing and dying. As in the case of top-of-the-line Japanese kimonos, silk clothing continued to signal true pres-tige. Yet, because cotton wearing was associated with commoners, and thus, more positively, seen as a sign of pious humility, urban manufacture of the textile became an important part of even the higher end of Japanese and Chinese consumer culture. In China, it played a growing role in the imperial economy as a whole, especially from the early Qing period on. Cotton growing produced far more fiber per acre of land than did sheep herding, and thus it could clothe more people. Thus, like the new food-stuffs, cotton released "Malthusian" constraints on the growth of the worlds' population, contributing to urban growth more specifically while propping up wages in select pockets of the world – thus stimulating more urban consumer commerce.[20]

Much of the stuff of global consumer culture passed from point of production to ports, to ships, to wharfs, to shops, to shoppers, ending up in yet another small but multitudinous urban place: the city's homes. Most households of the period – rural and urban, estate and plantation, peasant and artisan, and even merchant homes – remained places of work and production in addition to whatever consumption was possible. Only a few elite households could afford space for semi-public rooms designed to treat their guests to envy-provoking displays of the house-holders' purchases. However, widening access to income, urban

landowning, and building materials did allow the modestly more privileged members of the protean middle class to build solid brick and stone
houses – status-enhancing consumer items in themselves. Then they
added parlors, sitting rooms, and servant-managed dining rooms, all of
them separate from the kitchens and other living, working, and goods
storage spaces that a typical merchant house still needed to contain. The
new domestic spaces required furniture, curtains, dinnerware, porcelain
tea sets, decorative items including wall art and gewgaws, and oil lamps.
Cotton goods, noted Daniel Defoe, "crept into our Houses, our Closets
and Bed Chambers, Curtains, Cushions, Chairs, and at last Beds." Books
in impressive shelves could highlight a merchants' or a plantation
owner's learning – as could "cabinets of curiosity," filled with strange
and exotic items such as might give their owner a reputation for fashionable polymathy or "virtuosity," as well as cosmopolitanism.[21]

At the same time, an undercurrent of uneasiness about prideful
displays of wealth meant that the most tasteful décor often contained
gestures of understatement. In Japan and China, shoguns and emperors
were experts at expressing class superiority through modesty. Palaces and
aristocratic mansions – massive and impressive as they were – contained
lower-key interiors that mixed Confucian and Buddhist ideals of simplicity with a sense that power was most fiercely displayed through serenity.
The shogun's spare tatami-matted receiving rooms for different ranks of
supplicants in his castles in Kyoto, Osaka, and Edo very subtly reminded
guests of their place in society by the size of the rooms, the particular
animals or plants beautifully painted on the silk and paper screens that
served as walls, and the achingly simple artistry of furniture, notably the
wall shelves, which claimed alcoves in the corners of the rooms. In
Northern Europe, Protestants too professed "embarrassment" about
the region's especially lavish "riches." The consumer opulence of
Amsterdam or London bourgeois households sat poorly alongside their
critique of baroque Catholic extravagance. Dutch Calvinists at once
wondered at the wealth of goods they could afford and repented of
them, preferring sparer rooms in their stepped-gable houses. Yet they
also commissioned wall art from some of the greatest painters ever to
grace the planet. In the mid-1600s, they developed a mania for growing
tulips to display in vases on lavish bourgeois tables, a taste European

ambassadors in Istanbul had picked up from Ottoman princes. A wild period of speculation in contracts for tulip bulbs in 1634–37 ended in a crash in their value, often seen as the first modern financial crisis.[22]

Meanwhile, East Asian-style housewares, and in particular any housewares made of silk, porcelain, or lacquerware from China, became a common vehicle for Europeans to thread the needle between class pretension and modesty. In the newly forming West End, Londoners sipped their tea from cups on saucers and ate their big cuts of beef on plates all made of a substance they called "china." They got their china from China itself, until the mid-1700s when Josiah Wedgwood started making cheaper china in kilns he built in the English West Midlands villages that later became the city of Stoke-on-Trent. What the Parisians knew as *chinoiserie* – including porcelain vases, silk printing of East Asian and European scenes, painted *à la chinoise* by the artisans of Chinese port cities on curtains, screens, and wallpapers, and lacquered furniture of all types – became a staple of home decoration during this time. *Chinoiserie* – and its close cousin "japanware" – remained in fashion in Europe well into the twentieth century, expanding along with the bourgeoisie itself and the gradual transformation of its homes into places solely devoted to consumption. As growing numbers of historians have made clear, the growing adornment of the interior spaces of the Urban Planet reflected the growth of a new sphere of female decision-making, one that would have its own political consequences in the revolutionary age to come.[23]

CONSUMING THE EARTH ... AND THE OCEANS

Shops, streets, and homes were the most important spaces for the new consumer culture to put itself on display and thus to ignite its driving furnaces of desire, envy, and sociability. Much less visible to urban consumers, even in an Age of Enlightenment, were far larger spaces that provided the raw materials for the things themselves, and the still slowly growing spaces that served as dumping grounds for consumer cities' mounting waste. Also invisible and largely incomprehensible, even in Cities of new scientific Light, were the microbes that repeatedly turned Cities of Delight into Cities of Misery, most notably in the pandemics that struck the Americas, but also in repeated visitations of poxes and plagues in cities across the world, notably during years of climatic cooling. The devastating fire that followed the London plague was only one among many similar disasters; Edo suffered so many fires that they earned the nickname the "Flowers of Edo." However, such city-amplified catastrophes only temporarily halted the production of new urban energies. The strong recovery of Native populations in Lima and Mexico City, Edo's rise to a million-plus metropolis, and London's rise to the world's largest city after 1800 all underscored the era's Ocean-amplified forces of urban resiliency.[24]

Meanwhile the number of human mouths and stomachs kept rising – even doubling, as we know, from 1500 to 1800. Coupled with the massive increase in the number of merchant ships made of large forest trees and the take-off of discretionary consumer culture, human impacts reverberated upon larger parts of the non-built habitats of Earth. While the Columbian exchange of foodstuffs supplied the diverse nutrients needed for the doubling of the world's population, it also expanded the particular forms of agricultural activity that were most associated with deforestation. To feed the enormous cities of China, for example, the acreage devoted to rice growing tripled during this period, pushing the paddy-lands into remoter Chinese forests and other parts of East and Southeast Asia – while pushing greater quantities of methane into the atmosphere. Yet Asian rices also reached growing areas of Africa, where they soon replaced an indigenous variety, and the Americas, where they became central to the rice-and-beans cuisines of Mexico and the Caribbean. Maize growing expanded in its native habitat of the Americas, but also in certain bands of the Chinese uplands that had previously remained forested because they were unsuited to rice or wheat. Wheat and other staple grains, meanwhile, took over huge previously forested areas in Central and Eastern Europe, steppe Asia, and the Americas.[25]

Among the crops that contributed most to the consumer revolution, it is true that caffeinated tree plants, namely coffee, tea, and cacao, came at a much lower price in soil depletion or runoff than that which accompanied forest clearing for grain and other starches. By contrast, sugar and cotton, the two crops that expanded the most in response to discretionary consumer desires – and tobacco, which came close behind – were among the worst soil-depleters and forest-levelers of all, as well as the biggest taxers of water systems. Humanity's ever more ravenous sweet tooth and our nicotine habits must be blamed for the earliest beginnings of our now relentless destruction of the Amazon rainforest (though a mania for brazilwood, an ingredient, along with Chinese lacquers, of fine furniture during this period, did not help). Our weakness for the caress of cotton on our skin soon would prove even more momentous both for the Urban Planet and for the un-built environment, even if its early-modern impact was still modest.[26]

As urban consumers forced agriculture to push fiercely outward on the forest boundary, they also put market pressure on forest-dwelling villagers to increase the discretionary mass killing of the animals they had previously hunted only for their own needs. A global "Great Hunt" began in the mid-1600s. The first of its two main thrusts led deep into the forests of northern North America and Siberia. Many settler–colonial bastion cities that later became prominent parts of the Urban Planet first came into being as fortified fur-trading posts: Quebec, Montreal, Albany, Buffalo, Detroit, Milwaukee, Chicago, Kazan, Omsk, and Irkutsk among many others. As the comings and goings of fur-trapping season dictated, settlers built temporary shelters on the edges of the "white" sections of these towns to meet up with Native fur trappers or, in Canada, mixed-race *coureurs des bois* (forest runners). There they traded the basics of European urban consumer culture – pots, pans, axes, guns, tobacco, and alcohol – for skins and furs. Beaver, mink, and sable populations plunged, forcing their trappers deeper into the forests and increasing the need for more distant trading posts – and forts, later cities. The Qing dynasty, in a nostalgic effort to celebrate its origins in the Manchurian forests, hired hunters to fetch skins from the dwindling populations of Siberian tigers and other large animals from the region, so they could be used as exterior decorations in the palaces of the Forbidden City as well as for clothing. Bannermen in the surrounding districts followed suit, and Chinese tiger populations, threatened since Han times, declined even further. The same region supplied furs to wealthy *daimyō* in Edo. Artisans who transformed beaver-skins into hats for European gentlemen ignited a fashion that lasted for several centuries on the streets of New York, Amsterdam, and Milan – it was as long-lived as the fashion for *chinoiserie* in the parlors of their homes.[27]

While the Cities of the Oceans drew harder on land-based plants and animals to fuel and warm growing numbers of human bodies, urban consumer demands also spurred a second thrust of the Great Hunt, into the World Ocean itself. In great part, this new hunt aimed to nourish the bodies of the sailors so essential to the operation of the giant, wind- and wave-driven, floating wooden habitats that transported raw materials to craft shops and finished goods to all the parlors of the world. Early explorations of the Atlantic led to the discovery of enormous populations of codfish off Newfoundland and New England. Adapting techniques of Dutch herring fishermen, cod-fishing ships harvested vast tonnages of the animals, then salted and barreled them on board, for resale as the main source of unspoilable protein for long-haul ships' crews. In short time, cod-fishermen transformed the North Atlantic into a hinterland for the floating precincts of the Urban Planet – and thus, indirectly, for global consumer culture as a whole (salted cod became a delicacy in the port town cuisines of the Caribbean and Lisbon). Cod stocks plum- meted, on their way to virtual exhaustion by the end of the 1800s.[28]

9.2. A Danish Whaling Station in the Arctic
In 1634, on Danskøya Island in Arctic Spitzbergen, whaling ship owners built a blubber- rendering station to provide oil for lamps in homes in Copenhagen and elsewhere. A Great Hunt was afoot – there and in distant fur-trapping camps and trading posts – that pushed the boundaries of Earthopolis to the farthest corners of Earth. The consequences were felt across larger spaces too, as whale populations declined along with many other species, and as cities incubated the first global pandemics of disease. With structures like these, humanity also began a "Scramble for the Arctic" that has intensified as sea-ice melts in the twenty-first century, opening up new mines, oilfields, shipping lanes, and large circumpolar cities built on the tundra. Painting by Abraham Speeck.
Fine Art/Corbis Historical/Getty Images.

Meanwhile, the search for nighttime illumination of bourgeois dining rooms and salons – an all-important amenity for hosts-of-households who were eager to impress their party guests – landed on the virtues of whale oil. In New York, the fashion came from the very top: George Washington himself set the trend, when, as president, he owned a convivial mansion, staffed by enslaved people, in what was then the temporary capital of the new USA. While a fishy stench limited the longevity of the urban fashion for whale-oil lamps, the virtues of the slippery material for machine lubrication and in the manufacture of various consumer items sustained yet another new shipborne oceanic industry devoted above all to the needs of cities. In this way, the wealth and desires of the Urban Planet underwrote whale killing in the remotest reaches of the Arctic Ocean, creating also a need for temporary on-shore encampments for oil rendering and whale-flesh drying at the foot of bleak ice fields from Greenland to Spitzbergen, and from to Novaya Zemlya to the Kamchatka Peninsula. The impact on the whales of the World Ocean was as severe as cod fishing, with several species nearing extinction by the mid-1800s.[29]

More important than the need to illuminate households was the need to heat them. The rapid expansion of agriculture still left plenty of forest-land standing near cities, so that woodcutters could make a living hauling firewood or charcoal to urban markets on carts or canal boats. There they sold their bundles to householders for burning in hearths or, in China, the ingenious radiant heating systems known as *kangs*. In some cities, agricultural waste or peat supplemented wood. In China the *kangs* were also designed to heat homes with another substance – coal, yet another crucial practice that goes back to Song dynasty Kaifeng. Yet, for reasons we need urgently to think through next, a similar home heating habit arrived in London during Shakespeare's time, in a way that disrupted the Urban Planet, and Earth, far more extensively. Sipping exotic brown liquids in a 1660s coffeehouse, the "virtuoso" John Evelyn noticed how horrible the air of London had begun to smell. His keen, early environmentalist nose provided us with one of the first pieces of evidence – of the newfangled empirical sort, no less – that, by burning coal in London, we were using our cities to do something very big, new, and drastic.

PART THREE

CITIES OF HYDROCARBON

III.1. An Auto-Rickshaw Navigates the Smoky Air of Delhi
Hindustan Times/Getty Images.

"It has badly affected our eyes. It causes redness and they become watery. This is what happens. Secondly our lungs. Because we don't get clean air, it affects our lungs. We have chest pains. We cough, right? And the grime shows on our faces." Day in and day out, just as on this November morning in 2018, Suresh Karma Sharma drives one of Delhi's 200,000 three-wheeled auto-rickshaws – green, with a bright yellow top, propelled by an engine that burns liquid hydrocarbon and puffs smoke through a tailpipe behind. The smoke of the auto-walla's engine merges with smoke of all kinds from across the city: from over ten million other gas- and diesel-powered vehicles; from thousands of factories, dozens of power plants and cement works; from hundreds of construction sites; from 10,000 tandoori ovens, millions of home hearths, and hundreds of waste fires, including self-combusting ones on the city's mountainous landfills; from hundreds of thousands of fireworks celebrating the festival of Diwali and thousands of enormous Delhi weddings; from tens of thousands of acres of distant farmland where peasants burn the stubble from their rice crops so they can plant wheat so that they can feed the inhabitants of a "megacity" – Delhi's twenty-plus million people, headed fast toward thirty million and beyond.[1]

Weather forecast: smoke. Amidst all the burning, Delhi makes its own milky-gray, face-darkening, eye-stinging, lung-clogging winter weather. Delhi's smoke in turn helps make weather worldwide – and year-round. The city's burned carbon merges with the burned carbon of thousands other great cities and their own world-engulfing hinterlands, creating gases that trap heat from the Sun in the Earth's atmosphere. By summertime in Delhi, the smoke has dispersed, but Sharma Karma grumbles about the heat instead. Who can blame him? Delhi lies at the midpoint of a band of potential "Fifty-Degree Cities" stretching from the Persian Gulf to the Deltas of the Ganges and Brahmaputra, where urban temperatures increasingly threaten to top 50 degrees Celsius (125 Fahrenheit) – reaching a threshold beyond which people simply cannot sweat enough to survive the day.

Sharma calls himself "the Pandit," the scholar. Though his machine is little, his local knowledge is large. As he ferries us though his immense city, he bears witness to a tumultuous panorama of transformation. During the age of the Cities of the Oceans, our realm of action took a truly planetary dimension for the first time. Since then, all realms of Earthopolis have exploded in size – first in a great surge in the nineteenth and early twentieth centuries, then in the Greatest Acceleration of all from 1945 to today.

As the human population exploded, the population of cities exploded even more rapidly. So did the size and number of cities, and the scale of urban destruction and even more rapid reconstruction of cities. Urban peripheries have grown fastest of all, whether through single-family suburban homes, endless rows of tower blocks, or, as in Delhi and other megacities, the self-built shacks of hundreds of millions of poor people. In city centers, "gentrified" luxury districts and business districts have grown too. In the face of explosive demand, the value of urban land has escalated to unheard-of heights. For the first time, more than half of humanity, as best as we can count ourselves, lives in cities.

As our cities exploded, so did our realms of action, the ease of our ability to act worldwide, and the sheer energy of our spaces of politics. At times, the imperial, authoritarian, and totalitarian power of states reached unprecedented scope, sometimes accelerating the fierceness with which we waged world war, at other times escalating into fearsome "superpower" rivalries. At other times, urban polities exploded in revolution. At their most hopeful moments, these revolutions spread the idea of "People Power" along with all the virtues and vulnerabilities of democracy to more corners of the Earth than ever before. At the same time, the speed of technological revolutions also accelerated, starting with the rise of coal-fired factories. They, along with new states, gave a boost to the power of capitalists, soon enshrined in state-enabled corporations that run global industrial assembly lines, that dominate all-powerful "global city" financial districts, and that develop most urban land. In their shadow, professional urban planners gained Pharaonic powers. So did public health officials, who used new techniques to fight the still un-won wars against the diseases that our Urban Planet so prolifically incubates.

Meanwhile, the realm of human habitat has expanded far beyond cities. Infrastructures of transport, communication, energy, and power encase the globe. Farm and pastureland have gobbled up half the soil-covered surface of Earth. Our cultures of consumption have become insatiable, requiring massive new landscapes of mining and extraction, none larger than that devoted to petroleum.

Yet our realm of impact has accelerated fastest of all, now above all thanks to our rising mountains of solid, liquid, and gaseous waste. To dispose of it, Earthopolis has effectively annexed Earth's entire lithosphere, hydrosphere, and atmosphere. We now make much of our own weather. Yet, more than that, in an Urban Planet's worth of cities, we sit in the cockpits of all life and all life-energy-producing spaces of our planet Earth; many are convinced that we have decisively annexed Earth-time itself, threatening the remarkable 11,700-year old equilibriums between Sun and Earth that made Earthopolis thinkable. Surely, we face a question of both Anthropocenic and Epochal dimensions that we have never faced before: will our Urban Planet's accelerating realms of action, habitat, and impact succumb to the deathly realms of consequence that metastasize within them? Or, can we redesign Earthopolis as a force of human power capable of reanimating these imperiled zones while dependably nurturing our own futures and those of other life forms?

How, first off, did we become capable of all of this? Because, from the 1780s on, the people of Earthopolis, in one region after another, accepted a new wager with Sun and Earth, this one with the highly potent underworld of fossilized sunshine. As Pandit Karma hints, the Promethean audacity of the hydrocarbon bargain exceeded that of the great gambles of earlier times – the goddess Inanna's with the Rivers, and Christopher Columbus's with the World Ocean. To understand what we have done, just put a foot on the gas pedal. Feel the momentum surge, in all of the Urban Planet's many unpredictable dramas. Then, as we reach the culmination of two and a half centuries of increasing acceleration, take up Pandit Sharma Karma's offer. Settle into the back seat of his rickshaw, feel its petroleum-burning engine buzz below, and survey our Urban Planet as it has become in our own time. Breathe in, if you dare, the Cities of Hydrocarbon.

CHAPTER 10

Chimneys to Smokestacks

Many of us like to tell the story of hydrocarbon-fueled machines, including the Pandit's auto-rickshaw, as a single, predictable narrative of ever-increasing technological progress – from the clunky steam engines of the 1720s to the textile mills of the 1780s, to the locomotive engines and steamship engines of the 1820s, to the cars, planes, and blazing rocket engines of the twentieth century. Sometimes we throw in heroes too: the inventors, the industrialists who had the foresight to invest in the inventions, the nation states where the inventions occurred, and the civilization of "the West," Europe and its settler colonies, where many of these things first came into being. As ever, cities – those places filled with "energized crowds" – get plenty of credit for the industrial revolution too.

Things look very different to a historian telling the story of the Urban Planet as a cause and consequence of big historic transformations, including the transformation represented by atmospheric overheating. In this re-telling, the consequences of the story remain just as Earth-shattering – though the narrative of "progress," let alone heroism, becomes much less clear. As for the causes of the hydrocarbon revolution, their story simply does not follow any kind of straight line, upward or down. Were there moments when technological changes fed upon each other? Absolutely, and cities with their "energized" crowds helped make those spiraling "synergies" and sometimes-even-unstoppable "processes" possible. Yet, spirals of hydrocarbon-fueled transformation required many other historical ingredients. The built setting of the story – cities and the bigger built habitats they relied upon – was crucial. So was, as always, the urban polity, with its highly contingent negotiations and conflicts over power. So unpredictable were these urban parts of the story that, at any given time and place, the plotline of the industrial revolution might have twisted in completely different directions. Tell the story from the perspective of people living in most of the places and at most moments in time along the way – and who knows? The industrial revolution might never have happened, hydrocarbon might not have become the fuel of choice for our cities, and today, we might be taking the Pandit's tour of Delhi on a very different vehicle on a very different kind of Urban Planet.

Of course, things did go the way they did. Coal- and petroleum-powered engines did come into being, as did gas home heating and cooking and dozens of other uses of fossil fuels. Hydrocarbon Cities did explode into being. They eventually did get as big, as smoky, and as dangerously overheated as Delhi. Many cities played a role, including many outside the West. Yet one Western city in particular played the biggest role, a city that lies in a strange hinterland unlike any other: the city of London, on the island of Great Britain – a small piece of the Earth's surface laced with the most astonishing amounts of easily access-ible coal – including some that spilled from the earth directly onto its drizzle-swept beaches.

WHY LONDON? AND OTHER QUESTIONS

Instead of starting in the late eighteenth century and going upward in a straight line, the local story of London and coal starts with a corkscrewing tangle of backstories going back to the 1580s if not before – long before steam engines and factories, let alone internal combustion engines. This jerky succession of changes began when Londoners started building coal furnaces in their kitchens and brick chimneys on their roofs. Only much later did the story begin to pick up some of its own steam, so to speak, with the building of the first smokestack factories in the 1780s. But even then, still other dramatic plot twists had to happen (Chapters 11–14), before we can move from the late eighteenth century into even the beginning of the nineteenth, let alone into the twentieth – or to arrive, on the back seat of a rickshaw, into our own day. In recounting that story, we must divide a multi-century epic into shorter, overlapping and plot-twisting episodes, each of which solves one of the smaller riddles that – only when piled upon each other – collectively explain the whole.[1]

Even before we get to "Why London?," we need to note that the entire herky-jerky story of hydrocarbon is wrapped up in a bigger enigma that historians have yet to fully unravel. Londoners were not the first urbanites to heat their homes with coal. Once again, the honor – if we can still call it that, given what we now know about fossil fuels – goes to the capital of China's Song dynasty, Kaifeng. In the year 1008, Kaifeng's population was far larger than London's in 1580 – historians say anywhere from 400,000 to a million – and shortages of firewood due to agricultural deforestation that had been required in order to feed the city and a series of cold winters resulted in deaths of thousands of inhabitants each year. Riots often broke out as people fought over dwindling wood shipments. In 1068, after decades of trouble, a new emperor named Shenzong stepped in decisively. He abolished the tax that his dynasty collected on coal to bring the price of the black fuel down, and he later instituted a royal monopoly on coal shipments from mines up the Yellow River to keep speculators from withholding the fossil fuel from the market to get even higher prices. Because of Shengzong's policies, 100,000 households in the city switched to coal for heating and cooking. Even the city's poorer residents engaged in this early urban experiment with hydrocarbon, for they could buy cheap briquettes that hawkers fashioned from mud mixed with coal dust swept out of the bottoms of barges. After the Jurchen armies seized Kaifeng in 1127, coal home-heating did not disappear in China. It remained a substantial part of the fuel mix in ensuing dynasties' colder cities. Some of the million-plus inhabitants of Beijing burned coal throughout the Ming and Qing periods – that is, well into the era when a relative handful of Londoners made their own switch to coal. That leads to the unsolved enigma: why, despite all of Song-era technical prowess, did China did not develop smokestack factories until the late nineteenth century, at which very late date, a few Chinese industrialists copied British, American, and Japanese textile mills and a steel plant in cities like Shanghai, Wuhan, and Chongqing?[2]

Some of the answer may lie in the reasons why coal came to London. If so, a built place – a city, its growth, its location within bigger built spaces, the bigger actions and impacts that *made it* possible and that *it made* possible – in short, Urban Planetary dynamics – were essential to that answer. London in 1580 was not remotely as big as Kaifeng or Beijing, but it was growing fast nonetheless. The ultimate power source for this growth was, as elsewhere in the Urban Planet, the World Ocean. The city's merchant ship-owners used the winds and currents of the seaways to enrich themselves, first by benefiting from their direct access to English artisans' higher-quality wool goods and outcompeting Flemish merchants in the European market (Chapters 8 and 9). The wealth from that endeavor helped the city's merchants to embark on an ultimately successful project to outflank the main Flemish port at Antwerp, then to outpace Amsterdam, Paris, Madrid, Venice, and Genoa in tapping the wealth of global commerce, and by 1700 or so, come out on top as *the* capital of global capital.

As in all other Cities of the Oceans, London's wealth created large numbers of jobs in merchant houses, docks, shipyards, warehouses, and craft-shops, as well as retail shops that sold local and overseas goods. London was also the capital of an increasingly aggressive Ocean-fueled gunpowder empire whose ferocious capacity to wage war derived from King Henry VIII's Royal Dockyard in nearby Deptford, the Board of Ordinance (headquartered in the Tower of London itself), and a sprawling armory in the suburb of Woolwich. In a nearly never-ending search for better ships, cannons, and above all guns, the imperial state in London encouraged a fiercely competitive artisanal and commercial economy. That included merchants who sourced ship timbers, masts, and iron ore in Russia, Scandinavia, and North America, and an increasingly complex set of relationships between specialized artisans who developed a "culture of tinkering" in the workshops of London and other European cities that was essential to the continual redesign of parts for guns, other consumer objects, and – much later – industrial machines. The workshops and shipyards drew in peasants and artisans from the countryside as well as immigrants from across the continent and beyond. House builders, makers of household goods, and suppliers of food and fuel all needed to meet the demand, further increasing employment and migration to the city. Wages for ordinary workers increased too – never equaling the pay for similar jobs today and certainly not enough to allow families to avoid hunger or early death – but certainly higher in commercial and military capitals like London than the generally decreasing wages in most of the rest of the world during this time. Consumer culture blossomed, as we know, further increasing the economy and the allure of the city.[3]

In London, the Oceans, plus the trade they allowed, plus the gunpowder imperialism they enabled, thus set in motion a spiral of urban growth, economic growth, and more urban growth – despite devastating epidemics of plague in 1563 and 1665, the massive citywide fire of 1666, and the huge deathly toll of the Little Ice Age. Soon, though, London's growth began mysteriously to outpace that of other cities in Europe and in the world as a whole. From a depleted port town of 55,000 in 1520, when its size still reflected the devastation of the earlier, much larger, Black Death, London's population nearly quadrupled in size by 1600, surpassing Amsterdam and Paris. By 1700, London was the first European city since Rome to exceed the population of a major Asian capital – the Mughals' splendid Shahjahanabad, or "Old Delhi." British merchant companies, meanwhile, outclassed those of the Dutch and French. British kings allowed business interests in Parliament leeway to establish the Bank of England so that the state could enhance its ability to spend on warfare by tapping the fruits of supercharged capitalist activity. A hundred years later, in 1800, London's population outstripped that of Edo, Istanbul, and Beijing, surpassing a million people and becoming the world's largest – a position it would hold until New York and Tokyo surpassed it in the 1950s (Delhi caught up with London in the 1990s).[4]

Something was going on here besides better local wool, access to the World Ocean, and gunpowder. To explain London's unique acceleration, historians increasingly focus on the new source of energy that had quietly entered into the city's life: cheap, abundant coal. Already in the mid-1500s, it was clear that supplies of firewood and another wood-based fuel, charcoal, which Londoners had used for home heating and cooking since the foundation of the city in Roman times, could not grow rapidly enough to keep up with the city's redoubling population. London's home fires did not completely deplete the forests that supplied them. However, woodcutters and wood haulers did struggle to keep up with the demand, and firewood grew more expensive. When they tried to bring wood from forests further away, their transport costs rose, further pushing up the price. Soon poorer Londoners, then people with gradually increasing incomes, were obliged to forage the city's marketplaces for whatever they could find as a substitute. If the growth of the city was to blame for unaffordable firewood, a second factor, the unique geology of London's regional hinterland – that is, the island of Great Britain – led shivering Londoners toward coal.[5]

Coal was abundant in Great Britain, as in China, but it seems to have been even more accessible to London than it ever was to Chinese cities like Kaifeng. In the area near the small town of Newcastle upon Tyne in northern England, coal harvesters could pry black nuggets out of rain-swept cliffs on the beaches, thus explaining the contemporary name for coal in London – "sea-coal" – and for the fuel market on Seacole Lane. The location of early coal seams made it especially easy to transport by wide-bottomed grain ships down the coast to London. Coal shippers could make a profit from their black cargo even when it sold at a low price per calorie relative to wood. Other actors in London's growth encouraged the coal transport business. Smiths in the city had long used coal to forge iron household implements for London's growing numbers of homes, and helped build the Royal gun and cannon industries among others. Lime-burners used it to cook limestone for the mortar needed to build the proliferating brick homes and industrial shops in the growing city. The noxious smell of artisans' coal smoke was well known, and wealthy residents of the city, including Queen Elizabeth I herself, had long sought to banish smiths and lime-burners to places downwind of the city, without much success. When poorer Londoners began buying bits of coal to heat their homes, the grumbling increased. Soon, though, wood and charcoal prices climbed out of reach of even middle-class purses, and "sea-coal" entered into the heart and hearths of the city's consumer economy. In 1580, England's coal merchants sold about 50,000 tons of coal in London. That amount tripled by the early 1600s, then, spurred by Arctic winters of the mid-1600s, it tripled again by 1700, to about 450,000 tons. Modest Newcastle upon Tyne became the "New Peru," fueling London, not with silver "pieces of eight," but with "black gold."[6]

SPIRALS OF CITIES AND COAL

Urban expansion thus helps explain hydrocarbon burning, but coal also explains further urban and economic expansion. Coal allowed London to shed the "growth barrier" posed by scarcities of wood, and it cut the price of doing almost everything in the city. One consequence of burning all those tons of cheap coal was a new pattern of urban destruction and creation that increased the size of London and stimulated its economy. In the context of European house-heating technologies, burning coal required different urban spaces than burning wood. As the historian Robert Allen put it, the hydrocarbon revolution in London "was a matter also of the design and technology of grates, hearths, flues, and chimneys." Europeans had long abandoned the efficient central home-heating devices of Roman times, known as hypocausts, that worked by radiating heat under the house's floors. Similar devices, called *kangs* in China, with exterior furnaces, could be fired with coal as well as wood, whether in eleventh-century Kaifeng or seventeenth-century Qing Beijing. In Medieval Europe, householders had reverted to a form of campfire, a hearth situated in the very middle of the room of single-room houses, whose relatively light wood smoke rose into the rafters and out through a hole or vent; those who could afford wood-burning fireplaces built them wide and tall with relatively straight chimney flues. Switching to coal in Europe obliged householders to remodel completely, because burning coal required a raised grate in a confined space. Iron panels around the fire were needed to reflect its heat outward. Coaxing coal fires' heavier smoke out of the room without loss of home heat required fussy narrow tapered flues made of brick that extended through the roof into a chimney, preferably a tall one.[7]

The city's builders, drawing heavily on the art of coal-burning iron-smiths, lime-burners, and brick-makers, were happy to oblige. The smiths supplied London's houses and shops with iron grates and furnace-backs. The brickmakers dug up clay and limestone that the Thames River had deposited over the ages under the city, and used coal to bake millions of bricks and tons of mortar. Then, masons ran new brick-and-mortar flues through interior walls, sometimes redesigning whole rooms and buildings. Finally, the bricklayers topped off their work by festooning the city skyline with row upon row of chimneys. In 1666, as we know, disaster struck London when a bakery fire in Pudding Lane (we do not know whether it ran on wood or coal) spread throughout the historic center of town – where houses were still largely constructed of wood and plaster – and raged for five days. It engulfed 13,200 houses, the Royal Stock Exchange, government buildings, and an earlier version of St. Paul's Cathedral. As builders replaced the lost buildings and extended the city westward, they consolidated the domestic infrastructure of a hydrocarbon city, rebuilding London in brick and increasing its addiction to cheap coal. Meanwhile, coal soot blackened the inside of the fancy new flues of London, sometimes igniting and exploding, bringing down chimneys and whole houses. To prevent that, a new, iconic, character appeared on the city's stage. By as early as 1618, London already counted 200 chimneysweeps.[8]

Jump ahead to 1700, and, as climate historian John L. Brooke argues, "warming the city" of London "was literally driving the economy" of Great Britain as a whole. Coal and city growth increased the amount of work for London's many other artisans, like ironworkers, beer brewers, glassworkers, dye-makers, potters, woolens manufacturers, hat makers, fur-dressers, and even builders of new generations of iron-reinforced ships. Merchants drew on their own capitalist arts to invest in these urban businesses, pooling their money and transforming them into larger-scale enterprises – still located in small shops, and thus "pre-factory," but increasingly profitable. (Shipbuilding docks were already enormous – they expanded along the lower reaches of the Thames during this time.) From there, London's coal-supercharged urban-economic spiral sent swirls outward into its hinterland as well, into British towns that in 1600 were typically far smaller than those of other European countries. The householders and artisans in many of these towns – including Newcastle, but increasingly in towns near Great Britain's many other inland coal seams – could buy hydrocarbon energy even more cheaply than their colleagues in London. Pre-factory enterprises grew throughout the coal lands, allowing towns there to swell into cities. After 1700, Britain's urbanization rate exploded, surpassing earlier urban champions like Italy and Spain, where about one in five people lived in cities. By 1800, Britain even rivaled the Netherlands, where one in three lived in cities. Birmingham, in the Midlands coal areas northwest of London, grew relatively early, becoming Britain's second-largest city. Farther north, the substantial wool-cloth producing town of Manchester, close to still other coal seams, went through its own growth spurt a bit later; so did its neighbor, the slave and sugar port of Liverpool.[9]

London's growth spirals also reached deep into the countryside. To feed growing cities, Britain's large landowners and remaining smaller farmers needed to grow more food with fewer workers. They did so, in a remarkable transformation often called the British "agricultural revolution" (not to be confused with the Neolithic agricultural revolution after 10,000 BCE). Rich landholders became capitalist entrepreneurs in their own right. They used their own wealth and borrowed merchant capital from banks to amass larger tracts of land – a practice encouraged by the British Parliament's infamous "enclosure" laws – and financed experiments in new crops and tools. Historians have long drawn attention to the suffering that such profit-enhancing enclosure brought upon smaller farmers, but recent evidence shows that many smallholders were well placed to make innovations of their own. Either way, output per acre grew. Fast-growing hydrocarbon towns and cities, some historians suggest – not "enclosure" itself – acted as the principal stimulus for this agricultural innovation. Another urban synergy had gone into motion. The bigger food supply lifted yet another natural barrier to urban growth just as the countryside needed fewer farmers. More country-folk moved to towns and cities in larger numbers – not least to exploding London.[10]

Nowhere else in the world's most industrialized zones did urban growth spirals spin so quickly or intensely, nor was growth elsewhere so closely linked to coal. Amsterdam wiped out its forests, but turned to peat for fuel. Paris grew on Ocean-powered wealth and war making but continued to run on relatively abundant, if still expensive, wood – France's coal was difficult to deliver to the city, just as in Madrid and the big Italian cities. In China and in Japan, coal and wood both probably remained relatively expensive, never tipping cities fully to either fuel. Wood got more costly in the Ottoman Empire and in India, yet in places like Delhi, or in the massed textile villages of Gujarat and Bengal, the coalfields were too remote for inexpensive transport, until the railroads arrived in the mid-1800s. Only in the case of Antwerp, the Flemish powerhouse, was a City of the Oceans as conveniently located to coal-fields, just downriver near Liège. However, because London outcompeted Antwerp in commerce early on, neither its population, nor its ocean commerce, nor its war-mongering industries, nor its wood prices ever spiked strongly enough to prompt the city's householders and builders to redesign it as a coal-burning city until later. That said, Antwerp's closeness to coal helps explain why cities in the area we know today as Belgium were second in line, after Birmingham and Manchester, to adopt British factory technology.[11]

As London and its hydrocarbon hinterland spun out uniquely potent cycles of urban growth across Great Britain, it did one other thing that made the industrial revolution more likely on the island than elsewhere: it pushed the wages of British workers even further upward. Again, no artisan or journeyman in pre-industrial Britain made remotely as much as today in similar jobs. Yet there is growing evidence that by the 1700s, if not before, wages in London and Britain reached higher levels than in other societies with extensive pre-factory industries and oceanic commerce. One economic historian has recently explained these higher wages by means of an equation familiar to us as global urban historians: faster urban growth plus more farm output, plus cheaper energy prices, plus the extra economic churn of a city that had become the world's capital of Oceanic merchant capital and imperial war making.[12]

THE CALCULATIONS OF A COAL CAPITALIST

Add together the cheapest energy and the highest wages anywhere in the world and you get another sum. To make money, British capitalists had no choice but to use what they saw as the country's unique business advantage – coal – to deal with its unique business problem – wages. To make profits, in other words, they needed to burn coal to run machines that replaced as many workers as possible. Doing so set in motion a much choppier form of historical change. Capitalists had to invest in any early experiments with such machines that seemed promising. Then they had to make repeated reinvestments in those machines, sometimes over many decades, even at moments when long series of technical failures forced them to absorb big losses. Anywhere else but Britain, capitalists would perhaps think such investments theoretically interesting, but economically foolish. Coal there was too expensive for strings of failed experiments, and workers could do the work cheaply enough anyway. Outside Britain, there was simply no choice: industrial capitalists could not make money unless they used traditional, pre-factory, non-mechanized, usually non-coal-fired methods. In Britain, by contrast, capitalists *were obliged* to change.

By 1712, a coalmine owner named Edward Ward, Ninth Baron of the castle town of Dudley near Birmingham, cunningly demonstrated these sorts of capitalist calculations. His Conygree colliery had a problem that was typical of all coalmines: it was impossible to dig coal out of the earth without opening gushing streams of ground water and flooding the galleries, blocking miners from the coal seams. The Baron, like coal extractors the world over, used human bucket brigades, hand-dug drainage tunnels, or horse- or ox-powered pumping systems to extract the water. These solutions were all labor-intensive, and at British wages, very expensive. The Baron got word that a man in the port town of Dartmouth had perfected an idea to diminish the number of workers needed for mine draining. The Baron hired this man, Thomas Newcomen, to try out his strange idea.[13]

Newcomen was not a learned man. Of the hundreds of inventors of industrial machines that followed, the inventor of the steam engine was probably the least connected to the circuits of scientific knowledge then flowing between "Cities of Light" across Europe. He was quite wise, however, in the ways of merchants and, above all, he was a master-tinkerer. His ship-owning family contributed to Dartmouth's local spiral of British-style economic growth by plowing their Ocean-derived wealth into a specialty iron-mongering shop that made tools for coal miners. Note well: the Newcomen family, like the economies of entire British cities of the time, reaped its wealth in the Ocean and poured it into Hydrocarbon. In his milieu, Newcomen had learned exciting things about efforts to make mechanical pumps in France and England, and he took what he knew to Conygree in 1712. His idea was this. First, he set fire to some (very cheap) coal from the mine, to boil water in a domed copper vat, thus generating pressurized steam. He fed the steam into a cylinder containing a piston attached to a massive wooden pump arm.

With intermittent sprays of cold water, he condensed the steam in the cylinder, creating a vacuum that pulled the pump arm down and lifted water out of the mine-shaft – at twelve groaning, puffing pulses per minute. A machine to "lift water by fire" was born. Of course, to make the thing operable, Newcomen had to build an especially tall brick chimney above the firehouse to direct billowing coal smoke away from his invention – a smokestack.[14]

Newcomen's pumps were far from perfect; they could only raise water from so deep and they were slow and inefficient – only 1 percent of the power generated by all that coal went into the pump handle. Outside of Britain, no coalmine owner found Newcomen's engines worth their price for many years after he invented them. In Britain, by contrast, mine-owners bought dozens of them, replacing expensive crews of human mine-drainers and soon even some human haulers of coal wagons. Steam pumps soon became essential to making a profit in the coal industry, and capitalists were eager to find anyone who could come up with improvements. Fifty years later, after many successes and failures, James Watt, a former artisan turned inventor at the University of Glasgow in Scotland, came up with a few crucial tweaks to Newcomen's design, including a famous condensing cylinder that increased the machine's efficiency exponentially and soon gave steam the power to generate powerful rotating motion. In 1774, it was Watt's turn to visit the Birmingham area, this time at the behest of the local capitalist Matthew Boulton, who ran what he called a "manufactory" on the grounds of Soho, a nearby estate. The building housed an early version of an assem-bly line where workers stamped buttons and shoe buckles from metal sheets and assembled other household items, including "japanware" lacquer boxes. The manufactory ran on waterpower – it was thus a "mill," a not-too-distant descendant of the water mills of ancient Cities of the Rivers. Thus, the production of buttons, buckles, and beautiful boxes was subject to slowdowns during droughts and on winter days when the river froze. Watt's original commission was to use his steam engine to pump water upriver of the factory to stabilize the flow rate through the waterwheels. Soon, however, he built an engine that turned the machin-ery itself, by the power of coal and steam. Another smokestack pierced the English sky, and more puffs of black soot rose into the air.[15]

By 1774, cheap coal, high wages, growing cities, churning finance capital, the needs of the British war machine, and the "tinkering culture" that all of these factors encouraged in English cities had spiraled together into a full-blown industrial revolution. One crucial sign was the coke-fired iron-smelting furnace, the result of a century of experiments in the Birmingham area to burn off the sulfur in coalsmoke that otherwise contaminated iron melted in coal forges. Coke-smelting also went back to ancient China, but it was technically complex and not as economical as using charcoal in ironwork. Abraham Darby's furnaces in nearby Coalbrookdale solved the problem of cheap coke most successfully, allowing him to produce the higher-quality iron needed for dozens of more fine-tuned machines, including clocks, gears for textile machines – and increasingly deadly guns. Later improvements at Coalbrookdale included carts set on iron rails to transport heavy materials such as ore and coal between different parts of the industrial complex – an ancestor of railroads. Artisans in Birmingham's "Gun District" and the govern-ment-owned gun-smithies in Enfield, near London, supplied British mercantile companies, slave traders, and the British army and navy with weapons. They too became a source of constant incremental innovations in fine metalworking. The state's unquenchable need to deliver violence, particularly in its global wars against France, thus played a critical role in the industrial revolution – even though no British smiths made guns in actual factories until well into the nineteenth century (Chapter 13). Another indication of industrial revolution was the work of the potter's son Josiah Wedgwood, who, as we know, revolutionized the manufacture of porcelain "china" in six clay-rich, coal-rich villages in the Staffordshire countryside that later merged as the city of Stoke-on-Trent. By the early 1800s, his famous "bottle kilns," fueled with thirteen tons of coal at a shot, fired china tea sets that were far cheaper than the china that merchants brought from China.[16]

Most important of all, though, were the hydrocarbon-powered "fac-tory systems" we know as textile mills. Once again, several separate technical transformations needed to spiral together. Assembly lines had existed long before, such as in China's Jingdezhen pottery works and in shipyards from Nanjing to Amsterdam to London's own docklands. English capitalists such as the button-maker Matthew Boulton consolidated such systems further, bringing activities previously done in separate cottages or shops into a single, typically multistoried building with a single central power source. There, a single managerial hierarchy supervised workers who ran machines designed to accomplish individual steps in multi-step production processes. The owners of these factories could achieve more output from their investment in workers' wages than could any collection of independent artisan shops; they benefited from "economies of scale." The new machines, and the gears and belts that ran them, also required capitalists eager to invest in long strings of experiments designed to save on labor costs.[17]

Richard Arkwright's water-powered Cromford cotton mill, powered by the Derwent River in the north of England, pioneered the use of clockmakers, hired from near Manchester, to coordinate the motion of the river with a humming system of belts and gears powering his famous new carding and spinning machines. The art of clock and watch making, like that of gunsmiths, had also improved meanwhile as artisans got their hands on higher-quality iron and brass; better clocks had allowed ship captains to better calculate their longitude, and they fascinated consumers across the world, including as far away as the Qing court in Beijing. Arkwright applied time-telling machines to another invention crucial to global urban history, the first company town. His factory tower acted as a "clock" in its own right for the inhabitants of the small smattering of cottages he built for workers outside his textile mill: the tower had a loud bell that summoned workers to work at the start of two overlapping thirteen-hour workshifts. In this way, the place could run day and night, which was crucial if Arkwright was to get maximum profit on his investment. The bell also played a role in transforming farmers, used to days marked by the rise and setting of the Sun, into wageworkers, whose days were measured by the gears, belts, springs, and banging machines of the industrial revolution.[18]

THE TWISTING RISE OF THE SMOKESTACK

Even as the factory system came into its own, it was not a forgone conclusion that industry would do much to promote further use of hydrocarbon. Waterpower was easily as cheap as coal, and most early textile mills, including nearly all of those that soon appeared in the USA and elsewhere well into the 1860s, remained exactly that – "mills," run by flowing water. In the planned industrial town of Lowell, Massachusetts, where there was little coal, the textile mills ran entirely on the flow of the Merrimack River. Lowell dominated American textile production well into the 1860s, yet its greatest technological innovations involved canal systems, flood-proof millponds, and water-driven turbines. All of these items could be found dispersed across New England in small towns on the banks of dozens of fast-running streams named "Mill River" that had been refashioned into long strings of dams and small reservoirs.[19]

By contrast, back in Old England, the land of cheap coal, James Watt and Matthew Boulton had perfected their coal-fired steam engines by several notches more, and in 1785, they were powerful enough to run an entire Arkwright-style mill. Watt and Boulton built the first coal-fired textile factory near the city of Nottingham. However, Manchester's cloth merchants were even more avid buyers of steam engines. Not only did Manchester have readier access to coal, but its would-be factory owners could also tap the city's nearby specialty clockmakers and its advanced ironsmiths, whose coke furnaces, high-quality metal, and precision instruments could produce specialized parts for textile machinery; again, suppliers of parts to Birmingham's gun-makers also made contributions. Coal-powered factories did not shut down when the rivers stopped flowing. Also, because they could be located near each other, they benefited from a concentration of similar factories to attract a bigger whirlpool of laborers pouring in from the countryside. In Manchester, each of the factories themselves also grew in size. Some soon employed 1,000 or even 1,500 workers each, prompting the city's builders and landowners to invest in masses of new houses at cheap rent – the first industrial tenements. Hydrocarbon factories thus proved more efficient than river-powered ones in generating urban growth. Manchester – with 400,000 people by 1850, compared with, say, Lowell's 33,000 – at once created smokestack industry and was vastly enlarged by it. Soon Manchester also stimulated new technologies like canals, railroads, locomotives, iron-framed buildings to handle all the machinery, iron-framed bridges to handle the locomotives, and larger-scale iron and steel works to make machines, locomotives, buildings, and bridges. Coal-belching

10.1. Manchester, England: The "Satanic Mills" Viewed from the Idyllic Countryside
This painting from the early nineteenth century tells a story about cities and the
environment that still resonates with many people in the twenty-first: cities are the
problem; the countryside, where "nature" is intact, is the solution. True, by accepting the
hydrocarbon bargain, we refashioned cities to extend our realms of action, habitat, and
impact exponentially – with existential consequences. But the countryside – where millions
were exploited, where farming and meat production destroyed forests and other habitats,
and where fossil fuels soon dominated as well – was never so idyllic. Hydrocarbon is our
problem. Solving it requires the most powerful tools we possess – cities.
Hulton Archive/Getty Images.

smokestacks struck at the blackened sky, shocking even smoke-breathing
Londoners. The age of what the poet William Blake famously called the
"dark satanic mills" had begun.[20]

Even with all these twists and turns, we still have not fully explained
why the first Hydrocarbon Cities came into being. Coal had come to
homes and factory towns, with drastic implications for our own day.
However, cotton mills do not run on coal – or falling water – alone.
Cloth making also required vast amounts of raw fiber – and, to meet the
fashion needs of the day, that meant cotton. In 1785, it was unclear to
Manchester's factory owners where that cotton would come from. There
was also the question of people: How would factory owners get all their
workers? As the smokestacks multiplied, the same Cities of the Oceans

that struck the bargain with Hydrocarbon power were filling with crowds of people demanding a new form of political power, People Power – governments run upon the consent of the governed. Would the governments that came out of the looming age of popular revolution help factory owners meet their needs, not just for coal, but also cotton and equally large crowds of people willing to work in factories? Or would Manchester simply melt back into the Lancashire countryside?

As we know in hindsight, governments would in fact meet capitalists' needs, both for cotton and for workers, but not because "the West" inevitably brought democracy to the world, as some storytellers of the inexorable industrial revolution would have it, or because the West was just somehow "better." To get cotton to Manchester, some form of revolutionary People Power was necessary, but the "democracies" involved also had to engage in imperial war, expand slavery, and endow more forms of unequal power – not so much to "the People," but to new industrial capitalists, formed (thanks to People-Powered states) into even more powerful capitalist corporations. Only after many more uncanny historical intersections – most of them having to do with the great plot twists of urban political revolution and counterrevolution – would the hydrocarbon-fueled factory revolution finally stabilize as a permanent entity, with further spiraling consequences for the Urban Planet.[21]

CHAPTER 11

Planet of the People I: The Atlantic Cauldron

CITIES AND REVOLUTIONS

As smokestacks rose up in cities, so did "the People." Today, the Pandit Sharma Karma celebrates that fact by steering his rickshaw on a worshipful swoop around the circular Parliament Building in Delhi – the Lok Sabha or "House of the People." It is a monument to one of the great political victories of all time, the work of millions of ordinary people led by the Mahatma Gandhi and another self-described pandit, Jawaharlal Nehru. For decades, as part of a great people's movement, they marched in enormous crowds through the streets of Delhi and thousands of India's cities, towns, and villages. Wielding no weapons but the power of their own ungovernable numbers jammed into strategically chosen spaces, they slowly drained all legitimacy from the British colonial state – its authoritarian viceroys, its magnificent palaces in New Delhi, its armed soldiers, its grim prisons, unfair tax laws, and self-glorifying propaganda. In the Lok Sabha, the Indian independence movement rebuilt the very foundation of the country's governance, repositioning India upon what an earlier revolutionary, the American George Washington, called "the purest source and original fountain of all power": a "free people."

People Power is familiar to us from the earliest pages of our Urban Planet's long biography: it forms the heart of the idea that cities are places where we turn sunshine into politics. No state of any kind, from ancient times forward, ever wielded any form of power without the Sun-given energy of proximate people playing politics in cities. All along, a big part of People Power was its capacity to disrupt, even threaten, state rule. However, for most of the many millennia of global urban history, the story of city-spawned states can seem monotonous, nothing but a string of dreary continuities. Before the dawn of the modern "Age of Revolution" in the 1770s, most city-enabled states – even ones deemed heterarchies and democracies, and even the 500-year old Roman republic – seemed to devolve one after another into rigidly hierarchal governing institutions imposed *on* the People by a very small group of dynastic rulers.

These emperors and kings hoarded almost all forms of power available in cities: geo-solar energy, the power of monumental urban structures, weapons, wealth, bureaucracies, law, and even ideas; over and over, authoritarian rulers claimed legitimacy from gods. Gripping all the prime political chess pieces in their iron fists, emperors and kings checked the one source of power they could not depend on, the force of their own cities' teeming political communities, often supplemented by the force of the larger rural human majority who fed all cities. For such authoritarians, the job of the "People" was clear: they were to be loyal, subservient "subjects" of the dynasty's rule, not a force that ruled itself, let alone any part of the state. With the spread of gunpowder, authoritarian arrogance swelled further – and dictatorial rule became "absolute." For Louis XIV of France, a man who unequivocally equated state power with his person alone, all that remained was to seize absolute power's actual absolute source. Thus began – in the Versailles Palace twenty kilometers from Paris – the reign of the "Sun King."

And yet, the Sun King's château was barely 100 years old when massive crowds of restive People in one city after another – often joined by the rural majority – gave the long life of authoritarian Earthopolis an enormous jolt. The biggest of all People's revolutions rocked Versailles and Paris. Revolutions were always enormously improbable, unpredictable, deeply flawed, and enormously violent affairs – in that way very different from the ideal to which Gandhi aspired in the twentieth century. The road from "despotism to liberty," as the American revolutionary Thomas Jefferson noted amidst one of the revolutionary bloodbaths of Paris, was not one that you traveled "in a feather-bed." On top of that, many revolutionaries – Washington and Jefferson included – were enslavers of African laborers and conqueror-settlers of Native American land: dubious custodians of "free peoples," indeed. In fact, few of the early revolutions made any headway in solving inequalities of wealth of any kind – state-conquered, enslaved, or amassed by capitalists. Most early revolutionary states, as we shall see (Chapter 13), instantly pivoted to immense new acts of imperial conquest. Nonetheless, the main goal of popular revolutions was as lofty and promising as any proposed in human politics: to tear down states based on the will of a single person and rebuild their foundations upon the consent of the governed. Reviving the ancient ideas of *demokratia* and *res publica*, these states instituted regular elections and built dozens of new People's Parliaments entrusted with writing laws meant to be applicable to all.

When the People got such Power, how did they succeed? Cities were crucial. In the face of powerful absolutist adversaries, revolutionaries' strategies began with the elemental power of numbers in built spaces, especially cities. A typical first move was to gather crowds in popular neighborhoods and docklands or in new urban spaces like coffeehouses, bookstores, and intellectual *salons* or classrooms, and from there flood larger, strategically chosen spaces that were in one way or another crucial to the regime they were seeking to overthrow. Mobilizing large numbers in dispersed rural places, particularly on estates and plantations, or even on slave ships in the middle of the ocean, often helped. By surrounding monuments to dynastic rule and filling squares and streets with crowds, the People could undercut authoritarian propaganda and embody revolutionary ideology, starting with the sanctity of popular sovereignty and freedom from bondage. Yet such opening moves on the chessboard of built space always attracted the force of counterrevolutionary "crowds" of many types – whether in the form of armies, navies, police, spies, prison guards, or mobs loyal for one reason or another to the regime. To respond, the essential next step in the early Age of Revolution was the chanciest and messiest: to arm as many partisans of the people as possible for battle, while convincing the state's own weapons-bearers to honor any feeling of mixed loyalty by joining the revolution. Violence was an elemental part of early urban revolutions, yet it was (as Gandhi pointed out later) also a weakness, for it could generate fear as well as passion for the People's will, a fear that often took the specific name "*urban* disorder." Counterrevolutionaries fed on those fears, using promises of restored "order" to amass "populist" support of their own and to re-impose authoritarian rule. Their most enthusiastic recruits often came from city-fearing countrysides.

Cities alone – with their especially potent crowds and spaces – thus never determined the outcome of revolutionary conflict, which was always volatile and capable of sudden turns that urban space and the size of crowds only partly predicted. As always, cities are essential but never sufficient to explain any pattern of change – continuous, disruptive, or ambiguous and contingent. Still, revolutions could not do without cities in yet another way: the foundation of a new republic or a democratic state was impossible unless People's revolutionaries captured cities, capital cities in particular, and found a place there to build spaces essential to democratic rule, starting with a new House of the People.

When People's Revolutions did succeed, as they did after 1770 with greater frequency, in more places, and in ways that empowered greater numbers of citizens, they also did as much as the Hydrocarbon Revolution to completely transform cities in general – and our Urban Planet as a whole. Subsequent chapters will treat the ways the two simultaneous revolutionary forces, the People and Hydrocarbon, interacted, fed each other, threatened each other, and over time contributed to Great Accelerations in the size of our Urban Planet. That story culminates in our own time, when People's movements and democratic states, including many devoted to Gandhi's vision of non-violent revolution, make a bold claim that only an Urban Planet ruled by the People will be capable of guiding Earthopolis past the damage of the Hydrocarbon Era to a new era that is more just and sustainable for all.

Before we get there, we have another conundrum to unravel. If the most important ingredients of People Power existed in cities all along, why did humanity have to wait until the modern era, nearly 6,000 years into the biography of our Urban Planet, for democracies and republics to spread in a way they never did in ancient times? Explaining the still-ongoing birth of the Planet of the People requires telling a story more convoluted and more filled with unpredictable revolutionary plot twists than the story of chimneys and smokestacks. Although the two revolutions only tangentially touched off each other's births, they manifestly shared a common birthplace. Both emerged, like fraternal twins perhaps, from the same great cauldron of early-modern global urban history, the World Ocean. One Ocean in particular, that is. People Power, like Fossil Fuel, drew on tensions of power, wealth, and ideas that rose to an especially fierce boil in the Cities of the Atlantic.

THE CAULDRON BUBBLES

Four reasons explain why People's Revolution first bubbled up in the Atlantic. The first is a bit speculative: the oldest roots of Atlantic revolution may actually go as far back as the violent collapse of urban life in the Western half of the Roman Empire, a region that included the Atlantic-facing lands of Europe. For five centuries after the sack of Rome, that region could support only relatively small towns and weak states, and it was thus the site of frequent warfare. A general power vacuum in the area may have created especially good conditions for self-governing activity by the growing numbers of people who did trickle back into Europe's towns and cities – especially after about 1000 CE. These "burgers," that is, residents of "burgs," or fortified places, could purchase formal charters of "rights" from rival armed lords or relatively weak kings in their region. Some revived a version of the ancient Roman concept of "citizenship" (*Bürgertum* in German, also the root of the French word *bourgeois*) – a set of rights formally granted by a sovereign to people who inhabited a burg or in Latin, a *civitas*. In that context, merchant councils and artisanal guilds may have become – at least formally – more powerful during the European High Middle Ages (roughly 1100–1350 CE) than they did in the Golden Age regimes of the Islamic regions, China, and empires elsewhere. As we know, some European mercantile and financial towns, notably in Italy and in northern Europe where royal power was weakest, restyled themselves as "Free Cities" or even "Republics" – not true democracies, mind you, for they were run by elite merchant councils – but still largely free of royal soldiers. These included Venice, Genoa, Florence, Cologne, Strasbourg, Augsburg, Hamburg, Novgorod, and Pskov. In Holland, organizations of urban merchants and artisans successfully threw off the overweening imperial power wielded by Spanish kings from Madrid in a brutal war during the early seventeenth century. They created a "Dutch Republic" run by elite representatives of seven city-dominated provinces including Holland, the site of the Republic's capital, Amsterdam. In London, a Parliament of nobles had existed since the

High Middle Ages to review actions of the king, and the city's merchants founded the London Corporation, a town council that has since become accountable to a growing proportion of the city's inhabitants.[1]

A second, more palpable reason for the Atlantic birthplace of revolution has to do with the Ocean's two biggest cities: London and the Sun King's Paris, capitals of two imperial regimes that, as 1700 approached, outshone Lisbon, Madrid, and then even Amsterdam, building navies that dominated the north Atlantic world and beyond. These two cities were the first in Europe since ancient Rome to grow toward the million mark (both surpassed it in the early 1800s). During a time when gunpowder dynasties in Edo and Beijing reigned over "Long Peaces," kings in London and Paris fought each other, in and around most of the other Cities of the Oceans with unquenchable vehemence, not only in the Atlantic but also throughout the Indian Ocean even into the Pacific. Thus, their rivalry and violence far overshadowed newer European projects of absolutist imperial might that grew meanwhile in European capitals like Vienna, Berlin, and St. Petersburg, soon even eclipsing other war-mongering Afro-Eurasian gunpowder capitals like Istanbul, Isfahan, Delhi, and Benin.

Thirdly, though state investments in warfare stimulated wages in a few Atlantic cities, imperial rivalries imposed many heavy burdens on just about everyone in London and Paris's vast imperial spheres of influence. Across the British and French empires, anti-royal dissent grew among wealthy aristocrats and merchant capitalists, even as the People – urban artisans and the vast majority of poor and enslaved people – bore the heaviest burden of wartime taxes, military service, inflation, brute labor or care-work involved in sustaining armies on campaign and the economic depressions that often followed wars. The wars that London and Paris waged upon each other were particularly destabilizing to the long arc of Atlantic seaports stretching from Boston, New York, Philadelphia, and Charleston to the French Caribbean sugar ports of Cap-Français and Port-au-Prince, and soon to the far older cities of Spanish and Portuguese America. All of the many seaports and colonial cities of the Americas, unlike similar places in Africa and Asia, teemed with permanent European-descended settlers who ruled their local jurisdictions by means of particularly dangerous racial hierarchies and violence against

Native peoples, some of them stewards of venerable power-sharing traditions that inspired white revolutionaries. These settlers nursed grievances against tax collectors and recruiters whose authority was weakened by the long distances that separated them from imperial courts. Though often relatively small, American colonial cities, like the imperial capitals on the other side of the Ocean, contained many of the anti-hierarchical and even dissident spaces associated with global consumer culture. Some, notably in the British Atlantic, possessed their own municipal governments modeled more or less on that of London.

Fourth, last and by no means least, imperial power in the Atlantic rested not just on cities, but also on the brutal violence meted out in slave-ships on the high seas and on plantations in colonial cities' immediate hinterlands. "How much time will have to pass," prayed one white French plantation manager in Saint-Domingue, the greatest sugar and coffee colony of its day, "before the slaves forget that they set their master trembling?"[2]

Though ideas of rights and citizens had developed in many European cities, London in many ways set the immediate stage for the People's revolutions to come. As the growth in size of the British capital accelerated, on economic energy supplied by global mercantile capitalism and cheap hydrocarbon, the British royal houses wrestled mightily with the recalcitrant political energy of two of the city's resident representative institutions, the Houses of Parliament and the London Corporation. The British Parliament, at the time nestled in a jumble of old buildings in Westminster just outside London's walls, was hardly "democratic," in that it largely represented the landed elite (only a few rich merchants were allowed to participate), but it did keep its powers during a time when absolute monarchs elsewhere – particularly France's Sun King, Louis XIV – had discarded similar institutions. In 1649, Parliament even overthrew one British king, Charles I, when he sought to abolish its taxing power, then tried him for treason, executed him, and ruled the country on its own for four years until Charles's descendants seized power anew. In 1688, during the so-called "Glorious Revolution," Parliament deposed another would-be autocrat in favor of a more Parliament-friendly king, William III, invited in from "republican" Holland. Most of the populace of London welcomed William's invading fleet when it floated up the

Thames. Accordingly, the new king bowed to the city's "liberal" ethos by proclaiming a Declaration of Rights that formally placed Britain's sovereignty in the hands of Parliament.[3]

Indeed, British kings and queens found the city of London almost as intimidating to govern as Parliament. The Common Council of the London Corporation met in the Great Hall of the Guildhall in the heart of the city. After 1688, all of London's male taxpayers – about three-quarters of the city's total adult male population – were eligible to vote for representatives. As one historian put it, the Corporation's "elaborate infrastructure of wards, precincts and guilds … made participation in civic affairs a regular duty for many citizens rather than an occasional privilege." Yet London's polity also took energy from gatherings in hundreds of other spaces. In addition to the middle-class babble-and-grumble that flowed in London's 1000 or more coffeehouses and teashops, recall that the city was also home to dozens of sects of religious "dissenters." These included the Puritans, Quakers, and Levelers who abhorred all hierarchical institutions, including the Catholic Church, the High Church of England, and absolutist kings; the Levelers preached universal suffrage long before its time. These dissenters met in homes, conventicles, and Quaker meetinghouses that were often raided by the king's soldiery. The city's small but reviving Jewish population also maintained a handful of synagogues, whose members were likewise sympathetic to the desires of the urban majority.[4]

As Parliamentary revolutions lurched, Londoners honed another strategy involving space and the energy of their urban polity: they took their political activity "outdoors," into streets and squares and in front of the doors of grand buildings tied to oppressive power. Peaceful street processions could turn a traditional religious or artisanal fair in the town square into a little-disguised popular parliament, especially if the crowd unveiled public petitions there. If those strategies failed, crowds could express their anger in what the elite called "riots," collective violence against buildings and people. The word "mob," also an elite invention, first came into English at this time, from the Latin *mobile vulgus*, the "moving" (or "moved") crowd of commoners. London's mobile crowds, some tiny, some numbering in the thousands, could cross class in their composition, and many consisted mostly of women. Their assertions of power served many causes, including opposition to high prices for bread, tax hikes, merchant capitalists' takeovers of guilds, or the East India Company's cotton imports that endangered the livelihoods of 1,000 riotous weavers in the East End neighborhood of Spitalfields. At other times, the crowd turned on "bawdy houses," a favorite target of the pious conventicle crowd, to protest the disparity between the king's more vicious persecutions of dissident religious spaces than of what the dissenters deemed dens of sin. London "mobs" also engaged in national politics, seizing streets in support – and more rarely against – the armies of Parliament and the Glorious Revolution.[5]

A related form of urban-energized politics – this one from even "far deeper below," and farther out of sight of the state's radar, throbbed in the popular districts and extensive docklands in London's south and east. In this jumble of taverns, brothels, riverside wharves, and warehouses lived thousands of multilingual, multinational, and often mixed-race sailors and soldiers, enslaved African ship-hands, stevedores, sex-sellers, spirit-suppliers, and slit-throats with daily first-hand experiences of brutality and exploitation from their lives in London and in ports and plantations throughout the Atlantic and beyond. Docklanders lived lives of constant motion, some because they worked voluntarily for the low wages available on wharves and ships, others because captains, merchants, loan sharks, privateers, or naval officers pressed-ganged them into involuntary voyages across the entire World Ocean. Still others faced "transportation," typically from prisons in London to the colonies. That system expanded dramatically in 1788 with the first forced shipments of British convicts to Botany Bay, Australia that resulted in the founding of the city of Sydney. Some denizens of the docks reached London through prior experiences of capture in Africa and enslavement in the Americas. The politics of the docklanders, often enacted very locally in confrontations with police, employers, and each other, nonetheless benefited from their access to the decks, crew quarters, and slave-carrying holds of ships. A ship-bottom telegraph system arose – a century and a half before the first sub-ocean Morse-code cables – that allowed its users to exert popular counter-power everywhere along the Ocean's shores. As London docklanders traveled the world and mingled with compatriots from other places, they witnessed or partook in on-board mutinies, piracy, smuggling rings, tavern-hatched urban insurgencies, activism in informal free-Black neighborhoods or in runaway "Maroon" communities in the American countryside, and slave rebellions. At each place, the shipborne politics of this Atlantic sub-proletariat revealed weak threads in the ocean-spanning, city-connected textures of imperial and mercantile power.[6]

The cross-class, cross-color, cross-gender, and pan-Atlantic movement to abolish slavery formed at the intersections between London and all of these many fermenting polities in the urban Atlantic, reaching from there onto slave plantations. Enslaved people's own first-hand loathing of slave ships, plantations, and urban oppression of the enslaved was the touchstone for the rest of the movements' spatial politics. Enslaved people routinely sabotaged or destroyed the sugar mills that dictated the rhythms of their forced labor. In the fields, they used coded language, songs, and syncretic, African-inflected religious rituals to undercut the authority of their overseers. Many left their plantations for the surrounding mountains and forests, to meet rebels from other plantations clandestinely, or to create permanent settlements of their own. These included the great *quilombo* of Palmares, a free African city-like settlement in the Brazilian rainforest (1605–94), the jungle hideouts of the *Cimarones* in Panama, and the Maroon community of Trelawny Town, in the mountainous "cockpit" region of Jamaica, which actually wrested a charter for its own representative municipal government from the British colonial authorities who failed to subdue it. From places like these, temporary escapees, freed Black and mixed-race emissaries, and "higgler" merchants who supplied Maroon settlements moved information back and forth to seaport cities and into oceanic communication currents. News of outrages on slave ships made the rounds too, such as the famous incident on the *Zong*, whose captain ordered his crew to throw healthy slaves overboard in order to claim the cargo insurance. So did news of all-out slave revolts, such as those that arose from the taverns of New York in 1712 and 1741, the Stono Rebellion along the roads leading out of South Carolina toward Spanish Florida in 1731, Tacky's War in the plantation lands of Jamaica in 1760–61, and the Berbice River Valley uprising in Dutch South America in 1763, which was followed by decades of guerrilla war by Maroon communities in the hinterland of the seaport of Paramaribo, Surinam.[7]

Incidents like these pricked the consciences of the bourgeois coffeehouse set, dissenters, Quakers, and residents of popular neighborhoods throughout the Atlantic. The *Zong* case became a *cause célèbre* in the London law courts and dissenting congregations throughout the Atlantic. Narratives of slave abduction, the nightmarish "middle passage," and horrific treatment on plantations circulated from publication houses in Quaker Philadelphia to clandestine print shops in absolutist Paris. An African man named Olaudah Equiano wrote a memoir printed in London that told movingly of his childhood kidnapping, his enslavement as a plantation worker and ship crew-boy, the sordid life in the docklands of numerous ports, his precarious life as a freed Black in London, and his travels back into the Caribbean and beyond. In Philadelphia, the Quaker meeting announced its official opposition to slavery in 1754, and the eloquent pamphleteer Benjamin Franklin soon poured out anti-slavery propaganda from his print shop, joining Equiano's biography in an oceanic torrent of political pamphlets that made their way between Atlantic cities. In London, the abolitionist Thomas Clarkson embarked on a career as an early investigative journalist while renting an apartment above the "Baptist's Head" coffeehouse. He pored over records at a nearby customs office, met with Equiano and local Quakers in a former synagogue to raise funds, and used a sympathetic print shop nearby to publish accusations of murder against slave merchants. Slavers, in turn, gathered in their own London coffeehouses to grumble murderously about abolitionist protest. Clarkson then risked the wrath of his foes by stealing onto the docks of London, Bristol, and Liverpool to interview slave-ship doctors and crewmembers about their experiences of outrages in the Atlantic trade. The London Quakers formed an anti-slavery committee that sent Equiano and Clarkson out on speaking tours throughout the new factory towns of Britain. Abolitionists there drew up petitions to Parliament that, by the late 1780s, had attracted the signatures of thousands of ordinary people from all walks of life in Britain. In homes circumscribed by patriarchal rule, in embattled dissenting congregations, in publishing houses surveilled by censors, in docklands haunted by press-gangs, among inmates of debtors' prisons facing transportation, in weavers' cottages endangered by Indian imports or by new labor-saving machines, and in textile mills under the mastery of the factory bell, life veered far too close to slavery for comfort. Opposing the enslavement of human beings could feel like an act of deep self-interest to many people who felt only marginally "free" themselves.[8]

BOSTON VERSUS LONDON

Meanwhile, other radical revolutions erupted – the kind that not only replaced one king with another as in Britain, but sought to rid the world of kings altogether and place all power in the hands of the People. The British colonial port of Boston started it. The city's rebellious spirit drew on oppositional currents from throughout the Atlantic, including a large number of dissenting settlers whose ancestors had fled persecution in Britain to found the city, and a town council with a particularly democratic electorate. Boston's economy benefited from its busy harbor and its shipbuilding docks, but because it could not feed itself adequately from nearby fisheries and its rock-strewn agricultural hinterland (this was a century before the founding of nearby Lowell and other industrial towns), the city often swooned into recession, followed by bouts of paper-money printing and inflation. It had no high-and-mighty aristocrats as in London, but its wealthy ocean merchants, who always seemed to other Bostonians to profit from bouts of economic chaos, lived in arrogant houses a stone's throw from the peninsula-city's extensive docklands, packed with street-savvy – and Ocean-savvy – inhabitants. Boston's northern location made it especially attractive to British officials eager to impress its poorest residents into service as soldiers, sailors, and privateers in London's global wars against France – notably the conquest of nearby Canada. On the docks of Boston, grievances seethed accordingly.[9]

After seizing French Quebec in 1763, King George III famously sent waves of tax collectors and customs agents to Boston, and to American colonial cities further south, to cover his war debts. Multitudinous "outdoor" riots erupted in Boston. The king ordered the city's residents to pay for their own civic "order" by billeting British redcoats on the city's iconic Town Common, a symbol of Boston's tradition of collective self-government. In 1770, a multiracial mob that confronted a few red-coated soldiers outside a British Customs House on nearby King Street provoked a confused shoot-out later known as the Boston Massacre. In 1773, Bostonians enacted their most famous act of docklands spatial-political theater, the Boston Tea Party. In this case, the direct target was the British East India Company, whose debts Parliament in London had just bailed out with a fortune in tax receipts extracted from imperial subjects all around the world. After tipping dozens of chests of expensive Chinese tea into Boston harbor, docklands protestors led by the master agitator Samuel Adams threw British Parliamentary ideals into the face of Parliament itself, demanding settler representation in discussions of taxation in London. Boycotts of British goods spread to other increasingly ungovernable seaports like New York and Philadelphia. Wealthy merchants who broke the boycott there and in Boston found their proud houses hammered into rubble – and their beloved Birmingham-made *chinoiserie* hatcheted to lacquered matchsticks. King George and his Parliament responded to Boston's rebelliousness by shipping more red-coats into the city, this time billeting them in ordinary people's homes. In response, American seaport rebels and nearby farmers long accustomed to warfare with Native peoples organized themselves into a "Continental Army." A shooting war began outside Boston in 1775, and British battle-ships moved into the harbor to besiege the city by sea.[10]

The American Revolutionary War that followed teaches us several lessons about the Urban Planet as an aborning revolutionary space. The first lesson is the oldest: cities were at once critical tools of imperial power and empires' greatest points of weakness. Thus, they dominated the spatial rationale of imperial – and revolutionary – war strategy. The British naval commander evacuated Boston harbor when the rebel General George Washington pointed some cannons at his ships from an improvised hay-bale bastion on Dorchester Hill. However, squadrons of the world's mightiest navy quickly compensated by overrunning the wealthier and more strategically located seaports of New York and Philadelphia. With a fleet that looked like "all London afloat" the British took New York, giving official notice of the future importance of that city both to the Atlantic Ocean and to the continent's vast hinterland. In Philadelphia, their business involved political space. Taking what was then called the Pennsylvania State House (today's Independence Hall), they scattered the rebel Continental Congress that had met there to sign the American Declaration of Independence. The British would have soon consigned that document to the waste-bin of history – except that Britain's commanding admiral let Washington's army survive the ensuing winter in a small collection of log huts just up the river at Valley Forge.[11]

That brings up a second lesson: while both revolutions and counter-revolutions always needed cities, they did not run on urban spatial tactics alone. In the hands of a canny general like Washington, and with an opponent lacking the killer instinct, a tiny, ill-equipped revolutionary army could fight a war of retreat and attrition in a large, at least intermittently friendly countryside. There it could stretch the ability even of an empire headquartered and armed in mighty London to reassert the amphibious sort of power needed to reach through seaports into distant hinterlands. These tactics of fueling revolution from the countryside would become crucial to the far more radical revolutionaries of the twentieth century (Chapter 20).

Lesson number three: successful revolutionaries must look up from the streets (and their guerrilla retreats) to contemplate imperial politics on a global level. A small and crafty American lobby in Paris leveraged great-power rivalries to gain the support of the city's own revolution-minded aristocrats, like the Marquis de Lafayette, and even the absolutist King Louis XVI, driven above all by his hatred of Britain. Soon, France used its own rich slave ports to outfit a fleet powerful enough to bottle up British battleships in Chesapeake Bay.

This was only one French victory in what was otherwise a stalemate in naval battles fought with Britain, Holland, and Spain at the same time, in and around seaports from Canada to the Caribbean and from the African shore to India. It was enough, however, to allow Washington to lay siege to the tobacco-and-slave port and would-be British naval base of Yorktown, Virginia in 1783. When the defending British General Cornwallis flew a white flag from his still-rudimentary earthworks, he gave up an entire chain of what would soon become the richest overseas colonial fortress cities ever settled – then promptly shipped off to another fort city, Calcutta, to prosecute the British conquest of India instead. The

USA set up a Congress of the People – that is, its own version of an elite-dominated Parliament, in this case limited to white men with property – in a new capital city called Washington. Like Britain in India, the new USA used its own port cities, in its case the very birthplaces of its revolution, as bases for the conquest of a continent, and the spread of slavery across it. That should remind us of a fourth lesson of urban revolution: incubating People Power did not end cities' usefulness as tools for large-scale acts of colonial subjugation and enslavement, including that committed by so-called democracies or republics (more in Chapter 13).[12]

PLAYING PEOPLE'S POLITICS IN PARIS

As for Louis XVI of France, the price he paid for midwifing an anti-British republic in America was famously steep: that of his own head. By emptying his treasury on Washington's behalf, he lit one of many long fuses that led to an even more cataclysmic People's Revolution in his own kingdom. In 1789, Paris definitively took over from London and Boston as the global capital of violent popular revolution, a position it would occupy until Russia's St. Petersburg eclipsed the tumultuous French capital in 1917.

Louis XVI (reigned 1774–92) – like his family, the French absolutist Bourbon dynasty, the heirs of the great Sun King Louis XIV (1643–1715) – was even warier of the troublesome city of Paris than British kings were of London. Paris's connection to oceanic commerce mainly ran through slaving and spice-shipping ports like Bordeaux and Nantes, so the inland capital's docklands were somewhat tamer than London's. However, wages were high enough by global standards of the time, even without London's cheap-coal advantage. Large numbers of rural folk moved to Paris in search of livelihoods in the city's mercantile houses, artisan shops, eateries, marketplaces, theaters, and brothels, or as servants in the palaces of its urbane aristocrats and *haute bourgeoisie*, or as clerks or soldiers of the state. As of 1789, Paris was home to 600,000 people, a bit smaller than London. Like elsewhere in the Urban Planet, most of the city's people were poor, no matter the wage rate. "I saw only narrow, dirty and foul-smelling streets and villainous black houses," noted the revolutionary philosopher

Jean-Jacques Rousseau when entering the city through its notorious eastern *quartiers populaires* like the Faubourg St. Antoine, "with an air of unhealthiness; beggars, poverty; wagon-drivers, menders of old garments; and vendors of tea and old hats." The nightmarish thought that these neighborhoods' growing throngs, their concentrated misery, and the political potential of their largely impenetrable streets could one day scramble the power of the Bourbon dynasty filled the susceptible heart of the great Sun King's great-great-grandson Louis XVI with deep dread.[13]

In Paris, King Louis, like the Sun King before him, cultivated an absolutist spatial politics far more repressive than George III's in London and Boston. From every street in Paris, the dynasty's instruments of power were visible, resplendent, and fearsome. At the time, the massive Louvre palace had only one of the two magnificent wings it has today, but it already housed a sumptuous art collection featuring the *Mona Lisa,* and it already contained too many rooms to count. In 1789, the far end of the Louvre's single wing elbowed into an even more imposing baroque confection: the Tuileries Palace, officially the residence of the royal family. A long, rectangular series of gardens stretched out in front of the Tuileries toward the aptly named Place Royale. Louis XV (1715–74), Louis XVI's grandfather and the Sun King's grandson, had placed a statue of himself there, commanding everyone's view from high on a plinth. A long, straight, elegant, carriage path named after the Fields of Heaven, the Champs-Élysées, headed off into the woods from there. To win future victories against the British, Louis XVI built an École Militaire to train army officers on the opposite bank of the Seine River, next to a grand mustering ground for troops named after the Roman god of war – the Champs de Mars. Today, those grounds are the site of a certain very tall wrought-iron monument to the industrial era – but in 1789, neither the Eiffel Tower nor smokestack factories had arrived in France. Instead, the Paris sky was split by the steeples of Catholic churches from all epochs and styles, all of them overshadowed by the venerable gothic Notre-Dame Cathedral, nested on the island in the Seine where the city was originally founded in pre-Roman times. Church authority was largely an extension of absolute royal authority. Few London-style Protestant dissenters dared live in Paris, let alone gather in conventicles – for in

1685, the Sun King had expelled nearly a million Protestants, known as the Huguenots, at bayonet point to all corners of the Earth.[14]

In Paris, the Bourbons allowed nothing like London's Common Council to arise. Local authority resided not in the lovely renaissance Hôtel de Ville – the City Hall – but down the street in the grim medieval Châtelet, where the Provost of the Merchants Council and the Lieutenant General of the Police conducted most of the city's business. Paris's *gendarmes* were not as ubiquitous as Beijing's police forces under the Qing, but they were the most formidable in Europe, capable of slipping spies into high-society *salons* and the lowliest brothels, and conveying their reports to royal ministries lodged in various palaces around town. To prevent riots, the Lieutenant General kept his thumb on matters of both bread and circuses, impressing grain from farmers and merchants to keep the city's notoriously testy market women happy with the price of bread, and tolerating popular diversions along the boulevards as a kind of social safety valve for the poor. There was only one spatial limit to police power, the snarkily named Palais Royal – not a royal palace, as we know, but a shopping mall full of coffeehouses, bookshops, theaters, music halls, and speakers' corners across the street from the Louvre. Because the Palais Royal belonged not to the Bourbons, but to a dissenting line of the royal family named after their dukedom in the city of Orléans, it had immunity from incursions of the police and royal troops. Its shopkeepers and performers made their money by, among other things, peddling books on republican theory (such as those of Jean-Jacques Rousseau) and oceans of pamphlets mocking the royal family. To compensate, the Bourbons housed six elite companies of *Gardes Françaises* in barracks around Paris. The General Farm, a company employed by the king, collected royal taxes at each of fifty-four palatial tollgates in the city's twenty-four-kilometer stone wall. Then, there was the *Parlement de Paris*, across the street from the Notre-Dame in what is today called the Palais de Justice. Unlike Parliament in London, Paris's *Parlement* acted as a mere law court that rubber-stamped the king's decrees. Long before, in 1642–59, around the same time as Britain's civil war, the nobles of France had tried to stage a revolution, called the *Fronde*, against Bourbon rule in Paris, but the Sun King had trounced them. Since then, the kings arranged a special place for dissenters:

a prison-fort whose grim, crenelated towers rose above the same eastern popular neighborhoods that made Jean-Jacques Rousseau tremble and that gave sheer night-sweats to the royal court. That prison was the Bastille.[15]

Despite all of these well-designed built supports for Bourbon rule, the French king did not actually reside in his capital. In a way, the Bourbons thus resembled the British kings, who had also long eschewed central London, fleeing its "mobs" and coal smoke for palaces west of town. However, George III's magnificent abodes lay close enough to London that suburban development more or less filled in the intervening space. The Bourbons' use of self-segregation to enhance royal power was far more radical. In the 1660s, the Sun King famously moved his court a full two and a half hours' carriage ride from the Tuileries, through the bandit-filled forest of Boulogne, to the palace of Versailles. There, more than century later, protected by more *Gardes Françaises*, Swiss guards, and bodyguards, Louis XVI ruled a space exquisitely designed to pit former aristocratic rebels against each other in fights over the minutiae of palace life. Impotently, the noble class of France brawled over the right to occupy the château's most desirable apartments, or for coveted invitations to the king's daily procession, with his Queen Marie Antoinette, through the Hall of Mirrors. Mostly though, as one historian put it artfully, Versailles was not Paris: it "allowed monarch and the planet [to] traverse the course of the day serenely unoccluded by the havoc of city life."[16]

From 1789 to 1799, Paris's revolutionaries managed the unthinkable and overthrew this aloof dynasty, prying its carefully wrought absolutist habitat out of its hard fists, and finally turning the state's own guns, and then its head-chopping guillotine, against the king. The Old Regime's power reached beyond Paris and Versailles, of course, and hundreds of collective actions were required all across France – by townspeople in dozens of large provincial cities, by peasants at hundreds of estates and villages in the countryside – and in the docklands of seaports and the slave quarters of plantations in France's far colonies. The Revolution involved a wide spectrum of actors, from revolutionary aristocrats like Lafayette, inspired by the Americans, to bourgeois merchants fed up with royal taxes and regulations, to the Palais Royal's motley bohemian denizens, steeped in their Jean-Jacques Rousseau, to hundreds of lawyers newly empowered as constitution writers, to an early generation of feminists. Republican revolutions in Warsaw and other Polish cities, in Amsterdam and across Holland, and in the area around Dublin were inspired by events in French cities; all of these revolutions merged to some extent as they faced reprisals from royalists. An even more radical revolution, that of enslaved people in the far-off French colony of Saint-Domingue, also soon decisively interwove itself with the events in France (Chapter 12).[17]

No French Revolution would have happened, though, without dozens of spectacular battles over Paris's urban streets, squares, and monumental buildings. The main fighters of these battles were the capital city's own hundreds of thousands of artisans, shop owners, laborers, homemakers, prostitutes, street beggars, and *poissardes*, Paris's notoriously unruly market women. Also crucial were the ordinary soldiers and police officers whom the crowd convinced, at crucial moments, to defect to the People's cause. Emerging from their "narrow, dirty and foul-smelling streets," the *menu peuple* or humble folk of Paris – soon known as the "*sans culottes*" because they could not afford the silk breeches (*culottes*) of the elite – used their intimate familiarity with the political geography of Paris to flip the capital's absolutist spatial logic on its head.[18]

Well before the famous morning of July 14, 1789, when the people of Paris attacked the Bastille, ordinary folk across France had shown ample signs of aborning "modern" political sensibilities. As they mounted what looked like traditional bread riots in Lyon and Marseille, tossed tiles from roofs at the heads of soldiers in Grenoble, or wielded pitchforks in massive anti-tax attacks on rural estates, they increasingly identified themselves as "the people" or "the nation" – and demanded an institutionalized voice of their own in state affairs. As Louis XVI struggled to find a way to tax France out of the debts he amassed for the American war (among other adventures), he came under overwhelming pressure to reassemble a long-defunct Parliamentary institution called the Estates General, which included the so-called Third Estate, a body representing the commoners, the vast majority of France. Once this Parliament met in Versailles, the royal palace suddenly housed an institution at odds with absolutism, for "The Third" demanded representation proportionate to the population it served. Louis tried locking the delegates out, but 576 of them met in a nearby indoor tennis court instead. There, they renamed themselves the "National Assembly" and movingly vowed to write a constitution for the people who elected them, or die in the attempt.[19]

That is when the long series of Earth-shaking revolutionary spatial moves and countermoves began on the political chessboard of Paris. Fearing that a foolish conspiracy of Versailles courtiers would order the palace guards to slaughter the People's representatives, artisans and laborers in Paris convinced five out of the city's six detachments of *Gardes Françaises* to act first: to join the crowd from the neighborhoods in an all-out flanking assault, in Paris itself, against the Bastille. On July 14, 1789 and subsequent days, crowds tore the Bastille itself to the ground and seized its weapons, then dismantled forty of the General Farm's fifty-four tollgates. They turned the streets into popular law courts that tried the Bastille's commander and the Provost of Merchants, then decapitated them and paraded their heads on pikes throughout the neighborhoods, installing them for public viewing at the Palais Royal. In so doing, they also instantly sucked the power out of the once-feared Châtelet, relocating local control to the Hôtel de Ville, where ordinary Parisians, like urban "citizens" all across France, reorganized local government as a "commune" elected by the people. Meanwhile, lordly châteaux across the country met a similar fate to the Bastille, as peasants removed tax documents from their vaults, set fire to the turrets, and displaced authority from their local nobles to hastily elected village councils, also called communes.[20]

Versailles itself now came under withering pressure from the women of Paris. When the king refused to sign the Assembly's famous Declaration of the Rights of Man, detachments of *poissardes* marched six hours from Paris to Versailles, dragging Lafayette, his troops, and a few cannons in tow. Singing bawdy songs, they toured the National Assembly, then found their way into the palace. Someone slit the throats of a few royal bodyguards, allowing a crowd of women to enter the royal apartments, where they gave Marie Antoinette the fright of her life. A day later, in the pouring rain, the rebels escorted a carriage containing the king and queen back to Paris, this time with the entire National Assembly slogging behind. The royals were ushered into their disused apartments in the Tuileries. The Assembly took up residence down the hall in the palace theater, where it became the Constituent Assembly, empowered to tie the king to a permanent constitution. Back in Versailles, meanwhile, carpenters boarded up the Palace of the Sun King. Overnight, over a century's worth of absolute power had vanished from it absolutely.[21]

By contrast, in Paris itself, the space available for open public discussion now widened well beyond the Palais Royal. The Assembly itself developed its own political micro-geography, with the republican-leaning "Mountain" party in the highest benches of the theater, and moderates and royalists in the "Plain" lower down. This reflected a previous division in space in the chambers at Versailles, where republicans most sympathetic to the commoners sat to the left of the speaker, and monarchists to the right – the basis for the "left–right" spectrum in modern politics to this day. To plan legislative and protest strategies, delegates joined with others of like mind in political clubs, chapters of which spread throughout France. One club of high-Mountain leftists, which had originally gathered in a café in the town of Versailles, now identified themselves as the Jacobins, after the vacant monastery of the Jacobin Order a few blocks from the Tuileries that the club occupied as headquarters. Others in the Mountain took over a convent in a working-class neighborhood on the Left Bank called the Cordeliers. More moderate-minded "Girondins" preferred the *salons* run by rebel aristocratic women in their mansions. Meanwhile, the Commune divided Paris into twelve smaller municipalities, each divided into "Sections" with their own deliberative bodies. Some of these were renamed after revolutionary slogans – "Contrat Social" (Rousseau's Social Contract), "Droits de l'Homme" (Rights of Man), and "l'Indivisibilité" – to clarify their status as spatial tools for the gathering revolution. Though no women were eligible to vote in the Sections, a stinging male rebuke to the heroines of Versailles, the will of Paris's *sans culottes* nonetheless gained increasingly seamless access to the Hôtel de Ville, the Jacobins, the Cordeliers, and from there directly to the Mountain in the Assembly.[22]

More insurrections followed over the next six years, each built on strategic use and reuse of the city's spaces and their now rapidly evolving symbolic significance. In 1791, after revolutionary soldiers caught the king and queen dressed in servants' clothing fleeing for the Flemish border, the Jacobins and Cordeliers organized a mass petition drive in the Champs de Mars to force moderates to break off negotiations on a constitution that would include the duplicitous monarch. On behalf of the moderate Plain, Lafayette ordered his troops to fire on the radical crowd, killing somewhere between fifteen and fifty. The crowd counterattacked and forced the once-popular general to flee Paris; he cooled his revolutionary heels for a time in an absolutist Austrian prison. Meanwhile, Vienna's Habsburgs conspired with George III in London and Europe's other rising absolutist dynasties in Berlin and St. Petersburg to retake Paris for the Bourbons.[23]

11.1. What Should We Make of Democracy Born in an Urban Bloodbath?
For the "absolutist" Bourbon kings of France, cities were essential for wielding state violence but also a great threat. Claiming to ensure urban "order," they fostered a street culture inured to violence. Democratic revolutions arose on the idea that the People should run the state. They also required large – often unruly – urban crowds, self-defense against state massacres, and soldiers who switched allegiance to the revolution. All early revolutions were violent affairs, like this 1792 incident, when urban crowds and People's soldiers slaughtered royal troops at Paris's Tuileries Palace, later executing the king and queen. Yet fear of such disorder, along with revolutionary "Reigns of Terror," could fuel counterrevolution or bolster "populist" strongmen like Napoleon Bonaparte. Much later, the Mahatma Gandhi called for unarmed mass disorder as the only legitimate and effective route to democracy. Heritages Images/Hulton Archive/Getty Images.

In 1792, hundreds of French soldiers took time off from fighting these armies to join forces with the *sans culottes* in the neighborhoods. The armed crowd assaulted the Tuileries Palace and forced the king to hide among moderate delegates of the Plain in the Assembly. Louis ordered the Swiss guards to hold fire on "his" people, but the crowd slaughtered the guards, then locked Louis in one of his own remaining prisons to face treason charges. In January 1793, the guillotine came down on the king's neck – with throngs of spectators cheering in the now-renamed Place de la Révolution – next to the empty plinth that had formerly displayed the statue of Louis's grandfather. Even bigger crowds cheered when the queen lost her own head there nine months later. Incredibly, France had become a Republic.[24]

Still, the people did not remain quiet. In 1794, yet another Parisian insurrection targeted the Republic's own National Convention, leading to the arrest and execution of Girondist delegates deemed too moderate for the *sans culottes*. Spaces of free expression now contracted violently, this time under orders of radical *sans culottes* themselves in the Hôtel de Ville, who pushed the Convention's Jacobins under Maximilien Robespierre to wage a Reign of Terror against supposed enemies of the Republic. The Place de la Révolution and town squares across France became mass execution sites for people deemed traitors of the revolution. Soon the orgy of guillotine strikes consumed Robespierre himself, and the Reign of Terror mercifully faded.[25]

So did the People's command of the streets of Paris. In 1795, after another brutally cold winter, the price of bread rose once again, and paper money became worthless. The *poissardes* once again urged the crowd to take their grievances directly to the Convention. This time, though, their allies in the Mountain were under a cloud for their excesses with the guillotine. Fewer protestors joined, and the moderate executioners of Robespierre resolved to prevent a second Terror. This time, the army remained on the side of the Convention, forcing the *sans culottes* to retreat into the Eastern Sections, not to reemerge until Paris's next great revolutionary moment, in 1830.[26]

Paris's contingent of rightist royalists meanwhile felt secure enough to form their own mobs, often consisting of dashingly dressed young men, minor officials, and loyal servants in wealthier households located in neighborhoods to the west and north of the city center. In October 1795, they massed for their own march on the Tuileries, threatening civil war in France. The Convention entrusted its own defense to a twenty-six-year-old lieutenant colonel from the École Militaire named Napoleon Bonaparte. He loaded cannons with grapeshot and fired deadly volleys at the counterrevolutionary crowd as it poured from all directions into the Place de la Révolution. Three hundred protestors fell amidst rivers of blood. Some fled, ironically, to the Palais Royal, where Napoleon hunted them down the following day.[27]

Napoleon, a former Jacobin whose military training had since soured him on crowd politics, was suddenly a hero of the republic. As the Republican government in Paris mired itself in corruption and stalemate, Napoleon openly compared himself to nation-saving military men like Julius Caesar and Alexander the Great. The Republic encouraged this grandiosity by sending him to, of all places, Egypt, where he occupied Alexandria and Cairo in a swashbuckling gambit to outflank British influence in the Eastern Mediterranean. Another vision of People Power grew around Napoleon, in which popular sovereignty expressed itself through the larger-than-life character of a single person of action. In an age fatigued by the tumult of revolution, he appealed in his own way to the People of Paris, claiming that order, efficiency, and grandeur were as important as liberty, equality, and fraternity.[28]

That "populist" appeal helped Napoleon establish another precedent of modern politics: the military coup. Shrewdly, he applied his tactical genius to the all-important political geography of Paris. In 1799, fresh from Egypt, he convinced supporters in the assembly, now called the Council of Five Hundred, to move their meeting place from the Tuileries to the palace of St. Cloud on the wealthy western fringes of the city. There, far from any lingering support from the Paris crowd, republican or royalist, the Council proved defenseless when soldiers loyal to Napoleon cleared the chamber and endowed him with Julius Caesar's old title, Consul of the Republic. The route to his coronation as Emperor Napoleon I four years later followed a path that many military dictators and populist strongmen (and a few strongwomen) have taken since. Republican-style legislatures remained in place as showcases of popular sovereignty, stocked with regime supporters by means of sham elections, and bled dry of power by dozens of imperceptible and semi-constitutional knife-cuts. The "People" returned to their suppressed lives, most laboring hard on farms or plantations, in the poor sections of town, on ships, or on military duty. Still, many kept alert, as did the *sans culottes* of Paris, for another moment to exercise the power of their numbers at barricades in city streets.[29]

CHAPTER 12

Planet of the People II: Feminists, Abolitionists, and *los liberales*

Despite Napoleon, and because of him, People Power found growing numbers of habitats in city streets, coffeehouses, salons, religious spaces, town squares, and docklands elsewhere in the circum-Atlantic, as well as in the crucial capital-creating hinterlands of the Atlantic plantation system. In this widening archipelago of political spaces, the electricity of Paris's eventful *journées* resonated long after Napoleon's coup and auto-coronation. As Bonaparte and his generals subjected most of Europe to total war from 1803 to 1815, his armies destabilized absolutist capitals everywhere he went, in the name of the emperor's own "populist" rule. Amidst the chaos, practitioners of People Power inspired even more radical – and more uncertain – movements to emancipate women, European Jews, enslaved Africans, and the subjects of the largest empires in the world – those of Spanish and Portuguese America. As these movements spread, revolutionaries hurled the unpredictable and disruptive energy of urban polities – as well as rural and even oceanic revolts by enslaved people – against some of the most repressive and historically continuous forms of city-centered authoritarian power, while shifting bedrock institutions like patriarchy, Christian anti-Judaism, and Atlantic plantation capitalism.

Overall, feminists, emancipationists, abolitionists, and *los liberales* (as republicans called themselves in Latin America), remained in the minority, even in the "liberal cities" where they tended to cluster. Yet, their abilities with pen and printing press, the sympathies they could call upon at times in poor urban neighborhoods and among enslaved people, and their strategic understanding of urban spatial politics could give them moments of outsized power in key capitals as well as on plantations. In all of these places, as in Paris, they could at times counterbalance a better armed, wealthier, or simply a larger majority of politically more conservative fellow citizens, even if only for brief spells of time. Their precedents mattered greatly, even in defeat. The cause of People Power thrived in its urban haunts, nurturing its own historical continuity as a force that would reemerge in the streets again and again.

FEMINISM AND EMANCIPATION

Despite overwhelming male scorn, feminists used the revolutionary urban Atlantic to burst from the streets of Paris into world history in a truly significant way for the first time. At the same moment that the Parisian *poissardes* mixed a modern call for representative institutions into the traditional medium of a bread riot, the era's egalitarian ideas were being stretched by the city's *salon* activists, like Olympe de Gouges with her famous "Declaration of the Universal Rights of Women." De Gouges fell to the Terror's guillotine along with fellow Girondins, but the same Paris *salons* emboldened the visiting British philosopher Mary Wollstonecraft to launch a similar feminist manifesto into the English-speaking world.

Feminist resonances deepened over the next half century in liberal circles of urban Britain and the USA, where they joined anti-slavery crusades and gave birth to women's suffrage movements. The cities of Catholic Europe and Latin America were notoriously less fertile grounds for feminism, despite France's insistence on personifying its republican tradition by means of the bare-breasted, barricade-mounting Marianne. Yet the revolution in Spanish and Portuguese America could not have happened without *américana* feminist heroines like Manuela Sáenz of the Andean city of Quito, Simón Bolívar's pistol-waving, horse-riding, pants-wearing mistress. More demure, but just as courageous, were the dozens of conveners of *salons*, or *tertulias* across revolutionary Spanish America. They remained among the foundational doyennes of urban liberalism throughout the nineteenth-century Atlantic, even if their home cities only very slowly incubated feminist demands for equal political and economic power.[1]

For the Jews of Europe, the anti-clerical crowds of Paris gave a giant boost to the movement to end centuries of religious discrimination, including in the use of urban space. In 1791, the French Constituent Assembly passed legislation abolishing differential treatment of religious minorities. Napoleon proceeded to impose this writ on the rest of Europe. In 1797, while in Italy in service to the French republic combating Austrian absolutists, he entered Venice and ordered his soldiers to dismantle the gates of the 300-year-old ghetto. The walled *Judengasse* of Frankfurt fell to Napoleonic cannonballs a few years later. Similar emancipatory moves liberated Jews from constraining legal and spatial arrangements in Vienna, Hamburg, and Amsterdam, among other places with large Jewish communities. However, Napoleon's failure to hold Moscow and his subsequent defeat at Waterloo enabled various Christian absolutists to re-impose many discriminatory laws. Most notable was the Russian "Pale," a band of territory largely consisting of lands seized from Poland, in which the Tsar confined Jews to specific villages knows in Yiddish as *shtetls*, and forbade them from living in a number of the bigger cities in the area. In the Black Sea port of Odessa, home to a very old Jewish community, Greek Orthodox fanatics in 1821 launched the first of what would be hundreds of urban *pogroms* against Jews that grimly replicated themselves well into the twentieth century. By contrast, Jews in London, Birmingham, Paris, Amsterdam, and Berlin led movements for further emancipation that gained fruit in the years after revolutionaries upended Paris once again in 1830, and yet again in 1848 when barricades blossomed in dozens of European capitals during the "springtime of the peoples."[2]

REVOLUTION OF THE ENSLAVED

For enslaved Africans and other people of color, both the urban and the pan-Atlantic scales of the early revolutionary age were especially crucial. From distant plantations, millions of enslaved Africans looked to Paris for vindication of their own "universal" rights. On the especially rich French Caribbean sugar, coffee, and cotton colony of Saint-Domingue, no fewer than four separate French Revolutions broke out in 1789. The island's rich planters themselves rose up against against Louis XVI's policy of claiming all the colony's valuable plantation products for France, demanding "freedom" to sell them wherever they could get the highest price. The island's 30,000 "*petits blancs*" (little whites), who lived in the docklands of the colony's seaports, Boston-sized Cap Français and the then-smaller capital of Port-au-Prince, rose in solidarity with Paris's *sans culottes* – but insisted additionally on restricting their new legal privileges to whites only. The hated rivals of the *petits blancs* were the 25,000 free *gens de couleur* ("people of color"), mixed-race people typically descended from white slave-owners and their Black mistresses. The *gens de couleur* looked down on the *petits blancs*, but they too rose in revolution, demanding voting rights for themselves in exchange for the pivotal role they played on the island. That included service in the *maréchaussée*, a feared constabulary that tracked down escaped slaves, and in some cases as owners of coffee and cotton plantations in the hills, where they too owned slaves. Then there were the vast armies of "Black Jacobins": the 650,000 enslaved people who labored in the sweltering cane fields of the plains, outnumbering all others in the colony ten to one. When their bold guerrilla leaders left the plantations to coordinate their forces in the mountains, they had a single aim: to abolish forced bondage and, with it, the inequities of the plantation system as a whole. Soon their revolt became an anti-colonial one as well – for national independence. At that point, Saint-Domingue's four French Revolutions melted into a single, more disruptive one: the Haitian Revolution.[3]

The action began simultaneously in Paris, Port-au-Prince, and Cap Français on the island's north shore. In Cap Français, plantation owners owned elegant mansions and subsidized a full complement of urban amusements, including theaters and symphony orchestras, in addition to the portside jumble of their sugar, coffee, and cotton warehouses. Some of the wealthiest men in the French empire, these planters shuttled between the island and their families' country estates in France, but many spent most of their time in Paris's new mansion districts, in the royalist areas to the capital's north and west. In Paris, they formed a conservative political club at the Hotel Massiac to protest the Assembly's Declaration of Rights of Man, which they – and those they enslaved back in Saint-Domingue – saw as an abolitionist document. Meanwhile, the *petit-blanc* dockworkers and artisans formed communes in the towns across the colony, then convinced colonial troops to join them, then killed a royal governor at Port-au-Prince, then began hunting down local *gens de couleur*. In response, wealthier *gens de couleur* sailed to Paris to put a stop to the attacks. At the Club Massiac, they promised to enforce slavery in exchange for rights, but they also charmed the white abolitionists in Girondist *salons*, including the feminist Olympe de Gouges. The British abolitionist Thomas Clarkson rushed across the Channel to seize what he saw as a main chance to rescue the English anti-slavery movement, which was then sputtering in Parliament back in London.[4]

Meanwhile, back in Saint-Domingue, the enslaved African priest Boukman met with other bound and free Maroon leaders off plantation, high on the Morne Rouge hill above Cap Français, to plan a massive uprising across the colony's Northern Plains. Much of the highly capitalized built environment devoted to "white gold" went up in flames. Ticking off structures he lost to the slave rebellion, one white plantation supervisor mourned "the sugar refinery, the vats, the furnaces, the vast warehouses, the convenient hospital, the water-mill which was so expensive, all is no more than a specter of walls blackened and crumbled." Over 200 sugar and 1,200 coffee plantations lay in ruins, as did many lovely mansions and market-places in Cap Français, which only narrowly escaped capture and inciner-ation from embers of sugarcane ash that floated in from the plantations. Whites crammed the city's tiny harbor to retreat to safer slaving seaports like Havana, Cuba, Charleston, South Carolina, and French New Orleans.[5]

Reacting to these events with anguished deliberation, the Convention in Paris granted Saint-Domingue's wealthiest *gens de couleur* the vote, and sent a governor with the exquisite name of Léger-Félicité Sonthonax to Saint-Domingue to squash the *petit-blanc* revolution. To accomplish this task, Sonthonax had no choice but to employ rebel slaves as soldiers to do much of his military work. The same was true of the Spanish army headquartered on the eastern portion of the same island – in the Ozama fortress of Santo Domingo, the colonial city founded by Christopher Columbus's brother. That army soon invaded the French areas to reclaim them for the Spanish king's Bourbon cousins. One of its commanders was the free Black general Toussaint Louverture. In August 1793, however, Louverture received unbelievable news: at Cap Français, Sonthonax, a Girondist who had circulated in abolitionist cir-cles while in Paris, had emancipated all enslaved people in the Northern

VUE DES 40 JOURS D'INCENDIE DES HABITATIONS DE LA PLAINE DU CAP FRANÇAIS

12.1. The Plantation Revolution: Saint-Domingue Becomes Haiti
Most early revolutionaries focused on capturing cities and monuments to royal power, but they also relied on unrest on country estates and farms. The most radical revolution of all was in French Saint-Domingue, where thousands of enslaved laborers from industrial sugar plantations destroyed cane-crushing plants and boiling houses, thus also bringing the power of Oceanic capitalists into question. The armies and navies of every major Atlantic state – authoritarian and "democratic" – tried to stop the enslaved from seizing seaport cities, as here at Cap Français. In honor of the independence of the first "Black republic," the city changed its name to Cap Haïtien.
Universal History Archive/Getty Images.

Plains to thank them for their service in his army. Soon governors in Port-au-Prince and other sugar ports followed suit. For the first time, a formerly enslaved African resident of Saint-Domingue, Jean-Baptiste Belley, traveled by ship to revolutionary Paris. With the Terror rising around him, he successfully convinced the Convention to pass world history's first emancipation proclamation. In dubious celebration of the event, white Jacobins donned blackface in festivals that took place in town squares all across France.[6]

Impressed, Louverture switched to the French side and began fighting anti-abolitionist invasions by the Spanish, the British, and the USA. His opponents described Louverture's guerrilla warfare in utterly perplexed terms: "Often it was announced he was at Cap Français, and he was at

Port-au-Prince. When you thought he was at Port-au-Prince he was at Caye, at Môle, or at Saint-Marc ..." When Napoleon rose to power and reversed emancipation, Louverture convened a Constituent Assembly in the ruins of Cap Français to establish the independent nation of Haiti – the name that the Taíno had used for the island before Columbus. The city was renamed Cap Haïtien, and Port-au-Prince became the new national capital. Imperial France sent a massive force against Louverture, and the "Black Napoleon" ended his days in the White Napoleon's prison high in the freezing Jura Mountains of France. However, Louverture's protégé General Jacques Dessalines benefited from Europe's preoccupation with Napoleon's wars (and European troops' susceptibility to malaria and yellow fever), humiliating all of Europe's greatest imperial rivals, including a massive British naval force sent out from Southampton. He won independence for Haiti in 1804. Soon Dessalines installed himself, Napoleon-style, as the "populist" emperor of the new Black Nation.[7]

The Haitian Revolution redoubled and amplified the political turmoil in an Atlantic urban world already perturbed by Napoleonic chaos. In London, Parliament's increasingly racist West India Lobby had largely squashed the anti-slavery movement, but British military commanders returning to Southampton from their humiliating fight against the Haitian Revolution turned the political tide for abolition. These commanders had forcibly impressed countless soldiers and sailors from the docks of English cities to subdue Toussaint Louverture and the rebels he inspired in Jamaica. In the Caribbean, the same British commanders watched helplessly as two-thirds of their forces died from tropical disease and slave attacks, suffering more casualties than in the US Revolution. Practical necessity and grudging admiration for their opponents tilted these military men into the abolitionist camp, adding a certain conservative legitimacy to the anti-slavery movement.[8]

Napoleon's determination, meanwhile, to reestablish slavery in the Caribbean raised British abolitionists onto even higher moral ground. Clarkson and his ally in Parliament William Wilberforce could now square their arguments with the cause of imperial rivalry, for abolition would now strengthen Britain and weaken France. When Dessalines then defeated Napoleon's own army to win independence, he made sure that

France would not benefit economically from a British retreat from slavery, depriving the West India lobby of its best pro-slavery argument. Seizing this momentum, Clarkson and Wilberforce turned to their political ace in the hole, the growing working classes of Britain's new factory cities. In Parliament, workers' representatives unrolled massive petitions signed by thousands of Manchester cotton-mill workers that flatly countered their own employers' earlier support for an expansion of the slave trade to bolster cotton plantations in the Southern states of the USA. In 1807, Parliament rose to one of its finest occasions ever, reversing two centuries of state support for the world history's largest-ever slave-trading fleet. Under the Slave Trade Act, the legal status of the shipyards of Liverpool and Bristol, as well as London's own slave docks, transformed overnight from capitals of global capital to nests of pirates. Meeting amidst various construction sites of the new US capital Washington, D.C., the American Congress followed suit a year later.[9]

REVOLUTION OF THE *AMÉRICANOS*

The vast colonies of Spanish and Portuguese America contained well over a million enslaved people alongside a larger number of supposedly "free" subjects of European absolutist kings. Imperial courts in Madrid and Lisbon kept a far stronger iron grip than those in London and Paris on their American colonies through a much older, larger, and more elaborate transoceanic hierarchy based in the hemisphere's largest cities, many now several centuries old. Viceroys in Mexico City, Lima, Bogotá, and Buenos Aires, as well as a Captaincy in Caracas and Royal *Audiencias* in dozens of other cities, turned the king's word into law and enforced it with armed men. In grim ecclesiastical courthouses, the Catholic Inquisition rooted out "liberal" insubordination by declaring the whole Age of Enlightenment a vast form of heresy. Local governments in these cities met in beautiful baroque town halls called *cabildos*, and were strictly limited to the highest-ranking elites. During the French and Haitian Revolutions, the king and the Inquisition cracked down more severely on the circulation of books and printing presses. The colonial authorities hounded, imprisoned, or executed anyone with connection to revolutionary France, the "seductor nation." They also passed harsher laws to play various *castas* of ordinary people against each other and to squash any sign of rebellious behavior on the part of enslaved people. In Portuguese Brazil, the largest slave empire on Earth, similar arrangements operated in the colonial capital of Rio de Janeiro, as well as in the large towns of Salvador da Bahia, Recife, and São Paulo. Not a single printing press operated in any Brazilian city before 1808.[10]

Even political edifices of this magnitude, however, felt the pressures of People Power. As in France and Saint-Domingue, some early challenges arose in Spanish America's rural hinterlands, such as the massive rebellion of the Quechua nobleman Túpac Amaru II in the Peruvian Andes (1780–82). Taking the name of the last Inka emperor, Túpac assembled an enormous army of Native peasants eager to reclaim the empire's past and challenge the Spanish forced labor system in the mines. He laid siege to the former Inka capital of Cuzco, but the viceroy in Lima was able to muster a counterforce of loyal Indigenous troops, and kept the mountains in solid royalist hands, even as new independence movements brewed elsewhere.[11]

More threatening to the Iberian empires were cracks that opened at various subordinate points in their city-based colonial hierarchy and that soon shot back toward Madrid and Lisbon. At fault were the very shipborne circuits of transoceanic exchange that linked colonial cities to the power centers in Europe. Buenos Aires, in the distant South Atlantic, is a good place to see this dynamic in action. After centuries of neglect, the economy of the fortified seaport on the Río de la Plata estuary boomed after 1776 when it became the seat of a viceroyalty controlling not only the flat Pampas cattle-lands nearby but also the southern Andes and Potosí's still functional silver mines. Yet even the most vigilant viceroy, government official, and platoon of soldiers could do little to stop sensational rumors of revolution from filtering into the city's every ordinary household, artisan shop, and slave quarters. The city's harbor was to blame. "Every ship returning to the estuary from Cuba," writes one historian of the city, "brought news from the insurrection in Saint-Domingue and every ship arriving from Spain brought news of the French Revolution." Privately owned public places allowed breathless conversations about these matters, notably Buenos Aires's *pulperías* – dry goods stores that served food, coffee, and alcohol, and that also served as gambling halls, musical entertainment venues, and poor people's banks. Rumors of a "French conspiracy" among the town's mixed-race *pardo* artisans and slaves in 1795 earned the city an enormous vice-regal crackdown, but posters that proclaimed *Viva la Libertad* proliferated on the walls of public buildings over the coming years. Local slaveowners fretted that they controlled their human property less securely than the humiliated plantation owners of Saint-Domingue.[12]

In Buenos Aires and elsewhere in New Spain, urban elites, professionals, and even a few priests found ways of smuggling forbidden texts and ideas into their social circles, despite the viceroy's routine confiscation of books on the customs docks. By late in the first decade of the 1800s, Mariquita Sánchez, the wife of a Buenos Aires merchant, ran a famous republican *tertulia* (salon) in her substantial home on Unquera Street, and high-society women imitated her in the Chilean cities of Santiago and Concepción. In Bogotá, the aristocrat Antonio Nariño gathered with fellow *liberales* in his personal library, which he stocked heavily with banned books; he even possessed a print shop that allowed him to publish France's Declaration of the Rights of Man in Spanish. In Mexico City, the very belly of the absolutist beast, another revolutionary *tertulia* sprang up in the home of the courageous patrician Leona Vicario. In nearby Valladolid, the priest Miguel Hidalgo assigned enlightenment texts to his students in one of the colony's centuries-old Catholic universities. Many Iberian American elites had spent substantial time in London and Paris during their youth, imbibing revolution in person. The Caracas merchant's son Francesco Miranda traveled throughout Europe, and even took a stint as a general in the French revolutionary army. Simón Bolívar, heir to Venezuelan sugar and cacao plantations, grew up for the most part in Europe. He witnessed the self-coronation of Napoleon before embarking on a fervent pilgrimage on foot all the way to Rome, the ancient source of his newfound republican faith; both cities apparently also whetted his Caesar-sized military ambitions. Finally, from Santos, Brazil, the seaport that served São Paulo, the scientist José Bonifacio, son of a wealthy merchant and a Portuguese aristocratic heiress, traveled across Europe before becoming a professor at the Portuguese University of Coimbra, where he espoused abolitionism, justice for

(A)

(B)

12.2. Revolutionary *tertulias* and *pulperías* in Buenos Aires

Revolutions often incubated in small, private urban places. Mariquita Sánchez hosted revolutionary *tertulias* in her Buenos Aires parlor (A) for intellectuals and elites, like her merchant husband. Ordinary artisans, laborers, and caregivers gathered in neighborhood taverns and shops like Buenos Aires's *pulperías* (B). Cities earned a reputation as "liberal spaces" – especially when the countryside trended conservative. Yet divides grew within

Native peoples, and Brazilian independence. All of these figures of the urban Atlantic world are revered today as the founding fathers and mothers of independent Latin American nation states.[13]

From 1809 to 1812, the webs of authority that linked cities in *las Américas* with Madrid and Lisbon suddenly imploded, unexpectedly starting with their central command centers in Europe. Napoleon Bonaparte's armies precipitated the collapse by invading the Iberian Peninsula in 1809. He captured the Spanish royal family, and forced the mortified Portuguese court to retreat by ship, under protection of a British naval escort no less, from Lisbon to Rio de Janeiro. However, it was the collective actions of urban *américanos* themselves – elite monarchists and *liberales* alike, often pushed forward by crowds from popular neighborhoods – that opened out the otherwise unlikely path toward independence. As in Paris's revolutionary Hôtel de Ville, the city halls of the Americas, the *cabildos*, took the lead early on. Although the local elites that dominated local government were mostly staunchly royalist, they resented the authority of "peninsular" viceroys and privileges accorded to the European-born officials who skimmed off much of the colonies' wealth. To these *américano* elites, the collapse of the Spanish monarchy meant that sovereignty should shift into local hands – their own. They formed provisional executive councils or *juntas* – thus giving modern politics another key term. In smaller cities lower in the imperial hierarchy, *cabildos* often declared local autonomy from the *juntas* of the viceregal capitals, forming their own *juntas* and thus further fragmenting chains of urban authority.[14]

Caption for 12.2. (cont.)

urban revolutions, between bourgeois who opposed monarchy but restricted the vote, and more radical popular movements in places like the *pulperías*. "Liberal cities" could also hatch counterrevolutionary movements for "urban order," "national" might, and authoritarian empire. Human power augmented in cities thus remained dangerous, even as it raised new democratic hopes.

(A) Fray Pedro Subercaseaux Errázuriz, "El Himno Nacional Argentina se interpreta por primera vez en las casa de María Sánchez de Thompson, el 14 mayo de 1813," Alamy. (B) Watercolor by Jean Léon Pallière, "Pulpería. Interior," 1858. National Historical Museum, Buenos Aires, Argentina. Alamy.

The proliferation of deliberative bodies allowed a variety of experiments in self-rule, even if only for a tiny few. In Buenos Aires, the *cabildo* became a *junta*, deposed the viceroy, and hired generals to fight off attacks by the British navy on its own. The *junta* declared the independence of the United Provinces of Río de la Plata (later Argentina) in May 1811, and Buenos Aires became the only rebel city to resist the royalist counterthrust to come. Despite launching its own armed expeditions, however, the city's *junta* was unable to assert control over other prominent *cabildos* in its former viceroyalty, such as Montevideo, Asunción, and La Paz. All three later became capitals of separate independent nations. In Caracas, meanwhile, Bolívar and Miranda borrowed language from Thomas Jefferson's Philadelphia declaration to proclaim Venezuela an independent republic in 1811, but they too failed to convince other Venezuelan cities to follow suit. Nariño did the same in Bogotá, but also found himself stymied by autonomous *juntas* elsewhere in the Viceroyalty of New Granada. In the big capitals of Lima and Mexico City, viceroys remained in firm control, though the court in Mexico City had to repel a massive multi-colored peasant rebellion led by Hidalgo. He captured the silver mines at Guanajuato and threatened the capital before the vice-regal army trapped his rebels in a mountain pass and decimated them. Leona Vicario, whose bold *tertulia* in Mexico City had earned her a cell in the viceroy's prison, escaped to join the fleeing rebels, who soon regained force under revolutionary leaders José Morelos and Vicente Guerrero in Oaxaca and Acapulco. Meanwhile, in Rio de Janeiro, Brazil, the exiled King João VI reestablished the ruling institutions of the Portuguese empire in a colonial setting, but that very act expanded the influence of Rio's elite over the Crown, and soon the city's popular neighborhoods sought to have their say. João's British protectors also put pressure on him to end the massive trade in slaves from Portuguese slave forts like Luanda and Benguela in Angola across the South Atlantic.[15]

After Napoleon's defeat at Waterloo in 1815, the royal authorities in Madrid recaptured the initiative for a time, expelling or imprisoning Bolívar, Miranda, and Nariño among others, and reasserting their web of control in all of their colonial capitals except Buenos Aires. The Spanish king refortified Havana, Cuba to safeguard a new sugar colony that now leapfrogged Saint-Domingue as the world's greatest exporter of slave-grown white gold. Cuba, well-fortified Puerto Rico, and the distant Philippines all remained under Madrid's authority – until the Philippine Revolution of 1896 weakened Spain's remaining transoceanic ties, allowing American gunboats to take Manila, Havana, and San Juan two years later. Meanwhile, in 1821 João VI returned to Lisbon, leaving Prince Pedro, his heir apparent, in charge of the monarchical court in Rio.[16]

The counterrevolution sputtered, however, when popular neighborhoods in both Madrid and Lisbon caught their own versions of Atlantic revolutionary fever, and the various *juntas* and parliaments that had ruled Iberia during the Napoleonic interregnum rose from the dead. When a French army of the restored Bourbon King Louis XVIII briefly returned absolutist power to Madrid and Lisbon, detachments of Portuguese and Spanish troops rebelled in major cities, forcing both royal houses to call peoples' assemblies. In the Americas, these whipsawing motions from the imperial center opened enough of a fissure in imperial legitimacy for revolutionaries to start unraveling the transatlantic filaments of Iberian imperial power for good. Bolívar seized the royal naval base at Cartagena de Indias, marched to Caracas, and declared a new republic. Then he slogged back west, up into the freezing Andes to liberate Bogotá. Then he was in Quito, where the swashbuckling Manuela Sáenz fortified him with passionate love and fresh weapons for the assault on the vice-regal powerhouse at Lima. Meanwhile, far to his south, the former Spanish General José de San Martin executed orders from Buenos Aires to cross the Andes with an army of Native Americans and slaves to retake Santiago de Chile. Then, in the nearby port of Valparaíso, he built a fleet for his own attack on Lima. When news of soldiers' revolts in Madrid reached Mexico City at around the same time, royal authority in the northern Vice-Royalty of New Spain collapsed. Viceroy Agustín de Iturbide turned against Madrid, joined forces with the rebel peasant movement of Acapulco, and led the two armies triumphantly into Mexico City, proclaiming it the capital of a new nation. A year later, Lima too fell to rebel armies that poured in from the north and south, then chased the last Spanish viceroy into the Andes, capturing him at the battle of Ayacucho in 1824. In Rio, meanwhile, the Brazilian Emperor Pedro faced overwhelming pressure from the city's inhabitants to ignore his father's command to return to Lisbon and restore Portuguese colonial rule. Merchants in the town government issued proclamations, and ordinary people staged repeated demonstrations in the central Rossio Square and the city's marketplaces. Similar acclamations followed in São Paulo, as did rebellions by the emperor's own troops. Pedro not only agreed to stay in Rio, but soon fought off loyalist rebellions in northern cities, guaranteeing Brazilian independence by early 1824, a few months before the final demise of royal power in Spanish South America.[17]

City by city, the American *liberales* and People's movements unhitched webs of imperial power that once, long before, had inaugurated the truly planetary history of the human habitat. Across the Americas, "nations" came into being where colonies once existed. Most called themselves "independent" and some of them "republics" – governments for, by, and of the people. Yet in 1825, despite the life exertions of Louverture, Bolívar, San Martin, de Gouges, Vicario, Sáenz, and Washington, despite the courageous revolutionary crowds of actual "People" who rose up for republics in cities and the countryside throughout the Atlantic, we were still a long way from the Great Parliament building in Delhi and its 700 million voters. Almost all of the largest "democracies" on Earth restricted voting to male property owners. In the USA, where a few states did allow wider franchises, women, Blacks, and Native Americans mostly could not vote. Many of the new republics endured long spells of rule by dictators, some of whom rose by coup d'état, some of whom received acclamation from large popular crowds. Many more revolutions in urban streets, and some in countrysides, were necessary before long-lived republics could come into being that, on paper anyway, pledged their devotion to representing all of the People.[18]

Nonetheless, the people of many of the world's cities had thrown down a gauntlet. They had shown kings, emperors, and wealthy elites that they knew how to use the spaces they occupied, whether in the most powerful capitals or the most politically suffocated provincial or colonial cities, to challenge the power even of the harshest and furthest-flung of tyrannies. The future promise of People Power thus rested, in great part, on the large size, concentration, complexity, and diversity of space in cities – the same attributes that made urban space such an excellent tool for global empire in the first place. As this reality sank in, a grimly ironic attribute of modern politics emerged. On the one hand, cities became the founts of liberalism, abolition, anti-colonialism, and feminism – and soon radicalism and socialism too. The first "liberal cities" came into being, generators of cutting-edge political ideas that had a fighting chance, even if their adherents made up a tiny portion of the local urban population, let alone of their national polities' often more conservative-leaning rural populations.[19]

On the other hand, as their elites quickly realized, cities had hardly shed their utility as tools of tyranny and conquest. If nothing else, as Bonaparte proved, both strongmen and empires could find ways to sell themselves as expressions of People Power. The arrival of hydrocarbon power added to that prospect. We need look no farther than London, Paris, and Washington – at once the Atlantic's first capitals of "democratic" revolution and the seats of the three imperial polities that also benefited earliest from Cities of Hydrocarbon. These North Atlantic powerhouses showed the world how to do two strangely juxtaposed things at once. While continuing to incubate People's revolution, the worlds most advanced "liberal" cities also became weapons of conquest capable of projecting imperial power that for the first time subordinated the majority of the world's People, including the hundreds of millions of Africa and Asia.

CHAPTER 13

Weapons of World Conquest

CITIES AND EMPIRES (AGAIN)

As London, Paris, and Washington took leading roles as birth-sites both of the Hydrocarbon Revolution and of the People's Revolutions, they also became the spearheads of world history's most extensive exercise in violent imperial conquest. Berlin, Vienna, St. Petersburg, Brussels, Rome, and Tokyo followed suit as "Great Power" national capitals intent on global empire, widening the scramble for colonies across all of the world's continents for the first time. Cities, and the enormous political energies they contained, offered both very old and very new services to these conquering states, all of them essential. Just as always, capitals served as coordinating centers of conquest and administration as well as primary places to celebrate imperial might in stone and monumental space. Then there was the very old matter of projecting hot, hard metal into the bodies of enemies, which now required new industrial weapons-making cities that could transubstantiate hydrocarbon into unprecedented powers of death delivery. Earlier colonial Cities of the Oceans on all continents provided urban beachheads that were essential for dozens of new campaigns of amphibious assault by invading soldiers and for millions of new settlers. All of these cities also became grimly innovative propaganda workshops that made empire ideologically compatible with people's revolution, notably by embedding their polities and their unequally segregated spaces with the ideology of race.

If cities were essential to modern global empires, global conquest also dramatically transformed cities and the Urban Planet beyond. Conquest

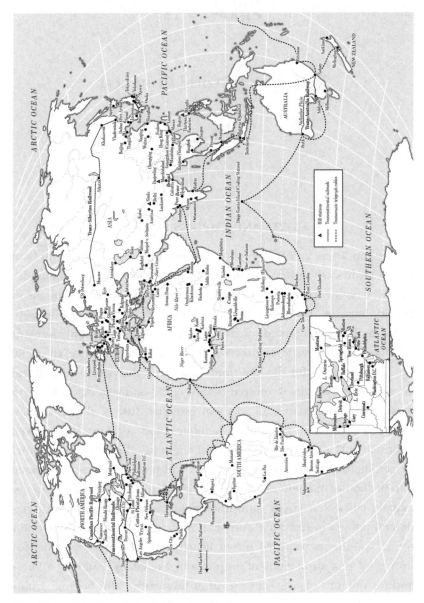

Map 13.1. Explosions of Empire and Capital
Map created by Joe LeMonnier, https://mapartist.com.

helped fuel the nineteenth-century acceleration in the size of cities and the human built environment more generally, while creating new inequalities between imperial metropoles and colonized regions. Empires help explain why their own capitals and arms-making cities exploded especially rapidly during this time, far faster than any cities before, and faster than cities with smaller roles in imperial conquest. Empires also explain the proliferation and uneven growth of brand-new colonial cities, not only along the coasts but deeper into continental interiors. Finally, imperialism helps explain the expansion of new hinterlands for exploitation of farmland, woodland, and mines, and large new additions to global infrastructures of transport, communication, and – of course – imperial power itself.

The most successful urban weapons of imperial conquest were capitals that ruled modern "nation states" – Great Britain, France, and the USA above all. These states defined the geography of their rule by means of a bordered "national" territory, a belief in the shared attributes of its citizen population, a body of law, a galaxy of legislative, executive, and judicial institutions, and an enlarged administrative apparatus staffed not solely by hereditary aristocrats but also by professionally trained civil servants. These bureaucracies aligned themselves closely with capitalist elites from cities across their national realms to assemble the financing, iron (soon the steel), gunpowder, cotton, soldiers' boot-leather, ship's timber, brick, mortar, and fuel required for conquest. They also prided themselves in precise inventories of the national territory, mapping out national, provincial, and city borders, and also surveying and registering the ownership of all of the nation's plots of land. This exercise helped the state to fulfill its obligation to protect private property, encourage its orderly sale and purchase, and enable a "modern" capitalist real estate market.[1]

The idea of a "nation" also did crucial ideological work, as a convenient catchall political tool to align large popular constituencies, including many otherwise inclined toward revolution, into celebrations of patriotism and imperial greatness. Cities were important incubators of modern nationalism. In multitudes of taverns, coffee shops, neighborhood festivals, circus side-shows, popular stages, election hustings, and homes, ideas of national superiority melded with popular and middle-class versions of racism. Many of these took legitimacy from academic notions such as the hierarchy of "civilizations" and "the races" that flowed from elite university lecture halls and laboratories into museums, international exhibition venues, public debating societies, and cities' growing number of public school classrooms. According to such magical lines of thought, superior racial attributes – associated with "whiteness" and male or "paternal" license to violence against "feminine" or "childlike" races of Asia, the Americas, and Africa – were re-imagined as inherited traits, the result of sex conducted exclusively between members of the same race. Soon, white supremacist propaganda achieved its culminant argument by equating conquest with the supposed biological duty of "white" men to subordinate "Black" men in order to preserve the racial and sexual "purity" of white women. Such ideas helped to animate, and then gained strength from, policies of urban racial segregation, a hallmark of city form that drew on practices in imperial capitals but became especially prominent in growing colonial and settler cities.[2]

Still, even as the new imperial powers honed the conquering vigor of these city-weapons, they knew perfectly well that cities could also put empire at mortal risk, even in an age when older existential threats from nomadic and ship-borne raiders had faded. Instead, as modern-era conquerors proceeded with their often bloody work, the strongest forces of resistance they faced everywhere, first in South and East Asia, then in Africa and Southwest Asia, came from states whose power relied heavily on armed force mustered in capital cities or city-states. As in Latin America, a few of these resistant states succeeded in establishing or expanding their own independent capitals during the imperial age – most notably in Bangkok, Kabul, and Addis Ababa. Yet the story of urban anti-imperialism was much larger than that, for even as world conquest proceeded, practices of mass resistance and street revolution linked to ideas of People Power and national independence bubbled out of their Atlantic crucible to *all* cities of our Urban Planet – world-conquering capitals and conquered colonial cities alike (Chapters 16, 17, and 20).

Amidst that rising tumult, though, world conquest still mattered, and profoundly. The new imperial capitals used their early bargains with Hydrocarbon to decisively end the "Age of Parity" between early-modern Cities of Oceans. In its place, modern world conquest opened a "Great Gap" of sharply unequal political power and wealth that redefined the shape of all realms of Earthopolis. As this gap first widened, it helped cause and took force from a highly skewed, two-centuries-long period of urban acceleration in which conquering capitals and industrial cities grew at unprecedented rates that left even the people who lived in them utterly confounded. The unequal shape of this, the first of two Hydrocarbon-induced, empire-skewed accelerations of our Urban Planet, can be most vividly perceived in differences between the lists of the ten largest cities in the world in 1750 and 1900. In 1750, eight out of the top ten were in the great gunpowder empires of Asia. Beijing, Edo, Istanbul, Guangzhou, and Osaka were the biggest of all; from Europe's Oceanic empires only London and Paris made the list. The highest estimates of the population of Beijing and Edo in 1750 range around one million, a threshold that cities had exceeded only a dozen or so times since ancient Rome. Fast forward to 1900, and London alone commanded the very top of the list with a precedent-shattering 6.5 million, New York was second with 4.5 million, Paris third with 3.5, Berlin fourth at 2.5, followed by Chicago, Vienna, Tokyo, St. Petersburg, Philadelphia, and Manchester, all home to between 1 and 1.75 million people. Other than the Japanese imperial capital Tokyo, the big Asian capitals had now all slid into a second tier, mixed in with other upstarts like Birmingham, Buenos Aires, Calcutta, and Shanghai – all industrial weapons cities or primary colonial sub-capital cities of European empires. Of course, we cannot attribute the explosive growth of, say, London or Paris to empire alone, since both commanded advantageous riverine and/or oceanic locations for centuries, and both were financial and hydrocarbon industrial centers in their own right. Water also explains why Washington, D.C. was the one imperial capital *not* to make the list. New York and Chicago grew at either end of the liquid pathway between the Hudson River and the Great Lakes, connected by the Erie Canal after 1825, that enabled the USA to conduct its own amphibious conquest of the richest city-feeding hinterland since the great river valleys of China. The presence of Manchester and Philadelphia on the list of the top ten – with Birmingham, Osaka, Pittsburgh, and many other industrial cities not far behind – demonstrates too that the capitalist factory revolution, stimulated by imperial arms manufacture to be sure, could also push a city well beyond the million mark (Chapter 14).

GUN CITIES

As in ancient and early-modern times, conquest depended on the weaponization of many other cities beyond capitals. Ironically, the world's largest empires came into being at a time when the oldest form of urban weaponization, the city wall, fell into disuse – most quickly, as a matter of fact, in the cities of those global empires' national heartlands. Partly that was because cities in those places were starting to grow too quickly for wall builders to keep pace (Paris did get a new, very long set of walls between 1841 and 1846, in recognition of France's vulnerability to attack across the flatlands to the northeast, but even these were removed after 1919). Walls also stood in the way of the ambitions of new professional urban planners who were eager to quicken movement within cities (Chapter 15). Mostly, though, walls fell because industrial cities were simultaneously developing new guns whose only effective military deterrent was other guns.[3]

Indeed, world conquest now required guns produced on industrial scales, and that meant empires could not do without gun-making cities – the nuclei of today's grim "military–industrial complexes." The use of Hydrocarbon to power these gun-cities is crucial to explaining the end of military parity based on pre-industrial cannons, battleships, and low, thick city walls. Thanks to coke-fired iron and bronze furnaces, the artisans and tinkerers of cities like Birmingham, London, the French cities of St. Étienne and Le Creuset, Belgium's Liège, and the American cities of New Haven, Connecticut and Springfield, Massachusetts began building much more lethal forms of cannons and guns – and built them in larger numbers – than anyone had ever deemed possible. Continuous warfare between France and Britain, including during the American revolutionary wars and the Napoleonic period, stoked the necessary urban energies involved. To defeat Britain, scientists in France pioneered experiments at military schools involving the drag on different-sized cannonballs and calculations about flight path and timing (Napoleon himself participated in these as a student at Louis XVI's École Militaire).

"Improvements" in death-dealing technology included bronze cannons and the incendiary shells that gradually ushered city walls into obsolescence. To defeat France, the British Board of Ordinance insisted on fostering competition between networks of gunsmiths in Birmingham and rivals in the London area that stimulated thousands of small, incremental, and ultimately terrifying refinements in rifles and guns of all kinds. Gunpowder-sorting machines created deadlier propellants. Meanwhile in the new USA, the federal government under George Washington subsidized industrial capitalists in New Haven and the US Armory at Springfield – including Eli Whitney, the famous inventor of the cotton gin. Whitney developed forges and machines that made guns from interchangeable parts, speeding production processes and easing battlefield repairs, further increasing lethality. Soon, hydrocarbon power boosted long-range killing technology even more directly with the launch of the first true coal- and steam-powered battleship, named the *Napoléon*, at the French naval base at Toulon. These ships also tied global imperialism to the construction of coaling stations in colonial cities, at the mouth of new canals such as those that pierced the isthmuses of Suez and Panama, and on remote ocean islands like St. Helena, Diego Garcia, and Pearl Harbor, Hawai'i. Meanwhile, Britain's new ironclad battleships perplexed cannoneers, forcing more innovations – such as cannons made of steel. The use of coal-fired railroads for military supply lines came only a bit later in the century. So did the direct application of mechanical motion to gunfire – the machine gun.[4]

As important as they were, deadlier guns and urban military industrial complexes did not change global geopolitics alone, for European and American merchants eagerly traded guns for goods overseas, including with the people they soon sought to conquer – Native American warrior bands, African kings and emirs, and the various sovereigns of India during the decline of the Mughal Empire. By contrast, the Chinese military had decidedly atrophied in the years after 1759 and received no weapons from Europe. The Qing emperor's historic conquest of the steppes that year and his subsequent victories over the sea people of China's long coastline gave the country decades of relative peace. As a result, China, the first of all gunpowder empires, lost its main incentive to develop new weapons, including a navy. In Tokugawa Japan, a similar "long peace" reigned under the iron fist of the shogun. Meanwhile, in the West, no matter the circumstances of their potential rivals, industrial gun-cities kept up such a fast pace of technological development, provided replacement parts and ammunition to battlefields so much more reliably, and so relentlessly increased the volume of production that the only way to defeat an empire with a weapon-building city was to build another city that built even deadlier weapons. Only a few states with access to factory technology were able to do that effectively in the nineteenth century. The Prussians who soon ruled Germany did so at the Krupp works in Essen; the Austrian Habsburgs at the Škoda weapons works in Plzeň, Bohemia; the Belgian King Leopold in workshops at Liège; the Russian tsars in the Putilov weapons works in their own capital of St. Petersburg; and the Meiji dynasty at Koishikawa Arsenal and Yokosuka Naval Base, both in the Tokyo Bay area. Such places did not allow imperial forces to win every battle they fought against less well-armed adversaries, but, on balance, they soon enabled very real, and very large, conquests.[5]

GATEWAYS TO CONQUEST, "STATIONS" OF RULE

Along with gun cities, Western imperialists also had the advantage of urban "weapons" previously stationed abroad – the chains of colonial seaports they controlled on the ocean shores of most regions of the world. As naval ports and sea-to-land mustering grounds, these cities provided wide-open gateways for new larger-scale projections of military power. In the Americas, Australasia, the Pacific, and a few large regions of Africa, they also served as entry points for massive new waves of European settlers and other migrant workers who were so important to the continued conquest of those continents. British and American warships even developed imperial advantage in the growing seaports of independent Latin America. When merchant ships bearing cheaper, higher-quality, factory-made goods from Boston or Liverpool entered factory-poor Rio de Janeiro or Buenos Aires, they could pry customers away from local urban artisans, re-igniting artisans' now well-established traditions of street politics. London and New York banks financed large-scale development projects such as cotton plantations, cattle ranches, mines, and railroads to transport locally extracted raw materials to port and generate at least some of the cash Latin Americans needed to pay for more imports. They opened branch offices in Latin American capitals, indebting elites and bringing proud declarations of national "independence" by liberal *américanos* into question. If local artisan insurrections or populist demagogues threatened to raise import tariffs or seize foreign assets, British and American warships moved in merchant ships' wakes into *américano* harbors to ensure that profits continued to flow outward. Washington's use of such "big sticks" to discipline Latin American governments increased over the course of the nineteenth century, amounting to a "second conquest" of the continent that slowed industrialization of its cities considerably until the 1930s.[6]

The greatest alteration in modern geopolitics, though, was the West's sudden domination of the great gunpowder empires of Asia. The central pivot-point of this power-shift was the British colonial city of Calcutta. When we last visited that city, in 1756, the British East India Company had learned, to its great humiliation, how costly a mistake it was to skimp on improvements to overseas fortresses during the age of global gunpowder parity. At the time, the Mughal emperor still ruled from his dynasty's formidable Red Fort in Delhi, but he struggled to control his provincial governors (*nawabs*), who had grown rich enough from local taxes to establish gunpowder power centers of their own. One of these was at Murshidabad, the stunning capital of the nawabs of Bengal. In the 1760s, the nettlesome Nawab Siraj-ud Daula ruled Murshidabad. His generals ignored Delhi, serially trading commercial favors with local British, French, and Dutch companies in exchange for weapons from Birmingham, St. Étienne, and Liège. When the British made a few small improvements to the slim Fort William at their thriving Bengali outpost at Calcutta, the Nawab's army spotted the threat and quickly overran the city. A few of the Nawab's subordinates jammed 200 British citizens into a small room in Fort William, locked the doors, and suffocated them to death during the night. To avenge the humiliating "Black Hole of Calcutta," the Company's General Robert Clive called in favors from his counterpart in the Nawab's army, Mir Jafar, who turned on his employer, allowing the British to defeat the Nawab and install Jafar as their puppet in Murshidabad. To stop this British coup, the French and

Dutch East India Companies quickly allied themselves with other Mughal governors and the emperor himself. However, the British forces, relying heavily on hired Indian troops called sepoys, defeated them all at the famous Battle of Plassey north of Calcutta in 1757. The Mughal had no choice but to grant the British Company the right to govern Bengal, levying taxes on it and two other rich provinces with a combined population far larger than Britain itself.[7]

With immense revenue pouring into British Calcutta, on top of the wealth from increased mercantile activity in the interior, the former trading "factory" quickly became a gleaming "City of Palaces." In the center of the new capital, the British governor general ruled from a Government House as imposing as the Tuileries – that is, whenever he chose not to stay at another palace a few miles out of town, at Barrackpore, which was often compared to Versailles. A massive star-shaped Fort William replaced the rickety affair that the Nawab had overrun. In addition, after 1775, Calcutta had its own Board of Ordinance, modeled on that at London's Woolwich. Gunpowder mills and gun shops sprouted in the near suburbs. Today's formidable Indian arms industry was a British creation that dates from this time.[8]

Soon, the British authorities at Calcutta repeated their bloody act of conquest all over South Asia, relying on the Mughals' increasingly shaky authority over their governors and on Anglo-Indian armies equipped in Birmingham, Enfield, and now Calcutta itself. Victories over the Nawab of Awadh, governor of a Mughal province further up the Ganges Valley with a lavish court at Lucknow, helped fuel longer wars against the Nizam of Hyderabad and sultans of Mysore in the south. Other campaigns followed against the Maratha Empire based in Pune and elsewhere in central-west India; the Burmese Empire based at Mandalay and other capitals in the Irrawaddy River Valley to the east; and the rising Sikh Empire to the north, centered on the Golden Temple in Amritsar. Beyond that, several massive invasions of Afghanistan, meant to counter Russian influence in the region, met with a succession of humiliations inflicted in part by kin-based armies sworn to Islamic *jihad* who occupied craggy fortresses in remote mountain valleys. An independent emirate governed these so-called "Graveyards of Empire" from an enormous palace in Kabul, giving headaches to the British – and then other

Map 13.2. Conquering a City, a River, and a Continent: Calcutta
European imperialism in Asia pivoted on control of Calcutta. After a humiliating defeat there (1756), the British conquered Bengal and ruled it from Fort William (lower left), the Government House (center), and the palatial "White Town" (lower right). It took more than guns and imposing buildings to control the majority "Black Town" to the north and the Hooghly River (Chapter 15), both blamed for global cholera pandemics. By 1854, the date of this map, urban "sanitarians" had straightened streets, hardened riverbanks, and installed sewers. As Calcutta mustered British conquests across India, the city's port funneled opium eastward, in a dastardly gambit to undermine China's Qing dynasty. Royal Geographical Society/Getty Images.

imperialists – into the twenty-first century. The Company's seaports at Bombay and Madras grew as they took on roles similar to Calcutta, martialing the Company's often ruinously expensive imports of weapons and allowing the disembarkation of tens of thousands of British soldiers and officers, many of whom would die of tropical diseases while leading armies that were otherwise mostly composed of Indian sepoys. Advances in weapons played an important role in the overall trend of conquest, though earlier sales to Indian princes like Tipu Sultan of Mysore in exchange for pepper or for help against the French minimized the British advantage. This resulted in especially bloody encounters, such as the epic siege of Seringapatam (1799), where the British killed Tipu and took Mysore after more than a decade of war.

In 1857, when the British conquest of India appeared largely complete, the introduction of a new rifle from the royal weapons factory at Enfield backfired badly on the new empire, sparking a rebellion of the Company's sepoys based at Barrackpore. The new cartridge casings, or so the sepoys had heard, contained sealant made of either pork or beef fat, offending both Muslim and Hindu troops. Their rebellion against British officers spread to garrisons in Lucknow and throughout the Valley of the Ganges. Various rebel princes soon elevated the last Mughal emperor, still in residence at the dynasty's Red Fort in Delhi, as their leader. Thus began the "Sepoy Mutiny," really the First War of Indian Independence. British cannons, however, had been increasingly successful in winning sieges against fortified Indian cities. In 1857, the British brutally stormed Lucknow, then turned their bronze cannons on the Kashmiri Gate of Delhi itself. British soldiers who survived the bloody assault on the gate overran the Red Fort, then looted and destroyed dozens of surrounding palaces owned by the Mughal court aristocracy. Buoyed by this victory, but skittish about the possibility of new rebellions, London abolished the Company's ineffective rule and invested Britain's own Queen Victoria as Empress of all India.[9]

To govern all India, the new "British Raj" supplemented its capital at Calcutta with a new form of weaponized built space. By the late nineteenth century, the British had constructed over 175 "cantonments" across the subcontinent, from the Afghan frontier to the Malay Peninsula, generally located five to ten miles away from the major cities they conquered. These were above all military bases, stations for British troops and far larger numbers of sepoys, though some cantonments also contained a "civil station" for administrators. In addition, to avoid disease and exhaustion from India's summer heat, British imperial officials and soldiers regularly rotated through dozens of "hill stations" they built at higher, cooler altitudes. Simla in the Himalayan foothills was the most famous of these; others included Darjeeling in the Eastern

Himalayas, and Ootacamund in the Western Ghats. At great expense each summer, the entire administration left steamy Calcutta behind to spend "the season" amidst the bracing breezes of Simla. These Indian hill stations mimicked one the Dutch had built in Java 100 years earlier at Buitenzorg. They also inspired similar retreats later in French Indochina (Ba Na and Tam Dao) and the American-ruled Philippines (Baguio); indeed, all of these examples showed the importance of hill stations for the conquest and administration of other extensive tropical territories that were similar to those under British rule in India.[10]

A few elements of these "stations" are worth noting. First, they were un-walled. Defense of British rule largely depended on placing its army and weapons depots at an aloof distance from town. When rebellious sepoys overran the giant British station at Lucknow in 1857, the local military commanders who retook the city, at great cost in lives, later simply built another station and cantonment further out. Secondly, this use of distance also translated into a form of racial segregation. The British depended upon provisions supplied by thousands of Indian shop owners who set up dense bazaars within the stations, at some distance from the houses of British officers, but accessible to the hundreds of Indian cooks and servants who lived in the bungalows alongside their white employers. Separate "lal bazaars" or Indian sex markets catered to largely single-male British soldiers willing to cross race lines from their nearby barracks. The majority of sepoys lived in distant "Native Lines," generally living in "hutments" with their families. Thirdly, in the stations, the houses of the British officers and officials were laid out with wide surrounding yards between them, in a way that exaggerated the placement of aristocratic households around the squares of London's West End. The tiny white credentialed minority thus took up by far the greatest share of the stations' real estate. In this way, these otherwise strange towns reflected a growing worldwide critique of urban density, which in India focused on the dangers of the teeming "Black Town" that surrounded Calcutta's palaces – and the stations' own bustling bazaars. Back in Europe and the USA, the same critique focused on alarmed descriptions of working-class "slums" (Chapters 15 and 16). In this way the spread-out "Officers' Lines" of the British stations helped pioneer a contrasting type of habitat deemed more "modern" – what we now rightly revile as suburban sprawl.[11]

CONCESSIONS IN THE EAST

In China and Japan, Britain possessed no urban beachhead like Calcutta. The Qing and Tokugawa emperors had devoted only a few acres of urban land out of their vast empires to the activities of the entire European and North American imperial project – and then to merchants only. We already know about one of these slivers of real estate, the tiny artificial island of Deshima in Japan's Nagasaki harbor that was restricted to Dutch traders under strict supervision by Tokugawa agents. Then there was the equally tiny "Thirteen Factories" section of Guangzhou (Canton), China – 350 by 200 meters of reclaimed land amidst the Pearl River docklands that contained the offices and warehouses (still called "factories") of all the Europeans and Americans who traded with China. Here the rules were very strict as well, reflecting the Qing dynasty's own predisposition for segregation. First, Qing bureaucrats opened the European neighborhood only during the October to April trading season. During those months, the monsoons allowed ocean ships to sail through the "Tiger's Mouth" of the Pearl River Delta up to an anchorage at Huangpo ("Whampoa") island. There they discharged their cargos onto ferries that made their way up the shallower parts of the river to the factories. Secondly, only men were allowed. When they came to the Factories in October, merchants had to leave their wives at the agents' off-season quarters at Portuguese-administered Macao on the far side of the Delta. Thirdly, while in the European quarter of Guangzhou, they could not leave their allotted premises, except for occasional promenades in the city's suburbs; it was strictly forbidden to pass through the gates of the third largest city in the world. Finally, foreign merchants had to negotiate prices with a single Chinese import-export Company, the Cohong, which worked under the supervision of the emperor's own governor general in the walled city.[12]

Yet, from that tiny speck of urban land, merchants were able to perform actions of enormous scope, profit, and, ultimately, world-altering importance. The Cohong assembled huge warehouses full of silk, porcelain, and tea from the Chinese interior nearby. The British East India Company shipped in cargos of their famous woolens from Leeds and increasing amounts of factory-produced cotton cloth from Manchester. American merchants from Boston and New York circumnavigated the Americas, exchanging their own factory goods for whatever silver they could acquire from the dwindling mines of independent Peru and Mexico, beaver pelts from Native traders on the Oregon coast, and sweet-smelling sandalwood from Hawai'i prized by Chinese customers. Once delivered to Guangzhou, the customs duties on these items provided the Qing court in Beijing with an increasingly crucial source of revenue at a time when its own internal system of fixed taxes on land could not keep up with its increasing obligations to China's fast-growing population. On the other end of the "Canton system," whenever British tea ships arrived back in London, they paid tariffs that were crucial to Britain's war budget; tea duties, for example, amounted to one-tenth of the revenues of the British Crown – and were essential to paying for the armed forces needed to defeat Napoleon. The tea itself also provided the caffeine that Manchester mill workers and Birmingham gunsmiths needed to get through their brutal workdays. As for the East India Company, two-thirds of its annual income came from tea sales. With that money, among other things, it bought guns in Birmingham that allowed it to conquer new parts of India.[13]

In the 1820s, the British conquest of the Indian countryside yielded a new valuable commercial hinterland for the European traders of Canton. The East India Company began growing opium poppies in Oudh and Bengal, assembling huge quantities of the drug in warehouses in Patna and Calcutta, and selling it to independent traders who shipped it from Calcutta's Kidderpore docks to the Pearl River Delta. Since opium was illegal in China, drug runners had to operate largely outside the Thirteen Factories and the Whampoa anchorage. To do that, opium ships heaved to further down the Pearl River at places like Lintin Island, where they offloaded their cargos onto clandestine British and American "receiving ships" which functioned as floating warehouses capable of evading the Qing authorities if needed. Chinese opium smugglers then appeared out of the vast maze of the Delta's muggy rivers on fifty-oar "fast crab" boats to buy opium. They paid in silver – another illegal act that drained the empire of the currency that Chinese subjects were obliged to use when paying taxes. The captains of receiving ships would then quietly deliver the silver to their own offices in one of the Thirteen Factories, from which it made its way back to Calcutta for more opium purchases.[14]

In Calcutta, opium revenues not only helped pay for further conquests in South Asia, but also spurred the colonial capital city's growth to a half million – easily among the world's twenty largest cities of the day. It also gave Calcutta a friendly rival in India, as opium produced on as-yet-unconquered Maratha lands in western India began flowing through the growing port of Bombay. Bombay's Parsi opium merchants soon established their own offices in Canton's Thirteen Factories, and the increased supply caused the price of the drug in China to plummet, allowing people of modest means to smoke it. Opium parlors proliferated in Chinese cities. Some court eunuchs in Beijing became hopeless addicts themselves. The heir apparent to the Qing throne even tried it in his chambers in the Forbidden City. Precious silver flowed out of the Celestial Empire, increasing its price in terms of other metals, and thus compounding the tax burden of Chinese peasants, whose copper coins bought less and less of the silver they needed to pay to the emperor. Such troubles sowed the seeds of future rebellion.[15]

By the 1830s, the formerly opium-curious Qing Crown Prince had become the Daoguang Emperor. After much debate, he adopted a hard line on European, American, and Bombay Parsi opium smugglers, many of whom had become chief merchants in some of the largest corporations in London, Boston, and Bombay. Daoguang's formidable envoy in Guangzhou, Lin Zexu, surrounded the Thirteen Factories with troops, forced all Chinese employees to leave, held the European residents of the quarter prisoner in their own offices, and frightened the British superintendent into purchasing, at British taxpayers' expense, all of the opium cargos then arriving in the Tiger's Mouth. In a major propaganda triumph, Lin Zexu dumped the contents of 20,000 chests of opium into the surrounding swamps, mashed it with mud and lye, and then let the narcotic sludge trickle out to sea.[16]

That moment of Chinese victory, like the Nawab's Black Hole of Calcutta, was short lived. The sensational blow that Lin Zexu delivered at the Thirteen Factories – both to the British Treasury and to London's imperial honor – gave Parliament the pretext to wage the one-sided Opium Wars of 1837–42 and 1858–60 against China. From the start, however, these wars focused less on revenge than on expanding Europeans' access to wealth in Chinese cities beyond the Thirteen Factories. The British, later with help from France, were able to seize this "right" to "free trade" because of another watershed event. China's city walls – the thickest and most formidable in global urban history – failed to protect Chinese soldiers and civilians from massacres caused by European guns, cannons, steamships, and ironclads. The British navy's unmolested trip in 1842 up the Yangtze to China's secondary capital at Nanjing highlighted what became twenty years of repeated mortifications of the Qing dynasty.[17]

At Nanjing, the British forced the emperor to sign the first of a series of "unequal treaties," this one giving Britain unimpeded control over the island of Hong Kong, and substantial "concessions" of port-front land in other Chinese coastal cities, to be governed by Europeans for the purpose of unmolested trade with Chinese merchants. These conceded territories included Shamen Island near Guangzhou, enclaves at the ports of Amoy (Xiamen) and Fuzhou, and the biggest prize of all, the British and French Concessions along the Huangpo River in Shanghai – soon the site of the impressive mercantile houses of the city's riverside "Bund." In 1860, British and French forces compounded the humiliation of the Qing when they arrived at the gates of Beijing itself. French soldiers scaled the walls of the imperial dynasty's own quarters in the Forbidden City, the Yuanminguan Palace complex, and touched off an orgy of plunder that ended only when a British general burned much of the compound to the ground. A new degrading treaty, this time signed in the smoldering imperial capital, gave foreigners access to still more portside concessions, including the port of Tianjin near Beijing.[18]

In the meantime, British and French merchants and warships meandered up the Chao Phraya River in today's Thailand to Bangkok, where they gained similar trading rights from the king of Siam and settled in a European District to the south of the walled palace and temple city. Nonetheless, the dynasty was able to keep Siam independent by playing the two European adversaries against each other, allowing Bangkok to industrialize faster than other cities in the region. A few years later, armed steamships from the USA made an even more consequential landing in Edo Bay, Japan. Laden with industrially produced goods, their Commodore Matthew Perry forced the Tokugawa shogun to abolish the Deshima system and open up Japan's ports in similar fashion, with concessions of dockside land for foreigners' use. Thus began the transformation of the swamp-side fishing town of Yokohama near Edo into Japan's gateway to world commerce, and later its second-largest city. Osaka and the nearby new port of Kobe had similar foreigners' districts, as did Nagasaki itself and several other Japanese cities. The Meiji also set aside land in the capital itself for foreign embassies and missionaries.[19]

In China and Japan, the foreign humiliation of centuries-old dynasties stirred up forces of rebellion. In China, the rebel leader of the so-called "Taiping Heavenly Kingdom" built a massive army against the Qing. He established a capital at Nanjing from 1853 to 1864 and ruled many of the Yangtze Valley cities, but failed to capture Beijing after one of world history's bloodiest wars, in which tens of millions died. In Japan, *daimyō* (nobles) from southeastern castle towns rebelled and entered the ancient imperial capital of Kyoto with armies of samurai equipped with European weapons, calling upon the emperor to end the now-feckless rule of the Tokugawa shogun and reassert Japan's power against the foreign menace. Commoners flooded into the streets of Kyoto, staging massive carnivalesque uprisings called *Ee ja nai ka* ("What the hell!") that satirized the shogun's weakness. Eroticized, gender-bending street theater, some of it based on *kabuki* characters, soon spread to cities from Hiroshima to Edo. Unable to control the rebels, the last shogun resigned, and in 1868, the Meiji dynasty took power in Edo, renaming the city "Western Capital" – Tokyo. Under the restored emperor, the rebel *daimyō* sent a delegation to San Francisco, Washington, Paris, London, and Berlin in search of the technologies and models of statecraft Japan required to prevent further colonization by the West and by Russian incursions into East Asia. The Meiji regime embarked on imperial projects of its own, first by intensifying Tokugawa conquests of the northern island of Hokkaido, seizing land from the indigenous Ainu people and founding the city of Sapporo as a magnet for settler colonists. In 1876, Tokyo forced the Joseon dynasty of Korea to grant Japan concessions of its own at the seaports of Incheon and Busan. In 1894, Japan turned on China, subduing the weak Qing navy and taking Taiwan and "treaty ports" at Dairen and Port Arthur. Japan also gained access to the concessions at Shanghai, and, with them, membership among the world's "Great Powers." By seizing their own segregated pieces of Chinese coastal cities, the Japanese also gained equal right to use river ship routes and to build railroads into the interior.[20]

LET LOOSE THE SETTLERS

Another, far more destructive form of nineteenth-century imperial conquest was settler colonialism: an accelerated, often genocidal, effort by the world's city-based imperial states to seize lands from people who lived primarily in villages or camps and replace them with large numbers of settlers from the national territory of the invaders. In earlier years, regimes in Madrid, Lisbon, Beijing, and St. Petersburg were the leading forces behind such settler-assisted conquests. In the nineteenth century, the British, the USA, the Empire of Brazil, and the Republics of Argentina and Chile took the lead – launching armies and waves of settlers across what they called "frontiers" in new armed assaults on the Native peoples of the Americas and Australasia. (Japan's annexation of Hokkaido involved similar dynamics on a smaller scale; it foreshadowed efforts to establish a Japanese settler colony in Chinese Manchuria during the 1930s.) Wherever it occurred, this "Great Land Grab" involved the massacre of hundreds of thousands and the death by disease of millions more. The built environment transformed radically across enormous swaths of the planet, as settlers' and soldiers' guns opened extensive new city-serving hinterlands that soon fell under the power of state land surveyors, the plow, and the railroad. Settlers' forts became the nuclei of some of the Urban Planet's youngest and most important cities.

In this type of conquest, nation states' "modern" insistence on precise land surveying played a critical role; surveyors' tents and land registry offices were crucial built structures of settler colonialism. Also important were the "pioneering" actions of squatter-settlers who were citizens of the colonizing state, who illegally or semi-legally claimed Native land by building small dwellings or pounding out a fenced perimeter beyond the reach of both state power and surveyors, and who then called for protection whenever Native peoples rejected their claims, sometimes with acts of armed resistance. While the state officially disapproved of settler squatting, both squatters and the state's frontier armies acted on a common vision of the built environment linked closely to ideologies of race. This vision held, first, that societies based on cities and farms with plowed fields were of a higher order of "civilization." Second, that building towns, cities, and individually owned farms represented necessary "improvements" to the natural environment. Third, people who did not "improve" the environment in these ways signaled their membership of inferior and unproductive races of humans with no title to the land that superior races were obliged to honor. Fourth, only one particular form of title to land held any merit, namely a title of individual proprietorship to a plot with fixed, state-surveyed boundaries, certified by a title registry, a body of law, and a system of property courts. Finally, lands beyond the frontier of "improvement" and land surveyors' tents were therefore empty, *terra nullius*. "Improvement" – building, settler style – was thus either the fulfillment of a covenant with God or the "manifest destiny" of the white race.[21]

In North America, already existing fortified cities on the coast, the rivers, and the Great Lakes provided the main conduits for westward conquests. In the 1820s, inspired by similar feats of canal building in France and Britain, the US State of New York financed the construction of the Erie Canal connecting New York City and the Great Lakes through a low point in the Appalachian chain, vastly easing movements of troops and settlers to the west. Over the course of the nineteenth century, the USA alone built no fewer than 500 forts and barracks west of the Appalachians to wage war against Native people in the interest of squatters and white settlers. A similar eastward pincer movement soon also began from the Pacific Ocean cities of California and British Columbia. In Australia and Aotearoa/New Zealand, meanwhile, the first white urban colonial outposts came into being later than anywhere in the Americas, with the 1788 transshipment of convicts from the streets of British cities to Botany Bay, the site of the future city of Sydney. The white-settled kernels of Brisbane, Melbourne, Adelaide, Perth, Auckland, and Wellington date from the years 1799 to 1840. In South America, urban centers had existed deep in the interior since the conquests of the sixteenth century, or, in the case of Brazil's interior "General Mines" (Minas Gerais) region, since the late seventeenth. New waves of conquest involved military campaigns southward into the Native lands of Patagonia and, in Brazil, deep into the Amazon.[22]

Weapons revolutions in Enfield, England and the American military-industrial complex in the Connecticut River Valley hastened the pace of nineteenth-century settler colonialism. Advanced guns made their way by trade, and by raids on armories, into the smaller settlements of Native peoples. These weapons enhanced the advantage Native military leaders shared with defenders of dispersed habitats throughout history, that wide spaces could weaken imperial power wielded from urban capitals. In response to conquest, Native peoples often fortified their villages and camps, as they had since the first arrivals of European settlers. Wooden palisades could be very effective against white settlers, notably the *pa* fortresses of Aotearoa/New Zealand, which the Maori built on prominent places that they carved out with steep step-like walls to repel attackers – the *pa* also had wells and food storage systems for outlasting sieges. Along the shores of the Amazon, formerly enslaved and Native people living in settlements of self-built huts (*cabanas*) united in a revolution called the *Cabanagem* in the 1830s, defying imperial and provincial forces. There, and in palisaded settlements elsewhere, resistance could hold out for decades, in many cases in the face of indiscriminate massacres, arson, and destruction of traditional ways of making a livelihood, such as when US soldiers mowed down whole herds of plains bison. Native people won numerous pitched battles against the invaders, engaged in guerrilla warfare, and, when military means failed, alternated strategic retreat with artful diplomacy. As settler numbers increased, so did the likelihood of deadly infectious diseases in Native settlements. Because of these epidemics, because white settlers were so numerous and so disruptive of traditional economies, and because both conquering soldiers and settlers had more direct access to the supply of industrial weapons and replacement parts, Native resistance fighters faced overwhelmingly unfavorable odds. For the survivors of the horrific acts of genocide that often followed, defeat took the form of peace treaties (often negotiated in bad faith by conquerors), and relocation to "reserves" or "reservations" which conquering states typically carved out of least desirable lands, sometimes far from traditional territories, supervised at an agency post by a state officer, and divided into individual plots that were largely useless for traditional foraging livelihoods, let alone farms. The conquering states also followed up by removing Native children from families to distant boarding schools aimed to train new generations for life in cities or on farms in city-serving agricultural hinterlands.[23]

Amidst wars of conquest, "frontiers" shifted and melted – and Native land became urban hinterland. Government surveying teams staked out orthogonal grids that they subdivided into farm-sized plots. Beginning in the 1860s, homestead laws passed by American and British authorities in both North America and Australasia granted new "open" land to settlers in farm-size plots free of charge in exchange for pledges of future "improvements." In the two continents' grasslands and mountain valleys, a thin but extensive new habitat came into being, made up of homesteader's cabins, sod houses, cattle and sheep posts, mining camps, then thousands of barns, silos, farmhouses, and spreading acres of plowed land or, in drier areas, immense livestock ranches. Some homesteaders turned their plots into "town-sites," subdividing their government-issued rectangles of land into many smaller ones, creating a grid of streets. Then they subdivided each street block into parcels for sale as building sites. The founders of these towns were betting on the fertility of the surrounding land and the richness of local forest or mineral resources. In Australasia, small interior towns grew within larger landscapes of settler farms, sheep posts, and mines that fed the cities like Sydney and Melbourne that, in turn, provided the jumping off points for conquest and arrival points for new settlers. In North America, the resources of the interior and the natural transport routes were unparalleled in any other lands conquered by nineteenth-century imperialists. Dozens of small town-sites and fortified outposts exploded into large cities over the course of the century of conquest, most notably along the rivers, the Erie Canal and the Great Lakes linking booming New York City to booming Chicago and from there via railroads toward the mountains and to growing settler cities on the Pacific (Chapter 14).[24]

STARTING GATES OF THE SCRAMBLE

As late as the 1860s, most of Africa remained beyond the reach of all three forms of city-based imperial conquest elsewhere: British Indian-style cities of conquest and colonial administration, East Asian style commercial concessions, and North American-style or Australasian-style settler cities. In the bloody "Scramble" for Africa of 1885–99, European empires unleashed all three of these urban weapons at once, engulfing the world's second-largest continent in colonial rule, expanding imperial control over existing colonial cities, seizing dozens of independent city states, and expanding cities everywhere, in many ways anticipating Africa's far more explosive African urban acceleration in the late twentieth century. As on most other ocean shores, Western conquerors had scouted the starting gates of conquest much earlier. These included, first, the former slave "castles" of West Africa, some of which had become minor merchant concessions in palm oil and other agricultural products as the slave trade waned. Second, there was the British-ruled "refreshment station" at Cape Town and its small Dutch-settler hinterland. Third, the sultan of Zanzibar had taken over the Portuguese colonial towns on the Swahili Coast, but they remained open for commerce – often still in slaves headed to Asia. Fourth, in Africa's north, Europeans found their way into the capitals of large Ottoman provinces. There, like in Mughal Murshidabad, governors in places like Algiers, Fez, Tunis, and Cairo operated mostly beyond the control of Istanbul. In so doing, they softened up the southern shore of the Mediterranean Sea for other would-be conquerors from Europe.

The city of Algiers was the first to fall to the new wave of European imperialism, ironically thanks to the latest People's Revolution in Paris, that of 1830. For years, the largely independent *bey* (governor) who ruled Algiers had annoyed imperial authorities in Paris, London, and even Washington by commissioning local corsairs to capture Western ships, sometimes selling their white crews into slavery. In Paris, meanwhile, the latest "restored" Bourbon King Charles X faced revolution from a restive urban bourgeoisie and from popular neighborhoods that had grown substantially since the toppling of the Bastille in 1789. Charles made a vain attempt in 1830 to distract the revolutionaries with a glorious act of national military might, sending 30,000 French troops to subdue nettlesome Algiers. Parisians saw right through the trick. During three "glorious" Paris days in July of that year, the descendants of the *sans-culottes* built 6,000 barricades to defy royal troops. Once again, they occupied the Tuileries, the Louvre, and the Hôtel de Ville. Fearing another Reign of Terror, General Lafayette, now seventy, intervened for a third time on an Atlantic revolutionary stage, this time to propose a "liberal" King, Louis Philippe – from the renegade wing of the royal family who had developed the bohemian shopping mall at the Palais Royal. Charles X fled France, forever extinguishing the dynasty of the Sun King. In Algiers, meanwhile, the French army sowed a true Reign of Terror, setting fire to the city's elegant seafront districts, Turkish *funduqs*, mosques and all, and chasing the *bey* out of town. The paradoxical result was that the so-called "People's King" of France inherited a bloody multi-decade imperial war against North African Arabs, who waged fierce resistance under the leadership of Emir Abdelkader in the mountains. As Parisians soured on Louis Philippe, then lurched toward an even bigger, European-wide republican revolution in 1848, the army of the People's King annexed "Algeria" directly to France. French land court judges invalidated Ottoman land titles and re-registered them according to legal guidelines set in Paris to settlers from France, Italy, and Spain. Thus, Europeans swiftly took over the colony's choice farms and urban neighborhoods, including Algiers's flattened Marine Quarter. Arab inhabitants of Algiers who did not flee to Abdelkader's lines huddled in the city's upper town, named after the *bey*'s castle on the peak of the hill – the Casbah. As in India's stations, the racial segregation of the Marine Quarter, rebuilt in this case in the style of a French provincial town, provided the empire with a built symbol of European superiority and a built base from which to conquer other cities, divide them, and administer the colony as a whole.[25]

Meanwhile, speaking of conquest and segregation, London encouraged settlers to flood the docks of Cape Town, capital of the Cape of Good Hope Colony, which had fallen under British rule since the Napoleonic wars. More whites piled onto the Colony's wharves further east at Port Elizabeth, East London, and then Durban, the capital of another new settler colony named Natal. As in the Americas and

Australasia, British troops fought redoubtable Native armies, first the Xhosa and later the Zulu, for decades, hoping to seize land for white farmers and herders. When Parliament abolished slavery in the British Empire in 1834, many longer-established Dutch Afrikaans-speaking farmers, known as the *Boers*, packed their ox carts and fled inland with their slaves and servants, where they established two white men's republics, with *Volksrads* (Parliaments) of their own in the villages of Bloemfontein and Pretoria. These white men's republics also fought imperial wars against African kingdoms for land.[26]

Decades later, in 1886, prospectors discovered the richest gold seam in the world near a low-lying ridge fifty kilometers south of Boer-run Pretoria known as the Witwatersrand. Mining tents, laid out on a classic settlers' street grid, blossomed on farms nearby, soon becoming wooden and then stone structures. Within a few years, the Witwatersrand had transformed into a forty-kilometer-long string of boomtowns, centered on the goldmines of the brand new city of Johannesburg. The tiny Boer republics now possessed a coveted asset of the highest order. After much skullduggery by British and French mine-owners, London declared war against the Boers in 1899. Three years of gruesome battle followed, during which the Boers resorted to guerrilla tactics and the British built some of the world's first concentration camps to keep Boer women and children from provisioning the guerrillas. The British won the Boer War in 1902, but Boers and British settlers joined the four colonies of South Africa in 1910 in a racist whites-only Westminster-style "democracy" called the Union of South Africa. Settlers then used their new Parliament in Pretoria to formalize a system of racial segregation that gave the white minority control over the vast bulk of the country's best agricultural land and urban real estate, putting in place many of the segregation laws that would undergird the notorious regime of apartheid after World War II. The British meanwhile pushed into the Rhodesias to the north, and imposed similar forms of settler rule on the countryside and in the divided cities of Salisbury, Bulawayo, and Livingstone. Settlers in all of these cities, as at Johannesburg, established "Native Locations" outside town to remind Blacks of their inferior status.[27]

Well before the Boer War, Europeans began "scrambling" in earnest for the rest of Africa. Leopold I, King of the Belgians, was the unlikely instigator. Disappointed with the tininess of his European realm, first founded in 1830, he set Belgium on its path to imperial glory in the early 1880s by hiring Henry Morton Stanley to reconnoiter several thousand kilometers of the Congo River watershed in Central Africa. From his desk in the Château de Tervuren, Leopold's "Versailles" near Brussels, the king contracted with merchants to ship guns from Liège, iron rails, locomotive parts, and even dismantled steam-fired paddleboats to a former Dutch slave port at the mouth of the Congo called Boma. Soldiers used the guns to press locals into a form of forced labor hardly distinguishable from slavery. At great loss of life, Leopold's enslaved laborers blasted a rail-line eastward through solid rock to bypass 100 kilometers of the lower Congo rapids. Sections of steamboats then made their way on railcars to the wider, flatter parts of the river at a place named after the king himself – Léopoldville, today's Kinshasa. Soon his colonial agents chugged far up the many rivers that feed the Congo, founding port-towns (one was called Stanleyville – today's Kisangani) where they forced villagers to compete against each other to meet Leopold's quotas of ivory and later rubber.[28]

Leopold's seizure of the Congo set fire to nationalist rivalries across Europe, in particular the old Franco-British one. Germany and Italy became unified nation states for the first time, and in Berlin and Rome, just as in Brussels, they too pursued the common wisdom that great nations required colonial conquests. In 1884, Chancellor Otto von Bismarck of Germany, fearing presciently that rivalries in Africa could lead to a world war in Europe, invited representatives of the major powers to Berlin to divide the continent into spheres of influence based on their supposedly pre-existing commercial and diplomatic ties in various African coastal seaports. To offset King Leopold's ambitions, the French government sent its own explorer Pierre de Brazza on a trip from Libreville, a coastal mission for freed slaves (and the capital of today's nation of Gabon), to the north shore of the Congo River, where, opposite Léopoldville, he founded Brazzaville. Bismarck, whose Germany had few ties in Africa, encouraged mercantile companies from Hamburg to lease segregated concessions at the West African port cities of Lomé and Duala. Following the mantra "merchants first, soldiers after," he used these supposedly peaceful beachheads to control the interiors of Togoland and Cameroon. The British government, which had purchased former slave castles along the "Gold Coast" from various companies over the previous half century, now invaded the Ashante Kingdom of the interior, capturing its court at Kumasi, but only after two bloody wars. From Lagos and other Niger Delta slave ports, British forces also seized the walled city of Benin, after a long war, and similar cities across Yorubaland including the port of Lagos itself, then besieged the powerful Sahel emirates capitals of Sokoto, Kano, Kaduna, and Zaria in the northern part of what they called Nigeria. The French outflanked the British further to the north by racing inland from Dakar on the far west coast, taking the adobe mosque cities of the Niger Bend in still more bloody wars with other emirs and consolidating control over most of the Sahel and the Sahara. Other West African slave ports and missionary stations provided starting gates for conquests of French colonies at Porto Novo (Dahomey) and at Grand-Bassam (near today's Abidjan), where subsequent wars against the powerful Baoulé Kingdom based at the interior city of Sakassie resulted in the foundation of the Ivory Coast. The port cities of the West African coast, like later ones in East Africa, all acquired small segregated European districts. They transformed from starting gates of the imperial scramble into centers of what their historian Frederick Cooper calls "gatekeeper" colonial states. European officials there financed the colonial administration by gathering tariffs in their harbors from exported agricultural and mineral goods destined for European markets, creating a strong disincentive to industrial development while still focusing urban growth on "primate" capitals like Dakar, Abidjan, Accra, Lagos, and Léopoldville. Such "underdevelopment" resembled sluggish industrial growth elsewhere in colonial world. Institutional underdevelopment followed, for gatekeeper cities also served for the offloading of European troops to maintain order. The soldiers withdrew when these cities became capitals of independent countries, and new governments struggled to keep order in places where imperialists had done little to foster any sense of popular loyalty to a state, least of all a "national" one.[29]

In Africa's northeast, the Scramble pivoted upon two great waterways: the ancient Pharaohs' Nile River and the brand-new Suez Canal (finished in 1869). The Canal – like many other expensive urban and rural development projects in Egypt, Buenos Aires, Rio, Bangkok, and Shanghai – was financed by a European company supported and partly owned by the independent-minded Ottoman khedives of Egypt, at first Khedive Said, and later his successor, Ismail "the Magnificent." In addition to increasing the European population of Egyptian cities, the net effect of these companies and their projects was to put the khedives in increasing debt to French and British banks. In 1882, Arab nationalists rebelled in the streets of Cairo and Alexandria and called on the khedival military to oust the Europeans. British and French forces shelled Alexandria, defeated the rebel army, and placed the British Chief Representative Lord Cromer in a supervisory position over the khedive in Cairo, establishing an effective colony there that remained under London's thumb until the 1920s and beyond.[30]

The Suez Canal – run by British authorities from a segregated administrative center called Ismailia (in a back-handed compliment to the khedive) and supervised at each end by newly built segregated port cities (Port Said and Suez itself) – created a vital new shipping corridor though the Mediterranean and Red Seas. Notably, it cut the distance between London and Bombay by almost 9,000 kilometers. To maximize control over the Canal's approach routes, British, French, Italian, German, Russian, and Ottoman imperialists proceeded to play chess with port cities that stretched from French Tunis on the Mediterranean, to Italian Asmara on the Red Sea, to German Dar es Salaam on the Swahili Coast. Each became a new gateway for colonial conquest, and most contained segregated administrative districts for overseas officials. Outside Egypt, the biggest colonial prize was the old Swahili city of Mombasa, which the British seized as the terminus of a railroad into the Kenya Highlands and Uganda, the source of the Nile River. The new colony of Kenya became yet another destination for European settlers, and its main railroad center at Nairobi grew swiftly – in a strictly segregated fashion that resembled South Africa.[31]

Control of the Nile, still as crucial to Egyptian agriculture as it was in ancient times, became an increasingly important strategic concern as Lord Cromer proceeded with plans to build the enormous Aswan Dam in Upper Egypt and expand cotton production downstream. Upstream of the dam, however, two expansionist African regimes remained in control of the Nile's two main tributaries and resisted European influence. High in the mountainous watershed of the Blue Nile, the Christian Emperor Menelik of Ethiopia, allied with Tsarist Russia, used cannons made in St. Petersburg to humiliate an Italian army that sought to expand its Red Sea colonies inland. After his victory in 1896, Menelik began building the city of Addis Ababa as a capital for the only African empire to resist Europe (that project too indebted him to European banks). Meanwhile in Sudan, a powerful movement led by a man proclaiming himself the Mahdi, an Islamic Messiah, killed the British governor at the colonial capital Khartoum. From this reclaimed capital, the Mahdi expanded his influence throughout the Upper White Nile. His project ended in disaster in 1898, however, when Anglo-Egyptian soldiers avenged the governor's death by mowing down the Mahdi's forces with machine guns across the Nile from Khartoum at the battle of at Omdurman. That year, a final face-off between Britain and France at the nearby town of Fashoda ended with France deferring to its rival's might in the Nile Valley, mercifully ending the Scramble for Africa.[32]

THE URBAN PLANET'S GREAT GAP

By the time of Fashoda, only a few cities on Earth had escaped the dominance of Western empires (see Figure 13.1) – and a new imperial power was on the rise in Asia, the Meiji Empire in Tokyo. The scale of conquest was unprecedented, and it was unthinkable without Hydrocarbon Cities of many kinds: the largest capitals up to that point in world history; weapons complexes; growing segregated colonial cities; and new settler boomtowns exemplified by Chicago, Vancouver, Johannesburg, and Sydney. Cities everywhere grew bigger, and so did the Urban Planet itself. Yet the biggest bouts of urban growth occurred in just a few places: imperial Europe, the Americas, and Japan. In Columbus's time, 81 percent of the world's total population lived outside those nineteenth-century Great Powers' national territories, most of them in China; by 1900, that number had fallen to 68 percent. The Great Gap thus replaced the Age of Parity with a truly novel axis of global urban inequality favoring the new imperialist nations over the rest of Earthopolis, most of it colonized, all of it deemed by conquerors inferior

13.1. Postcard from Addis Ababa: The Ethiopian Emperor Menelik and His Palace
Postcards like this typically depict subservient "natives" in "exotic" Western colonial cities.
Not this one: Menelik founded his own empire after defeating Europeans, building Addis
Ababa near Barara, an ancient capital of Ethiopia (Abyssinia). Other urban states in Africa
resisted colonizers too: the 1,000-year-old kingdom of Benin, the emirate of Sokoto, the
Ashante Kingdom at Kumasi, and the state of the Mahdi, an Islamic visionary who ruled
briefly from Khartoum, a colonial city seized from the British. Menelik's empire embodied
hopes for Black independence worldwide. Today, some call Addis Ababa the "Capital of
Africa" because it hosts the Organization for African Unity, but Ethiopia's diverse peoples
repeatedly contested the power wielded in Menelik's capital, launching anti-colonial
movements of their own.
Culture Club/Hulton Archive/Getty Images.

in terms of both "race" and the character of its built environment. That
said, while conquest *affected* everything in the Urban Planet of the nineteenth century, it does not *explain* everything about the abrupt nineteenth-century urban acceleration. For the rest, we need to explore the
next chapters in the biography of Earthopolis – those that tell the stories
of industrial capitalists, of urban planners, and of the millions of working
people that empires helped set in motion – from the world's farming
countryside towards newly conquered lands and, above all, to new and
accelerating industrial and colonial cities.[33]

CHAPTER 14

Capitalist Explosions

AN EARTHOPOLIS OF, BY, AND FIXED FOR THE CAPITALISTS?

Of all people on Earth, those who had the means to pool capital, invest it, and reap profit from it gained more than anyone from the era of Hydrocarbon, People Power, and global empire. During the nineteenth century, practitioners of the capitalist arts made profit from a much larger range of activities than before – most centered in cities, and most related to factories. Capitalist practice exploded in all dimensions. The numbers of capitalists themselves multiplied, as did their representation among the global elite, their personal wealth, the wealth of their newly chartered corporations, their share of global wealth, and their political, economic, and cultural power. The managerial classes and the workforces capitalists employed also swelled exponentially. Capitalists' political, economic, and cultural power within urban polities and the state overshadowed that of hereditary landholders and imperial dynasties for the first time, as did their contribution to human inequality and human immiseration. Capitalists set in motion new, far more turbulent cycles of economic boom and depression, while contributing decisively to the Great Gap between industrialized and colonized worlds. Their control over the human habitat exploded and so did the sheer geographical range of their activities. They seized vast tracts of urban land and gained decisive power over the size and shape of cities. The tentacles of their profit-making habitat spread worldwide, expanding the remotest outer boundaries of Earthopolis as a whole. From their commanding seats in all of these new spaces, capitalists radically increased humanity's impact on Earth. Much of today's expanding Urban Planetary realm of consequence too represents deferred costs that capitalists began shunting on to future generations in nineteenth-century cities.

The capitalist explosion involved an explosion of Urban Planetary construction that drew upon the era's global empires and extended them. Capitalists *themselves* did not build factories, skyscrapers, their own elite neighborhoods, worker housing for their millions of employees, ports, canals, railroads, pipelines, or sub-ocean cables – not personally, not with their own hands, exactly. Yet, as the poolers of the required capital, they controlled and managed much of what happened. This capital came from many sources: massive government subsidies above all; from the thin air of bank lending; by recruiting, paying, and often brutally supervising the labor of humans on vast new scales; from the swelling value of their own urban real estate holdings; by mining and burning tons of coal; by exploitation of the soil and the minerals of the Earth; and of course by accumulating more and more profit.

That said, capitalists could not set off all of these explosions on their own. Modern nation states, with their own anchors in urban polities and their vast extension of imperial power across all continents, were essential. Whether these states were "democracies," old-regime autocracies, Napoleon-style populist dictatorships, or global empires did not matter so much. Capitalists received support from nineteenth-century states of all kinds, though they benefited most from the world's most powerful ones. Even in a politically tumultuous age, capitalists fought and won far more political battles in imperial capitals than they lost. Meanwhile they also pushed states themselves to take on new powers and capacities that benefited the business of profit making.

The most important political victories of the capitalists – the real fuses of the capitalist explosion – involved important commitments by the world's most powerful imperial states to rescue the most fragile, riskiest, most expensive, and most powerful urban investment project in the capitalist portfolio: the hydrocarbon-fueled factory. Nothing about the industrial revolution was fated to happen just because coal-fired steam engines were so good at turning the wheels and gears of other machines. In an era of political upheaval, factory owners needed the help of imperial states to supply the vast cotton lands, the many other raw materials, the transport and communications infrastructure, the masses of customers, and above all the factory workers that transformed a factory into something that actually rewarded its investors with profit. All of these things were missing or at least uncertain when the first factory steam engines began belching smoke into the air of Manchester in the 1780s. Each involved its own unpredictable plot twist in the form of a political problem that only a growing empire, itself beset by revolution, could solve. The solutions to those problems, in turn, always meant building something new and often enormous: a new spatial "fix" for new problems faced by profit makers.

Was the nineteenth-century explosion of the world's Cities of Hydrocarbon the exact same thing as what theorists call the "process of capitalist urbanization"? Yes, and No. Yes, the nineteenth-century explosion of Earthopolis was at once the detonator and the fallout of the era's explosions of hydrocarbon industrial capital, and it would not have happened without capitalist factory owners, bankers, and real estate developers. Yet remember: capitalists needed empire, just as empire needed capitalists – every step of the way. Moreover, as imperial and capitalist cities grew, they needed planners to make those larger cities work, and – of course – they needed people, not only millions of industrial workers, but millions of people who lived in expanding urban hinterlands required by industry and industrial cities. The word "process" far overstates how smoothly things went, and building "capitalist" cities required many actors who were not accumulators of profit. It is no accident that this chapter on capitalist explosions is not the first, nor the last – let alone the *only* – chapter in the broader, multifaceted, highly unequal, and often interrupted story of the acceleration of Earthopolis of Hydrocarbon.[1]

MORE PLOT TWISTS IN SMOKESTACK CITIES

In our "global urban historical" explanation for the rise of coal and capital in cities, the first episodes (Chapter 10) led us through the many uncertain plot twists linking London's chimneys to Manchester's earliest smokestacks in the 1780s. Almost immediately, however, the Hydrocarbon Revolution and the People's Revolution collided. The owners of cotton mills – the factories attached to most of Manchester's belching smokestacks – faced a new life-threatening cliffhanger, for the Haitian Revolution wiped out the main supply of raw cotton they needed to feed into the maw of their mills.

At that moment of reckoning, one capitalist investor and one vigorous imperial state rushed to the rescue, offering various fixes involving technology, the law, and space. The capitalist was the American tinkerer and gun manufacturer Eli Whitney, whose famous cotton gin fixed a problem for large-scale cotton growers who needed to remove the plant's unwanted seeds from the fluff that made the money. Arguably even more important was Whitney's relationship to the empire in question, the expansion-minded federal government of the USA and its growing army. Eli Whitney, as we know, also made guns, and US President George Washington (no stranger to the difficulties of having too few guns) had personally made sure the new government lavishly subsidized the mass-production system Whitney developed in his New Haven gun factory. Whitney's weapons, added to those manufactured at the federal armory in Springfield, Massachusetts up the river, helped the new US conquer Native land west of the Appalachians. In the Northwest, that conquest resulted in huge losses of land for Native people and new farms for millions of settlers. In the Southwest – Alabama and Mississippi in particular – most of the Native land went to much wealthier people: capitalist investors who built hundreds of massive, slave-powered cotton plantations, the most important spatial fix textile industrialists could have wished for.[2]

As capital followed conquest into that region, countless trees fell, and millions of acres of thick Mississippi River bottomland shifted around plow blades to accommodate cotton plants. Some of the new plantations became home to over 1,000 enslaved people each. Since the slave trade from Africa was illegal after 1808, many of these bonded laborers came from now depleted tobacco farms near Washington's own plantation at Mount Vernon, Virginia. They arrived at the new cotton plantations chained together in "coffles," forced to walk over hundreds of miles of poor roads. Like sugar plantations, cotton plantations were industrial locations in their own right, dispersed across the countryside, yet complete with large ginning complexes and cotton presses that squashed the voluminous white fiber into compact bales for efficient transport.[3]

From such rural raw-capital-producing habitats, cotton bales made their way to river cities along the Mississippi River, in territory that the

USA purchased from Napoleon in 1803 (after his defeat in Haiti), and that US federal armies proceeded to empty of Native people by force and disease. In New Orleans, the greatest of the Louisiana cotton entrepôts, factors arranged transshipment from riverboats to ocean-going ships that increasingly ran on steam engines themselves, speeding the trade toward Britain and increasing its volume. In this very elaborate way, thanks crucially to the guns of the US army and the whips of plantation slavery, Manchester got its cotton, and that city's great experiment with Hydrocarbon power lived on.[4]

Not so fast! Big obstacles remained. Manchester lay thirty-five kilometers from the sea. How was all that cotton to get to the mills from the holds of ocean ships? Another imperial state, the British one this time, stepped in, to offer yet another series of spatial fixes for existential problems in the history of the urban factory. The first task was to resurrect the city of Liverpool, the closest seaport to Manchester, transforming a now-illegal center of the slave trade into a much larger port capable of unloading millions of bales of US cotton while *on*-loading tons of factory-finished thread and cloth onto other ships bound for customers all around the world. To make this possible, shipping company directors traveled from Liverpool to London to lobby Parliament for "Private Acts" allowing them to offer stock, and thus to pool the capital necessary to expand their port city's pioneering "enclosed" docks – sealed off from the rise and fall of ocean tides by a system of seawalls and locks. Over the course of the late eighteenth and early nineteenth centuries, dock-making companies continually reconstructed Liverpool's port, eventually settling on massive granite blocks from Scotland as a building material. Soon the Liverpool docks extended along twelve kilometers of the River Mersey estuary. In 1849, upon landing at Liverpool after a trip from New York, the American writer Herman Melville sputtered with superlatives. "Long China walls of masonry." "Equal to what I had read of the old pyramids of Egypt." "A chain of immense fortresses." Waterways that "recalled to mind the great American chain of lakes." How much more "wonder and delight" Liverpool presented to him than "the miserable wooden wharves, and slip-shod, shambling piers of New York."[5]

From the Liverpool docks to Manchester, incoming cotton and outgoing finished goods could move by the winding Mersey and Irwell

Rivers, but only when the water was high enough. When the water was too low, stevedores needed to transfer the cotton onto horse carts for a trip along miserable muddy turnpikes. To solve this problem, more capitalists took more trips to London to pass more Private Acts, this time chartering canal companies. The most famous of these factory-fixing spaces was that of the estate owner Lord Bridgewater. His canal connected the Mersey River to Manchester and, as a bonus, also ran north to coalmines on his estate. The coal-supplying end of the Bridgewater Canal actually tunneled deep into one end of his mine, allowing workers to load fuel directly onto barges while also draining water from the shafts above. At the Manchester end, the canal's elevated water level required Bridgewater's engineers to design an aqueduct that carried the canal, water, coal barges and all, *over* the River Irwell. The canal quickly cut the price of coal in half, making steam-engine-driven mills even more profitable, while also cheapening transport of cotton and goods both ways to Liverpool. "Canal mania" spread across the industrial lands of Britain, notably in the region around Birmingham, and soon gave inspiration to the builders of the much longer Erie Canal (1824), financed directly by New York State. The Suez (1869) and Panama (1903) Canals – later corporate ventures backed by imperial states – were the great-grandchildren of the Bridgewater Canal.[6]

All of these petitions to Parliament added up to enough legislative work that its Members soon passed a Corporations Law – imitated shortly afterward by the USA and France – that made it easier for capitalists to found a so-called Limited Liability Corporation. Once investors registered a company as an "LLC," or put "Incorporated" at the end of its name, their liabilities were limited to the money they invested in the company. The corporation's creditors, in other words, could not sue the company for any of its investors' own personal assets. This was another massive government-granted gift to capitalists, a certification that the state would accord to capitalists' wealth what the legal scholar Katharina Pistor calls an "exorbitant privilege" in all disputes. Although new corporations faced more competition than the chartered monopolies of the early-modern period, LLC laws allowed any group of capitalists to acquire what many in fact became: state-endorsed, privately owned, city-empowered vehicles of global power.[7]

In 1830, the first regularly scheduled freight and passenger railroad line began moving bales of American plantation cotton from Liverpool to Manchester, bypassing and underpricing the Bridgewater Canal. Its fifty kilometers of parallel iron tracks was the joint project of an LLC consisting of a merchant, a cotton mill-owner, and a land speculator who raised additional money by selling shares to the public at the Royal Exchange in London. Parliament enabled the company to take all of the land it needed, including pieces of estates owned by a pair of very dismayed dukes. The Manchester and Liverpool Railroad included built structures that would become commonplace in the Urban Planet of the future: a tunnel under a city (at the Liverpool docks), a long causeway through a wetland, a signaling system based on an early version of telegraphy, some of the first iron-reinforced bridges, several viaducts, including one that arched far over the worker's houses of factory towns near Manchester, and rail stations that grew more impressive as the century wore on.[8]

Thanks to various technical, legal, and above all spatial fixes engineered through imperial states, industrial capitalism began to explode on its own. All of the state-enabled, corporate-funded innovations in the built environment, from plantation to freight yard, allowed Liverpool to become the central pivot-point for a new set of large-scale activities that made up world history's first global, "unipolar," industrial sourcing and marketing system. At the Liverpool docks, the system's central "pole," merchants set prices for raw cotton – after 1809, they did so in a magnificent cotton exchange building. These prices in turn determined the amount of land that the American army expropriated and deforested for cotton, and the number of slaves that plantation owners sold "down the river" to newly cleared plantation fields. Meanwhile, Manchester mill-owners attracted buyers for their finished thread and cloth from around the world. Already in 1815, the city had over 1,500 showrooms designed to impress buyers with the virtues of its cotton goods. British mercantile houses set up dozens of shops of their own in Buenos Aires, Rio, Lima and other newly independent Latin American capitals, underselling local spinners and weavers, and riling up local crowds of unemployed artisanal spinners and weavers. Similar dynamics operated in post-Opium War China and, most momentously, in India, where the millennia-old village textile industry slowly collapsed due to competition from cheaper, higher-quality, Manchester-made imports.[9]

Profits available in the nearly inexhaustible global market in cheap mass-produced textiles quickly attracted manufacturing capitalists outside Britain. Though the British Parliament outlawed the sale of industrial technology abroad, profit had a way of speaking louder than the law. Factories – and not just factories, but all of the built infrastructure needed to sustain a factory system – began to spread. New "Manchesters" came into being at Mulhouse, France; Ghent, Belgium; Ratingen and Chemnitz, Germany; the Catalan valley towns in Spain; Puebla, Mexico; and – for a short time, under the energetic auspices of

COTTON BALES LYING AT THE BOMBAY TERMINUS OF THE GREAT INDIAN PENINSULA RAILWAY READY FOR SHIPMENT TO ENGLAND.—SEE SUPPLEMENT, PAGE 59.

14.1. Yet Another "Spatial Fix" for the Capitalists: The Cotton Pier, Bombay
The story of "capitalist urbanization" contains many political plot twists. As this woodcut from Bombay attests, imperial states often jumped in at moments of crisis to "fix" urban planetary space to keep private profits flowing. When the US Civil War disrupted cotton shipments to British textile factories, British India's colonial government subsidized new port facilities and warehouses in Bombay, and a rail-line into the interior, where state-seized land was converted to cotton growing. Manchester capitalists avoided the calamity we know today as "deindustrialization." Bombay grew to the largest city in India, soon with textile mills of its own.
Dinodia Photo/Getty Images.

the Egyptian Khedive Muhammad Ali (the predecessor of Said and Ismail whom we have already met) – in the Khumrufish quarter of Cairo. Mercantile companies in Le Havre, Bremen, Barcelona, Boston, and Alexandria sought to rival New Orleans and Liverpool in the import and export of this new form of "white gold," and railroad companies reaped overland transport fees.[10]

Then, suddenly, in 1861, this pulsing industrial revolution faced yet another moment of reckoning. In Washington, for years, senators from the Southern slave states of the USA had battled "free laborites" and abolitionists from the Northern states who opposed the South's dream to extend their plantation lands into Native and Mexican territory beyond the Mississippi. In 1861, the rival imperial projects of South and North came into collision, with the election of Abraham Lincoln and a political party devoted to ending the expansion of slavery. In the bloody Civil War that followed, Lincoln's Union navy blockaded Southern ports like New Orleans and Charleston, ending cotton shipments. Manchester's capitalists laid off thousands, and the unemployed rioted in the streets. An era of urban "deindustrialization" once again appeared imminent. In new corporate boardrooms, capitalists despaired at the unimaginable potential loss of all their enormous investments in built structures.[11]

Yet again, imperial states came to the rescue. The British Parliament passed legislation that encouraged Indian farmers to switch to cotton production, notably in the western province of Berar, which had recently been seized from the Nizam of Hyderabad. New roads and railroads brought bales from there to Bombay. Even as Bombay's raw cotton exports skyrocketed, the city's Parsi merchant families plowed opium money into their own textile mills, bringing a taste of the industrial revolution to a corner of Asia for the first time. Bombay soon outpaced Calcutta as the largest city in South Asia. Meanwhile in Egypt, Khedive Said, whose textile mills had fallen into ruins due to aggressive British tariffs, instead seized land from his own *fellahin* (peasants) and used new loans from London and Paris to cover the Nile Delta with cotton plantations, many worked by semi-enslaved laborers from Egypt's own colony in Sudan (the site of the future Mahdi rebellion). New railroads shipped cotton bales to Alexandria and from there to Liverpool. In Brazil, despite the opposition of sugar and coffee growers, more of the country's forests became cotton plantations, and a few textile mills opened in Rio, despite protest from local artisans and the Manchester lobby in London.[12]

In 1865, after the US South's defeat in the Civil War, American cotton planters resumed production, using debt-bound sharecroppers instead of enslaved workers. Texas, Oklahoma, and California became new centers of cotton growing, just as textile capitalists of all kinds had hoped before the war. Water-powered mills sprouted in towns in the Carolinas and Virginia, especially along the "fall line" of rivers that poured out of the Appalachian Mountains. In Japan, after Commodore Perry's visit to Edo Bay, the modernizing Meiji dynasty encouraged Japanese merchants in Osaka to build a huge concentration of spinning mills and smaller weaving shops, earning Osaka the nickname "Manchester of the Orient." Meiji Japan opened up cotton fields in the hinterlands of its treaty ports in Korea, and then conquered the entire peninsula (1911). Meanwhile, amidst the Scramble for Africa, French and German officials opened up still more cotton lands. Cities like Dakar, Lomé (in German Togoland), and Dar es Salaam took on some of the same raw-cotton-exporting role as New Orleans and Alexandria. In East and West Africa, imperial powers explicitly rejected setting up textile mills (to avoid competition with those back in Britain, France, and Germany). Yet they did run railroads between the ports and the cotton fields that to this day remain the sum total of West Africa's rail systems, largely useless for passenger networks and far sparser than those of Europe, the Americas, and Asia. These railroads also concentrated state power and wealth heavily in the port cities that, as we know, became collection spots for cotton tariffs that accounted for most of the colonial state's revenues: the "gateway city" system we have already met (Chapter 13).[13]

As new areas of the world's forest and grassland fell under the plow, as rivers came under increasing pressure to water cotton plants, and as growers resorted to hydrocarbon-based fertilizers to replenish taxed soil systems, the very Earth released enormous tonnages of carbon dioxide into its atmosphere. In that way, the actions of all types of cotton capitalists presaged the gigantic contribution that industrial monocrop agriculture makes to climate change in our own time (Chapter 21).

CITIES OF IRON AND STEEL

By repeatedly rescuing and supporting textile capitalists, imperial states went on to play a crucial role in the "second industrial revolution," an even more tumultuous force in the nineteenth-century urban explosion. By the 1850s, industrialists' need for cheap coal, rails, metal beams, trains, and steamship engines spawned a need for new built structures that could house much heavier industrial activities – iron and steel mills; locomotive and train car works; the first oil and gas wells, pipelines, and refineries; and power plants for electricity. Not incidentally, heavy-weapons-producing complexes also expanded during this time, often close nearby. Imperial states' assistance in creating new sources of raw materials did not stop at cotton. New colonies also provided iron and other metal ores, lubricants, rubber, leather, forest products, and other cash crops. Meanwhile, empires also remained the major clients for arms manufacturers' instruments of violence. Exploding second industrial revolution cities thus both encouraged and fed upon urban synergies of capitalism and empire.

The factory cities of northern England once again set off one of the crucial sparks for the second industrial revolution, in this case a particularly important development in metallurgy. France's Emperor Napoleon III, who took power in a coup d'état in Paris three years after the 1848 European revolution, nervously watched as metalworkers in the German town of Essen experimented with new ways to turn larger amounts of iron into steel. As he expected, they soon used that harder metal to cast terrifying new cannons. Louis Napoleon had mentioned his worries to the British inventor Henry Bessemer, then residing in Paris. Back in England a few years later, Bessemer found a way to scale up a technique first used (once again) in the Song period in China, and put this so-called Bessemer process to work at a huge steelworks in the city of Sheffield. It quickly attracted the attention of capitalists around the world. Money could be made not only from steel weapons, but also from longer-lasting steel rails for trains, and stronger steel beams to support bridges and the stouter buildings needed to house heavier steel machinery.[14]

The career of the Scottish-born American steelmaker Andrew Carnegie closely tracks the transformation of the built environment as the first industrial revolution led to the second. Born in a tiny weaver's cottage during the period when Manchester was making cottage-based weavers obsolete, Carnegie migrated with his family to Allegheny, Pennsylvania, near Pittsburgh, to work in a textile mill. Soon he was a telegraph boy for the octopus-like Pennsylvania Railroad Company, a job that allowed him to build contacts with prominent local capitalists who supplied the city's steel mills with coal. They introduced him to investment opportunities in other companies – builders of iron bridges, constructors of luxury Pullman train cars for intercity business travel, drillers of some the first petroleum wells in northwest Pennsylvania, and forgers of cannons and other steel weapons for the Union forces in the Civil War. The wartime industrial boom earned Carnegie enough wealth to buy the largest Bessemer steel mills in the Pittsburgh area. Soon he owned the railroad and steamship companies that supplied his mills with coal from Eastern Pennsylvania and iron ore from Minnesota.[15]

Meanwhile, in the German city of Essen, the career of Alfred Krupp followed similar lines. It was he who used a pre-Bessemer process to forge the steel guns that so frightened Louis Napoleon III. In the 1860s, the king of Prussia, Wilhelm I, whose domains included Essen, used Krupp's guns to defeat rival powers in Germany, with gimlet-eyed guidance from the "Iron Chancellor" Otto von Bismarck. Then, in 1870, Prussia humiliated the French army and its inferior bronze cannons, taking Louis Napoleon himself prisoner and ending the Bonaparte dynasty for good. In triumph, Wilhelm I had himself crowned Kaiser of all Germany in – of all places – German-occupied Versailles. Alfred Krupp and Co. soon possessed Dutch shipping companies and Spanish ore mines. A rich seam of coal under Essen and ten other nearby towns in the region of the Ruhr River helped Krupp and other heavy manufacturers build the Ruhrgebiet, a fifty-kilometer-long mass of nearly contiguous urban industrial development, stretching from Duisburg on the Rhine through Essen to Dortmund. As the region's furnaces poured out molten metal, they helped Germany begin its own hunt for colonies, in particular during the Scramble for Africa.[16]

Meanwhile, by the 1880s, in their respective headquarters in Pittsburgh and Essen, Carnegie Steel (later United States Steel), and Krupp Stahl took their places in the firmament of the world's largest corporations. They and other corporations invested in the construction of other extensive heavy industrial regions. Britain's East Midlands was joined by the coal and steel zone around the Silesian city of Katowice (today in Poland, then under German rule) and Belgium's Liège, connected to the coal and factory towns of Flanders. Pittsburgh spawned a metropolis of steel-mills that snaked through two deep river valleys that met in the city's center. By World War I, Pittsburgh occupied a central place in the largest heavy-industry archipelago in the world, stretching from Baltimore's Sparrow's Point through Syracuse, Buffalo, Hamilton (Ontario), Cleveland, Detroit, and Gary (Indiana), to Chicago. While the largest industrial districts were located in their birthplaces in Europe and North America, the weapons industry of British India helped spawn a steelworks in Bombay; the Meiji built another at Yawata near Nagasaki; and Qing officials yet another in Wuhan. Nonetheless, the unequal geography of heavy industry by World War I both reflected and helped to cement the Great Gap between the imperial "metropoles" of Europe, North America, and Japan, on the favored side of the chasm, and the far less developed cities in the colonies, on the other.[17]

THE TENTACLES OF CAPITAL: TRACKS, PIPES, AND CABLES

Railroad companies were steelmakers' biggest rivals for the title of world's largest corporation. While European and Japanese companies built the densest rail networks in the world, and the British Raj stretched rails across India, American tycoons like Cornelius Vanderbilt and Jay Cooke, like their counterparts in Canada, Australia, and later Russia, specialized in building rail lines of especially great length and tentacular reach. Imperial ambitions were foundationally important to these massive projects. In the USA, railroad companies were notorious for their skullduggery in acquiring continent-crossing bands of real estate from the federal government's vast inventory of conquests. Once built, the transcontinental rail lines, in turn, helped seal those conquests, by encouraging waves of new immigrant farmers to take up homesteads that the rails now tied more efficiently to urban markets. The Canadian Pacific Company's Trans-Canada railroad did the same after its construction between 1881 and 1885. In 1909, the Trans-Australia Railroad, with its famous 797-kilometer dead-straight line of track across the Nullarbor Plain, linked that continent's separate eastern and western colonies. In both Canada and Australia, railroads encouraged the foundation of unified, continent-sized settler dominions. Russia's Trans-Siberian Railroad (built from 1891 to 1917) was the longest single human-built structure on land in the railroad-era Urban Planet. It gave St. Petersburg and Moscow a much faster connection to former Siberian fur trading forts and far-east boomtowns like Khabarovsk and, at the far end of the line, the Pacific port at Vladivostok, fatefully intensifying the Tsars' rivalry with Meiji expansionists in Tokyo.[18]

No city boomed more spectacularly because of railroads than Chicago. In 1800, the site of the city's future soaring downtown was a tiny fort and fur trading post in the territory of the Potawatomie people. A hundred years later, despite a fire that consumed two-thirds of the city in 1871, it had 1,700,000 people and ranked fifth in the world. Chicago's spot on the southern tip of Lake Michigan not only positioned it best for the rail lines from the East Coast, but also made it the natural fulcrum for a fan of a dozen other rail routes toward the west. Thus, the city generated long necklaces of new cities radiating from its vast railyards to Minneapolis to Seattle in the northwest; through Kansas City westward to Denver and San Francisco; and southwest through Saint Louis (for a while a rival "Empire City") toward the oil cities of Texas and the Pacific port at Los Angeles. Chicago, "nature's metropolis," grew above all because of the enormity and variety of natural resources those rail-lines allowed Chicago capitalists to exploit, process, and transship eastward. Fur trappers yielded their forests to ravenous timber camps. Iron-ore and coal mines gashed Minnesota's Mesabi Range. Mineral resources of all kinds, including more coal, came from further west, including the immense Powder River Basin of Wyoming. Yet the most abundant product of the richest of the Urban Planet's hinterlands was the grain and meat from thousands of square-shaped homesteads and farms that Washington granted to white settlers across former Native lands. These homesteaders' tiny clusters of farm buildings, dispersed across a vast belt of rich loam, could give the families who worked them a living because they were connected by rail to Chicago.[19]

Chicago itself became home to a vigorous commodities exchange, to this day a major trophy of the capitalist Urban Planet. So were the lumber mills of Chicago and Milwaukee, where former trees became studs, joists, and clapboard siding that then made their way into the construction of countless wooden workers' houses throughout the American industrial belt. (The "skids" on which lumber was stacked lent their name to the "Skid Rows" or nearby homeless encampments that were another iconic feature of the American capitalist city.) As important were Chicago's tractor-assembling and farm-equipment plants that allowed thousands of farming homesteads to plow more acreage and eventually to consolidate into the larger factory-like, hydrocarbon-fertilized farms of the twentieth century. The grain silos of Toronto, Montreal, and especially Buffalo represent an even more monumental built manifestation of the wealthiest wheat and corn lands in the world; Buffalo's "secular cathedrals" and its grain transfer economy made the city's lake harbor and its adjoining rail yards into the world's eighth largest port by 1900. Similar "Prairie Castles" for grain storage punctuated the skylines of Great Plains towns from Saskatoon to Oklahoma City. Yet the greatest "shock space" of the entire North American network of capitalist cities was Chicago's Union Stockyards, the project of a cabal of railroad magnates led by Cornelius Vanderbilt himself. Twenty-five thousand workers in this great one-and-a-half-square-kilometer "Jungle" of pens, slaughterhouses, and meatpacking plants unloaded rail cars packed with hogs, sheep, and cattle from as far away as Montana. Some 400 million animals became chops and steaks amidst the screams and flowing blood of this death zone between 1860 and 1910. Though they were closed in 1971, waste from the Union Stockyards still causes a nearby tributary of the Chicago River to bubble with organic gas. Toxic wastes from the stockyards, combined with the city's capacious sewage, long threatened the city's water supply from Lake Michigan. In 1900, officials completed a 45-kilometer canal to reverse the flow of the Chicago River away from the Lake. Chicago's waste henceforth headed west, back into the Mississippi watershed that gave the city its great wealth.[20]

As railroads transformed tiny settlements into metropolises, much shorter filament-like iron structures had big urban impacts as well. Rail-guided urban streetcars go back as far as 1807, when the British Parliament permitted a company to run a horse-pulled version in the Welsh city of Swansea. Improved cars appeared in New York and New Orleans in the 1830s, across Europe in the 1840s (London did not get them until 1860), and in Alexandria, Santiago, Sydney, and Batavia (Djakarta) in the 1850s and 1860s. Because it was hard to harness a coal-fired engine to a streetcar without generating too much smoke for an urban neighborhood, horse traction remained the rule for urban trolleys until the end of the century. The Hydrocarbon Revolution in urban transport only began in the 1880s, with the first steam trolleys and cable-drawn cars; cleaner electric cars, fueled from central coal-fired power plants, came soon after. Yet street-car-pulling horses, the huge stables needed to house them, and the municipal networks of fodder-growing farms needed to feed them only fully disappeared in the 1920s. Companies often charged rates that only middle-class customers could afford, forcing municipalities to impose more order and equity on these companies, even buying some lines. However, street-cars' biggest contribution was to expand development on the urban periphery. As such, they contributed to urban growth, to the earliest waves of middle-class suburbanization, to segregation and urban sprawl, and to the Urban Planetary power of capitalist developers, estate agents, and issuers of mortgage loans (Chapter 19).[21]

Railroads and streetcars were not the only extensive tentacular structures created through corporate alliances with imperial states during this time. Oil and gas pipelines joined the Urban Planet only a few years later. The biggest builder of pipelines, John D. Rockefeller's Standard Oil Company, joined the exclusive group of the world's largest corporate titans in the 1890s. The pioneer petroleum magnate controlled the flow of oil as it emerged in a crude state from thousands of pumps and derricks in Pennsylvania to his riverside refineries in Cleveland. From there Rockefeller used commanding purchasing power to negotiate cheap rates with rail companies to transport barrels of kerosene and later gasoline; soon he owned a fleet of steamships that delivered the fuel throughout Europe and as far away as the cities of the Yangtze and Yellow River valleys of China. There he fought titanic battles with Russian, British, and Dutch companies which drilled, refined, and transported oil from the forest of derricks in and around the "Black City" of Baku on the Caspian Sea, and later from the Dutch East Indies. These European companies, eventually consolidated as Royal Dutch Shell, pioneered off-shore drilling, oil tanker ships, a pipeline (over the Caucasus Mountains to the Black Sea refinery port of Batumi), and massive oil spills on Caspian waters – due to tanker accidents and oil well blowouts. Meanwhile, Rockefeller faced competition from companies that built even-longer-distance pipelines in the USA, so he bought them up and commissioned new pipelines from Pennsylvania to Chicago, Buffalo, and New York. Such pipelines also increased the profitability of drilling for natural gas. Gaseous hydrocarbon, first produced as "coal gas," a byproduct of coal-fired steam engines, found its way into cast-iron piping systems as early as the 1810s for gaslights in high-end buildings and streets, then into bourgeois home heating. In the 1880s, the Pittsburgh capitalist George Westinghouse tapped methane gas from nearby oil wells, laying pipes under his city's streets and into enough houses to cut the city's gargantuan coal consumption by a third, that is, until the gas wells ran dry ten years later and the coal smoke returned.[22]

Meanwhile, the Westinghouse Electric Company in Pittsburgh fought another corporate titan, Thomas Edison's General Electric Company in Schenectady, New York to supply cities with coal-fired and water-powered electric turbines, distribution equipment, and a full array of electric appliances. These too spurred massive amounts of new building, and extensive new structures. Among them were coal-fired electric power plants almost as large as steel mills, hydroelectric facilities embedded in massive dams with enormous turbine systems, valley-swallowing reservoirs needed to turn the turbines, hundreds of thousands of kilometers of electric wires on poles or in pipes underground, transformers and elec-tric substations, and wiring systems in the walls of millions of buildings. Soon rooms in houses transformed as well, with the introduction of electric switches, lightbulbs, refrigerators, and washing machines. They joined plumbing systems that brought fresh water and evacuated human waste (Chapter 15).[23]

THE ROSE SERIES P. 5087
Copyright

CIRCULAR QUAY, SYDNEY N.S.W.

14.2. Circular Quay, Sydney Australia, *c.* 1900
By 1900, the human habitat encased Earth in a contiguous lacework of built structures –
even reaching the most recently urbanized continent. From Sydney's Circular Quay,
telegraph wires communicated instantly across all of the oceans. The harbor nearby
welcomed steamships filled with goods, tourists, and immigrants. Up the street,
transcontinental trains left the glass-roofed Central Railway Station (1906). Electric trams
opened new suburbs, and Sydney grew to a million people by 1920. Power and light flowed
to homes along pole-mounted wires from generating plants that burned coal from
Australia's enormous mines. Cities of Hydrocarbon and heavy industry soon put
humanity in command of Earth's entire halo of life.
Hulton Archive/Getty Images.

Earthopolis's most extensive tentacular structures grew out of mid-
nineteenth-century experiments by British army generals and rail companies with the telegraph. With obvious geostrategic interests at stake,
imperial states encouraged communications corporations to consolidate
their capital and connect cities at ever greater distances. The British
Eastern Telegraph Company became one of the largest in the world by
encasing copper wire from mines it controlled in Chile with pliable
insulating materials harvested in tropical forests that allowed the company to unwind enormous cables from ships onto the sea bottom. As early
as 1851, the Company spun such cables in Birmingham mills, insulated
them with *gutta-percha*, the rubber-like sap of a Malaysian tree, and laid
them onto the floor of the English Channel. The first trans-Atlantic cable
began operating in 1858, followed by extensions that linked Britain with

India, South Africa, and Australia. After 1879, the need for insulation of electric wires, among many other industrial needs, propelled a rubber boom in the Amazon rainforest – the largest region of the world still largely outside of the orbit of cities. As rubber plantations stretched across once remote native forestlands, the cities of Manaus, Brazil and Iquitos, Peru swelled deep in the heart of the forest. Like Léopoldville, Congo, they were outfitted with rubber-processing plants and riverside docklands devoted to shipping this increasingly valuable material to Europe and the USA. In 1903, a 10,000-kilometer rubber-insulated tele-graph cable connected San Francisco and Singapore via American-controlled Honolulu and Manila. The Urban Planet had reached a new threshold. By then, humans had built far more cities and far larger cities than ever before, but they had also untwisted a tentacular built structure of brick, stone, mortar, metal, and rubber that for the first time held all of Earth in its contiguous clutches.[24]

SKYSCRAPERS AND SMOKE: THE ASCENDANCE OF CARBON CAPITALISM

As the realm of human habitat became planetary, corporate and hydro-carbon power ascended rapidly – vertically upward in built space, and, through smokestacks, up through the atmosphere. Already in 1851, the booming cities of industrial capital were sparing little money to celebrate their exploding rule over the Urban Planet. That year, visitors to London's Hyde Park were astonished by the appearance of the "Crystal Palace," a building three times the size of St. Paul's Cathedral, made not of stone or brick, but entirely of iron – and astonishingly large panes of plate glass. Two Birmingham manufacturers built the thing, one a rail forger, the other a pioneering glazier, both of whose products relied on massive amounts of ignited coal. This was a monument not to gods and kings, but to human industrial ingenuity itself; the palace also contained a "Great Exhibition" of eye-popping machines and technologies. London hosted dozens of these celebrations in upcoming years, and Paris coun-tered with its own "*Exposition Universelle*" a few years later (it was there that Napoleon III got his first close look down the barrel of one of Krupp's steel cannons). In 1889, another spectacular fair in Paris featured

Gustave Eiffel's 324-meter-tall iron Tower – the most exalted celebration of metal girders ever conceived. Few expositions could top that, but national, regional, and imperial festivals of industrial might became *de rigueur* for cities eager to climb a notch or two in the hierarchy of urban civilization. Manchester, Rio, Osaka, and Nizhny-Novgorod (soon to become a Soviet-era automobile colossus) all held fairs; so did Atlanta (celebrating the growing industrialization of the cotton states of the US South), Buffalo (the first electrified festival, thanks again to those turbines in the Niagara Gorge), and Chicago (the especially well-attended World Columbian Exposition of 1893).[25]

Meanwhile, architects in Chicago and New York were the first to fuse steel girders and glass – along with traditional brick, stone, and, increasingly, cement – into a more permanent form of high temple to corporate industrial power: the skyscraper. Electricity and pneumatics were also essential, because buildings over ten stories tall – not to mention twenty or forty – were impractical without elevators; skyscraper builders adapted that novelty from the clunky so-called "upright tunnels" first used in cotton mills. Merchants since the Bronze Age had tried to imitate the palaces of kings. Nineteenth-century financial houses from London's Bank of England to the New York Stock Exchange to Shanghai's mercantile Bund typically adopted the solid and trust-inducing form of Athenian temples for their headquarters. The skyscraper gave corporate titans a new vehicle of built expression all of their own that soon completely overshadowed the urban architectural authority of royalty, states, and city governments – and even the high steeples of cathedrals. As company headquarters rose taller, and as they clumped together in stalagmitic central business districts, the urban skyline also gave corporations another space upon which to upstage their own capitalist rivals. Clustered skyscrapers also signaled another corporate asset, the expensive land that lay beneath them, which was only a source of profit if many stories of rentable space could be built above it. The proximity of so many piled-up offices, finally, intensified capitalists' use of urban environments as the ultimate fix they needed to coordinate their many logistical, legal, political, and above all financial affairs – allowing bankers like New York's J. P. Morgan to loan money everywhere in the world. Skyscraper districts in Lower Manhattan and Chicago's Michigan Avenue became the new model of the global capital of capital, a built form that has since spread to every city that wants to claim command over the Urban Planet as a whole. "It must be every inch a proud and soaring thing," the American skyscraper architect Louis Sullivan declared, "rising in sheer exaltation that from bottom to top it is a unit without a single dissenting line." Nothing better articulates the vertiginous rise of the power of profit-makers within the human habitat.[26]

In the meantime, coal had become king of the industrial world of the capitalists. By 1900, it is true that direct sunshine, wood, peat, falling water, and animal and human muscle power continued to fuel most human activities, notably agriculture. Hay-fed muscles propelled horse-drawn streetcar transport. The same was true of almost all activities in the many cities that still did not burn coal or petroleum – most of them in Asia, Africa, and Latin America. Flowing water remained an important source of power for textile mills and a slowly growing number of hydroelectric power turbines; Buffalo capitalists used the Niagara Gorge to generate hydropower for the first electric steel mill in 1902. All of that said, especially after 1870, rapidly growing numbers of cities were home to heavy industry that relied heavily on coal and coke. Moreover, wherever ships, trains, and pipelines connected coalmines and oil and gas fields to cities, most of their inhabitants followed in the now centuries-old path of Kaifeng and London by turning to coal instead of wood and charcoal for urban cooking and home heating.

For cities that embraced coal, there was an ascending impact and consequence: an urban atmosphere filled with eye-watering, lung-clogging smoke. As we know, London had been smoky enough in the thirteenth century to bother the king, and in the seventeenth century, coal chimneys inspired the first-ever environmental activist, the coffee-shop devotee John Evelyn. By 1870 in London, there was so much smoke in the air that torch-bearing peddlers charged a fee to pedestrians for help navigating pitch-dark streets in the middle of the day. By 1900, toxic gaseous brews like the ones that the auto-rickshaw driver Pandit Sharma Karma grumbled about in 2018 Delhi had been collecting for decades in the air of Manchester, Pittsburgh, the Ruhr, Chicago, Bombay, and Osaka. Great smogs – smoke trapped in fog or temperature inversions on windless days, killed 1,000 people in Glasgow 1909, sixty in the steel towns near Liège in 1930, and forty in the small town of Donora near Pittsburgh in 1948. London finally gave up on its 400-year dependence on coal for home heating after 1952, when a horrific five-day-long episode of smog killed 4,000 people and sickened 100,000. By 1960, the city had converted most home heating to natural gas.[27]

Choking smoke in cities made up only a small part of an increasingly aggressive human invasion of the larger planetary atmosphere. Amidst the sheer coal escalation after 1870, sulfur aerosols poured out of smokestacks across the industrial Atlantic and soon Japan. The same Greenland ice cores that registered grime from ancient Roman and Chinese mine fires now showed much thicker soot marks from industrial activity in the late nineteenth century. Dangerous greenhouse gases like carbon dioxide and methane rose upward too. "Between 1875 and 1880," the climate change historian John L. Brooke tells us, the level of CO_2 in the atmosphere "slipped past the highest ice-recorded measurement of the past 800,000 years." From an average level of 285 parts per million during the human era, it spiked toward 330 ppm in 1945. Even more dangerous methane levels followed suit. Anomalous peaks of both of these waste gases would soon become the bottom floor of a "new normal." Before 1900, the expansion of plow agriculture and cotton-growing in North America and the colonies – both to meet the needs of growing industrial cities – accounted for more greenhouse gas emissions than industrial smokestacks themselves. Yet, if methane emissions from rice fields may have softened cooling periods in pre-modern times, climate historians of the late nineteenth century detect a clear and entirely anthropogenic atmospheric warming trend for the first time. The trend affected the Arctic and the colonized lands of the tropics the most – for the ironic, and equally anthropogenic, reason that sulfur from coal smoke tends to refract the Sun's rays in industrial regions, cooling the air underneath. It would not be the first time that the industrial Great Gap conspired to exact a higher price from poorer regions as a consequence of the activities of the richest ones.[28]

Nor would it be the last time that advocates of hydrocarbon power ignored contemporary warnings about atmospheric heating. In 1900 – amidst the general celebration of humanity's domination of nature, the paeans to industrial progress, the skyscraping acclamations of corporate power, and the massive furnaces filled with hot burning coal – few listened to the physical chemist Svante Arrhenius of the University of Stockholm. That year, he published the first in a long line of dire prognoses about the effects of CO_2 on climate change. For now, the celebrations eclipsed all dire prophesies. After all, the real hydrocarbon capitalist ascendancy was just about to begin. In 1886, in the industrial city of Mannheim, Germany, the iron founder Karl Benz patented the first "automobile fueled by gas." In 1901, oil prospectors discovered immense new oilfields at Spindletop, Texas, followed by even larger ones in 1908 in the Persian desert at Masjed-e Soleymān. A third industrial revolution – complete with a new surge in the influence of profit-makers and a maximal hydrocarbon age – was at hand. So was the fulfillment of Svante Arrhenius's warnings of a too-hot Urban Planet.[29]

CHAPTER 15

The Pharaohs of Flow

TAMING FURIES WITH FLOWS (...AND SEGREGATION AND SPRAWL)

It should not come as a surprise that, when the empire-builders and profit-makers detonated the nineteenth-century explosion of Hydrocarbon Cities, they also let loose a Pandora's Box of furies across the Urban Planet. As in earlier times – and as today – humans had to face a realm of consequence that grew in tandem with urban acceleration, and we had to pay its prices and forestall its threats. The most dangerous fury to rise skyward, as we know, was largely ignored at the time: carbon waste and other greenhouse gases. Later generations were left to pay the price for these volatile forms of nineteenth-century human waste that inaugurated the era of anthropogenic atmospheric heating. Far less easy to ignore were the political furies of People Power. They exploded on a growing scale in 1848, inaugurating a century of soon globe-encompassing revolutions against state, imperial, and capitalist rule. These events will unfold in the background of this chapter and erupt in the following ones. Imperialists and capitalists made immediate responses to these crises, but hardly solved them, as we shall see: instead, imperial states dragged the entire Urban Planet toward a pair of cataclysmic World Wars in the twentieth century.

Before getting back to atmospheric heating, revolution, and war, we need to attend to another consequence of early Hydrocarbon Cities: new global episodes of global pandemic disease. The human habitat's unprecedented growth, and the simultaneously increased concentration and vast dispersion of our habitat, only further refined cities' ancient role as incubators for disease-bearing bacteria and viruses. The scourges of the nineteenth century were horrific, and they repeatedly crashed across all continents. Smallpox and typhus made repeated rounds of cities everywhere. Tuberculosis intensified, especially in cotton mills, worker's neighborhoods, and mines. Malaria and yellow fever haunted the colonial cities of the tropics, felling imperial officials and soldiers as well as millions of colonized people and tens of thousands of laborers on the massive canal and railroad works. Worst of all, a novel cholera bacillus hopped a ship between Calcutta and London in the 1830s. It set off no less than six global pandemics of this horrific disease that reverberated throughout the century. Finally, at century's end, the world faced its third global visitation of bubonic plague, transmitted by ship rats through Hong Kong to hundreds of port cities on all continents.

Overwhelmed by these events, imperial states and the new capitalist elites turned to a growing group of scientists and state officeholders for solutions. These "sanitarians," as they were called early in the century, began forming into a profession – a group of people with specialized training, who did research, published their work, and shared their ideas with other professionals at conferences that met in cities across the world. Until the scientific breakthroughs of scientists like Louis Pasteur and Robert Koch in the 1880s, professional sanitarians were not aware of the role microbiota played in disease. Instead, they blamed the new scourges on cities themselves, and, in particular, the pungent odors of sewage, rot, and smoke from urban waste that grew as profusely as the cities that generated it. The public health solution sanitarians offered to their employers in government and industry actually made some sense. Cities needed to flush odoriferous air, liquid, and solid wastes out, and they needed to open themselves up more to cleansing fresh air and water. To grow, in a word, cities needed to *flow*.[1]

Sensible as it may be, flow was expensive – extremely so in the fastest-growing cities. Huge projects of construction and destruction were required: buildings on narrow streets and giant city walls needed to come down to make way for wider air-clearing avenues, squares, and parks. Factories and dense apartment buildings, especially those housing factory workers, needed better internal ventilation systems, some requiring demolition and complete reconstruction. Someone needed to pay for large reservoirs, aqueducts, and piping systems to bring enough fresh water into urban homes. Vast sewer systems needed to run under the streets to remove the escalating tons of human waste. Enormous embankments were required to keep dirty, silty, and sometimes sewage-laden river and seawater out of cities during floods or storms. Urban building inspection, street-sweeping, and garbage removal systems needed improvement – and that required expansions of municipal authority, new sources of tax revenue, larger municipal workforces, and new office buildings to house city employees.

Projects like these also required power. Because flow was expensive, sanitarians dove headlong into the maelstroms of urban politics. There, they found some powerful allies and made many enemies, all of whom weighed public health alongside other considerations. Capitalists were divided on flow. On the one hand, industrialists, merchants, and even shop-owners noted that wide avenues promised not just flows of fresh air but faster flows of raw materials, goods, and laborers otherwise held up by urban traffic. Ventilation, water, and sewer systems could cut down on factory absenteeism caused by sick workers. On the other hand, rebuilding factories or mines along sanitary lines dipped very deeply into profits; thus, horrible working conditions persisted. Another group of capitalists, the real estate developers and builders who constructed the city itself, had similar concerns with flow. Setting aside potentially profitable urban land for purposes other than charging rent or speculative gain was anathema to them, and adding ventilation shafts to cheap worker housing that they never intended to maintain in the first place was out of the question. Indeed, capitalists generally found the upfront costs of urban flow too high. Thus, as they had done in the matter of conquering land for cotton plantations and financing transportation infrastructure, so they did in the matter of urban flow: they turned to the state for a fix. It was government's job, they maintained, to stuff the furies of urban disease back into Pandora's Box – as cheaply as possible – allowing industry and industrial cities to continue growing, unburdened by higher corporate taxes to government, let alone any worries about further human impact on Earth and the consequent costs.

Nation states, especially rich and powerful ones that ruled large empires, were more inclined to go with the idea of urban flow. In an age when revolution and empire coexisted uncomfortably, state elites saw an opportunity to at least appear to be promoting the "greatest good for the greatest number"; indeed this catchphrase from the work of the philosopher Jeremy Bentham inspired many sanitarians. Also, assuming that not every revolution-minded urban resident would be impressed by state sacrifices for the public good, wide avenues promised quicker movements of new police forces or soldiers to urban trouble spots, putting more of the state's eyes into revolutionaries' hiding places. Lastly, there was the matter of aesthetical flows: just as in Sennacherib's Nineveh, wider streets opened up longer, more awe-inspiring views toward monuments that inspired national pride – and thus, states hoped – more popular enthusiasm for the arrogant projects of imperial capitalist Earthopolis.

As the cause of flow grew in state circles, it expanded far beyond sanitarians' concerns with pandemic prevention alone. The professional writ of the flow-makers grew, and soon they took on the more exalted title "urban planner"; French planners emphasized their artistic side by styling themselves *urbanistes*. With growing state support throughout the cities of empires, planners emerged as Pharaoh-like forces of global urban creation and destruction in their own right. Their projects also set into motion substantial urban flows of their own: inward flows of construction workers, of brick, stone, iron, steel, cement, mortar, grout, and glass; and outward flows of rubble. Thanks, in part, to Pharaohs of Flow like Richard Wellesley in Calcutta, Baron Georges-Eugène Haussmann in Paris, Edward Bazalgette in London, Ali Mubarak in Cairo, Torcuato de Alvear in Buenos Aires, Paulo de Frontin in Rio de Janeiro, Daniel Burnham in Chicago, Henri Prost in Rabat, Morocco, and Edwin Lutyens in New Delhi, cities did gradually become more healthful places, even as they became faster-flowing, and far grander than before. The Pharaohs of Flow, meanwhile, proved themselves dead right in identifying flow as an essential element of livable large cities, a fact that microbiologists, and the planners' toughest critics, repeatedly confirm.

That said, planners also created their own realm of costly conse-quence. The expense of planners' undertakings and their own class position as bourgeois professionals meant that the greatest benefits of urban flow flowed above all to urban elites – and in colonial cities, to "whites." Sometimes planners blamed working-class people and colonial subjects of color for miasmas and other urban health hazards, tilting urban politics toward anti-egalitarianism. Too often, the great flow-makers also engineered greater inequality into the hard substance of urban space. It was they, for example, who set in motion the first instances of modern gentrification. They also segregated many cities by class and race in invidious efforts to "solve" urban problems for elites while skimping on the expense of ensuring flow in the city's majority neighborhoods. Some planners so abhorred the dense neighborhoods of cities' poorest inhabitants that they condemned all forms of urban density, setting the stage for anti-urban ideologies and the urban sprawl we face today. Planners of the nineteenth century were not the only people who engaged in these unequal practices. Still, the negative legacy of their professional endorsement of urban inequity, division, and sprawl meant that the positive legacy of their devotion to urban flow nonetheless extorted its own price from future generations.

The rise of the modern Pharaohs of Flow really consisted of two separate stories. The first, which best explains how flow encouraged sprawl and increasingly naked forms of segregation, began in synergies that developed as early as the late seventeenth century between London's West End and early "White Town" housing schemes for colonial officials in Calcutta (and across South and Southeast Asia). Trends that began there intensified during the twentieth century in the English-speaking settler colonies of Australia, South Africa, and North America. The second strand of the story, which began in France and preserved urban density to a greater degree, emphasizes the connection between flow, aesthetics, monumentality, and the injustices of gentrification. It too starts in the late seventeenth century, with Louis XIV's Versailles, but it achieved its apogee in Paris in 1851–69 with the *grands travaux* of the greatest of all Pharaohs of Flow, Baron Haussmann. His example set standards that influenced similar "great undertakings" – each in their own way – in dozens of large cities on all continents.

THE GREAT WEN AND THE PESTILENTIAL VAPOR BATH

London and Calcutta, the British Empire's two imperial capitals, are the best places to pick up the first strand of the story of urban planning. By

1800, early sanitarians themselves "flowed" back and forth between these two top cities (they also made side visits to Paris, where French flow-makers faced similar conditions). These were enormous places, swollen in size by imperial function and deluges of capitalist investment. Like most cities of the time, they were also previously "unplanned" or "organic" – that is, over long periods, their many different inhabitants jostled with each other over space, using various degrees of wealth and power to build solid things that helped them do what they wanted to do individually. Leftover public places – notably the streets between their buildings – writhed and snaked this way and that, and they were usually narrow. Indeed, this system was designed explicitly to give more space to buildings than streets, since, unlike streets, buildings actually generated rent.[2]

"Organic" cities, sanitarians complained, did not allow the efficient airflow of pre-planned cities, such as those with straight streets laid out at right angles into a grid pattern. There were fewer such cities in the world, but planned grids did have a long history, going back to the ancient capitals of China, the colonial cities of Rome and, more recently, those of New Spain. As in those cases, pre-planned grids were easiest to lay out in cities built from scratch on empty land. Recent examples also included Philadelphia (1682), St. Petersburg, Russia (1708), and New York City, where a commission of officials laid out a famous gridiron of numbered streets and avenues across three-quarters of Manhattan in 1811. Soon grids would appear across the various "frontiers" of the Americas, Australia, and Africa.

Of course, the streets of all cities, pre-planned or not, were replete with solid waste: rotting leftovers from kitchens, human and animal excrement that either dropped there or leaked there from cesspools, decaying vegetation, and even decomposing human and animal bodies that had yet to find a place underground or downriver. On top of that, both London and Calcutta, like other Cities of Rivers and Oceans, had bedeviling relationships to water: they lay on massive river mouths where ebbing and flowing tides met dozens of smaller tributaries mixing fresh water with seawater. There, natural silt washed from inland and mixed with liquid and solid waste, sometimes heedlessly sloshing through the middle of downtown streets. Water filled the air as well. London's air was a clammy dark mixture of salty mist, coalsmoke, and city stench. Its reformers called it the "Great Wen," using an old word for "cyst," implying that the city was a disease itself, not just the incubator of disease. As for Calcutta in the rainy season, the city's burning hot, intensely sultry tropical air turned the city into what one British governor general called a "pestilential vapor bath."[3]

None of these urban accumulations of nuisances – solid, liquid, or gas – were new. For thousands of years, most city dwellers, including those living on straight streets, had accepted daily nausea-inducing disgust as the price of all the advantages of urban living. There were also many periodic efforts to minimize these sensory nuisances. John Evelyn, whom we know as an early first urban environmentalist, not only complained about London's smoke in the 1650s, but also suggested ways to tamp it down. When the great fire of 1666 burned much of London to the ground, the great architect Christopher Wren took time out from rebuilding St. Paul's cathedral to suggest a new street plan for the city as a whole. He envisioned wide straight streets arranged in a grid overlain with diagonal avenues to add more airflow between London's buildings, and to spread the city to the less dense areas to the west of its walls. The city's speculator-builders were too quick for him, and the old twisted lanes reappeared downtown, but wealthier Londoners did seek out the relatively unbuilt West End for larger houses. There they "solved" the problem of urban nuisance in a different way, by putting restrictive covenants in their property deeds that preserved open space as "squares" and that discouraged anyone from building smaller, less architecturally distinguished buildings nearby that poor people might be able to afford. In so doing, elite Londoners followed the lead of wealthy merchants who fled to the more open peripheries of Manila, Batavia, Madras, Bombay, and Calcutta at the same time. Many of them returned to London with plenty of money to invest in the West End. In doing so, elites in all of these cities explained disease not so much by miasmas, but by blaming poor people or people of color whose lifestyles supposedly created urban stench and who were thus deemed morally, or, increasingly, racially inferior. The solution many of these elites preferred was less dense living, segregated in space from the urban majority. The square-studded wider avenues of London's elite West End spread out in the 1700s and 1800s.

Meanwhile, the southeastern districts of Calcutta sprouted their own semi-suburban area of bigger detached houses surrounded by wide lawns and walls called "compounds" in an area sometimes informally referred to as "White Town."[4]

Meanwhile, Governor General of Bengal Richard Wellesley appointed an "Improvement Committee" for Calcutta in 1804, among other things to straighten crooked streets in the city's northern neighborhoods – also known as "Black Town" – that went back to the days when the city was a collection of three Bengali villages. Over the next few decades, the English members of the Committee used imperial power to seize property in Black Town, deliberately taking more land than they needed so they could resell it at a much higher price once it was part of the frontage on more desirable straight streets. This practice – later known as "excess condemnation" – gave Calcutta a few long, fairly straight north–south avenues that vented more sweet breezes from the Himalayas down into the city's dense core (and into White Town) during the winter. They also allowed merchants to move their vehicles more rapidly through town, and made it easier for the governor general to move his soldiers and Indian sepoys (as well as their English guns) from Fort William toward new campaigns of conquest. As for Richard Wellesley himself, he got more flow too: his stately carriages could now convey him far more quickly out of steamy, smelly Calcutta to the breezier suburban "Versailles" he built for himself to the north of the city at Barrackpore.[5]

In general, the professional sanitarians who took up the work of urban flow from amateurs like Calcutta's Lottery Committee were less chauvinist toward urban majorities and more attentive to good things for the "greatest number of people." The great estuarine rivers that ran through London and Calcutta, the Thames and the Hooghly, caused as many problems of flow as they solved, and the many tributaries that snaked through town did the same. The Hooghly, which received a large part of the enormous rush of meltwater deposited by monsoons each year as snow in the Himalayas, was the worst of all. As the river's historian Debjani Bhattacharyya describes it, water from the Hooghly, amplified by the city's prodigious sheets of monsoon rain, seeped into almost all of the porous land that lay under Calcutta. This created swamps, puddles, and temporary creeks where dry spaces were supposed to be and mixed sewage and fresh water everywhere, including into the large rectangular "tanks" that Bengalis (and, following their example, Englishmen) dug to store drinking water. At the same time, the silt that the Hooghly washed into town repeatedly created dry spaces where boats were supposed to sail or dock, forcing the East India Company to move Calcutta's port facilities several times, at great expense. All that water and hyper-fertile silt helped feed profuse rainforest vegetation that alternately cracked building foundations and collapsed into piles of rotting mess, causing miasma theorists to blanch (and the occasional Bengal tiger to saunter into town). For most of the city's first 100 years, local authorities and wealthy Indians dug ditches to drain all this water and waste into the creeks that fed the Hooghly, hoping to re-channel all stench-producing stuff toward the Bay of Bengal. Still, floods, storms, and silt made them look like fools each time.[6]

So did the Hooghly itself. Its profuse siltation actually placed the river at the apex of the city's hydrological flows, not at the valley bottom like many other urban rivers. One very bad idea, to firm up the banks of the Hooghly by building an embankment out of the city's "night-soil" – human excrement – probably caused the world's first serious urban cholera outbreak in 1817. The disease revisited the city horrifically and often for the next century, adding to the misery caused by profuse malarial mosquitoes. Only in the 1850s did the successor to Wellesley's Improvement Committee come up with enough tax revenue to hire an engineer to build a system of drains and underground cast-iron pipes to channel the city's groundwater, rainwater, and waste downhill into the so-called Salt Lake to the city's east. White Town and Black Town were both served by this system, though direct connections to houses were always more common in elite – and whiter – districts. To this day, the city's self-built "bustees" of the poor continue to outpace new extensions to the overburdened sewers of Calcutta, now called Kolkata (Figure 13.1).[7]

In London, the River Thames and its tributaries toyed with the sanitarians almost as mercilessly. As the city grew, builders had buried dozens of streams that fed into the Thames under arches of masonry, over which they constructed houses. They also connected grate-covered holes in the streets via pipes to the now subterranean streams, creating a rudimentary storm-water drainage system that sometimes allowed rain to sweep waste from the streets. Londoners who could afford it buried their excrement in masonry-lined cesspits under their houses, which, similarly to Calcutta, received periodic cleanings from carters who delivered it to surrounding farms. As London ballooned, the distance to the farms increased, raising the price of human manure transport at a time when British ships were also providing the county's farms with a much cheaper, more effective fertilizer called guano, from seabird dropping deposits along the coast of Chile. The rising underground tide of waste rose even more after water-flushed toilets – some marketed by a shopkeeper with the excellent name Thomas Crapper – became more common in households. These washed waste through internal pipes into the cesspits, making the pits' contents soupier and more likely to overflow into the buried tributaries of the Thames.[8]

The tidal Thames, meanwhile, flowed majestically in and out each day according to the gravitational pull of the Moon. On its inward surges, it conveyed the city's rising river of sewage inland, from the tributaries upstream to a place higher upriver than the intakes of the city's drinking water pipes. Thus, when *Vibro cholera*, multiplying promiscuously in the bilge of some ship that steamed into London's India Docks from a prior berth in the Hooghly near Calcutta's waste dumps in 1831, the microbes found their way easily into the pumps on London's street-corners where the city's inhabitants drew their daily water. Within months, Western civilization plunged into the first of many moments of existential self-doubt that recurred every time cholera reappeared. That happened often in the ensuing fifty years. Tens of thousands of people died in cities from Paris, Berlin, and Vienna to New York, Tunis, and Tokyo from epidemics that even the greatest professional minds of the era were helpless to stanch.[9]

The theory of miasmas may look ridiculous in hindsight, but it spurred Parliament, and then one of the world's greatest professional sanitarians, out of despair and into actually effective action. In the hot summer of 1858, the Thames's utterly revolting fecal flow forced members of the British Parliament, the greatest imperial governing body in the world, to abandon debates on legislation that would place India under the rule of Queen Victoria. A year before, Britain had celebrated its soldiers' successful siege of Delhi and the suppression of the Great Indian Rebellion;

now the empire's own capital was under siege from the "Big Stink," a peak tide of its own sewage. Lawmakers quickly threw together a Metropolitan Board of Public Works for London, and empowered it to bypass the city's Corporation. The new Board hired the great civil engineer Joseph Bazalgette, and gave him Pharaonic powers to design what was essentially a new digestive tract for the world's largest city.[10]

Bazalgette's "intercepting" sewer system remains one of the unsung marvels of the modern world. It consists of an underground brick-and-concrete river-system totaling 131 kilometers. Eleven tributary sewers running parallel to the river "intercept" the flow of waste from the city's buried streams and pipes before it reaches the Thames. From there, gravity redirects the excremental flow along gently pitched tunnels that lead twenty kilometers downstream from Parliament. There, at two massive "outfall works" at the towns of Beckenham and Crossness, on opposites sides of the Thames, the sewage accumulates in reservoirs to wait for the tide to rise. At the right moment, teams of the largest Watt steam engines in the world pumped London's waste into the Thames to float far out into the estuary. Hundreds of millions of bricks went into these sewer lines and reservoirs before Bazalgette experimented with an especially hard form of Portland cement and built the rest of his structure with that material so beloved of the ancient Romans, effectively re-inaugurating its use as a primary ingredient of the Urban Planet. A massive temporary cement works went into operation to allow the project to continue. Thus the business of making London's colon flow also birthed one of Earthopolis's most important (and atmosphere-harming) new hydrocarbon industries.[11]

Meanwhile, because the principal north-side intercepting pipe ran right between the Houses of Parliament and the river, Bazalgette needed to construct new stone and concrete embankments along the Thames in central London. After leveling several miles of riverside docks and makeshift neighborhoods, he sank a line of empty bell-shaped wooden chambers called caissons into the Thames (these were similar to those used to pour foundations for the two towers of another contemporary experiment in urban flow, the Brooklyn Bridge in New York City). The caissons allowed workers to stay dry while laying concrete foundations on the riverbed. Over the next decade, a fifty-two-acre sweep of quayside

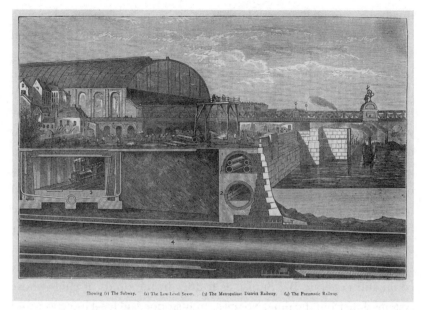

Showing (1) The Subway.   (2) The Low-Level Sewer.   (3) The Metropolitan District Railway.   (4) The Pneumatic Railway.

15.1. Into the Urban Underground
Cities needed to grow downward in order to grow outward and upward. Thus believed Pharaohs of Flow like London's Joseph Bazalgette, whose underground pipes and tunnels made a city of five million imaginable. His Victoria Embankment slowed the spread of cholera by separating the River Thames's brackish tidal flows from piped-in flows of safe drinking water (1) and outward flows of waste – the job of his masterpiece, the "Intercepting Sewer" (2). To move more people, carts, and trains faster, flow-masters widened streets, built bridges, and dug tunnels for subways like the London Underground (3). Communication flows even inspired a short-lived Victorian "internet," a driverless "pneumatic railway" (4) that carried mailbags of business correspondence – using still another tunnel under the accelerating city.
Print Collector/Hulton Archive/Getty Images.

avenues and parkland opened up on top of what had been sewage infested river beaches. The northern Embankment was a grand enough structure to be named after Queen Victoria herself. Underneath, the cavernous intercepting pipes shared space with a submerged set of pipes for fresh water, an electric rail line later called the London Underground, a short-lived "pneumatic railway" for mail trains, and soon gas and electric utility lines.[12]

While Bazalgette drilled this stupendous monument to urban flow underneath the first city of the empire, the older Calcutta Improvement Committee followed suit. In the 1850s, its nearly all-white membership finally expropriated enough land from the empire's Bengali subjects to drive the Strand Road alongside the Hooghly. Perched atop several kilometers of stout stone embankments, the Strand segregated Calcutta from the river's capricious flows of Himalayan water and silt, making the city a bit less soggy than before. A few decades later, the German microbiologist Robert Koch discovered *Vibro cholera* in one of Calcutta's many swampy ponds and reservoirs, launching the world upon a somewhat more fruitful conquest of the disease, focused more on excrement-laced water rather than stinky air. Nineteenth-century sewers, the conquerors of cholera, were not perfect. Even enormous tunnels like Calcutta's could not keep Himalayan silt out; they needed constant re-digging in the twentieth century. The practice of diverting sewage by pipe downriver naturally exacerbated sanitary problems in downriver cities. Finally, sewers' double duty as storm-water drains meant that combined overflow could still generate Big Stinks, as it does in hundreds of cities whose systems date from the time. No sewer fully stopped all fecal infection, and diarrhea remained a common complaint of urban life in even the best-sewered cities – as it does today for hundreds of millions living in cities without them. Nonetheless, drilling sewer pipes through many miles of the Urban Planetary subsoil remains a foundational imperative for our continued life on Earthopolis.[13]

BARON OF THE BOULEVARDS

These great early triumphs of British sanitarians coincided with the glory days of the single most Pharaonic of all urban planners – Paris's boulevard-building Baron Haussmann. Haussmann's work also represents the take-off point of the second globe-spanning story of urban flow making. In that story, the signature means of circulatory power were wide, long, straight, diagonal – very beautiful – tree-lined avenues driven through previously dense, labyrinthine popular neighborhoods, that also connected with wondrous squares and parks.[14]

Haussmann's ambitions were not new. French kings like Louis XIV had enhanced their absolute power by straight grids and diagonals when they built new cities – most luminously in the approach to the Sun King's palace at Versailles. Christopher Wren's diagonally crisscrossed gridiron design for post-fire London never came into being, but later planners sited the British monarch's Buckingham Palace quite grandly among diagonal suburban avenues, where it keeps calm and carries on to this day. The founding fathers of People's Republics liked this grand style too, as George Washington proved when he hired the French architect Charles L'Enfant to conjure a symphony of grids and diagonals on the patch of Potomac River marshland that became Washington, D.C. A grand boulevard like Pennsylvania Avenue, offering a straight shot between the Executive Mansion and the People's House on Capitol Hill, was just as capable of glorifying the democratic separation of powers as similarly radiant planning gestures could celebrate the unseparated power of Sun Kings. In Washington, D.C., avenues named "Independence" and "Constitution" added their own nationalist and democratic touches, and soon associates of L'Enfant offered similar grids overlaid with diagonal fans to largely unbuilt settler towns like Buffalo and Detroit. Meanwhile, the City of Washington celebrated each time the USA converted a new slice of conquered Native land into a US state by giving that state's name to yet another new diagonal street.[15]

In nineteenth-century Paris, the city's would-be re-planners were envious of these pre-planned cities, recognizing that, unlike ancient Paris, all had the advantage of being new-builds on "empty" land. Paris's labyrinthine streetscape was, by contrast, set in stone that went back to pre-Roman times; the only exception, as we know, was the Champs-Élysées, the broad woodland carriage road traced out on unbuilt land at a jaunty angle to the city's northwest. Haussmann's achievement was to realign all of Paris, hard and soft, along similar thrusting, connecting diagonals – and to do so, furthermore, in a manner where each individual *Grand Boulevard* was conceived as one part of a city-wide *réseau* – or connective network – of street-enlivened flows.

The greatest of all Haussmann's *réseaux* was the easiest to build: the symmetric convergence of twelve avenues at the Place de l'Étoile (today renamed for Charles de Gaulle) at the high point of the building-free Champs-Élysées. His most triumphant accomplishment, however, involved the same kind of massive destruction of existing neighborhoods that Wellesley's Improvement Committee had employed in Calcutta. Thanks to legal mechanisms rammed through Napoleon III's rubber-stamp parliament, Haussmann was free to "excessively condemn" just about any elongated slice of built space he wanted. He began by ramming a wider north–south axis that intercepted an earlier east–west route at the Châtelet, placing that intersection at the center of all of Paris's transport routes to this day. From this rectilinear cross, dozens of new diagonals and grand squares emerged out of the rubble of the former labyrinth, completing a veritable web of *réseaux* across the city.[16]

Why do all of this? Boulevards are among the most "multifunctional" of urban spaces, and the map of Haussmann's *œuvre* has given generations of admirers and critics alike a kind of Rorschach test by which to decode the otherwise inscrutable Pharaoh's full planning philosophy. Most simply, as Haussmann himself emphasized many times, boulevards allowed people and vehicles to move around the city far faster – once again, to flow. They enabled workers to get to work, merchants and shoppers to get to shops, travelers to get from one of Paris's stupendous terminal train stations to the other, raw materials to get to factories, and money to change hands more quickly and copiously as a result. Coal came in from distant mines to nearby freight-yards, thence via cart along the boulevards into the city's home furnaces – and out again as smoke through the millions of red clay chimneypots that sprouted from Haussmann-era Paris's romantic grey mansard roofs. On good days, free-flowing breezes along the boulevards ushered the smoke back out into the countryside. Goods of high quality poured out of factories and the city's high-end artisan shops, through the boulevards by horse-carts into the glamorous windows of new department stores like the Bon Marché. Still other boulevards allowed the city to ingest bigger shipments of France's fantastic foodstuffs, from the farms through the rail stations and city gates to the central market at Les Halles, immortalized by the writer Émile Zola as the "stomach of Paris." From there, the ingredients of long, languorous bourgeois luncheons flowed into distended bellies through hundreds of neighborhood groceries, butchers' shops, charcuteries, wine shops, bakeries, and *pâtisseries*. Every time Haussmann laid out a new boulevard, he dug deep into the limestone under the city and laid down new lengths of gently pitched pipeline. In them, fresh water flowed from a source fifty kilometers to the east, via a system of aqueducts and canals, into courtyard taps and later directly into home faucets and elite lunchers' drinking glasses. Separate sewers – hundreds of kilometers of them – delivered the city's gauzy April rainwater, along with the digested remains from all of the city's glamorous repasts, far downriver to the west. Later, engineers repeatedly ripped up the surface of the boulevards to bury other forms of urban flow underneath: gas pipes, electric and telephone cables, greywater systems for street washing, and then, over the course of the twentieth century, a dozen and a half fantastical metro lines and 245 underground stations with ceramic tile walls. Wide sidewalks aboveground allowed bohemian *flâneurs* to move from café to café and the first generation of mass tourists to line up around the monuments. Players of *pétanque* argued strategy for their next throw in the boulevards' tree-filled medians. Street entertainers found their audiences there, and beggars received tossed coins and snoozed on boulevard benches at night. Fans of musical theater strolled in their finery up the Avenue de l'Opéra to the global exemplar of all the nineteenth-century Urban Planet's opera houses. In the morning, tens of thousands of street trees brought fresh air and birdsong to all characters in the humming theater of Paris, luring serious promenaders and *pique-niqueurs* onto the lawns, lakeshores, and forest paths of the city's jewel-like parks. Meanwhile Paris helped stimulate the great sanitarian project toward its nineteenth-century climax. While Haussmann's sewers washed *Vibro cholera* from Paris toward towns down the Seine, its great university laboratories harbored the likes of the microbiologist Louis Pasteur, who pioneered systems to keep bacteria out of milk and wine, and invented new vaccines against disease. Pasteur set up a famous Institute in Paris that trained generations of public health researchers and officials who later worked in cities across the world. Haussmann added to the city's advanced health care system by leveling a large working-class neighborhood on the central Île de la Cité to make room for a modern hospital.[17]

Yet Haussmann's ambitions for his *grands travaux* were greater than even the most sublime sum of all improvements in *joie de vivre* and the public health. Under his watch, Paris also needed to become the true capital of a global empire, replacing what it had so often become before – a collection of hidey-holes for revolutionaries that regularly threatened the global order. Boulevards helped do this work of the state too. For one, they created the longest-sweeping sight lines in any capital city, re-setting its glamourous monuments to state glory onto a matchless urban stage. Under the July Monarchy, an Arc de Triomphe arose to celebrate Napoleon III's uncle Napoleon I. Once surrounded by the swirl of Haussmann's converging avenues at the Étoile, it was wondrously visible nearly two kilometers away from the gardens in front of the Tuileries palace, now the imperial residence of the latest Bonaparte. An obelisk from Egypt's Temple of Luxor occupied a crucial spot along that same glorious ocular flow-way, high on a plinth at the center of the Place de la Concorde once occupied by a statue of Louis XV. It offered a reminder in sweeping built space of Napoleon I's efforts to link France through the sweep of time to ancient empires via conquest of Egypt. It was no wonder that the Champs-Élysées also became a favorite place for world *Expositions Universelles* of industrial progress. Later, after 1871 when a republican regime returned to the city, the Champs-Élysées transformed into a triumphant way for parades of the French armed forces every July 14. Meanwhile, Haussmann and Napoleon III further obliged the memory of the greater Napoleon by naming the boulevards after all of his battlefield victories, and soon after that, all of his great generals.[18]

Speaking of battles and soldiers, Napoleon III seems to have hoped that at least some of Haussmann's boulevards would also make it easier for his soldiers to hunt down revolutionaries. Under the People's King Louis Philippe, a new east–west axis along the Rue de Rivoli gave soldiers with orders from the Tuileries much more direct access to the Hôtel de Ville, the capital of revolutionary rule in 1789, 1830, and once again in 1848. In the 1850s, Haussmann prolonged the street eastward to the new Place de la Bastille, with its central column giving an obligatory monumental nod to the first July 14. From there, however, Haussmann drove a *réseau* of diagonal boulevards through the most notorious of the revolutionary neighborhoods, prompting Napoleon III's indelicate remark that the Boulevard du Temple put him in position "to take the Faubourg St. Antoine from behind." Other networks that penetrated the old Cordeliers district on the Left Bank seem to have had a similar intention – to jackboot the most storied of all urban revolutionary traditions.[19]

That said, Haussmann's most sweeping counterrevolutionary act was to chase working-class people out of central Paris altogether – partly by destroying their neighborhoods but mostly by making it too expensive for them to live downtown. Boulevard building by Calcutta-style excess

(A)

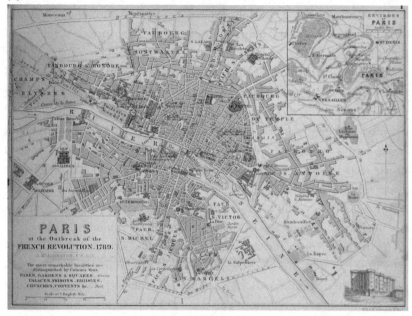

(B)

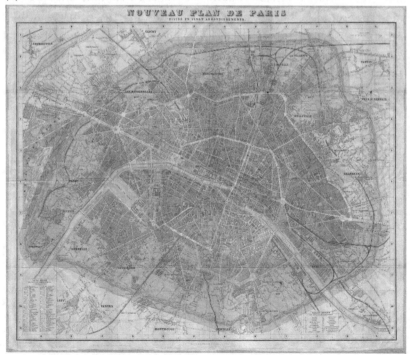

Map 15.1. Paris for the People … or Just the Bourgeoisie?

condemnation amounted to an act of synergy uniting the force of the state with that of capitalist speculation to make central-city housing less affordable. Today we call this synergy "gentrification." The very construction of the boulevards did far more than any "flows" of soldiers to change the political geography of Paris. As tenements fell, the boulevards attracted profit-seekers eager to capitalize on the new prestige addresses by erecting the long uniform rows of six-story bourgeois apartment buildings (those crowned by the gray mansard roofs and clay-pot chimneys) that give all of Haussmann's boulevards their visual sweep to this day. Smaller, untouched streets near the boulevards continued to conceal crowded tenements for a while, but as long as Paris kept attracting more poor people from the countryside, rents would rise there too, forcing tenement builders to speculate in cheaper land on the less-built frontiers, most often further east.[20]

In this way, the sprawling new tenement district of Belleville, situated to the east of the Place de la Bastille, became the heart of Paris's new "Red Belt." Boulevards, as gentrifying forms of flow building, also accentuated class segregation. Paris, much like London, split itself ever more definitively down the middle between a generally affluent west and a poorer east. That pattern held as working-class districts in both cities grew – soon inhabited by growing numbers of immigrants of color – fanning out to the north and south as well and creating racial divides that divide French and British society in our own time. Haussmann's preference for six-story buildings meant that the elite's

---

Caption for Map 15.1. (cont.)

During three revolutions in 1789, 1830, and 1848 the people of Paris chipped away at Louis XIV's chain of absolutist power-points connecting the Bastille and the Tuileries with his distant château at Versailles (A). After Napoleon III stifled the 1848 revolution, he hired Baron Haussmann to make the city governable again. Flow was essential: Haussmann's Pharaonic boulevards (B) moved people, traffic, air, water, and waste faster - while opening tangled revolutionary hotspots to imperial soldiers. Other popular neighborhoods fell to his wrecking ball, and land near boulevards became unaffordable. Ordinary people moved out to cheaper-rent towns like Belleville and Montmartre. From this class-segregated "Red Belt," the People led a fourth French Revolution, briefly taking Paris back under the Commune (1871), but the bourgeoisie's ownership of the central city survived. Today, we know Haussmann's acts of city grabbing as "gentrification." All of central Paris's neighborhoods are affected now – as are thousands elsewhere across the world.
(A) Niday Picuture Library/Alamy. (B) Sepia Times/Universal Images Group/Getty Images.

gradual flow westward took a denser built form than in London's generally more squat, spread-out West End, let alone Berlin's lakeside suburbs, even if both were far denser relative to later suburban "white flight" in South Africa, Australia, and the USA (Chapter 19). The denser downtowns of Paris and most other European cities – and the larger Latin American, African, and Asian cities that soon imported Haussmannian planning most faithfully – have typically remained bourgeois territory, though the edge of gentrification continues to expand into what, in Haussmann's time, were new working-class districts. Red Belt Belleville itself became *hyper-chic* and astronomically priced in the 1990s.[21]

Haussmann, as we shall soon see, was not able to contain the revolutionary force of Paris. A republican backlash ushered the mightiest Pharaoh of Flow into retirement even before Krupp's cannons and the bloodiest of all Parisian revolutions, the Commune of 1871, humiliated the last Bonaparte and ushered him off the stage of history (Chapter 16). Yet, in a bigger twist of the plot, Haussmann lived on. Once all the revolutionary blood washed into the drains and the dynastic pretensions collapsed, the diagonal boulevards of Paris continued to scaffold a consumer culture based on hydrocarbon industry and the exotic products of empire with finely graded elite, bourgeois, bohemian, and even a few working-class accents. As the nineteenth century gave way to the even more turbulent twentieth, a genteel era blossomed in between whose name could have only come from the boulevards of Paris: *la Belle Époque*.[22]

A PLANET OF FLOWS

Haussmann's Paris, meanwhile, became the finest bauble in the shop window of the globetrotting professional *urbaniste*. For elites in cities elsewhere, all it took was a visit to the Avenue de l'Opéra, or to the Parc des Buttes Chaumont, or to the Galeries Lafayette department store – located on the Boulevard Haussmann no less – or even on one of the new tourist barges that plied the sewers of Paris by torchlight. The result was the same: inspiration for a *Haussmannien* makeover of a capital back home.

Such inspiration struck Ismail the Magnificent, the khedive of Egypt, in the 1860s, on his second trip to Paris. He had visited the city as a child twenty years earlier, and the full thrill of Haussmann's transformations brought him to his knees with envy. Similar improvements were coming to Istanbul, the Ottoman capital whose pretensions of governing Egypt Ismail resented above all others. At the time, dignitaries from across the world were scheduled to arrive in Egypt to celebrate the opening of the Suez Canal, and Ismail could not bear the humiliation of receiving them in what European Orientalists referred to as "Old Cairo," with its tiny twisted lanes and crowded *souqs*. However, just as planners had tamed the Thames and Hooghly, Ismail had built embankments that channeled the annual floods of the Nile into a more predictably directed flow, leaving a giant expanse of former floodplain in between the river and Old Cairo. Ismail turned up the taps of credit that he enjoyed at banks in London and Paris, dragged the Egyptian *urbaniste* Ali Mubarak to Cairo, and set him to work laying out wide diagonals and greenspaces on the reclaimed floodplain, soon reorienting the city toward the west (and the West) as well as toward the pyramids of the original Pharaohs.[23]

The cattle elites of Buenos Aires and the sugar and coffee elites of Rio de Janeiro had meanwhile successfully turned back popular caudillos and the Brazilian emperor to run ascendant republican regimes designed to cement bourgeois power. They too borrowed European (and Wall Street) money to hire *planificadores* like Torcuato de Alvear in Buenos Aires and Paulo de Frontin in Rio to sweep away restive (and mixed-race) working-class neighborhoods near downtown – known by such contemptuous terms as *conventillos* (little convents) and *cortiços* (beehives) – and replace them with facsimiles of the Champs-Élysées. In short time, Buenos Aires became the "Paris of the South," complete with a dense bourgeois downtown penetrated by boulevards that led to squares and parks, that were underlain with the finest sanitary equipment, and that sharply segregated downtown from growing red belts and a growing number of shantytowns on the periphery. Rio earned its own Parisian accolades shortly after, by destroying *cortiços* and chasing their inhabitants to the Fluminense districts to the north. The elite laid down trolley tracks and lovely light fixtures to the south, allowing the city's elite access to the resplendent beachfront suburbs at Copacabana and Ipanema that many inhabit to this day.

Back in Europe, Otto von Bismarck's capital in Berlin gained prestige when Prussian forces captured Napoleon III on the battlefield, but the city's designers too knelt in fealty to Haussmann, scratching the city's magnificent avenues, fulminant parks – and its very first sewers – out of the marshy flatlands of Brandenburg. Vienna followed suit by replacing its bastion walls and glacis with the great Ringstrasse, a space we will return to soon, to see how Vienna's own *Belle Époque* revealed Europe's far darker side (Chapter 17).[24]

The flash of French urban planning continued to sparkle at the dawn of the dangerous twentieth century as students in the École des Beaux Arts, another legacy of the Sun King, digested the lessons of Haussmann and sought to improve on them. One strand of thought, which we explore in the next chapter, critiqued Haussmann's callous attitude toward worker housing and gave planning more of a social conscience focused on building better homes for the urban majority. Another sharpened the lessons of the boulevard. Despite himself, Haussmann had thankfully left plenty of Paris's smaller, more intimate streets intact. A *Beaux Arts* style of street planning emerged after 1900 that more intentionally merged these two features – the grandiose with the intimate, perhaps even village-like. Some of these impulses made their way into other cities in France and Europe, but the Scrambles for Africa and Asia opened up opportunities for *urbanistes* to let their imagination roam in the colonies. There they benefited from acres of "empty" ground and could operate free of meddling from local landowning elites, let alone republican parliaments.

Thus it was that "no man's land" in the suburbs of Rabat's medieval *medina* – actually seized under questionable legal standards by French judges from Moroccan aristocrats – became the canvas upon which the *Beaux Arts* great Henri Prost built a resplendent *Ville Nouvelle* (New City) to house the new French colonial "Protectorate." Segregation was built into the project: a lovely park under the walls of the *medina* set off a much larger space largely for European speculators and settlers along a lovely mixture of boulevards and smaller streets. Similar projects later came to Dakar in Senegal, and to Saigon and Hanoi in French Indochina, among other colonial cities.[25]

All of this French *grandeur* left British planners a bit in the shadow. During the *Belle Époque*, the British Empire's greatest achievement in

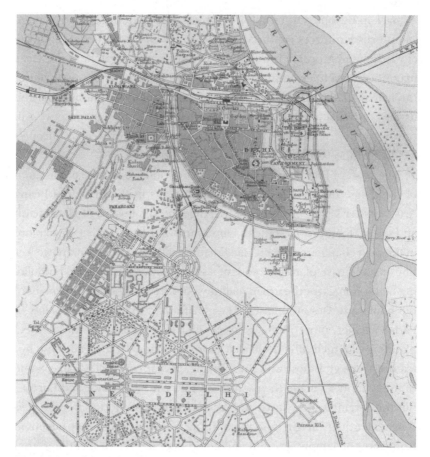

Map 15.2. Delhi: New vs. Old

In New Delhi (lower half of map), the British extravagantly deployed modern urban planning to serve imperial power. Designer Edwin Lutyens's long, straight boulevards converged at angles along the central Kingsway, culminating in a "Government House" (lower left) for the viceroy. On its far end lay the ruins of Indraprastha ("Indarpat" on this map), the first of seven earlier imperial capitals sited in Delhi. Mostly, though, New Delhi dismissed walled Old Delhi (upper half), contrasting a dynamic, modern design with the sinuous streets of a fading, unchanging "Oriental" city. No sooner did the British inaugurate New Delhi than their empire fell too. India's new leaders repurposed the round "Council House" (next to Government House) as the world's largest democratic parliament.

Antiqua Print Gallery/Alamy.

transforming its Asian and African colonial cities involved the cheapest and least effective form of sanitary reform: urban segregation. Local officials, under direction from the Colonial Office in London, placed (or at least tried their best to place) well-ventilated "white towns" or

"European Districts" on the higher ground of cities like Hong Kong, Nairobi in Kenya, Lagos in Nigeria, Accra in the Gold Coast, and Freetown in Sierra Leone. This system was meant to keep officials and soldiers at a distance from the cities' majorities and their supposed propensity to spread plague, yellow fever, and malaria (Chapter 16), but it was hardly a statement of imperial glory set off in magnificent urban space.[26]

By 1900, the British authorities had long felt that Calcutta – the original colonial "City of Palaces" – simply would no longer do as an imperial capital. The city's Bengali majority had formed into an increasingly militant anti-colonial movement, and its White Town remained as soggy and moldy as ever, especially during the "vapor bath" monsoon months of summer, when the administration decamped in any case for the cooler Hill Station at Simla.

In 1911, the Raj decided to move its headquarters to Delhi. There it could assume the mantle of the Mughals, another dynasty that had conquered India from outside, while shortening the relief voyage to Simla. The tombs and ruins of seven earlier dynasties covered the area south of the Mughal city. British officials expropriated forty-two square kilometers of this land for their new imperial capital. Still, the reference point was another imperial capital altogether – Paris, France. Edwin Lutyens, the planner in charge of New Delhi, pulled out all the Haussmannian stops, striking one thunderbolt of a boulevard against another at 30-, 60-, and 90-degree angles, allowing each intersection to explode into plazas resembling hexagonal and circular fireworks.[27]

Today, a rickshaw driver, perhaps the Pandit Sharma Karma himself, could take you to the culminating point of the imperial ensemble, the Raisina Hill. At its summit, Lutyens raised a great half-British, half-Indian Viceroy's Palace that makes Buckingham Palace in London seem frumpy by comparison. From there, the flowing view along the Kingsway – a tree- and lawn-lined boulevard that shares a name with a far-shorter Haussmann-era avenue in London – stretches the eye two and a half kilometers to British India's own "Arc de Triomphe" – the All-India Gate – not far from the spot where ancient Hindu gods supposedly built Indraprastha, their own mountainous capital.[28]

Yet, for all that, New Delhi purposefully retained the spirit of British suburbs. Lutyens's avenues are lined not with six-story Haussmannian apartment buildings that abut the sidewalks, but with detached bungalows on wide lawns hidden behind shrubbery. New Delhi thus severely rejected Haussmannian Paris's urban density; even more pointedly, it rejected the density of Muslim Old Delhi to the north. The message from the New "flowing" Delhi to the sclerotic Old was as clear as it was dangerous: the modern city – just like Western "civilization" more generally – should spread out, segregated from the historic Urban Planet, in direct opposition to outdated and inferior traditions of urban density everywhere in the world. This toxic sentiment in favor of sprawl, which only grew as the automobile age dawned, is one that we, and our new generation of flow-making professionals, will need to confront head on in order to survive in the Earthopolis of the future.[29]

CHAPTER 16

Planet of the People III: An Urban Majority Takes Its Space

THE PEOPLE AND THE URBAN ACCELERATION

It is time to return to the most numerous characters in the nineteenth-century biography of Earthopolis. Certainly, no urban explosion could happen without increasing numbers of people – one billion of us on Earth in 1830, on our way, with increasing velocity, to 2 billion by 1930. Of those billions, most lived ordinary lives of heavy labor. Most had little or no property, most spent long days hungry or sick, most died in their thirties if they survived childhood, and most were vote-less. In cities, most lived not on glamorous boulevards lined with cafés, but in shacks or grim, quickly constructed, unventilated buildings filled with tiny apartments whose resident families shared cold-water taps, courtyard outhouses, and tawdry neighborhood wine bars or beer cellars. About half lived as colonial subjects of an empire ruled from across an ocean. Most people on Earth, of course, still lived on farms and villages – most of them ever more precariously so, since most rural livelihoods became, incrementally then irreversibly, more dependent on cities, especially as capitalist landowners consolidated farms to make more profits by feeding cities. For those reasons, far more people than ever before were on the move. At least 200 million people between 1830 and 1930 ended their lives somewhere other than their birthplaces, often on the far shore of an ocean. Many moved to new countrysides, but most by far now ended up in cities. Cities, accordingly, grew faster than rural areas almost everywhere, even as imperial capitals and industrial cities grew fastest by far. In some regions – Great Britain first, around 1850, and in the USA and France after 1900 – urban populations did something unprecedented: they actually grew larger than those in the countryside, part of a trend that soon replicated

387

itself across Europe and the Americas, hastening our voyage to the urban-majority planet of today.[1]

These urban majorities did more than anyone else did to translate their own bodily strength, their own hands, arms, backs, and sweat – as well as their willingness to uproot and re-plant themselves – to make the Urban Planet the ever-denser, ever-more extended built structure it became by 1900. They personally redesigned the countrysides that fed the Urban Planet, did the labor of expanding the commercial farms or scratching out the new farmsteads needed to feed bigger cities. They felled more trees than before, and mined many more minerals and much more hydrocarbon fuel. In cities, they constructed new buildings and neighborhoods, raised new urban monuments against the sky, laid cobbles for the new boulevards, built factories, and tended factory machines. In between, they laid the iron rails, drove the trains, dug canals and built docks, hung the wires and cables, crewed the steamships, and filled ships' steerage holds as immigrants. In millions of homes, caregivers, most of them women, somehow renewed the energies of a billion laborers, preparing them for work the next day, typically in built spaces dangerous to the health of their inhabitants. Imperialists, capitalists, and Pharaonic planners may have envisioned, designed, financed, and supervised the biggest Urban Planetary projects of the era, but none could have any success, reach, or impact without the mobility and labor of the human majority.

In the midst of all that, the workaday human majority also put up an enormous political fight. Demands for People Power became fiercer and more radical. As always, built space was crucial. Exploding working-class districts, docklands, and colonial "Black Towns," often constructed with social pacification in mind, actually provided cover for popular resistance, as did, sometimes, farms and plantations. Streets and squares remained central places of public protest. Revolution spread across Europe in 1848, and in the ensuing half century, calls for People Power spread east and south from there, touching Istanbul, Cairo, Johannesburg, Calcutta, Tokyo, and then dozens of the great cities of China. Meanwhile, new volatile urban battlegrounds opened up in factories, at rail junctions, in the docklands once again, and in the mines. Labor strikes became a favored means to assert majority power, and they proliferated by the thousands from Chicago to

Shanghai. New urban police forces, largely established to quell such uprisings, faced street protest too, that targeted their often-abusive behavior and their complicity in authoritarian and corporate power. As the raging 1848 revolutions in the capitals of Europe had first made clear, new demands for equity and power were possible, and those demands now included socialist, anti-colonial, and more radical feminist ones than ever. In 1871, Paris detonated yet again and, for seven short weeks, the city became a socialist republic called the Commune. In cities across China in 1911, the massive republican Xinhai revolution, an affair consisting of hundreds of urban protests, deposed the Qing dynasty. The big news, however, came in 1905, and especially in 1917, when the world capital of cutting-edge radical politics shifted from Paris eastward – with help from street politics in Tokyo – toward St. Petersburg, Russia.

The multi-pronged and often chaotic political struggle for a more equitable, representative Urban Planet was fierce and only ambiguously successful by the early twentieth century. Still, well before 1900, it had its own effects on the growth and the shape of the Urban Planet. States slowly bowed to Urban Majority demands for an expanded vote. Despite many reversals, more in the propertyless majority and even many colonial subjects gained a voice in government; after 1920, the global voting public included more and more women. Peoples' parties arose wherever parliamentary routes to power opened. Protests, strikes, elections, and the specter of revolution all added gradual but generally relentless upward pressures on wages in industrial societies from the 1850s on, raising the pay of many workers of the world to levels higher than in even the most thrumming of early-modern Cities of the Oceans. These wage victories – though still limited or in some cases nonexistent, especially for women and children – paralleled incremental progress on working and housing conditions, better water, sewers, and hospitals – all of which led to better health and nourishment in worker households. Infant mortality fell and average human stature increased for the first time since the agricultural revolution, increasing life expectancy in industrial cities closer to forty years and then longer still. The fight for urban equity, along with the more fortuitous advances in urban planning, thus explains much of the unprecedented doubling of Earth's population between 1830 and 1930.[2]

A MAJORITY ON THE MOVE

Between 1830 and 1930, more than 200 million people moved from one part of Earthopolis to another. This too was unprecedented. The size of nineteenth-century migration was several orders of magnitude larger than the three million white settlers and the twelve million enslaved people who made the passage to the Americas during the entire early-modern period. Why did this happen? Because global conquest and capitalist industrialization transformed countrysides as well as cities. Rural life changed dramatically during the hydrocarbon and industrial revolutions, and so did the rural built environment and the way people related to land. In particular, farmers and villagers in all three of the most populated agricultural regions of the world – Europe, India, and China – faced enormous new pressures "pushing" them away from the rural places of their birth. Meanwhile, conquest and industry as well as the tentacular reach of new roads, railroads, and telegraphs also transformed gigantic new rural territories, most notably in North America, into farming, timbering, and mining hinterlands for cities for the first time. In the wake of abolition, plantations once worked by enslaved people throughout the Americas now needed new cohorts of "free" migrant workers. Such new rural lands exerted their own strong "pull" pressure on farming people dispossessed elsewhere, even if many more felt even stronger pulls toward industrial jobs in exploding cities.[3]

Over fifty-three million people left Europe between 1840 and 1930, mostly to the Americas, but also to Australasia and points in Africa. Meanwhile, another fifty million Asians left their birthplaces, most for other parts of the continent, but also by the millions to the Pacific shores of the Americas, the Caribbean, Australasia, and Southern and East Africa. As many as another 100 million – maybe more – people on all continents left the countryside for towns and cities nearby or farther away, or to enormous construction sites for canals and railroads.[4]

Some ordinary migrant households and communities could control their own decisions about when and how to move, even if the pressure to leave itself largely lay out of their hands. For most, however, poverty, debt, wealthy land-consolidators, state policies, or even violent attacks on their communities made it impossible to remain. As labor migrants and refugees moved, they ran a complex, unequal gauntlet through state- and corporate-controlled spaces that were alternatively designed to encourage their movements and to restrict them. On the whole, people of Asian, African, and Latin American descent had less control over their movements. They also faced larger obstacles along the way and were more likely to face exploitation and even death at their destination.

Constraints on choice began in the villages and farms where most migrants were born. In all of the largest agricultural regions, cotton factories undercut local cottage production of textiles that many rural households depended upon to sustain their farms. Across Europe, landowners responded to the larger profits available from the business of provisioning growing cities by buying up farmland from peasants and closing off common grounds – an extension of the "enclosure movement" in Britain that spread continent-wide throughout the nineteenth century. In Ireland, land consolidation went back to the English conquest; absentee owners of enormous estates hired middlemen to extract as much rent as possible from peasants, reducing them to tiny plots only suitable for one crop: potatoes. When a horrific blight struck potato plants in the 1840s, a million Irish crofters died and two million left the island. In Russia, laws that emancipated the serfs from the customary bondage to the estate where they were born also forced them to pay for land and access to other rural resources, indebting many former serfs to former lords, and forcing emancipees to face harassment from creditors or move. Russian Jews, confined to their *shtetls* in the Pale, faced increasing persecution, as tsars distracted their Russian subjects from their misery by whipping up horrific anti-Semitic mob attacks – the *pogroms* – that devastated the populations of many *shtetls* and Jewish neighborhoods. This violence forced many Jews to join a large westward exodus to the Americas and smaller streams of migration to the Ottoman province of Palestine, where small communities of Jews lived in Jerusalem, Jaffa, Gaza, and other ancient cities long home to Arab majorities.[5]

In India, the British conquerors mercilessly increased the power of landowners to squeeze villagers for tax income. In Qing China, imperial policy had long limited state revenues to fixed land taxes even as the population exploded, meaning that local officials got lower salaries and had greater incentive to exploit farmers who had previously been the most generously supported in the world. British wars of conquest in India and the Qing dynasty's bloody twenty-five-year war to suppress the Taiping Heavenly Kingdom devastated millions of farming families. Amidst growing rural destitution, British officials in India and in the Chinese treaty ports cheated hundreds of thousands of Indian and Chinese peasants into signing contracts of indenture that consigned them to hard labor as "coolies" overseas. To make this system work, officials built a system of collection stations in small towns that led to prison-like processing points in port cities. At the end of interminable voyages in the bellies of ships, many of these indentured laborers found themselves working in the now British-owned silver mines of Latin America, in the deep, hot gold mines of Johannesburg, or on Caribbean or South African sugar plantations, replacing formerly enslaved Black laborers, halfway around the world.[6]

Across Africa and Asia, food growers faced new colonial taxes that needed to be paid in cash, forcing them to shift to crops like cotton, cacao, palm oil, or rubber that put their livelihoods at the mercy of commodity exchanges in Liverpool and Chicago. New "gateway" colonial towns (Chapter 13) attracted migrants from the countryside. When the British seized the city of Lagos from its ruling Oba, the city absorbed formerly enslaved migrants from Sierra Leone, Brazil, Cuba, and the USA. Colonial officials in these cities use their military might to impose labor taxes (known by the French term *corvée*), forcing villagers to leave their fields or herds for extended periods of work on distant colonial building projects. The biggest of these was the Suez Canal. The French corporation that financed it contracted with Khedive Said of Egypt for enormous armies of *fellahin* (peasants) from up and down the Nile Valley. Whether under *corvée* obligations or wage contracts, these now-former peasants reported to foul tented camps along the isthmus for seventeen-hour shifts digging a massive ditch through hot desert sand and malarial mud flats, where thousands died. Later, similar conditions, in this case worsened by yellow fever, greeted over 150,000 former slaves and British-indentured migrants from the Caribbean recruited by the USA to dig another isthmian canal in Panama.[7]

From 1848 to 1890, a series of gold strikes reverberated around the Pacific Rim. Migrants from southern China to California or Australia met waves of white "Gold Rushers" in unruly mining camps. Racial violence exploded, often resulting in the death of Asian miners or the theft of their claims. In North America, rail companies happily scooped up expelled Chinese miners to lay steel tracks across blistering deserts, hack rail-beds out of sheer mountain cliffs, and stretch iron trestles above bottomless gorges. Anti-Chinese sentiment grew among white settlers in San Francisco, Vancouver, and Melbourne, who stoked claims that Chinese workers were stealing white men's jobs and championed national laws restricting Asian entry.[8]

As global migration grew, state officials and corporations built larger spaces of transit while also expanding spaces designed to restrict movement in discriminatory ways. Some European and Asian migrants could negotiate the terms of their departure, route, and communication back home through networks based in their own households, houses of worship, and village associations that sprang up at their destination. Modern migration, however, depended heavily on corporate-owned, coal-fueled spaces like trains, rail stations, docks, and the massive steerage holds of ocean-going steamships. These built structures funneled migrants, no matter their destination, from dispersed locations into teeming, concentrated transit areas in port cities on both ends of their ocean voyages. This funnel-like geography of mass transport allowed states to pinpoint new sites for facilities designed to control human movement. Modern national borders came into being above all in urban ports. There, officials had waged a century-long fight against cholera, plague, and other microbial diseases, relying at first only on the slim knowledge that outbreaks started in ports and appeared to have a link to steamship traffic. At first, they revived the medieval Italian practice of quarantining – sequestering arriving passengers on their ships for forty (*quaranta*) days. Shipping companies bristled at the expense, though, and by later in the century ports around the world were equipped with a more advanced system of onshore quarantine stations, lazarettos, and sanitaria to store infected arrivals until they posed no threat.[9]

In New York Harbor, which received larger numbers of immigrants from outside its national territory than any other port, the US government consolidated these health facilities into the famous immigrant inspection station on Ellis Island. Its massive, Renaissance-style processing hall, which on its own handled twelve million migrants over eighty years of operation, has achieved mythic status as a symbol of the USA's openness to outsiders, perhaps enhanced by the Statue of Liberty that holds its welcoming beacon high on the next island over. This myth should not distract us from Ellis Island's function as a young empire's population filtration system – let alone the frequent use of the Statue of Liberty as an icon of "nativist" anti-immigrant movements. In New York, passengers in the first- and second-class cabins of incoming ships debarked without fuss directly onto the streets of Manhattan. Only the "unwashed" majorities of steerage passengers needed re-routing to Ellis Island for further inspection. Officials there sorted out those deemed too diseased or mentally or "morally" unfit – including homosexuals and many political radicals – for detention and deportation. Indeed, to avoid such screening, many immigrants to the USA preferred to pass through the Canadian port of Halifax, Nova Scotia, whose arrival station at Pier 21 was far more lenient. On Angel Island in San Francisco Bay, by contrast, the USA transformed the city's quarantine station into a processing center to screen Asian immigrants according to the far stricter terms of various Asian immigration restriction acts. Medical exams were notoriously invasive, and migrants denied entry who wished to appeal their cases often spent prolonged time in cage-like detention cells. As nativists across the USA convinced Congress to restrict migrants from other parts of Asia, and then southern and eastern Europe, Ellis Island took on many of the same summary functions of Angel Island. Similar restrictive dynamics operated in Vancouver. Meanwhile, Brazil and Argentina pursued policies of racial "whitening" by encouraging European migrants to flow freely through *Hospedarias dos Imigrantes* in Rio and São Paulo and a similar "immigrant hotel" in Buenos Aires. Officials there refused visas to Africans and Asians, and rejected all labor activists and socialists.[10]

The especially strong "pull" of migrants toward North America was partly due to rural homesteading laws passed by US and British authorities there in the 1860s and 1870s; similar laws also drew migrants to Australia and New Zealand. Migrants from northwestern Europe made up a disproportionate number of homesteaders, and they got the most fertile land nearest the railroad lines that allowed them to market their crop. By contrast, Native Americans and aboriginal peoples who survived genocidal war were confined to reservations later subdivided into plots that had little use, either for farming or for traditional hunting and foraging; these plots often ended up in the hands of white cattlemen who could afford to buy them by the hundreds and consolidate them into ranches. As for freed Black formerly enslaved people in the US South, the federal government reversed its Civil War-era promise to offer forty-acre plots of confiscated plantation land, and many freed people negotiated contracts as sharecroppers instead, some on the plantations where they were born enslaved. Old slave quarters were replaced with scattered single-family sharecropping cabins planted "up to the hustings" with cotton. Some Black farmers were able to purchase land, but many more sharecroppers fell into debt to landowners for seed and supplies, and thousands fell victim to a convict-lease labor system on prison plantations that was little different from slavery. As racist lynch mobs attacked Black landowners, business owners, voters, and officials, some freed families moved west to claim homesteads, often facing more violence there. Meanwhile, in rural Southern Africa, very similar racial dynamics played out, where white migrants, helped by colonial armies, seized the vast majority of fertile farmland and passed laws consigning the country's majority Black population to overcrowded, increasingly infertile, reserves. In the Union of South Africa, this system effectively turned the reserves into pools of cheap farm labor for white settlers who passed a law in 1911 that gave them exclusive control of 85 percent of the colony's land.[11]

INTO THE "SLUMS"

Cities themselves, of course, were the greatest of all nineteenth-century magnets for migrants. That fact explains their much higher growth rates compared with the world population as a whole. In cities, migrants faced new, epic struggles over space, beginning with the landlords who owned most of the housing in colonial "native towns" and factory districts. Some of these landlords were professional masons and carpenters who constructed most of the new urban spaces, sometimes by pooling resources themselves to lease land (typically on short terms). More often, these artisans worked for local merchants or industrialists able to amass larger plots, tenement districts, and rents. Industrialists also sometimes commissioned local builders to construct "company towns" for their workers, an investment that could reap extra profits for the corporation, not only in rent, but also in sales at company stores. No matter the landlord, the easiest way to make the most money out of an apartment building was to pack as many people as possible into the smallest space possible, and to skimp on the long-term solidity and livability of structures – especially those built on land leased for short terms.[12]

The deteriorated urban places that resulted were bigger than any popular neighborhood before, and they horrified observers – whether elites, or those of the popular majority who rose in protest at their own housing conditions. On a visit to Manchester in the 1840s, Friedrich Engels, heir to a German textile fortune turned Communist, tromped through working-class communities like Ancoats, Medlock, and Salford that were filled with recent migrants from the English countryside, as well as "Irishtown" and "Little Ireland," neighborhoods occupied by migrant from further afield.

> [I] wandered ... from one court to another ... through innumerable narrow dirty alleyways and passages. ... The area is full of ruined or half-ruined buildings. ... In the houses one seldom sees a wooden or stone floor, while the doors and windows are nearly all broken and badly fitting. And as for the dirt! Everywhere one sees heaps of refuse, garbage, and filth. There are stagnant pools instead of gutters and the stench alone is so overpowering that no human being, even partly civilized, would find it bearable to live in such a district. The recently constructed extension of the Leeds railroad which crosses the Irk [River] has swept away some of these courts and alleys, but it has thrown open to the public gaze some of the others. So it comes about that there is to be found immediately under the railway a court which is even filthier and more revolting than the others. ... This whole collection of cattle sheds for human beings was surrounded on two sides by houses and a factory.[13]

In writing passages like this, Engels drew on dozens of earlier similar blow-by-blow reports from Liverpool, Glasgow, Edinburgh, Birmingham, and other British cities, included those of the great slums of

London – St. Giles, the festering embarrassment in the very heart of the elite West End, and the larger Whitechapel and Bethnal Green slums in the East End. Engels's goal was to condemn "the greed of the builder for profit," but the writers he quotes, and even he himself, often swerved into language that condemns the residents of "slums" themselves for the horrible conditions in which they lived. The cry "slum!" also equated horrific housing with other difficult urban problems, such as unemployment, homelessness, begging, prostitution, racial mixing, crime, overcrowding, fire, filth, smells, "miasmas," disease, worries about urban property values – and, as always, fear of labor strikes, political agitation, and revolution. Amidst all that shock-talk, it was easy to sidestep the huge role of the profit system in generating urban inequity, and indulge instead in malicious theories about the inherent "degradation" of the working classes, women, "the Irish race," Jews, "natives," Asians, Africans, or African Americans.[14]

"Slum"-talk became a global language in the late nineteenth century, its mixed messages just as well understood in elite circles in Chicago as in Rio, Johannesburg, Bombay, and Hong Kong. It also gave state officials – most notably those urban planners who had the least sympathy with popular politics – a reason to go after slumlords in ways that only compounded the housing problems of the majority. For many of these officials, the solution to bad housing was simple: move slums as far as possible out of eyesight. Baron Haussmann had little regard for what he called Paris's "floating mass of workers . . . who have no mind of their own." Like most officials and elites, he saw no contradiction between, on the one hand, his support of massive government intervention in urban space when it allowed him to destroy slums to make way for bourgeois neighborhoods, and on the other hand, his absolute opposition to any government role in re-housing the displaced, let alone guaranteeing better conditions for them. When he cleared slums for boulevards, as we have seen, he simply moved them, and expanded them, to the city's east – to the great profit of real estate speculators.[15]

In a very similar way, the coffee-growing elite of Rio de Janeiro, allied with their British financiers, supported the planner Paulo de Frontin's destruction of the Brazilian capital's "*cortiços*" – which the elite press described as dens of "sordid promiscuity" and racial "miscegenation,"

16.1. Hong Kong, 1894: British Soldiers Invade Homes in the Taipingshan "Plague District" The Earth-spanning human habitat bred disease on an planetary scale. Beginning in 1894, a new global pandemic of bubonic plague killed twenty million people. Anti-plague measures were partly at fault: by destroying "slums" like Taipingshan, these soldiers sent rats scurrying across the city. Fleeing eviction, huge exoduses of people infected villages across the countryside. Quarantines did not apply to ship rats, which disembarked in dozens of seaports, sometimes hopping on troop trains to inland cities like Johannesburg. Even after urban research laboratories developed vaccines, "slum clearance and relocation" remained a favorite disease-fighting tool. In colonial cities like Hong Kong, that translated into a worldwide epidemic of urban racial segregation.
Sir James Cantlie, *Illustrations of Tropical Diseases* (1894–1907), p. 123, MS.6938, courtesy of the Wellcome Library.

and "nests of yellow fever, . . . vice, and crime." Re-housing, likewise, was the business of the slumlords of the city's distant northern districts. Alternatively, in-bound migrants built shacks, called *"favelas,"* for themselves on the surrounding mountain slopes – as they do by the millions today. There, the displaced poor faced long and expensive commutes to their jobs in the city center, for streetcar companies preferred servicing the elite neighborhoods in the beach districts to the south. Meanwhile, in Hong Kong in 1894 and in Bombay in 1896, officials were surprised by a massive epidemic of bubonic plague. In Hong Kong, officials destroyed many of the homes and belongings of residents in the Chinese Taipingshan neighborhood and soon led a campaign to create a separate "reservation" for Europeans only on the very summit of Victoria Peak. In Bombay, officials blamed the plague on the poor of the city's "Native Town," whom they saw as "the great filth producers of the city." House-to-house searches for plague victims ensued. Police carted many off to "isolation hospitals," among other summary public health measures, crossing religious taboos of all kinds in the increasingly polyglot city. Later, officials empowered the Bombay Improvement Trust, a board composed of British officials and local elites, to seize and destroy slum properties, especially those near upscale neighborhoods. The Trust did little to provide replacements, thus allowing slums to spread along much of the island on which the city sits. The city's already large population of sidewalk dwellers grew as well.[16]

In Johannesburg, municipal officials linked slum clearance directly to something even more troubling, a regime of state-sponsored racial segregation. The discovery of the world's richest seam of gold on the Witwatersrand attracted thousands of male mineworkers from the country's depleted Black reserves. Johannesburg mine-owners enmeshed these migrants in a contract-labor system that required them to live in guarded hostels near the mines eleven months out of the year. Many other migrants, including Black women, formerly indentured Indian laborers from the sugarcane fields, and poor white farmers, were attracted to other commercial and employment prospects offered by the new city, settling in huge dilapidated neighborhoods in and around Johannesburg's downtown. When the plague arrived in the city, the local Municipal Officer of Health Charles Porter ordered one of these neighborhoods, the "Coolie Location," burned to the ground. He then removed its Black and Indian inhabitants fifteen kilometers away – to a new government-built "native location" at the fly-blown outflow-pipe of the city's sewer system. In this way, he gave birth to what, after 1948, grew into Soweto, the largest of apartheid's Black townships. Porter's efforts fit into a broader push among British, French, German, Italian, and Belgian officials in colonial cities who blamed plague and above all malaria not on germs, rats, fleas, or mosquitoes, but on Africans, Asians, or mixed-race people. These officials embarked on public health campaigns that some urban historians call "Segregation Mania," dividing cities by race in many parts of Asia, in the Canal Zone of Panama, and in most of the colonial cites of Africa, including Lagos, which sprouted a "European" District called Ikoyi to its east. Such segregationist measures caused protests by these cities' non-white majorities, who demanded equal access to health care – and, for those with the means, equal access to real estate opportunities in White Towns. Black Lagosians slowly infiltrated white Ikoyi as their movement for independence from Britain grew (Fig. 20.2).[17]

THE FIGHT FOR THE CITY

What could inhabitants of majority neighborhoods do, faced with the hostile power of wealthy landlords, the wrecking balls of the state, racist public health officials, and the gentrifying and segregationist pressures all of these set in motion? Urban elites were right to suspect that majority neighborhoods' growing size, density, and spatial separation could make them into incubators of autonomous political action. Some of these neighborhoods even came into being as acts of defiance, for many new arrivals eschewed the slumlord-dominated rental market for life in squatter shacks that they erected themselves on as-yet undeveloped property. We already met Rio's *favelas*, but squatter shacks appeared everywhere. As the city of New York climbed north along the ladder-like rungs of its pre-planned street grid, crews who paved new streets and constructed formal buildings often began their work by sweeping away shacks like these. Servants in Calcutta's "palaces" and laborers on its docks typically lived in "*kachcha*" huts they built out of bamboo and thatch on the city's swampiest real estate – though new building codes urged them to rebuild "pucka," that is, out of brick and mortar.[18]

In some cities, workers who earned higher wages had a more stable option, first put into practice in Britain, then spreading as far afield as Chicago and Buenos Aires: they used their artisanal associations or labor unions to organize cooperative Building Societies. Members who contributed deposits could take out small loans to buy land for themselves and build homes of their own. Some families opened boarding houses on these plots and grew vegetables on small scraps of remaining land. Such small businesses could supply extra income, typically thanks to grueling double shifts worked by women. None of these autonomous strategies guaranteed better housing conditions. However, self-owned property could lay the foundation for small shops, saloons, wine bars, township *shebeens*, cabarets, theaters, and multifarious religious establishments. In popular neighborhoods, these businesses continued a long tradition of providing out-of-sight gathering spaces for more subversive popular action.[19]

Before we get to subversion, another service that the urban majority could provide autonomously to its own fellow members was a warm welcome to migrants arriving in strange new urban places. In nineteenth-century Beijing, some 400 *huiguan*, or native-place lodges, run by veteran Beijingers born elsewhere in the country, welcomed new migrants from the same provinces, offering regional religious services as well as aid to the unfortunate. Similar institutions in the industrializing treaty port of Shanghai offered compatriots leads to jobs that workers from their region monopolized. Overseas migrants to Osaka, New York, São Paulo, and Buenos Aires typically made their way from steamships or border posts to what sociologists call "vestibule neighborhoods" inhabited by previous arrivals from their regions of origin or even their home village. There the newcomers could visit independent ethnic institutions for help with housing, work, and language barriers. In Osaka's Koreatown (Tsurahashi), Chicago's Old Ghetto, Greek Town, and "Polonia," or São Paulo's "Little Italy" (Mooca), religious establishments offered services in familiar languages, and grocers sold ingredients for familiar dishes. In the big American cities, ethnic associations grew powerful enough to print newspapers, operate gathering places, found small banks and insurance companies, and even offer widow's benefits or pensions, creating a kind of autonomous "welfare state" all their own.[20]

For the most part, the residents of these neighborhoods did not harbor sufficient collective desire or power to keep other groups of migrants out of their territory. Chicago's Polonia, for example, housed a majority of non-Poles; it was typical for dozens of languages to echo in the streets of such vestibule communities. That said, "ethnic neighborhoods" in the USA did find ways of organizing bands of toughs to keep their "turf" free of Chinese migrants, meaning that the substantial Chinatowns that grew up in San Francisco and Vancouver were organized more acutely around the protection of their inhabitants from working-class white mobs than other similar "vestibule" neighborhoods. When things got too dangerous on the West Coast, some Chinese migrated east to form new defensive Chinatowns in cities from Montreal to Washington, D.C., including the still thriving center on New York's Lower East Side. Meanwhile, increasing numbers of Black migrants fled indebtedness and violence in the US South to cities across the Midwest and Northeast and as far away as Los Angeles. There and in cities across the South, they met new rounds of white mob violence, especially when they sought to move into white neighborhoods, no matter their ethnic mix. After 1910, whites in Baltimore, other Southern cities, and even some Midwestern ones passed "segregation ordinances" to keep Blacks in different parts of town from whites. Real estate hucksters used scare tactic to convince white home-owners that a "Black invasion" of their neighborhood was imminent, leading to merciless "neighborhood protection" riots in some cases, and, in others, the first instances of panicked selling and "white flight." By all of these means, residential color lines began to solidify in US cities. The first "Black Belts" appeared in Chicago's South Side and Manhattan's Harlem by 1900 – predecessors of the African-American "ghettos" that would soon grow throughout the country (Chapter 19).[21]

On a more hopeful note, poor tenants also used their bases in their neighborhoods to band together to fight landlords and the state. Their resistance to these especially powerful forces took what one of their historians, in the context of Tokyo, called an "enormous variety ... of tactics, strategies, goals, alliances, political calculations, political alliances, compromises, and ideologies." Most often, protests of slum housing and slum clearances also fit into a longer list of concerns of equal urgency: wages, working conditions, the vote, police violence, the price of bread and meat, tax hikes, transit fare hikes, high-handed public health initiatives, and, in pointed reference to the gendered dimensions of domestic space, the emancipation of women.[22]

The biggest political explosion to come out of working-class neigh-borhoods during this time was the Paris Commune of 1871. It followed more than two decades of simmering resentment on the part of industrial workers, who had led the French version of the Europe-wide revolution in 1848, only to see the Second French Republic fall to Napoleon III in a coup d'état a few years later. By the late 1860s, Haussmann-era displacement had transformed small villages like Belleville and Montmartre on the eastern and northern peripheries of the city into large popular neighborhoods. In this new "Red Belt," a vibrant associational life centered on wine bars and cabarets. Radical speakers, including envoys from Marx and Engels's First International Workingmen's Association in London, spread socialist and anarchist ideas. The spark for the new revolution was the capture of Napoleon III himself by Bismarck's Prussian army in 1870. In desperation to fight off Krupp's guns from bombarding Paris, a hastily assembled French Government of National Defense inducted tens of thousands of Bellevillois into a National Guard, including radicalized cohorts of women and a good handful of radical bourgeois bohemians, giving them plenty of guns and dozens of cannons. When elite republicans then turned tail and, at the Versailles palace, signed a humiliating surrender to the new Kaiser of the Germans, Red Belt National Guard detachments hauled their cannons to the heights of Montmartre and aimed them at the French Government's army. Soon the People of Paris seized the usual monuments, the Tuileries and the Hotel de Ville. They crowbarred the paving stones out of the roadbeds of Haussmann's boulevards and built barricades, reclaiming central districts that the planner had wrested from them. One of the Commune's first acts was to abolish all rent owed to landlords during the siege, a move that horrified bourgeois observers. Given more time, perhaps, the most radical government up to that point in world history would have gone farther and abolished all private property, as Marx and Engels eagerly urged it to do.[23]

That was not to be. The regular army rolled into Paris a few weeks later and slaughtered most of the Commune's National Guard during the bloodiest week ever in the city's revolutionary history. Between 17,000 and 25,000 people lay dead on the barricades or in a trench dug in Paris's Père Lachaise Cemetery. In retreat, Communards filled a large hall in the Tuileries with gunpowder, and blew the Sun King's palace to the ground. Other buildings associated with the "Old Regime" caught fire too; the 1871 Revolution succeeded in forever banishing kings from France. The slumlords, by contrast, quickly re-established their rule over housing in Belleville and Montmartre, soon stretching their influence into dilapidated suburbs further to the east and north. Still, revolutionaries the world over watched carefully, noting the moment of contingency that allowed the Communards of Paris to strike.[24]

Indeed, working classes elsewhere arose in their beleaguered neighborhoods dozens of times in the years between the Commune and a chain of even more explosive events in Russian cities beginning in 1905. Many of these flared out as quickly as the Commune did, yet likewise managed to live on as examples. In Bombay and Calcutta, the taboo-crossing plague measures of the 1890s caused massive revolts and the wholesale exit of tens of thousands of laborers back to their home villages. This show of popular force encouraged radical nationalists in both cities to dream of a Britain-free India for the first time. In Rio de Janeiro in 1893 and 1904, inhabitants of the doomed *cortiços* of downtown rose up amidst similar public health measures. As a sign of their opposition to the planners, they destroyed the fancy new lampposts that planners had installed on the new boulevards. They also targeted the swank trolley cars of transport companies that allowed elites to commute towards Copacabana and Ipanema.[25]

In Johannesburg around the same time, Blacks challenged the native location system, winning exemptions for better-off migrants to live in the city, and allowing Sophiatown, the "Harlem" of South Africa to emerge nearer downtown. Gathering in a similar neighborhood in Bloemfontein in 1912, delegates from Sophiatown and elsewhere founded the precursor to the African National Congress, which became the principal organization in the fight against apartheid after 1948. Indians in Johannesburg also anointed a local immigrant lawyer named Mohandas Gandhi to lead their struggle against segregation and immigration restriction. He would rise to leadership of the Indian independence struggle when he returned to Bombay after 1915. Meanwhile, in the original Black Harlem – the one in New York – W. E. B. Du Bois helped found the National Association for the Advancement of Colored People (NAACP), giving new life to a growing Black-led civil rights movement that, among other things, would fight against segregation ordinances and for open housing throughout the next century and beyond.[26]

Amidst all of these momentous events, representatives of the urban majority often found common cause with liberal and radical middle-class reformers whose specialty was drafting policies for improved and affordable urban housing. The motives of these liberal "housers" varied. A few were openly sympathetic to labor and anti-colonial struggles. Most hoped that their ameliorative policies would blunt enough of the miserable edge of slum life to save the capitalist system from more Paris Communes. Like the international community of urban planners, housers traded ideas with colleagues across the world. Early inspiration included the efforts of "enlightened capitalists" to build model industrial communities, like Robert Owens's cotton-mill town at New Lanark in Scotland (founded in 1790), which provided what were then considered state-of-the-art one-room apartments to workers' families, inspiring similar schemes near cotton mills in Jena, Germany and Nantong, China. Housing activists used philanthropic funds to build "model tenements" in London, New York, and elsewhere, hoping that they could inspire private owners to improve their buildings too. Other reformers founded "settlement" houses, where the ancestors of today's professional social workers lived in working-class districts, among other things helping to spread knowledge among policy makers about the parlous state of the surrounding neighborhoods.[27]

The city of Calcutta, the British Parliament, the City Council of New York, and the post-Commune French Third Republic all passed building codes aimed to improve conditions in working-class neighbor-hoods. In 1890, the British Parliament passed the landmark Housing of the Working Classes Act, giving the London City Council power to seize slum sites it considered irredeemable, clear them, and build new housing on site, thus avoiding some of the disruption of Haussmann-like removals. The idea of government-owned housing also arose during this time, with London's first municipally owned working-class estates; so did a few government-owned tramlines designed for working-class commutes. Working-class housing activists, usually led by women, mean-while also clamored for lower rents and repairs from private owners. They staged the first rent strikes during the early twentieth century in Glasgow's grim tenements and among 10,000 tenants of New York's Lower East Side, thus sparking a broader movement for government-enforced controls on rent (Figure 16.2). None of these actions made a huge dent in the system of for-profit slum housing until after the World Wars and the Great Depression. Then, new "welfare states" and Marxist

16.2. Working Women Strike the Slumlords: Harlem, New York City
Working-class women worked many shifts. Long days at the factory alternated with cooking, cleaning, and caregiving at home. Here, some worked a third shift, in the streets as rent-strikers, protesting the appalling conditions in tenements. They helped convince governments to enact building codes and construct public, or "social," housing. Harlem was a "vestibule" neighborhood, where immigrant women also took shifts running shops, churches, and community organizations that made newcomers from overseas feel at home. Whites were less welcoming to African Americans who arrived in northern US cities in

regimes began implementing many of these nineteenth-century proposals, building massive public housing estates that transformed the landscape of many of the world's popular neighborhoods.[28]

WORKERS OF EARTHOPOLIS, UNITE!

Meanwhile, the urban majority also used their concentrated presence in cities to launch a global labor movement. The usual neighborhood haunts remained critical crucibles of these movements, but industrial worksites were even more important – factories above all, but also railyards, docks, mines, construction sites, and in some cases municipal office buildings, hospitals, and universities. In these places of work, small and very large, the political game-board was much the same as in the tenements. Owners, largely supported by the state, had their hands on all the strongest chess-pieces. With only themselves as pawns to play, workers had to do the best they could with their sheer numbers, mustering in spaces where they could congregate out of sight of the owning class and the state, and calling on help from a few trustable elite allies.

This unequal political game-board had its origins in another one of the uncanny plot twists that punctuated the rise of the factory system in the late eighteenth century. How did factory owners persuade hundreds or thousands of workers to enter hot, noisy, unhealthful, stressful, and dangerous places, there to watch over machines day after day, sometimes literally on their knees, for exhausting sixteen-hour shifts – when the only incentive consisted of wages low enough for the owner to make a profit? What should owners do about the possibility that all those people in such constrained spaces would find ways to assert their own collective interests?

New forms of state power, pioneered once again in late-eighteenth-century Britain, were essential to resolve these uncertainties

---

Caption for 16.2. (cont.)

increased numbers during World War I. As Harlem transformed into a majority Black neighborhood, it became the epicenter of a civil rights movement, calling on Black women for extra shifts of their own – protesting urban racial segregation. Bettmann/Getty Images.

emphatically in employers' favor. Landowners in Parliament passed legislation that weakened farmers' grip on land and gave them little choice but to sell farms to consolidators and head into factory cities. Unemployed spinners and weavers, once again including majorities of women, moved to the mills and mines for some way of sustaining their families. Local municipalities rounded up "vagrants" and orphans from the streets, incarcerated them in workhouses, and made deals with big employers for daily delivery of especially exploitable labor forces, including children as young as five years old. Parliament passed "Combinations Acts" beginning in 1790 to make it illegal for workers to organize unions and thus to collectively withdraw their labor. Strikes proliferated nonetheless, as did work slow-downs. Disaffected cottage spinners and weavers broke into factories and sabotaged machinery. In response, the British state built no less than 155 military barracks before 1815 to suppress industrial strikes. Nonetheless, in the 1842 "Plug Riots," coal miners across the Black Country and Lancashire mill-hands forced a general strike that stretched to Wales and Scotland, simply by pulling plugs on the pressurized steam chambers of the engines that ran the mines and mills. The rise of modern urban police forces and prisons during the mid to late nineteenth century was closely tied to control over restive workforces.[29]

All along, workers recognized the complicity of the state in their subordination. They linked their workplace struggles to the acquisition of the vote and Parliamentary representatives of their own. It was not for nothing that the bloodiest early instances of urban class warfare occurred at massive rallies for parliamentary reform. In 1819 in St. Peter's Square, Manchester, soldiers wielding swords mowed down dozens of protestors at a massive working class rally for the vote. Journalists evocatively christened this event the "Peterloo Massacre," after the bloody battle of Waterloo where Napoleon had met his final defeat a few years earlier. Workplace protest also deeply infused movements for universal suffrage in England, such as the massive Chartist protests in London's squares and parks in 1848, and the republican revolutions that rocked cities across Europe that same year, including Paris as we know, but also Milan, Berlin, Frankfurt, Copenhagen, Stockholm, Budapest, Vienna, and many other places.[30]

In the mines, the iron forges, the steelworks, the docks, and the rail-yards, strikes took on larger dimensions, and class war got bloodier. Owners of these enormous built spaces had much more at stake in labor compliance than did owners of cotton mills, who tended to diversify their investments in other enterprises. Investments in steel works could involve sinking whole fortunes, not only in order to build the massive mills themselves, but also thousands of houses in large company towns. Examples of these include the Schneider family steel town at Le Creusot, France; Krupp's worker housing in Essen; Bethelehem Steel's Sparrow's Point in Baltimore; the city of Pullman, Illinois near George Pullman's railcar factory; and US Steel's entirely new city of Gary, Indiana, southeast of Chicago. The profitability of these industries, meanwhile, also meant far more to the economic basis of the state. Because of the large number of workers involved, including large numbers of skilled artisans, strikes were also bigger and more disruptive. When 100,000 workers struck in the coalmines of the Ruhr in 1889, they won little in immediate concessions, but they founded lasting labor unions, complete with new meeting halls. State repression was brutal, yet it also had a rebound effect, building further support for universal suffrage and some of the first workers' political parties, in this instance the German Social Democrats, who turned the city council of Berlin "red" in 1890 after their earlier street protests forced the Kaiser to lift a ban on their activity. The Paris Commune, and unsuccessful but enormous strikes in Britain, such as on London's docks in 1889, set similar boomeranging dynamics in motion.[31]

Cities in the USA were among the biggest and bloodiest class battle-grounds, as they were home to the world's longest rail networks, the biggest mines, and almost half of the world's steel production. "Robber Barons" like rail magnates Jay Cooke and Cornelius Vanderbilt and the Pittsburgh steel king Andrew Carnegie did not hesitate to request federal and state armed forces to crush strikes. Carnegie also famously hired his own private force of detectives and shop-floor spies, the Pinkertons. In 1877, over 100,000 rail workers shut down Cooke and Vanderbilt's rail junctions in Baltimore, Pittsburgh, Buffalo, and Chicago and burned down big parts of Philadelphia, sparking fears of an American Paris Commune. State and federal troops took several weeks to crush the strike, killing dozens of strikers in the process. However, the uprising fueled the rise of the 800,000-member Knights of Labor, the largest confederation of unions in US history.[32]

Frightened city governments built forbidding armories for their new police forces, as did states for their militias and National Guard troops, explicitly in order to quell strikes. These moves emboldened employers to resist strikers' demands. The fury of class war escalated, notably in 1886 as part of international protests for the eight-hour day, when bomb blasts echoed in Chicago's Haymarket Square, and in strikes across the industrial belt during the years 1892–94. Hundreds of workers lost their lives during state repression of new nationwide rail and coal strikes and at Pullman's company town near Chicago – a place he intended as a monument to his benevolence toward the working class.[33]

In 1892, Andrew Carnegie launched a vicious anti-union campaign by locking his workers out of his enormous mill at Homestead near Pittsburgh. His chief union fighter Henry Clay Frick surrounded the plant with a fence and gun turrets, then tried to insert a force of Pinkertons by barge across the Monongahela River. Workers turned their wrath against the stooges, firing their own cannons, then pouring petroleum on the surface of the river and setting it alight. The Pinkertons retreated in face of the flames, but 8,000 Pennsylvania National Guard soldiers stormed the plant, allowing Carnegie to hire replacement workers – the hated "scabs" – and force the union to capitulate. That did not stop workers in other large-scale American industries from going on strike, including in Chicago's railyards and stockyards several times, in most of the country's coalmines in 1905, at several large Pittsburgh steel plants again in 1909, and, in a strike entirely led by women, across New York City's archipelago of shirtwaist factories the same year. Homesteaders turned farmers meanwhile erupted in the Populist Movement against monopoly railroad shipping rates and the high interest rates of New York banks. Policy victories accelerated, including a worker's compensation system for the families of the thousands of workers injured on the job each year, the first attempts at state arbitration of strikes, and legislation breaking up the massive corporations called trusts. Momentum grew in the USA, and elsewhere in the industrialized world, for the eight-hour day, minimum wages, and the formal right to organize.[34]

These biggest of the urban class battles are the most widely remembered, but the labor movement became a global phenomenon only because of hundreds of thousands of much smaller or spontaneous workplace actions, including in cities far from the heartlands of heavy industry. In Rio de Janeiro, for example, protests against slum clearances drew on veterans of work stoppages at construction sites, on the docks, and among skilled craftspeople who still worked in smaller shops, as well as in the city's textile mills. In the huge belt of gold mines surrounding Johannesburg, perhaps the largest urban industrial area in the colonized world, African workers "struck" in 1904 simply by refusing to take mine contracts at reduced wages and by remaining in the rural reserves. Owners had to import thousands of indentured "coolies" from China just to keep the mines running. Black mineworkers, excluded from white unions, nonetheless soon built on the shared experience of compound life to build the labor organizations that later proved indispensable to the fight against apartheid.[35]

A wave of twenty-five strikes in Bombay and Madras textile mills prompted the foundation of the Bombay Millhands Association in 1890, the first of many enormous labor unions that would later join the Indian nationalist cause. In the "treaty port" of Shanghai, Chinese and European merchants invested in some of China's first modern silk and cotton mills, and the Qing dynasty built the modern-style Jiangnan Docks and Armory, attracting skilled artisans from other nearby cities and as far away as Guangzhou. These artisans expanded the local native-place lodges and transformed them into job pipelines for compatriots who moved to the city, then into vehicles for mounting militant strikes. From 1890 to 1919, the city's foremost labor historian counted thirty-seven strikes by skilled artisans, including Cantonese carpenters at the Armory, butchers, metalworkers, silk dyers, barbers, and tofu makers. Unskilled workers, many of them recent migrants who depended on gang-like protection societies to establish themselves in the city, struck a further fifty-four times, most often at silk and cotton mills and on the docks. Even the city's night-soil removal crews struck twice at moments when sewer-building projects threatened their age-old livelihood. All of this militant activity underlay Shanghai's crucial role in the Chinese Xinhai Revolution of 1911, when Nationalists led by Sun Yat-sen overthrew the last Qing emperor and proclaimed what was at that time world history's largest-ever republic. Among other things, members of the Shanghai union of carpenters, a preserve of migrants from Guangzhou, opened the gates of the Jiangnan Armory to Republican troops, allowing them to launch their final assault on the Qing's southern capital Nanjing, and end 2,000 years of dynastic rule in the most fertile city-growing region of the world.[36]

By 1900, the urban majority – the sum total of the scattering and coalescing migrant millions, the colonial subjects of the world's empires, and the often radical "Workers of the World" – had established a firm, if radically transformed, place across much of the Urban Planet. Labor, community, farmer, women's suffrage, anti-racist, and anti-colonial movements had all become forces to reckon with. None ceded the geographical space it occupied – as grueling as life in the transformed rural stretches of Earthopolis remained, as dilapidated and overcrowded as their neighborhoods may have been, and as grim and hostile as work in factories remained.

What happened next to the exploding Urban Planet? And what next for all the imperialists, the capitalists, the planners, the high-minded *Belle Époque* bourgeois, and the fired-up urban majorities who caused Earthopolis to explode, both in size and in its politics? Leif Jerram lays it out best, as only a historian gifted at juggling events on small urban and large global scales could: "What did the tsar care what the workers of the No. 6 Shop, Trubochnaya Metal Works in St. Petersburg thought? Not much, perhaps. But he would soon come to care, when they went on strike in 1916 and 1917, destroyed his world, and transformed global politics for our time."[37]

CHAPTER 17

Lamps Out

BRIGHT LIGHTS AND POWDER KEGS: THE *BELLE ÉPOQUE*

The goddess Inanna had warned us, back when the Urban Planet was first born. Cities would allow us to accomplish big things, yet among them would be brutal acts of urban annihilation. That thought is terrifying enough, but even Inanna would have to wonder at the events of August 6 and 9, 1945, when, in a pair of blinding sun-like flashes delivered from the air, humans vaporized the Japanese city of Hiroshima, killing some 100,000 of its inhabitants – then repeated the act three days later at Nagasaki. What kind of horrific plot twist in the history of cities' capture of geo-solar energy and their potent polities made this possible? What role did the modern Hydrocarbon Urban Planet play in the most destructive chapters of world history – the leveling of hundreds of cities, yet another murderous global pandemic of disease, and the slaughter of over 100 million people, at the hands of fellow humans, from 1914 through that awful day in August 1945?

"Cities of Light." Back in 1900, the era's notoriously giddy prophets of human progress could not have remotely imagined the blinding atomic suns over Hiroshima and Nagasaki. "Vienna!," they would be more likely to sigh. "The Ringstrasse is lined with the lamps of human glory!" A modern miracle, indeed, the Ringstrasse: a necklace of some the most beautiful boulevards and monuments in Europe, an arching embrace of one of the continent's loveliest city centers, one of the best symbols of Europe's "beautiful years" – the *Belle Époque*. Also, a fitting symbol of forward-looking courage, for building the Ring required the Viennese to take down the city's enormous bastion walls and glacis – once protectors of Europe from the Turks, now symbols of a supposedly outdated, war-hungry age. True, even in 1900, relics of Vienna's warlike, authoritarian past lingered on. The medieval Habsburg dynasty still ruled from the many-winged Hofburg palace at the keystone of the Ringstrasse's grand arc. Old aristocrats still stuffed themselves and their large retinues in mansions throughout the city center. Barracks for the emperor's massive army pinned down key flanking points of the Ring, ironically where the boulevards caressed a channel of the city's romantic river, immortalized by the city's Waltz King Johann Strauss II as the "Blue Danube."

However, the Ringstrasse was the masterwork not of royalty but of Vienna's new "liberal" bourgeois elite – its Promethean industrialists, capitalists, upper civil servants, professionals, and Haussmann-inspired planners. The *Reichsrat*, the temple-like parliament that the new ruling class had called into being in the years since Vienna's version of the 1848 revolution, rose majestically next door to the Hofburg, transforming the once-absolutist Habsburgs into mere constitutional monarchs. The Ringstrasse also had a vibrant city hall, a stock exchange, a university, an opera house, a state theater and a city theater, art museums, and hospitals. Middle-class apartment buildings filled the old city inside the Ringstrasse's embrace, and a fantastical new department store supplied those apartments with luxury goods. Speaking of light, glorious wrought-iron street lamps made the whole Ringstrasse glow at night, even more so when electricity replaced gas. Vienna also displayed plenty of light of another kind. Statues to all of the geniuses of Central European culture filled the streets near the Ringstrasse: Haydn, Mozart, Beethoven, Schubert, Schiller, Goethe, and Richard Wagner, the Mastersinger of the German world's operatic national soul. All owed their immortality to the audiences and readers of Vienna.[1]

To be sure, not everyone in Vienna shared the bourgeoisie's high opinion of its own enlightenment. The opposition, in fact, started with the middling classes' own children. As bohemians, students, artists, scientists, or – as Émile Zola first called their Parisian counterparts – "*les intellectuels*," they used long stretches of family-funded disposable time to light all sorts of lamps and fires, whether in Vienna's cake-and-whipped-cream-filled cafés, its university classrooms, in laboratories and psycho-therapists' new sitting rooms, or in artists' garrets. Some revolutionized their fields with world-altering consequences: Sigmund Freud in psychology, Gustav Mahler and Arnold Schönberg in music, Gustav Klimt in painting, and Camillo Sitte and Otto Wagner in sanitation works, social housing, and architecture. They also absorbed waves of transformative discoveries across Europe: the discovery of the microbiological roots of disease in Pasteur's Paris and Koch's Berlin; Niels Bohr's modeling of the atom in Cambridge and Copenhagen; Marie Curie's experiments with radiation in Paris; Albert Einstein's theory of relativity, conceived in part while he was a professor at Austro-Hungary's own University of Prague. Thus was born the physics that underlay the bright suns that flashed years later over Japan.[2]

Others in "Young Vienna" thought their parents' revolution far too tame, and sharpened the radical edges of middle-class politics. What, they asked, of the spreading neighborhoods just outside the Ringstrasse, home of the city's majority – the working classes? What kind of City of Light left the human majority in its own urban shadow? Was the Ringstrasse still a glowering city wall after all, a fancified firebreak against surrounding sparks of discontent? Others pressed the "woman question," particularly as suffragists marched in American cities or, like the Pankhurst sisters in London, planted bombs in public mailboxes. Either way, by 1900, university students, inhabitants of the very core of the City of Light, had become a force in the new century's global urban mass politics.[3]

Vienna's workers, meanwhile, lit lamps of their own. Outside the Ringstrasse, in their hundreds of thousands, they built labor houses, union halls, and the headquarters of a new Social Democratic Party, complete with a newspaper print shop often raided by the police. Such spaces amplified thousands of conversations in the city's beer-cellars, the unions' new reading and sports clubs, and the shop floors of Vienna's factories. Visions emerged of city spaces that offered healthier lives to all, not just to the bourgeoisie – by providing workers with higher pay, safer workplaces and housing, greater dignity, and a sense of equality, belonging, and collective effectiveness. Strikes, mass rallies, and banner-waving May Day parades multiplied in the streets and at the factory gates, and sometimes flowed directly into the Ringstrasse itself. In 1905, when a would-be revolution detonated against the tsar in far-off St. Petersburg,

Russia, thousands of Social Democrats, feminists, and a smattering of student allies marched peacefully past the Hofburg and planted their red flags on the steps of the Reichsrat. It was a gentle reminder to the ruling family that, among Old Regime relics, the Habsburgs were almost as far behind as the Russian Romanovs in granting the vote to people who did not meet minimum tax thresholds for eligibility. Only universal suffrage, they argued – and Vienna's feminists insisted that meant *truly* universal – would allow the Social Democrats to take their rightful place in the parliament, maybe even supplanting the emperor, the factory bosses, and the bourgeoisie as a whole.[4]

What could go wrong in the *Belle Époque* Viennas of the world? What did the bright lights of this most advanced of cities have to do with the blinding suns of death at Hiroshima and Nagasaki? Unfortunately, Inanna would not have to search very far in Vienna to find lit fuses hissing far too close to explosive urban political forces. First, of course, Vienna was the capital of a rampant, conquest-hungry empire – like all the world's empires at the time, armed to the teeth. Historians sometimes pooh-pooh Austria-Hungary, run by a "dual" monarchy with one capital in Vienna's Ringstrasse and another at a splendid parliament building in Budapest 200 kilometers down the Danube. This cumbersome leadership structure and Austro-Hungary's lack of distant colonies seemed pale in comparison with empires run from Berlin, St. Petersburg, and Tokyo, let alone Washington, Paris, and London. Nonetheless, the empire of the Habsburgs remained a force of great potential violence. Its generals and admirals were empowered by the Reichsrat to conscript and arm up to 800,000 soldiers and sailors – the equivalent of an entire Vienna under arms. Each of the army's twenty-six corps was assigned a different barracks, commanded by the ones on the Ringstrasse but spread across the empire's archipelago of Central and Eastern European colonial cities, including Prague (Bohemia), Kraków (Poland), Lviv (Ukraine), Timişoara (Transylvania), and Zagreb (Croatia). Mostly landlocked, Austria-Hungary nonetheless possessed a navy with very big guns, docked at another colonial city it controlled, the Italian port of Trieste. The empire's latest conquest was admittedly small by comparison with the Scramble for Africa: the nearby former Ottoman province of Bosnia-Herzegovina in the Balkans. Sarajevo, the new colony's capital, soon got the twenty-sixth imperial barracks. Because the colony had a large Slavic population, the conquest put Vienna and Budapest in conflict with a fierce Russian-allied nationalist regime in neighboring Belgrade, Serbia. Because Sarajevo also had a large Muslim population, and many mosques and minarets, the Habsburgs likened it to other conquered "eastern cities" like French Algiers or British Cairo. Like the ruling classes of rival European "Great Powers," the Habsburgs longed to take Istanbul itself, feast on the whole of the Ottoman empire's revolution-wracked carcass, and, in the longer term, drink deeply from new oil wells in the Caucasus and Persia, now ruled by the Qajar dynasty in the new capital of Tehran.[5]

Indeed, a second light-darkening feature of Vienna was its role in Europe's arms races, which also increasingly involved thinking about sources of oil. In this matter, the Viennese bourgeoisie, and in particular its high elite of industrial and financial capitalists, was a critical partner to the empire. Borrowing capital from banks in Vienna, Paris, London, and even New York, raising even more on the Ringstrasse's stock exchange, industrialists continually updated the killing technologies produced by their metal shops in Bohemia and their dry-docks at Trieste, then ran rail-lines to connect all of these to the emperor's armories, barracks, and battleships. Hydrocarbon power ran the whole apparatus. Coal remained king at first, but in the 1910s, the British Navy Secretary Winston Churchill decided to refit Britain's dozens of steel-sided "Dreadnought" battleships with oil-burning furnaces. That sent signals to Austro-Hungarian Trieste and to admirals across the world that petroleum would soon become the fuel of choice to exert dominance of the oceans. Acquiring oil also meant practicing even greater global dominance, for oilfields were more distantly located to most Great Power capitals than were coal seams. In pursuit of objectives like these, the court in Vienna signed an alliance of mutual protection with its counterpart in Berlin against all of the world's biggest empires, notably Britain, France, and Russia. A Berlin-to-Baghdad railway that would exert Germanic domin-ance in Southwest Asia was high on the alliance-makers' list of projects.[6]

Third, there was the dark side of all of that light produced in univer-sities such as Vienna's. Almost all university students in *Belle Époque* Europe and the Americas learned of the "science" of race. In Vienna, middle-class students were taught that they were members of one of the "superior" races of the world, possessed of even higher energies of the super-racial German "nation" or *Volk*. The imperial hierarchy of Germans over Slavs, Hungarians, Romanians, and Muslims was reflected in the Austro-Hungarian polity – just as other imperial powers rested on the supremacy of Europe's "white" races of Europe over Asians, Africans, and "mixed-race" Latin Americans. Yet, warned some of Vienna's "ethnology" professors, racial superiority also came with racial vulnerability. World-spanning empires were thinly spread. Europe was threatened by what one theorist called a "rising tide of color," evident in the large-scale migration of Asians to white settler colonies and in rising anti-colonial movements. In Vienna, that rising tide meant angry "Slavic nationalist" crowds in the streets in Prague, Kraków, and Sarajevo. Even if soldiers from the barracks could control that particular problem, some theorists fretted about another dilemma much closer to home – something they called the "Jewish question." For homework on this subject, students might peruse the writings of the German composer Richard Wagner. An "alien" Semitic race, he wrote, had taken advantage of emancipation to assimilate itself into positions of power throughout the German-speaking liberal bourgeoisie, including its state bureaucracies, industrial headquarters, banks, the professors' own university departments, and even the lecture halls they addressed. To anti-Semites, Vienna faced racial subversion from within the very monuments of the Ringstrasse.[7]

All of this "race science" was fabricated nonsense: there are no "races" of humankind, let alone an existential "conflict of the races"; nor has there ever been a Jewish conspiracy to rule the world. However, racism and anti-Semitism – just like imperialist nationalism and the masculine strength of "great men" like the Bonapartes and Latin American *caudillos* – had a way of infecting "liberal" Europe's most promising innovation: People Power. True, that promise remained real enough – as attested by a worldwide Parliament House-building spree, and, after 1920, tumbling economic and gender restrictions on the vote. Industrial workers like those in Vienna were not the only ones pursuing the dream of popular sovereignty. So were tens of millions of colonial subjects: ethnic social democrats in Prague, other Slavic colonial capitals, and Trieste; anti-Ottoman movements stretching from Balkan, Romanian, and Greek cities to Armenian and Arabian capitals in the east; anti-British movements in Dublin, Cairo, Johannesburg, and Calcutta; and the fiercely anti-Western Boxer rebellion in and around Beijing.[8]

However, the streets of cities like Vienna also smoldered with popular counterforces that were anti-egalitarian and even anti-parliamentary. We cannot forget that the industrial and republican revolutions left many of the residents of European cities deeply embittered, even crushed; Japanese cities harbored many similarly humiliated by the Meiji, notably the old samurai class. In Vienna, these embittered classes included a declining group of aristocrats and monarchists, but also larger numbers of military officers, religious people skeptical of science, a few gangs of conservative students and bohemians, and a much larger group that Marx derided as the *"petite-bourgeoisie"*: lower-level state or corporate clerks, and small-shop artisans and retailers unable to compete with factories or department stores, often deep in debt to bourgeois banks. Their assorted resentments often entered the public discussion in the form of nostalgia for the grandeur of the old Imperial Catholic order, militant German nationalism and imperialist racism, and a hatred of capitalism, liberalism, and socialism, which many deemed the work of Jewish power.

In Vienna, the former liberal politician Karl Lueger tapped into these deeply poisoned wells of popular sentiment as early as the 1880s. Since his shop-owning *"petits bourgeois"* paid enough tax to acquire the vote earlier than factory workers, Lueger was able to upstage Social Democrats in a series of electoral victories in the popular districts of Vienna. Soon his Christian Social Party seized the City Hall on the Ringstrasse, and Lueger became the city's mayor. From that perch, the "Lord God of Vienna" cemented a pharaonic social legacy by hiring planners to expand Vienna's waterworks, sewers, parks, schools, hospitals, and social welfare institutions. Mercifully, Lueger did not stoop to discrimination or violence against Vienna's Jews, but the success of his anti-Semitic campaigns caught the eye of one of the Ringstrasse's shiftiest bohemians. Drifting between various garret apartments and cafés from 1908 to 1913, Adolf Hitler made his living painting postcards of Vienna's monuments, frittering away the proceeds on cake and whipped cream, and nursing idle dreams of becoming a great architect. Only later – in Munich, another German-speaking "city of light" – would Hitler draw up the blueprints for the murderous edifices for which he became famous. His "Führer Party" would use a street-based coalition similar to Lueger's to create a pan-German "Third Reich" whose first conquest, the 1938 *Anschluss* of Austria, was made possible by Vienna's city's own armed anti-Semites. The path to Hiroshima, we know in retrospect, opened largely because of his megalomaniacal fantasies.[9]

EXPLOSIONS TO THE EAST

Back in the early 1900s, however, the dual monarchy in Vienna and Budapest was still able to stanch the city's portentous fuses short of explosion. By contrast, the palace and bourgeois elites of Tokyo and St. Petersburg found their cities harder to govern. In Meiji Tokyo in 1904, the dynasty's ruling oligarchs had purchased a dozen British and French warships, added a few copies from Japan's own shipyards, and then sank much of the Russian tsar's Pacific Fleet at anchor in the Chinese treaty city of Port Arthur. A few enormously bloody battles later, some fought in trenches fortified by a newfangled product of Japanese steel mills known as barbed wire, the Japanese army marched north through the Liaodong Peninsula, and then mowed down 80,000 Russian defenders of the coal city of Mukden in Manchuria. A few weeks later, Japanese admirals completed the tsar's humiliation by sinking three-quarters of Russia's vaunted Baltic fleet, which arrived after sailing 33,000 kilometers from St. Petersburg to the Sea of Japan. (Problems fueling the Russian ships with enough coal gave Japan an advantage, and helped encourage Churchill to convert the British navy to lighter petroleum.) Victory celebrations in Tokyo, however, quickly led to rancor. In peace-talks hosted by US President Theodore Roosevelt in Portsmouth, New Hampshire, Meiji negotiators failed to secure war reparation payments from Russia like those that Britain and France had extracted from the Qing after the Opium Wars. Humiliated Japanese nationalists gathered in Tokyo's Hibiya Park. Police officers tried to pin the protestors there, but they broke loose and rampaged across the city, attacked hundreds of the city's new "modern" police boxes, and then gathered threateningly at the gates of the Imperial City. This was only one instance of what one historian called "unprecedented crowd violence" in Tokyo

(A)

(B)

17.1. *Belle Époque* Cairo: Between Café, Colonialism, and Mosque

and many other Japanese cities over the next few decades. As in Vienna, much of it involved labor militancy from the left; at several points, strikes dangerously paralyzed Tokyo's Koishikawa armory and the nearby Ishikawajima naval yards. As at Hibiya Park, though, much of it also came from Japan's version of Karl Lueger's populist right wing. Nationalist militarists repeatedly hounded the Meiji oligarchy anytime they appeared weak toward Russia, China, and Korea – or the USA. As in Russia and the USA at the same time, assassination of political leaders became a dangerously common tactic.[10]

In St. Petersburg, the tsar's defeat in 1905 enraged Russia's own Slavic nationalists and anti-Semites. There the violence was far worse, for the revolutionists took much of their rage out in unspeakable pogroms against Jews in the capital and across the Pale. In the Black Sea port of Odessa, mobs killed 2,500 members of the city's very old Jewish community. Meanwhile, tens of thousands of workers from St. Petersburg's particularly enormous metalworking and munitions plants left the factory to stage peaceful protests, along with substantial cadres of feminists, in front of the tsars' Winter Palace. There, Nicholas II's troops fired on the crowd, killing several hundred people in the infamous December Massacre. In response, strikes and protests reverberated throughout the Russian empire, at one time involving nine in ten workers. Murderous reprisals by troops killed hundreds of protestors in Russian-controlled Riga (Latvia) and Warsaw (Poland), igniting anti-colonial fury there and in Russia's Central Asian colonies. Students left the universities and cafés

---

Caption for 17.1. (cont.)

In 1900, at a sidewalk café almost anywhere, a white male bourgeois could bask in the satisfactions of global power and the thrills of modern city life. Nearby lurked tension, anxiety, and hatred – in Europe from rebel bohemians, feminists, workers, and right-wing radicals who deemed cafés a louche threat to virility, military might, and white supremacy. In Cairo, educated Egyptians sit in European-style cafés (A) beneath advertisements in French. Their *tarbush* hats may signal membership in a nationalist middle class eager to liberate Egypt from expatriate capitalists and colonial officers at the next table. Nearby, at another coffee shop (B) under advertisements in Arabic, people in "traditional" dress live to the rhythms of the minaret's calls to prayer – and in the mosques, Muslim *'ulamā'* despair of the boulevard life. Back in Europe, such mixed urban emotions led toward World War. In Cairo, they presaged mass protest against colonial rule and, later, conflict over the role of Islam in Egyptian society.

Roger Viollet/Getty Images and Hulton Archive/Getty Images.

for the streets, joining workers. Former serfs invaded noble estates and began a movement to redistribute acres of unused farmland there. Rail workers shut down the still-unfinished Trans-Siberian Railroad with help from mutinying Russian soldiers stumbling home from the Japanese siege of Mukden. Naval officers and sailors rebelled in Vladivostok on the Pacific, and in Sebastopol on the Black Sea. A militant activist from Georgia named "Koba" helped launch general strikes in the oil-refining port of Batumi, and then in the "Black City" of Baku, where dozens of oil derricks went up in flames in an ensuing ethnic war. Then, more ominously, sailors rose up in the home of the Baltic fleet itself – Kronstadt, on an island a mere twenty kilometers from the tsar's palaces in St. Petersburg.[11]

To coordinate worker strikes in the tsar's capital, socialist leaders called on factory workers to elect representatives, one for every 500 people on the shop floor. Hundreds met at St. Petersburg's Technological Institute, and the first worker "soviet" (council) was born, lasting three months until the tsar's henchmen arrested its leader, Leon Trotsky, and squashed the near-revolution of 1905. For Vladimir Lenin, the widely read Russian Marxist intellectual, 1905 was the "dress rehearsal" for something far bigger, a proletarian revolution and dictatorship led by his own extra-parliamentary "party of a new type," the Bolsheviks. Nonetheless, Lenin was aware that ruling a vast multiethnic empire like Russia would be just as difficult for Marxists as for Tsars. In 1913, he dispatched the oil-belt Bolshevik "Koba" to Vienna to study how the Habsburgs kept the ethnic peace. Once again, events in Vienna foreshadowed the world to come: Koba's report came out under his even snappier pseudonym Josef Stalin.[12]

URBAN PLANETARY WAR

Historians agree: the popular uprisings of 1905 highlighted the fragility of imperial and capitalist rule in the very streets of its capital cities. Yet imperialists and capitalists themselves built their own, much greater, explosive forces into the Urban Planet. In the wake of imperial conquests, military leaders gained influence in important ministries in these nations' capitals. The size and numbers of army barracks and seaport naval yards increased. Financial centers grew richer on loans for purchases of armaments. In weapons-making cities and shipyards, tsunamis of capital set off synergies of weapons "improvements" – as rifles gave way to machine guns, cannons to enormous non-recoiling artillery pieces, and as coal-fired battleships transformed into oil-fueled, all-steel dreadnoughts. Entirely new platforms for death-delivery emerged: petroleum-powered automobiles, submarines, airplanes, blimp-like airships like Germany's Zeppelins, and soon tanks. In an age of multi-million-plus armed forces, railroads became the ultimate machine of war mobilization, as the German strategist Helmuth von Moltke the Elder had noted as early as the 1880s: "For national defense, it is far more profitable to spend a few million on completing our railways than on new fortresses." For Germany, canals were weapons too: the navy dug an expensive one between its ports on the Baltic and North Seas so they could shuttle their battleships back and forth, as needed, against enemies in Russia to the east, and France and Britain to the west. The French responded by aiming more railroads of their own toward Germany's western borders, while investing heavily in the much sparser Russian system, hoping to endow the French Republic's unseemly absolutist ally in St. Petersburg, Tsar Nicholas II, with the ability to draw German forces away from France by moving his vast peasant armies toward Berlin from the east. Meanwhile these rivalries festered across the Oceans in too many European colonial cities to count. It is a cliché to call *Belle Époque* Europe an "armed camp." Yet the metaphor ably highlights the very real role played by the built environments of the imperial capitalist Urban Planet in touching off the combination of explosive synergies and sheer historical flukes that led to World War I.[13]

In August 1914, the "lamps went out" over Europe, its *Belle Époque* engulfed in total and soon global war. Why one assassination among many in the period, this one of a Viennese archduke in the streets of the colonial city of Sarajevo, Bosnia-Herzegovina, could set off such a calamity is a question that has no single answer. Clearly much hung on the fluky chains of diplomatic chess moves played by elites in European capitals' supreme "rooms where it happened." Yet the "total" part of total war – the weaponization of every aspect of most of the world's most advanced urban–industrial societies – also reflected massive shifts in the relationship between weapons and the built environment.

As Moltke hoped, mass mobilization by railroad and powerful new artillery pieces did quickly overwhelm stout fortress towns, including reinforced Vauban-era forts around Liège and Antwerp, Belgium. From there, the Germans nearly succeeded in a dastardly plan to outflank Paris from the west by moving hundreds of thousands of soldiers and wall-breaking guns by rail across flat northern France. However, thanks to the tsar's countermoves against Germany in the east, some last-minute hesitation by German generals, and the decision by Joseph Gallieni, a former colonial official turned Prefect of Paris, to deliver thousands of French soldiers to the front via the city's taxi cabs, an unexpected new reality set in. Once in battle, generals found that 1914-era gunpowder weapons could create much larger zones of death than ever before. In battlefield environments saturated with machine-delivered bullets, grenades, and shrapnel-filled exploding artillery shells, no train – nor horse, nor any new gas-powered automobiles – could move soldiers quickly enough to escape. The age-old flanking maneuver temporarily lost its efficacy, and frontal assaults became far deadlier than ever before. Neither the Germans nor the combined French and British armies found ways through or around each other. Soldiers were compelled to dig trenches to avoid the guns, and within months, Moltke's theory about trains supplanting fortifications dissolved in a fashion already presaged in Korea during the Russo-Japanese War. Soldiers on both sides became construction workers on a grim built environment designed to kill and bury millions of them. In the October muck of French farm fields, they improvised the largest and crudest fortification system ever: the trenches of the Western Front.[14]

Within a year, the front stretched from the English Channel to the Alps. Each opposing side consisted of three or more parallel ditches, connected with perpendicular communicating passageways to facilities in the rear, separated by a "no man's land" of varying width from the enemy lines the entire way. In the Alps, French soldiers carved more trenches through glacier ice against the possibility of hostile Italian moves over the passes. Machine gun points and concrete pillboxes punctuated trench-lines. Coils of barbed wire fresh from steel mills in Essen and Le Creusot ran throughout no man's land and rendered another venerable act of war, the cavalry charge, equally obsolete. The trenches themselves were death-dealing microbe traps as much as they were sources of protection. Even here, though, new urban sanitary measures, such as delousing stations against typhus, limited death by disease until the waning days of the war, when the flu overtook the war and the world. The only way to push opponents' trenches backward was through massive suicidal infantry charges through no man's land: the Battles of the Somme and Verdun were the deadliest as well as the least decisive in world history to that point. New technologies of armed mobility made some difference in breaking the stalemate by 1918, notably tanks that could overrun barbed wire and even trenches. Giant Zeppelin "airships" dropped bombs on Liège and Antwerp in the sieges of 1914, thus expanding a devastating new form of warfare pioneered in 1911 by Italian air pilots who bombed a site near Tripoli, Libya during Rome's conquest of that Ottoman province. German Zeppelins soon similarly delivered quiet floating death to civilians in London and the English port of Hull. More important to the outcome was Britain and France's enlistment of troops from across their African and Asian empires. So was North America's enormous archipelago of foundries, automobile assembly lines, and dry-docks, retooled by factory owners to serve the hot global market in weapons. By the time the USA entered the war in 1917, ocean-going troopships delivered soldiers from all continents to fight Germany on the Western Front. As the "Second" German Reich melted away in Berlin, and as Habsburg rule vanished in Vienna, revolution-minded urban protest spread throughout Central Europe and much of the world.[15]

Meanwhile, the new influenza virus, probably brought to the front by American soldiers from an army base in Kansas, outflanked the sanitary measures in the trenches, sickening hundreds of thousands of soldiers on both sides. Demobilization from World War I, itself an affair of still more ocean-going troopships and rail-lines, was thus likely more deadly than mobilization. The concentration and extension of a war-fighting built environment that killed ten million soldiers and as many or more civilians now metamorphosed into a super-incubator of deadly disease. Soldiers brought the flu home with them, spreading it throughout the large cities of the world and countrysides beyond. Despite pioneering public health measures like business closures, public event cancellations, social distancing, and even mask wearing, three waves of the virus infected a third of all people on Earth, killing at least fifty million people and possibly tens of millions more. The influenza pandemic of 1918–19 thus rivals "Justinian's Plague" of the sixth century CE as the second most deadly in history after the Black Death.[16]

RED PETROGRAD

A year before that, in February 1917, the biggest revolution of them all ended the 500-year rule of the Russian tsars. Like other revolutions, Russia's consisted of many events, not only in cities, but also on thousands of rural estates and on war-fronts stretching from Finland to the Caucasus to the Pacific Ocean. However, as always, the battle for the capital was decisive.[17]

At the beginning of the war, officials had toughened St. Petersburg's Slavic martial demeanor by renaming the city "Petrograd." However, Tsar Nicholas II's first city was a uniquely vulnerable space from which to operate a twentieth-century war machine. For one thing, Russia's measureless flat borders with Germany and Austria-Hungary required the capital's war ministries to recruit far more soldiers than those of its enemies. Some twelve million Russians, most heavily indebted former serfs, answered the tsar's involuntary call over the four years of the war. Several million more needed to leave the countryside to join the factory workforces that produced the weapons, uniforms, and boots needed by all those soldiers and sailors. Some headed to Moscow and other textile manufacturing cities, but the largest number, possibly as many as 400,000, moved to Petrograd, because the Russian arms industry was uniquely – and, it turned out, dangerously – concentrated in the capital. Railroads, and the city's rail stations, arguably mattered more to Petrograd than to other World War I capitals as well, because the distances from the arms factories to the sprawling Eastern Front were so much greater. Yet, despite French investment, the Russian rail network was sparser and more vulnerable to shell attack than that on the Western Front.[18]

While Petrograd's location on the Gulf of Finland had suited it well for its original mission as Russia's conduit to Europe, the city was distant from Russia's great food-producing lands to the south. As the city exploded in size to meet war needs, its reliance on rail-borne grain transport only increased. Meanwhile as peasants moved to the front and the cities, Russia's breadbaskets produced less for city dwellers to eat. As industrial output switched toward weapons, factory-made consumer items that, in peacetime, farmers would have bought eagerly with their grain money now became rarer and too expensive. Officials in Petrograd found it impossible to convince peasants, who were hungry themselves, to part with their grain at lower prices, and as a result the price of bread rose for the hundreds of thousands of war workers in Petrograd. By 1917, there was little bread in the city at all.[19]

Otherwise, downtown Petrograd was a standard old-regime absolutist capital. The tsar's own Winter and Summer Palaces spread-eagled themselves along the south shore of the Neva River. Aristocratic mansions surrounded them, as did statue-filled grand squares, dozens of police and army barracks, including two that housed the loyal horse-mounted Cossack regiments, and the headquarters of the Okhrana, the tsar's murderous secret police. Petrograd's "Bastille," the thorny Fortress of Peter and Paul, provided the semblance of protective order to the royal district from a small island to the north. The city's vast naval yards once more bristled with battleships, thanks again to French investment since the 1905 debacle in the Sea of Japan.[20]

Well before 1917, however, the first city of the tsars was effectively besieged by revolutionary spaces. Russia's weapons plants were not only concentrated in Petrograd, but also far larger on average than factories anywhere else in the world, including in such "arsenals of democracy" as Detroit and Chicago. Big plants could be found everywhere along Petrograd's outlying network of rivers and islands, and they were packed with restive workers who developed strong ties of solidarity based on the hundreds of smaller metal shops that made up the factories. The factory neighborhoods also teemed with worker tenements that aroused further grievances, including from working women. It did not help at all that Tsar Nicholas II had done so little to respond to the would-be revolution of 1905. True, he conceded his magnificent Tauride Palace downtown to representatives of a parliament, called the Duma, but a tight franchise requirement confined that space to Russia's male bourgeoisie, a large proportion of which resided alongside aristocrats in Petrograd's lovely apartment buildings nearby. The Duma had little power and the city's bourgeoisie was small by European standards – befitting owners of especially large factories, concentrated as they were in relatively few hands. Though this owning class profited maximally from the war, many hankered to remove the tsar themselves. The city's gigantic and largely illegal socialist parties, supported by bourgeois students, hundreds of thousands of hungry working families, large numbers of single men living far from their farms, and – in the distant hinterlands – millions of angry peasants, wanted revolution even more.[21]

The Eastern Front was a longer and sparser built environment than the Western one, less marked by contiguous trenches. It was equally deadly, however, partly because urban sanitary measures were harder to implement in its irregular geography. Additionally, the tsar had to engage in a fight against Vienna's allies, the Ottomans, in the oil belts of the Caucasus, straining supply lines for guns and bread even further. By early 1917, Russian armies were in full retreat from enemy soldiers who poured by rail from Austrian, German, and Turkish barracks. Petrograd's weapons manufacturers pushed their workers harder. When that did not work, they invited them into councils to try coopting them to labor more for even less. When the workers' soviet at the massive Putilov weapons works instead directed 26,000 workers to go on strike, the owners locked them out. A hundred thousand sympathizers, bread rioters, and women's activists slipped across the frozen Neva into the city's central royal district from working-class neighborhoods in the north, outflanking soldiers posted on the bridges. Soon those soldiers and even some Cossacks joined the crowd. Twenty-five kilometers offshore, the 50,000 sailors of the Kronstadt naval base killed their notoriously brutal officers and joined the revolution from their island base. Power devolved to the Tauride Palace, where the Duma forced the tsar to abdicate and renamed itself Russia's Provisional Government. Yet the new government did not rule alone. Down the hall, in another room of the same palace, socialists of many stripes, workers, soldiers, and sailors reconstituted the Petrograd Soviet of 1905.[22]

17.2. Vladimir Lenin Addresses Workers' Soviets at the Putilov Iron and Munitions Works, Petrograd
So often, world-changing events start in cities, where our most powerful political institutions are born. Here, in 1917, Lenin urges factory workers to join his "political party of a new type," the Bolsheviks. His goal? To topple bourgeois capitalist power – in the factories and in Russia's Parliament – and replace it with the power of workers' soviets. During Petrograd's tumultuous October Revolution Lenin himself seized power, then passed it to his protégé Stalin who launched a totalitarian global superpower called the Union of Soviet Socialist Republics. Meanwhile, similar events proliferated – starting with ruthless anti-parliamentary power-grabs by far-right forces in Tokyo, Rome, and Berlin. Totalitarians' conflicts against each other and against liberal capitalist empires led to World War II and the Cold War.
Corbis Historical/Getty Images.

The turbulent period from the February Revolution to the October Revolution – when Vladimir Lenin's Bolsheviks seized power in the Soviet and then Russia as whole – offers a primer on the ways that the urban geography of revolution had changed since 1789 in Paris. The separate workshops in Petrograd's large factories were intended to divide and conquer their workforces, but they did the opposite, creating tight cells of solidarity. Only a few of these, like the No. 6 Shop of Trubochnaya Metal Works, were sufficiently well-read in Bolshevik revolutionary theory to dream of seizing the state from the bourgeoisie, especially now that it was ensconced in a revolutionary parliament. Most of the shop-floor soviets focused on simpler economic issues like wages and hours. Soon, the need to defend their protests from counterrevolutionary agitators led the Soviets into alliances with solders from nearby barracks. Militias gathered, including the first elements of what later became the Red Army. Rival middle-class socialist party leaders, typically meeting in cast-off aristocratic mansions, lived apart from these worker cells, but continually sought connection to them through their printing presses and by giving speeches in the streets and in meeting halls, as well as in the Petrograd Soviet itself. The Finland Rail Station, where Lenin famously debarked on his return from exile, served as grand reception room for his shocking call, in front of a vast crowd of workers and intellectuals, to end the war against Germany, and instead to fight the bourgeois Provisional Government to the death.[23]

Despite the name Bolshevik ("The Majority"), Lenin's radical program doomed his party to the minority in the factories, barracks, and in the hundreds of soviets that proliferated across Russia throughout the summer. By autumn, though, the Provisional Government had frittered its legitimacy away on the losing war effort and a bungled counterrevolutionary scheme to sic a general on the Petrograd Soviet. Into the uncanny vacuum slipped the untainted Bolsheviks, supported by just enough of a passionate base in shops like the one in the Trubochnaya, as well as the Red street militias, to steal power. The location of their final victory was telling as well. The seizure of the government's new quarters at the Winter Palace on October 26, 1917, amidst shellfire from a Bolshevik garrison at the St. Peter and Paul Fortress, was largely an afterthought – unlike Parisians' capture of the Bastille and Versailles. Real power in Petrograd had fallen into Bolshevik hands earlier, when Red soldiers bloodlessly seized all of the city's telegraph offices and rail stations. As the spectacular news from Petrograd, as well as new orders and soldiers, radiated along these "sinews of power" outward across Russia's vastnesses, Bolsheviks seized dozens of other cities, even as "White" counter-revolutionary armies massed to shoot down the Reds. Lenin, however, would not make the tsar's mistake and fight on from the untenable geographical position of Petrograd. To spread his revolution throughout Russia, and soon across much of the world, he needed to occupy the city that had given birth to tsarist Russia in the first place. By March 1918, the Reds waged ruthless war on the Whites from the Kremlin in Moscow.[24]

HIGH TIDE OF GLOBAL URBAN RADICALISM

The Red Army, led by Leon Trotsky from an armored train that sped between Moscow and sixteen simultaneous fronts, brought hundreds more cities under Soviet control amidst a civil war that killed as many as ten million people from 1917 to 1923, and nearly completely dispossessed the Russian middle class and aristocracy. The Russian revolution, however, was only the most tumultuous crest of a worldwide tsunami of urban protest during the same period. As in Petrograd, the earliest waves swelled largely from the left. Workers in almost every industrial city of the world flooded the streets, notably as their wages eroded due to wartime inflation. In Vienna at war's end, the last Habsburg abdicated, and Vienna's Social Democrats once again seized the Ringstrasse, soon becoming the majority in the Federal Parliament of a new Austrian Republic. In Germany, forces modeled on the Bolsheviks came very close to seizing power. Sailors at the North Sea naval base at Wilhelmshaven set the stage by taking over battleships steaming toward what they knew to be pointless suicide missions against the British. Their resistance forced their admirals to retreat through the canal leading east to the navy's Baltic port at Kiel. There, thousands of soldiers mutinied and joined urban workers' councils called *Räte*, the German version of the soviets. Within days, workers flooded the streets of every major city in Germany, including Hamburg, the Ruhr, Cologne, Frankfurt, and Berlin itself. In Munich, Communist-dominated *Räte* established a *Volksstaat* : a "People's State." In Berlin on November 9, 1918, the Kaiser abdicated and Karl Liebknecht, leader of Germany's Communist Party, mounted the balcony of Berlin's City Palace to declare all of Germany a socialist republic. Unlike Lenin in Petrograd, though, Liebknecht did not get the support of workers' *Räte* in Berlin's largest factories, who preferred parliamentary parties under moderate socialist leaders. Within weeks Liebknecht and his fellow Communist Rosa Luxembourg were dead, murdered by an ominous right-wing militia called the *Freikorps*, first assembled by humiliated German officers along the crumbing Eastern Front. Blood flowed in Berlin and other cities for several months in 1919, requiring parliamentary leaders to retreat to the quieter town of Weimar. A shaky German republic was born there, even as street warfare between groups of partisan toughs became endemic to urban life.[25]

These revolutionary events ran in parallel to a worldwide wave of "General Strikes" involving tens of thousands of workers and all of the labor organizations of a city or even multiple cities across an entire country. In Mexico City, enormous worker strikes and various conflicts between radical and moderate labor unions played out against the backdrop of the Mexican Revolution (1910–17). An uprising in the capital that overthrew the dictator Porfirio Díaz and established a republic then devolved into a series of coups and assassinations by rival generals. Their armies fought a civil war against two agrarian uprisings, led by Pancho Villa and Emiliano Zapata, while fending off armed interventions by the USA. During the war, Mexico City swelled toward the million mark with refugees from the countryside and a continuing stream of peasants left landless as *hacienda* owners consolidated small farms into massive commercial operations. Zapata himself invaded the capital in 1914, laying waste to large neighborhoods. Only after his defeat and ongoing violent repression of leftist unions did republican leaders, allied crucially with moderate workers' movements in Mexico City, establish rule under a constitution that promised social justice for laborers and peasants. Elsewhere, workers launched general strikes in Australian, Brazilian, and Spanish cities in 1917, in Swiss cities in 1918, and in Seattle, Winnipeg, Barcelona, and Zürich in 1919. In that same year, steel workers in Pittsburgh and all of the largest mills in the USA struck in an attempt to regain momentum lost at Homestead a quarter century earlier. In Nagoya, Tokyo, and across Japan, tens of thousands of "rice rioters" protested rising food costs in the country's largest street demonstrations ever, forcing a prime minister to resign. German and Romanian cities erupted in general strikes in 1920, and most Italian cities erupted similarly in 1922.[26]

Colonial cities also rose up during these years. The World War had strained the power of their distant imperial overlords to the limit. For many diverse groups in these cities, that situation brightened the prospect of national independence, in part because of widespread anger that wartime service did not lead to the vote. In some cases, brutal urban warfare with oppressors was involved, as in the Easter Uprising of 1916 in Dublin, Ireland and the 1918 uprising in the city of Poznań that began the Polish war of independence from defeated Berlin, Vienna, and Moscow. The same year, Budapest's Chrysanthemum Revolution inaugurated a People's Republic that fell to a Soviet-style regime and then lurched back to a monarchy. The new nations that emerged from the collapse of the Habsburg Empire prompted US President Woodrow Wilson, upon his arrival in Paris for postwar diplomatic gatherings, to press the victorious powers to honor the "self-determination of peoples." That declaration helped ratchet up hopes across the colonial world, which then turned to fury as it became clear that delegates from London, Paris, and Tokyo intended to use the peace talks to justify further imperial scrambles in the Middle East and China. The West's protracted and bloody dismantlement of the Ottoman Empire that followed World War I followed many of the patterns of the Scrambles for Asia and Africa. Multiple European armies established beachheads in port cities from the Black Sea to the Persian Gulf and plunged into the interior from there, typically into the teeth of fierce resistance.[27]

Crowds of civilians in many of these cities played crucial roles in the resistance, with varying success. In May 1919 in Istanbul, the Association of Modern Women, students, and Turkish nationalist leaders organized mass rallies in front of the great Sultanhamet mosque to protest the city's occupation by British, French, and Italian forces. Their actions presaged the creation of a secular Turkish state under Kemal Atatürk, which adopted women's suffrage early on. In Cairo and Alexandria, massive crowds protested British efforts to solidify colonial rule in Egypt, winning a so-called "Universal Declaration of Independence" that nonetheless left British authorities mostly in control. In Jerusalem and other cities of Palestine, Arabic-speaking residents took to the streets in 1920 and 1921 against British promises to establish a "national home for the Jewish people" in the province it had seized from Istanbul. This promise, the famous Balfour Declaration, was a victory for the World Zionist Organization (WZO), an organization dedicated to Jewish protection founded in 1896 in the wake of Karl Lueger's victories in Vienna, as well as anti-Semitic rioting in pre-war Paris and the pogroms in Russia. The WZO had sponsored Jewish migration to Palestine, and in 1909 organized the settlement of a new colonial town exclusively for Jewish settlers – Tel Aviv. In 1920, Arab protestors in Jerusalem targeted the houses of Zionist immigrés, ending the long era of Ottoman peace in the most contested of ancient holy cities. In 1922, another wave of violence overtook Tel

Aviv and the nearby Arab-majority city of Jaffa. Zionist settlers organized a militia known as the Haganah, one of the nuclei of the Israel Defense Forces that continues to battle Palestinians to this day.[28]

In South and East Asia, post-World War I anti-colonial urban revolts had similarly thunderous impact on world politics. The most momentous was Mohandas Gandhi's call on Indians for a *hartal* – or cessation of all daily activities – in protest of new British laws allowing summary arrests of dissidents. Hundreds of thousands answered his call for non-violent disruption – *Satyagraha* – notably in Bombay, Ahmedabad, Delhi, Lahore, and Amritsar. Despite Gandhi's insistence that resistance remain unarmed, protestors at the Delhi rail station attacked the police. When the British arrested Gandhi as he raced to the capital to stop the bloodletting, even larger crowds filled the streets of Lahore, while saboteurs across the surrounding Punjab region dismantled rail lines and telegraph poles. In Amritsar, the holy city of Sikhism, a mob attacked a white female schoolteacher. Shortly afterward, British troops massacred several hundred people at a multi-faith protest that had gathered in a walled garden in the city called the Jallianwala Bagh. The brutality of the Amritsar Massacre catapulted Gandhi into national prominence and delivered a mass base to the movement for Indian independence.[29]

Meanwhile, in Baghdad and across Mesopotamia in 1920, massive rebellions led the new British Royal Air Force, on orders from the now War Minister Winston Churchill, to bomb dozens of villages into submission, foreshadowing the indiscriminate aerial bombings during World War II. In the Dutch East Indies, communist sailors at the Surabaya naval base failed to form Petrograd-style soviets in 1917, but they gained a large following among Javanese activists who launched rebellions in Batavia, Padang, and Surabaya in 1926. They were crushed again, but helped spur a movement for the independence of a nation they now called Indonesia. Back in 1918, thousands marched in Seoul and other Korean cities against Japan's increasingly brutal settler colonial rule. Then, on May 4, 1919, tens of thousands of Chinese students occupied the great Tien An Men Square in front of Beijing's Forbidden City to protest the decision made by negotiators in Versailles to award former German colonial territory in China to Japan. The "May 1 Movement" is credited for a growing radicalization of thought among Chinese anti-colonial intellectuals, including an obscure activist turned Marxist named Mao Zedong.[30]

THE RACIST COUNTERREVOLUTION

As many-shaped and far-reaching leftward waves of urban protest crashed across the Urban Planet in the years after World War I, equally important waves of popular protest arose from the right, often in the very same streets. In Chicago, for example, during the summer just before the Great Steel Strike of 1919, hundreds of white men launched a week of random armed attacks against the city's "Black Belt." The Chicago Race Riot began when a Black man crossed an ambiguous racial boundary on a Lake Michigan beach. It quickly transformed into an urban war targeting the tens of thousands of African Americans who had moved to the city to work in armament factories and who had sought housing in white neighborhoods just beyond the Black Belt's boundaries. Similar murderous events had shaken the city of East St. Louis in 1917. Historians have since counted thousands of bombings of Black-owned houses in white neighborhoods across the USA during the half-decade after the war. This violence culminated in 1923, when white mobs, the police, and even a few local pilots who dropped incendiary devices from the air set fire to the prosperous Black business district of Greenwood in the city of Tulsa, Oklahoma, killing at least thirty and possibly hundreds, later interred in mass graves. Large crowds of white-hooded members of the Ku Klux Klan rallied in city streets across the Midwest, electing anti-Black and anti-immigrant officials in large cities like Indianapolis and Detroit. In Chicago and elsewhere, realtors spread the practice of "restrictive covenants" in property title deeds that forbade resale of white houses to Blacks, the beginning of a movement that would segregate the American suburbs after World War II. White so-called "nativists" succeeded in passing restrictive immigration laws that decisively transformed Ellis Island into a segregationist institution that severely restricted entry of Italian, Slavic, Jewish, and Caribbean migrants.[31]

During the same period, street violence in support of segregation arose in other settler colonial cities. In Johannesburg, white mineworkers staged the 1922 Rand Revolt against their employers' increased use of Black miners in skilled jobs. In its wake, agitation grew for housing segregation measures across South Africa. The Natives (Urban Areas) Act passed in 1923; it set aside separate neighborhoods for Blacks in all cities of the Union and laid the foundation of later apartheid legislation. In Belfast and Derry, Northern Ireland, British Protestants descended from centuries-old settler families attacked Catholic households to weaken the growing movement to reattach Ireland's six northern counties to the now semi-autonomous Irish Free State in the south. Hundreds were killed, thousands were displaced, and the segregation of these cities into sectarian neighborhoods began, foreshadowing the "Troubles" of the 1970s.[32]

FASCISTS ON THE MARCH

Of more immediate consequence for the torturous route toward Hiroshima and Nagasaki were anti-parliamentary and racist movements in Tokyo, in Italian cities, and in the German city of Munich. Just before noon on September 1, 1923, tectonic plates under Tokyo and Yokohama shook violently, leveling buildings across both cities and then setting off fires that destroyed nearly all of Yokohama and 60 percent of Tokyo, killing some 130,000 people in one of the worst natural disasters ever to visit a city. As always in cities, natural energy compounded into chaotic political force. Rumors swirled that young Korean immigrant men, angry at Japanese colonial practices, had taken advantage of the earthquake to destabilize the country, and soon Japanese gangs, helped by police and soldiers, began slaughtering Koreans, sometimes by tying dozens of people together and setting them afire. Three thousand people died, revealing racial antagonisms that would resurface again when Japanese soldiers attacked Korean and Chinese cities in the later 1920s and 1930s.[33]

Meanwhile, in the industrial cities of northern Italy, powerful socialist parties who had wanted the country to remain neutral in World War I and who led waves of general strikes after the war became the targets of right-wing nationalists. Soldiers and toughs from the countryside organized into armed *squadri* to disrupt socialist rallies. The former left-wing journalist Benito Mussolini defended the actions of the *squadristi*. Their commitment was proof, he argued, that the true force of revolution was not Marx's proletariat but leaders from any class who espoused the historic vigor of the Italian nation. For him, this "national revolution" was best understood through the Roman symbol of authority known as the *fasces*, a symbol carved in stone throughout ancient Rome's forums consisting of an axe handle fortified by a leather-bound bundle of rods. Seeing these carvings as proof of Italy's primeval national unity and conquering spirit, Mussolini's "Fascist" party rose in influence in Parliament, abetted by a liberal government that feared a Bolshevik revolution more than they did the *squadristi*. In city streets across northern Italy, the black-shirted goons attacked Labor Houses, socialist bars, and striking workers at factory gates, such as at the Alfa Romeo automobile factory in Milan. Soon the Blackshirts controlled local government in several large cities, including Bologna. In 1922, they threatened a "March on Rome" to force parliament to appoint Mussolini Prime Minister. Thus, in hopes of stopping a revolution from the left, Italy's liberals fell to a coup by an anti-egalitarian right-wing dictator. Mussolini abolished elections, ruling through a would-be totalitarian Grand Council of Fascism. He began a massive program to restore Rome to its glory as an imperial capital and relaunched a scramble for colonies in Africa, starting with a brutal "Pacification" campaign to shore up Italian conquests in Libya that involved the ethnic cleansing of Bedouin communities and the death of maybe a quarter of the population of the former Ottoman province. Mussolini's goal was to assemble a modern Roman Empire with plenty of "Vital Space" to satisfy Italy's supposedly renewed racial destiny. Addis Ababa, capital of the independent Ethiopian Empire that humiliated Italy during the imperial Scramble, was next to fall into his sights.[34]

For Adolph Hitler, the path from chaotic postwar city streets to a far more ambitious fascist German "Reich" was longer and even more improbable. After a stint as a German soldier in the trenches of the Western Front, he resumed his drift amidst the cafés and pastry counters of Munich, once marching aimlessly in support of Munich's leftist People's Republic. He discovered his true calling, however, in the city's less pretentious right-wing beer cellars – amidst twilit gatherings of fellow army veterans, disgruntled small shopkeepers, splinter-party organizers, and assorted street bullies. Striding atop improvised speaker platforms, Hitler the actor and orator regaled his subterranean audiences with full-throated, one-man Wagnerian theater pieces on the aggrieved state of the German nation. With victory in Germany's grasp during World War I, he bawled, Bolsheviks, liberals, capitalists, and treasonous generals stabbed the *Volk* in the back. France and Britain then brutally kicked Germany while it was down, using the Versailles talks to demand enormous war payments from an industrial economy that they had all but destroyed. Behind these grievous machinations lay a Jewish conspiracy that infected the *Reich* like an inhuman, deadly "microbial" infection. All of these strands of what historians call Hitler's "big lie" gathered into a simple way forward. Instead of a divisive workers' revolution, Germany needed a unifying "national socialist" revival born of the blood of martyrs willing to emerge from cellars into the streets to destroy the hapless Weimar parliament and remove the Jews from Europe. To get there, Hitler concluded, all should raise their arms in a straight salute to the "authority of personality" of Hitler himself, the *Volk*'s essential leader, the *Führer*.[35]

To contain his growing audiences in the urban underground, Hitler's handlers in the "National Socialist" movement – the Nazis – booked him more cavernous spaces in Munich, monitored by growing bodies of intimidating individuals decked in brown shirts: the Nazis' *Sturmabteilung* (SA) – the storm troopers. As Hitler ranted, postwar inflation worsened, and then French and Belgian troops occupied Germany's Ruhr cities to extract unpaid war indemnities. Egged on by various Left parties, workers on the Ruhr and across Germany erupted in rolling general strikes. The Nazi SA and other right-wing mobs prowled the factory gates, seeking left-wing victims and right-wing converts. Thus it was that, on November 9, 1923, the fifth anniversary of Germany's capitulation to its World War I foes, Hitler muscled himself in front of a standing-room-only crowd at one of Munich's premier beer gardens, the Bürgerbräukeller, and exhorted his machine-gun-wielding storm troops to launch him into power. A coup against the authorities in Munich, he promised, waving his pistol, would give the Nazis support from local army detachments, which he would then lead in a triumphant "March on Berlin."[36]

The beer-hall putsch sputtered when the army failed to show up, and Hitler instead spent the next year in Munich's Landsberg Prison. After nursing his humiliation there for a time, he revived himself by scrawling his infamous testament *Mein Kampf*, with its sky-darkening call to destroy Europe's Jews and open up Slavic lands to the east, creating the perfect racial *Lebensraum* for the chosen German *Volk*. For the moment, such acts lay far beyond the ken of an imprisoned agitator widely seen as a washed-up political force. However, by 1923, humans' capacity to use cities to coordinate acts of mass extermination had been very recently tested and grimly proven – not in Germany, but several thousand kilometers to the east in the flailing Ottoman Empire. There, the Sultan and nationalists of the "Young Turk" movement fanned a longstanding hatred of the empire's Christian residents into a genocide that targeted Armenians above all. From the concentration camp system of Turkish cities, we will resume our trudge, amidst darkening lamplights, down the ghastliest backstreets of the Urban Planet – toward Hitler's "Final Solution," Hiroshima, Nagasaki, and the closest we have ever come to global urban Armageddon.[37]

CHAPTER 18

The Labyrinths of Terror

THE TRANSGRESSIVE TWENTIETH CENTURY

Even on the threshold of some of its awfullest days ever, we must remember that the early-twentieth-century Urban Planet had, in its paradoxical way, also become more benevolently capacious than ever. Before the World Wars, between them, and once again after them, many of Earthopolis's multiplying human-built spaces swelled and pulsed, as if in expiation for all the horror, into new sub-worlds of human expression, hope, and pleasure for millions. "Progress" is a difficult thing to measure for any large group of people, whether citywide or worldwide. Still, many cities allowed large numbers of women, people of color, and same-sex loving people new opportunities to occupy and benefit from urban space, and to do so more visibly than ever before. For that, many suffered horrific persecution, especially in places where forces of total terror were victorious. Yet they also laid resilient foundations for wider, more promising collective experiences of urban space to come.

The best-known stories about women and built space in twentieth-century cities focus first on the successful fight for access to voting booths and parliaments, and secondly on the longer march of middle-class women from homes to workplaces. As we already know, these stories barely scratch the surface, for women of all classes were active in a very wide spectrum of public affairs throughout the nineteenth century, in organizations of all kinds, on the streets and barricades, and even, like the militant socialist suffragists Sylvia Pankhurst or Emma Goldman, in prison cells or the holds of immigrant deportation ships. Working-class women, peasant women, female colonial subjects, and enslaved women, meanwhile, had all lived lives of labor, paid and unpaid, for centuries, and one of their most prominent political roles, sometimes joined by middle-class reformers, involved improving conditions in workplaces outside the home. Yet during the twentieth century, the design of domestic space too would transform in revolutionary ways, as industrialists touted labor-saving appliances like refrigerators, washing machines, and dishwashers to those with enough credit to buy them. The triple shift of caregiving, paid work, and politics continued to strain women's lives, yet the collective energies women exerted to redesign workplaces, homes, and other spaces of power represent a massive force in the shaping of the contemporary Urban Planet.[1]

Women's actions in a fourth urban arena – public spaces of leisure – were equally significant to global history. "Eight Hours for Work, Eight Hours for Rest, and Eight Hours *for What We Will,*" countless May Day protestors have chanted since the international workers' holiday came into being in Chicago in 1886. As social historians rediscovered a generation ago, young unmarried women, particularly from working class communities or communities of color living in large cities, played a crucial role in expanding the scope of urban leisure activities of the early 1900s into the global mass entertainment culture we know today. In their large numbers, with their slight wages or with money they negotiated into being among friends and dates, they collectively bankrolled the dramatic pre-war expansion of urban dance halls, and the growth of urban "cheap amusements" of many other kinds, including vaudeville theaters, circuses, and amusement parks. They also encouraged the rise of new technologies like nickelodeons and silent movie cinemas that made possible a new global urban capitalist enterprise – the film industries in cities like Los Angeles, Bombay, and later Lagos and Seoul. When the phonograph and recorded music burst into young women's lives, they bought piles of records, and when radio emerged, they were among its most avid listeners. Shopping districts, department stores, and later malls could not have come into being without purchases of many types that enhanced their leisure hours, most visibly in women's fashion. Advertisers took note. So did social commentators who wrote incessantly – in admiration and fear – of the rise of the "Modern Girl" in large cities on all continents.[2]

Young workingwomen, it is true, had less influence than their male counterparts on the resurrection of another large built space, the sports arena and the stadium – though women were numerous among the crowds, and a surge in women's athleticism was part of the ethos of the "Modern Girl." Sporting venues designed for mass audiences conquered huge amounts of urban acreage. Stadium building also got a boost from the revival of the Olympic Games in Athens in 1896. Parks around the world spawned ordinary playing fields, racecourses filled with gamblers, football and cricket pitches, and baseball diamonds. Less formal playing fields sprouted on dusty lots in cities everywhere. Boxing rings grew into real arenas, and commentary on prizefights was especially amenable to "broadcast" through telegraph stations worldwide. Clerks who relayed the dot-and-dash progress of boxing matches could attract huge crowds outside their offices. In the days and weeks after the great fight, silent films, such as those of the much-ballyhooed victory of the Black American champion Jack Johnson over the "great white hope" Jim Jeffries in 1910, attracted enormous crowds in cinemas across the world. Enthusiasm about Johnson's victory even sparked anti-colonial revolts outside theaters in Johannesburg, Calcutta, and Manila among many other places. Nervous officials there sought to ban the films. Meanwhile, white racists urged white men to join new gymnasiums, play sports, and embrace a "vigorous life" to counteract what they saw as urban forces of racial weakness. Anti-colonial activists counseled very similar training in response.[3]

Whether small and ubiquitous or large and globally connected, new spaces of leisure allowed ordinary people to act in ways that accumulated into cutting-edge, class-, race-, gender-, and continent-crossing cultural experiments. Performers of African-inflected musical traditions opened cracks in the era's otherwise tightening racial urban boundaries, all the while developing the essential stylistic ingredients for all global popular music to come. In small towns of the US South like Clarksdale, Mississippi, rural roadhouses incubated the blues, a form that spread quickly to urban leisure districts like Beale Street in Memphis and Maxwell Street in Black Chicago. In the Storyville "red-light" district of New Orleans and elsewhere, Jazz emerged from a mixture of blues, Habañera rhythms from Cuba, African-American ragtime and parade music, and the churchier sounds of Gospel music.[4]

World War I drew American Blacks into a "Great Migration" to northern cities, and then to the Western Front. The "crossover" appeal to whites of the blues and Jazz began early on, sometimes in places one historian has called Chicago's "Interzones." These included the "Black and Tan" clubs such as the boxer Jack Johnson's Champion's Club, where whites, both men and women, shared tables, dance floors, and back rooms with Blacks. When the USA prohibited the sale of alcohol in 1920, Jazz and the blues flourished in illegal speakeasies. Performers embraced microphones, inaugurating the age of amplified music, capable of reaching audiences in far larger venues. The daughters of "respectable" bourgeois women followed their working-class compatriots, developing sexualized identities such as the "flapper" in the Jazz clubs and clandestine women-only dancehalls of the 1920s. Urban recording studios and wartime mobility helped Jazzmen and Jazzwomen conquer the Urban Planet during the 1920s more rapidly than any global empire. Paris was especially well-known as a haven for Black American performers eager to breathe an atmosphere less tainted by racial violence. Yet Jazz clubs became critical urban hardware elsewhere: in Little Burgundy, Montreal's "Harlem of the North," in "red" European capitals like Berlin and Vienna, as well as the "White Towns" and many "Black Towns" in just about every colonial city in the world, notably in Kingston, Dakar, Cairo, Lagos, Johannesburg's Sophiatown, Bombay, Shanghai, and Yokohama. "Latin" music in its many forms emerged at the same time, as blues and Jazz mingled with Punto Guajiro from Cuba's sugarcane fields and other local African traditions in the clubs of Havana, Rio, and Buenos Aires. Indian movie music drew on mixtures of Bombay Jazz and Goanese traditions. Thanks to all of these fused innovations, the "thrill of the urban," as historians of human emotions call it, took on an altogether new energy. Billions of people since have found pleasure in exhilarating city-made mashups of sound, sight, touch, movement, and highly charged boundary crossing.[5]

Spaces of public sexual and racial crossing also helped create new highly visible gay and lesbian "worlds" in cities. George Chauncey, the pioneering historian of New York's gay community, lists "saloons, speakeasies, … bars … cheap cafeterias and elegant restaurants" as the nuclei of one of these worlds, which grew to include several "neighborhood enclaves" inhabited by gay men of different classes and colors. Gay men "organized male beauty contests in Coney Island and drag balls in

Harlem; they performed at gay clubs in the Village and tourists traps in Times Square." Other historians have rediscovered similar early-twentieth-century worlds for gay men and women and transgendered people in London's Piccadilly, in dozens of gay and lesbian bars in the basements of Berlin, along the central Nevsky Prospekt in St. Petersburg, and in the interwar clubs of Shanghai among many other cities. Gay and lesbian sexuality, like public female desire and cross-racial encounters of all kinds, faced the wrath of officials, political campaigners, and enraged bullies or mobs in the streets. Mobsters and bootleggers controlled its transgressive spaces in some cities. Many times, same-sex love had to occupy shadowier corners of cities, such as the alleyways of the *Passazh* in St. Petersburg or "Queer Way" in Berlin's Tiergarten, darkened cinemas and public toilets in almost all cities, and clandestine pick-up zones known only to initiates in city parks and on beaches. Yet the modern identities of gay, lesbian, queer, transvestite, and transsexual could not have come into being without the accommodating embrace of cities – not to mention the many inter-city connections that allowed those small worlds of widened love to, in turn, widen their arms worldwide.[6]

Sadly, these stories of hope come with a nasty paradoxical back-twist, for many of the spaces of new urban pleasures could also generate white-hot fears and hatreds. In part, this was about efforts by scandalized state officials to clamp down on what they correctly saw as important early manifestations of the twentieth- century sexual and racial revolution. The state's counterrevolutionary acts ranged from police raids to early closing times, shut-offs of tram service between clubs and factory girls' dorms, a general targeting of young women as potential prostitutes, moral uplift programs of all kinds, wars on alcohol and drugs, and police sweeps that criminalized people that "Vice Commissions" deemed morally suspect. The efforts to cancel Jack Johnson's fight films were also among these acts, as was a particularly nasty legislative campaign conducted in Washington and Chicago whose main goal was to put the great boxer in jail. Justifications drew heavily on imagery of dissolute biblical cities like Sodom and Gomorrah, as well as fears of racial and moral "degeneracy." Such propaganda could also easily serve as preludes to right-wing mob attacks, systematic police raids of gay clubs, and mass imprisonment.[7]

THE "KING OF MUNICH" TAKES "RED BERLIN"

Adolf Hitler did the most of anyone to incite such counterrevolutionary attacks. Once he left prison in the late 1920s, he resumed sowing his Pandora's politics of resentment and hatred in Munich. The rise of his anti-parliamentary "Führer's Party" adopted some of the same urban spatial strategies as Lenin's and Mussolini's "anti-parties" before, but it also relied heavily on the growing spatial apparatus of experimental urban leisure that he otherwise excoriated in his propaganda. This stood to reason, for his political movement depended crucially on putting a theatrical speaker in front of big, agitated audiences. After his release during the late 1920s, to his Nazi lieutenants' chagrin, Hitler kept up his café lounging ways between speaking gigs – his way of relieving the frustrations of leading a fringe terror group during a short period of economic promise for the Weimar regime. That put him in frequent proximity to Munich's flappers, gay men and women, and "decadent" Black Jazz performers, whom he otherwise lumped together with liberals, socialists, and Jews as emblems of "Red Berlin," the soft, morally dissolute seat of the bourgeois Weimar Republic.[8]

The Nazis mined their most potent seams of political rage in working-class and *petit-bourgeois* bars and beer cellars, where they also had plenty of opportunity to knock heads with rival Social Democratic and Communist toughs. The party's membership grew again after 1929, when the stock market crash on Wall Street led to a new catastrophic implosion of the German economy. The number of storm troopers also rose, as did their success in attacking union and Left party headquarters. To accommodate Hitler's growing rallies, Nazi henchmen regularly rented bigger performance spaces, such as Munich's celebrated Circus Krone. Like Left parties in Petrograd, the Nazis took over an aristocratic Munich mansion as a party headquarters, known as the "Brown House," after the color of the storm troopers' uniforms. The Führer's beloved Mercedes automobiles, and soon airplanes, whisked him to larger venues throughout Germany – Nuremberg's Market Square, for example – and then to repeated performances in front of tens of thousands in Red Berlin itself, at the city's gigantic *Sportspalast*.[9]

Organized Nazi street thugs, including the SA and an elite unit under Heinrich Himmler called the *Schutzstaffel* or SS (originally formed as a

(A)

(B)

18.1. Berlin: The Urban Foundations of Nazi Power
The rise of the Nazi Party warns us how potent and horrific city-born political forces can become, even seemingly improbable ones. In Munich barrooms, Hitler awakened a paramilitary force called the *Sturmabteiling* (SA) that attacked headquarters of other parties, like the German Communist Party in Berlin (A). Leveraging a threat of civil war, Hitler gained power in 1933, then empowered his ultra-loyal *Schutzstaffel* (SS) to escalate street violence, targeting shops owned by Jews on Kristallnacht in 1938 (B). Meanwhile the "Hitler cult" required larger urban gathering spaces: the Nuremberg Party Grounds and

(C)

(D)

18.1. (cont.) even Berlin's Tempelhof Airfield (C). The SS built dozens of concentration camps to imprison regime opponents, then captured and enslaved millions of Jews and others, transporting them by rail to city-like industrial death camps, where most transportees perished in gas chambers and crematoria like those at Auschwitz (D).
(A) Picture Alliance/Getty Images. (B) Hulton Archive/Getty Images. (C) ullstein bild/Getty Images. (D) Galerie Bilderwelt/Hulton Archive/Getty Images.

beerhall bodyguard), played a crucial role in the party's only slightly politer rise as an electoral force. Street fights at once increased urban chaos and convinced many voters that Hitler alone had the power to restore order. The SA and SS also acted as a weapon in Hitler's negotiations with other aristocratic and high-capitalist right-wing party leaders over government offices, allowing him plausibly to threaten civil war if they did not appoint him chancellor. After many rejections that nearly ended his career, his bullying campaigns uncannily succeeded in January 1933.[10]

As chancellor, Hitler gained the support of the regular army, the *Reichswehr*, and he reorganized his street militias. After disbanding the SA and personally directing the assassination of its leaders to prevent any putsch against himself, he ordered Himmler's ultra-loyal SS to metastasize into a totalitarian force that suffused the army as well as the streets. When a Dutch leftist set fire to the Reichstag in Berlin, the SS overran Depression-beleaguered party headquarters in the Red neighborhoods of cities like Hamburg and Berlin, then abolished rival right-wing parties too. The SS rounded up dissenters for imprisonment in a growing archipelago of "concentration camps," beginning with Dachau outside Munich. Soon Hitler called on the SS to enforce the infamous anti-Jewish Nuremberg Laws of 1935. A year later, he stared down France and Britain by marching troops into Cologne and other demilitarized Rhineland cities, increasing his popularity among nationalists. In 1938, he let the SS loose in a nationwide wave of street pogroms against Jews and their businesses known as Kristallnacht, after the shards of shop-window glass that littered the streets of every major German city in the wake of unspeakable violence.[11]

Equally vicious was the violence that soon ripped through Vienna. The SS enabled Austrian Nazi thugs to emerge from the Austrian capital's own darkest undersides and lay waste to the Ringstrasse and middle-class Jewish neighborhoods in support of Hitler's 1936 *Anschluss* of Austria to the Third Reich. In the meantime, Hitler's ally Benito Mussolini further destabilized the international order when he invaded Ethiopia in direct violation of League of Nations condemnation, captured Addis Ababa, and in 1937 massacred 19,000 people in the city suspected of rekindling the country's legacy of anti-colonial resistance. Mussolini's acts of impunity encouraged Hitler to turn his techniques of intimidation upon the French and British prime ministers again, at a meeting in Munich, where they gave him a free hand to invade the German-majority Sudetenland of Czechoslovakia and its industrial and weapons-producing towns. Advance SS troops helped suppress Czech resistance, and a few months later, they swept Hitler into the Castle of Prague itself. From there, an informal, utterly ruthless armed force honed in city streets prepared for missions of total destruction, particularly to the east, where the Nazis planned an invasion of Poland as step one in clearing a *Lebensraum* for the German *Volk*.[12]

In the meantime, Hitler's propagandist Joseph Goebbels and his architect Albert Speer collaborated on even more grandiose urban venues for the Führer's performances of personality-power. The most famous involved Speer's transformation of a former park in Nuremberg into the Reich Party Rally Grounds, a complex of mustering fields for the SS and the *Reichswehr*, a landing zone for Zeppelin airships, a two-kilometer parade route, a monumental Tribune of Honor for the Führer, and a gigantic arena for 50,000 modeled on Rome's Colosseum. The amplification systems were strictly of the modern world: they allowed Hitler to project hate through dozens of loudspeakers to hundreds of thousands of saluting subjects. Films of these events, notably those of Leni Riefenstahl, circulated widely in German theaters. In 1936, when the Olympics came to Berlin, Hitler tried to use spectacular mass events held in newly built arenas and stadiums to promote German racial superiority to a global audience. The great victories of the Black track star Jesse Owens blunted Hitler's message. So did the victory two years later of the African-American boxer Joe Louis over Max Schmeling, a German fighter the Nazis had proclaimed the greatest "white hope" of all. Undeterred, Hitler worked closely with Speer to draft plans for new spectacular urban spaces, including a 400,000-person stadium in Nuremberg, and a grandiose remake of Berlin. Had Hitler's "Thousand-Year Reich" come into being, Berlin would have transubstantiated into "Germania," a triumphant boulevard-crossed capital city studded with monuments to fascist gigantism that, as Hitler put it, would rival "Ancient Egypt, Babylon, and Rome!" "What is London," he taunted, "what is Paris compared to that!"[13]

THE LABYRINTHS OF TOKYO AND MOSCOW

By the time Hitler's tanks rolled into Poland to conquer the racial hinterland for a greater Berlin, regimes in Tokyo and Moscow were farther along in very similar plans of interlinked conquest, brutal destruction, and construction of new urban-serving rural spaces. A mere ten years after the Great Kantō Earthquake of 1923 leveled Tokyo's "Lower City" along the Sumida River, the city was thriving as never before. The country's large corporations, known as the *zaibatsu*, rebuilt their skyscraping headquarters in Marunouchi, two thronging shopping districts returned to Ginza and Asakusa – each packed with teahouses, jazz clubs, cinemas, and brothels – and hundreds of factories large and small sprouted in the vast, canal-lined, Nankatsu working-class district of the Sumida River Delta. Tokyo's municipal boundaries meanwhile widened into the hillier area to the west, swallowing Shinjuku, Shinagawa, and Shibuya. These gateway towns, once known as the "mouths of Edo," became elite housing and shopping districts in their own right, as throngs of youthful fashionistas and tourists know today. By absorbing this now-contiguous "High City," Tokyo instantly joined New York and London among the three largest cities ever built.[14]

The ferocious construction activity, however, helped trip off a financial panic in 1927, followed by a devastating depression that deepened after New York's even bigger stock market collapse two years later. Japanese male workers meanwhile briefly gained the right to vote, and a Social Democratic party surged. The Tokyo Federation of Women's Organizations hailed the "Modern Girls" so evident in the streets and clubs of Ginza, and demanded female suffrage. Labor strikes crested once again, and textile workers, including thousands of women who worked in notoriously awful conditions, poured into the streets, confronting police and even the family members of factory owners. They sacked police offices again, and surged toward the Japanese Diet and the Imperial Palace.[15]

This ferment from the left was short lived, for Japan's right-wing ultra-nationalists responded with a series of "catalytic" acts of terror in the streets of Tokyo, soon giving the military leverage to abolish political parties and unions and squash the civilian Diet – all with the full

compliance of the new Emperor Hirohito in the old castle of the shoguns. In Tokyo, the terrorists were army soldiers and officers, not members of any informal street militias as in Milan or Munich. They did
inspire some grassroots support by claiming a role as guardians of social
order in the face of what they deemed as workers' class divisiveness and
women's moral decline, and some nationalist workers formed right-wing
unions to resist left-wing strikes, notably at the Ishikawajima naval base.
However, the soldier-terrorists justified their violence with far loftier
ideas. For them, the Japanese represented a superior "Yamato" race
distinguished by the martial spirit of the shogun and the samurai, blessed
by the spiritual rule of the emperor, and destined to rule all Asia and the
Pacific in defiance of the West. Like the Nazis, they thought of themselves
as national redeemers, expunging a series of humiliations by the West
that went back to the unequal treaties of the nineteenth-century and that
had persisted since Versailles, as Britain and the USA repeatedly con-
nived to limit Japan's naval strength.[16]

The militant nationalists' goal was to build a "Greater East Asia Co-
prosperity Sphere" – a wider hinterland for Japan's industrial cities
centered on China, crisscrossed with railways and telegraph wires,
designed to supply the cheap labor, agricultural products, coal, iron,
and above all the oil that were unavailable in Japan itself. This grand
spatial strategy started in smaller places, with armed uprisings in Tokyo's
many army barracks – again contrasting with the actions of the
Blackshirts and Brownshirts in bars and streets. Their targets were the
stately homes of middle-class civilian and military leaders who seemed to
the rebels to show insufficient manliness and Yamato strength in
response to Western demands. Killing squads assassinated these figures
in their parlors, and then fanned out to ransack party headquarters,
banks, or even parts of the imperial city. The goal of these coups,
repeated in 1931, 1932, and 1936, was to provoke martial law and receive
the blessing of the Emperor for their patriotism. Though Tokyo's putsch-
ists all ended up in prison, their subsequent court hearings allowed them
to enlist considerable popular sympathy. That, in turn, gave like-minded
generals and admirals more leverage to ratchet up their total control of
Japan's institutions.[17]

These right-wing projects in Tokyo depended crucially on political fuel supplied by other military coups carried out at the same time by Japanese officers in colonized zones of China. In 1931, outside of Mukden, the Manchurian city where Japan had humiliated the tsar in 1905, Japanese troops acting on the orders of junior officers, without authorization from Tokyo, dynamited a few yards of railway track, blaming it on Chinese saboteurs. Japanese generals used these high-jinks as a pretext to launch an offensive that secured Japanese control over the coalfields and farmland of Manchuria. Emperor Hirohito placed Pu Yi, the heir to the Qing empire, in nominal control of what became a Japanese settler colony called Manchukuo. In 1932, Chinese residents of Shanghai's working-class districts attacked five Japanese Buddhist monks from an order known for its ultra-nationalist beliefs. Japanese officials stationed in the city's International Concession demanded restitution from the city council, then called in battleships, a newfangled aircraft carrier, bombers, and amphibious troops. The Chinese Nationalist Army of Chiang Kai-shek fought back, but Japanese commanders refused local Western officials' efforts to broker a ceasefire. The Japanese army burned whole neighborhoods of Shanghai and its fighter pilots unapologetically targeted the city's civilians from the air. In 1937, another incident manufactured by Japanese officers near Beijing led to a full-scale invasion of China, during which Japanese troops captured the Forbidden City. Shanghai came under relentless bombing again. Combined with weeks of street-by-street fighting, large parts of the city were reduced to rubble. Worse was to come when the Japanese reached Chiang's capital at Nanjing. Japanese officers gave their soldiers open license to pillage, rape, and murder the city's inhabitants. As many as 200,000 people lost their lives in the Rape of Nanjing. As Japanese bombers strafed Wuhan and then pummeled Chongqing further up the river, the Urban Planet teetered decisively toward the era of its great undoing.[18]

In Moscow, similar synergies of mass destruction and lightning-fast urban and rural rearrangement were under way at the same time – this time in a Bolshevik key. In 1918, Stalin's move, along with Lenin and Trotsky, from Petrograd to apartments in the Kremlin helped the new Soviet regime repel its enemies in the civil war. However, as the new state seized the "means of production" from the Russian bourgeoisie, factory production plummeted. The country's vast peasant majority had meanwhile seized Russia's estates and divided them into privately owned farms. Accordingly, they persisted in their annoying refusal to part with their grain in exchange for payments that were worth nothing in industrial goods. Moscow lost a million people during the Civil War, because they starved to death, died on the war's many fronts, or returned hungry to farms they had only recently left. In the Kremlin, the new Politburo of the Union of Soviet Socialist Republics (USSR) fretted that "capitalist" peasants had put Moscow and other Russian cities under siege – weakening any effort to expand Russian industry and leaving the Red Army underequipped.[19]

Over Trotsky's veto from the left, Lenin and Stalin tried appeasing the peasants with market reforms that jumpstarted the economy for a time and allowed Moscow's population to recover. By the late 1920s, though, poor harvests stymied the Kremlin again, raising worries that, with its industrial plant in tatters, Western armies would quickly defeat the Bolshevik experiment. When Lenin died in 1924, Stalin used his power to appoint loyalists to seize key parts of the Soviet bureaucracy, ousting Trotsky and other Politburo rivals. He described his First Five-Year Plan (1928–32) as a "Revolution from Above" – not from the streets that is, but from within the labyrinthine corridors of various new "People's Commissariats" in Moscow.[20]

Peasants were the plan's primary target, especially the richer ones called "kulaks." By erasing all property lines between their farms, Stalin hoped to consolidate the land into gigantic collectively owned fields suitable for higher-yield mechanized grain production. Following his commands from Moscow, the Black Earth country and Western Siberia would outcompete the growing commercial farmers of the US Midwest – with their Detroit-built Fordson tractors and Chicago-built McCormack reapers. Enough grain and livestock would make its way to the cities to feed their current inhabitants – plus the millions of former peasants no longer needed in the countryside. They would flood into town and become an expanded working class that would build thousands of new factories – among other things, to supply tractors to the collective farms.[21]

In 1931, 25,000 party stalwarts, Red Army soldiers, and the ruthless secret police of the GPU (soon renamed the NKVD, later the KGB) fanned out to impose Stalin's decrees upon 100 million peasants. Fearing a "second serfdom," farmers rebelled, leaving their fields unplowed, killing their livestock, or burying their harvests in the forests and graveyards, hoping to starve the corridors of Moscow into submission. By winter, though, the protest backfired when peasants' own larders ran out. Many resorted to meals of tree-bark and even the bodies of their own sickened children. Some twelve million died of hunger and disease. To this day, Ukrainians and Kazakhs refer to Forced Collectivization as a Stalinist genocide because their regions were worst hit. Surviving protestors faced arrest, execution, or deportation to a growing, sinister complex of forced labor camps in Siberia, known by the grim initials of its coordinating office in Moscow: the Gulag.[22]

Millions more peasants survived Stalin's calamity in the countryside by moving into cities. Moscow quadrupled in size during the 1930s, to over four million. In a move hard to fathom in light of the Cold War to come, the People's Commissariat for Heavy Industry purchased machines built in Detroit and Chicago by selling Russian grain abroad for hard cash. Stalin even hired the American industrial architect Alfred Kahn to build factories in Russian cities, and consulted with the arch-capitalist Henry Ford on assembly lines deemed essential for the march to Communism. The small city of Tsaritsyn on the Volga River became Stalingrad, home to *Traktorstroi*, the largest tractor plant in the world. Automobile factories built on blueprints similar to Ford's massive River Rouge Plant in Detroit arose in Nizhni Novgorod and in Moscow itself. The world's largest dam harvested electricity from the Dnieper River. Canals connected the Baltic with the White Sea, and Moscow with the Volga River. The Baku oilfields began production again thanks to refining equipment sold to Stalin by the American Koch Corporation. Even more important for the future of the USSR were the industrial complexes that arose in Siberia. Near a pair of iron-rich mountains east of the Ural Mountains, Stalin built Magnitogorsk, a steel complex modeled on Gary, Indiana that dwarfed the large metal shops of Petrograd – now renamed Leningrad. Rail lines connected Magnitogorsk to the enormous coal deposits at Kuznetsk further east, and to a giant rail-car factory in Nizhni Tagil and other vehicle plants in the west. Meanwhile, as Moscow grew, a General Plan for the city envisioned huge districts downtown for state office buildings and apartment blocks on the outskirts. The war and scarcity of resources delayed the Plan for decades (Chapter 19), but Stalin brought in forced laborers to drill new Metro lines and palatial stations deep under Moscow. Dynamite leveled most of the city's onion-domed churches, silencing the bells of the Tsarist era. The great Cathedral of Christ the Savior was destroyed to make room for a proposed skyscraper Stalin called the Palace of the Soviets. The war nixed that project too, but in later years Moscow acquired much of the grim gigantism envisioned by Hitler's plans for Germania.[23]

All of this ambitious destruction and construction relied above all on the coercive power of the Soviet state. Building, in turn, also increased state power, including the iron rule of Stalin himself. Workers at the car and tractor plants received bare subsistence wages, sometimes taking the form of a free bed in a drafty dormitory and a meager canteen lunch. Most of the builders of canals, dams, subways, and industrial complexes were peasants caught up in mass roundups of rebels, filtered through the Gulag, and redeployed as forced laborers. Some of the Gulag's camps themselves grew into cities, such as Norilsk, a nickel-smelting center hundreds of kilometers north of the Arctic Circle. Norilsk and the expanded ice-free Soviet Arctic port of Murmansk represent the most substantial extensions of the Urban Planet into circumpolar regions to this day. Thousands died on the massive construction sites involved in all of these projects, particularly during Russia's excruciating winters. As the First Five-Year Plan morphed into the Second and Third during the late 1930s, Stalin refocused the Soviet industrial machine on weapons building. Tractor and train-car plants retooled their assembly lines to make machine guns, tanks, and airplanes, all fueled with petroleum from Baku. The Russian military–industrial complex spread far beyond its origins in Leningrad throughout former agricultural towns in European Russia and growing cities along the Trans-Siberian Railroad.[24]

Meanwhile, the strains brought on by Stalin's lightning-fast socialist industrial revolution ricocheted through the commissariats and party bureaucracies. Arming himself against dissent both real and imagined, Stalin gave the NKVD more power to spy on rivals, try them, imprison them, and execute them. On the twentieth anniversary of 1917, some of the revolution's great heroes faced disgrace at elaborate "show trials" where they read forced confessions about conspiracies with Britain, Japan, or the hated Leon Trotsky. A "labyrinth of terror" metastasized in secretive buildings surrounding the People's Commissariat for Internal Affairs in Moscow's Lubyanka Square. The membership of entire councils, office corridors, or housing blocks disappeared mysteriously into its torture chambers, prisons, secret execution sites, and mass graves around town. Some 700,000 people perished in the "Great Terror" of 1937 and 1938 alone, and the "Gulag Archipelago" bulged with new inhabitants. In 1940, NKVD agents murdered Stalin's archrival Leon Trotsky in Mexico City, where he had taken shelter amidst an international community of socialist and anti-colonial activists. By then, though, Stalin had firmly imprinted his personal iron fist on the entirety of the expanding anti-capitalist realm of the Urban Planet.[25]

ARMAGEDDON OF THE HYDROCARBON CITY

As an event in the global history of the built environment, World War II was, like most wars, a conflict between empires orchestrated in their capital cities. Street-, barracks-, and corridor-born totalitarian movements in Rome, Berlin, Tokyo, and Moscow aggressively taunted older empire-building regimes headquartered in London, Paris, and Washington into a war that pitted every sinew of their rival multi-continental projects of conquest against each other. Even more than World War I, World War II was a "total war," fought by means of opposing military–industrial cities and urban complexes supplied and fueled by the fields, mines, and above all the oilfields of these empires' conquered and partly disciplined hinterlands.

The cities at the centers of these imperial realms once again spurted in growth to meet the challenge of war, drawing in larger working-class majorities that were also increasingly female, since the armed forces sucked away millions of men. Urban working classes in many places also became more diverse by race, particularly in the USA, where African Americans migrated into factory towns in far greater numbers than in World War I. Factories large and small, many of them home to rapid assembly line systems, retooled operations that built civilian products like automobiles, rail cars, and merchant ships to produce a prolific new generation of weapons and armed vehicles – guns and cannons of all kinds, new destructive projectiles, jeeps, armored cars, tanks, fighter planes, bombers, battleships, aircraft carriers, and submarines. As mobile built environments in themselves, these weaponized vehicles far outpaced their World War I counterparts in the level of defensive built shelter they could make available on battlefields and the speed of evasion from enemy fire, but also the speed of projectile delivery, and thus the geographical range of death-production. The swift early success of Hitler's tank- and plane-led *Blitzkrieg* attacks on Poland, the Low Countries, and France attests to this revolution. So did the Japanese attack on the American naval base at Pearl Harbor, which involved aircraft carriers positioning planes to drop bombs on a target more than 6,000 open-ocean kilometers away from Tokyo.[26]

Thus, World War II was also a war waged by oil and for oil – and thus by and for the world's widely dispersed petroleum mining and refining facilities. The black blood that guzzled through the crankcases and exploded in the piston chambers of Hitler's infernal war machine had two main sources. One was the archipelago of hydrogenation plants run by the chemical corporation IG Farben, headquartered in Frankfurt, which turned coal from beneath the Ruhr Valley into various forms of engine lubricants and fuels. The other, under the control of Hitler's ally, right-wing military dictator Ion Antonescu, was an oil-pumping and refining center sixty kilometers to the north of the Romanian capital, Bucharest, at the city of Ploeşti. This "taproot of German might," as the arch-petro-strategist Winston Churchill put it, fueled half of the 600,000 war vehicles that Hitler flung at the Soviet Union in 1941 in the largest military operation in history. That was enough oil for Nazi tanks to blast through Russian and Ukrainian villages, compact vast acreage of farmland beneath their treads, overrun Kyiv, lay devastating siege to Leningrad, and advance to within sight of the towers of the Kremlin in Moscow. However, late fall rains turned battlefields into quagmires. Then, hoary Russian blizzards froze the Romanian engine oil in German tanks. As the fuel gauges of the mighty *Wehrmacht* began to dip, Hitler turned his conquering sights even further, toward the hydrocarbon-pumping lands of Baku and the Caspian Sea. Hitler's winter halt, however, gave Stalin enough time to fire up his trans-Siberian industrial plant and to restock the Red Army with fresh recruits. Throughout 1942 and into another Russian winter, the two vast opposing forces burned countless gallons of petroleum, hurled untold tonnages of explosives at each other, then fought over every roofless house, every bombed-out factory, and every sniper-raked alley of the city of Stalingrad. A ruthless Blitzkrieg transmogrified into a macabre urban "Rattenkrieg" – War of the Rats. Two million lost-lives later, the defense of Stalingrad switched the momentum of Armageddon toward the anti-fascist side. The plot of the great oil war meanwhile twisted elsewhere: to the outskirts of the Polish town of Auschwitz (Oświęcim), where SS units were rushing Jewish slave laborers to the construction site of a new IG Farben fuel and rubber plant; and in Romania, where allied bombers lifted black clouds into the atmosphere above the burning oilfields of Ploeşti.[27]

Japan's petroleum dilemmas were even more acute, for its conquest of China and its oil-thirsty fleet in the Pacific depended almost exclusively on oil shipped from new fields in and around the American city of Los Angeles. That gave Washington considerable veto power over Tokyo's ambitions, and an embargo on oil supplies was imposed after Japanese troops occupied part of French Indochina in 1940. This embargo hindered the Japanese army's march up the Yangtze, and allowed Chiang Kai-shek to survive, barely, at Chongqing. Mao Zedong had escaped Chiang's Nationalists on his fabled "Long March" of 1934–35 that allowed him to regroup in the remote northern city of Yan'an. Ultimately, dependence on US oil led to Japan's simultaneous attack on Pearl Harbor and a massive campaign against French, British, and Dutch colonial capitals in Southeast Asia. There Japan secured British rubber plantations in Malaya – essential for tires on its war vehicles – and Dutch colonial oil towns like Palembang on Sumatra in the East Indies. Yet the Co-prosperity Sphere's declaration of hydrocarbon independence came at the price of a radical and even more oil-dependent reorientation of the Japanese war effort – against the US in the vastnesses of the Pacific Ocean.[28]

By contrast, Britain had a much firmer grasp on the new oilfields of the Middle East, thanks to concessions from the Pahlavi dynasty, which in

1925 took power in Tehran over a realm they renamed Iran – and the discovery of the great Kirkuk oilfields in the Ottoman territory of Iraq that Britain had seized after World War I. The oil metropolises around Kirkuk and Mosul, Iraq and around Abadan and Ahwaz, Iran date from the 1920s and 1930s. As for the USA, production declines plagued the original North American oilfields in Pennsylvania, but the discovery of oil at Spindletop, Texas in 1901 and then elsewhere in the US southwest gave American oil companies the chance to develop the world's most extensive urban infrastructure devoted to petroleum. This included boomtowns devoted to extraction such as Beaumont, Texas, and Tulsa, Oklahoma. More important for the urbanization of the region was a ship channel dredged through Galveston Bay that transformed the refinery and tanker-port complexes of Houston and Port Arthur into one of the largest industrial zones in the world. To get fuel to the East Coast and Europe, however, oil companies needed to circumvent German submarines that plied the Gulf of Mexico. Thus the war provided the occasion for the lightning-quick construction of the twin 2,000-kilometer Little-Inch and Big-Inch pipelines from Texas to the East Coast, the longest and widest ever built to that point. Huge new refineries sprouted at the other end, in Philadelphia and Northern New Jersey. More oil was discovered along the Pacific shoreline of Los Angeles. Los Angeles's famous beaches sprouted forests of derricks, and the port at Long Beach became a premier refining and oil transport hub for trans-Pacific shipments not only to Tokyo but to the American fleet at the former coal station in Pearl Harbor, Hawai'i. Even more important to the history of petroleum was the discovery by American oil prospectors of the world's largest oilfield, in the deserts adjacent to the pearl-fishing port of Damman, Saudi Arabia (Chapter 24).[29]

In the meantime, the US government subsidized experiments in petroleum-based synthetic rubber that allowed factories that made tires, engine-belts, and cooling hoses to multiply across the Midwest from their historic center in Akron, Ohio. The American plastics and nylon industries grew fivefold to supply fiberglass, body armor, and parachutes among many other wartime uses. All of these Allied-controlled "petroleumscapes" lay far beyond the range of enemy attack. They provided uninterrupted support both for the brutal island-hopping campaign against Japan in the Pacific and for the immense petroleum-fired armada that seized the beaches of German-controlled Normandy on D-Day in 1944. Oil made up half the tonnage of supplies that the US Army shipped to Britain in preparation for the assault. In the final days of the war, American oil fueled the aircraft carriers and planes that delivered another, more destructive, form of energy to Hiroshima and Nagasaki.[30]

CONCENTRATION AND GENOCIDE

World War II was also a race war. As such, it relied upon numerous institutions that could only operate in cities, and it resulted in the construction of some of the grimmest built spaces devoted to racial extermination ever conceived. Racist state propaganda during the era was hardly limited to Hitler's Reich Party Grounds. It drew on "eugenical" theories propagated in universities and by influential academic research institutes in London and near New York that encouraged funding for similar facilities in Rio de Janeiro and Mexico City as well as Berlin. Standard Oil's Rockefeller Foundation, which later played such an important role in postwar medical and agricultural science, was a major funder of eugenical experimentation. During the war, racial propaganda spread rapidly as combatant states deployed state-owned or private radio transmission stations, filmmaking studios (Los Angeles's Hollywood chief among them), and cinemas, now complete with sound systems, to pitilessly dehumanize their opponents.[31]

This mass culture of hatred amplified the racism that was already festering in urban streets, and it undoubtedly accounts for some of the extreme brutality and unprecedented death tolls on the war's battlefronts, particularly in Eastern Europe and the Pacific. Yet hatreds also scoured the war-spared cities of the USA and Canada. There racist propaganda fueled a vast operation to dispossess and imprison Japanese immigrants living in West Coast cities. This project was coordinated from the new Pentagon in Washington and various military or immigration facilities in Ottawa, Ellis Island, Los Angeles, and Vancouver. All told, these efforts involved the transport of 150,000 people to a gulag consisting of dozens of isolated and poorly equipped "internment camps" hastily constructed in some of the most desolate regions of North America.[32]

The most diabolical front of the race war was Hitler's mass murder of six million European Jews and five million Slavs, Roma, homosexuals, psychiatric patients, disabled people, and opponents of the Nazi regime. Nowhere in world history was the practice of "concentration," vital as it is to acts of city-building more generally, so grimly married to an urban industrial complex devoted to racially motivated mass slaughter. As extreme as Hitler's death camps were in global urban history, precedents for them did exist, both in the German Kaiser's earlier "Second" Reich and in the Ottoman Empire.

In 1905, in the German settler-colonial regime of Southwest Africa (today's Namibia), officials built a *Konzentrationslager* – a concentration camp – at Shark Island in the colonial port town of Lüderitz. The governor of the colony had earlier faced an outcry from liberals in Germany over the regime's genocidal war against the Herero and Nama peoples. German soldiers under General Lothar von Trotha had slaughtered tens of thousands of herding families who had rebelled against land seizures for a railroad designed to increase German settlement; many more families were forced into the Namib and Omaheke deserts, where they and their cattle died of hunger and thirst. Shark Island was intended to appear more humane, but as many as 3,000 inmates died there of the physical toll from forced labor in harsh conditions. Some perished after enduring forced medical experiments meant to confirm theories of African racial inferiority. Others were simply tossed offshore to the circling sharks that gave the island its name.[33]

During the same period, the Ottoman Sultan Abdulhamid II and a cadre of ultra-nationalist Turkish officials who later seized power in Istanbul led a decades-long series of public outcries against the forced migration of Muslims into Turkey from the empire's former Balkan provinces, including Austro-Hungarian Bosnia-Herzegovina. Their solution was to escalate longstanding attacks against Christian inhabitants of Turkey using Shark-Island-like techniques on a much larger scale. Thousands of Christian Greeks and Armenians died in massacres in Istanbul and later in the cities of Adana and Van. During World War I, officials constructed twenty-five urban prisons and concentration camps across Anatolia. Armenian intellectuals were the first to go to their deaths there, but thousands more descended though the system's labyrinths into forced labor camps on the war front against Russia, or, once again, died at the hands of physicians in experimental medical labs. Cattle cars delivered women and children to port towns like Izmir and Trabzon, where officials packed them onto rafts and launched them to their deaths by drowning in the Aegean and Black Seas. Many thousands more endured rape and forced marches into the hot deserts around the encampment of Deir ez-Zor in the Syrian Desert where many perished of thirst and hunger, or drowned in the Euphrates under deliberately capsized riverboats.[34]

How much direct inspiration the Nazis took from these precedents remains a matter of debate. Either way, the SA and SS had begun building the architecture for the Final Solution even as they ushered Hitler into power in 1933, by imprisoning leftists and patrons of Berlin's gay bars in "wild camps" made up of locked sheds, cellars, and beer cellars throughout the urban underworld that gave birth to the Nazi movement. Dachau and other formal *Konzentrationslager* opened months afterward, to absorb the massive overflow of political and "moral" prisoners from these places and Nazi-hijacked municipal prisons. Meanwhile, Hitler unleashed another force of death in Germany's advanced psychiatric institutions, where doctors had absorbed British and American eugenicist views that the greater interest of racial "fitness" demanded sterilizing or even euthanizing human "defectives." On the day he invaded Poland, Hitler signed a law permitting the complete destruction of all disabled German people. Accordingly, attendants at the Brandenburg asylum near Berlin led twenty inmates to their deaths in "shower rooms" connected to lethal exhaust pipes of gasoline engines. Over 200,000 people died in similar facilities in Germany throughout the war, and many more were sterilized.[35]

During the conquest of Poland, meanwhile, elite SS units known as *Einsatztruppen* began to move Poles and Jews out of neighborhoods, towns, and farms that the Nazis promised to German settlers. Amidst the chaos that ensued, Heinrich Himmler and his deputy Reinhardt Heydrich orchestrated the gun-point removal of Poland's millions of

Jews into fenced "ghettos" in Polish cities like Łódź, Lublin, and Kraków. In Warsaw's ghetto, the largest all, 400,000 people were crammed into a fenced zone occupying a mere 2.4 percent of the city's area. Many thousands died in the roundups; others died of hunger, disease, or exhaustion as laborers in textile mills that were ghetto inmates' only legal source of income. After the Nazi invasion of the Soviet Union in 1941, similar ghettos came into being in occupied cities of the former Russian Pale, like Riga, Vilnius, Minsk, and Lviv. On the outskirts of Nazi-occupied Kyiv, SS extermination squads massacred 37,000 Jews at the Babi Yar ravine in 1941, then, together with Romanian troops, killed over 30,000 more later the same year in Odessa. Warfare in the "Bloodlands" on the Soviet front was genocidal in its own right, and countless Slavic towns and Jewish *shtetls* were destroyed. Some twelve million people lost their lives in this region alone.[36]

In January 1942, Heydrich convoked a conference of Nazi officials at a villa in the Berlin suburb of Wannsee to launch the "Final Solution," a plan for the deliberate and systematic mass killing of Jews from all Nazi-controlled areas of Europe. Long lines of boxcars soon rolled up to collection points (*Umschlagplätze*) in the ghettos. There, SS officers loaded human cargos for delivery to top-secret rail sidings in small Polish towns like Chełmno, Bełżec, Sobibór, and Treblinka, where new detachments of armed men led inmates into barns, sealed the buildings shut and pumped them full of toxic gas, delivering agonized deaths to hundreds of thousands – 750,000 died at Treblinka alone. At Majdanek near Lublin and Auschwitz near the new Nazi fuel plant, Heydrich's operatives forced Russian and Polish prisoners of war to construct far larger, industrial versions of these death camps. Captives from across Europe arrived on crowded train platforms where they met the diabolical likes of Dr. Joseph Mengele, the student of a student of the medical researcher who conducted racist experiments on Africans at Shark Island. Mengele's staff led inmates into what amounted to an assembly line of family separation, material dispossession, psychological humiliation, toxic "medical" procedures, slave labor in dozens of nearby factories including I.G Farben's synthetic oil and rubber plants, death by firing squad or gassing in fake bathhouses modeled after those in the psychiatric hospitals, cremation of bodies in industrial-strength furnaces, and forced digging of mass graves. Eighteen thousand Jews went to their deaths at Majdanek on a single particularly grim day in 1943; over a million perished in Camp B of Auschwitz-Birkenau before the Red Army stormed the sprawling facility in 1945.[37]

"URBICIDE" FROM THE AIR

In the meantime, the bombers wheeled overhead in ever more menacing flocks. World War II was also a war of planes and bombs, of their mass production in cities, and of the devastating cruelties they could inflict on cities – nothing less than a mass "urbicide." Since the previous world war, the creators of new air forces argued extensively about the relationship between these things. Bomber pilots, they argued, should target cities' factories, transport infrastructure, fuel installations, and the people who worked there. Killing large numbers of people and destroying many built things, they argued, would not only inhibit the production of weapons and fuel, but also ignite mass uprisings against the enemy state, and thus forever end the bane of long, stalemated wars such as World War I that killed far more people. Such a brutal form of "pacifism" validates key points in this book about the centrality of cities to war and politics, but it overlooked another crucial argument, that urban politics is foundationally unforeseeable. Flaming urban rubble guarantees death, but beyond that, it does little to determine what surviving urban residents will do next. On top of that, bombing cities from the air involved its own abstractions of brutality that could just as easily feed escalations of carnage, not reductions. When bombardiers in planes saw cities below – assuming even they were flying in daytime and that their view was unobstructed by clouds or the smoke from other explosions – they could not see the living, thronging people they were about to kill. Perhaps these abstracted viewpoints help explain how it was that some of the strongest critics of city bombing, including Presidents Franklin D. Roosevelt and Harry Truman of the USA, became some of its most destructive practitioners during the course of the war.[38]

Whatever the case, the Axis powers clearly set the stage. Japan's attacks on the great Yangtze Valley cities in the early 1930s had normalized an unprecedented increase in the scale of air war, especially its relentless bombing of Chongqing from 1938 on. German pilots gained international notoriety in 1937 when they bombed the small Basque town of Guernica during the Spanish Civil War on behalf of Hitler's ally General Francisco Franco, but the *Luftwaffe* outdid even Japan's bombers during a massive attack on Warsaw in 1939. Aerial blitzes in 1940–41 followed, on the European oil refining port of Rotterdam, then on London, Manchester, Birmingham, and dozens of other British cities. Late in the war, Germany's V-1 and V-2 rocket attacks on London gave the Urban Planet its first taste of long-range missile warfare. Sixty thousand civilians died in Britain and two million urban houses became piles of rubble.[39]

Joseph Goebbels predicted that the Blitz would undermine the British will to fight, but nothing of the kind happened, as civilians streamed gamely into the London Underground for protection, hailing Winston Churchill's inspiring words to fight on. Yet Churchill himself had been an early advocate of aerial bombing, against rebels protesting the British seizure of Iraq in the 1920s; he even advocated use of mustard gas bombs there. Despite his knowledge that the Iraqi campaign had been largely ineffective and that German bombing only increased Britain's military resolve, he too insisted he could sap German war morale through even larger retaliatory attacks, adding blood-curdling rhetoric of revenge to the rationale for airborne urbicide.[40]

In 1942, US bombers joined the British in a two-and-a-half-year assault on German cities. Britain took the lead in killing civilians by dropping petroleum-based incendiary devices on the largely wooden and militarily insignificant medieval port of Lübeck. Air force pilots then used the fires to guide low-flying bombing raids at night, aimed to avoid anti-aircraft fire. The USA followed at higher altitudes during the day on raids theoretically designed to target military and industrial infrastructure. Bombs dropped from these heights often missed their targets, though, killing innocents; American raids also increasingly included working factories filled with civilians. As the raids escalated, city destruction increased exponentially. One thousand planes reduced much of Cologne to rubble (sparing the Gothic Cathedral), and a combination of bombs and incendiaries dropped on Hamburg immolated 45,000 people in a horrific, self-feeding firestorm. Thousand-year-old built

(A)

(B)

18.2. Tokyo: Into Ashes and Out

Few cities have experienced more destruction, sown more destruction, or emerged from the ashes of more destruction than the largest of all: Tokyo. As Edo, the city's wood and paper neighborhoods often burned to the ground. Earthquakes visited regularly, including the big one of 1923 (A) which leveled most of Tokyo, and touched off racial violence against Koreans and Chinese. That political quake set off chains of atrocities like the Japanese army's enslavement of 50,000 Korean "comfort women" on military bases across East Asia, the brutal "Rape of Nanjing" (1937), and aerial bombardments of Chinese cities and elsewhere that killed millions. During World War II, generals on all sides downplayed

(C)

(D)

18.2. (cont.) the human toll of bombing, so visible in this image from Chongqing (B), preferring the more abstracted view from planes like this American B-29 bomber that helped incinerate Tokyo once again (C). After 1945, Tokyo rose from the ashes, resuming its historic role as an amplifier of cosmopolitan pleasures, as in this cabaret (D) where American soldiers danced with young Japanese women. Today, Tokyo is known as one of the "most livable" cities on Earth – as its thirty-five million inhabitants perhaps attest.

(A) Bettmann/Getty Images. (B) Hulton Deutsch/Corbis Historical/Getty Images. (C) Corbis Historical/Getty Images. (D) Keystone/Hulton Archive/Getty Images.

structures, like the Old Town of Nuremberg, went up in flames – though many there saved themselves by hiding in the sixteenth-century network of sandstone beer-storage tunnels underneath the city. When Germans demonstrated little diminishment in morale and instead launched rocket attacks on London, the USA loosened its standards on civilian deaths further. Redoubled attacks on Berlin followed, as did the infamous and gratuitous attack on the lovely baroque city of Dresden in 1945, and random attacks on villages and towns equally insignificant to the German war effort.[41]

Six hundred thousand Germans in 131 cities and towns lost their lives in the barrage, and half a million buildings in German-occupied France were also destroyed. Perhaps the most "useful" outcome in military terms came when airplanes bombed actual battlefields. However, attacks on industrial installations and transportation infrastructure too were devastating. For example, a concerted attack on German-controlled French railways hindered the *Wehrmacht*'s resistance to the Allied ground campaign after D-Day, as did the destruction of Ploeşti, leaving Nazi tanks and aircraft with empty fuel containers. On the Eastern Front, as Soviet tanks and planes forced the Nazis into retreat westward after their defeats at Stalingrad and Kursk in 1943, German forces left Soviet cities like Kyiv and Minsk in smoking ruins, and, according to historian Tony Judt, leveled another "70,000 villages, 1,700 towns, 32,000 factories, and 40,000 miles of railroad track" in the Soviet Union. Ninety percent of Warsaw was reduced to rubble after no less than three separate assaults: the first in 1939 by the Luftwaffe, the second in 1943 when the Nazis destroyed the city's Jewish ghetto after its inmates rose in revolt, and the third in 1944 after a Polish uprising inspired Hitler to organize a special annihilation corps to dynamite the city off the face of the Earth.[42]

The American attack on Japanese cities further escalated all of these trends, normalizing mass urban destruction for the ages. Air-bombing converts like Harry Truman went even further, musing about the "revolutionary change in the relationship of man to the universe" involved in exploding atomic bombs on cities. American anti-Japanese racism – involving a further abstraction of bombardiers' human targets as "beasts," to use Truman's widely shared language – now also demonstrably played a part in the severity of the attacks. That said, so-called "conventional" bombing attacks, using petroleum-based explosives and inflammatory jellies (including a new substance called napalm) killed far more people in Japan than atomic bombs. Though American strategy spared the imperial city of Kyoto, US bombers leveled close to a half or more of Osaka, Kobe, Nagoya, Yokohama, and some sixty other Japanese cities. Above Tokyo, pilots dropped more bombs than anywhere before.[43]

As usual, the bombardiers saw only the funnels of rising smoke they left behind. Eye-witnesses in the streets, by contrast, described "rivers of fire ... flaming pieces of furniture exploding on the heat while the people themselves blazed like 'matchsticks' as their wood and paper homes exploded in flames. Under the wind and giant breath of fire enormous incandescent vortices rose ... swirling, flattening, sucking whole blocks of houses into their maelstrom of fire." Even before the atomic attacks, American warplanes killed 300,000 people, injured 400,000 more, and levelled 180 square miles of built-up space. By that point, the American commitment to city bombing had crossed a new existential threshold, thanks to a 20-billion dollar investment in the research facilities and factory buildings in places like Los Alamos, New Mexico and Oak Ridge, Tennessee needed to open the nuclear age. Underneath the menacing mushroom clouds and the flashing, unreal, suns that announced the new era, another 200,000 lives were lost amidst the vaporized buildings of Hiroshima and Nagasaki.[44]

In 1945, Inanna's paradox of urban creation and destruction stretched to extremes that befuddled all earlier imagining. An American general, surveying the damage in Germany wrought by his own country's air force, likened the collapse of the Third Reich in 1945 to the fall of Rome in 410. It was even worse, in many ways, for the force of destruction created in cities was of an exponentially greater scale than what a few Visigothic raiders could accomplish, as was the sheer volume of rubble. Yet for all of the transoceanic political force, the vast sums of capital, the millions of gallons of burning hydrocarbon fuel, and the split atoms that we threw against our own habitat in the 1940s, we also held enough of these assets in reserve after 1945 to – very tenuously to be sure – avoid the half-millennium of "dark ages" that followed the debacle of 410. Thanks to the un-bombed parts of the advanced industrial world and its oil hinterlands – the US East, Midwest, and Southwest above all, but also Stalin's forcibly industrialized Soviet Siberia, soon home to a second manufactory of atomic bombs – Hydrocarbon Cities survived the labyrinths of terror, only to enter a nuclear Cold War dictated by the two remaining superpowers. Indeed, "survival" does not capture all the paradoxical twists Inanna still had in store, for the white-hot moment of the Urban Planet's awfullest episode of destruction – the "Zero Hour" of 1945 – also marked the dawn of its Greatest Acceleration – and of still greater reckonings to come.

CHAPTER 19

Gathering Velocities I: Tailpipe Tracts and Tower Blocks

A COLD WAR IN THE KITCHEN

Few moments during the Cold War say more about the relationship between the most intimate parts of the human habitat and the propulsive edge of its postwar Urban Planetary whole than the great "Kitchen Debate" of 1959. The site was an exhibition at Moscow's Sokolniki Park, where the US government, taking advantage of a slight "thaw" in its postwar nuclear standoff with the Soviet Union, had built a typical American home, including a fully equipped kitchen. Staking out rival positions in front of the dishwasher were two of the era's master propagandists, US Vice-President Richard Nixon and First Secretary of the Soviet Communist Party Nikita Khrushchev. Their half-joking, half-acidic interchange soon played on television sets in real homes across the USA, the USSR, and the world.

Nixon was in boasting mood: America's capitalists, he trumpeted, had produced a superior cornucopia of consumer goods, and their private financial and real estate industries had spectacularly fulfilled the human needs for a self-owned home. At the bargain price of $10,000, miracles of domestic bliss like the one on display in Moscow were fully available to all American World War II veterans; all they needed to do was to take out a bank mortgage "on a contract running 25 to 30 years." Not only that, but modern appliances such as dishwashers made "life easier for our housewives." American women could leave the factories where they worked during World War II, and happily resume their role as home-based caregivers and cooks.

Khrushchev gave Nixon no quarter. "We have such things," he snipped, in an oblique reminder that, dishwashers or not, the Soviets had soundly beaten the USA in the race to launch a human-built structure, the Sputnik satellite, into space. The world's first intercontinental ballistic missile was also a Soviet device, tested the year before. Besides that, "in Russia, all you have to do to get a house is to be born in the Soviet Union. . . . In America, if you don't have a dollar, you can choose between sleeping in a house or on the pavement." Then he added a parting jab: "Your capitalistic attitude towards women does not occur under Communism."[1]

Both were feinting and posturing, caricaturing each other and themselves. In fact, both faced a new global reality that was far beyond their depth – let alone that of the rival systems they were selling to the world. The worst period of destruction in world history had given way to the Greatest Acceleration in the population, size, and impact of the human built environment. Builders of the Urban Planet faced the challenge of providing enough shelter for a surge in Earthly population that far eclipsed that of the nineteenth century. In 1959, our numbers had exploded from 2 to 3 billion in a mere thirty years – despite the mass slaughter of World War II. We reached 4 billion only fourteen years later, and after that, a billion new humans emerged on Earth every twelve years, on our way to nearly 8 billion total in 2020. Everywhere, cities continued to grow far faster than countrysides, and growing countrysides were emptying into cities. In the 1950s, this was especially true in the "First World," the part of the Urban Planet now dominated by the USA. In 1959, New York City and its now sprawling conurbation exceeded an unimaginable twelve million. Even as London fell to second place, its inhabitants filled in hundreds of craters left by the Blitz and grew their city past ten million. Although 60 percent of Tokyo burned to the ground in 1945, it rose from the ashes – *once again* – into third place in the world by 1950; by 1965, it had leapfrogged New York into first. Meanwhile, Philadelphia and Chicago passed the three million mark even as they faced rivalry from fast-growing oil and armaments upstarts like Houston and Los Angeles. The bombed ruins of the Ruhr, Hamburg, and Berlin filled back up, rebuilt themselves smoldering brick by smoldering brick and spilled beyond their pre-war populations. Osaka was half obliterated, but it soon rejoined the world's top ten; other Japanese giants like Yokohama and Nagoya grew into the top twenty.

Meanwhile, cities also gathered velocity in the Soviet "Second World." Thanks to Stalin's and Khrushchev's harsh Five-Year Plans, Russia's famous peasant masses had left the countryside, precipitously, and by the tens of millions. In 1959 – unthinkably – half of all Soviet citizens were city dwellers. Over the previous two decades, Moscow's population nearly doubled to seven million. Leningrad, besieged into starvation for three years by the Nazis, now had four million people, three times as many as when it was tsarist St. Petersburg. Warsaw and Kyiv rebuilt themselves from complete ruination, regaining their pre-war million people within a decade.[2]

Finally, in the "Third World" of Latin America, Africa, and Asia, cities that had substantial pre-war industry showed signs of the explosive growth that would become the main driver of the Greatest Acceleration after 1960. Shanghai was heavily bombed, but under Mao it quickly rejoined the world's top ten, with Beijing not far behind. Cities that escaped the bombs grew too. Buenos Aires and Calcutta had over five million by 1950. Rio, São Paulo, Mexico City, Bombay, and Cairo all topped two million. All told, in 1960 there were some seventy million-plus cities in the world, up from fifteen in 1900. An even bigger acceleration was to come, but there was no mistaking the gathering velocity of Urban Planetary growth.[3]

As Nixon and Khrushchev circled the model dishwasher like feral cats, neither could predict that megacities of ten and twenty million were a mere quarter century in the future – even though both had already helped set off the forces that would bring them into being. That did not stop the top two superpower spin-doctors from lecturing the world about how it should go about housing so many people. For Nixon, kitchens should nestle in detached homes surrounded by substantial grassy yards. For Khrushchev, kitchens should instead squeeze inside in high-rise apartment buildings, at the end of hallways where multiple families could share the appliances. In America, private developers would construct homes, and sell them through private real estate agencies to families who qualified for a government-supported mortgage at private banks. In the USSR, by contrast, the state would finance and build almost every single new apartment and communal kitchen; local officials would allocate them to eligible households and their descendants forever at nominal cost. In the USA, cities would sprawl outward with vast, repetitive low-density suburban tract homes. Soviet cities would grow by means of dense peripheries consisting of equally monotonous rows of tower blocks, separated by alleys of green space. In America, homeowners would get to work by private automobile, combusting great gulps of liquid hydrocarbon in six- and eight-cylinder engines manufactured in Detroit and releasing the fumes through a tailpipe. In the Soviet Union – as in the USA – factories would burn plenty of hydrocarbon and generate devastating pollution, but most people would walk or take public transit, such as Moscow's elegant Stalin-era subways, to work.

ANTI-URBAN PLANNING

Tailpipe tract homes in the low-rise suburbs? Or city-circling regiments of tower blocks? The contrast became something of a built symbol of Cold War rivalry. At first glance, Cold War Chicago and Moscow did indeed look just as different as the systems that built them – especially on the urban periphery where the accelerating growth of our habitat was most evident. Yet, both of the grand visions in Sokolniki Park were the off-spring of radical impulses that swept planning and architecture from earlier in the century – impulses so iconoclastic they even deserve the name anti-urban.

The leading iconoclasts were three utopian visionaries, the Londoner Ebenezer Howard, the American Midwesterner Frank Lloyd Wright, and the Swiss-French architect Le Corbusier. Between them, they rejected such foundational urban design features as concentration, proximity, and even the juxtaposition of diverse activities. Howard thought humans would be better off if all of us moved out of large cities like his native London into much smaller "Garden Cities," each home to about 30,000 people or so, spread throughout the countryside. He would divide these small, attractive, collectively managed hubs into sub-districts devoted to homes and gardens separated by green belts from others devoted to industry and offices. Railroads would connect garden cities with each other, doing away with the need for concentrated density that Howard linked to unequal power, disease, and the horrific conditions of the industrial working classes. Town planners have since built dozens of places following at least some of Howard's principles near bigger cities on all continents. Most garden cities were quickly swallowed by peripheral sprawl, and they have obviously failed to convince us as a species to abandon big cities. Yet, their juxtaposition of density with green space remains an important imperative as we think about how to build habitats that allow us to sustain eight or even twelve times as many people on Earth as lived in Howard's day, amidst renewed pandemic and intensifying climate change.[4]

For Frank Lloyd Wright, Garden Cities did not decentralize our habitats nearly enough. In his vision of "Broadacre City," urban hubs would disappear altogether, replaced by a habitat consisting entirely of dispersed single-family homes, worksites, shopping centers, and small entertainment zones. Only separation in space would give individual households the independence Wright thought they needed to control their own destinies. Rather than meeting chaotically in the streets, family members would make deliberate trips by car to zones designed for specific types of human interaction. His vision, of course, most closely anticipated the American tailpipe sprawl that Nixon celebrated in Sokolniki Park, and that quickly made Americans into the world's heaviest per-capita contributors to climate change.[5]

Of the three, Le Corbusier was the least anti-urban, but he nonetheless hated cities the way they were, and shared Howard and Wright's especial loathing for jumbled "chaotic" neighborhoods, especially "slums." His famous *Plan Voisin* for Paris elevated planners to god-like status. Olympian thunderbolts, delivered by wrecking ball, would level Paris's neighborhoods, boulevards and charming side streets alike, and relocate people into "vertical streets" – towering, cruciform apartment buildings of his own design that allowed far more sunlight into dwellings than dank, street-oriented homes. Because such structures put far more people on far smaller plots of land, planners would get rid of space wasted in streets and slums. Instead, greenery would flood the space between the buildings, delivering fresh air and leisure opportunities to all city dwellers' doorsteps. Workplaces, as in the other two visions, would occupy separate districts to keep smoke and effluents at bay. Transport, in the form of expressways teeming with automobiles (Voisin, the man who commissioned Le Corbusier's plan, was a carmaker) would occupy their own dedicated spaces too, along the far edges of the parks and in tunnels connecting the towers underneath. Like Howard and Wright but in a radically different way, Le Corbusier's plan pigeonholed the city's "four functions" – residence, leisure, work and transport – into distinct and segregated, if interconnected, zones.[6]

Thankfully, Le Corbusier never got the opportunity to actually raze Paris's neighborhoods to the ground and replace them with regiments of "towers in the park." However, his image of a city fit well with equally iconoclastic contemporary trends in architecture, which Le Corbusier himself championed as the "international [read "universal"] modernist" school. Modernists believed that unnecessary ornamentation had cluttered all earlier schools of design and that designers should consign it to the waste dump of architectural history. Instead, they championed "functional" designs, such as Le Corbusier's towers, emphasizing materials like steel, glass, and concrete often pre-assembled in factories as panels, and assembled into buildings with smooth surfaces and flat roofs. Masters of this genre have designed many structures of great merit and variety. Yet critics are right: in practice, modernists have inundated streetscapes across the world with thousands of drab office buildings, apartment buildings, and, saddest of all, state-owned housing projects. Many, such as those in Khrushchev's Moscow, surrounded themselves – in ways that Le Corbusier would have hated – with soulless open spaces. Meanwhile, in part thanks to cheap modernist imitations of Frank Lloyd Wright's otherwise ingenious innovations in domestic architecture, similar design principles spawned tens of millions of repetitious single-family prefab homes in American suburbs – including the American "model home" that developers shipped in pieces to Moscow in 1959.[7]

CRISIS, CARS, AND THE OUTSKIRTS

Three other pre-World War II contexts were relevant to the shape of the built Urban Planet as its growth gained velocity after 1945. One was a catastrophic, near-global housing crisis. In capitalist First World economies, the insufficient supply of housing was the product of the Great Depression and World War II, both of which slowed down the construction industry as urban populations rose. Bombing raids on residential neighborhoods did not help matters, notably in Britain, Germany, and Japan. In the Soviet Second World, the crisis was the result of forced collectivization and industrialization as well as similarly horrific wartime destruction in cities stretching from Leningrad to Stalingrad to Warsaw. In the still largely colonized Third World, it reflected population increases due to new public health, medical, and agricultural technologies (Chapters 21 and 22). Shortages were exacerbated by war in China, Korea, Vietnam, Palestine–Israel, and soon elsewhere. Overshadowing everything was Cold War-era imperial rivalry itself. Later, capitalist financiers and real estate developers extended their power in ways that increased urban real estate values in First, Second, and Third Worlds alike – a phenomenon we abbreviate as "gentrification" – making it much harder for lower-income people to afford safe, healthy housing in cities everywhere.

Secondly, the Great Acceleration of the Urban Planet came into being in great part because of the "automobile revolution" that Wright and Le Corbusier celebrated from the 1920s on. During those years, millions of cars and trucks demanded space in a built habitat not designed for their bulk or their speed. Motor vehicles reinforced modernists' calls for a new generation of wider roads, and entailed yet another exponential leap in cities' dependence on hydrocarbon. Nowhere was the car revolution more pronounced than in the USA, whose automobile factories reverted to peacetime use after 1945 and produced 80 percent of all cars in the world by the 1950s.

Thirdly, the emphasis of postwar construction across the Urban Planet shifted distinctly toward the peripheries of cities. Although already existing dense central cities also experienced enormous amounts of rebuilding along modernist lines – straight upward in skyscrapers and condominium towers, or in social housing towers that arose from the rubble of razed tenement districts – much of the Great Acceleration occurred because of our habitat's unprecedented appetite for gobbling up rural land and swallowing small towns on cities' peripheries. Cities grew, in other words, by acquiring what the ancient Romans knew as the *suburbium*. The world's twentieth-century urban outskirts grew with such a diversity of rates, densities, principal functions, architectural styles, degrees of separation and diversity, degrees of nucleation and polarity, and degrees of distinguishability from the urban core and the rural landscapes beyond that they continue to perplex every urban theorist who has tried to describe them. Tailpipe tract homes and tower blocks are only two ways that urban peripheries accommodated the accelerated arrival of new urban residents. Self-built shack cities are the third, arguably most explosive, way to expand urban habitats, perhaps rivaled only by China's more recent version of sprawl – an infinite spread of densely packed thirty-story apartment buildings.[8]

With these contexts in mind, we can set the record straight on the kitchen debate in Moscow. Truth be told: both Nixon and Khrushchev were sweeping huge amounts of global urban history under the living room rug. To get the right facts, we need to go back as far as the end of World War I, first in the USA and then in the post-revolutionary USSR.

FROM CRISIS TO SEGREGATED SPRAWL IN THE USA

In 1918, as again in 1945, the USA returned to peacetime with an intact, war-expanded industrial plant that was the envy of war-exhausted Europe. World War I allowed American capitalists to inaugurate the so-called "Fordist age," named for Henry Ford, the greatest exponent of huge assembly-line-based car factories. His first plant, at Highland Park in Detroit, was followed by an even more spectacular factory nearby, at River Rouge, where workers could unload Minnesota iron ore at one end and spit out fully operational, petroleum-puffing automobiles at the other. Ford famously paid his workers what was then a substantial $5 per day, in part to purchase labor peace in a tumultuous era of global class warfare (Chapter 17), and in part to convince his workers that spending their days repeating the same dull task was nonetheless worth the "good life" that their paycheck granted to their families. Ford wanted urban workers to use his "high" wages to buy expensive things such as kitchen appliances – or, better yet, one of Ford's automobiles, perhaps with extra help from a bank loan. A family house was in reach too, if a worker could get a mortgage with low enough down-payments and long enough repayment periods from a worker-run Building and Loan Society. Since such Societies had limited capital, most American workers in the 1920s still rented their homes. Nonetheless, during the 1920s,

(A)

(B)

19.1. Global Geopolitics on the Prefab Periphery

As Earthopolis's Greatest Acceleration gathered velocity after 1945, cities became taller and denser in the middle – and far more spread out on the edges. Urban peripheries varied enormously: just compare the outskirts of New York with Moscow. In the USA, capitalist developers like the Levitt Brothers built thousands of dispersed low-rise single-family homes reachable only by car (A). The Soviet state preferred five-story tower blocks (soon much taller), with communal amenities, including public transport (B). Both shared international consumer culture expanded in the USA, thanks to credit and wages that rose enough to cover a growing number of workers' loan payments.[9]

Most American industrialists, however, were not as generous as Henry Ford. The wages they paid limited the purchasing power of buyers for the escalating mountains of goods that their assembly lines produced in larger numbers than before. Soon, capitalists who pinched their workers' paychecks faced large bills from their warehousers for storing unsold items. Drains on profits like these caused owners of corporate shares to ring alarm bells on New York's Wall Street, and in September and October 1929, shareholders sold off catastrophic amounts of corporate stock. Without access to capital and nowhere to sell their merchandise, companies closed factories and laid off workers by the millions. Unemployed factory hands and middle-class holders of worthless corporate paper rushed to their bank branches to withdraw their savings. Many also held back on their monthly bank payments. Those banks that did not shut their branches began foreclosing on car and house loans, evicting millions of their customers, and forcing them into cheaper and over-crowded rental housing. For a vast army of homeless "hobos," that meant hopping on empty freight cars in search of any work available anywhere in the country. Many built their own shack towns outside of American cities. As Khrushchev reminded Nixon thirty years later, thousands simply slept rough on the pavement.[10]

By 1932, it was already clear to millions of foreclosed and homeless Americans that US President Herbert Hoover had failed to end the Great Depression. His favorite problem-solving technique, summoning capitalists to conferences in Washington, did not help. The homeless began calling their shack towns "Hoovervilles," and soon joined a landslide of voters who elected Hoover's opponent, Franklin D. Roosevelt as

---

Caption for 19.1. (cont.)

modernist architects' cult of prefabricated concrete panels, like the ones piled at the site in Moscow (center). Elsewhere these impulses varied and mixed – and both coexisted with another great force of urban peripheral expansion, self-built houses of the urban poor. Permutations of periphery-making explain why "the suburbs" resist any single definition. (A) Getty Images. (B) Newsday/Getty Images.

president. Over the next decade, Roosevelt fulfilled his campaign pledge of a "New Deal" in part by enacting dozens of long-shelved social welfare policy ideas that had circulated among urban reformers across the world since the late nineteenth century.[11]

One of these ideas involved putting the credit of the US government behind millions of affordable thirty-year house mortgages similar to those offered by British and American Building and Loan Societies. Combined with another government program that rescued many home-owners from foreclosure, the new Federal Housing Administration (FHA) slowly convinced mainstream bankers to lend ordinary people money to buy new homes. That trend took off after World War II, when a special program for veterans gave them access to FHA-backed loans – the "contracts" that Nixon boasted about in the kitchen with Khrushchev in 1959. Note how completely Nixon had repackaged a government-financed solution to a capitalist disaster as a triumph of profit-seeking private enterprise.[12]

FHA loans did not end the housing crisis of the Great Depression, and Roosevelt imported a second type of reform from Europe to the USA – state-owned, "social," or as Americans call it, "public," housing. In the 1920s, British authorities had adapted legislation first passed in London that substantially expanded funding to municipalities which wanted to replace nineteenth-century slums with modern, sanitary shelter. American housing reformers like Catherine Bauer were impressed with Britain's large tidy "council housing" estates, such as the one at Becontree outside London, and she wrote a similar public housing law for Roosevelt. Even then, only a handful of "projects" sprouted in US cities before World War II, and the housing crisis increased in intensity after Pearl Harbor.[13]

As American automobile and home-appliance factories retooled to make weapons, they drew large numbers of women out of homes, and hundreds of thousands of new migrant workers from the countryside, especially from the over-cultivated "dustbowls" of the Great Plains and the sharecropping plantations of the South. In the South, owners of plantations had begun evicting their predominantly Black tenants in favor of new cotton-picking machines. In cities across the East and Midwest, and now in Southwestern industrial cities like Los Angeles, working-class neighborhoods filled far beyond capacity, straining already poorly maintained tenements. "Black Belts" in places like the South Side of Chicago were worst off, for white opposition to African-American neighbors meant that these segregated slivers of the city had to absorb the largest group of new migrants. Slumlords in the Black Belt subdivided tiny apartments into tinier ones, built new ones in dingy basements, and crammed whole extended families into a few rooms, thus creating the squalid capitalist enterprise known as the "kitchenette." After the war, unsafe and overcrowded living spaces continued to expand. Black activists now called their neighborhoods "ghettos" – provocatively using the medieval term recently revived by the Nazis to draw attention to the involuntary nature of racial segregation aggravated by slumlordism. When Richard Nixon bragged about the spatiousness of American capitalist kitchens compared with cramped Soviet ones, he pointedly overlooked the "kitchenettes" – and the ghettos – of Chicago.[14]

As the housing crisis intensified, automobiles took decisive command of urban streets across the USA and to a growing degree across the rest of the industrialized world. Car factories spread far beyond Detroit. The Soviets, as we know, adopted Ford's assembly line technology at Nizhni Novgorod (renamed Gorky in 1932). Ford built his own plants in the United Kingdom at Old Trafford near Manchester and Dagenham near London. A Renault plant in Billancourt near Paris sprawled onto an island in the Seine. Hitler built the massive Volkswagen works at Wolfsburg, and the Toyota textile-loom company built a car plant near Nagoya, Japan. As these hyper-efficient factories churned out tens of thousands of new automobiles, drivers careened through city streets already packed with trolleys, delivery carts, bicycle riders, pedestrians, and children at play. Even Haussmannian boulevards, where they existed, were too narrow for this denser, and far faster, traffic.[15]

Deadly accidents were inevitable, and pedestrians, including darting children, were far bigger victims than drivers. That did not stop car manufacturers, influential automobile-promotion societies, or car-loving traffic planners from blaming the newly mortal dangers of street conviviality on its victims, especially focusing on the inadequate supervision of mothers. Pro-car forces lobbied for laws prohibiting "jaywalking" – as Americans renamed the millennia-old practice of walking in city streets – and relegated pedestrians to sidewalks and crosswalks at intersections.[16]

The first traffic police, traffic signals, parking meters, parking lots, repair garages, car parts stores, car junkyards, traffic engineers, sub-grade street crossings, limited access expressways, and cloverleaf interchanges all followed during a short period in the late 1920s and early 1930s. As petroleum-fired cars won out over promising electric ones, gasoline became the main fuel for urban transport and the main source of tailpipe-enhanced urban air pollution, and filling stations began their spread across the Urban Planet, as did roadside advertisements and traffic jams. Companies that specialized in laying down hard pavements offered their wares to cut down on the mud and road dust that car tires churned into the air. As asphalt largely won out for this purpose over cement and other materials, petroleum became a ubiquitous component of the built environment itself.[17]

Governments built wider, longer pavements – including Hitler's *Autobahnen*, and Route 1 in the USA, a dreamy four-lane divided highway between New York and Trenton, New Jersey. Paved roads began to supplant steel rails as the primary land-based transportation conduits of the Urban Planet, especially in the USA. Car parking became an urban issue for the first time, and the acreage devoted to paved surfaces for storing empty cars quickly equaled that devoted to driving them. By war's end, traffic engineers, now anointed as modernist heroes by Le Corbusier and others, looked for ways to drill wide habitats exclusively designed for automobiles and trucks directly into what had become traffic-choked, exhaust-filled central cities.[18]

In the USA, postwar policymakers like the Pharaonic New York City planner Robert Moses joined forces with downtown capitalist elites to "renew" cities with full doses of modernist medicine, focused above all on the flow of cars. On the outskirts, real estate developers built broad acres of single-family suburbs for a growing middle class, joined by white factory workers whose union activism during the Great Depression and the New Deal allowed them to command robust salaries alongside FHA mortgages. Nearer downtown, Moses and other planners rammed wrecking balls through poorly maintained tenement neighborhoods and replaced them with Le Corbusier-inspired tower blocks for the poor, especially people of color.[19]

The prime targets for planners like Moses were the overcrowded, under-maintained properties of slumlords in majority-Black neighborhoods, most of which were tucked into dense zones directly within the shadows of rising downtown corporate skyscrapers (New York's Puerto Rican migrants and Mexican migrants in Houston, Chicago, and Los Angeles occupied similar places). The corporate elites who owned Downtown believed that neighbors of color brought down property values and scared middle-class white customers away from their expensive offices, hotels, and department stores. After 1949, when the federal government began offering cities "urban renewal" funds, downtown corporate elites and their "pro-growth" allies in City Hall seized their main chance to bulldoze large chunks of neighboring Black Belts. Traffic engineers used the cleared space to run moats of elevated expressway around the skyscraper districts, such as Moses' West Side Highway, Roosevelt Drive, and the Brooklyn-Queens Expressway. (These and many other similar expressways also blocked American city residents' access to riversides and lakeshores.) From there, planners drove a web of divided highway spurs heading out to ring roads in the suburbs, often first traversing zones that had been thriving Black business districts, as in the case of Robert Moses's Cross Bronx Expressway and many of his famous parkways. In this way, white office employees could live outside the city but still make it to work downtown on time, while ignoring the increasing deterioration in the older neighborhoods they zipped by *en route*. Le Corbusier had envisoned this earlier, in another (thankfully) unbuilt plan for Algiers in which an expressway viaduct lifted on cement columns far above the Muslim Casbah would carry suburban cars into the largely European downtown Marine Quarter. America's "ghetto flyovers" became the most prolific embodiment of that vision.[20]

To people of color displaced by slum clearances, urban renewal looked far more like "Negro Removal" – or removal of Puerto Ricans and Mexicans. As their neighborhoods fell to planners' thunderbolts, many sought new houses in adjacent white neighborhoods where they were not wanted. In city after city, white residents' anti-Black movements ignited new "rings-of-fire" mob violence along outward-moving racial boundaries. The only victory Black home-seekers could claim for their bravery was to acquire older housing that whites left behind and that typically declined in value precisely because of white flight itself, aggravated by subsequent discrimination by banks. Meanwhile, New Deal public housing programs expanded for several decades after the war. Yet intense opposition from private developers meant that, relative to postwar Europe, American municipalities built relatively little mass housing. Wherever municipal authorities did build public housing in the USA, they, like many of their European counterparts, imported Le Corbusier-like designs.[21]

In this way, many US inner cities did get a *Plan Voisin*. Utopias, however, they were not. Many lower-income residents of these municipal apartments did welcome their new homes as a step up from the kitchenettes in older neighborhoods, but cities trimmed construction budgets to the minimum, and few of the projects had much green space between the tower blocks. In the USA, the number of new public housing units rarely exceeded the number destroyed, so the program did little to alleviate the housing shortage. Local housing authorities also typically baked racial segregation into their plans, by using the prevailing racial composition of the destroyed neighborhood to determine the occupants of the new projects. Additionally, American federal policy, unlike its European models, limited public housing to the very poor. Thus the "projects" became warehouses for the most destitute and further segregated Black neighborhoods by class. More importantly, public housing never developed a broad political constituency in the USA. Absent strong political pressure, city halls found it easy to defer funding for maintenance.[22]

In Chicago, the public housing program went from hope to tragedy very quickly. First, the largely Black neighborhoods along South State Street – the legendary birthplace of the urban blues – fell to wrecking balls to make space for the "Chicago Wall," a five-mile parade of city-owned tower blocks that actually reduced the number of units in the area. Deferred maintenance quickly degraded the projects into "high-rise slums" owned by the city; after emptying out and becoming high-crime areas, they were demolished in the late 1990s. One of the worlds' most faithful renditions of the *Plan Voisin* was built in the largely Black area of North St. Louis. The Pruitt–Igoe complex, consisting of thirty-three eleven-story towers in the park almost exclusively inhabited by the city's poorest African-American residents, deteriorated so quickly during the 1960s that the housing authority could not find tenants, and in 1972, the city dynamited the whole thing. In the USA, only New York City sustained its investments in social housing. There, enormous public housing towers rose in the South Bronx, Harlem, the Lower East Side, Bushwick, and Coney Island among other neighborhoods, and they remain in place, if in chronically poor condition, until this day.[23]

Meanwhile, downtown banks and real estate firms collaborated with the FHA to produce maps advising the federal government where to invest its new mortgage guarantees. They drew red lines around Black neighborhoods and zones of "racial transition," effectively sanctioning lenders' longstanding practices of starving older working-class neighborhoods of capital. Other FHA regulations privileged funding for newly built single-family homes surrounded by yards.[24] In doing so, federal policy reflected a mixture of anti-urban and sexist ideologies that went back to the earliest middle-class suburbs in London, and that Frank Lloyd Wright had infused into his visions of "Broadacre City." According to these lines of thought, women and children thrived best when they lived apart from the corrupting moral influences of cities and instead confined themselves to homes nuzzled in the uplifting lap of nature. In response to FHA guidelines, developers like the famous Levitt Brothers bought up large chunks of farmland on the urban fringe, and subdivided it into plots suitable for building long rows of Wright-inspired ranch homes and assorted other "little boxes, all the same" as far as the eye could see. These subdivisions, including several "Levittowns," typically incorporated themselves as separate municipalities. That gave residents the power to pass zoning codes that prohibited construction of rental apartment buildings that might attract lower-income people and people of color. By contrast, the new towns eagerly signed off vast acreage of their bucolic countrysides to developers of shopping malls and garish commercial strips, reforested in brightly lit signage meant to elicit desire from people driving cars at fifty miles an hour.[25]

Richard Nixon's dishwasher speech washed away thousands of nightmares that scoured the dark side of the "American Dream." Meanwhile a new urban crisis grew in the USA that would touch the entire capitalist

First World. As Nixon stumped for the presidency back home, his campaign took strength both from the American Dream and the American Nightmare. On the one hand, he continued to sing the praises of suburbs with houses and yards where upright male homeowners commuted to work in their Fords and where glorified female homemakers, enthroned in the most advanced kitchens on Earth, tended to husbands, children, grammas, grandpas, pet cats and dogs, and vast roomfuls of consumer goods. On the other hand, he continued to ignore the malignant effects of the FHA on American Blacks. Instead, he vilified crumbling public housing tower blocks and the deteriorating "inner cities" that surrounded them as a rightfully neglected zone for men and women of color who were adverse to work and prone to crime or fraudulent misuse of misguided state social programs.

In the middle was the white working class, those whose scant racial privileges included discriminatory access to factory work, Ford-sized wages, and FHA mortgages. Just barely, these privileges allowed them to both assemble and purchase the dishwashers and automobiles that made the suburbs and the malls possible. Nixon's black-and-white view of American cities was directed at them, aimed above all to inflate workers' racism and their sexism. In that way, he hoped to lure white workers away from Roosevelt's center-left New Deal coalition that they shared with Americans of color and the growing number of middle-class feminists who rejected their real or rhetorical assignation to model kitchens. In the meantime, though, industrial capitalists in Nixon's camp were eager to leave the age of Henry Ford behind, to move factories away from the world's greatest industrial cities to new locations where wages were lower and where white and Black workers' nettlesome labor unions were less powerful. Automobile plants began leaving Detroit, as had New England textile mills, Pittsburgh and Chicago steel mills, and other factories across the Midwest and Northeast. Some rebuilt in suburbs themselves, others shifted southward to US states hostile to unions, and many soon reopened in even-lower wage factory and sweatshop districts in the developing world.

"Deindustrialization" – the movement of factories away from their First World urban birthplaces – had threatened many times before; now it was truly at hand. As white working households' incomes stagnated and loan payments escalated, Nixon sought to fill their ears with a new propaganda that blamed the erosion of their livelihoods not on corporate paymasters, but on people of color, feminists, and soon gay rights and environmental activists. It was a powerful ploy, and by 1968, the conservatism Nixon supported in the suburbs and some urban working-class households was powerful enough to engulf the egalitarian New Deal and its base in the "liberal cities" of the most powerful empire in the world. Deindustrialization meanwhile gained momentum in the 1970s, and similar rightward swings affected the politics across the American Bloc, with enormous consequences for the Urban Planet as a whole.[26]

CRISIS, CONCRETE, AND MORE CRISIS IN THE USSR

As for Soviet Party Secretary Khrushchev, his performance at the dishwasher overlooked easily as many buried bodies as Nixon's did. From 1917 on, the Soviet system virtually guaranteed the majority of its citizens – everyone, that is, other than the highest-ranked Party *nomenklatura* – a permanent housing shortage that lasted until the fall of the USSR in 1989 and beyond.

In the 1920s, the Russian Revolution had sharpened the edge of Soviet planners' modernist iconoclasm. In their minds the mission to radically remake cities was folded into the mission to eradicate all traces of "bourgeois" influence in the built environment. Abolition of private homeownership went a long way toward that goal – though the state often raised needed cash by reselling expropriated private homes to former owners. Once in control of urban land, however, Stalin's Kommissars shunted the most ambitious ideas for socialist housing toward the bottom of a long list of pressing priorities. Thus, Soviet planners could only dream of a day when all citizens inhabited collective "housing combines," which theoretically emancipated women from housework (and removed kitchens from homes altogether) by offering assembly-line-like canteens that did all the cooking and centralized daycares that raised all the children.[27]

A few of these combines did come into being, notably near new factories, but from the First Five-Year Plan on, most of the country's resources went into building factories themselves, then tanks and planes to defeat the Nazis, then the postwar reconstruction of industry. In the early years of Stalin, the Party *nomenklatura* elite got lovely apartments in modernist buildings called *Staliniki*, and some acquired weekend retreats in the forests called *dachas*. Ordinary families, by contrast, crammed themselves into a room or two of an expropriated bourgeois apartment building where they shared bathrooms and kitchens with other tenants. Far greater numbers of less fortunate migrants made do with factory dormitories or even shoddier barracks without plumbing. Still less fortunate citizens, of course, faced the harsh conditions of the Gulag or perished on camps for construction workers in new factory towns. Even after the Nazi retreat in 1944–45 left a staggering twenty-five million Soviet citizens homeless, and until he died in 1952, Stalin persisted in focusing on building factories over houses, meanwhile adding swank skyscrapers across Moscow largely for elites. The average square footage of shelter occupied by Soviet citizens fell by a third during that time.[28]

Nikita Khrushchev, by contrast, bet his own historical legacy on resolving the Soviet housing crisis. In his "Secret Speech" denouncing Stalin's "cult of personality," the new party secretary bemoaned the "huge sums" Stalin had spent on a statue of himself over the ruins of Stalingrad in 1951, "when people in this area had lived since the war in huts." Even so, Khrushchev admitted it would take even him at least until 1980 to give every citizen an adequate home. As he out-boasted Nixon on the global stage at Sokolniki, he tamped down expectations among his Soviet audiences. "Would a citizen rather settle for an adequate apartment," he reasoned, "or wait ten to fifteen years for a very good one?"[29]

In the years after the Kitchen Debate, Khrushchev ordered every city in the Soviet Union to establish a new type of factory whose entire purpose was to prefabricate concrete panels for apartment buildings. In so doing, he expanded yet another "modernist" assembly-line production process pioneered in the USA. Khrushchev's regime rewarded the construction crews that met quotas for cementing these panels into housing units, and soon tens of thousands of squat, five-story apartment buildings, known as *Khrushchyovki* in honor of the Party Secretary, sprang up around every city in the Soviet Union. Families occupied their own individual apartments, unlike in the housing combines, but they shared kitchens and toilets with others on their hallway. Social services of various sorts were available on site, but Soviet women hardly experienced any sort of promised emancipation. Though women famously worked in factories at similar rates to men, they also shouldered all the bother of cooking in tiny, shared kitchens, raising children, and caring for elders in cramped spaces – while orchestrating the maintenance of communal spaces in often-tense negotiations with other families. Automatic appliances, including dishwashers, were – Khrushchev's Sokolniki debating points to the contrary – rare. Broken stoves and refrigerators were common, as were dead lightbulbs; waits for maintenance crews were long. Those who had an apartment paid next to nothing for it and could pass it on through the generations. However, for a growing family, moving to a new larger place was extremely difficult – and moving to another city was virtually impossible. For all his bold ripostes to Richard Nixon, Khrushchev suffered the same ridicule from his people in 1959 as Herbert Hoover had in 1932. Soviet citizens, known for a dry wit that substituted for forbidden protest, renamed the dark, drafty, wet, and often poorly finished buildings where they lived as the *Khrushchoby*, snarkily adding Khrushchev's name to the Russian *trushchoby*, meaning slums.[30]

By the 1970s and 1980s, prefabricated apartment blocks in larger Soviet cities grew taller, to over eleven stories, then over twenty stories in big cities. An especially dense ring of cement giants thudded around Moscow. During those years, the Soviet Union built millions of units of housing, yet the grim Soviet tower block, set amidst indifferent green space, became an enduring symbol of a dreary absence of virtually all comfort and consumer culture. "There are neighborhoods like this in each big city of the Soviet Union," wrote one commentator, "– depressing, identical apartment buildings, with identical roofs, windows and entrances, identical official slogans posted on holidays, and identical obscenities scratched into the walls with nails and pencils. And these identical houses stand on identical streets with identical names – Communist Street, Trade Union Street, Peace Street, the Prospect of Cosmonauts, and the Prospect or Plaza of Lenin."[31]

Private cars were even rarer than apartments and spare lightbulbs. Soviet motor vehicle factories multiplied after World War II, but as late as 1957, they produced only a half-million vehicles annually, two-thirds of them trucks. In that same year, their American counterparts built over eight and a half million private cars, accounting for nearly two-thirds of the world total. On the other hand, the subway systems in Moscow, Leningrad, and many other Soviet cities were cheap and very fast, as was the bus service – in sharp contrast to most cities in the USA. Car use helped keep the Americans well ahead of the USSR in both per-capita and overall carbon emissions despite the Soviets' parlous record on the environment.[32]

THE IRON CURTAIN ON THE URBAN PERIPHERY

In postwar First and Second World societies on both sides of the Iron Curtain, postwar urban peripheries cut deeper into farmlands, wetlands, and forests. In the First World cities outside of the USA, the style of construction on the urban periphery was more mixed in character than on the outskirts of, say, Chicago. In Western Europe, France was the biggest user of Le Corbusier-style suburban tower blocks. Paris may not have gotten the *Plan Voisin* treatment, but its enormous periphery did. Thousands of bleak social housing projects radiate across former farm fields of the Île-de-France region, epitomized by the town of Sarcelles, an immense landscape of over 100 brute cement rectangles that were often compared to sugar cubes – some laid lengthwise on their sides, the so-called *barres*; some propped on end, reaching upward, the *tours*. The city's eastern and northern peripheries contain most of these projects, and indeed they represent extensions of Paris's own now-gentrified former Red Belt districts. Today they house a disproportionate share of immigrant families from North and West Africa as well as other former French colonies. Haussmann-era class segregation thus seeded some of the most racially segregated zones in Europe. Some residents even use the world "ghetto" to describe their complexes, despite their peripheral location and the dozens of immigrant groups that live alongside each other there. Others complain of the soul-sapping dreariness of these zones, blaming it for "Sarcellitis," a form of *anomie* suffered by inhabitants of modernist bedroom communities who shuttle *en masse* into their offices in Paris and back each day. Other European countries built similar behemoths, such as the endlessly zigzagging modernist apartment blocks of the Bijlmermeer on the southern periphery of Amsterdam, and the prefabricated low-rise blocks of Rinkeby outside

Stockholm, which were part of the Swedish state's successful "Milljonen" plan to build a "million" apartments, mostly in suburbs throughout the country. Other large-scale estates were located in town rather than in the outskirts, including the phalanx of high-rises that replaced the working-class Gorbals area in Glasgow, the now-infamous Grenfell Tower in London, and the *Plattenbau* (prefabricated panel) estates in the war-cratered neighborhoods of German cities.[33]

Outside France, however, truly large estates made up a smaller portion of state housing. European cities that suffered massive bombing had more room for scattered-site social housing inside the older core. There, it could take many forms, from mid-sized apartment blocks in downtown Cologne or Rotterdam that were indistinguishable from privately owned buildings, to more distinguishable brick council estates in former bomb craters in London. In Britain, much smaller council houses stretched across suburbs that were less dense overall than those on the Continent. Cooperative schemes, which were discouraged under US public housing law, gave labor unions and neighborhood associations the power to build and manage mid-sized affordable state-subsidized apartment complexes. In all of Europe, Canada, and even Australia, social housing made up a far greater percentage of all housing than in most cities of the USA. Because people of medium incomes qualified for housing, not just the very poor as in the USA, publically and cooperatively owned systems could count on more widespread political support. Thus, municipalities kept their estates in relatively good shape, and (outside France), there was considerably less segregation by class, national origin, or race – even as the number of migrants of color increased across Europe.[34]

In the meantime, Western European zoning and planning codes put more restrictions on the private housing market than in the USA. Although governments likewise subsidized mortgages, new private construction was generally limited to smaller plots and channeled into more clearly restricted growth areas, called New Cities in France. Zones of tail-pipe sprawl could be found across Europe, notably in the broad belts of single-family *pavillons* in the "Third Crown" of suburban Paris, or almost everywhere in the outer suburbs of London. Today, Western Europe's suburbs remain less dense than the historic city centers they surround, but they rarely sprawl quite so sparsely as those in the USA.[35]

Other capitalist settler-colonial cities, like Toronto, Melbourne, and Johannesburg, imitated American tail-pipe sprawl more faithfully than in Western Europe. Suburban developers on the rolling High Veldt north of Johannesburg were America's most slavish imitators. There, the Group Areas Act of 1950, the crown jewel of apartheid-era planning legislation, made it virtually impossible for anyone but those the state defined as "white" to own property in the northern suburbs, and the state granted lower-income whites, notably the Dutch-speaking "Afrikaners," an exclusive path to homeownership similar in scope to the American FHA. The apartheid state built public housing for poorer whites in low-rise suburban apartments (one project was called "Franklin Roosevelt"), but for Blacks, state housing took the unusual form of detached brick "matchbox" houses that spread outward from the historic nucleus of Soweto, among dozens of other sprawling Black townships.[36]

In the Soviet-dominated Eastern Europe, in strong contrast to the First World, cities were substantially denser on the peripheries than in the historical center, even after bombed-out centers were rebuilt more or less from scratch after the war. Prefabricated Moscow-style *Khrushchyovki* ballooned on the urban edge of every "Soviet Bloc" capital and, as in Moscow, higher-rise cement giants followed during the 1970s and 1980s. Over 80 percent of housing in Bucharest took this form, exceeding the rate in Moscow. Soviet-style governments in Warsaw (55 percent) and Sofia, Bulgaria (65 percent) were only slightly less prolific builders of prefabricated tower blocks. Single-family dwellings were rare, and even sometimes prohibited near big cities. The closest thing to low-density suburbs in Eastern Bloc cities were the pods of *dachas* that appeared, in imitation of Russian models, in exurban woodlands near Belgrade, near Warsaw, and even near the cities of East Germany.[37]

The disparity between Western and Eastern European cities was best visible in the divided city of postwar Berlin. In the bombed-out neighborhoods of the city's capitalist Western zone, housing took on a mix of high- and low-rise *Plattenbau* apartment buildings – both public and private – and smaller private single-family homes, especially in the city's less-dense lake districts. In Communist East Berlin, by contrast, squadrons of Moscow-style high rises, also built of prefabricated concrete panels, paraded across the periphery.[38]

In such a city of contrasts, the "Kitchen Debate" played out especially intensely in real people's lives – generally to the disadvantage of Khrushchev's position. For most of the first decade and a half after World War II, East Berliners avidly commuted across the largely un-policed boundary between the Zones into the humming sites of First World consumer culture along the Kurfürstendamm and other revived shopping streets of West Berlin. As many as three and a half million citizens of East Germany emigrated permanently to the West simply by walking through Berlin's streets or taking the subway.[39]

In 1961, however, Khrushchev and the East German Premier Walter Ulbricht put a stop to all of that with a novel use for prefabricated concrete panels: the Berlin Wall. One hundred and fifty kilometers long, it bisected the city's downtown and surrounded all of West Berlin, closing off connecting streets to the East and isolating the Western zone from surrounding towns. Subway lines were cut in two, and a dozen stations became "ghosts" of their former selves – the so-called *Geisterbahnhöfe*. Soon a fence ran parallel to the wall fifty meters to the east, creating a death zone in between, guarded by snipers mounted atop 186 observation towers and patrolled by dogs.[40]

With this heavy-handed freeze on urban flow, Khrushchev ended the short Cold War "thaw" on display at Sokolniki Park. Years later, in 1989, the Berlin Wall fell along with the USSR, and the West celebrated its triumph. Yet the Cold War's Kitchen Debates, about the density, flow, and juxtaposition of our habitats, the profusion of our consumer culture, and the use of hydrocarbon to fuel cities leave all of us – former First, Second, and Third Worlders together – with urgent questions for a far Hotter Age.[41]

CHAPTER 20

Gathering Velocities II: Liberation and "Development"

REVOLUTION DEEPENS AND WIDENS

As our long biography of the Urban Planet arrives in the very recent past and, inevitably, toward hesitant reflections about the future, it is time to return to the backseat of a Delhi auto-rickshaw, perhaps even one captained by the Pandit Sharma Karma himself. Savor once again the moment when, through the city's calamitous traffic, our driver sweeps us into orbit around India's grand, circular Parliament Building. "*Umbilicus Mundi*," ancient emperors used to call their capital cities – the Navel of the World. Today, Earthopolis has many, multifarious navels; there are reasons to put other cities ahead of Delhi as the primary planetary pivot point, even as the Pandit's megacity grows toward the largest in the world. Still, it is worth singling out the Indian capital's great, round, republican *umbilicus* for contemplation, for its halls echo with a pressing question for us all. What is the connection between the act of building new, extensive places for humans to harvest more Sunshine – "development," as planners in India and across the world called it, stiffly – and the highest hopes for human liberation?

On February 10, 1951, this same round parliament building embraced a more famous self-styled "Pandit" – Jawaharlal Nehru. Assembled delegates of the people anointed him as the first Prime Minister of the independent Republic of India. Over the previous five months, 173 million male and female citizens had cast their votes, often in makeshift village or crowded neighborhood polling places all across the new country. In its day, it was the largest election ever organized; since then, India's elections remain the world's largest as they accelerate in size, just like everything else on the Urban Planet.

Pandit Nehru's victory was the culmination of nearly a century of struggle for independence from British colonial domination. That movement, famously orchestrated by the Mahatma Gandhi with Nehru's help from 1917 through Gandhi's assassination in 1948, grew out of what the novelist V. S. Naipaul dubbed a "million mutinies" throughout the great cities of India and the countless rural villages that Gandhi loved so deeply. Even as decades of growing violence between Hindus and Muslims culminated in the catastrophic partition of India from Pakistan in 1947, Gandhi's call to "*Satyagraha*" – massive non-violent demonstrations of public dissent – deflated almost two centuries of British rule and left an unextinguishably eloquent legacy for all future practitioners of People's Politics, and, with it, "liberation" more generally.[1]

The dramatic severing of the umbilical cord between Delhi and London in a big round House of Parliament was only one of dozens of similar exclamation points in mid-twentieth-century anti-imperial politics. After World War I, as we know, the scope of People Power expanded dramatically and far beyond the oldest urban crucibles of revolution in the Atlantic. Then, after World War II, as Allied armies threw off the yoke of Nazi and Japanese expansionism, the revolutionary age became a truly global phenomenon for the first time – erupting in cities in all regions of the world, and, as always, reverberating in and out of immense rural places too. In Asia and Africa, revolution incubated in built environments that were rare in the Atlantic: ashrams, temples, mosques, bazaars, extended family compounds, and neighborhoods defined by lineage, religion, and caste – many of them filled with labyrinthine alleyways connected to hallowed processional avenues. Across the southern hemisphere, rural spaces – including remote villages, new kinds of plantations, and guerrilla basecamps – arguably became more important sites of revolution than before, partly because of the proliferating global trade in industrial weaponry. As liberation movements grew in scope and in boldness in many such places, they generated a bewildering array of internal divisions, to the grim delight of counterrevolutionaries meddling from London, Paris, Washington, and (cynically disguised as the purest of all revolutionaries) from Moscow.

Amidst the great din, some movements, like Gandhi's in India, mightily expanded the realms of anti-racist and democratic practice. Others devolved into guerrilla campaigns or merciless civil wars, and far too many transmogrified into one-party dictatorships and even kleptocracies – the rule of elites who transferred the wealth of their new nations into personal bank accounts in Zürich, Switzerland. For others, true liberation meant following some variation on the Soviet route to revolution, nowhere more consequentially than in Mao's China, Ho Chi Minh's Vietnam, and Fidel Castro's Cuba. In South Africa, Rhodesia, South West Africa, and the new country of Israel, it was white settler colonists who declared their independence from imperial control, in great part to gain more leeway to suffocate parallel local liberation movements run by Africans and Palestinians. In Latin America, leaders of long-independent states – elected and otherwise – took the lead in anti-colonial activism, hoping to shrug off a "second conquest" of the region, this one by British and "Yankee" banks and capitalists, backed by state gunboats, troops, or shadowy artists of the international coup d'état.

"Liberation" thus took many flavors in its many new homes. Almost everywhere, though, liberationists linked their dreams to some idea of "development." As a word, development is much drier than liberation, but in a way it cut far deeper, for it exposed imperial states' long comparative neglect of their colonies' cities and built infrastructure, and in particular their refusal to extend advanced industrial environments outside the exclusive realm of the imperial urban core. To cry "development!" then, was also to cry for Urban Planetary equality – to erase the Great Gap of the nineteenth and early twentieth centuries and raise the independent Third World to the level of the First and Second. Development meant building as many car plants in Delhi, Accra, and Buenos Aires as there were in Detroit, Nagoya, or Wolfsburg. It meant expanding Europe and America's dense networks of rails and superhighways to continents where tracks and asphalt were far sparser. Office towers needed to scrape the skies of financial centers in Dakar or Bombay or São Paulo that could rival those of the City of London or Wall Street in New York. Africa, Asia, and Latin America needed far more universities, schools, parks, subways, sewers, water systems, hospitals, vaccination clinics, public housing estates, and all the planned accoutrements of modern – or "developed" – cities. As in the industrial revolutions of the imperial core, urban development required rural development too, for no large cities were possible without thousands of villages and farms that could feed urban residents. Frankly, for most liberationists, "development" also meant equal access to longer coal trains and bigger tankers-full of refined petroleum. All should acquire the dubious right to emit just as much carbon into the atmosphere as Europeans and Soviets – if not the profligate Americans.

Today, seventy years after Nehru's triumph in the *umbilicus* of Delhi, projects of liberation, development, and global equity continue to face steep obstacles, especially as new forms of imperial power intervene and atmospheric heating accelerates. Nonetheless, once again, our city-dominated built habitat acted as both cause and effect of worldwide transformation. As cities – and villages – nurtured dreams of liberation and development after World War II, places like Delhi and other "Global South" capitals gathered new conflictual and collective energies that were as volatile as they were creative. Development, unleashed by multifarious projects of liberation and vice versa, became a key force of growing velocity toward the Urban Planet's greatest moment of Great Acceleration.

THE "PROTO-THIRD WORLDS"

Even before World War I, Mohandas Gandhi and Jawaharlal Nehru learned how important it was for a budding anti-imperialist to travel from the very bottom of the urban hierarchies that undergirded imperial power to the very top. In the provincial colonial cities of their birth, both men benefited from the empire's basic need to coax local people over to the conqueror's side – to create what British officials condescendingly called "the better sort of native." Both witnessed first-hand how limited British-supplied educational opportunities and privileges, even in the remote Gujarati towns of Porbandar and Rajkot where Gandhi grew up, could nonetheless lead towards a questioning of the entirety of empire. Nehru's father, a lawyer, was a particularly good model to the young Jawaharlal, for he had used professional opportunities available in the colonial court system of the larger city of Allahabad to rise into the presidency of the rebel Indian National Congress, the party that later carried his son to power in Delhi. As young people, the future Mahatma and Pandit leveraged their families' privilege within the system to travel to London for a legal education, with the goal to return to their hometowns and to use local colonial courthouses on behalf of fellow colonial subjects. Another path open to British-trained lawyers could include standing for election to rubber-stamp municipal governments that the British had established in growing numbers of Indian city halls.[2]

Life in London, the very "belly" of the greatest of the world's imperial beasts, ironically became essential to the formation of truly effective anti-imperialists. There, Gandhi and Nehru could speak directly with liberals and suffragists eager to expand the vote in Britain itself, and radicals, for whom true liberation required proletarian ownership of the factories, mines, railroads, and banks. In addition to glimpses of classic Atlantic revolutionary practices in action, London's multifaceted political spaces gave Gandhi the chance to mix his own family's Hindu spiritual practices with European bohemian notions like vegetarianism, theosophy, and environmentalism, all of which themselves drew on his new Western colleagues' fascination with India's classical Vedic texts. Such East–West mixtures had been critical to the foundation of the Indian National Congress back in India itself, and they helped Gandhi build his own concepts of non-violence, *ahimsa*, and direct action: *Satyagraha*.[3]

Then there was London's profuse displays of industrial wealth and consumer culture. These gave Gandhi and Nehru an easy gauge for measuring the greatness of the yawning gap between their far dustier colonial hometowns and places like the imperial capital. However, the two fathers of independent India left London with opposed views on "development." Gandhi was one of the few anti-imperial leaders to reject urban industrial consumer values, instead calling for a return to the noble simplicity – as he implausibly imagined it – of India's pre-imperial village life. The signature form of dress he later adopted, the homespun cotton *dhoti* of the Indian village, was a potent form of protest against the Manchester system that had undersold India's traditional cottage industry. Nehru, by contrast, embraced a socialist version of Manchester – and later of such war-winning cities as American Detroit and Soviet Magnitogorsk – insisting that only a fully fledged, urban industrial revolution, complete with Henry Ford-like assembly lines, buttressed by Soviet-style Five-Year Plans, would set India free.[4]

During the interwar years, a much larger cohort of anti-imperial leaders emerged out of similar odysseys from colonial cities to great imperial capitals and back again. In addition to revolutionary legacies, London, New York, Paris, Brussels, and Berlin also offered universities, jobs in local factories, cheap bohemian flats, all the cafés, jazz clubs, and red-light zones that young rebels could want, along with flourishing avant-garde arts scenes, and printing presses and newsrooms eager for edgy colonial viewpoints. These cities also had migrant enclaves that grew after World War I, as brown and Black soldiers and armament factory workers from the colonial hinterlands settled in the imperial center, opening restaurants, and founding ethnic associations and political clubs. In London's heavily African and Afro-Caribbean Camden Town and the nearby precincts of bohemian Bloomsbury, activists and thinkers from the British West Indies like Eric Williams, George Padmore, and C. L. R. James met students from British African colonies like Kenya's Jomo Kenyatta, the Gold Coast's Kwame Nkrumah, and Nigeria's Nnamdi Azikiwe. Some of these future African Presidents had also spent time in the USA, in a growing archipelago of African-American-run colleges inspired by the Black leader Booker T. Washington's Tuskegee Institute. In New York's Harlem, African leaders made further contact with more radical leaders of the Black civil rights movement. These included W. E. B. Du Bois and Marcus Garvey, the Jamaican-born leader of the Universal Negro Improvement Association, an organization with members throughout the Atlantic and Caribbean.[5]

In the 1920s and 1930s, Paris became perhaps the most important capital of what historian Michael Goebel calls the "Proto-Third World." Ho Chi Minh arrived there early from Hanoi, as a student turned steamship cook who had visited New York and London before his arrival. Later, he moved from Paris's thriving archipelago of Vietnamese restaurants to more Spartan quarters in Moscow so he could expand his Marxist-Leninist revolutionary contacts. Zhou Enlai and Deng Xiaoping, both future giants of the Chinese Communist Party, lived in Paris at the same time, courtesy of a "Diligent Work Frugal Study" program organized by Chinese radicals to acquaint young activists first hand with Western society. Deng worked in the steel mills at Le Creusot and the Renault Automobile Plant in Billancourt to support his education as a Marxist revolutionary and, more portentously, as a fanatical supporter of China's industrial development. These Asian activists shared the city's streets, cafés, and jazz clubs with African-American artists and radicals who shuttled between Harlem, New York and "French Harlems" in Paris's Pigalle and Montmartre. Léopold Sédar Senghor, the future president of Senegal, presided over a community of francophone African intellectuals in the rue Cujas, near the Sorbonne University, alongside West Indian counterparts like his fellow poet Aimé Césaire. A large contingent of dissidents from Algeria met in the so-called "Moorish cafés" run by members of the 100,000-strong Algerian community in Paris. Latin American dissidents came to Paris from revolutionary Mexico City. In that rapidly "developing" capital city, they had gathered from across the continent to rail against US imperialism in the cafés of the Calle de Bolívar, surrounded by the uplifting public murals of the socialist artist Diego Rivera. On the Left Bank of Paris, the Latin Quarter – long a bohemian hangout – became the unofficial meeting place of those who were ready to give their lives to free the three colonized continents. In 1927, drawing on their interactions in Paris, these activists, supported by socialists from Berlin and the Communist International in Moscow, gathered in Brussels with others from South Africa, Indonesia, Vietnam, and China to organize the League Against Imperialism. At the League's founding conference, speakers announced with clarity, many for the first time, that they were no longer willing merely to expand political opportunities for colonial subjects within the existing structures of their respective empires. No matter whether the road to true liberation led toward capitalism or socialism, national independence was the first stop along the way.[6]

Such manifestoes were important, and – thanks to the megaphone of Brussels and other imperial capitals – their authors' demands carried widely. The delegates at gatherings like this were well aware that the real fight could succeed only if the desire for independence took fire among the hearts and minds of millions back home. The vast majority of the world's city-dwelling colonized people had never seen the insides of a school classroom, let alone a university lecture hall. For most, cafés, jazz clubs, and even newspapers were located on a different Urban Planet. Few had access to basic spaces of urban working-class politics in the industrial world, like factory shop floors, docklands, railyards, bars, union halls, and left (or right) party headquarters. On top of that, even though Asia, Africa, and Latin America were home to many large cities, they were still the least urbanized parts of the world. As Gandhi repeatedly reminded people like Nehru, most of the billion colonized people – eight or nine out of every ten – were farmers and villagers. Whatever strategies anti-imperialists devised for their own Hindu, Buddhist, Sikh, Muslim, chiefly, or traditional royal colonized cities, they would also have to mobilize people who lived in remote, dusty built places that cosmopolitan leaders could often barely imagine – even if those places also lay, very potently, outside of the control of empires too.[7]

SATYAGRAHA VS. SOLDIERS IN COLONIZED SPACE

In India, the urbane Pandit Nehru, based in Delhi, and the village-worshiping Mahatma Gandhi, ensconced in his rural ashram, launched a lurching series of non-violent actions against the British Raj. These began with the Non-cooperation Movement in 1920–22, rose to a crescendo with the Salt Marches of 1930, and culminated in the 1940s with the Quit India movement that finally led to independence in 1947. Gandhi's immensely innovative *Satyagraha* was, among other things, a collection of non-violent spatial practices, collectively meant to demonstrate the movement's capacity to impose more deeply humane, spiritually infused and peaceful oppositional forms of control over the colonial built environment – and to highlight the contrasting violence and racism that undergirded the spatial politics of the empire. At Gandhi's signal, massive unarmed crowds swarmed into urban streets, squares, and village lanes. People stayed home from work, shops and factories closed, consumers burned British goods in bazaars, and lower officials publically destroyed evidence of honors and commissions the empire had bestowed upon them to purchase their loyalty. Yet nationalist leaders' control over Indian spaces was by no means complete. In 1922, when a mob in the village of Chauri Chaura burned a *chowki* (police office), killing twenty Indian officers, Gandhi was forced nearly single-handedly to bring his growing, nationwide Non-cooperation Movement to an end by threatening to fast to the death in penance. Nonetheless, such mob reactions to imperial violence continued throughout the quarter-century-long march to independence.[8]

Even more bedeviling to both Gandhi and Nehru was violence between majority Hindus and Muslims, which increased as India's different religious communities insisted on their own forms of nationalism. These conflicts were rooted in far older practices, many of them tied to urban neighborhood-based spaces that lay even beyond the reach of the spiritual sway of the Mahatma. "Communal violence" had become endemic to the movement since at least the 1890s. In the city of Pune (Poona), the capital of the Hindu Maratha dynasty that had resisted Mughal rule in the eighteenth and nineteenth centuries, the charismatic Hindu activist Lokmanya Tilak called on devotees to circumvent British restrictions on public gatherings by taking their worship of the elephant-inhabiting god Ganesh out of their homes and alleyways into great street processions. To this day, in nearby Mumbai (Bombay) hundreds of these processions culminate in the immersion of giant elephant-shaped idols of the cheerful "god for everybody" in the Arabian Sea. Yet these celebrations were not actually "for everybody" – for they often took an anti-Muslim tone, especially when they attracted ardent Hindu supporters of "cow protection" laws meant to honor the sacred herds that ranged freely in Indian city streets. Violent protests could arise against mosques and *hallal* butcher shops in Muslim *mohalla* (neighborhoods) that dealt in beef. Revenge attacks by Muslims often followed against Hindu shrines and deep into the labyrinthine *galli* (alleyways) of surrounding nearby neighborhoods.[9]

There was no arguing, however, with the deeply unifying impact of Gandhi's greatest mass action, the Salt Satyagraha of 1930. In this case, the strategy involved luring imperial force into spaces where it was weak, a landscape of dispersed villages and rural state installations. Tens of thousands of protestors and pilgrims of all faiths gathered around him as he set off from his village ashram along dusty roads of Gujarat on a two-week march toward the Indian Ocean. At an isolated beach in the village of Dandi, he performed the simple task of evaporating seawater – thus violating the anachronistic British state monopoly on salt production. News of his eloquent ritual ricocheted deep into the homes and hearths of the teeming lowest-caste urban neighborhoods and the small villages all across the subcontinent – Hindu and Muslim. Despite Gandhi's own sexist orders prohibiting female participation in *Satyagraha*, women in villages and increasingly the cities acquired a deep sense of belonging in the nationalist cause by purchasing illegal salt in the black markets that now flourished in every city or by evaporating it themselves in their hearths. The British once again clapped Gandhi in jail, but his marchers trudged onward toward an imperial salt-works at Dharasana down the coast, where imperial soldiers mercilessly pummeled the *satyagrahis'* non-violent bodies and arrested 60,000 more. As the cause of independence lit up across India, newsreels and a film of the one-sided battle of Dharasana ignited new mass protests in cities and sympathy for the cause across the world.[10]

British viceroys sent soldiers to administer beatings in the streets and to drag thousands into jail, but they also tried to redirect mass protest into various elected legislative assembly halls. Some of these gained jurisdiction over whole provinces, and soon a few hand-selected Indian representatives gathered in a big round building in Delhi that the British built to showcase the empire's willingness to accommodate Indian demands. Significantly, that Parliament House was located in the shadows of Raisina Hill where the viceroy's palace stood – for Britain sharply circumscribed the Indian delegates' authority. In the wake of the Salt March, however, the round chamber of cooptation, like similar provincial assemblies, instead became a platform for activists to demand more powers. Nor could rubber-stamp parliaments remotely contain the growing protest energy in the streets. When Britain called on India to help it wage war against Hitler, Gandhi and Nehru, once again in prison, determined to grant that favor, but only in exchange for independence. By war's end, masses of protestors in cities and towns across the subcontinent, striking textile workers in Bombay and Ahmedabad, and mutinous soldiers in the cantonments and naval bases all called on Britain to Quit India.[11]

Elections to provincial assemblies, meanwhile, also sadly intensified Hindu–Muslim animosity, particularly in areas with large Muslim populations in the cities of the northwestern Indus Valley and in the eastern province of Bengal. There, a Muslim League rivaled Gandhi and Nehru's Congress party, and took advantage of the two leaders' wartime imprisonment to demand independence for a separate state of Pakistan. In 1946, horrific sectarian violence, fanned by elected leaders and others, killed 4,000 people in Calcutta. A year later, as the last British viceroy prepared to board a steamship for London, the empire accepted a plan to partition the subcontinent into two countries. Amidst unspeakable violence, some twelve million people became refugees – Muslims fleeing India and Hindus fleeing Pakistan – and as many as a million people died horrific deaths. Whole villages went up in flames if they did not become sites of abduction, forced conversion, rape, genocidal infanticide, and mass murder. Lahore and Calcutta, both multi-sectarian cities located in provinces divided by Partition, saw long days of massacres and vast streams of refugees. Delhi, now capital of independent India, had been the base of Muslim dynasties going back to the early years of Islam. Tens of thousands of Muslim refugees found shelter in camps near some of the monuments these regimes left behind, notably around the Red Fort and behind the ramparts of the Mughals' Purana Qila fortress.[12]

Still, madness raged across the city, as Hindu mobs damaged or destroyed some 135 mosques and attacked Muslim shops on Old Delhi's Chandni Chowk, killing some 20,000 people all told. Gandhi protested the violence by traveling to Delhi in 1948 for his last hunger strike, demanding that Muslims be able to once again move freely, regain their religious sites, and hold religious festivals in the city's streets. However, as Delhi finally quieted and he broke his fast, a Hindu fanatic, angered by the Mahatma's pro-Muslim demands, assassinated Gandhi at a multi-faith prayer meeting. On the newly renamed Rajpath in Delhi – the two-kilometer "Kingsway" that Edwin Lutyens had designed to glorify British rule – rousing celebrations of Indian independence gave way to one of world history's longest and saddest funeral processions.[13]

THE "VILLAGE ROAD" AND THE "CITY ROAD" TO LIBERATION

As in Delhi – and as in the villages and cities of the Punjab and Bengal – so in the rest of the Urban Planet. To paraphrase Harlem's great revolutionary poet Langston Hughes, after 1945, dreams of liberation deferred by the World War now exploded – in a much larger, more dispersed version of the urban political upheavals of 1918–22. Neither states, nor armies, nor liberation movement leaders fully controlled the spaces where mass collective actions took place. Peaceful and violent disruptions commingled; uprisings in cities and remote places occurred at the same time – all of them far more explosive than after World War I. Unarmed protestors sought the high ground, laborers went on strike across the First and Third worlds, ideologues and religious zealots clashed, mobs wreaked havoc, and columns of soldiers faced off against guerrillas emerging from the hinterlands.

In China during the 1930s, the Japanese army had hammered most of the eastern and northern cities into submission with a level of brutality that far exceeded that of Britain in India. From there, they ran walls and blockhouses along thousands of kilometers of Chinese rail networks, and used that net of fortifications as a base for horrendous "kill all, burn all, loot all" assaults on villages that left uncountable millions of Chinese peasants dead. In part, that was to stop Chiang Kai-shek's nationalists, but by the end of the war, it was clear that Mao's Communists had become Tokyo's far wilier opponent. Ever since Chiang's army had killed thousands of Reds in Shanghai and Wuhan, the Chinese Communist Party (CCP) had become a guerrilla movement in the villages. After surviving off the barest countrysides during the Long March, the CCP re-established itself under Mao in the small city of Yan'an, where it fanned out into nearby towns and villages, offering rent reductions and protection to peasants and administering these policies from ramshackle municipal buildings and repurposed farmhouses. With armed peasant support, the party then began dispossessing landlords, shaming them in rituals held in public squares. Where it could, the Party instituted collectivized production. Mao also delegated guerrilla generals to take over a growing archipelago of "base areas" in rural areas between the razor-wire strands of the Japanese military net. Soon, despite the vicious attacks, Red troops in those base camps controlled dozens of large blotches of rural territory that collectively surrounded Beijing and reached south toward Shanghai. Villages in the more stable base camps contained cooperative workshops and small factories. Some were connected by intricate networks of defensive tunnels, complete with ventilation shafts to disperse the toxic gas Japanese soldiers pumped into them. These camps, Mao claimed, served as "the buttocks" of the revolution.[14]

(A)

(B)

20.1. Two Village Lovers' Visions of Urban Mass Politics
Two of Earth's largest concentrations of cities are in India and China, yet leaders there insisted that villages should lead the liberation struggle. Beyond that, Gandhi and Mao had

Once Japan drew back its net after 1945, Mao was in a commanding position to fight off the Guomintang, and his spatial strategy pivoted in a radical direction. Instead of "using the villages in order to surround the cities, and then taking the cities," Mao determined that "now the period of the city leading the village has begun." Needless to say, what he had in mind was not Gandhian "non-violent non-cooperation," but a horrific civil war against Chiang. The proliferation of weapons during World War II thus helped inaugurate an age of renewed deathly power wielded by insurgents in remote places that could not only stymie conventional armies, but also proved capable of outlasting postwar empires wielding new generations of nuclear and conventional weapons. In 1949, the Red Army's triumphant strike from its rural then urban strongholds in Manchuria into the Forbidden City of Beijing – and its use of weapons manufactured in the latest military-industrial cities of the time – played out, in both space and technique, very much like the blood-bathed births of earlier imperial dynasties in Chinese history. So did Mao's declaration of the founding of the People's Republic of China in front of massive crowds on Tien An Men Square.[15]

Mao's successful base-area spatial strategy did not go unnoticed by revolutionaries who faced other imperial forces that held an especially strong grip on colonial cities. In Southeast Asian cities, European and North American colonial armies reasserted enough control in the wake of the Japanese retreat to force nationalists to retreat to villages and towns. The Indonesian nationalist movement benefited from what were at first

---

Caption for 20.1. (cont.)

little in common. Gandhi wanted independence from Britain, but hated hydrocarbon industrial cities even more, and envisioned an India that returned to its villages. He also abhorred violence, insisting on unarmed civil resistance – *Satyagraha* – which took enormous, often tumultuous, dimensions in cities (A). Mao assigned China's rural peasants the historic role of destroying urban bourgeois rule. Villagers, however, would take power from the "barrel of a gun." The Red Army mustered at rural base camps then attacked cities. Like China's earlier conquering dynasties from the farms and steppes, Mao's Communist Party installed itself in the Forbidden City of Beijing (B) – soon after Gandhi's movement took power in Delhi. Both India and China have since embraced their gigantic cities – and heavy industry – to overcome the great colonial wealth gap.

(A) Gamma-Keystone/Getty Images. (B) Archive Photos/Getty Images.

relatively weak British, then Dutch forces in Djakarta to declare independence in 1945. Then it retreated into backcountry Java, making what were later seen as heroic, if usually unsuccessful, assaults on the island's large cities. The Battle of Surabaya (1945) was the most celebrated of these, but the Indonesian Republic held on to Jogjakarta as a capital for a longer period. The Dutch committed numerous atrocities in towns and villages, leading to international calls for independence that finally came in 1949. Philippine nationalists won a similar, if quicker, victory against the USA, whose army had fought brutal battles against Japanese occupiers in the archipelago with no regard for casualties inflicted on Philippine civilians.[16]

In Vietnam, meanwhile, Ho Chi Minh similarly retreated from Hanoi (only after blowing up the city's main power plant as a welcome to the returning French forces). In the heavily built-up Red River Delta nearby, Ho's revolutionaries, the Viet Minh, had little success, in part thanks to a system of walls built by a French general. Only in 1954, when Ho lured the colonizers into a remote heart-shaped valley in the mountains at Dien Bien Phu, were the Viet Minh able to exact enough of a price – thanks, in part, to Soviet weapons – to convince Paris to withdraw its forces. Then, over the next twenty-five years, Ho threaded the Ho Chi Minh Trail southward through the mountainous spine of Vietnam to feed and equip base-camps in villages and rainforest clearings for a guerrilla army called the Viet Cong that fought a US-backed dictatorship in Saigon.[17]

Meanwhile a similar, but much smaller insurgency run by Chinese Communists in Malaya used similar tactics against the British. In response the British military devised brutal "anti-insurgency" techniques that targeted villages, destroying many and removing their inhabitants to fenced "New Towns" that segregated them from the guerrillas. By spraying defoliants like Agent Orange on the forests, the British succeeded in uncovering camps and minimizing roadside ambushes on their way to crushing the revolt, though Malaysia became independent shortly after. The US Army used all of these techniques against Ho's far larger Viet Cong, including "search and destroy" operations against rebel base areas and villages; forced removals of suspected peasant collaborators to "strategic hamlets"; and massive airdrops of Agent Orange, napalm, and bombs. Unlike in Malaya, however, the Viet Cong kept the Ho Chi Minh Trail open. In 1975, after years of intensifying raids on southern cities, Ho's forces successfully captured Saigon, renaming it after its captor: Ho Chi Minh City.[18]

Long before then, dozens of liberation movements in Africa and the former Ottoman Empire had mostly reversed the late-nineteenth- and early-twentieth-century European "Scrambles" for colonies there. Between 1945 and 1962, forty-six new formally independent nations came into being across these regions – seventeen in 1960 alone, the "Year of Africa." Popular urban protest was crucial to igniting nationalist movements almost everywhere in the region. New waves of longstanding nationalist protest crashed over Cairo, Baghdad, and Jerusalem. General strikes by dockworkers shook Dakar, Accra, Lagos, and Mombasa; railworkers shut down much of French West Africa, and mineworkers showed enormous collective strength on South Africa's Witwatersrand and in the Copper Belt cities of Northern Rhodesia and the Belgian Congo. Across Africa, such protests provided a signal for well-known expatriate nationalists to return home from exile in Paris, London, or New York to take leadership of local popular movements. In the colonies' principal port or rail cities, people like Senghor, Nkrumah, and Kenyatta also gathered support among urban African merchants whose careers were stunted by white trading monopolies run from Liverpool and Bordeaux. Other recruits to the nationalist cause included the similarly stymied African owners of rural plantations who grew lucrative products – like coffee in Kenya, peanuts in Senegal, and cocoa throughout West Africa – that provided revenue essential to the functioning of the colonial state. Such rural leaders presented a strong counterweight to chiefs and other traditional rulers in inland cities, many of whom had been coopted into the imperial administration.[19]

Most of the centers of nationalist resistance in Africa and the Middle East did not face the fierce level of armed counterrevolutionary conquest by European armies that former Japanese-controlled capitals in Southeast Asia did. In Egypt and most of the Middle East, negotiations for independence had been ongoing since waves of urban protest dating back to the years immediately after World War I. In sub-Saharan Africa, the French and British states used a spatial strategy similar to that in India, mixing police violence in the streets, imprisonment of leaders, and representative bodies designed for cooptation. In cities, as the historian

Frederick Cooper puts it, "colonial policing and colonial neglect only made ... life harder – and more explosive."[20]

As elsewhere, nationalist leaders used the local and metropolitan press as well as speeches in colonial representative bodies to play effectively on the anti-racist rhetoric that colonizers had employed in their own campaigns against the Third Reich. Put on the defensive, London, Paris, and Brussels promised to loosen imperial control and to focus more on what they increasingly called the "development" of their colonies. Kwame Nkrumah and Léopold Senghor convinced many of their supporters, however, that building industry in Africa was a task best left to Africans themselves. That said, visions of a Pan-African state that Nkrumah and Senghor had developed abroad never prevailed, in part due to the divided economic geography of the colonial built environment. In each of the richest coastal colonies, the wealthiest elites focused their activity on producing and transporting the fruits of largely separate hinterlands along a rail or road system that radiated from different port towns along the coast and did not connect with that of its neighbors. Nonetheless, much as in India, the cause of independence did spread outward into villages, often bringing traditional leaders on board as well. In the Highlands of Kenya, especially large numbers of peasants had become landless squatters, displaced both by growing African-owned coffee estates and by a large white settler population that owned most of the fertile land. The squatters' violent guerrilla rebellion, known as the Mau Mau movement, provoked a brutal anti-insurgent military campaign by the British, but ultimately added to the momentum for independence. Meanwhile, once Nkrumah muscled Britain out of the Gold Coast in 1957, declaring the independence of Ghana in Accra, movements elsewhere became too potent for Paris, London – or, in the case of Congo, Rwanda, and Burundi, Brussels – to resist. Most of the new independent nations born in the Year of Africa established their capitals in the largest former colonial seaports of the continent's Atlantic coast. In Kenya, Jomo Kenyatta took power in the mushrooming rail hub of Nairobi.[21]

OVERTHROWING THE SETTLER CITY

Not all of the colonies in Africa and the Middle East followed this comparatively peaceful route to independence. As the case of Kenya hints, the biggest exceptions were colonies with large European settler populations who not only exerted strong control over cities but also dominated their agricultural hinterlands. Algiers was one of the first colonial cities to achieve a special aura as a heroic "David and Goliath" Third World capital – arguably even before Ho's Hanoi and Castro's Havana took on similar mantles. Algiers's reputation came from the *Front de la Libération Nationale* (FLN), a revolutionary guerrilla force known for its tenacity – and often brutality – in fighting off the even more lethal French Army as well as various paramilitary units of the European settler population and Algerians deemed less militant or outright traitors.[22]

The Algerian revolution began in the small town of Sétif, where French soldiers and settlers killed over 10,000 largely peaceful Algerian protestors. Much of the subsequent fighting occurred in mountain villages and the tangled scrublands known as the "*maquis*," where women threw aside many of their traditional roles to take leadership alongside men as guerrilla leaders. The violence, however, also spread to cities across Algeria and France, not least Paris, where the FLN and its rivals attacked each other's favorite gathering places in the so-called "café wars." The best-known battle, however, occurred in Algiers itself, where the FLN famously tasked young women of the Casbah, dressed alternately in traditional *haiks* and the latest Parisian fashions, to plant bombs in public places in the Marine Quarter. In response, French paratroopers mercilessly invaded the labyrinths, courtyards, and even the sewers of the Casbah to root out rebels, whom they tortured in hopes of uncovering further safe houses. As elsewhere, the FLN's success lay not in any military victory, but in its ability to provoke the army into techniques of suppression that whittled away its support among moderate locals, mainland French voters, and France's ambivalently anti-colonial allies in Washington. In 1962, after it won independence, the FLN succeeded, unlike revolutionary movements in other settler colonies, in inspiring enough fear to cause almost all of the European settler population to leave Algeria for France, and give up on hotheaded schemes for street-fights and military coups. The Harkis, Algerians who fought on the side of France, also fled – only to be thanked for their service by means of confinement to festering concentration camps in the French countryside.[23]

Compared with Europeans in Algeria, white colonial settlers in the British-run Mandate of Palestine and Union of South Africa mounted far stiffer resistance to local Arab and African liberation movements. There settlers formed armed independence movements of their own against London that tightened their grip on cities and countrysides as part of a strategy to form settler republics largely off-limits to majority populations. For three years (1936–39), Palestinian Arabs had rebelled in the British Mandate's cities against the colonizer's' policy of expanding Jewish immigration and territorial partition between the two communities. In response, the Zionist Yishuv, based in Tel Aviv, organized paramilitary forces, at one point in 1946 exploding bombs that left a massive gash in Jerusalem's King David Hotel, the headquarters of London's Mandatory officials.[24]

In 1947, as Jewish refugees from Hitler's atrocities streamed into Palestine, and as Britain retreated in favor of the new United Nations, the Yishuv's Shadow Prime Minister David Ben Gurion launched "Plan Dalet" to seize control of the Mandate. Zionist militias like the Haganah and the Irgun invaded Arab neighborhoods in all of Palestine's cities, leveled approximately 530 Arab villages to the ground, and killed 12,000 of their inhabitants; 750,000 people fled into eastern neighborhoods of Jerusalem, the city of Gaza, and the hills of what later became known as the West Bank. In 1948, as Ben Gurion celebrated the independence of a new State of Israel in the conquered lands, the Palestinian liberation movement reeled from its calamitous defeat, which they remember as the Naqba – the Great Catastrophe. It took its exiled leadership almost two decades to regroup in exile in Amman, Jordan, as the Palestine Liberation Organization.[25]

In 1948, the same year as Israel's independence, white settlers in Southern Africa likewise took new steps to solidify their control of urban space and farmland for their exclusive use. They too strengthened pass laws that regulated Africans' movements between crowded rural settlements in the native reserves and the city. The larger goal of their new policy of apartheid was a white "South Africa without Africans" independent of Britain. During World War II, African mineworkers had demonstrated growing power in a series of bold strikes along the Witwatersrand, and Black migrants had established huge illicit shantytowns around official "native locations," such as those southwest of Johannesburg. The apartheid-era Group Areas Act shored up the boundaries of Black locations, renaming them "townships," and for the first time forced colored and Indian people into townships of their own. Another law, this one the brainchild of the Afrikaner nationalist Prime Minister Hendrik Verwoerd, established a Native Resettlement Board in Johannesburg empowered to eradicate leftover "Black spots" in zones designated for whites. These included the so-called "locations in the sky," tent cities of Black servants that had grown on the rooftops of the city's new modernist luxury high rises. In 1957, the Board also razed Sophiatown, Johannesburg's "Harlem," to the ground and forced its inhabitants to relocate to new sprawling native townships to the southwest of the city. To stifle dissent, apartheid planners laid the streets in some of these new places in radial form so that police at the central junction could command a "panoptic" view of township activities. Official maps called the wide buffer zone between the townships and the white suburbs of Johannesburg a "machine gun belt."[26]

Nonetheless, peaceful protests swelled, inspired by Gandhi. In 1955, under the leadership of Nelson Mandela, the African National Congress (ANC), allied with other liberation organizations, unveiled its Freedom Charter in Kliptown, near the site of Johannesburg's first native location. In response, Verwoerd pressed forward on the larger goal of apartheid, to keep Africans from migrating to cities at all, using pass laws to concentrate the majority of the population on rural reserves he now called "Bantustans." As South Africa declared its independence as a white republic in 1961, Verwoerd committed the new state to "prepare" these Bantustans for their own sham independence. That same year, white police fired on a peaceful protest in Sharpeville near Johannesburg, killing sixty-nine. Verwoerd locked Nelson Mandela and other leaders in the notorious Robben Island prison, twelve kilometers offshore from the docklands of Cape Town. Other ANC leaders regrouped as a government in exile in newly independent capitals like Dar es

Salaam, Tanzania and Lusaka, Zambia as well as in London and New York. From abroad, the ANC led an armed guerrilla movement that gained little traction in the settler-dominated countryside, though its operatives destroyed power stations and other infrastructure. It would take a decade and a half before the mass movement revived itself in Johannesburg's "Southwestern Townships" – Soweto. At that point, Soweto would join the list of the world's great urban incubators of People Power – and national liberation.[27]

CAPITALS OF DEVELOPMENT

As liberationists in Asia and Africa traveled their many hard roads, they could ill afford to ignore what was happening in the great cities of Latin America. The bad news was that independence, which most countries on the continent had achieved over a century before Nehru's victory in Delhi, had not stopped new kinds of debilitating "dependence" on the biggest imperial powers. As we know, Latin America's small oligarchical elite class – most of them owners of coffee and sugar plantations, gold mines, huge cattle *estancias*, and other large *haciendas* – had found it virtually impossible to resist striking Faustian bargains with much wealthier capitalists in London, Paris, and, increasingly, New York. There, the Latin American oligarchs could draw large loans to expand their rural operations. British companies built the ports and railroads that delivered local products to the steamships; other foreign mercantile concerns took handsome profits. The money that did come in allowed Latin American elites to conduct major makeovers of Buenos Aires, Rio, and other cities where most of them lived, and to invest some of the leftovers in industry, mostly of the lighter variety. All of that was enough to stimulate urban growth, and the capitals, along with the coffee-processing center São Paulo, grew particularly quickly. Yet, dependence on loans from abroad, drawn against the value of shipments of coffee or beef, meant that the economy swooned each time prices for those commodities dropped in European exchange houses.[28]

Meanwhile, European and American warships regularly threatened the ports of Latin American countries that did not meet the needs of overseas creditors and rival imperialists. After 1898, the USA waved its "big stick" in the region with particular vehemence. Washington ruled Puerto Rico directly and Cuba indirectly. In 1917, its ships sailed into Veracruz harbor to stop German arms shipments to revolutionaries in the Mexican revolution. The US Marines took over the customs houses at Port-au-Prince, Haiti and Santo Domingo, Dominican Republic, effectively running the governments of long-independent nations for long periods from the 1910s through the 1930s.

Anti-*Yanqui* riots were common in the cities of Latin America, but the most brazen moment of resistance came during the Cold War on the US-dominated island of Cuba. American interventions in the affairs of sovereign nations had increased worldwide after World War II (Chapter 21). A notable example occurred in 1954 in Guatemala City after the democratically elected president Jacobo Árbenz announced plans to assign unused lands owned by the US-owned United Fruit Company to some of the country's peasant farmers. The Company complained to Washington, and the American Central Intelligence Agency organized a group of mercenaries to seize the Presidential Palace and eject Árbenz, substituting him with a dictator who canceled the land program. One of the witnesses of this coup was Ernesto "Che" Guevara, a revolutionary doctor from Buenos Aires, who briefly joined a militia in support of Árbenz before fleeing to the thriving community of fellow radical exiles in Mexico City. There, he joined Fidel Castro, who had recently arrived from Cuba after a failed putsch of his own against another American-backed dictator. The two launched a tiny amphibious force that commandeered Mao-like base camps in Cuba's Sierra Maestra Mountains in 1958. From there they built a peasant army in camps spread throughout the islands sugar plantations, seizing power in Havana the following year.[29]

In the 1930s, long before Castro's Havana became a Soviet-supported headache for Washington, Latin American nationalists elsewhere used different means to remove their cities from dependence on overseas capital. Their method was to seize control of their country's foreign-built infrastructure to jump-start new projects of "development," financed as much as possible by Latin Americans themselves. During the Great Depression, overseas demand for

Latin American raw materials dried up ruinously, and so did overseas credit. Fierce nationalist movements based in the middle and working classes of the largest Latin American cities turned to populist strongmen both on the left and on the right, such as Lázaro Cárdenas in Mexico, Getúlio Vargas in Brazil, and Juan Perón in Argentina. Leveraging their own personal popularity, they boldly employed their sovereign authority to nationalize railroads and oil companies, many of which were owned by corporations based in Britain, France, and the USA. They also had their customs officials charge high tariffs for imported goods arriving from the imperial center so that local capitalists could invest in factories to make similar goods without fear of cheaper competition. Then, as London and Washington took on Hitler, global demand for Latin American products revived, particularly for the fruits of its nationalized petroleum wells. With the proceeds from wartime sales, governments in Mexico City, Rio, and Buenos Aires began to construct a whole array of "third industrial revolution"-style built environments, heavily centered in the largest cities. The goal was to allow Latin Americans to generate First World levels of wealth in Latin America itself. Locally organized development, they hoped, would liberate the continent from the ravages of its second conquest.[30]

Latin America's urban and economic growth during the 1940s and 1950s – often described drily as "Import Substitution Industrialization" or more fervently as the "Latin American miracle" – drew both on Stalin-style "Five-Year Plans" and on Roosevelt's New Deal, in addition to Vargas's and Perón's dismaying flirtation with fascist command economies. Yet the policy's appeal lay in the fact that it used imperialists' tools to declare economic and political independence from both the US bloc and the Soviet bloc. As India and China freed themselves from Britain and Japan, Nehru and Mao adopted broadly similar paths to "catch up" with advanced imperial economies, even if they took different forms to suit Nehru's socialism and Mao's totalitarian rule. Very real transformations followed in cities like Buenos Aires, São Paulo, Johannesburg, Cairo, Bombay, Ahmedabad, Shanghai, Wuhan, Chongqing, and Mukden already by the middle of the 1950s. Steel mills, including the very first ones in Latin America and India – roared into production. Thousands of local factories produced consumer goods that replaced heavily taxed items from abroad. In Latin America, massive strikes by workers in these plants, often encouraged by the state, resulted in large wage increases that in turn created a consumer base for local products. New economic activity produced revenue that governments used to rebuild railroads on standard gauges, to extend port facilities, shipyards, weapons plants, water systems, and tramways, to expand schooling and university systems as well as clinics and hospitals, and to construct the continent's first subway lines, expressways, airports, hydroelectric dams, natural gas pipelines, and oil refineries. Nehru and Mao's first Five-Year Plans envisioned a somewhat shorter list of such big-ticket items, but it took less than a decade for many of India's and China's first-industrial-revolution cities to acquire a full range of gigantic, smoke-belching structures devoted to heavy industry. By the 1960s, Brazil celebrated its arrival as a modern nation in another way, by constructing a new capital for itself at Brasília, a modernist paradise whose wide spaces and glamourous concrete forms were arranged in a pattern suggesting a jet airplane lifting off from the brushlands of central Brazil. The city had over a million inhabitants within fifteen years. Other postcolonial regimes emulated this optimistic, and very expensive, urban gesture of liberation and development, moving national capitals from older colonial seaports deemed too congested and too entangled in commercial interests for efficient government. Thus Yamoussoukro, in the interior of Ivory Coast, replaced Abidjan; Dodoma, Tanzania replaced Dar es Salaam; Abuja, Nigeria replaced Lagos; and Naypyitaw, the military capital of Myanmar, replaced Yangon (Rangoon).[31]

Thanks to liberation and development, the industrial and hydrocarbon revolution took flight from its jealously guarded pre-World War II confines toward the Global South and East, in a halting, unequal, and soon a far more decisive way, bringing with it new and crucial extensions of the built environment. Understanding this apotheosis of Hydrocarbon Cities means turning to a fuller

20.2. A View of the Urban Future from Decolonizing Lagos
Looking across Lagos in 1929, we take in the city's past, and envision its megacity future. Directly below lies leafy the Ikoyi European Reservation and the Racecourse District, legacies of racist British segregation policies. Up the peninsula (center) is the city's historical heart, the once-independent realm of the Oba of Lagos. Encouraged by nationalists like Nnamdi Azikiwe in London, Lagos's African property owners, its powerful market women, its traditional rulers, and its growing working class used the colonial Town Council to reimagine their city as the modern capital of Nigeria, a dream fulfilled in 1960. Few, however, could picture Lagos exploding from 100,000 people to fifteen-plus million today – as oil wealth hoisted skyscrapers downtown and migrants from across Africa built homes and shops on the "Mainland" – filling this photograph's far horizon. Today, African cities – especially modest ones (like Lagos was in 1929) – are growing faster than all others on our Urban Planet.[32]
Colonial Office Image CO 1069_62_6. British National Archives.

explanation of the climactic moment in the long life of Earthopolis. As colonial cities threw off the yoke of Empire, all dimensions of our Urban Planet exploded simultaneously and at an unprecedented rate: the human population as a whole, our cities and all other habitats, our food harvests, empires, capitalist power centers, consumer culture, industry, mining, harvests of hydrocarbon, waste, atmospheric heat, and our impact on Earth. The Greatest Acceleration was under way – with the greatest of consequences not far behind.

CHAPTER 21

Greatest Accelerations I: New Empires, New Multitudes

ACCELERATION CONUNDRUMS

The driver of the green and yellow Delhi auto-rickshaw releases us from our orbit around the House of the People of India. With our nimble guide's help, we have negotiated the narrow alleys of Mughal Old Delhi. Along New Delhi's boulevards, we have watched the British imperial sun set. We have circled the parliament of Nehru's New India, examining its promises and perils from many angles. Meanwhile, in the interstices of the Old and New, we have already caught glimpses of the vaster realms where we are heading next. Small clusters of shacks tucked under railroad trestles and in traffic circles. Sidewalk tent villages that unfold at dark and vanish at first light. Apartment blocks built of precarious piles of prefabricated panels. Glimpses down side streets – the city's thousands of narrow *galis* – lined with ramshackle homes, shops, schools, clinics, Hindu temples, Muslim mosques, temples, Sikh *gurudwaras,* and Buddhist *dharamshalas.* Our Earthopolitan odyssey's climactic moment occurs when we burst all previous orbits – into the Newest New Delhi, likely the home of the auto-walla himself, a whorling 2,400-square-kilometer urban penumbra of people and structures, many built by their occupants, that has more than doubled in area and population between 1990 and 2020, that has grown tenfold since 1950, completely engulfing Delhi's capitals, Old and New. What we see around us is immense, eruptive, multiplicative, energized, and vulnerable – accelerating and filled with portent.

Old Delhi ended at its walls, more or less, and New Delhi vanishes beyond its boulevard vistas. So where are the limits of the Newest New Delhi? The last we looked, in 1947, Partition had cost the Indian capital

350,000 of its Muslim inhabitants; thousands died in the violence, many more fled to Pakistan. Yet Delhi grew nonetheless, because over a million Hindu refugees poured in from the other direction. Within five years of the calamity, the city doubled in size, passing the two million mark by Nehru's world-record election victory in 1952. Then, as India's total population careened upward, from 300 million at independence toward the billion mark in 2000, Delhi grew faster, and even its Muslim population recovered. The city surpassed five million in 1980 according to the Census of India, eight million in 1990, eleven million in 2000, and fifteen million in 2010, including nearly two million Muslims. By then, though, even the counters were unsure what they were counting. In 2016, census takers' best guess was twenty million at least, in a metropolitan area that had now swallowed the old "ring towns" of Gurugram (Gurgaon), Ghaziabad, and Faridabad – each of them million-plus cities in their own right. Former villages like Kirti Nagar, Munnirka, and Kusumpur Pahari had swollen with enormous self-built settlements. Laced into the Newest New Delhi are some 850 *jhuggi jhopris*, whole neighborhoods made up of small mud, wood, metal, or breezeblock shacks, home to possibly two million people, most characterized by lack of electricity, fresh water, and sewers. In stark contrast, clusters of glittering gated condominium towers jutted up from the sea of greater Delhi, bubbles of high living for wealthier Indians. In 2018, the United Nations reported counting twenty-eight million people in a still bigger conurbation, making Delhi the second largest in the world after Tokyo. The UN now asserts that Delhi will become number one by 2030, possibly topping forty million during the decade after that.[1]

Megacity! Hypercity! Maximal City! New words for "big" have struggled to keep up with the Urban Planet's Greatest Acceleration. Where *do* we draw the line on such a thing, and why draw it there? As in Chicago and Moscow, megacities' most dynamic zone is their periphery, but where does "peripheral" begin, and more importantly where does it end? Delhi's regional planners have repeatedly added territory to something they call "National Capital Region," which now stretches across 55,000 square kilometers from Meerut to Bharatpur and contains fifty-eight million people. What should we call the North Indian Plains, a region of a quarter billion stretching from ten-million-plus Lahore in

Pakistan to the twin three-million-plus Ganges Valley giants Kanpur and Lucknow? In Java, the word is "*desakota*," an extended mass of spreading cities, oversized towns, city-like villages, semi-continuous roadside development, and horizons packed with farm structures and punctuated with monumental dams. Some of these areas' swollen villages, reports the great urban critic Ananya Roy, have applied for state "slum clearance" funds, just as a megacity would. The overall built-up space is so dense compared with that of other regions that we are forced to ask not only "where does the city – or its suburban periphery – end?" but also "what, any more, counts as countryside?"[2]

Delhi is not the only place where one can witness such a relentless human-built panorama from the back seat of the rickshaw. In India alone, Mumbai (Bombay), Kolkata (Calcutta), Chennai (Madras), and Bengaluru (Bangalore) are almost as mega-sized as the capital; Mumbai's Dharavi lays claim to being the world's largest self-built *jhuggi jhopri* – except that Mumbaikars prefer the nineteenth-century English word "slum." Beyond the giants of India, the list of ten-million-plus cities in what we now call the Global South must also include at least Lahore, Karachi, Dhaka, Djakarta, Bangkok, Manila, Seoul, Beijing, Shanghai, Tianjin, Chongqing, Guangzhou, Shenzhen, Tehran, Istanbul, Cairo, Lagos, Kinshasa, São Paulo, Rio de Janeiro, Buenos Aires, Lima, and Mexico City. Growth rates in some of these cities were faster than Delhi's. Dhaka, for example had just over 325,000 people in 1950, Lagos 230,000, Kinshasa (then still Léopoldville) 250,000, and Shenzhen a mere 3,000. Dozens of other cities, most of them former colonial cities in Asia and Africa, are home to between five and ten million, most of them growing faster than the megacities. In 2018, the UN counted 548 cities with a million or more people, up from seventy-eight in 1945. Another 598 are home to between a half-million and one million. These too grow faster than larger cities; in Africa, smaller cities like Bujumbura, Kampala, Tete, Niamey, Ouagadougou, and Bobo-Dioulasso are growing faster than cities anywhere else. Like Delhi, many of the largest urban nebulas have engulfed other very large cities nearby. There, polycentric "urban regions" have burst into being: China's Pearl River Delta, Egypt's Nile River Delta, West Africa's Gulf of Guinea Coast, and the stretch of Brazil from Rio to São Paulo. Some of these have more people than Japan's Kansai (Osaka) or Kanto (Tokyo) megalopolises, the East Coast of the USA, or the Lower Rhine region of Europe. The term *desakota* originates in the nearly contiguous built space connecting Djakarta and Java's five other million-plus cities. Yet to the extent that that term also applies to the North Indian Plains, it also fits most of Bengal on both sides of the India–Bangladesh border, the entirety of China's Pearl River Delta, and across the even larger triangular swath of China, stretching 1,000 kilometers on a side from Beijing and Zhengzhou to Shanghai.[3]

Yet even that is not all. Like all cities from the last 6,000 years, these enormous, variously concentrated, multifariously shaped, and phenomenally energized habitats all rely on and help grow the much larger realms that define our Urban Planet: the realms of human action, habitat, impact, and consequence. These larger realms too have accelerated in size and density, all the while remaining grievously unequal and maximally diverse. Explaining cities – and the many breathlessly superlative forms they have taken – means explaining the entirety of an Urban Planet whose fields and pastures have annexed half of Earth's surface, whose tentacles of communication, transport, and power grasp all of the Planet's continents and oceans, and whose waste dumps spread across all states of the Earth's biosphere – solid, liquid, and gas.

Still, in some ways, these hypertrophic cities – and the accelerating Earthopolis they inhabit – have not changed. Explaining the conundrums of the Greatest Acceleration requires the same ingredients as all episodes of change in Urban Planetary life, just in far bigger quantities. The remaining chapters of our biography of the Urban Planet explore these ingredients one by one. First, in this chapter: bigger states and empires; bigger concentrations of wealth of all kinds; more people living longer lives; and more food, unequally distributed. Second: more houses and buildings (Chapter 22). Third: more production and more consumption of things (Chapter 23). Fourth: more geo-solar energy – above all more hydrocarbon – more waste, and more impact (Chapter 24). Fifth: more geo-solar blowback; an accelerating realm of consequence led by planetary overheating; and of course, more, far bigger questions than ever about the future of our potent urban communities and their ability to safeguard life on Earth (Chapter 25).

SUPERPOWER IN BRICKS AND MORTAR

Start with states and imperial power. During the Cold War, as the Newest New Delhi began to grow, no back-seat rickshaw passenger would have been able to see the Pentagon or the Kremlin, the White House, the US State Department, the Soviet Ministry of Foreign Affairs, the headquarters of the CIA or the KGB, or the defense ministries of the superpowers' most important allies in London, Paris, and Beijing. Nonetheless, the Cold War rivals' unprecedentedly forceful militaries, their diplomatic missions, their rival cutthroat spy agencies, and above all their rival "nuclear umbrellas" cast long shadows of overwhelming official force across all of Earthopolis, including Delhi. In so many ways, the Cold War was the cradle of the Greatest Acceleration.

As hypertrophied global empires, the Cold War superpowers mixed novel elements of statecraft with older ones, a formula reflected in their use of cities and other built environments to pursue their rivalry. One new thing, of course, was the power to swiftly destroy the Urban Planet with nuclear weapons. Also new, though, was the age of decolonization and especially of highly armed guerrilla insurgencies, which prevented and, in several cases, defeated efforts by the USA and the USSR to build anything resembling nineteenth-century empires of conquest. Amidst extraordinary buildups of military might, both waged a "soft" Cold War, using propaganda blitzes and development aid, designed to win credit for being the better "big brother" to national liberation movements. Their smiling anti-colonial masks, however, barely concealed the scowl of another new aspect of their imperialist practice. The superpowers, argues the historian Paul Kramer, were "international empires" – not states that rule colonies, but states that rule other formally independent states. Thus, instead of deploying tried-and-true hierarchies of colonial cities to administer conquered territories, Washington and Moscow projected their consummate military might into the streets, offices, and barracks of other sovereign national capitals, targeting proud new states with acts of infiltration, pressure, and outright overthrow.[4]

All of these newfangled qualities of Cold War superpower rested on older imperial territorial foundations. Both rivals' rooted their might in vast, continent-spanning postwar military–industrial construction projects that were possible only because the cities and large regions they controlled – thanks to settler-colonial conquests dating from the seventeenth through early twentieth centuries, including Alaska and Hawai'i, and the Soviet Socialist Republics in the Baltics, the Caucasus, Central Asia, and Siberia – all served as sites for huge weapons factories and military–industrial complexes, sprawling army and naval bases, vast airfields and air force bombing ranges, and dangerous sites of uranium mining and processing. The Semipalatinsk nuclear testing facility in the deserts of Soviet Kazakhstan closely resembled its rival facilities in the deserts of Nevada, not to mention the American test site on Bikini Atoll – one of a dozen of the USA's relatively small collection of more or less directly ruled "outlying possessions" in the Pacific. All three of these sites, and others, were test-bombed into radioactive wastelands. As such, they joined a much larger archipelago of permanently polluted Cold War-era landscapes devoted to military and civilian nuclear power, stretching from Rocky Flats, Colorado and Hanford, Washington State, to nuclear disaster sites like Chernobyl, Ukraine, to the British and French nuclear test sites in South Australia, the Algerian Sahara, and French Polynesia. Most importantly, Cold War superpower grew out of the submerged barrels of missile silos spread across thousands of secret rural sites: Nebraska, North Dakota, Estonia, Sverdlovsk Oblast in Siberia, and for thirteen frightening days in 1962, in a Soviet installation near the town of San Cristóbal, Cuba. By means of such concrete orifices, and the hellhound warheads that they threatened to spit aloft, the two superpowers spoke intercontinental menace to each other and the rest of the world.[5]

As the example of Cuba suggests, both superpowers also built habitats for both nuclear and conventional weapons abroad. By the late Cold War, American military spokespeople evasively claimed that the Pentagon directly administered a total of "around 5,000" military "installations," of which "around 600" were located in independent nations overseas. The overseas part of this shifting "pointillist empire" included numerous large army barrack cities in Germany, Japan, South Korea, the Balkans, and, after 2001, Afghanistan and Iraq; naval bases in the former Meiji stronghold of Yokosuka in Tokyo Bay, on the Japanese island colony of Okinawa, at Subic Bay near Manila, on the island of Diego Garcia in the middle of the Indian Ocean, at Bahrain in the Persian Gulf, in the Bay of

Naples, Italy, and on the southern tip of Cuba at Guantanamo Bay; and Air Force bases near Ramstein, Germany, İncirlik, Turkey, Yokota in suburban Tokyo, Dhahran, Saudi Arabia, and Thule, Greenland. Vieques Island off Puerto Rico, among many other doomed locations, served as a bombing range to train US fighter pilots how to rain "conventional" ordinance on enemies. The built structures of American military empire far out-reached similar Soviet facilities. Other than the fleeting moment in Cuba, most Soviet bases were located in the USSR itself and the European Eastern Bloc, excepting only the "anchorage rights" that Moscow's admirals negotiated in a dozen ports, including Mers-el-Kébir, Algeria, Latakia, Cyprus, Luanda, Angola, the Dhalak Archipelago, Ethiopia, Vishakhapatnam, India, and, after the American defeat in Vietnam, at the port of Da Nang.[6]

While these bases were not designed as colonial administrative cities, some US overseas installations did bear more than passing resemblance to the British "stations" of nineteenth-century India (Chapter 13). Before its closure in 2016, for example, the enormous Clark Air Force Base near Manila made up one-half of a kind of "officers' lines–natives' lines" relationship with the largely Filipino Angeles City, which, like the "Lal Bazaars" of British India, was notorious for its bars and sex markets. The officers who ran the base competed for American airmen's leisure hours with an officers' club called CABOOM, American-style vaudeville and movie theaters, shopping centers with American products, softball diamonds, a football field (named the Bamboo Bowl for a while), and a huge vaulted structure called the Coconut Grove Airman Open Mess, complete with its own indoor stand of palm trees. Nonetheless, Angeles City – and many similar places elsewhere in the Pentagon's Urban Planet – often reeled with incidents of sexual assaults by American servicemen against local women as well as reprisals from local inhabitants (venereal disease was less of a problem than in India, thanks to the invention of penicillin). The image of the "Ugly American" rested in great part upon these and similar forms of arrogance in military posts across the globe.[7]

American diplomatic and spy posts cemented that reputation for imperial hubris. The US State Department ran a second, more staid version of the archipelago of American power from its hundreds of embassies, many of which doubled as nests of spies and some of which became menacingly fortified swatches of American sovereign territory surrounded by hostile forces. One early example was the fortified embassy in Saigon that fell to the Viet Cong in 1975. Some of these became more elaborate as the "War on Terror" (Chapter 24) replaced the Cold War. The bristling US embassy in Baghdad, for example, is the largest embassy in the world. Its heavily fortified forty-two-hectare campus is surrounded by a further perimeter of blast-walls and a ring of advance checkpoints that limit ordinary Baghdadis' access to the International or "Green Zone" in the heart of their city. A similar district mushroomed in central Kabul, Afghanistan to command a two-decade war against the Taliban. In the twenty-first century, the CIA developed a third, much grimmer pointillist habitat, namely a network of several dozen shifting "black sites" – secret prisons near airfields, designed for the transport, incarceration, and torture of kidnapped suspects of terrorist acts. By design, the geography and secrecy of this system allowed the CIA to sequester suspects away from supposedly more lenient judiciary systems in their home countries and in the USA itself, sometimes while awaiting delivery into less scrupulous torture chambers in the Middle East or post-Soviet Eastern Europe. The Pentagon's best-known Detention Camp, at the Guantanamo Bay Naval Base in Cuba, became a poster child for the argument that terrorism justified the use of "extra-territorial" built spaces to incarcerate people indefinitely without trial.[8]

The USA and USSR expanded another older urban imperial practice of the British and French. They employed military forces, diplomats, and spies to intervene in formally independent capitals whenever local social movements or electoral campaigns seemed likely to install governments that either superpower deemed counter to their interests. In general, these imperial interventions in capital cities "succeeded" more often than superpowers' similar "anti-insurgency" campaigns directed against rural guerrilla camps; perhaps this suggests something about the ongoing effectiveness of overseas cities as instruments of imperialism. The USSR was bluntest in its tactics, sending tanks directly into the streets of Budapest in 1956 and Prague in 1968 to throttle popular uprisings in favor of mildly reformist régimes. In 1981, the Kremlin directed the Polish general Wojciech Jaruzelski to do similar dirty work against the

Solidarity uprising in Gdańsk and other Polish cities. Meanwhile, during the USSR's occupation of Afghanistan, Moscow came closer to building a formal colonial city when it planted a small district of *Khrushchyovki* called Macroyan Kohna for Soviet advisors in the heart of Kabul.[9]

The USA, and in particular the Central Intelligence Agency (CIA), was by far the most prolific Cold War-era interventionist in restive postcolonial capitals. From the CIA's unassuming corporate-park-style headquarters in the Washington, D.C. suburb of Langley, Virginia, the spy agency waged a ruthless rivalry against the Russian KGB, housed in a former tsarist palace (and a grim assortment of cement annexes) in Moscow's Lubyanka Square, Stalin's Labyrinth of Terror. A diverse array of unsavory partners joined CIA operatives in missions to overthrow governments in Damascus (1945), Tehran (1953), Guatemala City (1954), Damascus again (1956–57), Havana (repeatedly and in this case unsuccessfully from 1959 through 2000), Phnom Penh, Cambodia (1959), Léopoldville, in the former Belgian Congo (1960), Santo Domingo (1961), Saigon (1963), La Paz, Bolivia (1964), Rio de Janeiro and São Paulo (1964), Accra, Ghana (1966), La Paz again (1971), Santiago de Chile (1970–73), Buenos Aires (1976), and N'Djamena, Chad (1982). Cold War-era American aid also flowed to guerrilla forces like the right-wing *Contras* in Nicaragua and the anti-Soviet Islamist *mujahedin* in Afghanistan, among others. These interventions were punctuated in 1957 by a flash of British and French military might, when airborne paratroopers briefly occupied the Suez Canal in an unsuccessful attempt to topple the anti-colonial regime of Gamal Abdel Nasser and stop his plan to nationalize Europe's fastest sea route to Asia. The USA and USSR both opposed this intervention, and London and Paris were forced to call off their operation, but France pressed on with military incursions and coups throughout West and Central Africa in the ensuing years, including operations that aggravated the Rwandan genocide of 1994.[10]

In most of these imperial assaults, whether American, Soviet, British, or French, the targets were popular movements that supported democratically elected or anti-totalitarian leftists. The USA suspected that leaders of these movements intended to nationalize American corporate assets or land, stood in the way of oil pipelines, or leaned toward Moscow. The Soviets, for their part, punished Marxist reformists whom they deemed insufficiently committed to the Kremlin's overlordship. Few of the regimes that the superpowers so rudely interrupted ever had much time to implement their plans – for example – to keep farmers on the land, to improve health clinics, to build more government-owned housing in cities, or lay out new sewage or public transportation systems. Thus, we will never know exactly how the Great Acceleration might have proceeded had so many of them not been removed from power. In the wake of these coups, and under the rule of dozens of other superpower-supported military regimes, far too many capitals of recently liberated nations added their names to the long and dreary list of urban tools of single-party authoritarian regimes.

FROM PLENTY TO AUSTERITY: THE CAPITALS OF CAPITAL SHIFT IN SPACE AND MOOD

Despite the unprecedented firepower of the weaponry they harbored, enormous Cold War structures devoted to superpower rivalry only created a kind of radioactive cradle for other forces that sparked the Great Urban Acceleration more directly. Rival military superpower, first of all, translated directly into rival financial superpower. In this game, Moscow fought hard for a while, but it finally lost out to the capitalist First World. The main reasons for this were New York, London, and Tokyo. The socialist system simply could not spawn anything with the sheer money-generating power of these ultra-capitals of capital, cities whose financial activities became essential to the wealth, power, and growth of cities everywhere else – cities that urban theorists anointed as "global cities."[11]

The rise of global city capitals of capital represented a subtle shift in the geography of global finance over the course of the years since 1945 – the latest state-assisted "spatial fix" aimed to revive corporate capitalist power. In the early Cold War, the most important forces of international capital movement were located in the headquarters of various intertwined development aid programs run by governments, of a new raft of "multilateral" organizations founded after World War II, and of corporate-run philanthropies. The government agencies included the US State Department in Foggy Bottom, Washington, D.C.; a number of other federal agencies headquartered nearby; and the Soviet Union's Ministry of Foreign Affairs, headquartered in its Stalinist skyscraper in downtown Moscow. The new universe of "multilateral" power was centered in the headquarters of the United Nations – a celebrated modernist office building on the East River in New York City. Its affiliates were also very important: the World Health Organization (WHO) in Geneva, Switzerland, the UN Food and Agriculture Program in Rome, Italy, and, after 1978, the UN Human Settlements program, in Nairobi, Kenya. Back in Washington, meanwhile, the International Monetary Fund and the World Bank – the two "Bretton Woods Institutions" founded at a conference in that small New Hampshire town in 1944 – set up shop in cement office buildings, located a few blocks from the principal sources of their power and capital, the American White House and the US Treasury. These institutions were designed to lend money to member states during times of trouble, both to avoid a repeat of the Great Depression and to provide loans for development projects too large for the financial capacities of postcolonial states. Finally, in the USA, large corporations, most notably hydrocarbon giants like the Standard Oil Company and the Ford Motor Company, also played an immense role in the flow of development aid money – by creating "charitable" philanthropic foundations. The two most powerful of these, the Rockefeller and Ford Foundations, operated out of lavish headquarters in midtown New York. Later the Bill and Melinda Gates Foundation took the lead in similar activities from a bespoke headquarters next to the Space Needle in Seattle, Washington.

All of these organizations funded teams of experts in various development fields, including, as we shall see, such crucial stimuli of Urban Planetary growth as public health, agriculture, and housing. These experts built relationships between their own First and Second World research institutions and their counterparts in development ministries or university cities in the Third World. Although most of the decisions about actual funding took place in Washington, New York, Moscow, and a few sites in Western Europe, development aid took on an air of "North–South" collaboration. As such, development programs became enormously influential substitutes for the old unequal relationship between outside colonial administrators and local elites in colonial cities – a form of "soft" imperial power that at once concealed, justified, and depended upon the military power lodged in embassies, military bases, and missile silos.

After 1973, and more notably after 1980, financial power began to shift, from government, multilateral, and non-profit organizations toward global corporate headquarters, above all those in the emerging global cities. Like all increases in corporate power, this shift was ultimately a decision of state. After a decade of crisis in industrial employment and inflation blamed on hikes in the price of Middle Eastern oil in the 1970s, the US government, followed by Britain and Japan, took the lead in granting unprecedented authority over global money flows to multinational financial corporations and investment funds which specialized in overseas speculation and investment. The Ministry of Foreign Affairs in Moscow could not offer anything remotely as powerful in response, and the oil crisis played a strong knock-on role in hastening the death of the Soviet Union – as well as the entire Second World – in 1991 (Chapter 24).

The expansion of global financial power took the form of a spatial fix – a shift in its urban location from state bureaucracies to the headquarters of private banks, investment firms, and soon hedge funds. Most of the new power flowed to such vintage capitals of capital as London's City and New York's Wall Street, though Tokyo's Marunouchi District became the third member of a triumvirate of capitals of imperial capitalist power after 1980. A second circle in the financial firmament connects these big three to similar districts in Paris, Frankfurt, Zürich, Chicago, Singapore, Hong Kong, and, more recently, Shanghai. Financial firms there benefited from the close proximity of their headquarters to the head offices of other high-end industrial, insurance, accounting, consulting, asset rating, and high-end real estate firms, as well as immense telephone exchange facilities and, soon, internet servers. Nearby stock and bond markets enhanced the power of these districts, as did important nearby business schools, chambers of commerce, business lobbying groups, national banks, state regulation bureaus, and crucial courthouses. Access to specialized legal service was essential, just as it has been since the first corporations gained extraordinary powers as legal entities in the early nineteenth century. The world's top corporate law firms all cluster in global city business districts, offering extensive knowledge of international regulations and tax policies that anoints their clients' corporate interests with a kind of gold-star consideration in disputes that occur anywhere in the world. To top off this accumulation of corporate power, the International Monetary Fund (IMF) and the World Bank in Washington also shifted their roles after 1980 – offering a formidable new "multilateral" stamp of approval on global city financiers' certification of priority interest. For the Bretton Woods institutions, collection of corporate debts from postcolonial state treasuries became a top priority.[12]

The spatial and institutional shift in the world's foremost suppliers of money had enormous political and economic ramifications for cities and the built environment worldwide. Flows of early-Cold War "development aid" served soft superpower geopolitical interests above all. No matter how many humanitarian needs they actually met by lending and granting money, the directors of governmental, multilateral, and foundation-funded development programs intended above all to woo new developing states into alliances with their rival superpower sponsors. The imperial propaganda that accompanied humanitarian aid broadly followed a thread common to the otherwise opposing positions in the Kitchen Debate. The USA and the USSR, Nixon and Khrushchev had both argued, were justified in wielding nuclear superpower because their systems promised the rest of the world greater economic prosperity and fairness. The ideology of development from 1945 to 1973 was above all an ideology of plenty.

After 1973, by contrast, corporate financial districts reversed this emphasis on plenty, and instead demanded "austerity." This shift reflected constraints on both First and Second World economies during the oil, industrial, and inflation crises of the 1970s, but also on financial firms' longer-standing mistrust of government spending, which they linked to inflation, an economic phenomenon that threatened lenders' profits more than those of other capitalists. With state help, financiers infused austerity into their relationship with all government debtors, transforming self-interest into an economic theory and a political philosophy. Private foreign investment capital, this theory went, had to return, with interest, back to the headquarters of the financial companies that dispensed it, and from there to those corporations' executives, their high-paid employees, and their clients, the world's tiny class of hyper-wealthy investors. To make this upward money flow work, governments that received loans from the global cities needed to keep their costs down and concentrate on paying their debts back to the money-masters. Better yet, austerity theorists insisted, states could cut their own costs by letting private companies take on the role of development – "privatization." That could make it easier for large private developers and builders to acquire land in cities and elsewhere and construct far more privately owned profitmaking urban spaces, corporate farms, mines, and the like – multiplying capitalists' spatial "fixes" by widening the frontiers of potential exploitation. The World Bank, meanwhile, took over the biggest flows of development money, those required for especially large infrastructure projects like roads, pipelines, airports, and dams. Corporations were typically unwilling to finance these projects, but large corporate developers were happy to take on contracts for construction once the money was there. After they were built, railroads, dams, power lines, pipelines, and the like dramatically enhanced corporations' ability to make profit from new zones of investment. The Bank usually insisted on "cost recovery" for these projects, which often meant asking local states to focus their budgets on repaying the Bank's infrastructure loans rather than, say, regulating the companies that profited from them. Swelling corporate powers like these swelled even more after 1989 when the Cold War ended. Then, the power of New York, London, and Tokyo soared, as did that of the IMF, the World Bank, and their "Washington Consensus" on austerity.

Cities grew during the era of "plenty" in the 1950s and 1960s – when flows of money actually did increase the overall economic growth of what were then known as "Third World" countries. They also grew during the era of "austerity" – when most now-renamed "Global South" countries experienced debt crises, sharp economic recessions, "lost decades," uncertain recoveries, and greater inequality. Only during the crisis years of the late 1970s did the Greatest Acceleration taper off somewhat. The fact is that both public money and private money were capable of spurring growth in the global population, in explosions of migration from the countryside, and in rapid expansion of all four realms of the

Urban Planet. Both the pull of economic growth in cities and the push of economic contraction could cause megacities to grow, respectively by the increased attraction of cities and decreased attraction of the global countryside. The same was true of larger net money flows from North to South and the reverse. What changed, as "plenty" shifted to "austerity," was the contraction of hopes generated by early-Cold War liberation movements for more equality between the most developed precincts of Earthopolis and its poorest, "developing" ones. For this reason, for the first time in global urban history, the planet's fastest growing cities were no longer those that generated the most economic well-being for their residents. The Greatest Acceleration took its greatest velocity in the world's poorest cities. While megacities like Delhi grew to some extent on the prosperity of relatively small local elites and even a quickly grow-ing middle class, they grew much faster on the desperation of the major-ity in the countryside that led that majority to become an urban human majority after 2000. Before we explore that development, however, we need to start with the more basic fact that cities also grew just because there were so many more of us on Earth. Like other large-scale changes in global urban history, the population explosion was a matter of multi-directional causality, for we did not grow from a species of two billion to one of eight billion in a single century without first also changing the ways we built cities.

BUILDING FOR LONGER – AND MANY MORE – LIVES

A very small, fragile rivulet within the world's escalating global flows of money had especially important implications for the Greatest Acceleration: development aid meant to improve cities' public health infrastructure. This small stream is crucial to exploring answers to the first of the Acceleration's many conundrums, why Earth suddenly became home to nearly eight billion people. To explain that enormous historical surprise, demographers generally start by pointing to a dramatic decline in human death rates relative to fertility and birth rates. That trend began, as we know, in the original heartlands of the industrial revolution in the nineteenth century, but it spread to all continents during the 1930s, and especially after 1945. Child mortality rates plummeted, and human life expectancy increased at all ages. The number of births to each woman – the "fertility rate" – gradually fell as life expectancy rose, but only after a lag during which population overall exploded. These trends took unequal courses in different regions of the world. In Europe, industrialized East Asia, Australasia, and North America, population grew faster than elsewhere between 1850 and 1945. Lifespans doubled later in Latin America, Africa, and poorer regions of Asia, though never quite as quickly, and fertility declines lagged longer. In 1900, human life expectancies in poorer areas had remained more or less where they had been for 12,000 years, in the middle thirties. By 1970, most people born on Earth could expect to live to at least sixty years old. The biggest jumps in life expectancy and population by that point occurred in the Global South. Since then, fertility declines have spread to faster-developing regions like Latin America, India, and China, slowing population growth there somewhat and presaging a global demographic plateau that forecasters expect at around eleven billion people by 2100. In South and Southeast Asia, parts of the Middle East, and above all Africa, fertility currently remains relatively high, helping to explain the faster acceleration of cities there.[13]

These dramatic changes occurred above all, according to the environmental historian John McNeill Jr., because humanity temporarily "stole a march" on our greatest biological threat, the world of disease-causing microbiota. As we know, germs thrive on the human habitat's combination of dense urban incubators and far-flung hinterlands that give more of them the chance to jump to human hosts for the first time. The greatly accelerating Urban Planet thus created perfect conditions for microbiota to accelerate greatly too, while diversifying their deliverance of human misery and death. Yet, from the nineteenth century forward, cities also housed the universities, medical schools, laboratories, and health care facilities required by scientists to engage in revolutionary explorations of the biology of disease and develop new technologies to ease the existential pressure from microbiota. Urban planners and public health officials gradually took stock of this knowledge too.[14]

As cities helped generate this new knowledge, anti-germ knowledge remade cities, and, overall, cities became important generators of improved public health, longer life, and a larger global human population. Health got better in cities where planners and developers built better housing, plumbing, water systems, and sewers. Sometimes cheap things, like public latrines made huge differences. Also essential of course, were new clinics, dispensaries, disinfecting stations, quarantine facilities, sanitaria, and hospitals needed to isolate or treat sick people. Such facilities also helped with the difficult task of distributing new antibiotics and anti-viral vaccines, notably after 1945. Greater numbers of public schools, especially those that took the education of girls more seriously, brought into being a much savvier force of primary caregivers with knowledge about sanitation. Meanwhile, public health workers launched more aggressive human interventions into the habitats of disease-carrying animals like rats, fleas, lice, and especially malaria-bearing mosquitoes.[15]

Imperial governments invested substantial funds in expensive public health projects like these, especially after 1900. Though these investments typically prioritized the interests of their own soldiers, settlers, and administrators over those of their colonial subjects, new spaces designed to promote public health based on biological science did spread in colonial cities and beyond. There they merged, and sometimes conflicted, with other long-established medical and sanitary traditions in regions like the Middle East, sub-Saharan Africa, and both South and East Asia. During the Cold War, the race between the USA and the Soviet Union to win the "hearts and minds" of newly independent countries led both superpowers to expand health-related investments as part of their development aid packages and their ideology of plenty. In such classic exertions of soft superpower, they followed the lead of private actors like the Rockefeller Foundation in New York and multilateral organizations like the UN's WHO in Geneva.[16]

All of these new health-promoting organizations typically operated on a top-down model that belied their imperial sponsorship. Their high-profile teams of outside experts were trained to "fly into" the developing world as angels of bounty, engaging local partners in regional campaigns against single diseases. The Rockefeller Foundation pioneered this sort of work before the war, targeting hookworm and yellow fever in the US South and Mexico. After the war, the WHO collaborated with Rockefeller in funding teams of malaria experts who fanned out from Geneva to drain mosquito-breeding swamps in tropical countries and spray entire

21.1. Building toward Eight Billion
Cities grew because of the postwar global population explosion, but cities also helped ignite
their own acceleration, through proliferating structures like sewers, water systems, medical
research centers, hospitals, health clinics, and schools. Here, a clinic in San José, Costa Rica
participates in a vaccination drive that helped decrease childhood death rates and
dramatically increase human life expectancy. American volunteers who "flew in" to help
locals give kids their shots testify to the role of the "Soft Cold War," waged with development
money by rival imperial states, corporate foundations, and multilateral organizations like
the UN's World Health Organization. Today, similar geopolitical contests drive halting –
and highly unequal – measures against the Covid-19 pandemic.
Getty Images.

nearby human urban neighborhoods with DDT, a pesticide that, during
World War II, had also been effective in diminishing the habitats of the
louse-borne disease typhus. Another WHO–Rockefeller, cross-Cold War
collaboration during the 1960s targeted smallpox with great success. It
relied on funding from US federal agencies and new vaccines manufactured in the Soviet Union. Meanwhile, vaccines and antibiotics also made
their way around the world, following the geographically very uneven
infrastructure of clinics, dispensaries, and hospitals capable of distributing them. At a conference in Alma-Ata (Almaty), Soviet Kazakhstan in
1978, the WHO shifted direction from top-down single-disease campaigns to the broader goal of helping poorer countries build more of
their own permanent structures designed for the provision of basic
preventative medicine. In this, it took inspiration from such models as

Tanzania's village dispensaries, Cuba's socialist health care system, and Maoist China's "barefoot doctors."[17]

After 1980, however, the WHO's new goal of "Health for All" whistled into the adverse economic winds of the age of austerity. As with all global money flows, much changed during the Oil Crises of 1973 and 1979, when Middle Eastern oil producers dramatically increased prices. The bank accounts that Saudi Arabian and other Persian Gulf elites maintained in the global city financial districts brimmed with so-called "Petrodollars." Banks in London and New York joined the World Bank in increasing loans to Latin American, African, and Asian governments. It was a bad time for those governments to go into further debt, because their increased collective exports of agricultural and mining products caused prices for many of these raw commodities to decline, thus drying up their main source of local development money even as rising oil prices brought down import substitution industries built up since the 1930s. Meanwhile, rising oil prices ignited both inflation and greater unemployment across the developed world, a situation that the US Federal Reserve Bank chose to combat by radically raising its influential Federal Funds Rate of interest. Repayment bills for debtor nations across the developing world rose rapidly, and many of their governments quickly plummeted toward bankruptcy.[18]

It was amidst this Debt Crisis in the 1980s that global-city elites and the US Treasury demanded that the IMF become an international debt-collection police force. The IMF sent its agents into finance ministries in capitals across the Global South, there to enforce infamous "Structural Adjustment" policies designed to free up government cash for loan repayment by imposing "austerity" on other expenditures. Among other things, these measures mandated cuts to spending on public health.[19]

If that were not bad enough, the world of microbiota fought back at the same time, mutating into forms that were resistant to antibiotics, and hitching rides in the guts of insects that could survive the assaults of pesticides. Economic austerity and the accelerating Urban Planet provided this mass of improved vector lifeforms with a larger pool of weakened human hosts within which to propagate. More humans interacted more frequently with animals beyond the urban frontier, exposing themselves to new zoonotic microorganisms. Anti-malaria programs lost ground just as drug-resistant malaria plasmodium and new pesticide-resistant strains of mosquitoes evolved. The budgets of the WHO and national governments were slashed; DDT came under criticism for its environmental effects; and rising mountains of discarded automobile tires and plastic trash provided new places for mosquitoes to breed in the heart of cities where they had previously been rarer. New viruses, meanwhile, emerged in the more generally enlarged global human habitat and its expanded transport arteries, which had increased the interaction of humans with other animal species and new microorganisms. HIV first jumped to people in marginalized farming settlements whose inhabitants increasingly relied on "bush meat" in previously uninhabited places like the Central African rainforests. Then the virus embarked on its horrific killing spree in gay clubs of First World cities and among needle-users in poor neighborhoods nearby. Soon it boomeranged back across the developing world, in part transmitted by long-distance truck drivers and their sex partners. New vaccine-resistant influenzas percolated in the world's growing poultry and hog farms and in mines that double as bat caves. SARS and Covid-19 likely emerged there, possibly first infecting humans at "wet markets" in cities like Wuhan, China that deal in live exotic creatures. Impoverished farmers' "bush-meat"-hunting and wild-animal-poaching camps, increasingly common in the world's savannahs and rainforests, likely also delivered SARS and Ebola to the bodies of their first human hosts. These tiny places, which have expanded in tune with demand for their products in cities, could easily thrust new zoonotic diseases on our Urban Planet as a whole.[20]

In recent years, the UN has released hopeful statistics that suggest that – even amidst the Covid-19 epidemic and the yawning vestiges of the Great Gap revealed by unequal vaccination rates between the Global North and South – access to primary health care, fresh water, and sewer systems is slowly catching up with population and urban growth. The World Bank and the Gates Foundation have made widely publicized commitments to vaccination for all, renewed anti-malaria campaigns, large-scale financing for water systems, and investments in on-site waste-water-recycling machines that do not rely as much on expensive underground piping and enormous treatment plants.[21]

Our visit to the Newest New Delhi, the capital of one of the richest of all developing nations, gives us plenty to think about on this subject, starting with the sharp stench in the air. Only slightly over half of the households in today's Delhi have formal connections to water and waste pipes. Cheaper public latrines are available to some the city's poorest, but open-air defecation is very common. Much of the city's human waste collects in streets and streams, and mingles with water also used for drinking and bathing. Human waste also contaminates ground water, including the water in private wells drilled by the wealthy Diliwalas who are eager to avoid drinking the city's piped supply. Contaminated streams and aquifers feed Delhi's sacred Yamuna River, a primary tributary of the even holier Ganges. As the Yamuna enters the city from the north, no less than seventeen outfall drains dump raw sewage into the river. In 2012, the Indian Supreme Court, in an opinion about water rights, fumed that Yamuna's water was just as foul as the sludge flowing in the city's main sewage pipes.

Under some pressure from international creditors, India has embraced the World Bank's mantra that profit-making solutions are the best way to solve urban problems. One such "solution" is the Delhi Jal (Water) Board (DJB) of 1998, which the Indian Parliament authorized to charge increasing rates for water and sewerage, including a fourfold increase between 2010 and 2012. These higher fees are supposed to offset the cost of providing new services to poorer communities, but most of Delhi's poorest people still pay private tank-truck providers even higher prices for water. Their advocates in the Water Privatisation and Commercialization Resistance Committee have tried, so far unsuccessfully, to remind the DJB that "water is a naturally occurring public good. ... our society has, over centuries, recognized its obligation to provide water to the needy and thirsty through the establishment of *piaos* at temples, mosques, *gurudwaras*, and *dharamshalas*, as well as by individuals in front of their homes and in public places."[22]

Access to safe drinking water and sewerage is even worse in most other Indian cities, and worse still in rural villages. Progress worldwide remains even more uneven by country and within poorer countries across the urban–rural divide. Advances that the UN tabulates on the global level are heavily balanced on the positive side by the wealthier countries of

South and East Asia and to some extent Latin America. In eighty-five out of 132 developing countries in the world, most in Africa and Southeast Asia, sanitary improvements are either falling behind urban development or declining in quality. Meanwhile, India has become a major force in the manufacturing of essential medicines and vaccines, but its primary care system still struggles to deliver these to the poor, even in cities. "Big Pharma" drug companies in the First World charge premium prices for the newest medicines that Indian "generic" producers are forbidden from manufacturing at lower cost. As a result, distribution of medicines and vaccines is worse in poorer countries where cities are now growing the fastest – as evident in the unequal rollouts of Covid-19 vaccines. Meanwhile, a million and a half people die each year of diarrhea, the disease of befouled water systems. Malaria is an even bigger killer – reversing it requires more preventative nets, drugs, wider-spread drug manufacturing facilities, and caregivers trained in medical schools. Simple hand washing, meanwhile, remains out of the question for millions who face the scourge of new viral epidemics.[23]

The expanded but uneven global scope of built environments devoted to health embodies great hopes and ongoing despair. We now know more than ever before about designing cities to counteract their built-in tendency to incubate disease. Yet we still deprioritize investments in public health infrastructure that can stop the miseries we know best – even as the human habitat's planet-wide reach generates new diseases we know nothing about. If we want to build a healthier Urban Planet for all, global flows of money will need to run far more smoothly and copiously. Its lenders will have to insist far less on private companies as a solution to problems and resort far less to austerity mongering as an excuse for lack of progress. All of us will need to listen better to social movements of the urban majority, starting with Delhi's brave water activists.

FEEDING THE MULTITUDES?

The same is true if we want to feed everyone. The post-1945 fight against hunger involved a cast of powerful characters similar to those who fought the fight against disease – and it suffered from the same savage whipsaw in money politics. Like other episodes of urban growth in the past, the Greatest Urban Acceleration at once took strength from and helped to expand a revolution in farming – in this case, the so-called "Green Revolution" that began in the 1940s. Its leaders prided themselves in extracting far greater yields of wheat, rice, and soybeans from existing farmland and thus their ability to spare forests from their age-old fate at the hands of farmers wielding axes and plows. Though the Green Revolutionaries gave public health experts credit for quadrupling of the postwar human population, they claimed to have found the way to feed those billions, lowering the risk of famine and malnutrition in the process.[24]

The Green Revolution began when the Rockefeller Foundation's pre-war experiments in high-yield wheat farming in Mexico attracted support from the UN's Food and Agricultural Organization, the USA's many development aid organizations, the new Ford Foundation, and the Mexican opponents of the land redistribution programs that had defined farm policy in the revolutionary years before the war. Funding poured into the International Wheat and Maize Improvement Center, based in a spanking new headquarters near Mexico City. Agronomists there con-ducted experiments breeding high-yield crops whose stockier stems could support the weight of more grain. In addition to bioengineered seeds, these varieties required expensive inputs: artificial fertilizer, pesti-cides, and more water. To build the capital needed for these expenses, it was best to operate on a larger scale, which required more land, tractors, and agricultural laborers. For those who could afford to build such larger mechanized farms, the results were dramatic. By the late 1950s, in Mexico's drier northwest, large farmers far out-produced poorer farmers. Wheat production per hectare nearly quadrupled in Mexico from 1950 to 1975, that of maize doubled, and the country began exporting foodstuffs that it had previously spent ruinously on importing. Wheat production in Argentina followed suit, as did that of soybeans in the heavily treated soils of Brazil's Sertão grasslands and, soon, in cleared expanses of the Amazon rainforest. Meanwhile, a similar Rockefeller-funded agro-institute in the Philippines, housed in a state-of-the-art modernist campus south of Manila, created a high-yield strain of rice. With similar inputs on larger farms, rice production there grew rapidly, as it did later across Southeast and East Asia, reaching as far as Iran, Afghanistan, and the Indus Valley of Pakistan. In India, memories of the Great Bengal Famine of 1943 and the threat of new food emergencies in 1960 convinced Nehru to adopt the Green Revolution wholesale. Among the world's great agricultural hinterlands, the North Indian Plains is one of the few to serve as both rice bowl (May to October) and breadbasket (November to April). Yields of both rice and wheat have increased steadily in the region.[25]

The color "Green" should not confuse this revolution with today's revolution in solar and wind energy: this was self-consciously a Hydrocarbon-industrial revolution in the countryside. The fertilizer required by the new plants was derived in part from natural gas, the pesticides from petroleum. The tractors ran on gasoline. The "miracle" plants were also thirstier, so the Green Revolution required a revolution in water use – and thus an exponential increase in the number and size of dams, reservoirs, and irrigation ditches, and hundreds of thousands of boreholes into aquifers, each surmounted by new gasoline-powered pumping stations. Such structures were dispersed across the countryside and represented yet another aspect of the industrial-scale redesign of the world's millions of acres of cropland. The greatest monuments of the Green Revolution were a new generation of mega-dams. They warmed the hearts of developmentalist nationalists because they evoked a renewal of the glory of ancient "national" pasts. Nehru called the hundreds of dams he authorized the "temples of modern India." Egypt's Nasser called his dams on the Nile the new "pyramids for the living," reserving pride-of-place for the massive Aswan Dam, financed by fees from the nationalized Suez Canal and with money from Moscow. The number of large dams (over fifteen meters high) rose from near zero in 1850 to 5,000 in 1950. Since then, the number has septupled to 35,000 worldwide, nearly half in the developing world. China's Three Gorges Dam on the Yangtze River (2006) dwarfs them all.[26]

Not surprisingly, the agricultural revolution was also intended as a 'soft' First World political counterrevolution. For the USA, the lofty mission to end famine served as a weapon against the frightening tendency among millions of the world's smaller farmers to congregate in guerrilla camps, demand bigger shares of farmland, and join "red" armies to seize the means of food production from the wealthy. That said, the Green counterrevolutionaries in Washington and New York shared at least one predilection with the chief of all Red peasant revolutionaries, Mao Zedong of China. When Mao enlisted Moscow's help in his First Five-Year Plan to industrialize Chinese cities, he insisted, as had Stalin, that only large, hydrocarbon-powered farms could possibly feed the giant working class he hoped to spawn in urban factories. Beyond that, his system was different in all respects from the American one. His big farms were to operate on Soviet collectivist principles, not under the control of profiteering private land consolidators. In 1958, Mao went even further. He called for a "Great Leap Forward" that would transform collective farms into true communes – forerunners of Karl Marx's most exalted utopian vision of the "communist" society. These would run their own local governments and militias, and would share duties for industrial production, in the form of rudimentary village iron furnaces, while they also grew more food, in part thanks to their own irrigation works. The Great Leap was catastrophic for the Chinese countryside. The communes were unable to take on all of their duties at once, in part because Beijing also saddled them with quotas to feed millions of new industrial workers engaged in a parallel Great Leap in the cities. On the land, commune officials eager to please Mao inflated their production figures, even after natural disasters and bad weather in 1959 heightened the conditions for disaster. Mao used the fake good news to flay the communes even harder, and between twenty-five and thirty-five million people, most of them rural, starved to death in one of the greatest preventable famines in world history.[27]

Despite the communes' dystopian birth, they persisted as an institution, largely thanks to the backbreaking labor of China's peasants, rural craftspeople, and soon millions of urban workers who were sent back to the countryside to help (Chapter 22). After 1970, many of the communes had their own agro-institutes that deployed Green Revolution-like techniques, as well as hundreds of thousands of small iron smelting operations and small dams, the diminutive grandparents of the post-Mao-era Three Gorges. By then, China's agricultural productivity had outstripped that of the USSR and India, and closed in on that of the USA. With help from the "barefoot doctor" system of rural health clinics, life expectancy in China rose from under fifty in 1964 to sixty-six at Mao's death in 1978.

When Deng Xiaoping took over the CCP, he abruptly returned the communes to private production, but Chinese agriculture had already regained much of its historic role as supplier of nutrients to the Urban Planet's greatest concentration of its very largest cities. As such, it also fueled the accelerated rise of industrial capitalism "with Chinese characteristics" that soon enabled China to launch a financial and military challenge to the victors of the Cold War and the triumphant power of their capitalist global cities.[28]

THE HARROWING OF THE VILLAGES

Back in the Newest New Delhi, a lunch stop features both rice, topped with one of the city's delicious curries, and wheat-based flatbreads – *roti, naan, chapatti* – cooked on the hot sides of a clay tandoori oven. The menu may tempt us to join the celebrations of late-twentieth-century agricultural development. Surely, the task of feeding over a billion Indians with both rice and wheat deserves all of the accolades that world leaders have heaped upon the Green Revolution. Surely too, as the US President Barack Obama vowed in 2016, India shows the way forward for Africa, where drier, more varied soils and generally less wealthy farmers have thus far prevented the creation of true continental breadbaskets like the Punjab, the Yellow and Yangtze Rivers, Ukraine, the Brazilian Sertão, or the American Great Plains.[29]

Why, then does our lunchtime perusal of the headlines in Delhi's newspapers shock us with reports that some 300,000 Indian farmers, including in fertile North India, have committed suicide since 2000 – many, horrifically, by drinking the pesticides that were supposed to bring them wealth? Why did hundreds of thousands of angry farmers converge in mass marches on Delhi in 2006 and again in 2018 and 2019? Why in 2020–21 did millions of Punjabi farmers fill the city's new elevated expressways with their massed tractors and protest banners, rally in a park where the old city walls used to stand – then, like the Gandhian *satyagrahis* of old, besiege India's round parliament, the world's largest – then even invade the Mughals' old Red Fort? Why, more ominously, have thousands of farmers joined Hindu and Muslim mobs to reignite India's baleful religious violence in the countryside? Why did that violence spill into Delhi itself in 2020, bloodily, when a mob once again raged through the streets of the capital, killing fifty-three Muslims, burning hundreds of shops and houses and four mosques, and forcing 1,000 to seek refuge in tents on the city's outskirts?[30]

There are two answers to these questions, a deeper one and an immediate one. The deeper one is that, in the name of feeding cities, the Green Revolution has disrupted geo-solar energies upon which all life depends, starting with the Earth and Sun's 2-billion-year-old nitrogen cycle. By the 1990s, the "brute chemistry" of industrial fertilizers knocked global nitrogen levels farther beyond Holocenic sustainability thresholds than those for atmospheric heating. Vast surpluses of nitrogenous nutrients wash into lakes, rivers, estuaries, and oceans, threatening aquatic life and the balance of other Earth-systems, including the climate. Meanwhile, the Green Revolution threatens its own increased yields of human nutrients. The use of grain and soybeans to feed livestock and poultry for the meat industry dramatically cuts down the calorie-producing efficiency of every acre of cropland and every liter of fresh water while expanding methane outputs. Meat also demands more acreage of pasture from forests – rainforests in particular – undermining another of the revolution's key missions while producing a form of food that is less affordable to the poorest, less healthy for all, and that adds greatly to the Urban Planet's risk of cross-species pandemics. Seventy-five years into the Green Revolution, approximately one billion people, many of them children, remain malnourished. Famine has not disappeared; in fact, atmospheric heating, amplified by the revolution's hydrocarbon and methane wastes and declines in carbon sequestration from lost forests, may soon make it more common (Chapter 24).[31]

The immediate explanation for India's farmer crisis is that the more productive global countryside we have built – sustainable or not – has become far less equitable for those who work there. Whatever it gives in food, it takes away in livelihoods for the poorest country-dwellers, the majority of a rural population that has now as a result become a minority of the majority-urban human species. Farmers who leave the countryside for the city, or who kill themselves – or kill each other – do so overwhelmingly because they cannot get themselves out of debt. These debts mounted in the years approaching the millennium. In India, they grew out of global money flows that connected their farms along many smaller financial streams back to Delhi itself, and from there to the global capitals of capital abroad.

As perhaps befits a "Green" Revolution, building its enormous structures required lots of money, especially "greenbacks" – American dollars. Many of the debts that developing nations have accrued since 1945 come from World Bank loans to finance the construction of irrigation systems and dams. Since the debt crisis of the 1980s, repayments to global city creditors, plus escalating interest bills have formed a roaring river of money flowing from South to North measuring in the hundreds of billions of dollars. Such reverse capital flows suck money out of the pockets of ordinary farmers too. All of the "inputs" that they need to grow their crops require loans – expensive tractors, fertilizer, and pesticides; deeper wells and new local irrigation ditches. So do the miracle seeds themselves, now overwhelmingly produced by multinational agriculture companies like Monsanto that demand royalty payments on what they consider their own intellectual property. Meanwhile, farm incomes have gone down too. In part because food supply has grown even faster than the human population, the price farmers get for their crops each year has fallen too low on average for them to cover their loan payments. On top of that, global-city financial instruments that incorporate crop futures have become big sellers among investment houses' wealthy clients; the rollercoaster values of these high-tech securities also play havoc with farm incomes. Under Nehru and many other Green Revolution developmentalist states across the world, the country's taxpayers were willing to subsidize farmers in times of falling prices, in part to sustain their good yields. Yet after 1991, India's own parliament, again following the lead of the IMF and World Bank, began its own austerity campaign against government spending. Farm subsidies fell, forcing farmers further into debt. Money is the basic demand of the hundreds of thousands of marchers who descend on Delhi in the twenty-first century: relief from debt and a renewed debate on India's obligation to the people who feed the nation.[32]

Yet these desperate money worries only give us a pinhole glimpse into a much wider universe of rural immiseration. The marchers, after all, are those who have enough land that they can even walk into a bank office.

21.2. A Green Revolution or a Black-and-Blue One?
At Kauli Village in the Punjab, near Delhi, a farmer burns the stubble of his rice crop to plant wheat. Double harvests allow the Punjab to feed Delhi's twenty-plus millions. The Cold War's "Green Revolution" expanded yields too, enabling global population growth. To go "Green," though, farmers needed more "Black" (hydrocarbon fuels, fertilizers, and pesticides) and more "Blue" (Himalayan river water diverted by dams into irrigation canals) – all requiring a different kind of "Green," bank money. Debt mounted in the Punjab, alongside farmer suicides, religious strife, city-ward migration, and mass protests in Delhi. Back to "Black": stubble-ash too drifts from fields like these into Delhi, exacerbating smoke pollution that kills millions in India and elsewhere each year.
Hindustan Times/Getty Images.

Many millions more across India – and across Asia, Africa, and Latin America – farm tiny plots on increasingly marginal land, on the eroding slopes of mountain ranges, on the advancing fringes of deserts, or on the retreating fringes of rainforests. They have no access to irrigation, they contend with much severer forms of environmental degradation, and are more vulnerable to natural disasters. Climate change threatens them most directly. They farm such unsustainable spaces because larger farmers and large commercial concerns have consolidated their control over the flatter, better irrigated, and more fertile lands that are easiest to plant with "miracle" crops and animal feed. Dams and reservoirs displace tens of millions of rural people each year according to the World Bank; its officials should know, since the Bank finances many of these projects. Other development projects like roads and mines also dislodge large numbers of farmers from their farms. Debt worries are much worse for the larger group of people who must leave their own little plots to work as tenants and manual laborers on larger farms. Women have less access to land than men, and all face particularly brutal lives in far too many of the world's countrysides, as do children. Many of these poorest of all villagers fall into the enormous class of the world's multiply exploitable people whose lives are hard to distinguish from those of the twenty-five million who live in outright slavery. Rural debt, often involving tiny amounts, is in fact the widest door into slavery itself – whether as bonded farmworkers, as internationally trafficked sex workers, or as child laborers in mines or urban sweatshops. Meanwhile, domestic violence and mob violence against women, or mob violence directed against perceived religious or racial enemies, regularly flares in rural towns, often ricocheting into much larger cities, as it did in Delhi in 2020. When political parties exploit such gendered and racialized fears, as do many members of India's parliament and the country's prime minister, they play with fire that feeds hungrily on destitution – rural especially but also urban. Genocides in Rwanda in 1994, Bosnia in 1995, Darfur in 2003, and Myanmar in 2016 all bear ample testament to where that game can lead.[33]

The rural crisis brought on by the Green Revolution is a foundational element in the acceleration of megacities like the Newest New Delhi. To see that fact, all we need to do is look up from the disturbing news we read at the tandoori stall – and just notice all of the people. The megacity's millions throng the city around us. Most of the city's annual growth, it is true, comes from the births of new children – all of them more likely to live into adulthood than 100 years ago. However, for years before the Covid-19 crisis caused many migrants to return to their villages, fully one-third of the newest Diliwalas each year were born outside the city, most on a village farm, most poor. That amounted to over 100,000 people every year, 8,000 every month – 500, relentlessly, each day. They represent Delhi's slice of the unimaginably enormous tide of three million people worldwide who move from the countryside to the city each week – as refugees from land consolidation, poverty, and debt, from climate change and natural disasters, displaced by dams, reservoirs, roads, and mines, and from violent conflict.[34]

These rural calamities, and the Great Acceleration they helped to ignite, could not have happened without the Cold War imperialists, the multilateral developmental experts, the philanthropists and experts they hired, and the surging imperial power of global city capitalists. Liberationist leaders bear some for the blame too, for their drive for development plunged them into the dangerous vortex of profit-driven global money flows – and from there too often into the political temptations of racial nationalism.

Yet the Great Acceleration of cities is also the result of the sweat and the movement of the billions of people who left the county to join the new – urban – human majority. That brings us to the most complex part of our Acceleration conundrum. What exactly do the world's poorest cities – with all their own problems with water, food, waste, disease, deteriorated built environment, and violence – offer to so many poor migrants that they could not find in the country? Why are places like Delhi, Kinshasa, and Lima growing so much faster than most far-richer cities? Answering that question forces us deeper into the streets of the Newest New Delhi, and deeper into the audacious wager that humans, and especially the most vulnerable of us, have made by hitching a ride in the vast new "slums" of the world – the fastest-accelerating habitats of our twenty-first-century Urban Planet.

CHAPTER 22

Greatest Accelerations II: Shacks and Citadels

THE PLANETARY URBAN LAND WAR

The Challenge of Slums. Lifted from the title of a 2003 United Nations report, these five syllables invite many re-readings, like the culminating line of an Urban Planetary haiku. *Slum*, the word, is a challenge of its own. Can a bit of slang from Victorian-era London meaning "back alley," since freighted with two centuries of moral contempt and shock, help us understand why over one billion people live where they do today, in hundreds of cities, in millions of self-built dwellings especially in Latin America, Africa, and Asia? If so, why have Earthopolitans invented such a profusion of synonyms for *slum*, as if we need as many words as we have of the thing itself? The UN had a different "challenge" in mind: a puzzle for humanitarians and technocrats. By what "best practices" should humanity deal with today's great cities of the poor – should we "clear," "upgrade," "notify," "regularize," "redevelop," "involve," "empower"? As for the one billion themselves, they present a bold challenge of their own. By gathering in immense numbers, by building hundreds of millions of small dwellings, and sometimes by launching improbable social movements, they have made a risky move on the political–economic chessboard of urban land, even as it became one of the highest-priced assets on Earth. Perilously, they press against the grand strategies devised for the same land in citadels of empire and capital, in government bureaus of all kinds, and on the ground by developers, "gentrifiers,"and speculators, some of them the wealthiest people in the world.[1]

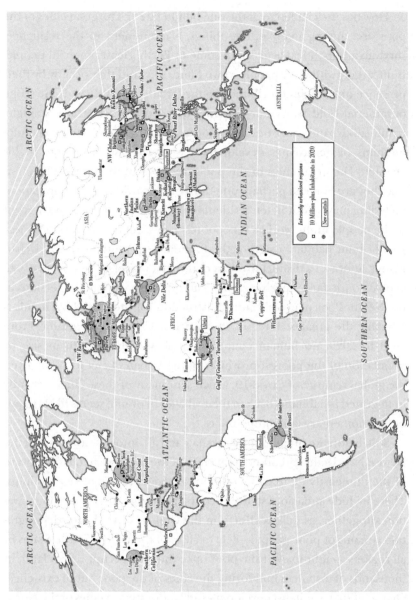

Map 22.1. Urban Superlatives: Megacities and Urbanized Regions
Map created by Joe LeMonnier, https://mapartist.com.

How has the challenge of the one billion fared? The great cities of the poor are, among many others things, a monument to the resilience, survival, and political activism of some of Earth's least powerful people. Built largely with poor people's own hands, on land they occupy by their presence only, their contribution to the Urban Planet exceeds the scope of imperial Cold War visions of cities that grow by accretions of single-family suburban homes or tower blocks, let alone the downtown condominiums of gentrifying developers – who will also re-emerge in his chapter. The great cities of the poor are *a part* of the Urban Planet, in that they are home to perhaps one-third of the world's urban population, including maybe four in ten residents of Delhi, and more than 80 percent of the people in the world's very poorest cities. Yet they are also *their own form* of built habitat, a sign of the foundational plurality of the Urban Planet, above all a distinct product of the sheer diversity of the post-1945 Global South, far outpacing earlier – and recently resurgent – versions in the North. Poor peoples' "auto-construction" of their neighborhoods is arguably the greatest force of the Greatest Urban Acceleration. From 1945 to 2020, no human counterforce slowed the growth in size or population of the poorest provinces of the Urban Planet for long. Even the global scourge of Covid-19, which sent many of these cities' recently in-migrated inhabitants back to their villages of origin, seems likely to put only a momentary tap on the brakes.[2]

Still, before we plunge, auto-rickshaw and all, into the vastnesses of the Newest New Delhi and other great cities of the poor, we need to be aware of the immensity of attacks *on* the urban poor: the challenge *to* slums. These include audacious state efforts to discourage rural-to-urban migration altogether, as well as efforts, in the Global North, to restrict migration streams of poor people solely to cities of the Global South. States in all regions sought to evict the poor once they did occupy urban land, in thousands of instances bulldozing the cities of the poor out of existence. On top of that, capitalist developers and landowners in cities of the North and South – also with state help – engaged in a great urban land grab on behalf of the world's wealthiest people that also limits poor people's options in the city. Challenge and counterchallenge: we should need no reminder by now that urban space is the product and the producer of political conflicts that play out locally and globally. Describing that drama, essentially a planetary war over urban land, requires more than five syllables – especially ones that include the parting expletive "slum."

HOLLOW ECHOES FROM THE KITCHEN

Where will an accelerating population of humans live, asked Richard Nixon and Nikita Khrushchev in Moscow, when countrysides no longer sustain the poorest of us? In 1959, both gave blustery answers. Yet in the years since, no one has found a way to coax either Nixon's capitalist "market" or Khrushchev's "state" – let alone any more typically inter-woven combination of the two – into providing safe, affordable, dignified shelter for the poor people who have thronged the world's cities. In the USA and Soviet Union, as we know, rural exoduses such as the Second Great Migration of African Americans to US cities (1940–70) and the enormous city-ward waves of Russian peasants found accommodation in inadequate – and in the USA racially unequal – swaths of substandard private and state lodging in the cities of both superpowers. The wealthiest and most egalitarian social democracies in Scandinavia, the Netherlands, and Canada have arguably come closer to a satisfactory answer, by build-ing far more comprehensive postwar public housing systems for their relatively small poor urban populations. Yet even they have faced enor-mous stress as sub-streams of the world's international rural-to-urban migrants, augmented by war and climate refugees, cross over otherwise hardened borders to reach the "most liberal cities in the world" – Copenhagen, Amsterdam, Toronto, and their kind.

For Delhi, Lima, Kinshasa, and other cities of the Global South large and small, the challenge has been orders of magnitude more daunting. Much larger flows of migrants and refugees flood their thresholds, and local and national governments have far less to offer. The first of the hemisphere's cities to face "the challenge of slums" at a truly large scale were those that were home to at least rudimentary pre-1945 factory districts. Perón's Argentina, postwar Brazil, Green Revolution Mexico, the FLN's Algeria, Kemalist Turkey, Nasser's Egypt, and Nehru's India did build substantial social housing estates as part of their development missions. Peripheral *superbloques* arose in Latin America. French-subsidized "*barres*" circled Algiers. Prefab state apartments sprouted in

(A)

(B)

22.1. Thrust and Counterthrust in the Planetary Urban Land War
Such obscenely unequal images attest to an Urban Planetary land war – waged by the world's wealthiest against almost everyone else, including a billion people whose basic survival depends on staking out tiny spots of space in the city for self-built homesteads. "Development states" once tried to level the battlefield, but their public housing programs faded as state support for high-end suburbs grew, like in apartheid-era Johannesburg (A). Now, as "promotional states," they compete to attract investment in gated communities, as

Fidel Castro's Havana, with help from Moscow. Mao's China was a special case, as we will see shortly. Yet all of these regimes – like the empires they fought – needed to keep the allegiance of their large numbers of civil and military personnel. Low-paid but economically far more secure soldiers, police officers, and other government workers "poached" most developmental states' public housing from the very poor.[3]

Meanwhile, Washington jumped deeper into the contest of homes and kitchens. In 1959 the Cuban Revolution stunned American anti-communists like Richard Nixon, and in 1960, Nixon himself lost the US Presidential election to John F. Kennedy. Yet Kennedy's response to the setback in Havana drew heavily on Nixon's act in Moscow. He expanded Washington's longstanding Cold War strategy to win "hearts and minds" abroad by peddling so-called "market"-driven homeownership programs that actually involved huge federal investments, including in public housing. Earlier, such programs had reached relatively poor people in Cold War hotspots like Taipei and Seoul, and in cities where the USA exerted historical colonial authority like San Juan, Puerto Rico and Manila. Now, however, Kennedy expanded an FHA-style mortgage guarantee program that encouraged American developers and foreign partners to build quasi-American style tailpipe suburbs near cities like Lima, La Paz, Bogotá, and Mexico City – and soon Tunis, Bangkok, and back around to Taipei. "Rhetorically, these programs were designed for the masses," writes their skeptical historian Nancy H. Kwak; "in reality, such housing remained out of reach for the vast majority of impoverished residents." In the 1970s, now-President Richard Nixon judged these programs too expensive and cut them, abandoning his promise of plenty in favor of the now fashionable doom-speak of austerity. The World Bank picked up where the USA left off, launching similar "market-oriented"

Caption for 22.1. (cont.)

in Gurugram (Gurgaon) near Delhi (B) – plus high-end financial districts, hotels, resorts, and malls that signal "World City" status. To make space, states routinely bulldoze "informal settlements" while also channeling corporate money into rural agribusinesses, forcing poor farmers off the land. That only swells the numbers of migrants seeking basic shelter in the great cities of the poor.

(A) Per-Anders Pettersson/Getty Images. (B) AFP/Getty Images.

lending programs aimed to spread individual homeownership among the world's poor. The Bank's insistence on "cost recovery," though, has priced its "good cop" loans largely out of poor people's reach. Meanwhile, next door in Washington, D.C., the "bad cop" IMF harassed debtor states to cut public housing programs, and urged demolition or sell-offs of older state-owned apartments.[4]

Among developmental states, only Mao's China succeeded in housing its poorest urban migrants – if only by brutally reversing rural-to-urban migration. Immediately after his victory in 1949, Mao curried favor with urban China's capitalist landowners by entrusting them with shelter for the country's growing working class. Results in Shanghai were no different from cities like Chicago or Rio de Janeiro. Rents skyrocketed and owners refused to invest in repairs, the classic instance of market failure. China's working class – the "Masters of the Country" – made do with slums and even shantytowns. After 1956, Beijing exerted far more Marxist muscle, placing most of China's urban rental housing stock under state management. Local party bosses set rents low and scheduled repairs more regularly. The shantytowns retreated, and state-owned industrial firms cleared many inner-city slums, replacing them with new housing for their "work units" – most in four-story modernist low-rises. Some factories moved to planned satellite cities, taking with their work unit housing with them and presaging the unprecedented expansion of Chinese urban peripheries in the 1990s. Modest low-rent apartments became part of the "iron rice bowl" welfare system that was the birthright of all city dwellers in China.[5]

Meanwhile, Mao's *hukou* registration system prevented all but a few of China's hundreds of millions of peasants from migrating off the land. Holders of rural *hukou* documents discovered by the police in the city faced forced return to their villages or worse. By contrast, urban *hukou* holders became a privileged "nation within a nation," entitled to first claim on the produce of the farms and on the party's stock of urban apartments. Few Chinese city dwellers suffered during the Great Famine of 1959–60 that killed tens of millions of peasants (Chapter 21). However, in the wake of the disaster, Mao revoked the urban *hukou* status of millions of factory workers and ordered them to relocate to rural communes – increasing China's food supply while diminishing the number of urban mouths to feed. Even before that, he expelled hundreds of thousands of owners of restaurants, clubs, cafés, opium dens, and houses of prostitution. Such "sugar-coated cannonballs of urban life," Mao thought, disrupted the discipline of revolutionary cadres. (His scruples did not extend to his own emperor-like cultivation of concubines in the Forbidden City.) Some of these purveyors of moral dissolution began their exile in China's version of the Gulag, the shadowy *laogai* re-education camps deep in the grimmest parts of the Chinese interior. During the tumultuous Cultural Revolution (1966–76), many more millions of urban residents followed similar paths "Back to the Countryside." China's urbanization rate fell from about 20 percent in 1960 to 13 percent by Mao's death, during decades when the Greatest Acceleration took off virtually everywhere else.[6]

GLOBAL APARTHEID

Few countries could muster the totalitarian clout needed to reverse a large internal rural exodus like Mao Zedong. Only South Africa's apartheid-era pass laws functioned similarly, authorizing police to deport Black people without an urban work pass to destitute, all-Black rural reserves – or to prison, or to forced labor on the country's vast white-owned farms (urbanization rates in South Africa too remained steady between 1960 and the 1980s). That said, the world's richest states – including First World countries and the rising petroleum-wealthy countries of the Persian Gulf – engaged in a far-larger project of global human movement control, successful enough that it deserves the nickname Global Apartheid. They too issued a version of a pass or a *hukou*, in their case visas or ID cards allowing relatively small streams of state-approved migrants to cross borders and to live and work in the wealthiest cities of the world. Like apartheid and the *hukou*, this system hardly stopped large waves of undocumented migration. However, because it channeled most country-to-city migrants away from the Urban Planet's wealthiest cities, Global Apartheid's relative success does help explain why poorer cities have grown faster than richer ones for the first time in history.[7]

Like all large-scale institutions in world history, Global Apartheid requires an extensive built habitat in order to operate. By 1945, the infrastructure of national borders had expanded far beyond nineteenth-century steamship-era port facilities like Ellis Island. The best example is the land border between the USA and Mexico, the longest of all between the Global South and North. During the early Cold War, while Washington dispensed health aid, agronomy expertise, and mortgage supports to prevent Mexico's peasants from forming Chinese-style revolutionary base camps, federal officials pursued the same anticommunist goals by offering tens of thousands of those peasants temporary work on the farms of the USA. The *bracero* (or guest laborer) program began with a network of recruitment centers in dozens of Mexican country towns. Screened candidates reported to border posts inside the USA to get their papers – and a DDT-laced disinfection shower – before proceeding north to distant locations like the fruit and vegetable farms of California's highly irrigated Central Valley. Thousands of undocumented migrants, meanwhile, slipped around the border posts into the USA. Anti-immigrant sentiment reignited among white "natives" of the "Immigrant Nation." The federal government bent to this racist pressure with a deportation program called "Operation Wetback," derogatively named after paperless Mexicans who swam the Rio Grande to get north. Raids occurred along the border and in Mexican neighborhoods in cities like Los Angeles, Houston, and Chicago. Some of these neighborhoods had grown as large as whole cities in Mexico itself. Over a million migrants were deported. Many turned back northwards across the border soon after.[8]

Guest worker programs similar to the *bracero* program existed in Europe at the same time. Post-1945 immigration from the "Global South" to the "Global North" has grown larger, in sheer numbers, than transatlantic migration in the nineteenth century. By 2020, between a fifth and a third of all residents of the USA, Canada, the European Union, the United Kingdom, and Australia were people born into families that had arrived recently from a different country, most from the developing world. Temporary foreign-born workers make up a large majority of the populations of Dubai, Abu Dhabi, Doha, and other rapidly growing cities in the Arab Persian Gulf States. The labor needs of host societies are responsible for these enormous streams of migration, as is undocumented immigration. Escalating movements of refugees from conflicts in the Global South add to the numbers.[9]

While specific labor needs of richer host societies help drive immigration, documented and otherwise, the bigger context is the great hemispheric wealth gap, which has widened during the age of austerity, intensifying all of the "pulls" and "pushes" that drive long-distance movements of people. Despite decades of development in many parts of the South, hemispheric inequalities in opportunities for employment, education, and health care have grown, pulling more migrants north. Meanwhile differential experiences of political repression, war, natural disaster, and climate emergency push many refugees out of their home countries in the South, sometimes in waves numbering in the millions, as from Syria after 2012.

Despite these basic facts, and despite the many benefits migrants bring to societies that welcome them, political parties of many stripes in the Global North escalated anti-immigrant rhetoric, especially after 1990. Large employers of migrants tacitly supported such campaigns because they keep their employees in a precarious bargaining position in workplaces often characterized by harsh and unhealthy conditions. Governments have responded by increasing migration deterrence measures such as border fences, armed patrol cars and boats, and other hard structures. Collectively, these form an intermittent but still globe-girdling Great Wall separating North from South. This vast structure first rises as a steel barrier off the beaches south of San Diego. As it heads east toward the Gulf of Mexico, its various segments – including a few put in place by the loudly anti-immigrant US President Donald Trump – force illegal migrants on detours into the blistering deserts of the Southwestern USA, often to their deaths. From there, patrol boats in the Straits of Florida and the Mediterranean Sea take over the task of turning back migrants who use small boats and rafts to move north. The on-land version of the global Great Wall picks up again south of Gibraltar, where two short fences seal off Spain's leftover colonial enclaves at Ceuta and Melilla, Morocco, from the rest of Africa. In 2014, Turkey began constructing a huge outwork of the Great Wall – an 826-kilometer concrete barrier along its border with Syria meant to slow the flow of war refugees. The European Union added money for enforcement, while Greece built its own wall along its land border with Turkey, and Hungary added yet another line of fencing to keep Syrian refugees from seeking asylum through intermediate countries in the Balkans. Meanwhile, Turkey then added another 144 kilometers of wall on its border with Iran to stop Afghan refugees. Since 2002, Israel has maintained fences around the Gaza Strip and a 700-kilometer "Security Barrier" around the West Bank. It has also peppered mines along the Jordan River near Jericho to stop the return of Palestinians from exile, most notably from nearby Amman, Jordan. The Gulf States have built thousands of kilometers of fencing to stop migrants on temporary construction work contracts, most of them from South and Southeast Asia, from moving across borders to neighboring states. India keeps Bangladeshis out with yet another long border fence, and Australia uses patrol boats in the Timor Sea and the Torres Straight to keep an eye on southward-moving rafts carrying destitute Indonesians and other Asians. Japan seals itself off nearly entirely from refugees, also relying on its island geography to deter illegal immigrants.[10]

To supplement this hardened hemispheric border, First World and oil-rich countries developed an enormous archipelago of immigrant prisons and detention centers. This collective structure too stretches from California and Texas across all of the countries of the European Union and the Persian Gulf, and from there as far east as the extraterritorial detention camp that Australia leases from the tiny Pacific island nation of Nauru. By design, the parlous, overcrowded conditions in these centers discourage both undocumented immigrants and asylum seekers, no matter how legitimate their claims. Under Trump, the USA brutally heightened those disincentives by using its detention facilities to separate migrant children from their parents. Since such centers everywhere are always filled beyond capacity, informal camps spring up in the Global North that resemble smaller versions of Global-South "slums." Most notable was the "Jungle" of Calais, France near the rail tunnel to Great Britain. Other camps grew in the northern suburbs of Paris, in squats and parks in Brussels, Amsterdam, Lisbon, Madrid, Athens, and in tents at "hotspots" for arriving Syrian refugees on the Greek islands nearest the Turkish mainland. One of the most notorious slum clearance operation in recent years was France's decision to level the "Jungle" in 2016. Meanwhile the USA, the EU, and Australia have deported millions of illegal migrants and rejected asylum seekers during the early twenty-first century, dwarfing "Operation Wetback."[11]

The United Nations itself enables Global Apartheid in another way, by siting nearly all of its camps for war refugees in the Global South itself. In the 2010s, there were over 120 of these worldwide, some housing over 100,000 people. Some have since become permanent cities or neighborhoods, the oldest being the camps housing Palestinian refugees from the 1948 Naqba on the West Bank and in Gaza. The UN reclassifies its "temporary" camps as "protracted" when they start to take on urban functions. The 100,000-plus Kakuma and Dadaab complexes in Kenya, first established in 1991 for refugees from wars in the Horn of Africa, and the vast Zaatari camp for Syrian refugees on a desolate plain in Jordan north of Amman all have utility systems, schools, hospitals, and local governments. The million Rohingya refugees from Myanmar who settled at Cox's Bazaar, Bangladesh and other nearby locations have far fewer such amenities, but are well on their way to "protracted" status. As of 2020, the largest concentration of refugee camps is located in Turkey, along its side of the border wall with Syria. In 2016, the European Union agreed to help fund these camps, along with the wall nearby, in exchange for a commitment from Turkey to prevent refugees from moving on to Greece – let alone Paris, London, or cities deemed among "the most liberal in the world," like Berlin, Rotterdam, or Oslo.[12]

THE GILDED URBAN LAND GRAB

As imperial states in the Global North filtered poor migrants away from the Urban Planet's wealthiest cities, they granted new powers to capitalists to profit from buying and selling urban land in any city and any hemisphere they pleased. As the gap between the rich and everyone else grew in the late twentieth century, the frenzied rush to capitalize on the accelerating worth of urban property – usually known by the abbreviation "gentrification" – put further obstacles in the way of poor people's claims to the city, not only in the Global North, but also in Global South cities like Delhi.

New York City was in many ways "ground zero" for this enormous grab of land and power, which began in earnest during the 1980s when the city re-committed itself to its reputation as one of the three premier homes of the imperial financial and real estate industry. The city's transformation from the most generous social democratic municipal state in the USA to a global playground of ultra-high-capitalist finance and austerity politics had its roots in the urban crisis that Richard Nixon sought to cover up in his debate with Khrushchev. After peaking as the largest city in the world in the 1950s, New York's population had declined, thanks in part to thirty years of FHA policy encouraging middle-class people to flee the city for tailpipe suburbs. In the 1970s, the city's economy wilted further amidst the "stagflation" caused by the Middle Eastern oil embargo. As in many other "deindustrializing" Global-North cities, New York factory owners closed hundreds of their operations in hopes of finding lower labor costs elsewhere. City Hall's revenues collapsed even as demand grew for its capacious services, which included city-owned day care centers, clinics, and hospitals, a vast portfolio of public housing units, some of the most celebrated public high schools in the county, and the city's own university system, available, European-style, to students tuition-free.[13]

The city's debt-service payments to Wall Street escalated in 1975, to the point where the city's bankers refused further loans. This was a crucial moment in the transformation of First World state priorities from economic plenty for all to austerity in the interest of profit makers. The State of New York in Albany, under pressure from the post-Nixon federal government in Washington, pioneered a role that the IMF would assume during the 1980s when it imposed austerity on entire developing countries. It appointed a Financial Control Board for New York City that served the interests of Wall Street tycoons by defunding the city's educational, social, and housing services and refocused New York's budget on repaying its debt to Wall Street.[14]

Soon after, Wall Street financial and real estate firms used their own swelling lobbying power – and the electoral victory of the pro-business US President Ronald Reagan – to convince the US Congress to loosen key regulations on their industry, widening the range of speculative investments they could make, including in urban real estate. London's City joined Wall Street's political project with help from the British Prime Minister Margaret Thatcher, and Japan's financial elite followed suit. Collectively, the global financial class also whittled away remaining legal barriers to movements of wealthy people's money across borders. Demand for ultra-high-end global financial services in New York, London, and Tokyo grew. Communication technologies improved as well, allowing swifter telephone-, computer-, and soon internet-enabled transactions between the three global cities, dividing the world's twenty-four-hour cycle of speculative betting into separate, increasingly frenzied, eight-hour shifts. Far more "hot" money changed hands in these markets in a day than in all global commercial transactions in a year.[15]

Salaries in these and other secondary global cities' complexes of corporate-service firms rose, attracting large numbers of young urban professionals back into cities like New York. One result was that former industrial districts like New York's Soho, whose emptying garment factories and machine shops had been settled by artists in search of large lofts for their work, began to attract Wall Street "yuppies" and the high-end estate agents who brokered sales to them. City Hall's coffers filled once again, thanks to elevated property taxes it collected from the city's new well-heeled residents. Soon, officials in New York and cities across the USA fought against each other to dole out tax breaks to high-end developers in hopes of augmenting revenue streams from even larger influxes of yuppies. Building prices in Soho skyrocketed. The state-enabled, market-enhanced force of real estate value inflation took the name "gentrification" in New York as it advanced into new Manhattan neighborhoods like Tribeca, Chelsea, and the immigrant precinct of the Lower East Side. "As soon as they said 'East Village,'" one anti-gentrification activist put it, "they tripled the rent." Soon, similar price-hikes spread to the nearby neighborhoods of Brooklyn, Queens, and New Jersey. By the 1990s, wealthier professionals were apartment hunting in previously redlined neighborhoods like Black Harlem and Fort Greene, Brooklyn.[16]

During these years, New York's poor faced some of the same trends as in Delhi and other developing world cities. The city's public housing deteriorated, rents rose, and more people were forced to squeeze into smaller spaces, including dilapidated "welfare hotels" converted into public shelters. The South Bronx, victim of an earlier "urban renewal" scheme – Robert Moses's Cross-Bronx Expressway – became a global symbol of urban apocalypse in the heart of the richest society on Earth. Owners of slum buildings set fire to their structures to claim insurance payouts far in excess of potential rental income. The numbers of homeless people exploded meanwhile. New York's streets, subway stations, and even some parts of the sewer system filled with residents, regularly inviting comparison to the sidewalks of Calcutta. New York's crime rate rose precipitously. Crack cocaine ravaged many families, and lifespans in Black neighborhoods diminished to "Third World" levels.[17]

New York has nonetheless attracted well over a million overseas migrants since 1980, both legal and undocumented, from almost everywhere in the world. Some arrived with enough family capital to start small businesses. Most took low-paying jobs similar to migrants' most common occupations in cities like Delhi – in construction, domestic service, childcare, dog-walking, laundry, restaurant service, taxi driving (later ridehailing), delivery, and small sidewalk stall ownership. Shantytowns never grew remotely as large as those in Delhi, but many undocumented migrants camped rough where they could in New York, some in the same subway tunnels and sewers inhabited by US-born homeless people. Most found cheaper housing far from their jobs, piled up in tiny apartments, slept in cars and delivery vans, or alternated shifts in dormitory "hotbeds" with others – for example in the basements of Chinatown restaurants. Informal markets such as the one established by African immigrant stall owners along 125th Street in Harlem grew, and then faced dismantlement and relocation by City Hall to less lucrative spaces.[18]

In gentrifying neighborhoods, meanwhile, poorer residents, and even some more well-off homeowners, faced sharp hikes in rent or property taxes, and many had to look elsewhere to live. Gentrification-driven displacement – like slum clearances by government bulldozer – can destroy social ties crucial to poorer people's survival and upend small neighborhood businesses. Unlike the "best" slum-clearance programs, gentrifiers do not typically provide affordable replacement housing. To the contrary, upward pressure on prices tends to diminish a city's overall stock of shelter for low-income people, and its quality. Like those displaced by slum clearances, victims of gentrification often face larger transport costs to get to work.[19]

Amidst the devastation of austerity, a new global "Gilded Age" had dawned. As the Earthopolis's wealthiest people sharply increased their share of the worlds' income and wealth, they also expanded their claim to the most expensive parts of the Urban Planet, even building "new addresses" for themselves, such as New York's Battery Park, built on land claimed from the Hudson River, and London's postindustrial Docklands. High rents and apartment prices are just as effective at keeping everyone but the wealthiest out as are the guard-shacks of suburban gated communities that the global real estate developers have built worldwide. In addition to creating a class of high-salaried employees, the world's foremost capitals of capital sparked the wealth grab in at least two other ways. Their increasingly powerful financial firms used their proximity to the necessary law offices and other services to devise new classes of financial derivatives for high-end investors only. The quickly rising value of real estate in those cities gave wealthier people from anywhere in the world a way to diversify their portfolios while hiding wealth from local tax collectors. By the mid 2010s, the value of all of the world's derivatives – despite a few spectacular roller-coaster dives along the way – exceeded an incomprehensible one quadrillion dollars. The value of the world's real estate also inflated in dramatic fashion in three waves during the 1980s, the late 1990s, and again after the financial crash of 2008, reaching 228 trillion dollars worldwide in 2019. This estimate, by one of the foremost real estate investment firms, is no doubt elevated for marketing purposes, but it remains the closest approximation we have of the price of the Urban Planet as a whole. While lower than the global traffic in financial instruments, the world's buildable hard ground and the structures it supports are worth almost three times as much as the world's annual income, plus the total value of all the world's stock and bond markets, plus all the gold ever mined.[20]

The twenty-first-century global urban economy pivots more tumultuously upon the whims and bubble-bursts of its most arcane financial casinos, and upon high-rolling investments in glittery trophy towers. Meanwhile it whipsaws the lives of the world's urban poor – putting the wealth of many middle-class people at risk as well. The most egregious example was the financial crisis of 2008. Wall Street banks and hedge funds subcontracted with ill-meaning mortgage companies to sell fraudulent "predatory" home loans to millions of ordinary home-buyers in the USA and Europe. Such mortgages bound homeowners to adjustable rates of interest, meaning that their monthly repayment bills were subject to abrupt upward fluctuations. In the USA, such predatory schemes disproportionately targeted people of color long ignored by the mortgage industry, giving the practice the apt name "reverse redlining." Financial mills on Wall Street nonetheless won approval from credit rating agencies located in neighboring office buildings to "securitize" the promise of future gains on these loans and to sell the resulting exotic instruments widely to wealthier clients. The same financiers sold elaborate insurance contracts on the same securities, essentially betting on their demise. When the original mortgagees' loan payments escalated, many found themselves "underwater" – possessing homes that were worth far less than the debt they owed. The value of the securities based on these loans collapsed as the insurance obligations soared. The resulting financial cascade in 2008 took down several Wall Street firms before the US Treasury stepped in to bail out the rest of the toxic mess. Within a year or so, Wall Street and the City were back at it, speculating on new shining slivers of refined, digitized, thin air. Defrauded mortgagees, by contrast, suffered foreclosure and lifetimes of collapsed personal wealth. African Americans' hard-won share of housing wealth from the redlined American Dream fell from one-tenth that of whites of similar incomes to one-twentieth.[21]

The 2008 crisis did little to stop the global urban land grab. Petrodollar investors from the Middle East, Russian oligarchs, Latin American tycoons, and wealthy Shanghainese and Hong Kongers have joined European and Japanese investors in pouring magnificent sums into real estate in Manhattan and elsewhere. The value of New York City, once famously purchased for twenty-four dollars by a Dutch ship captain, now stands somewhere close to two trillion. One Donald J. Trump, the world's most notorious salesperson of high-end architectural baubles in New York and elsewhere, used his financial leverage and an uncanny capacity for fraudulence to become president of the USA. A full three-quarters of the world's wealth in land and buildings is located in just 100 of the world's cities, most in North America, Europe, and coastal East Asia. In the 2010s, the new Gilded Age took its most arrogant built form in New York's 200- and 300-million-dollar-plus apartments, perched high in structures taller than the Empire State Building. Many imitations sprouted in London, Frankfurt, Toronto, Vancouver, San Francisco, Hong Kong, former-Communist Moscow, still-Communist Shanghai, and most improbably, in the former slice of Arabian Desert that became Dubai. Many of these properties remain vacant, as their main purpose is to shelter their owners' money from their home countries' tax officials. As such, they form part of a larger archipelago of built structures that the journalist Oliver Bullough calls "Moneyland," also consisting, in part, of smaller "off-shore" financial districts in Liechtenstein, the Cayman Islands, Panama City, and Taipei, Taiwan – perhaps the ultimate in boutique "spatial fixes" for the hyper-wealthy. Meanwhile, shelter in New York – like dozens of other cities that are similarly awash in this most orgiastic moment of "capitalist urbanization" – became ever harder to afford for the workers who make its "real" economy work. Population growth has slowed once again in many First World cities, including New York, due to a widening epidemic of urban unaffordability.[22]

By the 1990s, the leading edge of the Gilded Age land grab also sliced into "emerging" Global South megacities. In 1991, the Indian parliament ended Nehru-era restrictions on the entry of foreign money – as part of the same "austerity" legislation that, as we have seen, rolled back munici-pal ownership of water companies and cut subsidies to farmers. In the early 2000s, Delhi's Planning Board launched a campaign to transform Delhi "From a Walled City to a World City." Soon, global real estate service firms' glossy websites touted "the bright future" available in India to those with the right amounts of capital in the right forms. Savills of London enthused that "population growth, urbanization, accel-erating GDP, and the development of top commercial districts all con-tribute to India being in the spotlight for global real estate investors." In other words, partly *because* poor people's self-built houses were radiating outward into the periphery of Delhi, the city's newest wave of wealthy conquerors were being advised to seize portions of the same valuable peripheral land for far more scintillating habitats.[23]

In Delhi's case, the most spectacular transformation began already after about 1995 in the old village of Gurgaon (recently renamed Gurugram to suit Hindu nationalist fashion). Because the town sat on land zoned for agriculture, developers working for wealthy Indians applied to the local authorities for permission to build "farmhouses" that soon became luxury compounds instead. As in New York, many of these remained unoccupied most months of the year – the servant staff excepted – waiting for the cooler (if smokier) winter months when their owners jet in for family gatherings from their first homes, in tower condominiums in Toronto or Dubai. "World-class" luxury shopping malls based on American models sprouted up near the farmhouses. One of these boasts "more marble than the Taj Mahal." Most of the world's largest corporations maintain office space in the former village's new spiky crown of corporate office towers – often compared to Houston or, inevitably, Manhattan. Gurugram also gained its own ring of "slums" and a population that soared toward two million. Yet, just as the capital of India moved southward in earlier times – from the Mughals' Red Fort, to the British Viceroy's Palace, to the Parliament of the Republic of India – so Delhi's newest imperial capital, this one belonging to Gilded Age capital itself, has moved ten kilometers further south, to Gurugram.[24]

CHAI QIAN WORLDWIDE

"States," wrote the sociologist Erhard Berner bluntly, "have been far more effective in the destruction of mass housing than in its construction." Indeed, for newly independent developmental states, the most forceful form of discouragement to rural migrants is the old Haussmannian practice of bulldozing the urban neighborhoods that those migrants build for themselves. The practice has done little to stop inward flows of people, but it is gloomily persistent, perhaps because it disguises so many unsavory authoritarian or land-grabbing projects as high-minded crusades for public health, national "beautification," or glamourous "World City" status. In the 1940s, when truly large self-built shantytowns began growing on the peripheries of Latin American cities, governing regimes cleared slums to uproot opposition social movements that incubated there, or to remove what they deemed shameful signs of national poverty from the eyes of visiting foreign dignitaries. More often, states forged lucrative alliances with private developers to clear land for construction of up-scale real estate ventures. There, class segregation by means of slum clearance looked very similar to racial segregation conducted by the same means – as in many colonial cities, South Africa, and the USA. Indeed, American overseas housing aid often came in handy for clearance projects. In those cases, bulldozers became Cold War weapons.

Finally, as the historian Nandini Gooptu argued, poor people, especially people of color or, in India, of lower caste, make easy rhetorical scapegoats for elites. The "war against slums" in Northern India, she wrote, became the equivalent of privileged peoples' "offensive against the poor themselves."[25]

No matter the guiding passion involved, slum clearance has littered late-twentieth- and early-twenty-first-century global urban history with forlorn remains of bulldozed shacks and cinderblock homes. In the 1950s, powerful mayors like Ernesto Uruchurtu Peralta of Mexico City, or dictators like Marcos Pérez Jiménez of Venezuela and Rafael Trujillo of the Dominican Republic distinguished themselves in the art of trolling for middle-class support by flattening the houses of the poor. In Rio de Janeiro, Cold War housing aid from the USA supported repeated assaults on the city's hillside *favelas*. After 1970, the pace of slum clearance quickened as policies of plenty gave way to austerity. People's liberation movements in Africa and Asia, now transformed into ruling regimes, adjusted their calculations about the value of elite support and the expendability of slums. The socialist poet-president of Senegal Léopold Senghor betrayed his own way with words on the way to bulldozing the homes of some 90,000 "human encumbrances" near downtown Dakar. Indira Gandhi, daughter of Jawaharlal Nehru, seized absolute power in India for twenty-four months in 1975 to 1977, and evicted 70,000 slum dwellers from downtown Bombay and thousands from Old Delhi's Muslim Turkman Gate and Jamma Masjid neighborhoods, among many others across the country. The ruling Communist Party (Marxist) of Kolkata has harassed *bustee* and sidewalk dwellers continuously. From 1986 to 1989, Joaquín Balaguer of the Dominican Republic continued Trujillo's assaults on Santo Domingo's *colonias populares*, displacing 180,000 of their residents by bulldozer. Authorities in Seoul topped that by moving 800,000 from dilapidated neighborhoods to clean the city's face in advance of the 1988 Olympics; Rio did the same to 60,000 people in advance of the 2016 games. The Nigerian military leveled Lagos's fabled Maroko district in 1990; the Kenyan army did the same to large portions of Nairobi's Kibera the same year. The Burmese junta obliterated slums in Yangon (Rangoon) and Mandalay from 1996 on, affecting perhaps a million. A half-million were displaced in Djakarta in

2001–3, and the Zimbabwean dictator Robert Mugabe perfected the art of vengeful spatial politics in 2005 by destroying the homes of over three-quarters of a million of Harare's squatters in Operation *Murambatsvina* ("Drive out the Rubbish").[26]

The largest government clearances of all time, however, occur in the cities of post-Mao China as part of the policy of *chai qian* – "Demolish and Relocate." During the 1980s, Mao's successor, the former Paris autoworker Deng Xiaoping, reoriented China's industrial economy along Communist Party-driven capitalist principles. He and his successors selectively relaxed the *hukou* system to funnel more farmers into factories. Older housing in city centers filled up, and the specter of 1950s shantytowns rose again. Deng lifted bans on owning property, but Beijing later gave local officials sweeping powers to acquire land and lease it out, tying their careers to evidence that such leases maximized land value, increased municipal revenues, and promoted regional economic growth. The incentives to raze older housing downtown for corporate uses was overwhelming, as was the impulse to seize peripheral land for high-rise residential developments for downtown displacees and rural migrants. A few savvy home and farm owners held out for higher indemnification payments. Their "nail homes," single older houses in fields of otherwise leveled ground, became poignant symbols of resistance to *chai qian*. Large street protests also erupted, most fleetingly, before being smothered by the police. The CCP forcibly removed two and a - half million people from central Beijing and Shanghai alone from 1985 to 2000. Many of the capital's famous *hutong* (lane) districts were destroyed, along with the elegant *siheyuan* courtyard houses that lined them, to make room for skyscrapers, elite housing, and, once again, Olympic venues. The number of displaced people in China's four other megacities and its 124 million-plus cities are anyone's best guess. Many inner-city residential spaces in China remain in deplorable state, and thousands of illegal rural *hukou* factory workers live in barracks-like structures or in hidden slums. The official solution is more *chai qian* and more twenty- to thirty-story apartment buildings on the urban periphery. Tens of thousands of these buildings tromp across swaths of peri-urban farmland in staggering parades that totally eclipse anything Nikita Khrushchev could have ever imagined. Only one home-building program in world history rivals the Chinese one in size: the "planet of the slums" itself.[27]

CITIES OF THE POOR

Try as they might, no state, no global financial center, no gentrifying capitalist, and no army of bulldozers has succeeded in turning back the "challenge of the slums." The UN's tally of one billion slum dwellers in 2003 aligned well with the urban planner Patrick Geddes's prognosis from the early 1960s: "Slum, semi-slum, and super-slums, to this has come the Evolution of cities."[28]

Perhaps so, but the "s-word" poorly suits the task of telling us why this is so. The arch mix of Victorian contempt and shock that freight the word slum, leavened only perhaps with pity, remains too useful as a means to cover up the long chain of global power-plays responsible for the rural-to-urban acceleration and the gauntlet of obstacles migrants face on their way to cities and after they get there. Instead, "slum" most often serves to blame the poor themselves for the state of the places they inhabit, and, from there, to dislodge them from the land they occupy. "Slum," conversely, also confuses our understanding of poor people's very real part in the saga. A billion poor people truly did not just stand on the sidelines while rocket-like projections of elite power careened around the Urban Planet in their general direction. The great cities of the poor, like all urban majority neighborhoods, came into being through poor people's own audacious, multitudinous, collective acts as much as by their tragic victimhood and vulnerability. In grasping this contradiction of boldness and precarity, we need to avoid slandering urban poor people, but also avoid turning the one billion poorest urban residents on Earth into humanity's greatest heroes. The many synonyms we have invented for *slum* make this subtle work difficult, for they contain vast thickets of sensationalism and caricature – a proliferation of misleading images that can be difficult to un-see.[29]

Meanwhile, many synonyms for "slum" have come into circulation to describe the condition of poor people's urban environments, starting with words evoking the simplicity and improvisational nature of structures. The mid-twentieth-century French term *bidonvilles* ("oil-can cities") highlights the material recycled in the shack settlements that came and went in the suburbs of 1950s Paris, and that now sprawl around many cities of French-speaking Africa. So does the older Portuguese *caniços* for the "reed towns" of the Mozambican capital Maputo. Shantytowns, shack towns, Caracas's *ranchos*, Delhi's *jugghi jhopris* (JJs, roughly, "hut towns"), and the old French word *taudis* (a tent, derived from an old word for the covering of medieval siege works) all refer to modest, improvised structures. The *bustees*, or *basti*, of Kolkata and Karachi, and the *kampungs* of Djakarta are both older words for "village" that have since stuck as urban terms. Such words, along with "transit camp" or "squatter camp," imply that migrants bring less sophisticated forms of rural habitat into the city with them. Istanbul's *gecekondu* ("appear overnight") and the *villes champignons* ("mushroom towns") of francophone cities disparage neighborhoods that appear out of nowhere, spread rapidly, and often disappear. *Favela*, the term of art in Brazil, refers to trees that grow on Rio de Janeiro's steep mountainsides; it implies a kind of spontaneous profusion. The word "colony," or in Latin America *colonia*, likewise evokes large gatherings of shore birds. Indeed, animalistic imagery has been part of "slum" talk for over a century, from the "rookeries" and "dens" of nineteenth-century New York to more recent "rabbit coops," "cocklofts," and *cages à poules* (henhouses), to "slumdog," a word that entered the global slum-lexicon thanks to *Slumdog Millionaire*, the Oscar-winning 2008 film set in Mumbai.

Such words draw attention away from the diversity, the changing nature, and the ambiguous borders of the cities of the poor. Poor people often acquire collective economic resources and political connections needed to rebuild the places where they live, often resulting in sturdier, more permanent structures. Temporary structures (*kuchha* in Delhi) can support livelihoods that then help pay for more permanent ones, say, built in brick (*pucca*). A profusion of rubber hoses drawing drinking water to shacks from the city's official mains, the mass of electric wires atop teetering poles that draw power from municipal lampposts, or informal sewage dumps or garbage incinerators in streets can act as implicit and eloquent demands for more solid infrastructure. City planning departments that otherwise focus on demolition can sometimes be swayed to make at least piecemeal improvements, say, in exchange for votes. The urban poor also often reuse older structures for residential purposes. They have built new housing by subdividing the textile workers' *chawls* (dormitories) of Mumbai for example, or the warehouses of Manila's Port Three, the bourgeois high-rises of Johannesburg's Hillbrow, and the burial chambers in Cairo's massive cemetery, the City of the Dead.[30]

As space in such cities of the poor gains value, a class of speculators, many of whom may have been born in shacks themselves, buy up plots, subdivide, and build precariously upward in order to rent to poorer people. The urban critic Mike Davis sardonically referred to this type of urban evolution as "Manhattanized" slums. The oldest *favelas* in Rio are the easiest to see, for their four- and five-story apartments float impressively (and dangerously) up the city's mountainsides. Hong Kong's shanties grew into twenty- and thirty-story towers of "Kowloon Wall City" and its famous tiny "cockloft" apartments. Istanbul's *gecekondu* evolved as early as the 1970s from "over-night" tents into ten-story apartments, many of which now house the non-poor perilously on top of the city's twitchy earthquake faults. As Davis hinted, this form of Mahattanization is far from the kind that produced 100-million-dollar penthouses. Rather, think of turn-of-the-twentieth-century Manhattan's tenements – highly dangerous environments for all who live there, the epitome of housing market failure.[31]

Indeed, as in poor neighborhoods of the contemporary USA, Global South cities of the poor are filled with ambient asbestos, silica, and mold as well as cohabiting insects and rodents, and their airborne dried excrement. Microbiotic pathogens of all kinds and water-borne toxins including sewage are all central features of the built environments of the cities of the poor. The poor everywhere suffer greater exposure to industrial and environmental toxins brought on by their segregation on lower-valued land, near factories, refineries, power plants, plastics plants, construction sites, road dust, landfills, high-tension wires, flooding rivers, rising oceans, polluted air, and urban "heat islands," zones where the world's rising summer temperatures are particularly withering. House fires can be especially vicious, stoked by use of wood or cardboard building materials, by the sheer density of rooms and streets, and by

(A)

(B)

22.2. Do-It-Yourself Urban Infrastructure: A Manual from São Paulo
Residents of "Blocolândia," a *favela* in São Paulo's Eastern Zone, rebuild their shacks in brick, solidifying their "insurgent" claim to citizenship in the megacity. A merchant selling *blocos* (A) gives the place its name. Hoses from a city main supply fresh water (B). Electricity comes from streetlights via wires on makeshift poles (C). Sewage flows through plastic pipes directly into the river, whose repeated floods are fought back with sandbag retaining walls (D). This

(C)

(D)

22.2. (cont.) infrastructure insurgency may be winning, as indicated by the "formal" cement electric poles and a city bus (C). Since Blocolândia lies eighteen kilometers from downtown, its citizens, most from Brazil's distant northeast, will need to travel onward each day for work in South America's most explosive urban nebula.
Photographs from the author's collection.

the lack of water systems that could help douse them. Arson is a classic political weapon in the cities of the poor, sometimes wielded by corrupt officials, sometimes by owners in search of insurance payouts. All of these environmental dangers have been highlighted as Covid-19 rages through the self-built homes of the world's poorest people, since so few of these structures have access to clean water, and since dense conditions make distancing all but impossible.[32]

Another group of synonyms for *slum* emphasizes the shaky legitimacy of poor people's claim to urban space. The term "squatter camp" highlights the most rudimentary of such claims – occupation of space by the occupant's body alone, without title or payment. *Squatter* also carries a sense that the urban poor of the Global South share a heroic left-kinship with the mixed-class anti-gentrification "squats" of Berlin's Kreuzberg or New York's Lower East Side – as fellow soldiers in the war against landlordism and capital. In fact, however, land in most Global South megacities – even in the poorest ones, even on the farthest peripheries, and even in the city's most dangerous environmental zones – has gotten so valuable that true squatting is not sustainable for long. More often, new migrants' claim to the city resembles that of Bogotá's *urbanizaciones piratas* ("pirate settlements"), in which established "owners" – legitimate or not – sell "titles" to occupants, but in violation of local zoning ordinances, typically on land that authorities deem unfit for building and which are equipped most often with the barest of sanitary infrastructure.[33]

Far more common are rent arrangements, typically without leases, sometimes relatively non-exploitative, but too often augmented with protection payments to police or local criminal gangs. From the 1980s forward, the World Bank, eager for cheaper ways to house the poor, urged countries simply to grant poor people formal titles to the land they occupied. Some neighborhoods gained stability from this act, but just as many suffered onerous obligations stemming from legal disputes, taxes, and debt. Many simply sold their newly valuable plots to slightly wealthier speculators, explaining why some poor neighborhoods "Manhattanized" overnight. In those instances, titles only increased the number of dangerous places to live instead of improving them.[34]

The vocabulary of the slum also includes political words. Take the highly ambiguous term *colonias populares* from Mexico City – an early prime destination for massive country-to-city migration, a city that is now home to some of the world's largest cities of the poor, including the endless million-plus Nezahualcoyotl. Who are the "people" in this word *popular*? From the days when Parisians invented the phrase *quartiers populaires*, invoking "the People" could serve to do many things: pity the cringing, unwashed, illiterate masses; vilify shifting migrants as having no legitimate claim to the city (Haussmann's view); sound alarms about crime and disorder; or salute great right-nationalist and/or left-proletarian heroes. As examples of the latter, populist politicians left and right in Lima and Caracas celebrated the slums as "*ciudades jovenes*" (young cities). Other words evoke spiteful agendas of race, caste, and religion. The *musseques* of Luanda, for example, derive from Portuguese settlers' contemptuous word for the Black districts of town, perpetuating inaccurate and blameful equations of people of color with the poor. The widespread use of the racial word "ghetto" to mean some closer relative of "slum" does the same work. In Delhi, the word "ghetto" resonates dangerously alongside old colonial words like "location," and "colony" itself, to describe neighborhoods of lower-caste people ("Harijan colonies") or impoverished Muslims. Hindu nationalists – including many very poor urban people – equate "Muslim locations" with "slumdogs" more generally, dehumanizing both in the process.[35]

What political role do the billion poorest people of the Urban Planet play in the modern history of People Power? A very large one. They build diverse social movements much like other disadvantaged urban residents in modern history. Given the increasing press of government-led evictions and various versions of *chai qian*, many of these movements focus on defense of their claims to the space where they live. Yet they also fight for better public health infrastructure, affordable and safe food, environmental remediation, attention to climate change, and, as we shall see in the next chapter, better, safer, and more remunerative work. Since the 1980s, dozens of anti-IMF protests against austerity and structural adjustment have relied upon the leadership of people from the cities of the poor. Some local movements have built coalitions between cities, like the transformative Slum Dwellers International, which grew from connections between activists in Dharavi Mumbai and the "squatter camps" of Soweto and now has chapters across the Global South. By contrast, some movements of the poor also splinter badly along national, racial, caste, and religious lines – perhaps none more egregiously than in the repeated bouts of anti-Muslim violence in the cities of India. Class divisions also exist within the cities of the poor, between those who rent and those who own, and between those who work in factories and those who run them. As in all cities, criminal enterprises sometimes control whole neighborhoods. James Holston, the great chronicler of life in the *favelas* of São Paulo's massive Zona Leste, urges us to see the cities of the poor as places of "insurgent citizenship," but to remain well aware that the people's insurgencies there, as anywhere, can be "both subversive and reactionary, inclusionary and exclusionary, a project of equalization and one of maintaining inequality."[36]

For the poor themselves, the most dangerous political threat comes at moments when the state classifies their settlement as "informal," "unplanned," "unauthorized," or, worse, "illegal." While these terms have become nearly as ubiquitous as "slum," the fact is that very few developmental states have been able to impose planning, zoning, building, title registration, public utility, or tax regulations on most neighborhoods in their cities – whether in poor, middle-class, or even wealthy neighborhoods. The Delhi Department of Planning, for example, acknowledged in 2000 that only one-third of the city consisted of "planned settlements" – the rest, including big swaths of gilded Gurgaon, was "informal" to one degree or another. Despite this level of state failure, informality and illegality become effective weapons in state-led *chai qian* directed at the poorest and most vulnerable.[37]

The rash of slum clearances ordered by the Delhi Department of Planning after 1991 is a good example. These acts flew in the face of Nehru-era housing legislation that had emphasized the humanity of *in situ*, or on-site, rehabilitation of poor people's self-built neighborhoods, and recognized the sheer cost to the poor of destruction and removal. The premise of these earlier laws was that "slums" were vehicles for poor people to leave behind their status as impoverished or indebted farmers in the countryside and secure a marginally better livelihood in the city. Proximity to work sites is the most important asset that a self-built neighborhood can offer. In its 2003 *Challenge of Slums* Report, the United Nations similarly declared itself in favor of "comprehensive on-site renovation" – providing better housing and all utilities at the original site of settlement – as a way to guarantee continuity of employment and a chance for upward mobility. International movements of shack dwellers have emphasized that their "right to livelihood" and even their "right to the city" depend on a moratorium on both *chai* and *qian* – eviction and resettlement.[38]

After 1991, however, according to the Delhi-born sociologist Gautam Bhan, Delhi's Planning Department weaponized the derogatory slum-synonyms "illegal settlement" and "encroachment" to mobilize anti-slum sentiment among the near-poor and middle class – as well as grassroots anti-Muslim sentiment among Hindus – against the city's hundreds of *jhuggi jhopri* ("JJ") clusters. In 2004, the department destroyed Yamuna Pushta, a "JJ cluster" of 150,000 people, the homes of migrant construction workers whom the Indian state had recruited to build the venues for the Commonwealth Games in Delhi. The municipality justified this pitiless action on the grounds that the settlement drew too much attention to poverty at a moment when those very Games trained international eyes on Delhi's progress as a World-Class City. Altogether, the department destroyed the homes of some 300,000 people between 1990 and 2012. Relocations have since taken an increasingly anti-Muslim tone with the rise to power of the Hindu nationalist Prime Minister Narendra Modi. In Delhi, as elsewhere in India, evicted *jhuggi jhopri* inhabitants are not relocated to brand new tower blocks, as in China, or even to small township houses as in apartheid South Africa. The luckiest get title to empty sites or sometimes to rudimentary houses on peripheral land far from their work, rarely with full utility hookups. Displacees' incomes typically fall drastically the moment they are resettled – by 50 percent, Bhan calculates in the case of the Yamuna River displacees. Thus, eviction can result in an expansion of even poorer slums – not "eradication."[39]

THE CONUNDRUM OF "SLUMS"

Each year Delhi's Planning Board (DPB) counts its many forms of slums – using almost as many slum-synonyms. "About one third of Delhi," declares its 2019 report, referring to about seven million people, "lives in sub-standard housing." From there, drifts of slum words accumulate: "695 slum and JJ clusters, 1797 unauthorized colonies, [unnumbered] old dilapidated areas, and 362 villages"; unnumbered instances of "unauthorized regularized colonies infill" (the DPB's word for "Manhattanization"); 135 "Urban Villages" and 227 "villages not yet notified as urban." On top of that, the board also – somehow – counted 16,000 "Homeless and Pavement Dwellers" in the city; other estimates range above 50,000. Lastly, thanks to the DPB's *chai qian* there are no less than eighty-two "Resettlement Colonies," only some with "good shelter consolidation," all of these "still without adequate services."[40]

Piles of words like this only begin to account for the conundrum of the great cities of the world's poor. Since 1945, they have accelerated in size amidst an Urban Planetary war over mobility, land, and homes originally set in motion largely by the world's most powerful states and capitalists. These forces at once expanded the global population, immiserated the countryside, put obstacles in the way of streams of rural-to-urban migration, funneled much larger ones into poorer cities, then took huge amounts of urban land away from millions of the migrants who arrived there. The poor themselves responded to these deeds with countless acts of movement, settlement, construction, adaptation to defeat, rebuilding, resettlement, internal division, resistance, and bare survival.

Where does that leave us so far? Between 1945 and 2020 poor people's collective acts of city-building have outflanked all of the counter-challenges. Despite all of the bulldozers, the Newest New Delhi grew continually. So did places like Rochinha in Rio, Nezahualcoyotl in Mexico City, Ajegunle in Lagos, Kinshasa's immense Cité, Nairobi's Kibera, Cape Town's Khayelitsha, Mumbai's Dharavi, the enormous slum belt of Dhaka South, Manila's Tondo and Payatas, the vast riverside and rail line cities of the poor in Djakarta, and the settlements of hundreds of millions of the newest and most vulnerable city dwellers in countless places elsewhere. Only the arrival of Covid-19 in 2020 appreciably slowed the growth of the great cities of the poor, by blazing through so many self-built neighborhoods and forcing many recent migrants to return, at least temporarily, to the countryside. Time will of course tell, but if historical experience is any guide, the greatest pandemics on their own can only reverse urban growth for so long, especially if larger and longer-term forces – such as those driving twenty-first-century-style rural immiseration and climate migration – continue to make cities so essential to the survival of so many billions.

Survival, indeed. Exploring cities' capacity to deliver it, even in its most rudimentary forms, is an essential next step if we are to fully solve the conundrum of the urban poor. As advocates of "*in-situ* rehabilitation" have observed, poor city dwellers build houses in places where they can sell their labor and acquire the food and goods that keep them alive. During the Greatest Acceleration, our Urban Planet's workplaces and marketplaces have transformed as much as its giant, unfurling fans of new homes. Our next step is to pay these worksites and shops a visit too. They not only help us understand why so many of us moved from villages to cities, they explain why so many billions of us put such a high value on actually *staying* in cities, sometimes in apocalyptic circumstances, once arrived.

CHAPTER 23

Greatest Accelerations III: Pleasure Palaces and Sweatshops

ORBITS OF WANT AND WORK

Our ride in the auto-rickshaw teaches us many things, but one of the more valuable lessons is that an accelerating Urban Planet must satisfy a growing number of people's needs and desires while offering a growing number of people places to work. A rickshaw orbiting a giant city does these things, all the while doing its part to make the city grow even more. It is at once a workplace – a place where drivers like the Pandit Sharma Karma sell their time and labor behind the wheel – and it is a space that satisfies its passengers' transportation needs. The money that passengers pay the auto-walla for his work allows him and his family members to visit marketplaces to buy the food and household items they need, thus sustaining the marketplaces. It also allows both drivers and customers to earn what they need to keep their house in place on a piece of urban land, so that they can eat and sleep comfortably enough to give them the force for another day at work. Meanwhile the rickshaw allows the city to grow and function better, for an exploding nebula like Delhi needs vehicles that get people to work on time despite the city's traffic and the sclerotic congestion of its many small streets. Rickshaws also attract tourists by promising the thrill of a lifetime buzzing through the city's awe-inspiring rush hours and visiting its stupendous sites. Those tourists deposit more money into the pockets of many Diliwallas – thus feeding worldwide flows of cash that also drive Earthopolitan acceleration.

As the auto-rickshaw does on a microscopic scale, so Delhi does on a megacity scale – and so the Urban Planet does on a Greatly Accelerating scale. Since 1945, Delhi and cities everywhere have grown alongside new spaces of need and desire and new workplaces. Our Cities of Delight –

habitats for need-satisfaction, desire, entertainment, buying, and selling – grew everywhere in size, extent, variety, quantity, inventory, and impact. From countless stalls much smaller than a rickshaw and shops barely larger, they range upward in size to mega-malls, online shopping sites, luxury real estate markets, and the jet-borne global tourist industry. Today these spaces shelter an Urban Planetary consumer culture of a size and energy unimaginable in 1945. Our Cities of Toil have also grown. The world is covered with little workshops that, like rickshaws, often produce what they sell; some double as homes. Meanwhile, factories of all sizes – from tiny sweatshops to city-sized assembly plants – burst the old boundary that limited their growth in the Global South. Like short-hop auto-rickshaw rides across Delhi, Earthopolis's much longer-distance transport infrastructure – the world's many "Belts" and "Roads," to use boastful terminology from Beijing – connects workshops to factories, tax-free export zones to ports, container ships to railyards and trains, trucking hubs to overgrown warehouses, and fulfillment centers to fleets of delivery vans. Put all of these workplaces end to end, and you get today's "global assembly lines" or, as capitalists call them, "global value chains," the systems of work and production that provision most of the world's Cities of Desire while fattening profits ("value") each step of the way. Meanwhile, the Great Accelerations in spaces of desire, need, work, and production both gave their power to and took their power from Great Accelerations of people, food, health, buildings, urban land value, imperial power, capitalist power, and, of course, hydrocarbon.

Before we launch ourselves into these giddy orbits, three quick warnings from the back of the rickshaw. First, quickened circuits of consumption and production *connect* the rickshaw, the city, and the planet, but all of these spaces remain deeply unequal and divided. The canyon between the highest-price mega-malls and the lowliest sweatshops is just as obscene as the one between empty, tax-sheltering 300-million-dollar Manhattan penthouses and crowded Delhi shacks. Second, remember again, that, as with auto-rickshaws, repeated stops at the great Urban Planetary petrol station (Chapter 24) are necessary, with all the consequences. Third, where do we put all the stuff we desire and produce once we are done with it? Where is this wild ride heading, we must ask, and when will the riders' bill come due?

(A)

(B)

23.1. Pleasure Palaces and Sweatshops

What do we learn by juxtaposing a glittering fashion mall in Cairo (A) with a collapsed sweatshop in Dhaka where 1,132 seamstresses lost their lives (B)? First, we learn that both spaces have traveled far from their North American and European birthplaces. Second, we expose their hydrocarbon links: fashion gets to fashionistas thanks to coal plants, container ships, planes, trucks, and delivery vans, not to mention the cars that deliver most customers to malls. Third, we refute the glittering propaganda of the global advertising industry.

A PLANET OF DESIRE

Ever since we lived in villages, marketplaces have been our habitat's organs of desire. Markets give off pheromones from afar – via pulse-quickening word of mouth or seductive modern "marketing." Enter a good shop, stall, bazaar, or *souq,* and new cravings bloom while familiar ones re-ignite; satisfactions culminate in exchanges of goods, food, amenities, "experiences," currency, credit card taps, or smartphone scans. It is no secret – in a time when the political worship of "markets" is so fervent and when our cities are growing with such abandon – that the Urban Planet's habitats of desire have hypertrophied. Indeed, marketplaces also possess reproductive functions. The enticing pulse of commercial space acts as one of the most powerful gravitational forces drawing us to cities. The engorgement of Cities of Desire is essential to Urban Planetary acceleration more generally.

Getting consumer desires going – the initial act of arousal – arguably requires the largest of the built precincts of Cities of Desire. Advertising can seem to engulf whole cities and even large landscapes beyond them; more recently, it also suffuses, and largely finances, the brash, enormous, and accelerating realm of "virtual" space. We have come a long way from the days when shops in Edo and Paris, for example, supplemented small medieval-era artisans' "shingles" with larger woodcut shop signs, and when shop-owners hired people to distribute the first advertising flyers. Newspaper advertising brought the business of awakening consumer desire into seventeenth-century coffee shops, then into the very sanctuary of homes. In the streets, woodcuts gave way to mid-nineteenth-century "posters." Commentators in 1860s New York rued the "thousands of tons of paper and oceans of paste consumed in decorating the fences." Soon they could protest similarly about the cluttered sides of trams, buses, lampposts, the back and front panels carried by "sandwich men," and the ubiquitous billboards – "hoardings" in the British Empire – atop

---

Caption for 23.1. (cont.)

Plastered on urban surfaces everywhere and posted throughout the "virtual" world, its goal is to channel maximum desire towards one of these spaces while negating the existence of the other.
(A) Franz-Marc Frei/Getty Images. (B) K. M. Asad/LightRocket/Getty Images.

buildings and along roadways. Meanwhile, radio and television slipped consumer pheromones deeper into private spaces like living rooms, kitchens, bedrooms, and even bathrooms. Telephone books delivered to doorsteps served as domesticated encyclopedias of the urban marketplace's many allures; not so long ago, the urban theorist Jane Jacobs thought the thickness of the local phone book the best measure of the energies of a city's economic crowds. Neon signs, first developed in 1910s Paris to sell Cinzano vermouth, meanwhile blinked and blared in commercial districts everywhere. Times Square, New York, London's Piccadilly Circus, and Tokyo's Shibuya were overwhelmed with neon, as were America's car-based spaces of enticement like Los Angeles's Sunset Strip and *The* Strip in Las Vegas. In places like these, the density of human eyes brought on the density of advertising, but the Bright Lights also made these spaces into crowd-luring destinations in their own right. By the 1970s, the Neon Age had faded into nostalgic memory, eclipsed by standardized, lit-up corporate logos, hoisted high on lollipop poles and displayed in look-alike candy forests, notably on the banal peripheral commercial strips of almost every American town.[1]

Meanwhile, downtown, municipal governments opened new revenue streams by leasing out space for advertising on street furniture like park benches, bus stations, and tourist information kiosks. Corporate logos also saturate the privately owned spaces of streets, in shop windows but also on the bodies of passersby who wear brand-emblazoned clothing designed to boost the wearers' personal desirability while delivering corporate advertising at the wearer's expense. Giant plasma screens have replaced neon in the great advertising commons like Shibuya; similar screens distract drivers along expressways, greet customers at the entrance gates of shopping malls, and flash from "jumbotrons" and around playing fields in stadiums. "Smart" electronic billboards can shuffle video ads according to the collective "aspirational profiles" that they draw from smartphones in the pockets of people in the streets nearby. In those cases, the built infrastructure of "Outdoor Advertising" – just like urban space more generally – exemplifies the frantic marriage between the Earthopolis and the World Wide Web. It also lures us into drastically expanded labyrinths of corporate and state surveillance.[2]

Since the rise of the internet in the 1990s and 2000s, we have been tempted to see this "virtual town square" as a tool that rivals the brick-and-mortar Urban Planet in its capacity to enable large-scale human actions. Certainly no physical city plaza can match the internet's aptitude for "annihilating space and time" in nearly instantaneous deliveries of highly complex information to large audiences located on far ends of Earth. In reality, of course, the two "spaces" – virtual and physical – cannot do without each other: the combination of rivalry and symbiosis resembles that between cities and their rural hinterlands, or between Earthopolis and Earth more generally. The internet's need for built structures – Pentagon-sized server farms, tens of thousands of kilometers of new sub-ocean fiber-optic cables, and tens of millions of cell towers and wifi hotspots just to begin with – has grown prodigiously in tune with the volume of information that the internet stores and circulates. The circulation of virtual information, in turn, is now essential to all the elements of urban planetary acceleration – from the most humble movements of migrants, to global commerce and production, to the rarified circulation of global-city capital and imperial power, to the global transport of oil. Meanwhile malls' reign as the monuments of the twentieth century has been replaced by that of 100-acre online fulfillment warehouses, the clearest indication that the built environment is not going out of style in the age of the internet.[3]

The internet's special genius for eliciting consumer desire exemplifies its rivalry–synergy with the physical Urban Planet. No commercial district, no matter how festooned with flashing enticements, can compete with computers or smartphones in the race to dangle huge volumes of consumer bait to large publics, or to do so in such a targeted fashion, or in a way that so seamlessly connects desire via mouse-clicks or screen-touches to online purchase. By the early 2000s, the market value of advertising "space" on internet "sites," "rooms," and "posts" traded over "social" media far eclipsed that of mono-directional, less targeted, and less navigable spaces of print, radio, and television. By contrast, spending on "outdoor" advertisement – the form most dependent on hard urban space – continued to rise in the internet age, even surpassing print ads for the first time in many urbanized consumer marketplaces. In Delhi, dealers in the city's vast acreage of hoardings sell their space by emphasizing its command over the urban visual landscape and the sheer volume of human eyes it attracts. Or, they insist, outdoor ads can target the desires of specific audiences, by their location in neighborhoods segregated by one "psycho-graphic" segment or another. Or, they can escort shoppers from bus-stall advertisements directly to nearby shops. Or, they can guide the captive eyes of car drivers stuck in Delhi's epic traffic jams from expressway billboards to shopping "sites" on their smartphones, or to a "big box" adjacent to the next off-ramp.[4]

Similar virtual–physical relationships operate within real, hard shops. Physical shopping spaces have in fact accelerated everywhere on the Urban Planet in the internet age, amidst particularly perfervid rhythms of destruction and creation. Mushrooming shopping malls burst out of their postwar seedbeds in North American suburbs to spring up across Europe in the 1970s and 1980s. Monumental "international destination malls" like the Mall of the Americas in 1990s suburban Minneapolis then served as model for 2010s imitations like Manila's Mall of Asia, Johannesburg's Mall of Africa, and Cairo's Mall of Arabia, all of them located in Gurugram-like edge-city developments. Gurugram itself, along with Delhi's other upscale satellites, sprouted some seven shopping malls in the early 2000s. The one that boasts "more marble than the Taj Mahal" regularly comes up in the Delhi Planning Board's own advertisements touting Delhi's capital-luring claims to "World Class City" status.[5]

As malls grew more prominent in First World urban peripheries during the 1960s, commentators like Jane Jacobs countered with toasts, and then eulogies, to inner-city shopping streets, especially as so many vintage downtown department stores disappeared, notably in cities suffering from deindustrialization. Yet mall look-alikes have sprouted up in many of these same downtowns. "Mom-and-pop" grocery shops, convenience franchises, "ethnic" restaurants, and "Patel hotels" surged in many immigrant "vestibule neighborhoods" of First World cities, many drawing higher-income customers. Gentrifying developers sometimes price these lower-capital spaces out of the migrant ecosystems that first generated them, but they tend to supplant them with profusions of both corporate and independent coffee shops and high-end boutiques. Teeming outdoor marketplaces, meanwhile, continue to accelerate everywhere, from farmers' markets in middle-class neighborhoods, immigrant street stalls like the African market in Harlem, and gigantic, bustling informal market squares in Delhi and all of the great cities of the Global South. Although planning authorities often closed down the more informal versions of these markets (including Harlem's sidewalk African Market), informal stall owners and shopkeepers typically find plenty of spaces in megacities to reappear.[6]

It is important to acknowledge that the internet – and the giant corporations that dominate it – do compete vehemently with both malls and more "walkable" downtown commercial spaces. Much destruction and abandonment has followed, including vast "ghost malls" on the US urban periphery. Far too many small shops suffered in the 2000s from the unfurling tentacles of big-box Walmart and online Amazon.com. However, the social allure of physical shops, cafés, and restaurants is not replicable on the internet, nor can it satisfy the desire to walk out with your purchases in hand, packaged in yet another form of urban advertising, the shopping bag. Nor can a computer screen satisfactorily deliver most in-person services or "experiences" – such as those at salons, gyms, arcades, theaters, concert venues, sporting events, and tourist sites – that have replaced physical objects at the leading edge of millennial-era consumer cravings. Of course, smartphones smartly bring the internet into real shops; there, search engines become useful for navigating endless big-box shopping aisles or crowded commercial districts and for comparing prices. When quarantining measures for Covid-19 dramatically slowed shop and mall traffic in major cities, the internet was there as a substitute, as the ballooning of Amazon's profits demonstrated. Yet neither online shopping nor movie streaming dampened the city-induced (and internet-induced) craving for a return to shops, cinemas, restaurants, and bars, despite the dangers. The precipitous worldwide economic collapse of April 2020 paradoxically registered the immense value we place on the physical and social aspects of buying and selling.[7]

The rising value of the urban shopping "experience" is part of an accelerated transformation of cities themselves into consumable goods – a transformation also enabled by the internet. The multi-trillion-dollar travel and tourism industry is the supreme indication. Desire for travel to urban monuments, unfamiliar urban surroundings and histories, and the chance to shop, eat, drink, sleep, vacation, or have sex in another urban commercial district far from the one near home – all have a long history of their own. In the eighteenth century, English aristocrats (and Latin American republicans like Simón Bolívar) could not come of age without making a "grand tour" of ancient sites in Italy. The Hotel of England, built in 1845 near the Spanish Steps in Rome, is an iconic example of a structure designed to satisfy such desires.[8] Since then, cities have continually altered themselves to suit the longings of outside visitors, starting with expanded accommodation, tourist offices, souvenir shops, currency exchanges, ticket booths, and other infrastructure needed to transform historic buildings into "tourist attractions" – or tourist traps. Hotels – "boutique," or in corporate towers – became essential equipment to colonial white towns, and then for postcolonial "World-Class City" status. Corporate hotel chains often led the advanced guard of wealthy investors' gentrifying conquest of urban real estate in the developing world. So did retailers who commercialized transport infrastructure for tourists along highways, at airports, inside railroad stations, and at ports of call for giant cruise ships – "floating malls" or "floating cities" in themselves. City-like landscapes mushroomed in barren locations previously thought useless for humans, like vast, skyscraping beachside resorts and condo-filled high-mountain ski stations. National park infrastructure (including their vast systems of blazed trails) expanded in places prized precisely because of their "preservation" as wildernesses. Golf courses take up enormous amounts of peri-urban space, swallowing crucial animal habitats and draining urban water systems. So do the never-ending imitations of Disneyland theme parks – themselves often built, complete with ersatz Eiffel Towers and Taj Mahals, as "safer" imitations of other far-off tourist destinations. In turn, those who devote their lives to preserving real "Old Cities," "colonial districts," or historic towns that attract tourists are often accused of "Disneyfication" by giving a theme-park feel to the district, locating carnival furniture nearby (the "London Eye"), or building entire theme parks downtown as a supplemental draw for overseas dollars. Virtual space too contributes to the commodification of real cities, since air tickets, museum tickets, room bookings, and advertisements for choice tourist destinations are all easiest to acquire online. Online room booking services spurred the conversion of apartments into lucrative Air BnB units for tourists that has contributed directly to housing shortages and rent increases, propelling gentrification. Yet no other built habitat mattered as much as passenger airplanes themselves, which accelerated in size and number alongside the Urban Planet more generally. Wide-body jets like the Boeing 747 – as miraculous as any innovation in modernist architectural design – did as much as craving for ancient monuments did to massify and globalize tourism. Put tourism travel on top of business travel, and you get a "J curve" in jet trails that rhymes with all of the other upward spikes of the Greatest Acceleration. Several tens of millions of foreign arrivals by plane worldwide in the 1950s grew to a billion by 2010.[9]

The rising value of urban "experience" also plays a role in the rising value of urban land. Though we cannot forget the much harder influences of state and capital in spurring gentrification, analysts correctly note the important role played by "cultural factors" that explain the allure of certain initially devalued downtown neighborhoods to higher-end home-seekers and shop-owners. These factors can include: the lure of distinguished but neglected architecture; the cachet that artistic pioneers can give to a district like New York's Soho; the importance of cutting-edge musical venues like CBGB's in the neighboring East Side; or the chance to create new additions to gay-and-lesbian-oriented spaces. The allure of urban edginess, danger, and even decay – a kind of urban necrophilia that also so often underlies advertisements that rely on postindustrial "ruin porn" visual materials – also plays a role. This craving for urban spaces with "character" or "authenticity" also reflects a desire for relief from the standardization of urban space.[10]

Indeed, complaints about urban homogenization are fair enough, in light of the pervasiveness of corporate advertising imagery, the dreary repetition of modernist corporate headquarters with their pedestrian-unfriendly street-frontage, the replicative automobile-scapes of the suburbs, and even the cookie-cutter feel of "World Class" gentrified neighborhoods. It is impossible to deny the extent of Disneyfication, Cocacolonization, McDonaldization, the transformation of coffee-shop bohemianism into faux-bohemian Starbucks branches, or the tsunamis of camera-toting tourists that ruin "authentic" Amsterdam or Bangkok – as tour groups who seek exotic experiences at the end of fourteen-hour flights are often heard to gripe themselves. The pervasiveness of the

English language on tourist signage (and in the mouths of hordes of Anglophone tourists) is another sign of the homogenizing capacity of Urban Planetary consumer culture, especially at a time when indigenous languages are rapidly becoming extinct worldwide. The sheer privatization, corporatization, and surveillance of physical public spaces and the internet are cause for deep concern.[11]

In such moments of despair, however, it is good to acknowledge the countertrends as well. The human habitat – and cities in particular – remains too capacious to be ruled by one line of desire, no matter how lucrative. Whatever we think about consumer culture and tourism in particular, it has also inspired huge investments in preservation of vintage architecture that keep at least that element of global urban diversity alive. Yet cities do not only preserve their pasts, they also create new cultures. Communities of migrants bring their home cultures into new cities, and cities therefore continue to act as generators of complex hybrid identities, imaginations, and new cultural expressions – despite such obstacles as global inequality and the Great Wall between the hemispheres.[12]

Nor has the desire to purchase objects and experiences completely dumbed down the spiritual soul of Earthopolis. There are more urban churches, mosques, synagogues, and temples than ever before, and all of the Axial Age religions have become Urban Planetary in scope. While many of Europe's older churches attract far more tourists than worshippers, new arena-sized megachurches hold services for as many as tens of thousands of Christian devotees at a time in Dallas, Belo Horizonte, Lagos, Seoul, and Surabaya – broadcasting and real-timing to thousands of others over the internet. St. Peter's Basilica in Rome is no longer the largest church of all, for it was surpassed by the cathedral of Yamoussoukro, the new capital of Ivory Coast. Thousands of far smaller makeshift Pentecostal churches in the *favelas* of São Paulo or the squatter camps of Accra attend to larger total congregations. Participation at the Hajj in Mecca has accelerated alongside the global population of Muslims. The vast built environment of Hinduism has expanded along with South Asia's megacities, and its massive pilgrimages are larger than ever before – even as the color festival of Holi in Benares becomes a global tourist draw. Buddhism and Sikhism have become true world religions since 1945, spreading deeply throughout the Global West, and spawning a substantial environment of monasteries, Peace Pagodas, retreat centers, *gurudwaras*, and a massive parade of 100,000 Sikhs once a year in the streets of Toronto.

All world religions continue their long and conflicted relationship with the consumer culture's secular forms of fulfillment. Some, like certain Protestant fundamentalisms, celebrate the acquisition of status objects as divine rewards for economic striving. Some, including devotees of the Wahhabi strains of Islamic fundamentalism, deem urban commercial districts doorways to hellish temptations like alcohol, illicit sex, female "impiousness," and homosexuality – as well as signals of the ongoing creep of Western imperialism. Such bleak thoughts inspired such groups as the al-Qaeda, the Taliban, and Islamic State/Daesh to favor strict gender segregation in commercial spaces as well as religious ones, and even to launch terrorist bombings against nightclubs, cafés, shopping streets, and tourist destinations. These acts live alongside ongoing violence, such as that in Delhi, between religious groups and across lines of ethnicity and race. Yet most people of faith worldwide have been far more even-handed in balancing secular consumer cravings with spiritual uplift and awe. These include shops (and whole fashion districts) devoted to high-end Islamic women's "modest" fashion.[13]

A PLANET OF TOIL

Desire for goods, amenities, and consumer experiences may not completely dominate global culture, but producing them remains the primary mission of the Urban Planet's labor force – paid and otherwise. The livelihoods available within the world's highly segmented job market – fabulously remunerative for a relative few and brutally exploitative for far too many – are the main benefits most new inhabitants of Earthopolis seek when they migrate to cities with the goal of staying there.

Cities in turn, played the central role in the dramatic birth of the "new global division of labor" we know today – based around global assembly lines that involve far more factories and industrial cities, connected by far denser transport and communications infrastructure, and spread over far greater surfaces of the Urban Planet than ever before. The most striking

23.2. A New Arrival in Shenzhen
At the gates of the Foxconn assembly plant in the Shenzhen Special Economic Zone, another migrant from the Chinese countryside wonders what is next. For many workers at the largest factory in world history, the long hours, fast-paced, repetitive work, limits on movement, anti-migrant prejudice, frequent sexual assault, and low pay amount to an extreme version of dehumanization. Some end their own lives by jumping from upper floors; the owners responded by hanging out nets. Outside the gates, the global proletariat builds its own "informal" spaces of desire. The stall owners pictured here fulfill basic consumer desires while providing energy for another day's work in the massive factory beyond.
AFP/Getty Images.

feature of the Great Acceleration-era geography of production is the relative waning of factory building in the cities of the Global North, where the industrial revolution was born, and the sheer explosion of manufacturing in a select group of industrial empires' former colonies – places that previously had few factories or none at all. This fourth industrial revolution, based heavily in Asia, involves iconic structures from all three previous manufacturing eras: textile mills, steel mills, and automobile assembly plants. Yet today's fourth-wave industrialists spread out the business of production and assembly far more widely than before. Increasingly specialized factories send their individual pieces of complex goods to other facilities often located on several different continents assembling apparel, vehicles, and electronic devices, each acting as a subpart of the fourth revolution's distinctive "global value chains." As important to the functioning of these spread-out assembly systems was the expansion, mostly in First World cities but now also in China and India, of corporate headquarters, research and development facilities, advertising operations, and, of course, the highly concentrated "global city" financial industry. As we will see (Chapter 24), corporate control over the extraction and sale of the petroleum needed to run the whole system is almost as concentrated in a few cities as the control over global manufacturing.[14]

The accelerating Cities of Toil that exploded at the intersections of all of these activities are at once more connected and more unequal than they were in 1945; since 1980, both connection and inequality have intensified. We have already seen how the very wealthiest urban elites captured the top income- and wealth-producing activities in finance and urban real estate. Yet Cities of Toil also depend heavily on an expansion of a range of "middle classes" whose incomes allow them to purchase most of the world's consumer enticements. More important was an even vaster global working class that toils in the factories and various other netherworlds of the global economy, for these workers account for the bulk of cities' accelerating populations; combined, their far more modest incomes can also make or break the consumer economies that the global working classes bring into being. Thus the city-based systems of toil that produce the Cities of Delight add a crucial strand of explanation to the core conundrum of the Great Acceleration: why cities got so big in our time, and why some of the poorest cities grew the biggest of all.

The middle classes have defied any easy definition ever since they emerged from mercantile circles in the seventeenth century to become the liberal bourgeoisie of the nineteenth century – central players both in the "modernizing" rise of hydrocarbon industry and in the People Power revolution. Since 1945, if not before, expanded welfare states, including but not limited to mortgage-subsidies, have lifted many inhabitants of First and even some Third World industrial working-class neighborhoods into what, at the very least, could be called an "aspirational" middle class. Shop-owning "petit" middle classes, both locally born and immigrant, have continued to fight for their place in cities against the rise of mega-malls and gentrifying shopping districts and internet giants, sometimes adopting niche specialties or a bohemian or artisanal style to appeal to better-heeled customers. In national capitals and city halls, another middle class rode the expansions and contractions of workforces needed by different agencies of the state. Such public-service middle classes encompass a spectrum of Urban Planetary occupational groups ranging from unionized sanitation workers, police officers, and state railroad workers to high-level bureaucrats in the Foreign Service, the national treasury, or the citadels of the Armed Forces. A "professional" middle class meanwhile also expanded and contracted in tune with the fortunes of hospitals, law and accounting firms, and universities. All of these spaces included larger "white" and "pink" collar "service industry" staffs whose livelihoods can pass as middle class, though their jobs shade quickly into a much larger sea of poorly paid, contingent "service sector" employment, notably in hospitals or as home health aides. In the world's office towers, the managerial middle class itself diversified widely, as corporate firms took over new sectors of the world economy. In addition to more solid "white collar" careers in industry, mining, shipping, industrial agriculture, retail, consumer services of all kinds, and tourism, the corporate world has opened doors for a tiny few into the precincts of the ultra-rich – not just in finance and real estate, but also in the millennial internet-related technology sectors, and in energy, especially oil.[15]

In each segment of these middle classes, the range of salaries, real estate wealth, income from investments, and capacity to shoulder debt can accomodate a range of possible consumer lifestyles, each helping to define "middle-class-ness" in its own way. Taken as a whole, the purchasing power of the Urban Planet's many bourgeoisies has long supplanted that of the old aristocracy as the driver of worldwide production and trade in consumer goods and services. Middle-class politics, as we know from the first centuries of the age of revolution, has always been as slippery as it is influential, but it has become more so – just as likely to support rank authoritarianism as more People Power. Each of these middle classes has left a strong and distinctive imprint on the built environments where they live, work, and shop.[16]

The standard story of the twenty-first century's middle classes celebrates their overall growth and geographical spread. The focus is on global capital's miraculous creation of world history's largest bourgeoisies – in the cities of post-Maoist China and post-Nehruvian India. The flashier new downtown urban developments created by *chai qian* in

China and India's many private middle-class "bubbles" – culminating in places like Gurugram but including thousands of smaller "planned developments" – exemplify this acceleration-within-the-acceleration. Globally, the pattern is far more complex. In the North American, European, and Japanese heartlands of global capital, large inequalities have split "middle classes" into small very wealthy groups and much larger middling and lower groups whose grip on economic stability has waned. The grim gurus of austerity politics won more battles in the 1980s, and corporate-led attacks on welfare systems and unions slowed the increase in middle-class salaries and wages, while stunting incomes among poorer workers across the First World. In Latin America, urban middle classes that grew from import-substitution collapsed as the oil shocks and the IMF wreaked vengeance on that developmental strategy. Two incomes or even three became essential to maintain most middling and "aspirational" middle-class families' consumption standards in places like the older, "inner-ring" suburbs of the USA. Double and triple shifts for middle-class women, rare in the 1950s, became essential for many households in the 2000s, and women's workforce participation rates have expanded dramatically across class spectrums. Just as in the 1920s, the pursuit of consumption on stagnating incomes leaves many deep in debt, at no time more perilously so than during the Financial Crisis of 2008. These blows add to the intensifying difficulties middle-class families face in affording housing in the gentrifying cities favored by the enriched global elite.[17]

In the Persian Gulf, by contrast, states redirected income from the oil price hikes into the creation of substantial new urban middle classes and smaller hyper-wealthy elites. Governments and corporations also invested heavily in migrant service and construction labor from South and Southeast Asia. The real estate markets of Riyadh, Dubai, Doha, and Kuwait City generated a spiral of luxury urban amenities. These include the tallest skyscraper in the world, Dubai's Burj-Khalifa, lavish malls and hotels, branches of Global North museums and universities, mega-mall airports, uncanny refrigerated indoor ski-slopes in otherwise flat desert landscapes – all in the midst of the hottest zone on Earth and one of its greatest political tinderboxes. Similar government-boosted petroleum middle classes, capped by tiny billionaire elites, rule from penthouses perched above the shacks of such detonating African megacities as Lagos and Luanda. The petro-elites of Mexico City, São Paulo, Caracas, and in the twin Petronas Towers (the world's second tallest) of Malaysia's Kuala Lumpur rode considerably rockier boom-and-bust cycles – just as they have in Houston and in the spiraling new glass headquarters of the Russian petroleum giant Gazprom outside St. Petersburg.[18]

Thanks to enormous government and military subsidies in the internet that go back to the Cold War, the San Francisco Bay Area's Silicon Valley has meanwhile spawned the world's biggest "dot-com" bourgeoisie, capped by the world's flashiest billionaire class. A flotilla of spectacular "landscraper" suburban headquarters for the newest world's-largest corporations helped spur outrageous real estate prices throughout the Silicon Valleys of the world. High-Tech suburbs spread outside Seattle, Washington, D.C., Boston's Route 128 Corridor, the "Silicon Docks" of Dublin, the "Silicon Glens," "Fens," and "Roundabouts" in Britain, and many other European Technopolises. Brazil has a Silicon Valley in Campinas near São Paulo, Israel a "Silicon Wadi" near Tel Aviv. Bengaluru, India has its Electronics City, and both Chennai and Kuala Lumpur possess several long strings of tech-centers nearby. China has countered with the Zhangjiang Hi-Tech Park in Shanghai and the Zhongguancun center in Beijing.[19]

Factory districts however, are the most important generator of new middle classes – and, more importantly, the biggest generator of new working classes. As is often the case in the age of market hyperbole, the "global" in "global assembly lines" actually refers to a highly uneven, very diverse, urban geography. Earthopolis's Cities of Industrial Toil still include the otherwise slower-growing factory districts in North America, Europe, Japan, and Latin America, but they have expanded especially rapidly in so-called Special Economic Zones in East, Southeast, and South Asia. Within that region, the giant cities of China have become – by far – the largest workshops in world history. Within China, no industrial city grew more spectacularly than the city of Shenzhen. Finally, within Shenzhen, no factory grew bigger than the endless complex of electronics assembly plants contained in the Longhua Science and Industrial Park.

The story of Chinese factories "so large they make Manchester's textile mills look like mom-and-pop shops" typically begins in 1979, when Deng

Xiaoping and the CCP embraced ideas about global capital that were hard to distinguish from those of their contemporary ideological arch-enemies, Ronald Reagan and Margaret Thatcher. Yet the story has deeper roots in the region going back to the tariff-free-port status granted by the British to Singapore and Hong Kong in the nineteenth century. In the 1960s, the governments of these two city-states pursued vigorous development policies, pouring money derived from textile factories into transport and communications infrastructure as well as universities – a model imitated by Taiwan and South Korea after World War II. Meiji Japan's longstanding system of state rewards to its biggest corporate titans was also influential in stoking this model. So was American Cold War development aid that poured into Pacific Asia to counteract the influence of Mao's China. Tax breaks and other incentives wooed private American and Japanese capital across that region, and governments like South Korea's directed enormous resources to a few families who ran corporate conglomerates known as the *chaebol*, such as Daewoo and Samsung. Shipbuilding works, car factories, and hi-tech electronics plants helped cities like Seoul, Inchon, Busan, Taipei, and Kaohsiung became home to large middle and working classes. The largest cities of the so-called Four Asian "Tigers" soon all had multiple millions of inhabitants as well as hundreds of corporate skyscrapers. Seoul had just over a million people in 1950, but almost ten million in 2020. Singapore and Hong Kong – five-million-plus cities themselves – became global financial centers only one notch lower in importance than Tokyo.[20]

When Deng came to power in China in 1978, he imitated these capitalist "Asian Tigers" in many respects. He opened a Special Economic Zone in the provinces surrounding the former treaty ports at Guangzhou and Xiamen, wooing investors from the nearby "Tigers," then from Japan, Europe, and the USA, to pour money into factories while paying low taxes and benefiting from enormous investments in infrastructure and lax environmental regulation. Yet global capital's greatest reason for investing in the Chinese Special Economic Zones was the world's largest reservoir of potential factory labor – the immense population of China's villages. When Deng abolished Mao's farming communes, he allowed a growing stream of migrants to move to Chinese cities as long as they retained their rural *hukou* status, implying that their primary livelihood still came from their farms back home. On that principle, the migrant workers' new corporate paymasters could hire them to do factory work for far lower wages than Mao's "Heroes of the Revolution," workers in state-run enterprises who possessed urban *hukou* papers. Migrants, by contrast, were jeered at as "laboring boys," and – in even larger numbers – "laboring girls." They were mostly consigned to barracks and dormitories in the new factory complexes not too different from the labor compounds for seasonal Black workers in apartheid South Africa's gold mines. In the 1990s, there were some fifty million migrant workers in Chinese cities. In 2014 there were an astounding 270 million – the largest industrial working class ever assembled. Shenzhen – as late as 1950 a tiny fishing port of 3,000 people on the border with Hong Kong – had 59,000 residents in 1980 but over eleven million in 2020. Meanwhile, an enormous corporate middle class – also world history's largest ever – worked long hours downtown in some of the world's tallest buildings to keep production quotas on track and to speculate on the side in the stock of new Chinese corporations. Migrant workers in thousands of factories produced goods from all four industrial revolutions: textiles and shoes; steel, rails, and ships; cars and buses; and laptop computers, tablets, and cell phones. Another factory in Shenzhen makes shipping containers to carry all of these goods to consumers around the world. In the city's Longhua Park, the Taiwanese-owned company Hon Hai Precision Industries, otherwise known as Foxconn, operated the largest factory in world history. It consists of a fenced city-within-a-city stuffed with dormitories, shopping centers, and entertainment centers for as many as 400,000 workers who assemble, among other things, hundreds of millions of Apple's smartphones.[21]

Special Economic Zones like the one that roused a mega-boomtown like Shenzhen into being have sprouted up elsewhere in China, in Asia, and across the Global South. Shanghai's Pudong New Area, a former residential area on the opposite side of the Huangpo River from the old imperial Bund, sprouted a spectacular bouquet of skyscraping corporate headquarters. This activity allowed Shanghai to remain larger than Shenzhen and its neighboring commercial giant Guangzhou, while perhaps surpassing Hong Kong's claims to global-city status. The chain of industrial Yangtze River giants – Nanjing, Wuhan, and Chongqing –

topped the ten million mark each, in part because their huge factory districts benefited from cheap power from the mammoth Three Gorges Dam. Further upriver, another low-tax zone attracted the largest shoe factory in the world to the nine-million-plus Szechuanese capital of Chengdu. Hundreds of makers of plastic toys accumulated in smaller million-plus cities like Yiwu and Chenghai, which vied for status as the "North Poles" of the twenty-first-century; they also dominate the world's production of artificial Christmas trees. Smaller plastic parts making, electronics assembly, footwear, and textile plants abound in China's other million-plus cities, and have spread to Beijing's grim re-education camps for the Uighurs of Xinjiang. Similar factories have also spread, more thinly but still by the tens of thousands, across a global belt of export processing zones. That belt stretches throughout many of the cities of Southeast and South Asia, includes a more sporadic sprinkling in African port cities, picks up again in cities like Port-au-Prince and San Salvador, then culminates in the string of *maquiladora* cities that parallels the USA–Mexico border. China has expanded its reach over the value chains in all of these places with an immense "Belt and Road" program of transport infrastructure and raw materials extraction sites (Chapter 25).[22]

The "formal" factories of the world – places whose owners technically abide by state agreements on labor and environmental practices in exchange for the benefits offered by their location in the Special Zone – nonetheless shade into the much larger realm of "informal" workplaces. There, extreme exploitation has created a larger and poorer working class whose welfare the state, for the most part, simply ignores; the "informal-ity" of such workplaces serves largely as an excuse for employers and state actors to deny any demands for improvement. "Sweatshops" – or "illegal factories" as officials in Delhi call them – employ millions of informal workers. Most are located in cities of the Global South, though the "spot-market" fashion sweatshops of New York's Chinatown, the electronics plants along Los Angeles's Alameda Corridor, and meat processing plants across the USA have hired poor immigrants on similarly exploitative terms.

The boundary between a factory and a sweatshop is indistinct. Conditions in China's largest corporate factories are brutal by most standards. Long workdays, low pay, and a crushing of union organizing efforts caused dozens of Foxconn workers, for example, to jump to their deaths from factory buildings in the 2010s, forcing the company to erect miles of nets outside the windows to catch people tempted to follow suit. These factories are "legal" but their owners flout the law serially.[23] Still, most of these formal plants do not combine the low light, high heat, dangerous conditions, feverishly repetitive work-pace, toxic fumes, repressive supervision, summary firings of activists, sexual harassment and violence, widespread use of child labor, and frequency of factory fires and building collapses as do, say, the thousands of ready-wear clothing sweatshops of Dhaka, Bangladesh. Thousands of predominantly female workers perished there in building collapses in the early 2000s, and tens of thousands of sweatshop workers worldwide acquire permanent health problems after a few years of literally backbreaking, lung-lacerating, or cancer-causing work. Many others, including tens of thousands of sari embroiderers in Delhi, the soccer-ball assemblers of Lahore, or the legions of carpet-sewing children of Tehran, earn pittances doing exacting piecework in their homes, much like textile workers in the seventeenth century.[24]

THE SUB-PROLETARIAT OF WORK MAKERS AND CITY MAKERS

Somewhere along the spectrum, the new global industrial working class shades into a multiply exploitable "informal" sub-proletariat that contains an estimated seven to eight out of every ten people in Delhi, six out of ten in Lima, and almost nine in ten in Kinshasa. The story of this Global South majority is the foundational subplot of the fourth industrial revolution and the consumer culture explosion. In other ways, though, it is altogether a different story. In their extremely low consumer power as well as their distance from even the most marginal state benefits, the poorest sweatshop and informal workers of the world make up a distinct class. The space they occupy is distinct too, for they make up the vast majority of those who live in the Global South's massive self-built cities of the poor.[25]

Within the informal Cities of Toil, thing-making sweatshops are only one of many informal livelihoods that poor people cobble together for their own basic survival. Just as important are three other kinds of work, most of which lies in the least-well-paying realms of the informal sector: work that makes work itself possible; work that brings the city itself into being; and work that makes the city work well enough that it generates more work. Only by adding such extra-industrial work-making and city-making toil to the story of the Urban Planet can we finally and fully solve the conundrum of how twenty million people could gather in the often extremely unhealthy and dangerous self-built neighborhoods of the Newest New Delhi, yet stay there nonetheless.

Behind most sweatshop seamstresses – just as behind all other work-ers – is a home. Typically overcrowded, unsanitary and physically danger-ous, the homes of the poor nonetheless manufacture care, food, and rest – if they do not also do duty as a mini-factory for piece goods, a shop, a garage, a warehouse, a daycare center, a boarding house, or a real estate venture involving rents from poorer people who inhabit shacks out back. As has been the case since humanity's first days in villages, women still do most of that home-based work. They give birth to new potential workers, prepare them for work at a young age, and care for people too old for work. Meanwhile, they do the work of keeping whole households of workers (including themselves) in shape to work another day. Doing this work of making work possible is an especially laborious task in the great cities of the poor. Basic cleanliness, sanitation, and safety are often virtually impossible. Caregivers must haul water from distant standpipes, obtain food at unregulated marketplaces, and manage waste without sewer pipes. Patriarchal norms too often sanction violence against the same women who do most of this nurturing work. The same patriarchy makes remuneration for household care-work uncertain, since it relies heavily on male wages earned outside the home. For this reason, largely women-run home-based enterprises are crucial to homes' capacity to regenerate the bodies of workers who live there.[26]

If middle-class families of the Global North were only recently forced to take on their multiple shifts, poor women have always worked triple and quadruple shifts, whether inside or out of homes, whether in First, Second, or Third World cities. For some of Delhi's poorest women, one of the largest sources of extra-shift employment is work in other people's homes. Wealthier women in the Global South who are eager to subcontract their own patriarchy-delegated housework duties can take advantage of very low prevailing wage-rates for female labor to hire domestic servants – usually off the books. In Gurugram, domestic workers and their households often build their own neighborhoods close to the gates of elite communities in order to manage sharp shifts between penthouses by day and the family *jhuggi jhopri* by night. Men from the same households provide domestic service too, more often as gardeners, security guards, and drivers. Still other poor women do very similar domestic work in the city's large tourist hotels. In Delhi as elsewhere in the Global South, some of this housekeeping work is further subcontracted to enormous informal laundry operations – such as Delhi's famous *dhobi-wallas*. Pick-up and delivery, washing, drying, packaging, and overseeing the logistics all creates other very low-paying work – washing typically for women (often in polluted waterways), transport for men.[27]

To succeed in their task of regenerating the energies of workers, urban homes, meanwhile, need food and household items. By means of that marginal participation in global consumer culture, homeworkers collectively support yet another substantial world of informal work – the realm of the street vendors. Vendors' job is to generate income from the frenetic energy of the Global South's immense and shifting informal marketplaces. Often they fill the narrowest of market niches – selling low-cost tortillas in Mexico City, traditional medicines in Soweto's *muti* markets, fish and vegetables in Bangkok's river markets. Stall-owners in Delhi sell a single type of fruit arrayed on a wicker mat; wandering sales-women sell cheap crafts or mobile phone cards from heavy "head-loads." Delhi, like other Indian cities, also has vast informal "tiffin" delivery systems in which ultra-low-wage delivery-people supply tens of thousands of office workers with precisely made-to-order daily lunches. In Delhi, these informal caterers supplement the operators of the city's 10,000 tandoori stalls and other street-food stands, as well as countless Muslim *hallal* butchers whose hanging goat carcasses and tiny slaughterhouses grate on the nerves of vegetarian Hindus. The manufacture and sale of cheap alcohol sustains many an owner of a toddy shop, *shebeen*, or cantina, while offering many a chance to forget their miseries or take them out violently on even more vulnerable people.[28]

Street vending reminds us that the lowest-paid informal work often takes the form of self-run enterprises that also rely on extended families, home-based warehouses, and often-exploitative relationships to informal wholesalers. Such enterprises warm the cockles of right-wing free-marketers' hearts, and spawned dozens of left-leaning micro-loan programs, especially targeting female-run artisanal collectives. Some of these artisans benefit from this ideological or financial attention, and a few go on to sell their wares in international marketplaces – as fashion accessories or home decorations in First World condos or split-levels. For the majority, though, profit margins are often as slim as the chances of any "bootstraps" upward mobility. Bribes to police officers or protection payments to the markets' criminal networks are an often-ruinous cost of doing business, and poverty in the informal commercial sector remains the norm. For many, the far more dangerous and lucrative business of selling illegal drugs, guns, bush meat, ivory, blood minerals, or service in armed militias is the only route to a more solid income.[29]

If street vendors supply the homes that regenerate the city's workers, informal construction workers do the work of bringing the megacities themselves into being. Most numerous are those who spend much of their time building and rebuilding their own houses. Many others are recent migrants recruited by high-end developers from the countryside at small pittances to take on muscle-work such as lifting and carrying bricks, breezeblocks, and heavy bags of concrete mix. Many are women, especially in Delhi. They often inhabit the simplest of temporary dwellings, often downwind of dangerous silica- or asbestos-saturated worksites and cement plants. As we know, their neighborhoods are often the first to be identified for destruction by their own employers, high-end developers with closest ties to the planning boards and their bulldozers.[30]

Work in urban transport likewise makes the Urban Acceleration possible. The speed of vehicles has always been a crucial factor in determining the outer limits of urban size, and the work involved in moving fellow urbanites around the city requires increasing numbers of urbanites to drive those vehicles. Transport – like industry, commerce, and construction – has a glamorous formal side, dominated by private automobiles and limousines (with private chauffeurs), and a middling realm of taxis, trucks, public buses, and commuter rail systems like the gleaming Delhi

Metro. Subway systems – among other Pharaonic transport infrastructure, like expressway tunnels, soaring river bridges, helipads, touristic cable cars – figure prominently in megacities' hopes for "world city" status. Dozens of Global South city halls have contracts with the Paris-based global subway engineering firm SYSTRA, which has offices in, among many other places, suburban Delhi. These baubles of transport infrastructure are notoriously too expensive and poorly situated to serve the Global South's great cities of the poor, however. The complexities of a megacity's urban geography and its stark class divisions require other transport solutions that shade across the formal–informal boundary.[31]

The tens of thousands of minibus taxis of Johannesburg, for example, fill a need for long-distance intra-urban transport left over from apartheid. Soweto, and other southern townships where most workers live, are located an hour's drive or more from the still largely all-white northern suburbs, where most formal jobs – and many more informal ones – are located. Fearing a spoliation of their property values, elite neighborhood organizations in the north have resisted direct formal bus lines that might make it easier for Sowetans to get to work. That includes the thousands of domestic workers and security guards who live in Soweto but commute north to keep middle-class houses and corporate offices clean and safe. The lack of formal options consigns most Black commuters to over-crowded Toyota vans whose drivers depend on several trips back and forth to make payments for loans, protection, and gas. When the heavy traffic from so many small vehicles does not slow everything to a halt (especially on the hillier slopes of the expressways leading to the suburbs), drivers are obliged to careen across the spread-out city at top speed to make ends meet – often meeting their ends in terrible crashes as a result. Competition over routes has led to horrifically violent taxi wars, though the city did engage a consortium of mini-bus owners to run the city's first formal bus company during the Football World Cup of 2010.[32]

In Delhi, as in other historically denser cities of Asia, the rickshaw occupies a special place atop a universe of smaller vehicles that can negotiate both tiny alleys in old towns and the foot-tamped earthen streets of the far slums. From their invention in the 1860s streets of Yokohama and Tokyo, rickshaws were as one with low labor and fuel costs. The "engine" of the first *jinrikisha*, or "human-powered vehicles," was a single human rickshaw puller, far cheaper than the sedan chairs borne by two and four people that they replaced, let alone carriage horses. As one-person rickshaws were also more maneuverable in teeming streets, they spread across cities in Asia to African ones by 1900. After World War II, independent developmental states banned human-drawn rickshaws as backward symbols of colonial servitude; Kolkata's famous Bihari rickshaw pullers are only now phasing out of circulation. Yet the number of pedal, gasoline, electric, and even solar-powered rickshaws, auto-rickshaws, trishaws, tuktuks, mototaxis, babytaxis, and velotaxis has risen sharply in the twenty-first century as a cheaper, less polluting, less traffic-snarling alternative to four-wheeled cabs.[33]

As one of no fewer than 200,000 auto-rickshaw drivers in Delhi, a guide like Sharma Karma easily navigates not only the city's sinuous allies and preposterous traffic, but also the complex line between formal and informal labor, not to mention the complexities of the city's class structure and its consumer markets. Many certified drivers, like the Pandit, rent their machines out to non-licensed drivers on off-hours; some of them use the back seat as home. The price of a fare is regulated in theory but highly negotiable in practice. Though the price of auto-rickshaw rides is typically out of reach of the very poorest, who tend to rely instead on slower pedi-cabs, motor scooters, bicycles, or their own two feet, Delhi's legions of lower-middle-class people make up a large market for the Pandit and his colleagues. Overseas tourists who flocked to Asia in larger numbers after 1990 also helped drive the renaissance in such vehicles. For them, surfing Delhi's cresting waves of vehicular mayhem in an open-air yellow-and-green three-wheeler amounts to a "novelty" urban experience that they can purchase because they previously bought air tickets – possibly with the goal of slaking their desire for a tour of a "slum." Brazilian *favelas* and South African townships have become tourist destinations fed by similar transport chains. Would-be tourist-trappers in almost every First World city have cashed in on the rickshaw rush to launch their own three-wheeled tours of Amsterdam, Vancouver, and even their original Tokyo Bay Area birthplaces. Meanwhile, studies of megacity rickshaw pullers and drivers in places like Kolkata and Mexico City emphasize the work's evanescent profit margins and a grim toll in physical and mental health. Most of the reports start with the effects of inhaling the maximally polluted air of the streets that serve as primary workplaces for the transport industry.[34]

In that way, our auto-walla delivers us closer to the crossroads where Cities of Delight and Cities of Toil meet the last stops on our journey, Cities of Oil and Cities of Waste. To guide us into the last stretch, though, we must turn to the Global South's vast armies of trash sorters. You can find them if your rickshaw "slums tour" stops at their settlements, which in Delhi nestle dangerously near the slopes of the city's four monumental municipal landfills – Bhalswa, Okhla, Narela Bawana, and Ghazipur.[35]

Like most armies of the world's poorest workers, trash sorters, also known as waste pickers, are disproportionately women and children – in India, they predominantly come from the same "lower" castes who used to rake up night soil from the streets. You can call their work "informal," yet they are often the only people who allow municipalities in most cities of the Global South to remotely meet their own formal recycling targets. In Cairo in 2007, informal waste pickers recycled nearly a quarter of the city's daily garbage (twice as much as the municipality, the largest in Africa); in Lima, Pune, and Manila's Quezon City, municipalities relied almost entirely on informal workers for recycling. In Delhi, as many as a half-million waste pickers sort through the nine out of every ten tons of waste that regulations say must be winnowed through municipal recycling plants. All told, they return about a quarter of the city's daily dump into the city's economy in the form of reusable plastic, aluminum, cloth, glass, brick, and even gravel.[36]

Some virtually live on the great garbage mountains themselves. Others ride cargo tricycles around the city to scavenge areas where the municipal trucks do not go. Still others wake up in sidewalk tents near pre-arranged sites where informal truckers pull up with a day's worth of rank-smelling work. By afternoon, thanks to water from nearby fire hydrants, proud piles of freshly cleaned raw materials line the street. Delhi's *khacchra seths* (waste merchants) collect these piles of the city's spent consumer desires and resell them to formal and informal industries; there new objects of desire are born, and enter the consumer circuits again. Most sorters earn less than the equivalent of two dollars a day. Their work exposes them to rotting food (temptingly recyclable as cheap meals for hungry children), falling masses of masonry, discarded syringes, rats, disease-carrying insects and microbiota, toxic chemicals, and trash fires. Children are vulnerable to attacks from adult competitors desperate for more real estate on the slopes of the city's great refuse mountainsides.[37]

Our desires and our labors are intimately connected to each other, to all of our built spaces, and to the sheer momentum of Acceleration. Nowhere is this truth more gut-wrenching than on the limp, oozing, hot mountains of our ejected consumer longings, where some of Earth's poorest people toil under its worst conditions to harvest a rupee or two, returning the stuff we value the least back into the global chain of new "value." Our rickshawala has left us here at the great trash mountain of Ghazipur – perhaps to refill his petrol tank once again – giving us a moment to contemplate our sort. Time to sum up the bill for his labors, and those of so many others we pay so poorly, yet who make possible the impossible Urban Planet we all live on. Time too, to reckon the culminant costs of all our toils and cravings.

CHAPTER 24

Great Accelerations IV: Maximal Hydrocarbon, Maximal Waste

THE VIEW FROM GHAZIPUR MOUNTAIN

Take a breath if you dare. Pick through a megacity's worth of waste yourself. Sip from the Styx of effluent that seeps from the great Ghazipur garbage mountain into the sewers, the sacred rivers, the over-extended oceans. Where has our three-headed, three-wheeled rickshaw ferried us, its tailpipe shaking exhaust into the smoke-laden Delhi air? Have we rowed too close to hot Dystopia? Or, have we merely reached a shabby waypoint, a spot to re-reckon the Urban Planet's orbit onto more propitious pathways? The answer, our Pandit might say, is blowing in the smoke. Flowing on the discharge, oozing from the rot. Like archaeologists who bring the ancient Urban Planet back to life by sifting through Rome's Monte Testaccio – the ancient Eternal City's Eighth Hill of discarded wine jugs – so we must, like the humblest trash pickers, sort through the components of our cities' solid, liquid, gaseous, and caloric waste. The remaining riddles of the Greatest Acceleration are hidden here. In the smelly spoor we discard are scrawled maps for the ferry-wallas of the future.

The first lesson is quickest to grasp. We pile Planet Earth with so much detritus because we take so much from it. If waste is the Omega of the Urban Planet, the extraction business is the Alpha – and the oil extraction business is the Alpha of all Alphas. Earthopolis has become an incubus that ingests Earth's mineral, vegetal, and animal riches through multiplying, ravenous feeding tubes of our own construction. Both bookended orifices, of extraction and expulsion, are massive,

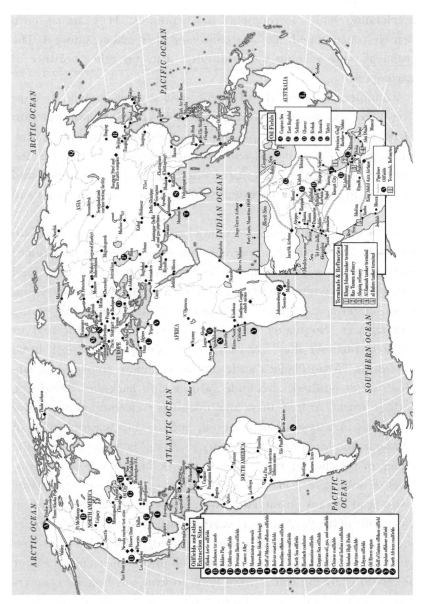

Map 24.1. Cold War to Hot Oil
Map created by Joe LeMonnier, https://mapartist.com.

accelerating built environments in themselves. They are at once densely concentrated, like our cities, and they extend outward. The realm of waste is more widely diffused than any other province of Earthopolis.

To understand the Urban Planet's waste streams, though, we must first follow the mauls of extraction as they suck deep into our host planet's flesh. The geography of extraction begins in broad farmlands, pastures, woodlands, and thirst-slaking rivers, but also in the dispersed but heavily built spaces where we tunnel our mines, and above all, in the ever more extensive places where we drill for oil and gas.

From there, Earthopolis consumes raw foodstuffs, basic materials, and fuels, and heaves them peristaltically through our Urban Planet's every other distended organ – populations, homes, buildings, food systems, health systems, power plants, vehicles, communication systems, states, empires, capitalisms, manufacturing chains, and desire-firing marketplaces. No matter how these materials are reprocessed or digested, whatever they create or destroy along the way – all lurch toward the Urban Planet's waste outlets: chimneys, smokestacks, tailpipes, sewer outflows, street-side garbage tips, back-alley dumpsters, garbage trucks. At first, these anal openings concentrate our massive droppings in a few urban locations, such as the towering piles of Ghazipur, the leach ponds in factory yards and downstream from the mines, or the choking smoke clouds over Delhi. From there the provinces of waste spread like hell's emissaries – as liquid slicks; as plastic micro-bead blooms on the land, river, and seas; as islands of trash in the middle of the Pacific; or as heat-trapping gases in Earth's ever more wrathful atmosphere. We have come to the edge of a global River Styx, where the final ferry awaits. It will take all of our cities and all of our powers to chart the course from here, to write any hopeful chapters that come next in the life of Earthopolis.

THE HUMAN LITHOSPHERE

In its globe-embracing infrastructural lacework and its extensive food and materials-producing hinterlands, the human-altered, human-built crust of Earthopolis mimics planet Earth's full spherical geological crust – the one laid down long before us over billions of years of geological time. Moreover, our own crust is made *from* that of Earth. For our habitat to accelerate, web-like yet unevenly, across the livable hard surface of Earth since 1945, we relied upon accelerating acts of plowing, felling, digging, drilling, removing, reprocessing, and redesigning of the natural lithosphere's minerals and its non-human habitats. Thanks to the Greatest Acceleration, our own crust now takes up over half of that of Earth's. It weighs, according to one estimate, more than the rest of the biosphere combined. The cascading impact upon Earth of such hard facts takes up far larger spaces still.[1]

Seven-tenths of the Earth's dry land is covered with fertile soil. Today over half of that is human-altered cropland and pastureland. The J-curve acceleration in agricultural land at the expense of forest and scrubland began earlier than other upwardly careening dimensions of the human habitat. In 1000 CE, the approximately 500 million hectares of crop and pastureland that we needed to feed the great Cities of the Rivers doubled to the one billion hectares needed in 1720 for the expanding Cities of the Oceans. After that, agricultural land doubled again far more quickly, reaching two billion hectares by 1880 (about 16 percent of all soil-covered land) at the first peak of the hydrocarbon revolution. The J-curve bent far more acutely in the twentieth century, rocketing toward the five billion hectares that we need to feed our majority-urban population today. After 1970, cropland growth stabilized or declined in places where Green Revolution technologies were deepest-rooted, but it accelerated in Africa, Southeast Asia, and the Brazilian Amazon. Meanwhile, pastureland devoted to the far less nutritionally efficient business of meat production remained high in the Americas while it exploded across the Global South. Land devoted to meat and dairy accounts for three-and-a-quarter billion hectares worldwide today, well more than double the acreage devoted to plant crops.[2]

Forests paid the biggest price in land, biomass, and sequestered carbon lost to the accelerating acreage of the agricultural provinces of our "anthrome." The forest historian Michael Williams has decried the "great onslaught" on trees and their understories that began between

1945 and 2000 when 555 million hectares of forest disappeared from the Earth; another 230 million hectares has fallen to clearing machines and to human-set fires since then. A full two-thirds of the over 300 million hectares of rainforests that were in existence in 1950 are gone. There was a slight reprieve in the rainforest collapse after 2000, but new assaults on the Amazon in the late 2010s have re-accelerated the catastrophe, even as palm oil plantations decimate rainforests in Southeast Asia. "In the whole history of deforestation," writes Williams, "there has been nothing comparable to this."[3]

In the croplands, growing Green Revolution crops drew less on new acres of soil but far more heavily on other kinds of human projects of planetary crust- and river-rearrangement. These included growing mining of the mineral phosphate, natural gas, and petroleum needed for our tenfold increase in use of chemical fertilizers since 1950, not to mention gasoline for the world's twenty-five million tractors. Other Pharaonic feats of earthmoving were required for the sixfold increase in dam construction during the same years. Dams, in turn, served as tools for the bigger project of re-engineering Earth's undulating surface to redirect freshwater flows toward irrigation channels, fields, and the drinking troughs of meat and dairy animals. All told, agriculture now absorbs four times the amount of water it did in 1950, amounting to 2,800 cubic kilometers each year, or 70 percent of all water consumed by humans.[4]

Meanwhile, our human crust contains far more hard structures and infrastructures since 1945 than ever before. We have not "paved the planet" yet, not quite, despite what our eyes may tell us on a drive around Delhi, São Paulo, or Los Angeles. Estimates of the sheer area occupied by human-built features vary as much as do urban population figures. By one measurement, the built part of our habitat covers one and a half million square kilometers, the size of the entire country of Iran; another puts the total closer to four million, considerably larger than India. Summing up the area of all of our stacked-up indoor floor surfaces adds another two million square kilometers – creating a total that is the equivalent of maybe 6 percent of Earth's land area. Even by the lowest estimate, built areas tripled in size since 1950, grew sevenfold since 1900, and increased fiftyfold since 1600. Other researchers focusing on very large cities alone found, startlingly, that they are growing faster in area than in population. In other words, despite gentrification and many taller buildings, our habitat is getting less dense overall – a very worrying sign for efficiencies in the use of energy for transport and home heating. Overall, the cities of the USA occupied more space by far per capita than the cities of any other country, because of their FHA-induced addiction to sprawl (Chapter 19). Although high overall land-coverage figures in the USA mask big variations in density, from very tight New York to very loose Houston, American cities covered twice as much land as a whole as Chinese ones in 2000, though China had twice as many urban residents. That difference in area has no doubt diminished since, though Chinese cities' suburban tower-building schemes are likely to sustain their higher density. Of all inhabited world regions, Southeast Asia was the most densely covered by cities, thanks in great part to the *desakota* of Java. Sub-Saharan Africa was sparsest in built-up area, but Kinshasa, Lagos, Accra, and dozens of medium-sized cities grew fastest in acreage as well as in people.[5]

As concentrated human habitats grew, so, as always, did extended ones. We now live in an uneven global lacework of over forty-five million kilometers of roads, one and a half million kilometers of railroad track, over forty million kilometers of suspended electric wires, and three-quarters of a million kilometers of sub-ocean cables. The human-built web on land, however, still takes its shape from the Great Gap of the nineteenth century. It is much denser in Europe and Japan, quite dense in North America, India, and China, and denser around the coastal Cities of the World Ocean in general. It is markedly less dense in interior Asia, Latin America, and Africa, but it is growing fast there thanks to logging and ranching in the Amazon and the enormous "Belt and Road" transport initiatives financed from Beijing. Meanwhile, the human-built lacework extends across the seas, through the air, and beyond. Shipping lanes wide enough for the largest fleets of the largest vehicles ever constructed connect thousands of the largest ports ever built; the big ships leave long heavy-fuel slicks in their oceanic wakes – that is, when they do not run aground in the middle of the Suez Canal, as one mega-ship did in 2020, instead backing up long lines of floating behemoths deep into the Red Sea. There are over 41,000 airports on Earth, about 17,000 capable of handling commercial jets and 1,500 equipped with customs offices for international flights. Before the Covid-19 pandemic shut down international travel in 2020, over 26,000 passenger airplanes filled the skies, leaving behind an ever thicker network of jet trails. Earth has just one Moon, but since Sputnik, Earthopolis has had over 8,000 human-made satellites launched into its orbit at different times, equipped to prop up the internet and other communications, spy on enemies, and track our ever more turbulent weather.[6]

No matter how we measure it, building an Urban Planet of this size requires colossal forces of extraction from the natural lithosphere and vast amounts of industrial processing of extracted materials. Long before the hydrocarbon age, city and village builders set aside the flimsier, typically plant- and animal-based materials we used to build temporary camps, preferring solider stuff like wood, stone, rammed earth, or some reworked form of clay: adobe, brick, and mortar. Much later, the industrial revolution spawned a construction revolution relying on factory-made materials. The Crystal Palace (1854) celebrated the first buildings made of iron girders and glass, and the Portland cement that Joseph Bazalgette manufactured in such large quantities for London's sewer system found its way into the first steel-reinforced concrete skyscrapers, giving rise to ever larger cement plants. Modernist architects so loved the sharp, unadorned look of concrete – held in place by steel reinforcements and accessorized only by glass – that cement factories and cement mixers followed them everywhere they designed and built. The Hoover Dam (1936) advertised the virtues of concrete as eloquently as the Eiffel Tower (1889) had done for iron girders. Concrete became the city-making material of choice for the Great Acceleration, notably in the "brutalist" period of modern architecture named after *béton brut*, French *urbanistes'* word for raw cement. Prefabricated concrete panels even made inroads in the self-built cities of the poor. Yet concrete, like meat in the food world, is the most resource-inefficient way to transform the Earth's crust into our own. It requires enormous mines of limestone, gravel, and gypsum, and, because steel-mill-grade heat is required to make the "clinker" that holds concrete together, cement plants burn colossal amounts of petroleum. The Burj-Khalifa in Dubai – the tallest building in world history upon its completion in 2010 – consists of 375,000 cubic meters of concrete, which required 100,000 barrels of

Persian Gulf oil to make and mix. Worldwide, the production of cement accelerated from about 133 million tons in 1950 to a billion in 1990. That accounts for all of the *Khrushchyovki* of the Soviet Bloc, the many mega-dams that followed in the Hoover Dam's heavy footsteps, all of brutalist architecture, the countless home foundations and towers-in-the-park elsewhere, the newest generation of concrete railway ties, and millions of expressway overpasses, concrete roadways, temporary road dividers, driveways, and sidewalks. The US Interstate Expressway system alone, as its greatest champion President Dwight Eisenhower famously boasted, contained enough concrete for "eighty Hoover dams or six sidewalks to the moon." And yet, just since 1990, concrete use has quadrupled again. Most of the newest batches went into building the cities, highways, and rail lines of China, which, according to the US Geological Survey, pro-duced more cement in the years 2011 through 2013 alone than the USA did in the entire twentieth century.[7]

The mining of metals likewise accelerated since 1950, keeping pace with the demands for skyscraper and bridge girders, all the stuff of global consumer culture, and the increasingly complex electronics technolo-gies that went into some of the things we buy most – cars, appliances, computers, and cell phones. With some exceptions – most notable being the gold-mining city of Johannesburg and the Copper Belt towns of Zambia and Congo – the mining of metal ores does not generate large neighboring cities; rather it contributes to Urban Planetary growth by requiring bigger and typically more dispersed processing plants as well as extended transport facilities in order to feed urban factories. Yet open-pit metal mines are among the largest things people have built on Earth. Their apocalyptic, roughly chiseled, and downward spiraling landscapes are also home to some of largest land vehicles ever built, and large workforces toil there in sometimes appalling conditions before returning home to squalid, often poisoned, homes nearby. Iron mines, by far the largest and most numerous of all metal mines, have also expanded the most in number, size, production, and global extent since 1950. While iron mining increased, then stabilized in legacy industrial homelands after 1945, it expanded even more rapidly after 1970 in Brazil and India, after 1980 in Australia, and after 1990 in China. Brazil is home to five of the largest iron mines in the world, topped by the Carajas open-pit mine in the country's northeast. An even larger number of enormous iron mines in China's provinces of Hebei, Liaoning, and Inner Mongolia drove a quintupling of the country's production from 2005 to 2020, making China the world's leading iron ore producer by far. Despite a waning demand for copper, largely caused by the advent of fiber-optic cables for communications, other giant pits, spread across the world, have expelled increased amounts of non-ferrous metals like zinc, lead, tin, nickel, and bauxite – needed for the perilous business of making aluminum. Uranium mining escalated along with the demand for Cold War weapons and nuclear reactor fuel. Dangerous new facilities opened up across the world outside the territories of the superpowers, notably in Canada, Kazakhstan, Niger, and Namibia. As the nuclear power industry declined recently, so has uranium production. By contrast, demand for cell phone and electronic vehicle batteries drove a doubling of cobalt mining after 2006 – over 60 percent of it from giant pit mines developed by Chinese capitalists in conflict-ridden southeastern Congo. Lithium mining, for batteries in electronic devices, tripled after 2012. It requires toxic evaporating pans, such as those in the deserts of northern Chile and western Bolivia; they should remind us of the dangerous mercury "patios" of sixteenth-century Potosí.[8]

On the Planet of Mines, coal remains more important than metal to the Greatest Acceleration. Coal mining has also torn a far larger gash in the Earth's surface, thanks to enormous pits and surface strips like the Hambach Open Pit Mine in Germany, and to the extraordinary practice of "mountaintop removal" in North America's Appalachian Mountains, where enormous excavators flatten peaks and dump toxic tailings into stream valleys. The acceleration of coal mining nonetheless closely mirrors the regional geography of iron. Relative declines in Europe, and more recently in the USA and the former Soviet Bloc, have been offset by enormous spikes in tonnage from new mines in India and China; China also burns most of the coal scoured from widening open-pit mines in Australia. Few factories run directly off coal as they did in Manchester, and coal home heating has dropped dramatically, again especially in the Global North. Nonetheless, coal still generates nearly 40 percent of the world's electricity – natural gas and petroleum add another 35 percent – even as nuclear power wanes and the share produced by solar panels and wind and water turbines begins to rise. That said, the global geography of coal-fired plants is highly uneven too. Most of the hundreds of plants in Europe, North America, and Japan are scheduled for closure within the next few decades. In post-Soviet Russia, old Five-Year-Plan plants continue to power most cities, particularly in central Siberia. By contrast, thousands of brand-new plants have opened in recent decades in India, in Southeast Asia, and above all in China. Kilometers-long coal trains file into Beijing, Delhi, and most of Asia's megacities on a daily basis to pour hard black fuel into giant furnaces that provide the majority of electric power there – and much of the smoky air. Far fewer coal-fired plants have ever been built in Latin America, the Middle East, and Africa outside of coal-rich South Africa (Soweto is still largely a coal-heated city). The highly centralized electric grids encouraged by coal-fired plants are notoriously unequal providers of power. Because of the expense of stringing electric wire from hubs to distant villages, let alone between rickety poles in self-built megacity neighborhoods, over a billion people still have no electricity in their homes.[9]

HYDROCARBON ZENITH: CITIES OF OIL

As coal, the pioneer fuel of the hydrocarbon revolution, refashioned itself as an electricity specialist in Asia, petroleum rose to the throne as "king of all raw materials." The "global petroleumscape" – as the planning historian Carola Hein calls the built environment dedicated to our hunger for oil – became the most ravenous of all of our lithospheric extraction systems. In tandem with a parallel structure designed for natural gas, its basic sucking and dispersing structures – derricks, fracking and offshore drilling platforms, field camps, flaring pipes, pipelines, tank farms, tanker ports, tanker ships, tank trains, tank trucks, refineries, gas stations, and vast municipal and household piping systems – lead in one way or another to virtually all other built spaces of the Urban Planet. At the consumption end of this black-blooded circulatory system are hundreds of millions of house-heating furnaces and kitchen stoves, and billions of combustion engines. From there, historically high urban real estate values rely foundationally on oil and gas, as vehicular technologies and land prices are intrinsically bound to each other. Concrete buildings, as we know from Dubai, are slaves to hydrocarbon inputs. Factories, it is true, no longer run directly on oil or gas like Manchester's did on coal, but the vehicles that bring raw materials in through the factory gates and that ferry manufactured goods back out to marketplaces do not operate without heavy fuel (ships), diesel fuel (trucks and most locomotives), jet fuel, and gasoline. The business of pulling trillions of dollars from the pockets of tourists and business travelers each year also relies existentially on airplane fuel and gas for vehicles, including auto-rickshaws. Most consumer items, finally, are made of plastic – or they are packaged in massive amounts of it – another pestilential progeny of oil and gas.[10]

Our appetite for oil and gas is governed from such twitchy imperial-capitalist nerve-centers as the Pentagon, the White House, the headquarters of oil companies and cartels, and the global city financial districts, many of whose prominent banks owe their very existence to loans they make to oil companies. Since the 1930s, imperialists have become far more obsessed with the control of the petroleumscape – or at least some kind of sway over oil production quotas and prices – than they were with earlier efforts to control spice islands, cotton fields, rubber plantations, goldfields, diamond mines, coaling stations, or, more recently, cobalt pits. In the 1980s petroleum displaced Cold War ideological differences as the pivot of global geopolitics, igniting world history's most cynical "resource conflicts" – the twin Persian Gulf Wars of the two American Presidents Bush. The price these oil warriors willingly paid for their particular "fixes" of the Urban Planet's maximal hydrocarbon addiction was a series of blindingly violent terrorist attacks, followed by a "War on Terror" that obscured the central role of oil and gas in unremitting suffering in the great cities of the Middle East and beyond.

If there is a central pumping station in the vast built realm of the global petroleumscape, it is located a few miles outside the Persian Gulf port city of Dammam, Saudi Arabia. There, after World War II, a small pre-existing settlement of American petro-prospectors blossomed into a scale-model of a California condo-complex called Dhahran Main Camp. This strange place owed its conception to a 1944 assignation between elected US President Franklin Roosevelt and the absolutist King Abd al-Aziz ibn Saud of Saudi Arabia on an American battleship moored in the Suez Canal. The American prospectors had discovered what turned out to be the world's largest oilfield not far from Dhahran, and the deal was simple. The king got American military support and oil drilling experts. The USA got oil. Dhahran housed the expat experts.

The same pen strokes drastically augmented the power of movements we now lump together as "Islamic fundamentalism," or perhaps more accurately, radical-right Islam. The Saudi dynasty's rule over Arabia originated in a walled cluster of oasis towns called Riyadh ("The Gardens"), fed by the Wadi Hanif, a seasonal river that runs through the heart of some of the driest deserts on Earth. In these same towns, the eighteenth-century cleric Mohammed al-Wahhab began a movement to restore Islam to what he deemed its original practices. The Saudi dynasty strengthened its power by patronizing his sect, for the Wahhabis' reputation for piety allowed the Saudis to win allegiance of various armed nomadic groups to fight off competing fortress-based dynasties on the peninsula. In the 1920s, ibn Saud managed to seize control of the holy cities of Mecca and Medina. Britain recognized his rule, and the new king massacred a nomadic Wahhabi army called the Ikhwan that had helped him win power but that began attacking British-ruled territories. To forestall resentment from Wahhabi 'ulamā' (scholar-preachers), the king redoubled his support of the sect's sway in the mosques and madrassas (religious schools) of cities in Saudi Arabia, and soon across the Sunni Islamic world.[11]

The key to ibn Saud's dynastic future and the power of Wahhabism, however, lay underneath the desert sands near Dhahran. Once the king and the president had signed their agreement, a consortium of four American oil companies headquartered in New York and Houston – all of them offshoots of John Rockefeller's dismantled Standard Oil – joined forces with venerable Wall Street banks to charter the Arab–American Oil Company, or Aramco, building its headquarters in Dhahran. Aramco gained exclusive drilling rights in the surrounding Ghawar and Safaniya oilfields, respectively the world's largest onshore and offshore deposits of easily tapped petroleum. This golden-black opportunity came at a crucial moment for the USA. Similar oilfields in Texas, Oklahoma, and California had produced copiously in response to the needs of World War II, but they strained to meet the escalating need for hydrocarbon in the booming postwar-era American tailpipe suburbs. With access to easily pumped cheap Arabian oil, Washington could expand the FHA's financing of vast racially segregated American subdivisions on which tiny Dhahran was modeled – together with the uniquely petroleum-dependent commuter- and consumer-driven "growth economy" that those suburbs brought into being. Houston, the American oil capital, became a global exemplar of low-density suburban living that has kept US per-capita petroleum consumption higher by far than in any other country on Earth. The family of the oilman George H. W. Bush was one of many that moved to Houston from declining industrial cities in the north. Forty years later, he would defend the "American Way of Life" exemplified by the suburbanites of Houston as a "non-negotiable" aim of oil war. Wealthy Saudis soon acquired a taste in upscale Houston real estate too. Private jets allowed quick commutes to mansions in Texas from mansions in Jeddah.[12]

Meanwhile, in Riyadh, untold oil revenues flooded the Royal Treasury. Ibn Saud and his successor contracted with the Jeddah-based bin Laden Construction Company to build an enormous royal palace fit for a theocratic despotism; nearby Deera Square (nicknamed "Chop-Chop Square") served as a site for public beheadings and even crucifixions. Yet the lavish lifestyle of Saudi princes and their contractors rankled the fundamentalists they had suppressed, and in the 1960s, the dynasty's successor King Faisal further angered Wahhabi *'ulamā'* by launching a developmentalist program of tax-free welfare benefits and schools that, among other sins, educated women. Yet the fundamentalists were irked even more by Dhahran Main Camp. With the king's permission and Aramco money, the US Army Corps of Engineers laid out an island of American-style ranch homes, condominium blocks, primary and middle schools, a hospital, shopping centers with American products, restaurants, gender-integrated dance clubs, a dedicated Persian Gulf beach resort for half-naked bathers, and soon another separate elite neighborhood for company executives. Uncannily green lawns, street trees, and even a grassy golf course sprouted from the scorched desert sands, much as they did in the far larger FHA suburbs around desert boomtowns like Phoenix and Las Vegas. Even as these US cities sucked the Colorado River dry, similar expatriate enclaves bloomed around Riyadh and Jeddah, the holy port used by *hajjis* arriving in Mecca. Though

Dhahran was a corporate-owned enclave, it was manifestly a space of empire. An American airbase spread-eagled next door, to protect the House of Saud and the suburban houses of Aramco "oil wives" and "oil brats." The threats that the base was designed to fight were very real. In Riyadh newer versions of armed anti-colonial fundamentalist Ikhwan warriors arose again in rebellion, and riots repeatedly flared around the gates of Dhahran Main Camp and other Aramco facilities. Oil-infused anti-colonialist and religious rivalries simmered between Riyadh and nearby Baghdad and Tehran, whose agents conspired to launch anti-Saudi uprisings during the Hajj in Jeddah and Mecca.[13]

The nervous sinews of hydrocarbon, corporate power, and overseas military might that intersected at Dhahran shivered throughout the global petroleumscape. During the 1950s and 1960s, the "Seven Sisters," consisting of Aramco's four partners plus three other oil giants, conspired in their headquarters in Houston, New York, and London to keep the world price of oil low enough to discourage competition from smaller "wildcatter" oil companies. The Seven Sisters' dominance over Middle Eastern production spread to the world's other "supergiant" oilfields, such as around Ahvas and Abadan, Iran, the Burgan field in Kuwait and the Rumailah field along its border with Iraq, the East Baghdad and Kirkuk fields, the Upper Zakum field near Abu Dhabi, and the rich coastal fields of Venezuela. In so doing, they minimized the costs suffered in Houston when import-substitutionists in Mexico City nationalized the country's oilfields around Tampico. With all that power, the Seven Sisters far out-produced Soviet oilfields in the Caspian Sea and Siberia, as well as those in Mao Zedong's model oil city of Daqing in Manchuria.[14]

Oil wells nonetheless multiplied in all of these places, as they did in the US Southwest. Thanks to the bin Ladens, Aramco built a vast oil processing facility in the sands of Abqaiq north of Damman; the company's tanker ports and refineries sprawled at Ras Tanura near Damman, at Jeddah, on Kharg Island, Iran, and at Basrah, Iraq. The "Ras Tanura Price" of oil set the standard worldwide, just as Amsterdam had done with pepper and Liverpool with cotton. The 1,200-kilometer Trans-Arabian Pipeline, flanked by fences and a dead-straight security road, stretched from Dhahran across the desert to Beirut in order to supply Europe. Ever larger oil ships clogged the Persian Gulf, the Suez Canal, and the Straits of Malacca, leaving miles-long wakes – and often tanker spills – behind. Receiving ports and refineries metastasized along the Delaware River in Philadelphia, along the New Jersey side of New York Harbor, in Tokyo Bay, at Fos-sur-Mer near Marseille, and downriver along the Maas River estuary in Rotterdam, where tank farms plunged far into the North Sea on reclaimed land. From 1950 to 1970, oil production grew from about ten million to sixty million barrels a day. Petroleum's share in Earthopolis's total production of energy grew from half to double that of coal. The manufacture of gasoline-powered cars and trucks more than doubled from fifteen million to thirty-three million from 1961 to 1971, a large percentage still from factories in Detroit, now supplemented by rebuilt auto-works in Coventry, Stuttgart, and Nagoya. Plants that made plastic from oil grew alongside refineries – notably in "Cancer Alley" along the lower Mississippi and upriver from Rotterdam, in Antwerp, Cologne, and the Ruhr. Plastic factories erupted with their uniquely non-degradable hardened petroleum, producing about one and a half million metric tons in 1950 worldwide and fifty million in 1976. Add all of these structures to the global petroleumscape, and we can unveil the final segment of our long-sought answer to the riddle of the Great Acceleration. Cities began to grow so fast after 1945 because they washed themselves in cheap oil – much of it slurped from the sands underneath the very same Mesopotamian and Persian Gulf regions where cities were born in the first place.[15]

New plot twists in this story of oil and cities were quick to materialize. In 1973, the military, corporate, and extractive edifice that created Dhahran Main Camp and its cheap oil shattered. In protest of American military aid to Israel during the Yom Kippur War that year, the Saudis broke with Washington and the Seven Sisters – and the royals of Riyadh took direct control over Aramco headquarters. Local rivals followed suit: the US-supported Shah of Iran and the secular Arab nationalists in Baghdad. Newly nationalized Middle Eastern oil companies joined with their Third World Latin American allies to create a price-fixing cartel of their own, the Organization of Petroleum Exporting Countries (OPEC), abruptly switching power over the global petroleumscape to OPEC's headquarters in Vienna. When the new cartel cut production in 1973, 1975, and 1979, Houston's car owners seethed in miles-long lines for fuel at suburban gas stations. Prices at the pumps quintupled. First World economies battled the inflation and unemployment that arose simultaneously from expensive oil, and the Greatest Acceleration slowed appreciably for a half-decade. Notably, a decade-long slowdown began in the growth of the world's fleet of passenger cars. All of Detroit's auto plants cut back production, and many closed forever. Detroit's losses in factories and its plummeting population were among the worst of those in the First World's deindustrializing cities. As the Greatest Acceleration picked up again elsewhere during the 1980s, industrial giants like Milwaukee, Buffalo, Pittsburgh, Baltimore, Glasgow, Essen, Leipzig, Turin, Donetsk, and Nizhni-Novgorod all joined the ranks of "shrinking cities."[16]

In Washington, the White House and the Pentagon "solved" the oil crisis by playing on tensions within Saudi society, and between Riyadh, Baghdad, and Tehran – in each capital wielding the USA's favorite form of superpower: weapons proliferation. In 1975, Wahhabi rebels assassinated King Faisal in Riyadh, and in 1979, another group briefly seized the holy Mosque at Mecca. In a tumultuous revolution, radical clerics took power in Tehran. Faisal's successor King Fahd assuaged his radicals by opening the country to fundamentalist exiles from prisons in Cairo, Damascus, and Baghdad, some of whom preferred the term Salafi for their practices. The prestige of Wahhabi and Salafi *'ulamā'* grew in Islam's birthplace. Religious police enforced gender segregation in Saudi cities, including a ban on women driving cars. Playing on the crisis, Presidents Carter and Reagan offered King Fahd advanced weapons in exchange for a commitment to reopen the oil-taps at Dhahran and thus to lower the price of oil. Fahd submitted, partly also to join forces with the USA to weaken the already tottering USSR. Moscow relied on sales of Caspian and Siberian oil to Europe as its main source of hard currency. As the last Soviet leader Mikhail Gorbachev later confirmed, the temporary return to lower oil prices – plus American opposition to a new Soviet–European pipeline – helped speed the decline of the Soviet economy during the 1980s and the implosion of the USSR in 1991.[17]

George H. W. Bush of Houston became US President a few years before the climactic moment in 1989 when the Berlin wall fell to the ground, taking the entire "Second World" along with it. Bush reversed Reagan's course on oil prices: dangling still more weapons, he convinced the Saudis to close the taps at Dhahran to a trickle and force the Ras Tanura price to rise again. George Bush's Houston-centric worldview was more subtle than Reagan's was, for as Bush knew intimately, the higher oil prices of the 1970s had actually been profitable for the Seven Sisters. Reagan's return to lower prices in the meantime had boosted the US economy overall, but several regional economic "busts" had occurred in previously booming Oil Patch cities, including Houston. (George Bush's son, a less successful oilman also named George, was one of the victims.) Fields in Mexico, Venezuela, Southeast Asia, and the Caspian meanwhile rose to their own "peak oil" moments and began slow declines. Coal made a resurgence, as did nuclear power. For oil companies to continue making profits, they needed capital to begin risky searches for new "unconventional" – that is, very expensive – sources of oil. For them, less oil from Dhahran, not more, meant higher oil prices and more profits in their own pockets, all the better to expand the frontiers of the petroleumscape to new extremes.[18]

Then, Iraq's Saddam Hussein invaded Kuwait to seize the southern end of the Rumaila fields; and Dhahran itself came into range of his huge fleet of Russian-made tanks. On behalf of Houston and America's tail-pipe suburbs, George Bush went to war in the Middle East. He pressed the Saudi king to invite a gigantic force of American troops, ships, and planes back into the vicinity of Dhahran. American bombers lifted from the runways at King Abdul Aziz Air Base, passed through thousands of columns of black smoke rising from Kuwaiti oil derricks ignited by Saddam's retreating troops, and pummeled Iraqi cities from the air. The bombs ruined power grids, factories, Green Revolution food systems, hospitals, and clinics, killing as many as a quarter million Iraqis and guaranteeing a half million premature deaths of Iraqi children during the 1990s. The four biggest sisters of the original seven began the new era of higher-priced Arabian oil by consuming their weaker siblings. One of the combined giants, ExxonMobil – formed in the suburbs of Dallas in 1996 – became for a time the largest company in the world. With Saddam constrained and the price of petroleum nicely elevated, the new corporate behemoths set out for the far frontiers of the oil and gas world.[19]

Meanwhile though, emboldened terror cells grew in villas near Cairo and on ranches owned by wealthy Saudis near Medina. In Palestinian cities like Nablus and Gaza, in chaotic Beirut, and in revolutionary Tehran, "jihadists" trained to fight Israel and the West. In the virtually ungoverned cities of Peshawar and Quetta in northwest Pakistan, the American CIA itself had supplied fundamentalist *mujahedin* with weapons to stymie the Soviet occupation of Afghanistan. That paved the road for the ultra-fundamentalist Taliban, named after the word for madrassa students, to come to power in Kabul and begin a regime that consigned Afghan women to their homes, to full-length *burqas*, and to street violence by squads of religious enforcers. In the wake of Bush's Gulf War, a smattering of especially radical militant *jihadis* came together as al-Qaeda, led and financed by Osama bin Laden, heir to the fortunes of the oil construction family. Bin Laden's allies in Kabul and Peshawar offered protection to al-Qaeda, which recycled oil money into explosives and terror training bases in the Afghan mountains, then, attacked US military targets, embassies in Nairobi and Dar es Salaam, and the Khobar Towers housing complex in Dhahran. Then on September 11, 2001 al-Qaeda militants, most of them Saudis, flew hijacked American airplanes into the uppermost nerve centers of the petroleumscape – Wall Street's World Trade Center and Washington's Pentagon.[20]

The new American President was George Bush the younger. He responded with massive bombing sorties on Afghan cities, including Kabul. The Taliban, allied with Saudi jihadis, fought the US just as Afghans had fought other superpowers such as the British and the Soviets before, from guerrilla sanctuaries and caves in the region's bleak mountains and from the streets of Peshawar on the other side of the ungoverned Pakistani border. Bush reopened Houston's war for high oil prices, now scantily disguised as a "War on Terror." Once again, the Saudi king offered Dhahran's military bases – and lots of fuel for military vehicles. In 2003, Bush the son far outdid his father's assault on Saddam's Iraq, complete with massive aerial bombings and indiscriminate civilian casualties. Entering Baghdad within a few weeks, American soldiers allowed looters to overrun such monuments to the Urban Planet as the Iraqi Archaeological Museum (they even stole the Warka Vase), making American priorities clear by seizing the Oil Ministry first of all. In Iraq, as in Afghanistan, years of strife followed. Sectarian militias split Baghdad and the Shia Holy Cities of Karbala and Najaf into warring Sunni and Shia districts whose streets echoed with car bombs. Iraqi resistance to the Americans resulted in horrific urban battles in cities like Fallujah. Soon an offshoot of al-Qaeda called Daesh seized the oil cities of Kirkuk and Mosul on its way to establishing an Islamic State that spread a regime of seventh-century law far into civil-war-wracked Syria. New bursts of urban warfare turned Mosul and the Daesh capital of Raqqah into smoldering ruins, even as the Syrian regime in Damascus bombed its own people in the massive cities they had liberated from its tyranny.[21]

Out of all of these calamities came new profits for the four remaining oil titans. Already in the 1970s, they used higher revenues to extend the petroleumscape to remote places, where getting oil to the surface required high-tech construction unimaginable two decades before. The Prudhoe Bay oilfield opened in far northern Alaska in 1977 after a 1,300-kilometer pipeline connected it to an ice-free port in the small town of Valdez after crossing wide rivers, mountain chains, and soon-to-be-melting permafrost. The Canadian oil town of Fort McMurray, Alberta arose amidst the Athabasca tar sand fields, a huge territory of forest and bogs now home to giant surface excavators, 400-ton trucks, and hundreds of venomous lake-sized tailing ponds that they left behind. A global archipelago of over 1,400 offshore platforms spread throughout the stormy North Sea, the ecologically fragile Gulf of Mexico, the politically contentious South China Sea, the Gulf of Guinea, the Angola Basin, the Mumbai High Fields off India, and above the three-kilometer-deep ocean floors off the coast of São Paulo, Brazil. Vast fields in the "Oil Rivers" region of Nigeria exploited by Shell and Chevron became the site of a low-level resource war in which state troops killed thousands of people who protested the devastation of traditional riverine food sources by oil spills.[22]

Seven thousand oil tanker ships, meanwhile, sailed the oceans, many so large they demanded superlative classifications like "Very Large Crude Carriers" (VLCCs, capacity two million barrels) and "Ultra Large Crude Carriers" (ULCCs, up to four million). The largest ULCC, the *Knock Nevis* – almost a half kilometer in length – was too big to enter any port. It spent most of its life as an offshore storage facility near new Persian Gulf oilfields off Doha, Qatar. Over three and half million kilometers of oil and gas pipelines expanded the Urban Planet's worldwide lacework of built structures, with an 8,000-kilometer behemoth planned to connect new oilfields in Xinjiang with Mao's oil city at Daqing – an homage in flowing hydrocarbon to the ancient Silk Road. Seven hundred oil refineries looped labyrinths of coiled pipe in port cities across the world, sending ominous gas-flares skyward above such "African Kuwaits" as Pointe-Noire, Congo, Libreville, Gabon, and Cabinda, Angola. The largest of all refineries, a twin complex at Jamnagar, on the Gujarati coast a few miles from where Gandhi made salt, connects via three parallel pipelines to gas stations in Delhi, fueling more than ten million vehicles including those 200,000 auto-rickshaws. In the USA alone, some 670,000 "fracking" wells have spread across wide regions – tapping gas in the original oil lands of Pennsylvania, and oil in the Permian Basin of West Texas and the Bakken fields of North Dakota. Each pad is surmounted with a high-tech drill tower and storage tanks for poisonous fracking liquids, surrounded by networks of access roads, trailer-park-type residences for drilling personnel ("man camps"), and associated "adult entertainment" districts. As human-built environments go, fracking patches are among the most fleeting, for their lifetimes are governed by profit-and-loss calculations tabulated in Houston, by production quotas set in Vienna, by spot-prices paid at Ras Tanura, by speculators in oil futures in Manhattan and London, by rattling sabers in Washington, Riyadh, Baghdad, and Tehran, and in multiplying terror cells worldwide.[23]

Taken together, imperial war and the construction of "unconventional" parts of the petroleumscape – both made possible by oil from "heritage" spigots such as at Dhahran – combined to rescue the Great Acceleration in human petroleum use after 1980. From under sixty million barrels per day in the early 1980s, production rose to over 100 million barrels in 2019. That year, as the desert city of Riyadh bloomed into a skyscraping financial center of over five million people, US shales and offshore rigs out-produced Saudi wells for the first time since the 1950s. Manufacture of gasoline and diesel-fueled vehicles more than tripled from twenty-seven million in 1981 to an astounding ninety-five million in 2018. Detroit's share fell from 80 percent to 5 percent of the new spiraling total, as car plants in Ulsan, Korea, in rings of new assembly plants around Mexico City and São Paulo, and in Gurugram outside Delhi took up even larger shares. By 2010, China's assembly lines in Yangtze megacities like Wuhan and Chongqing generated two and a half times as many vehicles as those in the USA. Plastics production meanwhile septupled, from fifty million metric tons in 1976 to 350 million in 2018, as new Cancer Alleys came into being in the coal lands of Pennsylvania and as plastics factories multiplied across China and East Asia. As China's overall oil consumption grew, the USA remained by far the highest per-capita gas-guzzling country, and Houston continued to sprawl, even after Hurricane Harvey flooded huge areas of the city's suburban real estate – and its vast port and refinery lands – in 2017.[24]

Still, the outer limits of the petroleumscape may be coming more sharply into view. Politically, imperial scrambles for oil have intensified counterforces capable of stymying even the worlds' most powerful "War on Terror"-era militaries. Persistent al-Qaeda knock-off groups in the Sahara and Somali deserts, and the Taliban's swift second conquest of Afghanistan in 2021 prove once again that sparse, inhospitable, road-poor mountain valleys and even caves can still act as "Graveyards of Empire," no matter how many "bunker-busting" bombs the Pentagon drops or how much counter-terror it delivers from its dozen-and-a-half regional drone bases. The fall of Kabul in 2021, of course, occurred despite the additional fact that the USA funneled a trillion dollars' worth of development funds through a fortified Green Zone in the Afghan capital with the goal of "building" a "nation" upon prisons, airfields, military bases, and a hierarchy of quasi-sovereign, quasi-liberal cities. Extracting a barrel of oil from the lithosphere now requires burning twice as much oil as it did in the 1970s, and explorations further into the Arctic have stalled, despite US President Trump's dogged efforts to open ecologically sensitive zones to drillers. Though the shale boom momentarily "emancipated" US oil supplies from OPEC, frackers pumped such a glut onto the global market that lower prices caused many operations to cease. This spread new oil patch recessions and scattered rusting derricks across places like the Bakken oil play in the northern Great Plains. During "Black April" 2020, the Covid-19 epidemic so depressed demand for oil that its price plunged into negative figures: paying the cost of storing oil was preferable to selling it. But most important of all are the limits we set by our own meddling in the relationship of Sun and Earth. The movement to halt global warming has correctly identified the petroleumscape for what it is: a cancerous tumor on the human habitat that has too long posed as its beating heart. Indeed, a Greatest Acceleration fueled by oil creates an Urban Planet ever more likely to choke to death on its own very dangerous waste.[25]

LAYING WASTE TO EARTHOPOLIS

At Ghazipur, an idling rickshaw engine chortles happily on its refilled gas tank, and beckons us onward, toward future Urban Planetary adventures. Yet the great garbage dump signals "No"! Remain here and contemplate the enormity of this place. We need a final and fulsome reckoning with our waste if we are to move forward with any hope. The evidence is piled high in front of us, monumentally in fact – for Ghazipur, local headlines scream, has grown "Almost as Tall as the Taj Mahal!" More smelly clues float in the inky moats that exude around the base of the great pile – human tributes to the Yamuna River that receives them a mere six kilometers away via the Ghazipur Canal and the stygian Shahadra Drain. The timing of our visit, on a smoky November evening, also suits us well as global urban historians, for the stench and the smoke in the air contain their own rich archive of human waste. Even more fruitfully, we could return at dawn in high summer, when the sun's rays ignite yet another tandoori oven of a Delhi day. By noontime on such days, when the heat sharpens the stink and attacks our bodies' waning capacity to cool ourselves, all the dirty secrets of the Greatest Acceleration leap out of Ghazipur, assaulting all of senses.[26]

Yet Ghazipur is just one tiny, hot, stinking tip of a much bigger human-piled monument, the largest thing we have ever "built," in fact, far larger than the megacities and the hard lacework of the Urban Planet itself, and far more mobile, even volatile. The Great Global Waste Acceleration, like the explosion of the built Urban Planet itself, consists of natural materials from across Earth, but it is a thing in constant motion: it erupts, piles up, flows, blows, rises aloft, and becomes one with the world's weather. It is solid, liquid, and gas, and it is virtually everywhere. Solid trash may accumulate in Ghazipur, but it also blows throughout the Urban Planet

(A)

(B)

24.1. Planet on Fire!
Black clouds signal distress: our Urban Planet faces ever direr consequences from amplified human action, habitat, and impact. In 2012, at Venezuela's Paraguana Oil Refining Complex (A) – the world's second-largest – a gas explosion killed forty, injured eighty, and launched a dark anthropogenic assault on the atmosphere. Oil spills, sub-ocean blowouts, well fires, fracking dumps, gas leaks, and the overheated heavens now form an integral realm of urban space. At the other end of our city-planet's alimentary canal, landfills like Delhi's Ghazipur Mountain (B) generate gases prone to spontaneous

and far beyond, into the wildernesses of all continents. The waste flow's wetter and more microscopic parts pervade the global hydrosphere as a whole – not just canals, drains, and the Yamuna but all rivers, lakes, and oceans – even the very rain and snow, even the water that makes up our bodies' very cells. Our waste planet's most mobile elements are gases from tailpipes, chimneys, and smokestacks that fly to the farthest reaches of the atmosphere – enough to trap planet-cooking heat. That not only raises the temperature in hot summertime Delhi, but also threatens the world's iciest stretches – the cryosphere, the quick-melting realm of water in its solid state. A rising World Ocean is the result.[27]

As a phenomenon in motion, the Waste Acceleration is best divided into three: an upstream of many capillaries and tributaries, a midstream of digestive tracts and rectal openings (in full obscene view at Ghazipur), and a vast, continental, oceanic, and atmospheric downstream – sometimes called the "pollution-shed," humanity's "environmental footprint," or, less reverently, the "global toilet bowl." Like other human-created things, the Waste Acceleration is unjust in its very structure: the poorest people in the world contribute by far the least upstream and suffer by far the most midstream and downstream. Like the Urban Planet that generates it, the waste acceleration is varied in composition, merging the dangerous byproducts of our use of biomass and mineral toxins. Of minerals, hydrocarbons matter most. Of hydrocarbons, petroleum remains "king" even after we burn it into waste. It is oil that transforms a waste stream that is merely a smelly, unhealthful, inevitable byproduct of acceleration into a planetary existential threat.

Plant and animal material – biomass – remains a ubiquitous part of the upstream component of our great waste mountain – as in refuse dumps going back to the first village middens that so delight archaeologists. Today there are tens of thousands of municipal landfills worldwide, some

---

Caption for 24.1. (cont.)

combustion, as in November 2020. Trash fires aggravate the city's smoky winters and interrupt the vital work of thousands of waste recyclers. Meanwhile, humans too haltingly renegotiate our underworldly bargain between Earthopolis and Hydrocarbon.
(A) AFP/Getty Images. (B) Hindustan Times/Getty Images.

on land, some on sea-bottoms near port cities. Garbage trucks – like the 600 that each day grind up the switchbacks they have compacted into the flanks of Ghazipur – and garbage barges feed these piles collectively by more than two billion tons each year. Most on-land dumps are located in poor neighborhoods. Partly this is because, thus far, no gilded land investor has succeeded in gentrifying neighborhoods near active land-fills. Also, as we know, trash sorters, who make their living at the dumps and who do indeed live nearby, are among the poorest people on earth. Other poor neighborhoods fester from uncounted tons of garbage that municipal services neglect to collect and that pile up in streets. Together these piles all at very least contain the scraps from billions of kitchens – to which we need to add the enormous tonnage of food we waste on farms, in transport, at sorting and processing plants, and at marketplaces. Wherever it accumulates, typically mixed with human sewage, food gar-bage also draws rodents, cockroaches, and other local vermin and dis-ease-carriers. Their feces adds to the threat of respiratory disease, as does mold, another biological toxin found above all in poor neighborhoods where ventilation is hardest to come by, where older buildings are more common, and where more garbage piles up. A final factor in these accumulations of bio-waste is our still largely mind-numbing lack of initiative in re-creating urban composting systems that pre-modern cities often managed far better than we do, even in the richest cities, today.[28]

Because organic waste gets compacted under tons of other garbage in landfills, anaerobic bacteria are the only available biota to break it down. Unlike their oxygen-breathing cousins, anaerobic species exhale methane, a particularly caloric contributor to planetary heating. In addition, according to climate scientists in Delhi who are equipped to sort through a city's gaseous wastes, spontaneous fires that break out on Ghazipur Mountain and the city's four other landfills, plus trash fires in the streets, contribute between 10 and 20 percent of the particulates that make up Delhi's November smoke. There they join other floating residues from biomass burning elsewhere. Wood and dung cooking or home heating fires are no longer allowed within Delhi's city limits, but biomass smoke from surrounding villages and towns floats freely into the megacity. During the high hydrocarbon era, two billion people worldwide still cook and heat with wood, peat, or cow-dung, accounting for 10 percent of all human energy use. Most people living in cities of the Global South breathe a lot of smoke from home fires, which account for poor peoples' single largest upstream component to the world's waste. A more important component of Delhi's November smoke-storms – 17 percent according to the climate scientists – comes from thousands of acres of surrounding fields where farmers burn wheat crop residue in time to plant rice (Figure 21.2). Biomass burning for agricultural purposes occurs on even larger scales in the Amazon and the Southeast Asian rainforest belts. There larger-scale commercial farmers do most of the waste-generating work – either burning sugar-cane residue, or setting fire to rainforest trees and understory plants to open palm-oil plantations or new fields for cattle-feed and pasture. The global population of cattle, concentrated on large-scale ranches and feedlots in the Americas, has accelerated to around one billion animals. The methane-laced flatulence from fermenting grass and grain in their stomachs accounts for a full 14 percent of anthropogenic greenhouse gas emissions.[29]

Rock and metal mines make up a second notorious foundational source-point for some of the most dangerous things that flow through our global accretions of waste. From the mines, the "value chains" that convert these materials into consumer goods and urban buildings acti-vate a chain of built dispersal points for multifarious forms of pollution. Industrial chemical spills have been part of the built environment since ancient times. They multiplied throughout the industrial revolutions, but they only truly gained the ability to shock us during the 1960s, when industry waned as the primary motor of the First World economy, and the environmental movement first took wing as a global phenomenon (Chapter 25). One of that movement's legacies is the discovery of some 450,000 "brownfields" in the USA alone. Some of these go back to nineteenth-century factory sites; many have been since overbuilt with schools and playgrounds. The famous Cuyahoga River Fire in Cleveland in 1969 – a scandal credited with energizing the US Congress's passage of the Clean Water Act – was actually the twelfth fire on that single beleaguered creek; the first was in 1868, when the Standard Oil Company was acquiring its first refineries along its banks. River fires were quite common elsewhere in the USA and Europe throughout the last century and a half.[30]

Since then, despite heroic clean-up efforts, plumes of dioxins, PCBs, and PFAS, known as "forever chemicals" for their stability as poisonous compounds, have become near-permanent features of many river-bottoms, including the Hudson downriver from the General Electric Plant in Schenectady, New York. In the 1980s, Europeans celebrated the clean-up of industrial wastes in the Rhine, only to watch in dismay when a chemical warehouse in Basel caught fire in 1986, loosing mercury and other horrific substances downstream. It gave the river a reddish human-made hue, and killed millions of its otherwise tenacious eels. Meanwhile, as we know, overused agricultural fertilizers and pesticides – industrial chemicals in their own right – have leached from farm fields into rivers and created their own near-permanent monuments in off-shore waters beyond major estuaries. Oxygen-starved "dead zones" have spread for miles around the mouth of the Mississippi, the Don and Dnieper deltas in the Black Sea, the Yangtze delta, and most other estuaries in Japan, Europe, and North America. An even bigger type of monument to chemical pollution was the "ozone holes" that opened up over the polar regions due to the release of household and industrial refrigerants. Here the story was somewhat more uplifting, since a multinational ban on these substances, agreed to at a UN conference in Montreal in 1987, has allowed the great wounds we inflicted on a key protective layer of the atmosphere to begin healing.[31]

As industry migrated Southward – partly because corporations hoped to avoid what they deemed profit-minimizing environmental protection costs – dumps and plumes of chemical waste have become ubiquitous features of our habitat globally. One early wake-up call was the most catastrophic of all industrial accidents, an enormous gas leak from an American pesticide factory at Bhopal, India in 1984, which killed as many as 15,000 people and sickened a half million more. Less well known are mass poisonings at the La Oroya lead smelter in Peru, the copper smelters of Kabwe, Zambia, the Soviet chemical weapons dump at Dzerzhinsk, the massive nickel smelter at Norilsk, the radioactive mine waste site on the Mailuu-Suu River in Kyrgystan that threatens the entire Ferghana Valley, and the Baogang Steel and Rare Earth Processing

Center in Chinese Inner Mongolia. Other, more diffuse, threats from minerals are posed by asbestos, silica, lead, and dust, thanks to mining industry campaigns that suppressed adverse research while these materials were incorporated into millions of homes and buildings. Again, older homes that shelter a disproportionate number of poor people make up another discriminatory delivery device of such toxins. Lung-shredding dust from various construction materials makes up a large portion of the air in Delhi, particularly in summer when the hot winds pick up around cement plants, construction or demolition sites, and poorly finished road surfaces. Informal construction workers, not surprisingly, suffer the most.[32]

Manufacturing corporations also feed global toxicity by subcontracting with informal factories in Global South cities like Delhi whose owners keep costs low by setting up shop in jurisdictions known for non-existent enforcement of existing pollution controls. The "urban villages" that surround Delhi are a utopia for this global nexus of sweatshop polluters. In 2000, the city's periphery housed some 100,000 informal factories that dumped untold volumes of toxins into local creeks and groundwater, which already seethed with sewage overflow and floating garbage. Much of this bubbling mess passes though the dangerous Najafgarh Drain into the Yamuna River north of the city, where it soon meets effluent from landfills like Ghazipur. On November 4, 2019, another horrifically smoky Delhi day, thousands of the Hindu devout celebrated the Chhath Puja on the sacred river's banks, thanking the non-visible Sun God Suriya and his sister Chhati Maya for all their graces by wading into four-foot drifts of thick, toxic, white foam that covered the river and floated for miles in every direction.[33]

Depressingly, the Waste Acceleration may be most dangerous to the small subset of very poor people who seek to recycle its mined components back into the value chain. We already know of the compounded toxins that endanger the waste sorters of Ghazipur, and residents of other high summits in the global cordillera of urban garbage mountains. Still other combinations of dangers face informal workers at the ship-breaking yards near Chattogram (Chittagong), Bangladesh. There, along kilometers-long stretches of open beach and with little or no protective gear, they scrap giant disused container ships, providing much of the raw material for their countries' steel industries. One worker dies every week at these places, crushed by heavy pieces of falling metal or slowly consumed by asbestos poisoning. Similar fates befall those who pull apart discarded motherboards, USB cables, electronic toys, refrigerators, smartphones, and other components of the world's annual forty-two million tons of e-waste. Premature cancers and a range of gastroenterological and respiratory illnesses are common among the often very young workers at large e-waste recycling yards such as at Guiyu, China, at New Serampore near Delhi, and, most famously, at the informal settlement of Agbobloshie near Accra.[34]

ANNEXING THE ATMOSPHERE

Of all the minerals we have sucked from the lithosphere, consumed, then scattered with abandon, none has left a greater monument of a waste problem than fossil fuels: coal, gas, and oil. In cities where we burned coal, first in Kaifeng, then in London, then across the industrialized world, coalsmoke was the first mineral waste to approximate the pervasiveness, within the urban fabric, of our own excrement and other biowastes. It was also the first new form of pollution to pose almost as many of the life-shortening dangers as sewage. After the great twentieth-century smogs in the Global North, environmentalists chased coal from homes and factories but not from the roaring furnaces of electric power-plants, and thus its plumes of particulates, sulfur dioxide, and nitrogen oxides continued to create region-wide waste monuments in the form of acid rain that devastated forests in eastern North America, the "Black Triangle" of central Europe, and southeastern China. Such human-induced mineral invasions of atmospheric rainclouds also helped acidify ocean waters off the coasts of these regions. Air pollution in Asian cities like Beijing, and other cities where domestic coal use is still heavy, like Soweto and Mexico City, is among the worst in the world. Micro-particles from Delhi's coal-fired electric plants alone make up over a third of that type of ingredient in the city's November smoke; many of the city's tandoori restaurants and some homes emit their own streams aloft as well. These particles cause much of the eye, nose, and lung irritation that Sharma Karma grumbles about, and rightly so, for they are a leading cause of pollution-related deaths in Delhi, as in many other Global South cities, disproportionately affecting the poor.[35]

Petroleum may reign as the king of raw materials but it is the veritable emperor of humanity's waste acceleration. Natural gas – its masquerade as a "clean alternative" notwithstanding – rules as oil's dirty deputy. From the beginning, industrial "accidents" involving leaks of oil and gas have been an intrinsic part of the very business of raising these materials from the depths of the Earth. Petroleum flowed freely in nineteenth-century Pennsylvania creeks and in the Caspian Sea off Baku and Astrakhan, especially when the best way to transport oil barrels was to float them in water currents – sharp rocks and shoals be damned. As Dhahran crowned itself capital of the petroleumscape, oil spills from tankers became a near-permanent feature of Persian Gulf waters and slicks spoil harbors at virtually every refinery terminal. Natural gas flares – set alight in places where oil is the priority and there are no pipelines to carry the gas to places where we could burn it more usefully – dump megatons of carbon into the atmosphere. Gas pipelines also spring multitudes of leaks wherever we lay them, sending millions of cubic kilometers of pure methane skyward. Fracking gas and other toxic compounds used in the shale-splitting process all make their way into aquifers. The search for "extreme" petroleum has escalated the range and destructiveness of oil spills, as amply testified by the Exxon Valdez spill in Alaska's pristine Prince William Sound (1989), British Petroleum's Deepwater Horizon explosion in a kilometer-and-a-half-deep ocean well in the Gulf of Mexico (2010), and the Norilsk diesel fuel spill in the Siberian Arctic (2020). An even larger range of oil and gas pollution, as we know, comes indirectly from the Urban Planet's vast production and use of fertilizer, asphalt, and concrete.[36]

Discarded plastic makes up an even larger downstream flow of the oil and gas waste empire. About half of the 359 million tons of plastic we make from fossil fuel each year is intended for a single, fleeting use – as a bag to carry groceries home, as packaging for a cellphone, or as a bottle that contains one-sixth of the fresh water needed to produce the bottle itself. Trillions of these single-use items make their way into waste dumps, most of them in China, but most per capita, by far, in the USA. Luckily for Delhi and other megacities, local waste pickers find plastic recycling lucrative. Although India's per-capita plastics use is still relatively low, the overall volume that gets by the trash pickers is nonetheless choking. Plastic bags float through the air; bottles finds their way into waterways. About a third of all plastic waste ends up in the oceans, in giant slicks of bottles, bags, and a slurry of tiny sun-degraded flakes. The Yamuna, by way of the Ganges, contributes to a growing plastic garbage pile tossed around by the currents of the Indian Ocean; the Atlantic and the North Sea have similar plastic islands; the Arctic and Antarctic seas contain the most flaked micro-plastic per gallon. The largest oceanic garbage dumps of all are located at the eastern and western ends of the North Pacific Subtropical Gyre, a giant ellipse made up of four clockwise rotating currents. This massive whirlpool traps river-borne plastic from the Yangtze and other Asian and American rivers, mixes that with miles of discarded nylon fishing nets, and whisks in more plastic items that fall from container ships. Even more terrifying is the explosion of plastic microbeads and microfibers, widely used in cosmetics, face creams, and synthetic clothing after the 1990s. Flushed into plumbing systems every- where, they mix with other flecks of degraded plastic in rivers and oceans and soak up all manner of other toxins. Soon enough, these largely invisible particles surface on floodplains and beaches, where they dry into dust and ascend into the clouds. A layer of microbeads joins the wood soot from Rome and the coal smoke of London in its own thick layer in the Greenland glacial ice (that is, in places where it has not already melted). In this way, we carelessly toss the petroleum that we pump at such great expense from the lithosphere into the entirety of Earth's hydrological cycle – liquid, gas, and solid.[37]

As it rains plastic and soot on cities across the world – streaking through smoky fog in far too much of the Urban Planet – Earth is, as we know well, also getting hotter. Once again, the principal instruments are petroleum and natural gas, with slightly more ambiguous help from coal, which emits Sun-refracting gases like sulfur dioxide alongside mas- sive amounts of more persistent planet-heating gases. Production of carbon dioxide (CO_2) – the most voluminous and most stable of the greenhouse gases – grew with the industrial revolutions, reaching some five billion tons by 1950. Since then, yearly production of CO_2 has septupled – as industry spread worldwide; as the amount of building construction accelerated, expanding the acreage of interior spaces requiring heating and cooling; and especially as the entire Urban Planet enslaved itself to petroleum-fired vehicles. Accumulation of CO_2 in the atmosphere rose along with production, from about 320 parts per million in 1955 to over 400 parts per million today, the highest levels in eight million years. Methane production – mostly from agriculture and especially meat production, but also from natural gas leakage, and increasingly from anthropogenic melting of permafrost – increased by a similar factor. In the upper atmosphere, these two gases, plus nitrous oxide and remaining fluoride-based refrigerants, have trapped solar heat ever more effectively than before. In most years, the heating action of our own Urban Planet-generated greenhouse gas accumulations outstrips the cooling effects of coal-related sulfur dioxide emissions and Earth's own sun-blocking emissions from volcanoes. Since 1950, average temperatures on Earth have risen by a dangerous 1 degree Celsius.[38]

The Greatly Accelerating Urban Planet has thus allowed us to complete the biggest thing we have ever done: As our gaseous wastes annex the outer atmosphere, geologists tell us that we also annex future time, by laying down a layer of harder substances – concrete, asphalt, steel, glass, thousands of new inorganic chemical substances, and even the skeletons of novel meat-animal species – that will forever send fossil "signals" of the dawn of a new Epoch in Earth Time, the Anthropocene. More terrifyingly, our cities put humans, the great planetary waste-spreaders, into the very cockpit of that future. Like the Greeks' Icarus, we have flown far higher than we should, becoming one with the creative–destructive goddess Inanna who first brought city-life to Uruk. Who will suffer the most from the wrath of the human-jiggered geo-solar energy system? Who will make off with the diminishing bits of loot generated in the slow-dawning new Epoch? Will we survive or not, and what about all other life? The answer that wafts from the hot stench of Ghazipur is unequivocal: it depends on the course we set as human political communities, mostly urban ones – and we must start with the conditions faced by the most vulnerable of Earthopolitan citizens, people who mass along the hottest front lines of our Urban Planet's fast-accelerating realm of consequence.[39]

CHAPTER 25

2020 Hindsight . . . and Foresight?

AN EARTHOPOLIS OF HOPE?

Twenty-twenty may seem like an outrageously nail-biting historic moment to choose as the endpoint of a 6,000-year biography of our Urban Planet. Even before the dystopic dawn of the Human Epoch's newest decade, the human home glowed far too hot with trapped energy from the Sun. Too many Cities of Rivers had become Cities of Inundation. Cities of the World Ocean faced rising surges of the very saltwater and smacking wind that gave them life. So carelessly have we piled the human lithosphere overtop Earth's tectonic faults that our planet's every shudder threatens mass live burials beneath toppled concrete and jangled rebar – if not under tsunamis hurled from disturbed Ocean deeps. Meanwhile, Cities of Hydrocarbon – and the Countrysides of Hydrocarbon that feed them – stoke the maximal storms, floods, mudslides, droughts, heat, ice-melt, wildfires, human-set rainforest fires, and multifarious waste build-ups that render our habitat by stages ever less habitable.

Then, of course, as New Year's Day 2020 approached, Earthopolis breathed in and out – for that is the wont of something so vastly concentrated and so infinitely extended. Through its immense airstreams and into a Yangtze Valley megacity slipped a tiny coronavirus new to humans from somewhere in wide zones where our Urban Planet overlaps with the habitats of other creatures – likely a mountain mineshaft filled with bats, though similar effects could be expected from a chicken farm, a distant savannah's poaching camp, or a hunting blind deep in the rainforest. From Wuhan, the microscopic menace hopped airplanes to cities on all continents. It sucked the social oxygen from our mightiest gathering places. It threw our nurses, doctors, and ambulance drivers directly into its reaping path, with auto-rickshaw wallas, bus drivers, human service workers, and factory workers not far behind. It sealed many billions of us in our homes, stressing families emotionally, economically, and multifariously. It obliged us, frantically, to inventory every infinite inch of all our most beloved urban spaces, assessing the potential of each to become a vector of horrid, gasping death. Sirens howled in the streets – sometimes punctuated by an impromptu pick-me-up from a portico accordionist, by remonstrances from an end-of-time sidewalk cleric, or by crowd-sourced bursts of applause for front-line heroes. Hospitals pitched tented wards in parking lots and stadiums. Gravediggers conjured cemeteries, cremation sites, and lonely mass funerals in city parks. The virus flew fiercest – as pandemics do – through the unpaved, crowded streets of the cities of the poor and of people of color. Then the Urban Planet exhaled again, as poor migrant workers fled to the bus stations and mobbed the trains. Death rode back out into the towns, villages, and far-off fringes whence the virus came.

Bit by bit, our urban streets coughed back into action. The pedestrian "ballet" of urban anonymity returned, its magnificent busy-ness awkwardly re-choreographed for social distances and covered faces. Then, defiant springs and summers of protest bloomed forth – rekindling energized proximity and urban contestation from Hong Kong to Minneapolis to Minsk to La Paz to Lagos to Jerusalem – with it spreading hopes for greater Urban Planetary justice. In the largest *Satyagraha* since independence, the farmers of northern India once again rode their tractors into Delhi, demanding a reversal of decades of rural immiseration and debt. Climate justice activists filled the streets too, while the Covid-19 recession gave us a tantalizing, if perverse, glimpse of a post-hydrocarbon, clean-air future. Oil prices went negative. Soot and smog failed to appear across the continents as traffic jams vanished, factories idled, and power plants powered down.[1]

Yet as disease rode across Earthopolis, rogue presidents in Washington, D.C., Brasília, Ankara, Manila, and in the old viceroy's palace on Delhi's Raisina Hill fired viral volleys of virtual disinformation and hate. A turbulent autumn came to the USA, and its elections took on Urban Planetary stakes. Were overpriced, covid-filled "liberal cities" adequate bases from which to fight against a counterrevolution that burned hottest in so many of the world's smaller, most dispersed and forgotten places? Or, do we face more chilly midwinter days like those of Delhi's bloody sectarian rage in February 2020, or the brutal attack on Washington's "Temple of the People" on January 6, 2021? Had the Urban Planet become too big, too complex, too accelerant, too sick, and too hot for deliberative democracies to manage – as the apex opponents of People Power in Moscow and Beijing chortled loudly, and for all on the global internet to hear? Worse, do such gas-lit anti-democratic ill wishes carry the whiff of nuclear, or robotic, or cyber-Armageddons to come?[2]

And what of the capitalists? Somehow, during a "Plague Year," the skyscrapers of global capital and the land-scrapers of tech monopolies managed to suck in new empires of wealth, taking untold trillions from a vertiginously unequal global economy that plunged into recession for the rest of us. Clearly, such unbalanced private profit-mongering could coexist with unbalanced authoritarian power-mongering, no matter how assiduously marketers "whitewash" or "greenwash" corporate missions in gauzy devotion to democracy, equity, diversity, or sustainability. Can global capitalism – arguably the single most potent city-aroused, city-making force of our day – play any trustworthy role in an Earthopolis of Hope?

For such existential questions, global urban history provides dependable hindsight, but, alas, only the foggiest of foresight. Still, here are seven things that are certain.

First: cities remain spaces where we bend time – where we stretch it into long continuities, spin it into spiraling synergies, curl it toward cliffhanger contingencies, and crack it with the force of our own disruptive experiments in geo-solar energy harvesting and human politics.

Second: Earthopolis remains as multifariously plural as it is singular and connected. Rebuilding our Urban Planet will have to happen in the same way we built it in the first place, with hundreds of millions of local impulses that have influence beyond their home city precisely because cities' role in world history is to transform smaller human acts into larger ones.

Third: as Inanna's riverboat, as Columbus's ocean-ship turned gunpowder-fort, and as the auto-walla's puffing tailpipe have taught us, cities are always instruments of destruction as well as creation. To expand actions, habitats, and impacts is – forever and always – to court expanded consequences, deathly ones for sure, less deathly ones possibly, life-affirming ones we can only hope.

Fourth: the coronavirus we inhaled into our streets in 2020 may be novel, but pandemics are endemic to the compacted yet stretched-out architecture of our planetary home. As World Health Organization epidemiologists repeatedly prophesy, our cities will need to cope with many "Disease Xs" to come, just as cities have always done in the past.

Fifth: the momentum of the Greatest Acceleration remains intense – Covid-19 be damned. Transforming Earthopolis today means channeling the force of ongoing explosions in our Urban Planet's four realms of action, habitat, impact, and consequence – all of them unprecedented in scope. As our numbers spiral toward eleven billion by century's end, Mumbai could outpace Delhi toward forty-five million people by 2050. We could see a Kinshasa of fifty-eight million by 2075, and a Lagos of eighty-eight million by 2100. All of that of course depends on the wildest card of all, for the realm of deathly consequence is growing – unpredictably as always – now in far faster and in far larger bursts than ever before that for the first time threaten to engulf all three other realms of Earthopolis permanently. Will Mumbai or Lagos even still be situated on dry land in 2050 or 2100, and what about hundreds of even faster-growing seaside cities like Dar es Salaam, Dhaka, or Mogadishu? How, exactly, will rainforest desecration and desertification affect Kinshasa, or Kabul, or Cairo – or Niamey, the now barely known capital of Niger that may be home to fifty-six million people in 2100? "Twenty-Twenty" is what it is: a crisis of our Urban Planet's Greatest Acceleration, one of the most dangerous of all of Earthopolis's 6,000 whirling orbits of the Sun. But even as we rebuild our Urban Planet, more dangerous years will come, and we can announce with certainty that they will arrive unannounced.[3]

Sixth: to build an Urban Planet capable of another 6,000 years, we must abandon our Cities of Hydrocarbon. That means redirecting the state power and corporate wealth that built them – along with all the other exclusive, unequal, overextended, and wasteful structures that make up too much of Earthopolis – toward new renewable, cleaner, and more equitable modes of harvesting energy from the Sun and Earth. To build true Cities of the Sun, fired on the power of sunshine and wind, we need an urban energy transition right away – in the 2020s – as momentous as those of the 3000s BCE, the 1500s CE, and the 1780s CE. The transition this time, however, needs to be far more just, transparent, and equitable. If not, make no mistake: it will fail utterly.

Seventh: as always, the foggiest view of the future concerns the alignment of the Urban Planet's states – and the diverse, anonymous, and fractious urban planetary political communities that created all of our most powerful institutions in the first place and ignited our species' Epochal power over Earth. Through the fog of 2020 politics, the opposing forces are easy to identify. The fate of Earthopolis, both as a thing of Earth and as a thing of the *polis*, hangs on a four-way, high-wire political struggle that is at once local, national, hemispheric, and Urban Planetary in scope. Authoritarian states jangle one of those high wires, hoping all others will fall under their sway. Global capitalists occupy a second wire, their eyes on the bottom line, far too ready to abandon anything useful to the rest of us if it interferes with the next few months or years of profit accumulation. (The fact that some of them are shooting themselves into space or eyeing Martian real estate is no consolation.) A third high wire swings wildly under the influence of raging mobs and terror organizations, many of which muster beyond city limits or in remote camps beyond the reach of the most powerful imperial capitals, amassing enough weapons to destabilize city-dependent democratic states as well as the internet, turning both into forces of gaseous misinformation, hate, and violence. A fourth and last wire supports the Urban Planet's most hopeful political force: those of us who have joined growing movements to deploy People Power toward a Just Transition, a new chapter when our majority urban species rejects its Underworldly deal with Hydrocarbon and negotiates a new bargain between Earthopolis, Earth, and Sun.[4]

Boil these seven certainties down and you get one big one: an Earthopolis of Hope will consist of true Cities of the Sun. To build the foundations of such cities, two millennia-old types of Urban Planetary space are more essential than ever. We need spaces where we can dependably produce and disseminate new, verifiable knowledge about our home and our planet: Cities of ever more probing Light. And, we need spaces that – much less predictably – enable assembly, discussion, negotiation, protest, contestation, and the political power of humanity as a whole, including its new urban majority: the *polis* of a truly democratic Earthopolis. Both of these spaces of hope, each a galaxy of many smaller spaces, have grown in unprecedented, if still uneven, ways alongside the many more cancerous realms of the Greatest Acceleration. Both suffered damage from the crises of 2020. However, in Cities of Light and in the *polis* of a resurgent Planet of the People, we can as a species once again gather the natural energy we need to compound the massive exertions of human power we need to disrupt time in the ways we must – and right now. As we end the long biography of our Urban Planet in the uncertain wake of an impossible year, we need to dwell a few moments longer, first in the knowledge-producing, and then the People-Power-producing shrines of our greatest possible dreams and yearnings.

EXPLODING URBAN PLANETARY KNOWLEDGE

How do we know that Earthopolis exists? How do we measure its crisis? Are cities, let alone an Urban Planet, worthy of our trust after 2020? Why should we invest hope for the future of all Earthly life in any type of space, least of all spaces built by humans? Our Urban Planet is immense and we are small. Yet our knowledge of our habitat, in its multifarious smaller parts and in its vast plural-yet-singular whole, has grown alongside all of its periods of acceleration, and especially during its greatest one. Thanks to today's urban archaeologists, historians, sociologists, anthropologists, political scientists, theorists, architects, designers, planners, public health specialists, engineers, geologists, Earth Systems scientists, and climate scientists, we produce more new academic knowledge about the built environment every month than any single human can possibly read in a lifetime. Urban knowledge production has also expanded among urban and environmental activists, government officials, journalists, bloggers, travel writers, tourists, and ordinary observers of streets and neighborhoods, who flood newsprint, magazines, and the internet with everything from official data to profoundly thoughtful perspectives to enlightening campaigns for urban environmental justice. As Covid-19 heaved through Earthopolis in 2020, urban knowledge makers mobilized an unusual species-wide re-examination of virtually every corner of our built habitat from the point of view of a virulent virus. Hallowed ideas like urban density were treated to a dismayingly skeptical second look. Yet so was "sprawl": decoupled from the merely "suburban," the dangers of the far-more-extended realms of the human habitat reinforced the import-ance of analyzing cities as components of an Urban Planet. All of these *savants* of the city have informed this biography, even if one book can give only tiny glimpses into the vast universe of knowledge they have collect-ively produced. Meanwhile, we have come a very long way since the first world atlas of cities in the sixteenth century. Thanks to online mapping software, most people with a cell phone merely need to press their thumb onto glass to summon the layout of every street in every city on Earth, and in many cases, tap a few more times to acquire an overhead satellite or street-level view. New innovative maps trace the scope of our actions, habitats, impacts, and their consequences with breathtaking creativity. Never has the Urban Planet been more visible, even in all of its acceler-ated complexity, to the naked human eye.[5]

Our window on the Urban Planet has opened wider in part because our Cities of Light have themselves accelerated in size. The growth is as uneven as it is spectacular. The world's adult literacy rate jumped uncan-nily from just over half to almost 90 percent during the Greatest Acceleration. But that still leaves 750 million people without basic literacy skills – more people on Earth who cannot read than ever before, most of whom live in a wide belt of cities and villages stretching from Casablanca to Manila and across explosively urbanizing Africa south of the Sahara. In an age of austerity and corporate dominance, spaces of knowledge every-where face increasing financial strain. Challenges to their democratic structure have mounted, and thus so have obstacles to their primary mission. In 2020, Covid-19 worsened all of these problems by imperilling the basic relationship between teacher and pupils, especially for learners who are most vulnerable to educational delays.[6]

Nonetheless, our Urban Planet consists of more classrooms, daycares, schoolhouses, high schools, universities, and teaching hospitals in more cities, towns, and villages than ever before. Those places served more students than ever before, and larger portions of them were people of color, girls, young women, or the first in their families to attend. There are more libraries than ever before, more museums, more performance venues of many more types, more urban festivals, and more rural ones.

Publication houses have declined in number under the weight of the internet and speculative corporate consolidations. However, they have spread across the Great Gap to a great degree, printing books in a wider range of languages than ever before. Research parks, spaces designed to put state power, corporate money, and highly trained brains behind innovative and potentially hopeful technologies, have sprouted up in more cities in more regions of the world than ever. They and other knowledge-creating spaces of the Urban Planet have launched their own Greatest Acceleration of discovery – including a series of break-throughs in 2020 itself, when a half dozen medical research centers used new techniques of gene sequencing and other advanced biotech-nologies to develop vaccines for Covid-19 within a few months of the pandemic's baleful beginnings. Then there is the internet itself. True, a handful of corporations headquartered in Silicon Valley and the Seattle suburbs distort its structures to their will – including those maps on our cell phones. True, access remains as unequal as access to our most hopeful schoolhouses. True again, knowledge competes there, more than elsewhere, with vicious lies. Still, the internet's promise remains: no technology has ever allowed us to transform so many other built spaces, whether our own kitchens, sidewalks, remote farmhouses, or Antarctic climate research stations into new places of knowledge con-sumption, production, and dissemination in their own right.[7]

Even in their many worst, 2020-like days, cities have always remained the primary sites for creative people to build and enthral their audiences. During the Greatest Acceleration, extraordinary amounts of wealth poured into vintage bourgeois venues such as art museums, art auctions, symphony halls, theaters, dance companies, film studios, high-fashion runways, and opera houses. The biggest story by far, though, is the explosion of popular arts, most often in urban spaces balefully disre-garded by state or corporate investors. Blues, jazz, merengue, and salsa led the way before World War II, but the enormous sonic universes they opened up since are unprecedented – in dance clubs, recording studios, on the radio, in film, on TV, in summertime parks, in enormous concert arenas, and on internet streaming services. As African-descended artists transformed earlier genres into Rhythm and Blues and Rock and Roll, they invented a basic sonic canvas upon which thousands of urban folk artists in dozens of cities and their overlapping Diasporas could deliver life-affirming pleasures to audiences numbering in the billions. Soul from Chicago and Philadelphia, and Motown from Detroit. *Bossa nova* from the beaches of Rio. British rock from Liverpool. Country from Nashville. Reggae from Kingston, Jamaica. Afro-pop in many genres from Kinshasa's Matongé arts district, Dakar's Médina, and Lagos's Ajegunle. *Raï* from Oran and elsewhere in revolutionary Algeria. Bhangra from the Punjab and London. Punk and Heavy Metal across the postindustrial First World. Techno from Frankfurt, and from Detroit again. K-pop from Gangnam, Seoul. Kwaito from Johannesburg. And dominating the sonic world as a whole: Rap and hip-hop from the South Bronx and every self-anointed "ghetto" in every corner of the Greatest Acceleration Urban Planet.

In many cases, popular musics provided the soundtrack to widespread urban visual cultures. Hip-hop's influence is best known: it inspired graffiti muralists to cover the walls of buildings, bridges, embankments, and of course subway cars with the single most extensive form of human creative expression outside corporate advertising and the built environment itself. Sartorial styles of popular performers and fans upended the dominance of high-couture and pervaded the fashionscapes of city streets. Break dance revolutionized the performing arts on stages everywhere, not to mention sidewalks. Most of all, knowledge of urban life in some of the most neglected corners of Earthopolis became far more accessible to far more people in far more places than ever before. As American rappers claimed the title "CNN of the ghetto," popular artists elsewhere could say as much for the fresh urban knowledge they delivered from their own neighborhoods, via their own genre of "World Music."[8]

Of course, critics of the biblical "Tower of Babel" were right: the volume of urban knowledge is no measure of its quality. This is especially true when it comes to such foundational knowledge as the relationship between Earthopolis, Earth, and Sun. During most of the hydrocarbon era, the greatest "Cities of Light" spouted fountains of academically endorsed nonsense about humanity's mission to conquer other species' habitats on Earth, to exploit them as infinite sources of human wealth and as an infinite sink for human waste. Few voices rose in opposition.

Those that did object saw themselves as fiercely anti-city, spokespeople for what they deemed cities' diametric opposite – "nature" (Figure 10.1). In the nineteenth century, British "Back-to-the-Landers" John Ruskin and William Morris, and – from his famously remote pondside cabin – the American philosopher Henry David Thoreau, condemned cities for despoiling the countryside and for transforming noble farmers and shepherds into degraded factory workers. Ruskin's acolyte Edward Carpenter even built a rural commune on a hill in sight of the "vast dense cloud" of coal-burning Sheffield to lure workers out of the city. Still, Cities of Light, notably their print shops and lecture halls, were necessary for this anti-urban, anti-hydrocarbon environmentalism to grow. When Mohandas Gandhi emerged from a few years of deep immersion in London's radical conclaves in 1891, the anti-city environmental movement gained its greatest global spokesperson, a living saint who insisted until his death that India's true independence rested on a return from its growing cities to its 600,000 villages. His critique of Hydrocarbon Cities was unsparing: "I wholeheartedly detest this mad desire to destroy distance and time to increase animal appetites, and to go to the ends of the earth in search of their satisfaction. If modern civilization stands for all of this ... I call it satanic."[9]

In Gandhi's time, as we know, modernist urban planners embraced various anti-urban sentiments of their own. Yet whether they hoped, like Ebenezer Howard, that London would dissolve into small "garden cities," or that Chicago would melt into Frank Lloyd Wright's dispersed homesteads, or that crowded Paris or Algiers would submit to Le Corbusier's regiments of cruciform towers, all embraced hydrocarbon – whether coal-powered trains or enormous fleets of private cars. That consensus broke thanks to two prominent city-loving dissenters familiar with Gandhi's work, the globe-hopping Scottish radical Patrick Geddes and his student, Lewis Mumford of New York. They pointed the finger at the real problem: not cities themselves, but their enslavement to what they called "carboniferous capitalism." In 1961, as American tailpipe suburbs sprawled explosively and the Greatest Acceleration ignited worldwide, Mumford warned presciently that Hydrocarbon Cities threatened to pave over their life-giving hinterlands, even "ruin whole countries and continents" in a catastrophic moment of ecological disequilibrium.[10]

For that prophesy to go global, it took a famous trilogy of blockbuster books written by American women during the opening years of the 1960s: Jane Jacobs's *The Life and Death of Great American Cities*, Betty Friedan's *the Feminine Mystique*, and Rachel Carson's *Silent Spring*. Jacobs argued that the real villain in the human story was not so much urban size, but modernist urban planning *à la* Le Corbusier. By destroying dense, diverse, lively, highly juxtaposed urban environments, planners deprived humans of the highly crowded spaces that generated the innovative imagination and economic prosperity needed to solve our biggest problems. By giving cities over to automobiles, modernists choked and poisoned the places where people still walked, biked, or took public transit to get around, minimizing "carboniferous" footprints.[11]

Jacobs, a resident of New York's then still un-gentrified, dense, walkable, Greenwich Village, did even more: she organized her neighbours to protest the modernist planner Robert Moses's plans to hack expressways through the squares and lively streets of Lower Manhattan. By holding Moses and other pharaonic professional planners accountable to the urban knowledge of grassroots community-based organizations, Jacobs's work resonated with the great democratic protest movements of the 1960s. As the American Black Liberation Movement won victories against Jim Crow in the Southern states, its leaders also protested segregation in New York and other northern US cities, with big knock-on implications for Europe and Latin America. Taking Jacobs a step further, they marched *en masse* against top-down modernist slum clearances like Moses's, accusing him of urban racial cleansing. In nearby universities, a New Left student movement embraced Jacobs's critique of the suburbs as inauthentic and sterile. On top of that, came Betty Friedan's electric call for a new feminist movement. Middle-class women's soul-dulling confinement in isolated single-family tailpipe-tracts, she wrote, amounted to a spatial tool of patriarchal oppression.[12]

Meanwhile, Jacobs's Greenwich Village blossomed almost as she theorized it would: as a nerve-center for the era's counterculture, including some of popular music's greatest bards. Leaders of an increasingly radical and soon global feminist movement lived there or planned their revolution there. When the police raided a gay bar in the Village's Stonewall Inn in 1969, a fierce protest inaugurated the modern gay liberation movement, another urban gift that kept on giving, as Pride Parades in streets and marches on parliaments spread worldwide. Student movements and countercultural ferment centered on similar places: the Latin Quarter of Paris, London's Notting Hill, central Prague's clandestine "Underground," Mexico City's Tlatelolco, Tokyo's Shinjuku, and San Francisco's Haight-Ashbury. Taking force from restive university campuses nearby, they confirmed Jacobs's dictum that dense urban places lay at the cutting edge of human consciousness, at least for bourgeois youth.[13]

Amidst protest and counterculture, Urban Planetary self-knowledge also grew thanks to a truly global environmental movement. Rachel Carson sparked it in 1962 with her electrifying warning, in *Silent Spring*, that chemical pesticides such as DDT threatened non-human habitats, including those of springtime songbirds. By the 1970s, the movement had already won its first victories, when the USA and other First World states created pioneering environmental protection agencies. They regulated chemical waste and achieved remarkable success in reversing industrial air and water pollution. Since then, of course, manufacturers have outflanked pollution controls by building more, even dirtier factories in cities in Asia and elsewhere in the Global South. Yet, thanks in part to the widening celebrations of "Earth Day," grassroots environmental protection movements have grown worldwide too in the years since, drawing on energies far beyond the First World middle class. In Delhi today, large protest organizations repeatedly call on city officials to make pollution reduction central to their "World City" pretensions. The highly unequal impact of environmental toxins on communities of color both in the Global North and in the Global South has become a central concern for today's global movement for climate justice. A new Urban Planet, they argue, will of course need to shift away from fossil fuels. Yet the "Transition" will only be "Just" – let alone possible – if it responds to the needs of all Earthopolitans.[14]

Meanwhile the environmental movement, like other protest movements of the 1960s, transformed the priorities of universities and research centers. In the 1980s, spurred by the trauma of the Oil Crises and a renewed wave of journalistic exposes tying fossil fuels to greenhouse gases, universities dramatically expanded the fields of climate science and Earth-Systems science. The extent of our hot conquest of the atmosphere became far clearer, confirming Svante Arrhenius's dire nineteenth-century prophesies. Researchers working simultaneously in a dispersed hinterland of climate monitoring stations, in concentrated university data-processing facilities, and in packed convention halls established new basic facts about Earthopolis, Earth, and Sun. Humanity is a main force of atmospheric warming, of desertification and rainforest retreat, of diminished biomass and carbon sequestration capacity, of nitrogen overload and fresh water depletion, of the melting of glaciers, permafrost, and polar ice, of sea level rise, ocean acidification, shifts in ocean currents and water masses, of accelerated waves of species extinction, and even the latest wobble in the Earth's axis. At the same time, Urban Planetary self-knowledge shed much of its historic anti-urbanism. Cities may indeed exacerbate "satanic" problems – including the howling crises of 2020 – but cities, properly redesigned and democratically run, are also the most useful tools we have left: the spaces where we can muster the power we need to recreate what Earth-Systems scientists deem a "safe operating space" capable of sustaining our multiplying billions.[15]

CITIES OF THE SUN

What should 2020's "Cities of Tomorrow" look like? As always, everything will start with the spaces we use for harvesting geo-solar energy. The sheer scope of the task of Transition requires the energy we gather in those spaces to be as abundant, as renewable, and as clean as possible. Justice also demands that these systems be more decentralized and relatively inexpensive. A return to Cities of the Rivers will only go so far, as we have tapped most hydroelectric power available on Earth, and because dams spread human inequalities as well as negative consequences for other species more widely than other renewable energy harvesting devices. A renaissance of Cities of the Oceans may be more promising, provided wave- and tide-energy harvesting technologies become much cheaper and less potentially impactful, though centralized versions of these harvesting devices could be very difficult for the least advantaged of us to build or control. As for post-Hydrocarbon Cities of the Lithosphere, further bets on radioactive minerals have huge disadvantages when it comes to the dangers of accidents, waste, and encouragement of nuclear

(A)

(B)

25.1. Cities of the Sun
The Just Transition, the great task of all Earthopolitans today, is to rebuild Cities of Hydrocarbon as Cities of the Sun – habitats run on the infinite energy of the breezes and the daylight. Such is the promise of the wind farm in a pasture high above Nairobi, Kenya (A), and the profusion of solar panels (B) sprouting amidst rooftop satellite dishes in Alanya, Turkey. A Just Transition depends on defeating threats to democracy in both of

arms races. Geothermal energy is far cleaner, completely inextinguish-able, more peace-loving, more decentralized, and thus more controllable by the least disadvantaged, yet it will need to become far less expensive if it is to do the job of running a whole Urban Planet fairly.

By far our best option is to turn more directly to the day's sunshine, and to the breezes the Sun quickens through every corner of Earthopolis. Building true Cities of the Sun will require new acts of extension to our habitat, above all consisting of photovoltaic cells and wind turbines. Both technologies benefit from decades of improvements in dozens of universities and research and development facilities across the world. The good news is that, as of 2020, both have become cheaper generators of electricity than coal, oil, and gas. The 800-fold increase in solar and the 1,000-fold increase in wind power between 2000 and 2020 are by far the most hopeful measures of the Greatest Acceleration. Admittedly, the vast new solar farms we have built in the deserts of Nevada, North Africa, or Tibet and the enormous windfarms we have planted on land and on seabeds do represent enormous invasions of non-human habitats. These are far smaller, though, than those of the petroleumscape. Cover Saudi Arabia's Ghawar Oilfield with solar panels instead of derricks, and you can power all of Japan, megacities and all, while happily leaving the hydrocarbon in the ground. We can also drastically reduce the built footprint of our renewable-energy harvests by transforming many more existing human spaces – notably rooftops and parking lots, especially urban ones – into solar and wind collectors.[16]

In fact, plugging our cities directly into the day's sunshine opens new options for urban planners and architects. Jane Jacobs-inspired planners' embrace of urban density and "multi-functional" neighbourhoods comes with increased attention to urban walkability, cyclability, the viability of

---

Caption for 25.1. (cont.)

these places and everywhere. It also depends on far more equitable control over the world's wealth. It will take enormous investments to plug our Greatest Acceleration-era Urban Planet more directly into the Sun. Yet the ability to harvest energy locally (such as on rooftops) can bring down costs of shelter, crucial for an Urban Planet of eight, soon to be eleven, billion. That number includes the modest apartment dwellers of Alanya – and the young shepherd whose livelihood lies directly in the path of exploding Nairobi.
(A) Getty Images. (B) Selimaksan/Getty Images.

public transit, creative reusability of defunct spaces, and reductions in buildings' carbon footprints. They also suggest new answers to crucial questions – first raised by park-makers like Frederick Law Olmsted and small-city advocates like Ebenezer Howard – about the juxtaposition of built density, channels of flow, and open green space. Meanwhile, architects have designed buildings that use renewable materials, that harvest all of the energy they use on site, that double as vertical food production, water filtration, or carbon sequestration sites, or that reuse most of their reduced waste streams. Other "green" architects have developed protocols for retrofitting old buildings to match these results.[17]

The largest task faced by designers of Cities of the Sun remains the construction of safe, healthy, affordable, energy-efficient housing, above all in the great cities of the poor. Yet solar and wind energy offers some new promise for this task as well, since neither its harvest nor its delivery depend on expensive centralized facilities like coal plants or extended ones like power grids. Built into homes, renewable-energy-harvesting systems like solar water heaters, neighborhood micro-grids, or networked urban heating or cooling systems can dramatically reduce the cost of shelter, especially at a moment when some form of electricity-driven domestic cooling systems will become essential to city life. Retrofitting, installation, and maintenance, meanwhile represent an enormous new realm of what Jacobs would celebrate as city-created "new work."[18]

Electric vehicles have received far more attention than solar homes, and the need to run urban transportation on a day of sunshine is a defining challenge of cities to come. Above all, we need to favor investments in sun-powered public trains, trams, and buses – supported if necessary by solar taxis and, yes, Rickshaws of the Sun too. Private vehicles, even electric and self-driving ones, simply need to take a far smaller role, despite huge incentives for expanded production that may come from cheaper energy. Cars run roughshod over dense spaces, waste our time in traffic jams, kill too many people, encourage sprawl, and use far more fuel per capita, blunting campaigns for energy conservation. Cities of the Sun cannot ignore the dangers of building the electric storage capacity needed for such vehicles, or the danger that lithium or other raw components of batteries could make up a new dangerous stream of toxic waste even in the most efficient of cities. Billions of used electric car batteries will make that waste far more difficult to manage. Either way, recycling and reuse of all renewable energy harvesting and storing equipment needs to be designed more deeply into its production.[19]

Meanwhile, as Covid-19 has reminded us brutally, urban density, for all of its overriding advantages, can make epidemics harder to combat, and thus deadlier. No matter how climate-friendly our cities become, we will need to build flexibility and flow into our dense spaces and into our lives within them. Cities will need to encourage movement of air, flow of water, and human movement while stopping the flow of viruses and bacteria between people – and between animals and people to begin with. As in 2020, practices such as face covering and social distancing will require that we rethink the ways we use the sides of our eyes, the flare of our nostrils, the set of our jaw, and the propulsion of our bodies to navigate anonymous spaces – even as we rely on electronic gathering spaces to compensate for periods of diminished urban proximity-power. Small businesses like cafés, barbershops, bars, and restaurants that incubate so much crowd-energy (and that provide much of a city's employment) need better government safety nets to keep them resilient during public health emergencies. Municipalities demonstrated this elegantly when they extended spaces for socially distanced outdoor eating into street and parking lot acreage previously devoted to cars. Far more important, though, will be investments in redesign of the true front-line trenches of any infectious pandemic: homes, schools, daycares, clinics, hospitals, eldercare facilities, shelters, jails, immigrant detention centers, small-scale workplaces, water and wastewater systems, and internet infrastructure. Larger-scale workplaces also need careful redesign, and relief funds for furloughed workers, to avoid the horrific outbreaks that occurred in places like meat packing plants and sweatshops. After 2020, the highly uncertain fate of Covid-19-emptied office towers, hotels, and high-end condominiums caused even the left-leaning mayor of London to despair for the highest-price urban districts of the world and the tax revenues they bring into City Halls such as his own. The future of gentrification, urban land prices, and the inequalities they generate all remain question marks in the 2020s – hinting at tantalizing silver linings for those who do not inhabit penthouses. Meanwhile, the same year of horrors reminds us once again of the beneficent value of parks – as guarantors of airflow, as sequesterers of carbon, as enablers of density elsewhere, and as spaces of public health, both physical and mental. In addition to offering resilience in the face of pandemics, parks that incorporate restored urban wetlands, floodplains, salt marshes, and forests can help to mitigate destruction from floods, storm surges, and rising seas. The Covid-19 crisis has opened up new conversations about restoring streets to walkers and bikers, thus extending the precious flows of parkland throughout cities.[20]

Both global warming and the coronavirus are scourges of an overextended human habitat as much as they are of large, densely concentrated central Cities of Hydrocarbon. As we rebuild them as Cities of the Sun, we will need to redesign their planet-encompassing hinterlands and larger connective infrastructures too. The first task, of course, is to defund and dismantle the distended global fossil fuel incubus. At the same time, we need to spark a second far more equitable and truly "Green" Revolution in the world's accelerating food-growing lands – notably its monocrop and meat-producing ones. States need to reorganize the capitalist agricultural financing system to encourage investment in smaller farms, new experiments in organic agriculture, drip irrigation, and flows of urban compost to the countryside. We need money to restore degraded farmland, diminish livestock pastureland, increase acreage devoted to creatively managed grazing, and expand research into new protein sources, including plant-based "meat." We need to encourage healthier mutual relations between food lands and more sustainably administered forestlands. Dams and nuclear power plants need to come down as irrigation and urban water systems become more efficient, and as the day's sun and wind energy fills our electric grids. Such renewable flows, meanwhile, will diminish the global crisscross of power lines in favor of more responsive smaller-scale systems. Mining companies and the industries they serve need to calculate remediation costs into their business plans. Concrete manufacturers need to find cooler substitutes for petroleum-cooked clinkers. Plastics engineers need to find degradable replacements for their material's basis in hydrocarbon. In all of these industries, wherever possible, we need to mine our own massive waste mountains instead of the lithosphere for primary materials. Each one of these revolutions could sharply disrupt global capitalists' Urban Planetary "value chains," whose fragility Covid-19 exposed in 2020. Future crises could be more tumultuous, yet with hope, our cities can encourage less distended sourcing systems that are more equitable and require less energy. Disruption must be part of any dream of reversing Earthopolis's biggest of all monuments, our Great Waste Acceleration. If we succeed, due credit should go to our own time's contribution to our Urban Planet's exploding knowledge of self.[21]

STATES OF JUST (AND UNJUST) TRANSITION

As Just Transition activists know well, our wisest answers to our largest questions matter little unless we harness truth to maximal exertions of human power. At today's crossroads, our recipe for power amplification is the same as at Uruk six millennia ago: funnel energy from Sun and Earth into cities and release it as states. Today's states are immense, unprecedented in both political capacity and in the spread of the built environments that their agency headquarters occupy within capitals and subordinate administrative posts. Predictions of the demise of the state in an era of quadrillion-dollar global-city moneymaking districts have repeatedly revealed themselves as hyperbole. Nonetheless, states will need to face radical political pressure – best delivered, as we will see next, largely through urban spaces that empower them – to disentangle their own tentacles from those of Earth-desecrating industries, lie-spreading internet algorithms, and global finance and real estate. The states we need now are those that respond creatively to the voices of all of Earthopolis's billions. To clarify: they must align their maximal releases of human power with maximal commitments to People Power.

By such measures of state-led justice and transformation, the years leading up to 2020 contain many flashes of hope amidst moments of high peril and grim portent. One of the most uplifting episodes took place in Paris in 2016, when representatives from the capitals of 194 nation states, between them responsible for 97 percent of all greenhouse gas emissions, gathered to sign the United Nations Climate Accords, the culmination of two decades of global conversations begun in Kyoto, Rio, and Copenhagen, and animated by regional conferences in between. In

Paris, signatories committed their governments to cap atmospheric temperatures "well below" a 2-degree increase over pre-hydrocarbon levels, by transitioning away from fossil fuel and rebuilding their portion of the human habitat to refocus human energy harvests on Sunshine. States in the Global North, moreover, agreed to earmark loans and grants to their counterparts in the Global South for such development – a promise to narrow the Great Gap even as we build new Cities of the Sun. In the meantime, states made pledges to invest in infrastructure that will make existing habitats more resilient in the face of the consequences of human impact, admitting that the furies we first awakened in the 1780s will continue spreading costly consequences well into the foreseeable future.

As each of the national delegations returned from Paris to their own capital city, each sought to build pro-Paris coalitions to combat formidable opposition to the Accords. Hopes for success there rested heavily on the spread of institutions of popular sovereignty. There, in 2016 at least, the news had been good as well. Since 1989, when a large cohort of representative governments replaced Soviet-style autocracies in the "Second World," the number of national capitals that have thrown off dictatorships and built thriving parliaments, election systems, and independent courts and printing presses has risen dramatically. By the time of the Paris Accords, for the first time, over half of all of the world's governments, home to a combined five billion citizens, claimed a basis on the consent of their own People.[22]

Yet no state will find the Just Transition easy, and many are committed to dangerous courses no matter what they promised at Paris. A full billion and a half officially designated "citizens" of popular governments actually live in what political scientists call "pseudo-democracies" where strongmen have, by various schemes and thousands of small cuts, stifled the power of legislatures, courts, elections systems, political parties, and the press. These regimes include such petroleum giants as those headquartered in Vladimir Putin's Moscow, the Luanda of José Dos Santos and his successors, and Nicolás Maduro's Caracas, all of whose climate declarations rest largely on the personal word of heads of state whose power rests on the support of hydrocarbon-industry oligarchs. Other state-owned fossil fuel establishments operating out of Riyadh, Kuwait City,

Doha, Manama, Dubai, and Tehran are controlled by absolute monarchies or barely disguised theocracies that make little or no pretence of democratic control and are among the biggest violators of the Paris Accords.[23]

Far more complex and worrisome is the story of the biggest polluter – and biggest city builder – of all time. As the tensions of autumn 2020 escalated, Chinese President Xi Jinping announced in a Zoom speech to the UN that, under his proposed Fourteenth Five-Year plan, China's vast industrial habitat, its hundreds of smoke belching power plants, and its coalmines (four times the size of any other nation's on Earth) would convert themselves to carbon neutrality by 2060. As fanciful as this may seem, Xi's claims to global climate leadership rested on some substance. Chinese cities have taken the lead in manufacturing solar panels and wind turbines, almost single-handedly creating the Great Acceleration in renewable energy-harvesting devices. Many of the largest solar and wind farms are located in China, generating far more green energy than all other countries in the world combined.[24]

Nonetheless, Xi's version of a green transition fits into a much larger bid for global prestige that involves enormous amounts of hydrocarbon and very little justice. Since 2013, China has touted the "Belt and Road Initiative," world history's largest construction project – in essence a vast extension of China's already unprecedented domestic urban building boom – as a generous "South–South" international development program rivaling those of the heavier-handed World Bank and IMF. Its plans for new infrastructure retrace the old Silk Road through Xinjiang into Central Asia, then across Afro-Eurasia and beyond. Overland, new rail lines connect Chinese factories with markets in Europe and oilfields in the Middle East. By sea and air, new container ports and airfields connect Shanghai and Shenzhen to commercial plantations and mines in Southeast Asia, Africa, Latin America, and even in the USA's Caribbean "backyard." The Initiative's pipelines, refineries, coalmines, cement factories, its dozens of new and massive coal-powered electric plants, and megaprojects like the liquefied natural gas facility at the remote Pakistani port of Gwadar represent the twenty-first century's largest additions to the global petroleumscape. Rail-lines transect sensitive ecological zones,

Chinese-owned palm oil and soybean plantations have taken over Southeast Asian rainforests and African village lands, and its new dams and mining facilities strain rivers, including what was until recently the last of the world's great free-running rivers, Southeast Asia's Mekong.[25]

Like all "Belts and Roads" of previous empires, Xi's are designed to spread state power far beyond China's borders. In Algiers, Maputo, Nairobi, and Kinshasa, recipients of Chinese loans for Belt and Road infrastructure worry about debt-entrapment to Shanghai banks that will exacerbate their already dire subservience to New York, Washington, London, and Paris. Others question whether new expressways, dams, power grids, or mining facilities actually benefit local majorities, let alone the climate. Meanwhile, the Chinese Huawei Corporation successfully peddles its inexpensive 5-G telecoms networks in many countries, raising concerns that this "Virtual Silk Road" will permit Beijing to extend its draconian forms of domestic surveillance based on cell phones and facial recognition software to new semi-colonies abroad. An ice-free Arctic could open a "Polar Silk Road" that will shortcut the Suez route to Europe, accelerate the scramble for the regions' minerals, and intensify global geopolitical tensions. Like many previous "Belts and Roads" projects in world history, Beijing's serves an autocratic form of imperial aggrandizement. Xi has transformed contested rock shoals in the South China Sea into human-made islands that serve as naval bases and airbases, including for the largest aircraft carriers ever built. Dams on the Upper Mekong allow China to "weaponize" water to the disadvantage of its far poorer Southeast Asian neighbors downstream. Within China, the Belt and Road Initiative involves an intensification of a settler colonization program in Xinjiang that goes back to the Han dynasty 2,000 years ago. To quell dissent among the region's Muslim Uighur people, Xi has incarcerated a million or more residents of the region's large cities into a gulag of re-education and forced-labor camps, many of which are connected, like sweatshops elsewhere, to global value chains. He has also tightened Beijing's control over Hong Kong in the face of massive and persistent urban protests. Observers in Taipei fear the implications of this sabre-rattling for democracy there.[26]

All of this authoritarian hubris has two primary targets: the now vintage empire operated from Washington, D.C., and the large, fractious, and often unwieldy transnational conglomeration of even older imperial European states run from Brussels, Belgium. The USA still encompasses the single most carbon-intensive built habitat on Earthopolis. Its petroleum and coal firms, ensconced in the tail-pipe corporate parks of Dallas and Houston, have used their wealth to wield outsized influence within many spaces of urban knowledge-production and state power. As early as the 1980s, oil executives built their own Cities of Disinformation in the form of "think tanks" such as that of the energy-services billionaire Koch Brothers in Wichita, Kansas, designed to drown the results of university climate research in campaigns of what we now know as climate denialism. They also financed angry spokespeople on talk radio, TV, and the internet to transform pro-Paris sentiment into a conceit of out-of-touch "globalist" elites and pencil pushers in New York, San Francisco, Brussels, and Ottawa. As such, they played on the fact that, by embracing a message of "austerity" emanating from global city financial districts for forty years, the world's formal democracies sharply widened inequality within their cities and between cities and their countrysides. It is no wonder that the political classes in democratic states face recriminations for ignoring those left behind in hundreds of beleaguered, climate-ravaged, and dispersed places, many of whose inhabitants have no faith in either the urban or the planetary dimensions of Earthopolis, nor a sense of our Urban Planet as a single (or plural) human ecosystem, nor a sense of the crisis of its Greatest Acceleration.[27]

One year after American negotiators returned from Paris, the New York real estate huckster Donald Trump thrusted a rising storm of internet thunderbolts directly into these beleaguered places, mixing climate denialism with settler colonial racism, misogyny, homophobia, and contempt for public health science, all framed as populist anti-elitism and anti-urbanism. Trump's gambit was not the first or the only one of this type. Even before Paris, democracy-mutilating strongmen in Warsaw, Budapest, Ankara, Brasília, Manila, and Delhi tapped support from similar longsuffering spaces to sweep their own burgeoning personality cults into electoral victory. It would be a mistake to ignore the size or power of these spaces of counterrevolution. Trump's appeal in the indebted hydrocarbon farmlands of the Great Plains, the used-up oil patches of West Texas, the poisoned coal "hollers" of Kentucky, and the gun-shows of Alabama mirrored authoritarian sentiments in the rusting steel towns of the former Warsaw Pact, the gated condominiums of São Paulo and Manila, the militarized police stations of Rio de Janeiro, the cattle-lands of the Amazon fringes, the Selimiye Army Barracks of Istanbul, and tens of thousands of reeling villages of Northern India. Thousands of fundamentalist tabernacles add the word of many gods to these voices, from the galaxy of Bible-Belt megachurches in the USA to self-built houses of evangelical worship in Brazil's *favelas*, to mosques in small Turkish towns, to temples and pilgrimage sites across the Ganges Plains.

Indeed, Islamic militants are not the only ones to sow armed terror in a world they find too impious to tolerate. In India, a Hindu fundamentalist mob attack on the Babri Mosque in the Ganges Valley city of Ayodhya in 1992 signaled an end to the relative sectarian peace that had prevailed since Partition, and the rise of *Hindutva* – the idea that multifarious India actually belongs to Hindus alone. In subsequent years, mobs killed thousands of Muslims in months-long rampages across the cities of Gujarat, in Mumbai, and elsewhere, forcing survivors to find protection in separate shack cities, the so-called Muslim "colonies" or "ghettos." In 2014, Narendra Modi, one of the mobs' early inciters, rode the rage of *Hindutva* into a majority in Delhi's Round House of the People. Then his troops assaulted Srinagar and other cities of the majority-Muslim autonomous region of Kashmir. Indian Army tanks shut down streets and soldiers threw up barricades on every block against protest. Modi's mobs have since celebrated this coup with flashes of violence across India, including, as we know, in Delhi itself in 2020, the year that the leader of *Hindutva* gave a warm welcome to a visiting Donald Trump. In fervor fueled by intolerant professions of faith, the massacre-mongers of Delhi echo Jair Bolsonaro's cheerleading of police violence against *favelados* in Rio de Janeiro, Rodrigo Duterte's paramilitary attacks on slum dwellers in Manila, Recep Tayyip Erdoğan's suppression of dissent in Istanbul's Taksim Square, the rising resentment among police and militias in the USA against the Black Lives Matter movement, police killings of people of color across the world, and Trump's mob in midwinter Washington.[28]

Such grim acts in city streets threaten democracy and they are the cutting edge of "popular" forces that could rescue fossil fuels companies and their financiers, and from there stifle hopes for a Just Transition. Already, the damage they have inflicted is significant, whether during Trump's rejection of the Paris Accords, Bolsonaro's active encouragement of Brazilian ranchers' flaming assault on the Amazon rainforest, or Modi's cavalier attitude toward India's deathly coal plants. In the meantime, this troika of would-be tyrants spurred the rage of the pandemic too, by ridiculing the common-sense measures public health scientists recommended for slowing Covid-19 deaths. Accordingly, the USA, Brazil, and India have traded off the unenviable title of number-one nations in coronavirus deaths, imposing the highest price on their citizens of color, the migrant urban poor, and their disproportionately female corps of caregivers. Such callous and incompetent behavior by leaders of formally democratic states only cheered the opponents of People Power in Moscow and Beijing, who happily, if very dubiously, claimed the mantle of the world's most efficient virus-killers and climate heroes.[29]

WHOSE STREETS?

Clearly, the Just Transition will only occur if states take their guidance not by hate-blinded mobs with no sense of the Urban Planet's crisis, but by hopeful visions of democratic Cities of the Sun infused into the energized, complex, and fractious urban polities that first gave birth to both cities and states 6,000 years ago. Now known as the "public sphere" or "civil society," this space of maximum Urban Planetary hope connects to Earthopolis's nearly infinite much smaller components, each pushing power through equally infinite connective "capillaries" in between them – and from there upward and outward.

Ultimately, we conjure most of our public power in spaces we usually think of as private, even intimate. In our homes, at kitchen tables, and in bedrooms, we negotiate questions of gender, sex, age, and domestic economics to supply ourselves with Sun-gifted water, food, shelter, rest, reproduction, care, and emotional strength. In the streets and shops where we provision our homes, we negotiate still other lines of identity

(A)

(B)

25.2. Justice and Transition, at the Heart of the Urban Planet and on Its Far Horizon
No exaggeration: city streets are the fulcrum for the next 6,000 years of life on Earth. Unarmed urban protests do not always win victories for Justice and Transition, but they are our best tool to hold states, corporations, and counterrevolutionaries accountable for prolonging authoritarianism and the Hydrocarbon bargain. In 2019, two million marchers gathered at Hong Kong's Government Complex (A) against Beijing's iron fist before Covid-19 and armed state force took back the streets. In Port-Louis, the mid-Indian Ocean capital of Mauritius (B), environmental justice activists protested an oil spill that destroyed pristine beaches on the far fringe of our Urban Planet. Earthopolis's future orbits of the Sun depend on our eagerness to hoist new generations of human protestors into the streets – and from there into power.
(A) Stephan J. Boitano/LightRocket/Getty Images. (B) Fabien Dubessay/AFP/Getty Images.

in public. Pausing on street-corners, in neighborhood meeting places, and in places of worship we build a sense of place, belonging, and spiritual strength – often in the face of vexed questions of race, culture, and religious practice. In the world's cafés, bars, restaurants, gyms, dancehalls, and art spaces we experience the social and bodily pleasures so crucial in a world where so many of us suffer from isolation, sickness, hunger, or hard labor. In schools, campuses, libraries, union halls, community-based organizations, and online sites we hone our analyses of broader spheres of power. In millions of workplaces, we contemplate our odds for control over the time and energy we sell to our employers, making strategic decisions about the possibilities of collective action in the face of ruthlessly effective and ubiquitous corporate attacks on workers' organizations during the austerity era. From all of those places, we make strategic and tactical decisions: whether to entrust our fates to states, through voting booths, by petitioning officials, by going to court, by going on strike, or by launching our own political candidacies.[30]

Or, instead, we turn to the streets, the greatest space of direct People Power we have ever built. Protest: marches in the boulevards or along dusty roads, demonstrations, processions, rolling mass actions, rallies, strikes, boycotts, mock trials, solemn funerals. Streets festooned with signs, banners, murals, graffiti, buttons, leaflets, petitions, candles, cellphone flashlights, umbrellas, tent cities. Streets echoing with chants, bullhorn speeches, costumes, guerrilla theater and dance, carnival, protest music, deafening silence, muffled drums, or raucous hammering on pots and pans. Crowds – some summoned retail-style, door-by-door, others assembled in community gathering spaces or union halls, and others mustered wholesale through organizing apps or by mass outrage at heinous state or corporate acts. No matter its origins, the rich language of "blessed unrest" has become the language of pure numerical power transubstantiated into the highest of all moral authority – at its best a source of hopeful sovereignty that rivals that of states or corporations and that re-charts the way they use their power.[31]

During the Greatest Acceleration, non-violent varieties of protest have grown alongside our cities. It is true that many revolutionaries have also turned more readily to weapons, barricades, urban riots, guerrilla bases in the countryside, and border-defying terror cells. But no protestor today can overlook the history lessons taught by Mahatma Gandhi. Whether marching weapon-less in downtown Johannesburg, on the dusty backroads of Gujarat to make salt on a beach, or in mass processions in huge Indian cities like Delhi, Gandhi's *Satyagrahis* faced many of the same opponents on Earthopolis's urban chessboards as do all democratic revolutionaries. The state's basic checkmate moves are these: to flood protest spaces with armed police, soldiers, and spies; to move protestors by force from the streets into cellblocks, interrogation chambers, or morgues; and to find any way possible to discredit protest in available media. On top of that, cameras mounted virtually everywhere in cities now give their secretive monitors eyes on everyone. Surveillance malware designed to silently infect cell phones has become a global commodity with deeply chilling potency that has already allowed some states, corporations, and even criminal organizations to de-power the *polis* of some of Earthopolis's most active streets. Too many protestors have been forced "underground" or out of the city, and state crackdowns of all kinds increase the attraction of armed struggle. Nonetheless, nonviolent protest still offers democratic forces the widest and most adaptable vocabulary by which to employ built space to transform the raw power of numbers into an unassailable form of civic spirituality – or, as Gandhi's greatest disciple, Martin Luther King, put it, "to meet the forces of hate with the power of love."[32]

Scholars who study the hundreds of thousands of twentieth- and twenty-first-century urban street protests, and the smaller number of similar actions in the countryside, tell us that Gandhi and King were right – most of the time, and at least so far. The moral clarity and wide diversity of unarmed protest practices are more effective than other techniques for unifying large varied protesting communities, for drawing the largest numbers of people into action, and for gathering the broadest sympathy from the non-protesting public. Non-violent protestors also most efficiently deprive the state of its primary political argument for crackdowns, namely that it is acting against chaos in the name of public order, or in defense of a broader majority of non-protesting citizens. This is doubly important for urban protest, because counterrevolutionary states regularly demonize protest through familiar anti-urban tropes – that cities are the source of all corruption, mayhem, and the greatest enemy of the innocent countryside. As Gandhi and King acknowledged frankly, non-violent protest is most successful when it elicits violent state reprisals, even with "softer" weapons like water cannons, tear gas, stun grenades, or phalanxes of shielded police in riot gear. The beatings of Gandhi's Salt Marchers bore witness to the global potential of power unleashed in this way, as did in the police violence against King's 1963 desegregation marchers in Birmingham, Alabama and in the 1965 voting rights campaign on the Edmund Pettus Bridge in nearby Selma. As King wrote from his jail cell in Birmingham, state violence in response to non-violent protest "dramatizes" injustice so that "it cannot be ignored" in the larger society. It also casts the People as David against the Goliath of the counter-democratic state.[33]

City streets are not the only space where the *Satyagrahis* of the future will gather to build hope for our Urban Planet's future. Strikes may once again sweep the workplaces of the world, despite surveillance systems that corporations have installed in big factories and warehouses – and despite the anti-union laws they have passed in parliaments. Gandhi's Salt Marches, King's marches on backroads of the Deep South, and the "Freedom Rides" organized by American civil rights activists on interstate buses all suggest that protest in the spaces between cities can have strategic advantages too, since the state often operates more awkwardly there. Most protestors, though, rightfully choose to knock directly on the front doors of power. That means gathering in big public spaces in front of big buildings in big cities: the very places where the state delivers its carrots and sticks, where corporations amass wealth, where shop and mall owners aggrandize desires and sublimate them, and where universities and other Cities of Light generate the power of knowledge. Urban neighborhoods segregated by race, class, nation, and religion function in their own way as monuments to unjust power; they too serve as effective mustering grounds for protest, just as their boundaries make good protest targets.[34]

During the 1960s, young leaders stepped into these protest spaces in greater numbers and diversity than before, bringing new creativity to the theater of street politics. Black college students in southern cities of the USA drove a wedge between business owners and white supremacist state governments by "sitting in" at Jim Crow lunch counters, providing a model for some of King's tactics in Birmingham. The grace and bravery of these non-violent protests in the face of mob reprisals at soda fountains and the attack dogs and water cannons of Birmingham Police Chief Bull Connor inspired white students in the USA and elsewhere. They called out Cold War weapons research at universities, protested the Vietnam War in greater numbers and with increasing militancy, then demanded that society adopt new forms of consciousness to replace what they saw as stultifying Cold War bourgeois and institutional cultures that underlay white supremacy, class intolerance, patriarchy, homophobia, warmongering, and assaults on the Planet.

By 1968, another momentous year of global urban upheaval, young American protestors led the way toward such a revolution in sensibilities, staging "live-ins" and "be-ins" in San Francisco's Haight-Ashbury during the previous summer that spread to other cities. In March 1968, French students on the university campus at Nanterre near Paris launched a revolution demanding "the impossible" that caught fire in the Sorbonne and Left Bank cafés and encouraged no fewer than eleven million workers to go out on strike. In May, revolutionaries once again flocked to barricades in Paris, fighting *gendarmes* with Haussmann-era cobblestones and bringing the French state to a temporary halt. Later that summer in Chicago, anti-war protestors battled the Chicago police outside the Democratic Party Convention. In Prague particularly brave protestors confronted Soviet tanks that squashed a "Spring" of reformist sentiment led by writers, journalists, and a few Communist Party officials. In October, students in Mexico City aptly chose the Avenida de los Insurgentes for their peaceful protest of the state's increasing authoritarianism, but while mustering for a repeat march in the city's Tlatelolco section, they met with a withering hail of bullets that left scores dead. The Tlatelolco Massacre was not alone: state violence and poorly armed but violent protestor reprisals were part of all of the events of 1968. In the USA, five "Long Hot Summers" of violent rebellions in the Black sections of big cities culminated in Spring 1968, in the aftermath of King's assassination. Police violence often sparked these events, which were squashed with armed force from National Guard troops and even tanks. Soon similar uprisings would echo in the "ghettos" of the French *banlieues*, and in postindustrial Manchester, Liverpool, and London.[35]

"The arc of the moral universe is long," Martin Luther King Jr. was fond of saying, "but it bends toward justice." Since 1968, protest has brought much previously thought "impossible" into being. In 1968, the "Whole World" was, in fact, "Watching," and new variations on the theme of mass protest spread worldwide. Inspired by King's March on Washington that filled the National Mall with a quarter million people in 1963, marches in the US capital since gave energy to many of the social movements that spun out of the 1968 era – including a moratorium on the Vietnam War that sapped the strength of a rampant empire. Similar protests in large monumental squares of capitals or in neglected spaces of great explosive power have pushed the envelope of People Power to places previously thought hermetically sealed in authoritarianism. In Soweto, schoolchildren massed in the streets to protest apartheid-era education policies only to meet squads of gun-toting soldiers delivered in armored cars called hippos. A decade and a half of growing protest in the townships, supported on university campuses across the world, led to the release of Nelson Mandela from Robben Island Prison in 1989 – yet another signal year of global urban democracy. By then, the spirit of the Prague Spring had gamely and repeatedly reincarnated itself, first in the shipyards of Gdańsk, Poland in the early 1980s, then a few years later when Soviet leader Mikhail Gorbachev's reforms encouraged people to flood Eastern Bloc streets once again. In 1989, the city of Leipzig, East Germany erupted with protestors who soon inspired thousands of Berliners to sweep into the Alexanderplatz and take out their fury on the Berlin Wall. Similar revolutions, "Velvet" and otherwise, swept other Eastern-Bloc capitals, and in 1991, the people of Moscow mounted barricades around a newly invigorated parliament in the city's "White House" to face down the tanks of hardline generals, bringing the Soviet Union to an end.[36]

As the Berlin Wall fell, though, the "one percent" in global city capitals of capital claimed the victory as their own. "There is No Alternative," some of them crowed from the skyscrapertops, to the finance industry's embrace of austerity. Others declared the "End of History," implying that 6,000 years' worth of city-energized political contestation had dissolved within the all-enticing brew of global capitalist power. City streets, soon hitched to the crowd-sourcing genius of the internet, swiftly debunked this "Washington Consensus." Protests against IMF and World Bank austerity programs that had proliferated in the great cities of the poor since in the 1970s expanded during the 1980s and 1990s. In 1999, vast moats of "Blue and Green" protestors from unions and environmental groups, summoned by early email chains, converged on Seattle's convention hotels to disrupt meetings of the World Trade Organization, as the police department's percussion grenades and teargas cannons echoed nearby. A year later, the "Battle in Seattle" resumed in front of the IMF and World Bank headquarters in Washington, D.C., then spread to increasingly fortified meetings of global elites in Quebec City, Canada, Göteborg, Sweden, Genoa, Italy, and Davos, Switzerland. In 2003, the winds of worldwide protest turned against George Bush's oil war in Iraq as crowds totaling in the millions gathered in hundreds of cities. Later, a broader critique of capitalism and hydrocarbon resurfaced in the vast Occupy Wall Street movement in 2011, which flooded global cities and business districts everywhere in the world with protestors and months-long encampments.[37]

Anti-authoritarian, anti-austerity, and anti-hydrocarbon protests have, of course, not always won. Urban activists will always bear searing memories of the tanks that killed thousands in Tien An Men Square in 1989 while repressing the massive Chinese Democracy Movement; the disproportionate Israeli repression of the *intifadas* in Palestine; the razing of the Zucotti Park tent city near Wall Street in 2011; the Egyptian military's reconquest of Cairo's Tahrir Square in 2012 ending the largest of the Arab Spring revolutions; the aerial bombardment and gassing of protestors in Syrian cities from 2011 to 2019; and the crushing of mass protests in Minsk, Yangon, and Hong Kong amidst the Covid-19 epidemic. Not all states care one bit whether their monopoly of violence, even used in crowded spaces filled with unarmed people, rests on any moral standing whatsoever. Non-violent protest, as we know well, can at times draw violent militants or armed counter-protestors into the power vacuums it creates in streets, and police reprisals can lead to violent forms of self-defense – even, as in Syrian cities like Aleppo, Homs, and Hama, in catastrophic civil war and in cities once again laid waste from the air. Commercial cyber-spyware has proven effective in rounding up of revolutionaries in Minsk among other places, and in tagging the journalists who are indispensable to protest organizers. Dictatorship may soon get too high-tech to resist from old-fashioned streets alone.

That said, the aroused streets of Earthopolis have delivered plenty of good tidings too. We have enormous urban crowds to thank for the rise in the number of democratic governments worldwide – going back to the 1974 Carnation Revolution in Lisbon through the "People Power" protests in mid 1980s Manila, to anti-authoritarian protests and overthrows of dictators in Santiago de Chile, Quito, Buenos Aires, Santo Domingo, Port-au-Prince, the small towns and cities of Mexico's Chiapas region, Beirut, Baghdad, Belgrade, Tbilisi, Yerevan, Warsaw, Kyiv, Bamako, Ouagadougou, Khartoum, Bishkek, Ulaanbaatar, Khabarovsk, Moscow, Kathmandu, and Bangkok, among many others. Even colossal defeats can transmit the courage of convictions from the streets of one part of the Urban Planet to many others. Cutting through all the vicissitudes, scholars of resistance movements have shown that the success of non-violent campaigns has increased in the twenty-first century, with some 60 percent of non-violent campaigns achieving some sort of substantial victory by one count. Contrary to the received wisdom of some, unarmed protest campaigns are also twice as likely to result in democratic outcomes as violent protests – though the effectiveness of wildcat acts targeting high-symbolic-value shop windows, urban buildings, on the fringes of peaceful crowds needs closer measurement, as does the dismantling of statues or monuments commemorating historic injustices. The same conclusion is borne out by the converse fact that rural guerrilla wars have established so many of the world's most persistent dictatorships. The senseless acts of urban terrorism that have also proliferated in the same period suggest much the same.[38]

Hope. Generated by crowds in city streets. Televised or Tweeted and transmitted everywhere else. Even as the police, goons, and spymasters of counterrevolution gathered menacingly in some of the very same streets during the 2010s, hopes born of People's Protest will be essential to lift Earthopolis into new orbits around the Sun. It was thus that, even in the depths of 2020, globally connected movements for democracy showed a capacity to spur action on all the biggest crises of our time: climate change, a new pandemic, and resurgent authoritarianism. The Paris

Accords, after all, did not materialize solely out of state benevolence. They were encouraged into being by protests that in 2014 alone involved hundreds of thousands of people in New York City, Bogotá, Rio, Johannesburg, Lagos, Istanbul, Paris, and Delhi among many other cities that launched the global climate justice movement. In 2019, the Climate Strike movement led by schoolchildren across the world gave Earthopolis another shining addition to a global culture of unarmed unrest. So did deeper discussions in community-based organizations elsewhere about the need to supplement the Transition envisaged at Paris with more attention to Justice. Meanwhile, record numbers of democracy protests exploded in 2019 and 2020, capped by the two million people and the countless unfurled umbrellas that took part in the doomed yet surely arc-bending Hong Kong uprisings against Beijing. The American Movement for Black Lives spread its massive wings too, in anguish over the murder of George Floyd in Minneapolis. As videos of a police officer's nine-minute street execution of a defenseless Black man flooded the internet, millions more people took to their own streets, most masked against Covid-19, most by far peacefully, filling public spaces of thousands of smaller cities, including majority-white towns and suburbs in the USA. From there, the telegraph of urban civil ungovernability resonated once again across the Urban Planet, this time in the shape of a pan-continental general strike against abuses of state violence. In the USA, this outpouring of People Power generated more than enough votes from America's "liberal" cities, from energized neighborhoods of color, and even from some typically conservative white suburbs to end the reign of America's most authoritarian president. As fraught as the cities of 2020 were, they managed to deliver a precious moment of respite after all.[39]

Of course, "the Revolution," as one protestor in Minsk ruefully reminded us a few weeks later, "does not always go according to plan." Uncertain urban futures have a long past; they date back to the very beginning of Earthopolis's life story, when, we are told, the goddess Inanna rolled the dice of city-hood at Uruk's Lapis Lazuli Quay. Still, since then we have built some certainty into our cities and into the potent *polis* of Earthopolis: by virtue of our built habitat, humans possess unprecedented power to guide our Urban Planet's next trips around the Sun wherever we collectively choose as our destination. Just as certain is that any responsible use of that daunting power requires us to embrace all of the hardest lessons from the long and large biography of our home on Earth, and of the life stories of all of its teeming cities. Only as deeply informed Urban Planetary *citizens* can we imagine a fairer human habitat, which allows the urban majorities who will harvest the new energies needed for new centuries of human power to reap greater measures of power themselves. Only under the light cast in these juster Cities of the Sun can we read through the ledgers of six millennia's acts of urban creation and destruction, and honestly account for the exploitative price non-human lifeforms have paid for humanity's achievement of species supremacy. Only then can we pray, in long solemn processions toward our great temples, schools, libraries, and universities if necessary, for an Earthopolis whose citizens use our generous space under the Sun to repair and regenerate our home planet's much older, larger, and far more prolific life-giving habitats, while bowing to the deep understanding that they too make our own ongoing life histories possible. And only then can we gamble, godlike perhaps, on building new cities and a new Urban Planet – a human space endowed with the power to nurture Earthly life everywhere, and across longer-bending arcs of time to come.

Acknowledgments

The perspectives in this book arose from a course on world history that I have taught for over a quarter-century as a Professor of History at the University of Massachusetts and the State University of New York at Buffalo. I owe a debt of gratitude to the thousands of students who took the class and the dozens of TAs who helped me teach it. Over time, this course transformed into a new guise as "Cities of the World." I am particularly grateful to my graduate students Guangzhi Huang and Shengkai Xu for helping me make that transition, and for reading and correcting some of the early chapter drafts of this book as I tried them out as course readings. Among other things, I hope *Earthopolis* can function as a quick-service source of basic knowledge upon which instructors and students can draw for similar courses.

If so, *Earthopolis* owes much larger debts to thousands of other scholars who make their living researching cities. The book's primary scholarly mission is to connect urban studies scholars in general with the enormous but often neglected labors of urban historians – and in particular the work of global urban historians. Putting that mission into play meant drawing on what I call, in Chapter 25, the "explosion" of Urban Planetary knowledge – really a "greatest acceleration" in urban research that more or less coincides with the Greatest Acceleration in the Urban Planet's growth since 1945. No single scholar can come close to reading that entire body of work or even keeping up with the weekly output of new urban research today. My footnotes, extensive as they may be, acknowledge only a tiny proportion of scholarly work on any of the more specific subjects the book strives to cover. I have no doubt missed the chance to alert readers to many crucial titles, including ones that contain discoveries that made many others possible. To all of the scholars who have inspired me over the years – named and unnamed – I can only hope that my debt to you is obvious enough, as is my deep gratitude for the chance to learn from you.

That said I must highlight one group of scholars whose inspiration literally saturates these pages. These are the 500-plus historians who have joined the Global Urban History Project since its birth in 2017. For anyone interested in learning more about any subject in this book, one quick route to learn about dissertations and new work in progress is to become a member of GUHP and peruse the "Meet Other Members" feature on the website. I have drawn extensively on these scholarly profiles when I needed information for *Earthopolis* and I thank all GUHP members for the opportunity to know what you are up to! Thanks too to all the contributors to the *Global Urban History* blog, another great source of newly minted knowledge in the field, and to its editors, who now also shepherd a series of Elements in Global Urban History from Cambridge University Press.

Among GUHP scholars, I owe the most to those who have served with me on the Board of Directors, and who have collectively made up one of the kindest and most supportive academic communities imaginable. I can only hope you find this book's good parts and its faults (mine alone) worth wading through. Kristin Stapleton read early drafts and helped me with several sources in Chinese. My enduring thanks to blog and Elements editors Michael Goebel, Tracy Neumann, and Joseph Ben Prestel, and especially to Michael and Joseph for meeting with me to discuss their thoughts on the manuscript at a critical time. Enduring gratitude to Emma Hart and Mariana Dantas for their big role in bringing GUHP into being, to GUHP's first Presidents Carola Hein and Rosemary Wakeman, to Nancy Kwak, Su Lin Lewis, Li Hou, Anindita Ghosh, Andra Chastain, Yunus Ugur, Debjani Bhattacharyya, Cyrus Shayegh, Alexia Yates, and Titilola Halimat Somotan. Dr. Somotan is part of an especially inspirational group of "Emerging Scholars" who gathered in Zoom workshops with more established mentors during the challenging 2020–21 academic year, then presented their work in public forums. To Bernard Keo, Archa Neelakandan Girija, Camille Cordier, Aishani Gupta, Ernest Sewordor, Rustam Khan, Chester

Archilla, Ingy Higazi, Yingchuan Yang, Stephen Pascoe, and Amanda Waterhouse, thanks for all for your company and inspiration during that otherwise trying year – and best wishes as your work lights up the Urban Planet. Deep thanks too to GUHP Mentors and other especially supportive colleagues, including but not limited to Constanza Benavides Castro, Michael Vann, Trevor Burnard, Guadalupe Garcia, Micah Muscolino, Katherine Zubovitch, Annelise Orleck, Mark Healy, Camilo Trumper, Ademide Adelusi-Adeluyi, Abosede George, Devika Shankar, Saheed Aderinto, Dries Lyna, João Júlio Gomes dos Santos Júnior, Kristie Flannery, Seamus O'Hanlon, Isabella Jackson, Eric Ross, Prashant Kidambi, Simon Gunn, Anna Ross, Weifang Lu, Samuel Grinsell, Bronwen Everell, Christian Schmid, Lynn Hollen Lees, and Richard Harris. Thanks to Ayan Meer for handling GUHP's communications systems so ably and for his own fascinating work in the field. Thanks to Michael Watson at Cambridge University Press for recognizing the importance of this new field, commissioning this book, then supporting the project as it grew and transformed. Thanks to Emily Plater, Ruth Boyes, Madelon Naninga-Fransen, and Steven Holt for shepherding it through the production process.

Earthopolis is a product of its perilous time. As I wrote this book, a triple crisis in global politics, public health, and planetary climate grew in intensity, culminating in the *annus horribilus* of 2020–21. The crises of these years are the direct result of the shape of spaces humans have built on Earth. However, moving our Urban Planet out of harm's way depends mostly on how people choose to inhabit and rebuild those spaces going forward.

I know no better model for how to make such choices than that of another group of longtime dear colleagues, the activists who brought People United for Sustainable Housing (PUSH Buffalo) into being over the past fifteen years. In a city that has endured all of the mounting crisis of Urban Planetary History – and in particular the exacerbated version of that crisis in the USA – PUSH Buffalo has provided a place of safety, purpose, power, and hope. Not just any hope, but the determined, daring, practiced, and continually revised form of hope that is the only kind that will suffice for the challenges all of us face, especially those on the front lines of inequality and planetary overheating. That form of hope is the ultimate form of urban knowledge; it is also the only form of human power capable of propelling our Urban Planet toward a Just Transition for all generations to come. For firing up that kind of hope, none of us on Earthopolis can thank any one of you enough. The culminating dedication of this book goes to you: Rahwa Ghirmatzion, Aaron Bartley, Dawn Wells-Clyburn, Harper Bishop, Clarke Gocker, Jen Kaminski, Sarah Gordon Halawa, Whitney Yax, Eric Walker, Nicolalita Rodriguez, Tyrell Ford, John Washington II, Christian Parra, Geovaira Hernandez, Emily Terrana, Kelly Camacho, Theresa Watson, Ramone Alexander, Tori Kuper, Phawmu Nar Thaw, John Buckley, Shirley Sarmiento, Bob Jahnke, Maxine Murphy, Micaela Shapiro-Shellaby, Da'Von McCune, Andrew Delmonte, Luz Velez, Providencia Cintron, Felicita Cintron, Emily Louis, Bryana DiFonzo, Genise Thomas, John Bono, Ben Siegel, Steve Freeburn, Heidi Jones, Nakia Hock, Maribel Rodriguez, Delta Wilson, Samantha Peterson-Borins, Meghan Zickl, Cole Adams, Muna Abdirahman, Bonko Ba, Kawiye Jumale, Aweso Malande, De'yron Tabb, Angel Rosado, Jennifer Mecozzi, Ismail Johnson, Aminah Johnson, Saint Rodriguez, Eddie Ice Cream Jones, Asim Johnson, Keith Kristich, Josh Smith, Sergio Uzurin, Marshall Bertram, Kristin Rose, and hundeds of other PUSH members and staff who have filled the streets of the West Side with brilliance and courage.

Like all things with a purpose in the public spaces of Earthopolis, this book also took its primary energies from smaller, more private places: the homes I have been so enormously lucky to inhabit over the course of a lifetime. For sharing all the cheer, work, tough times, and sustenance of my family's household over the past twenty-something years, I thank my daughter Mbali McCluskey-Nightingale and my spouse Martha McCluskey – both of you, from the bottom of my heart. These last few years have been big ones for all of us, and I have deeply enjoyed sharing intellectual and political journeys with you! Along the way, Martha's parents Dorothy and Donald McCluskey made our home possible in many other ways, and they inspired us by their example as environmental activists and pioneering solar energy adopters. Dorothy left us a decade ago, but not before she and Don took their own home off the grid. Don continues to urge us on, his hundredth birthday behind him, toward new frontiers of hydrocarbon drawdown and climate repair. Meanwhile, as always, I also appreciate all the warm and steadfast love from my dearest siblings, siblings-in law, nieces, nephews, and cousins – as well as the huge, adoptive embrace of Mbali's South African relatives.

This book's dedication starts where I started off, in the home of my parents: Dale Husemöller and Jeanne Nightingale. *Earthopolis* draws deeply on my childhood, shaped not only by the immense amounts of love my parents packed and unpacked (along with everything else) from one to another of the homes they built in many cities of the world – but also by a generous flow of books, maps, and transport tickets. Always, they gave such gifts with eager, maybe too-open-ended, anticipation for what I would do next. Those gifts remain piled up all around me as I write – as does all the stuff I learned about cities and the world because of them. I hope this book can at least begin to seal the circle of a lifetime of gratitude to you, mom and dad.

Notes

INTRODUCTION OUR URBAN PLANET IN SPACE AND TIME

1. This biography of "Earthopolis" is my own response to the challenge offered by Charles Tilly, the great sociologist of cities and states. He argued correctly that "in principle urban historians have the opportunity to become the most important interpreters of the ways that global social processes articulate with small-scale social life." His parting words served as an impetus: "No use talking about it; someone will have to *do* it!" (Charles Tilly, "What Good Is Urban History?," *Journal of Urban History* 22 (1996): 702–19). Of course, I am not the only one "doing it." The phrase "Urban Planet" represents a gesture of both respect for and engaged puzzlement with the theorist Neil Brenner's phrase "planetary urbanization," formulated in collaboration with the geographer Christian Schmid. While accepting their central idea that "the urban" cannot be limited to cities, my goal is to offer a critique of the monolithic conception of change – "capitalist urbanization" – underlying their analysis by focusing on the sheer plurality of projects of urbanization, the sheer unpredictability, contingency, and primal power of energized urban polities, and the bidirectional causality of urban and planetary history. To do this, I divide the larger-scale reach of urban influence into specific geographies of action, habitat, impact, and consequence. Of course, I also establish the far longer and larger historical contexts of our use of cities as tools of larger-scale and planetary influence. This book also relies on several collective efforts on behalf of urban historians to pave a road toward Tilly's goal: Peter Wood ed., *The Oxford Handbook of Cities in World History* (Oxford: Oxford University Press, 2013); Andrew Lees, *The City: A World History* (Oxford: Oxford University Press, 2015); Nicholas Kenny and Rebecca Madgin, *Cities beyond Borders: Comparative, and Transnational Approaches to Urban History* (Farnham: Ashgate, 2015); A. K. Sandoval-Strausz and Nancy H. Kwak eds., *Making Cities Global: The Transnational Turn in Urban History* (Philadelphia, PA: University of Pennsylvania Press, 2018); Mariana L. R. Dantas and Emma Hart, "Historical Approaches to Researching the Global Urban," in *Doing Global Urban Research*, ed. John Harrison and Michael Hoyler (London: Sage, 2018), pp. 211–24; the special issue of the Brazilian Journal *Esboços* edited by Mariana L. R. Dantas, João Júlio Gomes dos Santos Júnior, and Carl H. Nightingale entitled *Dossiê: História urbana global, Esboços* 28 (2021); and Cyrus Schayegh's concept of "transpatialization" in Cyrus Schayegh, *The Middle East and the Making of the Modern World* (Cambridge, MA: Harvard University Press, 2017). It also draws heavily on the collective work of the 500-plus members of the Global Urban History Project (GUHP), a networking organization the author helped found with colleagues in 2017 and has helped to coordinate since. The GUHP website at https://globalurbanhistory.org and the *Global Urban History* blog at https://globalurbanhistory.com, edited by Michael Goebel, Joseph Ben Prestel, and Tracy Neumann, allows specialists to learn more about members' work. Cambridge University Press's series of "Elements in Global Urban History" is a result of that collaboration. In writing *Earthopolis*, I benefited greatly from the first two of these Elements to appear, Richard Harris's *Why Cities Matter*

(Cambridge: Cambridge University Press, 2021) and Alexia Yates's *Real Estate in Global Urban History* (Cambridge: Cambridge University Press, 2021).

2. As I hope I signal here, this book affirms Ananya Roy's critiques of the original idea of planetary urbanization that faulted it for paying insufficient attention to what she sees as "undecidable" distinctions between cities and other human and non-human spaces. Ananya Roy, "What Is Urban about Critical Urban Theory?," *Urban Geography* 37 (2016): 810–23 and Aiwha Ong, "Introduction," in *Worlding Cities: Asian Experiments and the Art of Being Global*, ed. Ananya Roy and Aiwha Ong (Chichester: Blackwell, 2011), pp. 1–27. See also Neil Brenner, "Introduction: Urban Theory without an Outside," in *Implosions/Explosions: Toward a Study of Planetary Urbanization*, ed. Neil Brenner (Berlin: jovis, 2014), pp.14–34; Brenner and Christian Schmid, "Toward a New Epistemology of the Urban?," *City* 19 (2015): 151–82; Brenner and Schmid, "The Urban Age in Question,"*International Journal of Urban and Regional Research* 38 (2014): 731–55, and Christian Schmid, "Journeys through Planetary Urbanization: Decentering Perspectives on the Urban," *Environment and Planning D* 36 (2018): 591–610 (this last article is in a special issue of the journal that includes many other perspectives on the concept). In this book, I follow a method from my own *Segregation: A Global History of Divided Cities* (Chicago, IL: University of Chicago Press, 2012). Planetary observations about actions, habitat, impact, and consequence are counterbalanced by an effort to understand the specific location where these were set in motion, often from many different places, and with many different intentions, thus adding longer-term historic specificity to Roy and Ong's idea of "worlding practices." Also see my "The Seven C's: Reflections on Writing a Global History of Urban Segregation," in Kenny and Madgin eds., *Cities beyond Borders*, pp. 27–42.

3. In "What Is Urban?" Roy argues that rural and other non-urban areas are cities' "constitutive other." This formulation emphasizes both difference and mutuality, yet implies a preference for a plural conception of the human habitat over a singular one. My concept of the Urban Planet seeks to retain plurality and mutuality – or even "symbiosis" – between city, country, and unbuilt space while focusing on the increasing (and often decreasing) dominance of actions that we take in cities and that have done the most to connect our habitat on a planetary scale. The Urban Planet is thus a phenomenon whose checkered history as a singular, whole, interconnected human habitat is worth interrogating as deeply as the histories of its undeniably *constitutive* city-influenced parts – urban, rural, and otherwise. The same goes for the histories of the relationships between the "realm of human habitat" as a whole and other interconnected singular-yet-plural realms of action, impact, and consequence.

4. Erle C. Ellis and Navin Ramankutty, "Putting People in the Map: Anthropogenic Biomes of the World,"*Frontiers in Ecology and the Environment* 6 (2008): 439–47. Again I prefer "Urban Planet" and "Earthopolis" over "anthrome," because the latter does little to name the singular types of space that over time became the existential pivot-point of our habitat: cities.

5. Quotation from Richard Overly, *The Times Complete History of the World*, 9th ed. (London: Times Books, 2010), p. 80.

6. Julia Adeney Thomas, Mark Williams, and Jan Zalasiewicz, *The Anthropocene: A Multidisciplinary Approach* (Cambridge, UK: Polity Press, 2020), pp. vii–40.

7. Edward Glaeser, *Triumph of the City: How Our Greatest Invention Makes Us Richer, Smarter, Greener, Healthier, and Happier* (New York: Penguin, 2011); Ben Wilson, *Metropolis: A History of the City, Humankind's Greatest Invention* (New York: Doubleday, 2020).

PROLOGUE BEFORE AND BEYOND: BIG THINGS IN TINY PLACES

1. These quotations are from photographs of the fountain, located behind "Temptation" restaurant in Jericho, taken by the author in January, 2015.

2. Kathleen Kenyon, *Archaeology in the Holy Land* (New York: Praeger, 1960), pp.36–57.

3. Jerry D. Moore, *The Prehistory of Home* (Berkeley, CA: University of California Press, 2012), pp.1–115.

4. Moore, *Prehistory of Home*, p. 46.

5. A compelling new exploration of these modes of collective life is David Graeber and David Wengrow, *The Dawn of Everything: A New History of Humanity* (New York: Farrar Straus and Giroux, 2021).

6. Elliot M. Abrams and Anncorinne Freter, *The Emergence of the Moundbuilders: Archaeology of Tribal Societies in Southeastern Ohio* (Athens, OH: Ohio University Press, 2005); Thomas Knopf, Werner Steinhaus, and Shin'ya Fukunaga, *Burial Mounds in Europe and Japan* (Oxford: Archaeopress, 2018); Avi Bachenheimer, *Göbekli Tepe: An Introduction to the World's Oldest Temple* (Ardross: Birdwood, 2018).

7. On the causes of climate and habitat change over this period, see John L. Brooke, *Climate Change and the Course of Global History: A Rough Journey* (Cambridge: Cambridge University Press, 2014), pp. 55–108. For a quick summary of early human accomplishments and environmental impacts, see J. R. McNeill, "Global Environmental History: The First 150,000 Years," in *A Companion to Global Environmental History*, ed. J. R. McNeill and Erin Stewart Mauldin (Chichester: Wiley Blackwell, 2012), pp. 3–17.

8. Peter Bellwood, "Neolithic Migrations: Food Production and Population Expansion," in *The Encyclopedia of Global Human Migration, Volume 1. Prehistory*, ed. Peter Bellwood (Oxford: Wiley-Blackwell, 2013), pp. 79–86.

9. Ofer Bar-Yosef, "The Natufian Culture of the Levant, Threshold to the Origins of Agriculture," *Evolutionary Anthropology* 6 (1998): 159–77.

10. Jane Jacobs, *The Economy of Cities* (New York: Vintage, 1969), pp. 3–48. For a similar analysis of Jericho see Edward W. Soja, *Postmetropolis: Critical Studies of Cities and Regions* (Oxford: Blackwell, 2000), pp. 12–49.

11. Moore, *Prehistory of Home*, pp. 57–59; Bar-Yosef, "The Natufian Culture of the Levant"; Alexander Weide, "On the Identification of Domesticated Emmer Wheat *Triticum turgidum* Subspecies *doiococcum* (Poaceae) in the Aceramic Neolithic of the Fertile Crescent," *Archäologische Informationen* 38 (2015): 1–44, esp. Table 2, p. 13; Ryszard F. Mazurowski, Danuta Michczyńska, Anna Pazdur, and Natalia Piotrowska, "Chronology of the Early Pre-pottery Neolithic Settlement Tell Qaramel, Northern Syria, in the Light of Radiocarbon Dating," *Radiocarbon* 51 (2009): 771–81. Also see Michael E. Smith, Jason Ur, and Gary M. Feinman, "Jane Jacobs's 'City First' Model and Archaeological Reality," *International Journal of Urban and Regional Research* 38 (2014): 1525–35. A response to this refutation is given in Peter J. Taylor, "Post-Childe, Post-Wirth: A Response to Smith, Ur, and Feinman," *International Journal of Urban and Regional Research* 39 (2015): 168–71.

12. Archaeologists refer to these developments as the "secondary products revolution." A. Sherratt, "Plough and Pastoralism: Aspects of the Secondary Products Revolution," in *Pattern of the Past: Studies in Honour of David Clarke*, ed. Ian Hodder, G. Isaac, and N. Hammond (Cambridge: Cambridge University Press, 1981), pp. 261–305; Richard Evershed et al., "Earliest Date for Milk Use in the Near East and Southeastern Europe Linked to Cattle Herding," *Nature*, 455 (2008): 528–31. See also John L. Brooke, *Climate Change and the Course of Global History: A Rough Journey* (Cambridge: Cambridge University Press, 2016), pp. 191–94.

13. Kent Flannery and Joyce Marcus, *The Creation of Inequality: How Our Prehistoric Ancestors Set the Stage for Monarchy, Slavery, and Empire* (Cambridge, MA: Harvard University Press, 2021); Timothy A. Kohler and Michael E. Smith, *Ten Thousand Years of Inequality: The Archaeology of Wealth Differences* (Tucson, AZ: University of Arizona Press, 2018); Merry Wiesner-Hanks, *Gender in History: Global Perspectives* (Chichester: Wiley Blackwell, 2011), pp. 12–20. For a counterpoint see Graeber and Wengrow, *Dawn of Everything*, chapters 3–8. Their treatment of the Trypillia "megasites" is on pp. 288–97. On Banpo village, see Alfred Schinz, *The Magic Square: Cities in Ancient China* (Stuttgart: Edition Axel Menges, 1996), pp. 16–23.

14. Flannery and Marcus, *Creation of Inequality*, pp. 187–338; Graeber and Wengrow, *Dawn of Everything*. Brooke, *Climate Change*, pp. 213–42.

15. See Brooke, *Climate Change*, pp. 286–87; William F. Ruddiman, "The Anthropogenic Greenhouse Era Began Thousands of Years Ago," *Climatic Change* 61 (2003): 261–93; and William F. Ruddiman, *Earth Transformed* (New York: Freeman, 2014).

PART ONE CITIES OF THE RIVERS

1. Quotations from Diane Wolkenstein and Samuel Noah Kramer, *Inanna: Queen of Heaven and Earth* (New York: Harper and Row, 1983), pp. 11–28.

1 MAKING POLITICS FROM SUNSHINE, EARTH, AND WATER

1. Annette Zgoll, "Inanna – City Goddess of Uruk," in *Uruk: First City of the Ancient World* (Los Angeles: J. Paul Getty Museum, 2013), Nicola Crüsemann, Margarete van Ess, Markus Hilgert, and Beate Salje, eds., pp.51–59. Quotation from Roderick J. McIntosh, *Ancient Middle Niger: Urbanism and the Self-Organizing Landscape* (Cambridge: Cambridge University Press, 2006), p.144. On LiDAR, see, for example, Arlen F. Chase, Diane Z. Chase, Christopher T. Fisher, Stephen J. Leisz, and John F. Weishampel, "Geospatial Revolution and Remote Sensing LiDAR in Mesoamerican Archaeology," *Proceedings of the National Academy of Sciences, USA* 109 (2012): 12916–21; Damian H. Evans et al., "Uncovering Archaeological Landscapes at Angkor Using LiDAR," *Proceedings of the National Academy of Sciences, USA* 110, (2013): 12595–600.

2. Marc Van De Mieroop, *The Ancient Mesopotamian City* (Oxford: Oxford University Press, 1997), pp.1–41; Mario Liverani, *Uruk: The First City* (London: Equinox, 2006), pp. 25–27; Crüsemann *et al.*, Uruk; Bruce Bower, "Dawn of the City: Excavations Prompt a Revolution in Thinking about the Earliest Cities," *Science News* 173 (2008): 90–92; Salam al Quntar, Lamya Khalidi, and Jason Ur, "Proto-urbanism in the Late 5th Millennium BC: Survey and Excavations at Khirbat al-Fakhar (Hamoukar)," *Paléorient* 37 (2011): 151–75; Ruth Shady Solis et al., *Caral, the Oldest Civilization in the Americas: 15 Years of Unveiling Its History* (Lima: Gráfica Biblos, 2009); Nancy S. Steinhardt, "China," in *The Oxford Handbook of Cities in World History*, ed. Peter Clark (Oxford: Oxford University Press, 2013), pp. 105–26; Nancy Shatzman Steinhardt, *Chinese Imperial City Planning* (Honolulu: University of Hawai'i Press, 1990); Paul Wheatley, *Pivot of the Four Quarters: A Preliminary Inquiry into the Origins and Character of the Ancient Chinese City* (Chicago: Aldine, 1971); George Erdosy, "City States of North India and Pakistan at the Time of the Buddha," and "Early Cities and States Beyond the Ganges Valley," both in *The Archaeology of Early Historic South Asia: The Emergence of Cities and States*, ed. F. R. Allchin (Cambridge: Cambridge University Press, 1995), pp. 99–122; David M. Carallo, *Urbanization and Religion in Ancient Central Mexico* (Oxford: Oxford University Press, 2015); John S. Henderson, *The World of the Ancient Maya* (London: John Murray, 1997), pp. 65–113; David Mattingly and Kevin MacDonald, "Africa," in *The Oxford Handbook of Cities in World History*, ed. Peter Clark (Oxford: Oxford University Press, 2013), pp. 66–82; Roderick J. McIntosh, "Different Cities: Jenne-jeno and African urbanism," in *The Cambridge World History, Volume 3. Early Cities in Comparative Perspective, 4000 BCE–1200 CE*, ed. Norman Yoffee (Cambridge: Cambridge University Press, 2015), pp. 364–80; Timothy R. Pauketat, Susan M. Alt, and Jeffery D. Kruchten, "Cities of Earth and Wood: New Cahokia and Its Material-Historical Implications," in *The Cambridge World History, Volume 3. Early Cities in Comparative Perspective, 4000 BCE–1200 CE*, ed. Norman Yoffee (Cambridge: Cambridge University Press, 2015), pp. 437–54; Elena Krapf-Askari, *Yoruba Towns and Cities: An Enquiry into the Nature of Urban Social Phenomena* (Oxford: Clarendon Press, 1969), pp. 39–62; Bill Sanborn Ballinger, *Lost City of Stone: The Story of Nan Madol, the "Atlantis" of the Pacific* (New York: Simon and Schuster, 1978). On the possible connection by sea between ancient South American and Mesoamerican cultures, see Lincoln Paine, *The Sea and Civilization: A Maritime History of the World* (New York: Knopf, 2013), pp. 22–28.

4. Van De Mieroop, *Ancient Mesopotamian City*, pp. 1–41; Guillermo Algaze, "Initial Social Complexity in Southwestern Asia: The Mesopotamian Advantage," *Current Anthropology* 42 (2001): 199–233; Gwendolyn Leick, *Mesopotamia: The Invention of the City* (London: Penguin, 2001), pp. 1–60.

5. John L. Brooke, *Climate Change and the Course of Global History: A Rough Journey* (Cambridge: Cambridge University Press, 2016), pp. 188–91 and Table II.4, p. 115; Leick, *Mesopotamia*, pp. 19–22.

6. Clemens Reichel, "Hamoukar," in *Annual Report* (Chicago: Oriental Institute at the University of Chicago, 2011–12), pp. 69–76, https://oi.uchicago.edu/sites/oi.uchicago.edu/files/uploads/shared/docs/ar/11-20/11-12/11_12_Hamoukar.pdf (accessed July 18, 2021); al Quntar et al., "Proto-urbanism"; Patrick

Roberts, *Jungle: How Tropical Rainforests Shaped the World – And Us*" (New York: Basic Books, 2021), pp. 153–72.

7. Timothy Beach et al., "Ancient Maya Wetland Fields Revealed under Tropical Forest Canopy from Laser Scanning and Multiproxy Evidence,"*Proceedings of the National Academy of Sciences, USA* 116(43) (2019): 201910553 (9 pages); Stephanie R. Simms, Evan Parker, George J. Bey III, and Tomás Gallareta Negrón, "Evidence from Escalera al Cielo: Abandonment of a Terminal Classic Puuc Maya Hill Complex in Yucatán, Mexico," *Journal of Field Archaeology* 37 (2012): 270–88; Mattingly and McDonald, "Africa," pp. 72–77.

8. Nancy Evans, *Civic Rites: Democracy and Religion in Ancient Athens* (Berkeley, CA: University of California Press, 2010), p. 19; Simon Keay, "Portus in Its Mediterranean Context," in *Ancient Ports: The Geography of Connections*, ed. Kerstin Höghammar (Uppsala: Uppsala Universitetsbibliotek, 2016), pp. 291–322.

9. Jane Jacobs, *The Economy of Cities* (New York: Vintage, 1969), pp. 49–84.

10. Spiro Kostof, *The City Shaped: Urban Patterns and Meanings through History*, p. 37; Jan Brueckner, *Lectures in Urban Economics* (Cambridge, MA: MIT Press, 2011); Edward L. Glaser, "Introduction," in *Agglomeration Economics*, ed. Edward L. Glaser (Chicago, IL: University of Chicago Press, 2010), pp. 1–14; Edward Soja, *Postmetropolis: Critical Studies of Cities and Regions* (Oxford: Blackwell, 2000), pp. 12–16; Michael E. Smith, "Energized Crowding and the Generative Role of Settlement Aggregation and Scaling," in *Coming Together: Comparative Approaches to Population Aggregation and Early Urbanization*, ed. Attila Gyucha (Albany, NY: State University of New York Press, 2019), pp. 37–58.

11. Jacobs, *Economy of Cities*, pp. 3–48; see other citations in the Prologue above. On "the capitalist city" see David Harvey, *The Urbanization of Capital: Studies in the History and Theory of Capitalist Urbanization* (Baltimore, MD: The Johns Hopkins University Press, 1985); Michael Peter Smith and Joe R. Fagan, *The Capitalist City* (Somerset, NJ: Blackwell, 1987); Richard Sennett, *The Fall of Public Man* (New York: Norton, 1992), p. 62.

12. Liverani, *Uruk*, pp. 19–25; Solis et al., *Caral*; Wheatley, *Pivot of the Four Corners*; Steinhardt, *Chinese Imperial City Planning*.

13. Quotations from Diane Wolkenstein and Samuel Noah Kramer, *Inanna: Queen of Heaven and Earth* (New York: Harper and Row, 1983), pp. 11–28; Van de Mieroop, *Ancient Mesopotamian City*, pp. 31–33, Liverani, *Uruk*, pp. 23–25.

14. Margarete van Ess, "The Eanna Sanctuary in Uruk," in *Uruk: First City of the Ancient World*, ed. Nicola Crüsemann, Margarete van Ess, Markus Hilgert, and Beate Salje (Los Angeles: J. Paul Getty Museum, 2013), pp. 205–11; David Graeber and David Wengrow, *The Dawn of Everything: A New History of Humanity* (New York: Farrar, Straus and Giroux, 2021), pp. 276–327; Liverani, *Uruk*, pp. 15–52.

15. Liverani, *Uruk*, pp. 15–31; Graeber and Wengrow, *Dawn of Everything*, pp. 297–304.

16. Liverani, *Uruk*, pp. 53–66; Van de Mieroop, *Ancient Mesopotamian City*, pp. 215–47; Margarete van Ess, "The Clay Cone Mosaic Technique," in *Uruk: First City of the Ancient World*, ed. Nicola Crüsemann, Margarete van Ess, Markus Hilgert, and Beate Salje (Los Angeles: J. Paul Getty Museum, 2013), pp. 108–10; van Ess, "Eanna Sanctuary"; Daniel T. Potts, "Trade in the Early Ancient Near East," in *Uruk: First City of the Ancient World*, ed. Nicola Crüsemann, Margarete van Ess, Markus Hilgert, and Beate Salje (Los Angeles: J. Paul Getty Museum, 2013), pp. 235–41; Brooke, Climate Change, pp. 205–7.

17. Hans J. Nissen, "Uruk's Beginnings and Early Development," in *Uruk*, Crüsemann *et al.* eds., pp. 87–94; Ricardo Eichmann, "Uruk's Early Monumental Architecture," *Uruk*, Crüsemann, *et al.*, eds, pp. 97–107.

18. Van de Mieroop, *Ancient Mesopotamian City*, pp. 33–38, 217–22; Leicht, *Mesopotamia*, pp. 40–44, 66–69. Petr Charvát, *Ancient Mesopotamia: Humankind's Long Journey into Civilization* (London: Routledge, 2002 [1993]), pp. 98–160; Liverani, *Uruk*, pp. 21–22, 53–66. Quotations from Wolkenstein and Kramer, *Inanna*, pp. 16–18; and Wu Jing, *The Essentials of Governance from the Reign of Constancy Revealed*, ed. Hilde De Weert, Glen Dudbridge, and Gabe van Beijeren (Cambridge: Cambridge University Press, 2020), pp. 21–22.

19. Graeber and Wengrow, *Dawn of Everything*, pp. 328–59. On the complexities of this evidence see Deborah Nicholas, "Teotihuacan," *Journal of Archaeological Research* 24 (2016): 1–74.

20. Rita P. Wright, *The Ancient Indus: Urbanism, Economy, and Society* (Cambridge: Cambridge University Press, 2010); Monica L. Smith, "Early Walled Cities of the Indian Subcontinent as 'Small Worlds,'" in

The Social Construction of Ancient Cities, ed. Monica L. Smith (Washington, D.C.: Smithsonian Books, 2003), pp. 269–89.

21. McIntosh, *Ancient Middle Niger*, pp. 10–44, 144–91, 209–29; McIntosh, "Different Cities." Similar arguments have been applied to Mayan cities: Carole L. Crumley, "Alternate Forms of Social Order," in *Heterarchy, Political Economy, and the Ancient Maya: The Three Rivers Region of the East-Central Yucatán Peninsula*, ed. Vernon L. Scarborough, Frank Valdez Jr., and Nicholas Dunning (Tucson, AZ: University of Arizona Press, 2003), pp. 136–45; Marshall Joseph Becker, "Maya Heterarchy as Inferred from Classic Period Plaza Plans," *Ancient Mesoamerica* 15 (2004): 127–38.

22. Evans, *Civic Rites*, pp. 1–62; Ian Morris and Alex R. Knodell, "Greek Cities in the First Millennium BCE," in *The Cambridge World History*, Volume 3. *Early Cities in Comparative Perspective, 4000 BCE–1200 CE*, ed. Norman Yoffee (Cambridge: Cambridge University Press, 2015), pp. 353–54; Amy Russell, *The Politics of Space in Republican Rome* (Cambridge: Cambridge University Press, 2016).

23. Readers may note that my list of city-making components overlaps with those in classic definitions of a city proposed by Louis Wirth, in "Urbanism as a Way of Life," *American Sociological Review* 44 (1938): 1–24; and V. Gordon Childe, "The Urban Revolution," *Town Planning Review* 21 (1950): 3–17. Michael E. Smith meditates thoughtfully on the adequacy of these classic definitions in "Cities, Towns, and Urbanism: Comment on Sanders and Webster," *American Anthropologist* 91 (1989): 454–61. On anonymity, see Sennett, *Fall of Public Man*, p. 62.

24. This paragraph expresses my own long-standing suspicions of urban historians' willingness to import theoretical tools from the social sciences that seem to me to sanitize the radical complexity we perceive in routine readings of primary historical evidence from cities, not to mention the immense and largely lost underlying past realities we cannot see. At the same time, it values the expanded definition of power and politics imagined by such concepts as political economy, cultural politics, "infrapolitics," "biopolitics," and the politics of intimacy. In that vein, I appreciate Ananya Roy's insights that the urban is "undecidable" and foundationally a "political subject" (Roy, "What Is Urban?," pp. 9, 13). Insights from explorations of "complexity" in the natural sciences may also be helpful, such as Warren Weaver's classic description of "situations in which the essential important quantities are either non-quantitative, or have at any rate eluded identification or measurement up to the moment," notably where "the number of variables is very large." Yet "in spite of this helter-skelter, or unknown, behavior of all the individual variables, the system as a whole possesses certain orderly and analyzable average properties." Warren Weaver, "Science and Complexity," *American Scientist* 36 (1947): 536–44. My rejection of the exclusive role of "capitalist urbanization" reflects that of Manuel Castells in *The City and the Grassroots* (Berkeley, CA: University of California Press, 1983), pp. 13–14 and many others. Also, see the Introduction, to this book, notes 1 and 2.

2 IGNITING EMPIRE

1. Quotation from Guillermo Algaze, *The Uruk World System: The Dynamics of Expansion of Early Mesopotamian Civilization*, 2nd ed. (Chicago, IL: University of Chicago Press, 2005), p. 5.

2. Algaze, *The Uruk World System*; Joan Oates, "Trade and Power in the Fifth and Fourth Millennium: New Evidence from Northern Mesopotamia," *World Archaeology* 24 (1993): 404–23; Augusta McMahon, "Mesopotamia," in *The Oxford Handbook of Cities in World History*, ed. Peter Clark (Oxford: Oxford University Press, 2012), pp. 31–48; Mario Liverani, *Uruk: The First City* (London: Equinox, 2006), pp. 48–49; Bruce Bower, "Dawn of the City: Excavations Prompt a Revolution in Thinking about the Earliest Cities," *Science News* 173 (2008): 92.

3. David W. Anthony, *The Horse, the Wheel, and Language: How Bronze-Age Riders from the Eurasian Steppes Shaped the Modern World* (Princeton, NJ: Princeton University Press, 2007); Clemens Reichel, "Hamoukar," in *Annual Reports* (Chicago: Oriental Institute at the University of Chicago, 2005–6, 2007–8, 2011–12), http s://oi.uchicago.edu/research/projects/hamoukar-expedition (accessed July 19, 2021).

4. See, for example, Michael E. Smith, "Sprawl, Squatters, and Sustainable Cities: Can Archaeological Data Shed Light on Modern Urban Issues?," *Cambridge Archaeological Journal* 20 (2010): 229–53.

5. Quotations from Adelheid Otto, "Neo-Assyrian Capital Cities: From Imperial Headquarters to Cosmopolitan Cities," in *The Cambridge World History, Volume 3. Early Cities in Comparative Perspective,* ed. Norman Yoffee (Cambridge: Cambridge University Press, 2015), pp. 482, 486.

6. Quotations from *The Epic of Gilgamesh,* trans. Andrew George (London: Penguin, 1999), p. 145; Otto, "Neo-Assyrian Capital Cities," pp. 481–87.

7. Victor Cunrui Xiong, *Sui–Tang Chang'an: A Study in the Urban History of Medieval China* (Ann Arbor, MI: University of Michigan Center for Chinese Studies, 2000), p.11; Toby Lincoln, *An Urban History of China* (Cambridge: Cambridge University Press, 2021), pp. 15–44.

8. Xiong, *Sui–Tang Chang'an,* pp. 8–14; Tonio Andrade, *The Gunpowder Age: China, Military Innovation, and the Rise of the West in World History* (Princeton, NJ: Princeton University Press, 2016), pp. 96–102.

9. Nicola Terrenato, "The Archtypical Imperial City: The Rise of Rome and the Burdens of Empire," in *The Cambridge World History, Volume 3. Early Cities in Comparative Perspective,* ed. Norman Yoffee (Cambridge: Cambridge University Press, 2015), pp. 513–31.

10. Compilations of competing estimates of urban populations of the largest cities in periods throughout history can be found in Tertius Chandler and Gerald Fox, *3000 Years of Urban Growth* (New York: Academic Press, 1974); Tertius Chandler, *Four Thousand Years of Urban Growth: An Historical Census* (Lewiston, NY: The Edwin Mellen Press, 1987); George Modelski, *World Cities: –3000 to 2000* (Washington, D.C.: FAROS, 2003); and Ian Morris, *Social Development,* Stanford University, October 2010, at https://web.archive .org/web/20110726164950/http://www.ianmorris.org/docs/social-development.pdf (accessed July 19, 2021). The results of all four of these studies are presented conveniently in four parallel columns as part of the Wikipedia article "List of largest cities throughout history," at https://en.wikipedia.org/ wiki/List_of_largest_cities_throughout_history (accessed July 19, 2021).

11. Lincoln, *Urban History of China,* pp. 45–75.

12. Miko Flohr, *Urban Space and Urban History in the Roman World* (London: Routledge, 2021); Ray Laurence, Simon Esmonde Cleary, and Gareth Sears, *The City in the Roman West, c. 250 BC–c. AD 250* (Cambridge: Cambridge University Press, 2011); Josephine Crawley Quinn and Andrew Wilson, "Capitolia," *Journal of Roman Studies* 103 (2013): 117–73; Robert B. Marks, *China: Its Environment and History* (Plymouth: Rowman & Littlefield, 2012), pp. 77–83; Alfred Schinz, *The Magic Square: Cities in Ancient China* (Stuttgart: Edition Axel Menges, 1996), pp. 175, 205–12; Valerie Hansen, *The Silk Road: A New History* (Oxford: Oxford University Press, 2012), pp. 141–243; Nancy S. Steinhardt, "China," in *The Oxford Handbook of Cities in World History,* ed. Peter Clark (Oxford: Oxford University Press, 2013), pp. 105–26; Hilde De Weerdt, "China 600– 1300," in *The Oxford Handbook of Cities in World History,* ed. Peter Clark (Oxford: Oxford University Press, 2013), pp. 292–309; William Rowe, "China 1300–1900," in *The Oxford Handbook of Cities in World History,* ed. Peter Clark (Oxford: Oxford University Press, 2013), p. 310. I am grateful to Professor Kristin Stapleton for providing information on Chinese place names via personal communication.

13. Kirk Grayson, "Assyrian Rule of Conquered Territory in Ancient Western Asia" in *Civilizations of the Ancient Near East,* Vol. 2, ed. Jack Sasson (Peabody, MA: Hendrickson, 1995), 966; S. F. Starr, "The Persian Royal Road in Turkey," in *Yearbook of the American Philosophical Society 1962* (Philadelphia, PA: American Philosophical Society, 1963), pp. 629–32.

14. On Roman roads, see Raymond Chevalier, *Roman Roads* (Berkeley, CA: University of California Press, 1976); Victor Wolfgang Von Hagen, *The Roads That Led to Rome* (Cleveland, OH: World Publishing Company, 1967); Susan Raven, *Rome in Africa* (London: Evans Bros., 1969), pp.51–54; Robert B. Jackson, *At Empire's Edge: Exploring Rome's Egyptian Frontier* (New Haven, CT: Yale University Press, 2002), pp. 95–107; and T. P. Wiseman, "Roman Republican Road Building," *Papers of the British School at Rome* 38 (1970): 122–52. On China, see Marks, *China,* pp. 77–89, 97–99, 103–42; and Lyn Harrington, *The Grand Canal of China* (Chicago, IL: Rand McNally, 1967).

15. Duncan Campbell, *Roman Auxiliary Forts 27 BC–AD 378* (Oxford: Osprey Publishing, 2009), p. 4; Guy de la Bédoyère, *Roman Britain* (London: Thames and Hudson, 2010), pp.189–301.

16. For example, see the location of the military barracks on the map of Han Changan in Schinz, *Magic Square,* p. 122.

17. Gwendolyn Leick, *Mesopotamia: The Invention of the City* (London: Penguin, 2001), p. 34. Quote from Edward H. Schafer, "The Last Years of Chang'an," *Oriens Extremus* 10 (1963): 133–79; Diane Wolkenstein and Samuel Noah Kramer, *Inanna: Queen of Heaven and Earth* (New York: Harper and Row, 1983), p. 17.

18. Marc Van De Mieroop, *A History of the Ancient Near East, ca. 3000–323 BC* (Oxford: Blackwell, 2004), pp. 74–75, 78, 84, 250.

19. Benjamin Isaac, "The Meaning of 'Limes' and 'Limitanei' in Ancient Sources," *Journal of Roman Studies* 78 (1988): 125–47; Raven, *Rome in Africa*, pp. 55–59; Søren M. Sindbæk, "Networks and Nodal Points: The Emergence of Towns in Early Viking Age Scandinavia," *Antiquity* 81 (2007): 119–132; Søren M. Sindbæk, "Urbanism and Exchange in the North Atlantic/ Baltic, 600–1000 CE," in *The Routledge Handbook of Archaeology and Globalization*, ed. Tamar Hodos (New York: Routledge, 2017), pp. 553–65; Johannes Fried, *Charlemagne*, trans. Peter Lewis (Cambridge, MA: Harvard University Press, 2016), pp. 91–163, 317–72.

20. Marks, *China*, pp. 82–83, 133–34; Arthur Waldron, *The Great Wall of China: From History to Myth* (Cambridge: Cambridge University Press, 1990); William Lindesay, *The Great Wall Revisited: From the Jade Gate to Old Dragon's Head* (Cambridge, MA: Harvard University Press, 2008); Julia Lovell, *The Great Wall: China against the World 1000 BC–AD 2000* (Sydney: Picador Pan Macmillan, 2006).

21. Ulambayar Erdenebat and Ernst Pohl, "The Crossroads in Khara Khorum: Excavations at the Center of the Mongol Empire," in *Ghengis Khan and the Mongol Empire*, ed. William Fitzhugh, Morris Rossabi, William Honeychurch (Washington, D.C.: Arctic Studies Center of the Smithsonian Institution, 2009), pp. 137–51; Morris Rossabi, *Khubilai Khan: His Life and Times* (Berkeley, CA: University of California Press, 1988), pp. 29–34; Lincoln, *Urban History of China*, pp. 76–104. On Dadu, see Lillian M. Li, Alison J. Dray-Novey, and Haili Kong, *Beijing: From Imperial Capital to Olympic City* (New York: Palgrave, 2007), pp. 8–24.

3 WEALTH FOR A FEW, POVERTY FOR MANY I

1. Jane Jacobs, *The Economy of Cities* (New York: Vintage, 1969), pp. 7–18.

2. Toby Lincoln, *An Urban History of China* (Cambridge: Cambridge University Press, 2021), pp. 76–104; Robert B. Marks, *China: Its Environment and History* (Plymouth: Rowman & Littlefield, 2012), pp. 26–27, 113–16, 135–37, 166–67. Figures on Chinese urbanization in Hilde De Weerdt, "China 600–1300," in *The Oxford Handbook of Cities in World History*, ed. Peter Clark (Oxford: Oxford University Press, 2013), pp. 293, 306; and William Rowe "China 1300–1900," in *The Oxford Handbook of Cities in World History*, ed. Peter Clark (Oxford: Oxford University Press, 2013), p. 310.

3. Mario Liverani, *Uruk: The First City* (London: Equinox, 2006), pp. 32–52.

4. Bert Hostelitz, "Generative and Parasitic Cities," *Economic Development and Cultural Change* 3 (1955): 278–94; David Graeber, *Debt: The First 5,000 Years* (Brooklyn, NY: Melville House, 2011, pp. 80–87.

5. Marks, *China*, pp. 99, 106, 126, 187–89, 235, 243.

6. Alberto Angela, *A Day in the Life of Ancient Rome*, trans. Gregory Conti (New York: Europa Editions, 2009), pp. 179–94.

7. Orlando Patterson, *Slavery and Social Death* (Cambridge, MA: Harvard University Press, 2018 [1982]), pp. 20–40, 100–44, 188–221, 270–308.

8. Dieter Kuhn, *The Age of Confucian Rule: The Song Transformation of China* (Cambridge, MA: Belknap Press, 2009), pp.11–13; Patterson, *Slavery and Social Death*, pp. 470–91.

9. For evidence of a Mesopotamian slave revolt see Andrea Serri, *The House of Prisoners: Slavery and State in Uruk during the Revolt against Samsa-Iluna* (Boston, MA: de Gruyter, 2013).

10. Diane Wolkenstein and Samuel Noah Kramer, *Inanna: Queen of Heaven and Earth* (New York: Harper and Row, 1983), pp. 17–18.

11. Quotation from Romolo Augusto Staccioli, *The Roads of the Romans* (Los Angeles, CA: Getty Museum, 2003), p. 22.

12. Excerpt from Meng Yuanlao, "Reminiscences of the Dreamland Glories of Dongjing" (1147), quoted in Alfred Schinz, *The Magic Square: Cities in Ancient China* (Stuttgart: Edition Axel Menges, 1996), pp. 223–24.

13. Passage from Juvenal's *Satires* quoted in Jeremy Hartnett, *The Roman Street: Urban Life and Society in Pompeii, Herculaneum and Rome* (Cambridge: Cambridge University Press, 2017), p. 1.

14. Juvenal quoted in Harnett, *The Roman Street*, p. 37.

15. Angela, *Day in the Life of Rome*, pp. 87–118.

16. See the section on "Proximity Power" in Chapter 1 for a fuller discussion of cities' role in economic growth.

17. Merry Wiesner-Hanks, *Gender in History: Global Perspectives* (Chichester: Wiley Blackwell, 2011), pp. 58–62, 66–68.

18. Liverani, *Uruk*, pp. 32–50. Quotation from *The Epic of Gilgamesh*, trans. Andrew George (London: Penguin, 1999), p. 145.

19. Victor Cunrui Xiong, *Sui–Tang Chang'an: A Study in the Urban History of Medieval China* (Ann Arbor, MI: University of Michigan Center for Chinese Studies, 2000), pp. 165–94; David Nicholas, *The Later Medieval City, 1300–1500* (London: Longman, 1997), pp. 47, 80–83, 274–77; Ira M. Lapidus, *Muslim Cities in the Later Middle Ages* (Cambridge: Cambridge University Press), pp. 86–87.

20. Xiong, *Sui–Tang Chang'an*, pp. 165–94; Anthony Jerome Barbieri-Low, *Artisans in Early Imperial China* (Seattle, WA: University of Washington Press, 2007); Charles Benn, *Daily Life in Traditional China: The Tang Dynasty* (Westport, CT: Greenwood Press, 2002); Maartin Prak, *Citizens without Nations: Urban Citizenship in Europe and the World, c. 1000–1789* (Cambridge: Cambridge University Press, 2018), pp. 83–160, 253–62.

21. Andrew Wilson, "Machines, Power, and the Ancient Economy," *The Journal of Roman Studies* 92 (2002): 1–32; the waterwheels in Rome are described on pp. 12–14.

22. Michael Williams, *Deforesting the Earth: From Prehistory to Global Crisis, An Abridgment* (Chicago, IL: University of Chicago Press, 2006), pp. 74–80, 122–24.

23. Wilson, "Machines, Power, and the Ancient Economy,"; G. D. B. Jones, "The Roman Mines at Rio Tinto," *The Journal of Roman Studies* 70 (1980): 146–75; Marks, *China*, pp. 142–46.

24. Anne Gerritsen, *The City of Blue and White: Chinese Porcelain and the Early Modern World* (Cambridge: Cambridge University Press, 2020); Robert Hartwell, "A Cycle of Economic Change in Imperial China: Coal and Iron in Northeast China, 750–1350," *Journal of the Economic and Social History of the Orient* 10 (1967): 102–59; Tim Wright, "An Economic Cycle in Imperial China? Revisiting Hartwell on Iron and Coal," *Journal of the Economic and Social History of the Orient* 50 (2007): 398–423.

4 WEALTH FOR A FEW, POVERTY FOR MANY II

1. Quotation from Meng Yuanlao, "Reminiscences of the Dreamland Glories of Dongjing" (1147), quoted in Alfred Schinz, *The Magic Square: Cities in Ancient China* (Stuttgart: Edition Axel Menges, 1996), p. 223.

2. Guillermo Algaze, *The Uruk World System: The Dynamics of Expansion of Early Mesopotamian Civilization*, 2nd ed. (Chicago, IL: University of Chicago Press, 2005), pp. 23–41, 72–74.

3. Mario Liverani, *Uruk: The First City* (London: Equinox, 2006), pp. 40–44. Also see the essays in J. G. Dercksen, ed., *Trade and Finance in Ancient Mesopotamia: Proceedings of the First MOS Symposium* (Leiden: Nederlands Instituut voor het Nabije Oosten, 1999) and Jonathan Williams, ed., with Joe Cribb and Elizabeth Errington, *Money: A History* (New York: St. Martin's Press, 1997). Also Marc Van De Mieroop, "The Invention of Interest: Sumerian Loans," in *The Origins of Value: The Financial Innovations That Created Modern Capital Markets*, ed. William N. Goetzmann and K. Geert Rouwenhorst (Oxford: Oxford University Press, 2005), pp. 17–30; Christopher Mounfort Monroe, *Scales of Fate: Trade, Tradition, and Transformation in the Eastern Mediterranean, ca. 1350–1175 BCE* (Münster: Ugarit-Verlag, 2009), pp. 40–103; Anja Slawisch, ed., *Handels- und Finanzgebaren in der Ägäis im 5. JH v. Chr./Trade and Finance in the 5th C. BC Aegean World* (Istanbul: Ege Yayınları, 2013); Alberto Angela, *A Day in the Life of Ancient Rome,*

trans. Gregory Conti (New York: Europa Editions, 2009), p. 69–70; Neil Coffee, *Gift and Gain: How Money Transformed Ancient Rome* (Oxford: Oxford University Press, 2017).

4. Philip Curtin, *Cross-Cultural Trade in World History* (Cambridge: Cambridge University Press, 1984); Richard L. Smith, *Premodern Trade in World History* (Abingdon: Routledge, 2009); Valerie Hansen, *The Silk Road: A New History* (Oxford: Oxford University Press, 2012), pp. 94–106; Samuel N. C. Lieu and Gunner B. Mikkelsen, eds., *Between Rome and China: History, Religions and Material Culture of the Silk Road* (Sydney: Ancient Cultures Research Centre, 2016).

5. Marc Van De Mieroop, *A History of the Ancient Near East, ca. 3000–323 BC* (Oxford: Blackwell, 2004), pp. 89–93; Dercksen, ed., *Trade and Finance in Ancient Mesopotamia*, pp. 55–100.

6. Mogens Trolle Larsen, *Ancient Kanesh: A Merchant Colony in Anatolia* (Cambridge: Cambridge University Press, 2012), pp.67–87; Monroe, *Scales of Fate*, pp. 39–150.

7. Monroe, *Scales of Fate*, pp. 56–150, esp. 65–69.

8. Monroe, *Scales of Fate*, pp. 73, 282.

9. Monroe, *Scales of Fate*, pp. 151–205.

10. Maria Eugenia Aubet, *The Phoenicians and the West: Politics, Colonies, and Trade* (Cambridge: Cambridge University Press, 2002 [1993]); David L. Stone, "Economy," in *The Oxford Handbook of Cities in World History*, ed. Peter Clark (Oxford: Oxford University Press, 2013), pp. 127–46; K. N. Chaudhuri, *Trade and Civilization in the Indian Ocean: An Economic History from the Rise of Islam to 1750* (Cambridge: Cambridge University Press, 1985), pp. 9–62; John Julius Norwich, *A History of Venice* (New York: Vintage, 1982); Carrie E. Beneš, ed., *A Companion to Medieval Genoa* (Leiden: Brill, 2018); Helen Zimmern, *The Hanseatic League: A History of the Rise and Fall of the Hansa Towns* (San Diego, TX: Didactic, 2015).

11. Monroe, *Scales of Fate*, pp. 105–7; 125–26.

12. Carl H. Nightingale, *Segregation: A Global History of Divided Cities* (Chicago, IL: University of Chicago Press, 2012), pp. 27–39.

13. Curtin, *Cross-Cultural Trade*, p. 3; Nightingale, *Segregation*, pp. 27–39; Richard Belsky, *Localities at the Center: Native Place, Space, and Power in Late Imperial Beijing* (Cambridge, MA: Harvard University Press, 2005), pp.21–26; Jean-Christophe Lefevre, *Histoire de l'hôtellerie: Une approche économique* (Paris: Publibook, 2011), pp.15–137; Olivia Remie Constable, *Housing the Stranger in the Mediterranean World: Lodging, Trade, and Travel in Late Antiquity and the Middle Ages* (Cambridge: Cambridge University Press, 2003), pp.1–13, 64–66, 107–57.

14. Robert B. Marks, *China: Its Environment and History* (Plymouth: Rowman & Littlefield, 2012), pp. 81–83, 119–21; Hansen, *The Silk Road*, pp. 6–20, 103–11, and throughout; Lyn Harrington, *The Grand Canal of China* (Chicago, IL: Rand McNally, 1967).

15. Roderick J. McIntosh, "Different Cities: Jenne-jeno and African urbanism," in *The Cambridge World History, Volume 3. Early Cities in Comparative Perspective, 4000 BCE–1200 CE*, ed. Norman Yoffee (Cambridge: Cambridge University Press, 2015), pp. 376–78; Robert B. Jackson, *At Empire's Edge: Exploring Rome's Egyptian Frontier* (New Haven, CT: Yale University Press, 2002), pp. 95–107; Roberta Tomber, *Indo-Roman Trade: From Pots to Pepper* (London: Duckworth, 2008); Vimala Begley and Richard Daniel De Puma, *Rome and India: The Ancient Sea Trade* (Madison, WI: University of Wisconsin Press, 1991); Gary K. Young, *Rome's Eastern Trade: International Commerce and Imperial Policy, 31 BC–AD 305* (London: Routledge, 2001); Wilfred H. Schoff, ed., trans., *The Periplus of the Erythrean Sea: Travel and Trade in the Indian Ocean by a Merchant of the First Century* (New Delhi: Munshiram Manoharlal, 2001); Marie-Françoise Boussac, Jean-François Salles, and Jean-Baptiste Yon, eds., *Ports of the Ancient Indian Ocean* (Delhi: Primus Books, 2016).

16. Russell Meiggs, *Roman Ostia* (Oxford: Clarendon, 1973); Giulia Boetto, "Portus, Ostia and Rome: A Transport Zone in the Maritime/Land Interface," in *Ancient Ports: The Geography of Connections*, ed. Kerstin Höghammar (Uppsala: Uppsala Universitetsbibliotek, 2016), pp. 269–90; Simon Keay, "Portus in Its Mediterranean Context," in *Ancient Ports: The Geography of Connections*, ed. Kerstin Höghammar (Uppsala: Uppsala Universitetsbibliotek, 2016), pp. 291–322; Marie D. Jackson et al., "Phillipsite and Al-Tobermorite Mineral Cements Produced through Low-Temperature Water–Rock Reactions in Roman Marine Concrete," *American Mineralogist* 102 (2017): 1435–50.

17. Bérénice Bellina, "The Inception of the Transnational Processes between the Indian Ocean and the South China Sea from an Early City-State on the Thai–Malay Peninsula (Fourth–Second Centuries BCE)," in *Ports of the Ancient Indian Ocean*, ed. Marie-Françoise Boussac, Jean-François Salles, and Jean-Baptiste Yon (Delhi: Primus Books, 2016), pp. 481–510; Dilip K. Chaudhuri, *The Archaeology of Ancient Indian Cities* (Delhi: Oxford University Press,1995), pp. 170–262; Dieter Schlingloff, *Fortified Cities of Ancient India: A Comparative Study* (London: Anthem, 2013), pp. 11–56; F. R. Allchin, ed., *The Archaeology of Early Historic South Asia: The Emergence of Cities and States* (Cambridge: Cambridge University Press, 1995), pp. 187–220; Cameron Petrie, "South Asia," in *The Oxford Handbook of Cities in World History*, ed. Peter Clark (Oxford: Oxford University Press, 2013), pp. 99–101; Chaudhuri, *Trade and Civilization in the Indian Ocean*; Róbert Simon, *Meccan Trade and Islam: Problems of Origin and Structure* (Budapest: Akadémiai Kiadó, 1989).

18. John Hyslop, *The Inka Road System* (Orlando, FL: Academic Press, 1984).

19. Edward L. Dreyer, *Zheng He: China and the Oceans in the Early Ming Dynasty, 1405–1433* (London: Pearson Longman, 2007); Sally Church, "Nanjing's Longjiang Shipyard Treatise and Our Knowledge of Ming Ships," in *The Ming World*, ed. Kenneth Swope (London: Routledge, 2019), pp. 34–70; Lillian M. Li, Allison Dray-Novey, and Haili Kong, *Beijing: From Imperial Capital to Olympic City* (Houndmills: Macmillan, 2007), pp. 18–27.

5 HOW KNOWLEDGE BECAME POWER

1. Lewis Mumford, *The City in History: Its Origins, Its Transformation, and Its Prospects* (New York: Harcourt Brace and World, 1961), p. 30. Quotations from Diane Wolkenstein and Samuel Noah Kramer, *Inanna: Queen of Heaven and Earth* (New York: Harper and Row, 1983), pp. 16–18, and "The Marriage of Martu, Part II," translated and quoted by Marc Van De Mieroop in *The Ancient Mesopotamian City* (Oxford: Oxford University Press, 1997), p. 43.

2. Quotation from Dieter Kuhn, *The Age of Confucian Rule: The Song Transformation of China* (Cambridge, MA: Belknap Press, 2009), p. 204; Erich S. Gruen, *Rethinking the Other in* Antiquity (Princeton, NJ: Princeton University Press, 2011); Benjamin Isaac, *The Invention of Racism in Classical Antiquity* (Princeton, NJ: Princeton University Press, 2004), pp. 190–92; François de Polignac, *Cults, Territory, and the Origins of the Greek City-State* (Chicago, IL: University of Chicago Press, 1995).

3. Quotation from Wolkenstein and Kramer, *Inanna*, pp. 16–18; Marc Van De Mieroop, *A History of the Ancient Near East, ca. 3000–323 BC* (Oxford: Blackwell, 2004), pp. 42–62.

4. Marc Van De Mieroop, *Philosophy before the Greeks: The Pursuit of Truth in Ancient Babylonia* (Princeton, NJ: Princeton University Press, 2016), p.145; Nancy Evans, *Civic Rites: Democracy and Religion in Ancient Athens* (Berkeley, CA: University of California Press, 2010), pp. 21–26, 220–26.

5. Nigel Cawthorne, *Public Executions* (Edison, NJ: Chartwell, 2006).

6. Joseph Watts, Oliver Sheehan, Quentin D. Atkinson, Joseph Bulbulia, and Russell D. Gray, "Ritual Human Sacrifice Promoted and Sustained the Evolution of Stratified Societies," *Nature* 532 (2016): 228–31; David Carrasco, *City of Sacrifice: The Aztec Empire and the Role of Violence in Civilization* (Boston, MA: Beacon Press, 1999).

7. Karl Jaspers, *The Origin and Goal of History*, trans. Michael Bullock (London: Routledge and Kegan Paul, 1953 [1949]); Robert N. Bellah and Hans Joas, eds., *The Axial Age and Its Consequences* (Cambridge, MA: Belknap Press, 2012).

8. Karen Armstrong, *The Great Transformation: The Beginnings of Our Religious Traditions* (New York: Knopf, 2006); Shmuel Eisenstadt, "The Axial Age: The Emergence of Transcendental Visions and the Rise of Clerics," *European Journal of Sociology* 23 (1982): 294–31; Evans, *Civic Rites*, pp. 1–11, 208–44.

9. Charles Benn: *China's Golden Age: Everyday Life in the Tang Dynasty* (Oxford: Oxford University Press, 2002), pp. 243–64; Kuhn, *The Age of Confucian Rule*, Chapter 6; Karen Armstrong, *A History of God: The 4,000 Year Quest of Judaism, Christianity, and Islam* (New York: Ballantine, 1993); Karen Armstrong, *Islam: A Short History* (London: Phoenix, 2000), pp. 3–96.

10. Robert P. Kramers, "The Development of Confucian Schools," in *The Cambridge History of China, Volume 1. The Ch'in and Han Empires, 221 BC–AD 220*, ed. Dennis Twitchett and Michael Loewe (Cambridge: Cambridge University Press, 1986), pp. 747–65; Kuhn, *The Age of Confucian Rule*, pp. 120–37.

11. Hans Bielenstein, "The Institutions of the Later Han," in *The Cambridge History of China, Volume 1. The Ch'in and Han Empires, 221 BC–AD 220*, ed. Dennis Twitchett and Michael Loewe (Cambridge: Cambridge University Press, 1986), pp. 491–519; Kramers, "The Development of Confucian Schools."

12. Toby Lincoln, *An Urban History of China* (Cambridge: Cambridge University Press, 2021), pp. 76–104; Alfred Schinz, *The Magic Square: Cities in Ancient China* (Stuttgart: Edition Axel Menges, 1996), pp. 179–82; Kim Won-Yong, "Kyongju: The Homeland of Korean Culture," *Korea Journal* 22 (1982): 25–32 (quotation on p. 28); Nguyen Van Ky, "A City That Remembers," in *Hanoi: City of the Rising Dragon*, ed. Georges Boudarel and Nguyen Van Ky, trans. Claire Duiker (Oxford: Rowman & Littlefield, 2002), pp. 12–14; William S. Logan *Hanoi: Biography of a City* (Sydney: University of New South Wales Press, 2000), pp. 19–66.

13. Spiro Kostof, *The City Shaped: Urban Patterns and Meanings through History*, pp. 171–73; William L. Rowe, "Caste, Kinship, and Association in Urban India," in *Urban Anthropology: Cross-Cultural Studies of Urbanization*, ed. Aidan Southall (New York: Oxford University Press, 1973), pp. 211–14.

14. Robert B. Marks, *China: Its Environment and History* (Plymouth: Rowman & Littlefield, 2012), pp. 139–41.

15. Mary Boyce, "On the Zoroastrian Temple Cult of Fire," *Journal of the American Oriental Society* 95 (1975): 454–65.

16. Karen Armstrong, *Jerusalem: One City, Three Faiths* (New York: Ballantine, 2005), pp. 56–124.

17. Evans, *Civic Rites*; Peter Thonemann, *The Hellenistic Age* (Oxford: Oxford University Press, 2016), Henning Börm and Nino Luraghi, eds., *The Polis in the Hellenistic World* (Stuttgart: Steiner, 2018); Amstrong, *Jerusalem*, pp. 103–52; Roy McLeod, ed., *The Library of Alexandria: Center of Learning in the Ancient World* (London: Tauris, 1995).

18. Nathan T. Elkins, *A Monument to Dynasty and Death: The Story of Rome's Colosseum and the Emperors Who Built It.* (Baltimore, MD: Johns Hopkins University Press, 2019), p. 23; Mary Beard, John North, and Simon Price, *Religions of Rome*, 2 vols. (Cambridge: Cambridge University Press, 1998).

19. Armstrong, *Jerusalem*, pp. 125–73; Martin Marty, *The Christian World: A Global History* (New York: Modern Library, 2007), pp. 103–231.

20. Armstrong, *Jerusalem*, pp. 174–193.

21. Armstrong, *Jerusalem*, pp. 217–71; Róbert Simon, *Meccan Trade and Islam: Problems of Origin and Structure* (Budapest: Akadémiai Kiadó, 1989).

22. Vernon Egger, *A History of the Muslim World to 1790* (New York: Routledge, 2018) pp. 220–50.

23. Armstrong, *Jerusalem*, pp. 271–322.

24. Olaf Pedersen, *The First Universities: Studium Generale and the Origins of University Education in Europe* (Cambridge: Cambridge University Press, 1997).

25. Roy McLeod, "Introduction: Alexandria in History and Myth," in *The Library of Alexandria: Center of Learning in the Ancient World*, ed. Roy McLeod (London: Tauris, 1995), pp. 10–12.

26. William V. Harris, *Ancient Literacy* (Cambridge, MA: Harvard University Press, 1989); Alan K. Bowman and Greg Woolf, eds., *Literacy and Power in the Ancient World* (Cambridge: Cambridge University Press, 1994).

6 THE REALM OF CONSEQUENCE

1. John L. Brooke, *Climate Change and the Course of Global History: A Rough Journey* (Cambridge: Cambridge University Press, 2016), pp. 288–316.

2. Brooke, *Climate Change*, pp. 288–428; Rita P. Wright, *The Ancient Indus: Urbanism, Economy, and Society* (Cambridge: Cambridge University Press, 2010), pp. 312–13; John S. Henderson, *The World of the Ancient Maya* (London: John Murray, 1997), pp. 201–59.

3. William McNeill, *Plagues and Peoples* (New York: Doubleday, 1977), pp. 36–43; Brooke *Climate Change*, pp. 221–23.

4. Brooke, *Climate Change*, pp. 343–49; quotations from p. 280, and from McNeil, *Plagues and Peoples*, pp. 56, 57.

5. McNeill, *Plagues and Peoples*, pp. 61–64, 87–93; Brooke, *Climate Change*, pp. 279–81.

6. McNeill, *Plagues and Peoples*, pp. 61–64, 87–93; Brooke, *Climate Change*, pp. 279–81.

7. Monica H. Green, "The Four Black Deaths," *American Historical Review* 125 (2020): 1601–31; McNeill, *Plagues and Peoples*, pp. 97–108; Robert B. Marks, *China: Its Environment and History* (Plymouth: Rowman & Littlefield, 2012), pp. 126–32, 215–20.

8. A concise introduction to the salinization debate can be found in J. Donald Hughes, "The Ancient World, *c.* 500 BCE to 500 CE," in *A Companion to Global Environmental History*, ed. J. R. McNeil and Erin Stewart Mauldin (Chichester: Wiley-Blackwell, 2012), pp. 25–27.

9. Brooke, *Climate Change*, pp. 261–69, 328–39; Marks, *China*, pp. 83–90, 97–98, 132–41. Markus Dotterweich, "The History of Human-Induced Soil Erosion: Geomorphic Legacies, Early Descriptions and Research, and the Development of Soil Conservation – a Global Synopsis," *Geomorphology* 201 (2013): 1–34; Michael Williams, *Deforesting the Earth: From Prehistory to Global Crisis, An Abridgment* (Chicago, IL: University of Chicago Press, 2006), pp. 3–124.

10. Williams, *Deforesting the Earth*, pp. 3–124.

11. Hughes, "The Ancient World," 28–29; Robert Hartwell, "A Cycle of Economic Change in Imperial China: Coal and Iron in Northeast China, 750–1350," *Journal of the Economic and Social History of the Orient* 10 (1967): 114; Marks, *China*, pp. 111–18, 132–41; Williams, *Deforesting the Earth*, pp. 62–86.

12. Williams, *Deforesting the Earth*, pp. 62–124.

13. Williams, *Deforesting the Earth*, pp. 87–124.

14. Simon Keay, "The Site and the Portus Project," www.portusproject.org/about/ (accessed July 23, 2021).

15. Marks, *China*, pp. 89–90, 132–37, 150–62.

16. Andrew Wilson, "Machines, Power, and the Ancient Economy," *The Journal of Roman Studies* 92 (2002): 26–28; J. R. McNeill, *Something New under the Sun: An Environmental History of the Twentieth-Century World* (New York: Norton, 2000), pp.55–56; Sungmin Hong, Jean-Pierre Candelone, Clair C. Patterson, and Claude F. Boutron, "History of Ancient Copper Smelting Pollution during Roman and Medieval Times Recorded in Greenland Ice," *Science* New Series 272 (1996): 246–49.

17. Anina Gilgen, Stiig Wilkenskjeld, Jed O. Kaplan, Thomas Kühn, and Ulrike Lohmann, "Did the Roman Empire Affect European Climate? A New Look at the Effects of Land Use and Anthropogenic Aerosol Emissions," *Climate of the Past: Discussions* Online publication at https://cp .copernicus.org/articles/15/1885/2019/cp-15-1885-2019.pdf (accessed July 23, 2021).

18. William F. Ruddiman, *Earth Transformed* (New York: Freeman, 2014); Marks, *China*, pp. 121–41; Brooke, *Climate Change*, pp. 286–87, 477–79.

PART TWO CITIES OF THE WORLD OCEAN

1. Quotations from *The Journal of Christopher Columbus during His First Voyage, 1493–93*, trans. Clements Markham (London: Hakluyt Society, 1893), pp. 90, 132–33, 137–38; and Laurence Bergreen, *Columbus: The Four Voyages* (New York: Viking, 2011), pp.188–219.

2. This image of this period as a "hinge" in human impact on climate represents a variation on John L. Brooke's insight that "The epoch between the Black Death and the onset of the Industrial Revolution was the fundamental hinge of human history." See John L. Brooke, *Climate Change and the Course of Global History: A Rough Journey* (Cambridge: Cambridge University Press, 2016), p. 413.

7 BASTIONS, BATTLESHIPS, AND GUNPOWDER CITIES

1. Hugh Thomas, *Conquest: Montezuma, Cortés, and the Fall of Old Mexico* (New York: Simon and Schuster, 1993).

2. James L. McClain, John M. Merriman, and Ugawa Kaoru, eds., *Edo and Paris: Urban Life and the State in the Early Modern Era* (Ithaca, NY: Cornell University Press, 1994), pp. xv–xvi, 3–41, 68–69.

3. Michael Gomez, *African Dominion: A New History of Empire in Early and Medieval West Africa* (Princeton, NJ: Princeton University Press, 2018), pp. 315–54; Ebru Boyar and Kate Fleet, *A Social History of Ottoman Istanbul* (Cambridge: University of Cambridge Press, 2010), pp. 6–71; Yunus Ugur, "Mapping Ottoman Cities: Socio-spatial Definitions and Groupings (1450–1700)," *Journal for Early Modern Cultural Studies* 18 (2018): 16–65; Sussan Babaie, *Isfahan and Its Palaces: Statecraft, Shi'ism and the Architecture of Conviviality in Early Modern Iran* (Edinburgh: University of Edinburgh Press, 2008); Syed Ali Nadeem Rezavi, *Fathpur Sikri Revisited* (Oxford: Oxford University Press, 2013); Stephen Blake, *Shahjahanabad: The Sovereign City in Mughal India, 1639–1739* (Cambridge: Cambridge University Press, 2002); Abishek Kaicker, *The King and the People: Sovereignty and Popular Politics in Mughal Delhi* (Cambridge: Cambridge University Press, 2020).

4. Toby Lincoln, *An Urban History of China* (Cambridge: Cambridge University Press, 2021), pp. 105–34; Lillian M. Li, Allison Dray-Novey, and Haili Kong, *Beijing: From Imperial Capital to Olympic City* (Houndmills: Macmillan, 2007), pp. 22–39.

5. Geoffrey Parker, *The Global Crisis: War, Climate Change and Catastrophe in the Seventeenth Century* (New Haven, CT: Yale University Press, 2013); Li et al., *Beijing*, pp. 35–39, 71–81, 84–86; Geremie R. Barbé, *The Forbidden City* (Cambridge, MA: Harvard University Press, 2008).

6. Mark Ravina, *To Stand with the Nations of the World: Japan's Meiji Restoration in World History* (Oxford: Oxford University Press, 2017) pp. 40–49; James McClain and John M. Merriman, "Edo and Paris," in *Edo and Paris: Urban Life and the State in the Early Modern Era*, ed. James L. McClain, John M. Merriman, and Ugawa Kaoru (Ithaca, NY: Cornell University Press, 1994), pp. 3–41; Louis Beik, "Louis XIV and the Cities," in *Edo and Paris: Urban Life and the State in the Early Modern Era*, ed. James L. McClain, John M. Merriman, and Ugawa Kaoru (Ithaca, NY: Cornell University Press, 1994), pp. 68–69.

7. Peter C. Perdue, *China Marches West: The Qing Conquest of Central Asia* (Cambridge, MA: Harvard University Press, 2005), pp. 51–302; Tonio Andrade, *The Gunpowder Age: China, Military Innovation, and the Rise of the West in World History* (Princeton, NJ: Princeton University Press, 2016), pp. 219–30; John F. Richards, *The Unending Frontier: An Environmental History of the Early Modern World* (Berkeley, CA: University of California Press, 2003), pp. 242–73, 517–45; James Millward, Ruth W. Dunnell, Mark C. Elliott, and Philippe Forêt, eds., *New Qing Imperial History: The Making of Inner Asian Empire at Qing Chengde* (London: Routledge, 2004); Dittmar Schorkowitz, John R. Chávez, and Ingo W. Schröder, eds., *Shifting Forms of Continental Colonialism: Unfinished Struggles and Tensions* (Singapore: Palgrave Macmillan, 2019).

8. Andrade, *The Gunpowder Age*, pp. 34–35.

9. Lincoln, *Urban History of China*, pp. 76–104.

10. Andrade, *The Gunpowder Age*, pp. 34–47.

11. Kelly de Vries, *Medieval Military Technology* (Peterborough, ON: Broadview Press, 1992), pp 143–280; Philippe Contamine, *War in the Middle Ages*, trans. Michael Jones (Oxford: Basil Blackwell, 1984), pp. 101–14, 345–53; Andrade, *The Gunpowder Age*, pp. 88–102.

12. Andrade, *The Gunpowder Age*, pp. 90–102; William E. Wallace, "'Dal disegno allo spazio': Michelangelo's Drawings for the Fortifications of Florence," *Journal of the Society of Architectural Historians* 46 (1987): 119–134; Roger D. Masters, *Fortune Is a River: Leonardo da Vinci and Niccolò Machiavelli's Magnificent Dream to Change the Course of Florentine History* (New York: Plume, 1999), pp. 32, 117–19, 137–38.

13. Andrade, *The Gunpowder Age*, pp. 211–34; José Eugenio Borao Mateo, "Renaissance Fortresses in the Far East: The Case of Taiwan," paper presented at the conference "The Birth of a Global

Society: Circulation of Knowledge, Goods and People between Europe and Asia", Tsinghua University, Beijing, April 21, 2012, available at http://homepage.ntu.edu.tw/~borao/2Profesore s/Fortresses.pdf (accessed July 24, 2021).

14. Martin Van Creveld, "Technology and War I: To 1945," in *The Oxford History of Modern War*, ed. Charles Townshend (Oxford: Oxford University Press, 2000), p. 212.

15. Andrade, *The Gunpowder Age*, pp. 196–210.

16. Malyn Newitt, *A History of Portuguese Overseas Expansion, 1400–1668* (London: Routledge, 2005), p. 43; Carl H. Nightingale, *Segregation: A Global History of Divided Cities* (Chicago, IL: University of Chicago Press, 2012), pp. 55–56; Gomez, *African Dominion*, p. 7.

17. Newitt, *Portuguese Overseas Expansion*, pp. 76–86.

18. Newitt, *Portuguese Overseas Expansion*, pp. 58–91; Andrade, *The Gunpowder Age*, pp. 55–56, 124–31; Liam Matthew Brockey, *Portuguese Colonial Cities in the Early Modern World* (Farnham: Ashgate, 2008); C. R. Boxer and Carlos de Azevedo, *Fort Jesus and the Portuguese in Mombasa, 1593–1729* (London: Hollis and Carter, 1960); Archa Neelakandan Girija, "Movement of Spices, People and Faith: Role of the Indian Ocean in the Making and Unmaking of Calicut, c. 1400–1750 AD" (M.Phil. Thesis, Jawaharlal Nehru University, 2016).

19. Newitt, *Portuguese Overseas Expansion*, pp. 58–91; Charles R. Boxer, *The Portuguese Seaborne Empire, 1415–1825* (New York, A. A. Knopf, 1969).

20. Laurence Bergreen, *Columbus: The Four Voyages* (New York: Viking, 2011), pp. 188–219; Kathleen Deagan and José María Cruxent, *Archaeology at La Isabela: America's First European Town* (New Haven, CT: Yale University Press, 2002); Hugh Thomas, *Rivers of Gold: The Rise of the Spanish Empire, from Columbus to Magellan* (New York: Random House, 2003).

21. Thomas, *Conquest*; John Hemming, *The Conquest of the Incas* (Boston, MA: Mariner Books, 2003); Camilla Townshend, "Burying the White Gods: New Perspective on the Conquest of Mexico," *American Historical Review* 108 (2003): 659–87; David Graeber and David Wengrow, *The Dawn of Everything: A New History of Humanity* (New York: Farrar, Straus and Giroux, 2021), pp. 346–58.

22. René Chartrand and Donato Spedaliere, *The Spanish Main 1492–1800* (Oxford: Osprey, 2006); Charles Gibson, *The Aztecs under Spanish Rule: A History of the Indians of the Valley of Mexico, 1519–1810* (Stanford, CA: Stanford University Press, 1964); Adelaida Sourdis de De La Vega, *Cartagena de Indias durante la Primera República 1810–1815* (Bogotá: Banco de la República, 1988); Joseph Mulder, "Lima Ciudad de los Reyes," map available at www.leventhalmap.org/projects/mapping-a-world-of-cities/?fbclid=IwAR15H6YnWD9VSZpxpzkQGP1qjnGxEPYrLOQGWJNk5zGG0l6en7RFbP7bLAw; Nightingale, *Segregation*, pp. 49–51.

23. Robert Ferry, *The Colonial Elite of Early Caracas: Formation and Crisis, 1567–1767* (Berkeley, CA: University of California Press, 1989), pp. 1–44; Mary P. Ryan, *Taking the Land to Make the City: A Bicoastal History of North America* (Austin, TX: University of Texas Press, 2019), pp.173–217; Robert R. Reid, *Colonial Manila: The Context of Hispanic Urbanism and the Process of Morphogenesis* (Berkeley, CA: University of California Press, 1978), p.49.

24. Maarten Park, *The Dutch Republic in the Seventeenth Century: The Golden Age* (Cambridge: Cambridge University Press, 2002), pp. 45–60; Andrade, *The Gunpowder Age*, pp. 216–19; Stephen R. Platt, *Imperial Twilight: The Opium War and the End of China's Last Golden Age* (New York: Knopf, 2018), pp.112–14.

25. C. R. Boxer, *The Dutch Seaborne Empire, 1600–1800* (Harmondsworth: Penguin, 1965) pp. 219–30; C. R. Boxer, *Jan Compagnie in Japan: An Essay on the Cultural, Artistic, and Scientific Influences by the Hollanders in Japan from the Seventeenth to the Nineteenth Centuries* (Oxford: Oxford University Press, 1969).

26. Jean Gelman, *The Social World of Batavia: European and Eurasian in Dutch Asia* (Madison, WI: University of Wisconsin Press, 1983), pp. 3–32; Robert Ross, "The Cape of Good Hope and the World Economy, 1652–1835," in *The Shaping of South African Society, 1652–1840* (Middletown, CT: Wesleyan University Press, 1988), pp. 243–80.

27. John Keay, *The Honourable Company* (London: Harper Collins, 1991).

28. Keay, *The Honourable Company*, pp, 72–146.

29. Nightingale, *Segregation*, pp. 54–71; Keay, *The Honorable Company*, pp 69–73, 125–53.

30. Nightingale, *Segregation*, pp. 47–49, 54–71.

31. Thomas, *Rivers of Gold*; Michael Williams, *Deforesting the Earth: From Prehistory to Global Crisis, An Abridgment* (Chicago, IL: University of Chicago Press, 2006), pp. 127–49; Andrew Lipman, *The Saltwater Frontier: Indians and the Contest for the American Coast* (New Haven, CT: Yale University Press, 2015); Allan Greer, *Property and Dispossession: Natives, Empires, and Land in Early Modern North America* (Cambridge: Cambridge University Press, 2018).

32. Maurice Miles Martinez, *The Great Wall of Africa: The Empire of Benin's 10,000 Mile Long Wall* (Orlando, FL: Journal of African Diasporic Civilizations, 2020); John Vogt, *Portuguese Rule on the Gold Coast, 1469–1682* (Athens, GA: University of Georgia Press, 1979); Robin Law, "Ouidah as a Multiethnic Community," in *The Black Urban Atlantic in the Age of the Slave Trade*, ed. Jorge Cañizares-Esguerra, Matt D. Childs, and James Sidbury (Philadelphia, PA: University of Pennsylvania Press, 2013), pp. 42–62; Kristin Mann, *Slavery and the Birth of an African City: Lagos, 1760–1900* (Bloomington, IN: Indiana University Press, 2007); Roquinaldo Ferreira, "Slavery and the Social and Cultural Landscape of Luanda," in *The Black Urban Atlantic in the Age of the Slave Trade*, ed. Jorge Cañizares-Esguerra, Matt D. Childs, and James Sidbury (Philadelphia, PA: University of Pennsylvania Press, 2013), pp. 185–206.

33. Marcus Rediker, *The Slave Ship: A Human History* (New York: Viking, 2007), pp. 41–72.

34. Thomas, *Rivers of Gold*; Rodolfo Segovia Salas and Jorge Mario Múnera, *The Lake of Stone: The Geopolitics of Spanish Fortifications in the Caribbean (1586–1786)* (Bogotá: Áncora Editores, 2006); Lawrence N. Powell, *The Accidental City: Improvising New Orleans* (Cambridge, MA: Harvard University Press, 2012), pp. 60–128.

35. Lipman, *The Saltwater Frontier*; Greer, *Property and Dispossession*; Mary Maples Dunn and Richard S. Dunn, "The Founding, 1681–1701," in *Philadelphia: A 300-Year History*, ed. Russell Weigley (New York: Norton, 1982), pp.1–32.

36. Ann Durkin Keating, *Rising Up from Indian Country: The Battle of Fort Dearborn and the Birth of Chicago* (Chicago, IL: University of Chicago Press, 2012); William Cronon, *Nature's Metropolis: Chicago and the Great West* (New York; Norton, 1991), pp. 23–30. The online encyclopedia Wikipedia offers a convenient list of the some 215 coastal forts built in what became the USA along with the dates of their construction and the different strategic projects that brought them into being: https://en .wikipedia.org/wiki/List_of_coastal_fortifications_of_the_United_States (accessed July 24, 2021). This does not include hundreds of forts built to protect the colonies from the French, Spanish, and Native Americans. These are listed in the article https://en.wikipedia.org/wiki/List_of_forts_in_the_ United_States (accessed July 24, 2021).

8 WEALTH FROM THE WINDS AND WAVES

1. For example see Santhosh Abraham, "The Keyi Mappila Muslim Merchants of Tellicherry and the Making of Coastal Cosmopolitanism on the Malabar Coast," *Asian Review of World Histories* 5 (2017): 145–62.

2. John E. Willis Jr., "Introduction," in *China and Maritime Europe, 1500–1800: Trade, Settlement, Diplomacy, and Missions*, ed. John E. Willis Jr. (Cambridge: Cambridge University Press, 2011), pp. 19–23.

3. My use of the phrase "spatial fix" is an application of a theoretical concept associated above all with the geographer David Harvey. For a useful summary, see David Harvey, *Spaces of Capital: Toward a Critical Geography* (New York: Routledge, 2001), pp. 284–311.

4. Kenneth Pomeranz, *The Great Divergence: China, Europe, and the Making of The Modern World Economy* (Princeton: Princeton University Press, 2000), pp. 3–68; Jürgen Kocka, *Capitalism: A Short History*, trans. Jeremiah Riemer (Princeton, NJ: Princeton University Press, 2016), pp. 50–51

5. Pomeranz, *The Great Divergence*, pp. 114–65.

6. Kris Lane, *Potosí: The Silver City That Changed the World* (Berkeley, CA: University of California Press, 2019), pp. 20–45.

7. Lane, *Potosí*, pp. 45–91.

8. Lane, *Potosí*, pp. 45–91; Nicholas Robins, *Mercury, Mining, and Empire: The Human and Ecological Cost of Silver Mining in the Andes* (Bloomington, IN: Indiana University Press, 2011).

9. Lane, *Potosí*, pp. 45–91; Robins, *Mercury, Mining, and Empire*, pp. 15–92.

10. Quotation from Robins, *Mercury, Mining, and Empire*, p. 75. Robins is also the source for the estimate that half of all the silver mined in Latin America came from Potosí (p. 39). For volumes of silver, and smuggling to Buenos Aires, also see Dennis O. Flynn and Arturo Giráldez, "Born with a 'Silver Spoon': The Origin of World Trade," *Journal of World History* 6 (1995): 201–21.

11. John E. Willis, Jr., *China and Maritime Europe, 1500–1800: Trade, Settlement, Diplomacy, and Missions* (Cambridge: Cambridge University Press, 2011), p. 4; Flynn and Giráldez, "Born with a 'Silver Spoon'"; Kenneth Pomeranz, *The Great Divergence: China, Europe, and the Making of the Modern World Economy* (Princeton, NJ: Princeton University Press, 2000), pp. 159–62, 189–91, 271–74.

12. Flynn and Giráldez, "Born with a 'Silver Spoon.'"

13. María Elena Martínez, *Genealogical Fictions: Limpieza de Sangre, Religion, and Gender in Colonial Mexico* (Stanford, CA: Stanford University Press, 2008).

14. Barbara E. Mundy, *The Death of Aztec Tenochtitlan, the Life of Mexico City* (Austin, TX: University of Texas Press, 2015); Charles Gibson, *The Aztecs under Spanish Rule: A History of the Indians of the Valley of Mexico, 1519–1810* (Stanford, CA: Stanford University Press, 1964), pp. 289–99.

15. Gibson, *The Aztecs under Spanish Rule*, pp. 32–97, 220–99; John F. Richards, *The Unending Frontier: An Environmental History of the Early Modern World* (Berkeley, CA: University of California Press, 2003), pp. 334–76.

16. Gibson, *The Aztecs under Spanish Rule*, pp. 99–133, 147–50, 370–81, 395–40.

17. Gibson, *The Aztecs under Spanish Rule*, pp. 225–26, 236–42, 368–402; R. Douglas Cope, *The Limits of Racial Domination: Plebeian Society in Mexico City 1660–1720* (Madison, WI: University of Wisconsin Press, 1994); Vera Candiani, *Dreaming of Dry Land: Environmental Transformation in Colonial Mexico City* (Stanford, CA: Stanford University Press 2014).

18. Quotation from Clifton Ellis and Rebecca Ginsburg, "Introduction," in *Slavery in the City: Architecture and Landscapes of Urban Slavery in North America*, ed. Clifton Ellis and Rebecca Ginsburg (Charlottesville, VA: University of Virginia Press, 2017), p. 15.

19. Marcus Rediker, *The Slave Ship: A Human History* (New York: Viking, 2007), pp. 14–72, 132–57; Adelaida Sourdis de De la Vega, *Cartagena de Indias durante la Primera República 1810–1815* (Bogotá: Banco de la República, 1988), p. 16.

20. Ana Lucia Araujo, *Shadows of the Slave Past: Memory, Heritage, and Slavery* (New York: Routledge, 2014), pp. 84–112; Gregory E. O'Malley. "Slavery's Converging Ground: Charleston's Slave Trade as the Black Heart of the Lowcountry," *The William and Mary Quarterly* 74(2) (2017): 271–302; Trevor Burnard and Kenneth Morgan, "The Dynamics of the Slave Market and Slave Purchasing Patterns in Jamaica, 1655–1788," *The William and Mary Quarterly* 58(1) (2001): 205–28; Walter Johnson, *Soul by Soul: Life inside the Antebellum Slave Market* (Cambridge, MA: Harvard University Press, 2001).

21. Richards, *Unending Frontier*, pp. 388–90; Stuart B. Schwartz, "Colonial Brazil, c. 1580–c. 1750: Plantations and Peripheries," in *The Cambridge History of Latin America, Volume 2. Colonial Lstin America*, ed. Leslie Bethell (Cambridge: Cambridge University Press, 1984), p. 424.

22. Carl H. Nightingale, *Segregation: A Global History of Divided Cities* (Chicago, IL: University of Chicago Press, 2012), pp. 49–53.

23. Cope, *The Limits of Racial Domination*, pp. 15–21; Mary C. Karasch, *Slave Life in Rio de Janeiro, 1808–1850* (Princeton, N.J.: Princeton University Press, 1987), pp. 59–66; Anne Pérotin-Dumon, *La ville aux îles, la ville dans l'île: Basse-Terre et Pointe-à-Pitre, Guadeloupe, 1650–1820* (Paris: Éditions Karthala, 2000), pp. 462–70, 641–718; Pedro Welch, *Slave Society in the City: Bridgetown, Barbados 1680–1834* (Kingston, Jamaica: Ian Randle, 2003), pp. 39–40, 158–63; Richard C. Wade, *Slavery in the Cities: The South, 1820–1860* (New York: Oxford University Press, 1964), pp.55–79; Emma Hart, *Building Charleston: Town and Society on the British Atlantic* (Charlottesville, VA: University of Virginia Press, 2010), pp. 56–57, 79–80; Ira Berlin, *Many Thousands Gone: The First Two Centuries of Slavery in North America* (Cambridge, MA: Belknap Press), pp. 58–59, 61–63, 162, 204, 249–50, 287, 318–21, 339.

24. Mariana Dantas, *Black Townsmen: Urban Slavery and Freedom in the Eighteenth-Century Americas* (New York: Palgrave Macmillan, 2008); Hart, *Building Charleston*, pp. 187–88; Welch, *Slave Society in the City*; João José Reis, "African Nations in Nineteenth-Century Salvador, Bahia," in

The Black Urban Atlantic in the Age of the Slave Trade, ed. Jorge Cañizares-Esguerra, Matt D. Childs, and James Sidbury (Philadelphia, PA: University of Pennsylvania Press, 2013), pp. 63–82; Matt D. Childs, "Re-creating African Ethnic Identities in Cuba," in *The Black Urban Atlantic in the Age of the Slave Trade*, ed. Jorge Cañizares-Esguerra, Matt D. Childs, and James Sidbury (Philadelphia, PA: University of Pennsylvania Press, 2013), pp. 85–100; David Gegus, "The Slaves and Free People of Cap Français," in *The Black Urban Atlantic in the Age of the Slave Trade*, ed. Jorge Cañizares-Esguerra, Matt D. Childs, and James Sidbury (Philadelphia, PA: University of Pennsylvania Press, 2013), pp. 101–21; Trevor Burnard, "Kingston, Jamaica: Crucible of Modernity," in *The Black Urban Atlantic in the Age of the Slave Trade*, ed. Jorge Cañizares-Esguerra, Matt D. Childs, and James Sidbury (Philadelphia, PA: University of Pennsylvania Press, 2013), pp. 122–45; Jane Landers, "The African Landscape of Seventeenth-Century Cartagena and Its Hinterlands," in *The Black Urban Atlantic in the Age of the Slave Trade*, ed. Jorge Cañizares-Esguerra, Matt D. Childs, and James Sidbury (Philadelphia, PA: University of Pennsylvania Press, 2013), pp. 147–62; Mariza de Carvalho Soares, "African Barbeiros in Brazilian Slave Ports," in *The Black Urban Atlantic in the Age of the Slave Trade*, ed. Jorge Cañizares-Esguerra, Matt D. Childs, and James Sidbury (Philadelphia, PA: University of Pennsylvania Press, 2013), 207–31; Mary C. Karasch, *Slave Life in Rio de Janeiro, 1808–1850* (Princeton, NJ: Princeton University Press, 1987); Richard C. Wade, *Slavery in the Cities: The South 1820–1860* (New York: Oxford University Press, 1964); Leslie M. Harris, *In the Shadow of Slavery: African Americans in New York City, 1626–1863* (Chicago, IL: University of Chicago Press, 2003); Ira Berlin and Leslie M. Harris, eds., *Slavery in New York* (New York: New Press, 2005).

25. Jill Lepore, *New York Burning: Liberty, Slavery, and Conspiracy in Eighteenth-Century Manhattan* (New York: Vintage, 2005).

26. Nightingale, *Segregation*, pp. 54–65.

27. Nightingale, *Segregation*, pp. 54–65.

28. Nightingale, *Segregation*, pp. 54–65.

29. Nightingale, *Segregation*, pp. 54–57; Willis, *China and Maritime Europe*, pp. 42–43.

30. Nightingale, *Segregation*, pp. 57–60; Pedro Luengo, *Intramuros: Arquitectura en Manila, 1739–1762* (Madrid: Fundación Universitaria Española, 2013); Robert Cowherd, "Spices, Spies, and Speculation: Trust and Control in the Early Amsterdam-Batavia System," in *A History of Architecture and Trade*, ed. Patrick Haughey (New York: Routledge, 2018), pp. 44–61; Willis, *China and Maritime Europe*, pp. 54–58. For a description of the rituals at the Dutch factory at Deshima in the late Tokugawa period, see C. T. Assendelft de Coningh, *A Pioneer in Yokohama: A Dutchman's Adventures in the New Treaty Port*, ed. and trans. Martha Chaiklin (Indianapolis, IN: Hackett, 2012), pp. 3–34.

31. Nightingale, *Segregation*, p. 60–74; Dries Lyna, "Ceylonese Arcadia? Colonial encounters in mid-eighteenth-century Dutch Sri Lanka," in *Building Bridges: Scholars, History and Historical Demography. A Festschrift in Honor of Professor Theo Engelen*, ed. Paul Puschmann and Tim Riswick (Nijmegen: Valkhof Pers, 2018), pp. 157–72.

32. Carlo Taviani, "Companies, Commerce, and Credit," in *A Companion to Medieval Genoa*, ed. Carrie E. Beneš (Leiden: Brill, 2018), pp. 427–47; Larry Neal, *A Concise History of International Finance: From Babylon to Bernanke* (Cambridge: Cambridge University Press, 2015), pp. 28–51.

33. Malyn Newitt, *A History of Portuguese Overseas Expansion, 1400–1668* (London: Routledge, 2005), pp. 44–45, 64–68; Patrick O'Flanagan, *Port Cities of the Iberian Atlantic, c. 1500–1900* (London: Routledge, 2016), pp. 59–67.

34. Robert Goodwin, *Spain: The Centre of the World, 1519–1682* (London: Bloomsbury, 2015), pp. 391–479.

35. Lodwijck Petram, *The World's First Stock Exchange*, trans. Lynne Richards (New York: Columbia Business School Publications, 2014), pp. 5–34.

36. Petram, *The World's First Stock Exchange*, pp. 102–8; Russell Shorto, *Amsterdam: A History of the World's Most Liberal City* (New York: Doubleday, 2013), pp. 106–14; Neal, *Concise History of Finance*, pp. 52–71.

37. C. F. Smith, "The Early History of the London Stock Exchange," *The American Economic Review* 19 (1929): 206–16; quotation from p. 208.

38. Christine Desan, *Making Money: Coin, Currency, and the Coming of Capitalism* (Oxford: Oxford University Press, 2014), pp. 295–329; David Kynaston, *Till Time's Last Sand: A History of the Bank of England 1694–2013* (London: Bloomsbury Publishing, 2017), pp. 59–64; Neal, *Concise History of Finance*, pp. 72–99.

39. James A. Rawley, *London, Metropolis of the Slave Trade* (Columbia, MO: University of Missouri Press, 2003); David Richardson, Suzanne Schwartz, and Anthony Tibbles, *Liverpool and Transatlantic Slavery* (Liverpool: Liverpool University Press, 2007); Madge Dresser, *Slavery Obscured: The Social History of the Slave Trade in an English Provincial Port* (London: Continuum, 2001); Robert Fishman, *Bourgeois Utopias: The Rise and Fall of Suburbia* (New York: Basic Books, 1987), pp.18–72; Peter Thorold, *The London Rich: The Creation of a Great City, from 1666 to the Present* (London: Viking, 1999), pp.43, 52–53; Jerry White, *A Great and Monstrous Thing: London in the Eighteenth Century* (Cambridge, MA: Harvard University Press, 2013), pp. 27–36; 76–81; Shorto, *Amsterdam*, pp. 117–25; Roger Chartier, "Power, Space, and Investments in Paris," in *Edo and Paris: Urban Life and the State in the Early Modern Era*, ed. James L. McClain, John M. Merriman, and Ugawa Kaoru (Ithaca, NY: Cornell University Press, 1994), pp. 132–52; James L. McClain, "Edobashi: Power, Space, and Popular Culture in Edo," in *Edo and Paris: Urban Life and the State in the Early Modern Era*, ed. James L. McClain, John M. Merriman, and Ugawa Kaoru (Ithaca, NY: Cornell University Press, 1994), pp. 105–31; John Archer, "Colonial Suburbs in South Asia, 1700–1850, and the Spaces of Modernity," in *Visions of Suburbia*, ed. Roger Silverstone (London: Routledge, 1997), pp. 26–54.

9 CONSUMING THE EARTH IN CITIES OF LIGHT . . . AND DELIGHT

1. Vikram Lall, *The Golden Lands: Cambodia, Indonesia, Laos, Myanmar, Thailand & Vietnam* (Kuala Lumpur: Abbeville Press, 2014); André Alexander, *The Temples of Lhasa: Tibetan Buddhist Architecture from the 7th to the 21st Centuries* (Chicago, IL: Serindia Publications, 2005).

2. Gülru Necipoğlu, *The Age of Sinan: Architectural Culture in the Ottoman Empire* (London: Reaktion Books, 2007); Richard Yeomans, *The Art and Architecture of Ottoman Istanbul* (Reading: Garnet, 2012); Elias N. Saad, *Social History of Timbuktu: The Role of Muslim Scholars and Notables, 1400–1900* (Cambridge: Cambridge University Press, 1983), pp. 108–20; Michael Gomez, *African Dominion: A New History of Empire in Early and Medieval West Africa* (Princeton, NJ: Princeton University Press, 2018), pp. 278–97.

3. Ross King, *Brunelleschi's Dome: How a Renaissance Genius Reinvented Architecture* (New York: Bloomsbury, 2000); Henry A. Millon, *The Triumph of the Baroque: Architecture in Europe 1600–1750* (London: Thames and Hudson, 1999); Martin Marty, *The Christian World: A Global History* (New York: Modern Library, 2007), pp. 27–102.

4. Susan Naquin, *Peking: Temples and City Life, 1400–1900* (Berkeley, CA: University of California Press, 2000), pp. 128–249, 499–678; Nishiyama Matsunosuke, *Edo Culture: Daily Life and Diversions in Urban Japan, 1600–1868*, ed. and trans. Gerald Groemer (Honolulu, HI: University of Hawai'i Press, 1997), pp.76–93; Robin Law, "Ouidah as a Multiethnic Community," in *The Black Urban Atlantic in the Age of the Slave Trade*, ed. Jorge Cañizares-Esguerra, Matt D. Childs, and James Sidbury (Philadelphia, PA: University of Pennsylvania Press, 2013), pp. 42–62; David Gegus, "The Slaves and Free People of Cap Français," in *The Black Urban Atlantic in the Age of the Slave Trade*, ed. Jorge Cañizares-Esguerra, Matt D. Childs, and James Sidbury (Philadelphia, PA: University of Pennsylvania Press, 2013), pp. 101–21; João José Reis, "African Nations in Nineteenth-Century Salvador, Bahia," in *The Black Urban Atlantic in the Age of the Slave Trade*, ed. Jorge Cañizares-Esguerra, Matt D. Childs, and James Sidbury (Philadelphia, PA: University of Pennsylvania Press, 2013), pp. 63–82.

5. William E. Burns, *The Scientific Revolution in Global Perspective* (Oxford: Oxford University Press, 2016); H. Floris Cohen, *The Rise of Modern Science Explained: A Comparative History* (Cambridge: Cambridge University Press, 2015).

6. James Mosley, "The Technologies of Print," in *The Book: A Global History*, ed. Michael F. Suarez S.J. and H. R. Woudhuysen (Oxford: Oxford University Press, 2013), pp.130–53.

7. C. R. Boxer, *Jan Compagnie in Japan: An Essay on the Cultural, Artistic, and Scientific Influences by the Hollanders in Japan from the Seventeenth to the Nineteenth Centuries* (Oxford: Oxford University Press, 1969); Jonathan D. Spence, *The Memory Palace of Matteo Ricci* (New York: Viking, 1984).

8. Rodney W. Shirley, *The Mapping of the World: Early Printed World Maps, 1472–1700* (London: Holland Press, 1984); Thomas Reinersten Berg, *Theater of the World: The Maps That Made History*, trans. Alison McCullough (London: Hodder and Stoughton, 2018); Henry D. Smith II, "The History of the Book in Edo and Paris," in *Edo and Paris: Urban Life and the State in the Early Modern Era*, ed. James L. McClain, John M. Merriman, and Ugawa Kaoru (Ithaca, NY: Cornell University Press, 1994), pp. 332–52; Georg Braun and Franz Hogenburg, *Cities of the World* (Cologne: Taschen, 2019), reprint of *Civitates Orbis Terrarum* of 1572; Sakıp Sabancı Museum, *From Byzantion to Istanbul: 8000 Years of a Capital* (Istanbul: Sakıp Sabancı Museum, 2010), pp. 317–27; Naquin, *Peking*, pp. 24–34, 252–71; Nishiyama, *Edo Culture*, pp. 64–75.

9. On contestation over urban marketplace regulation in American colonial cities, see Emma Hart, *Trading Spaces: The Colonial Marketplace and the Foundations of American Capitalism* (Chicago, IL; University of Chicago Press, 2019).

10. On the urban–rural connections involved in production of new consumer items, see Jan de Vries, "Purchasing Power and the World of Goods," in *Consumption and the World of Goods*, ed. John Brewer and Roy Porter (London: Routledge, 1997), pp. 85–132; Kenneth Pomeranz, "Political Economy and Economy on the Eve of Industrialization: Europe, China, and the Global Conjuncture," *American Historical Review* 102 (2002): 425–46.

11. John F. Richards, *The Unending Frontier: An Environmental History of the Early Modern World* (Berkeley, CA: University of California Press, 2003), pp. 309–33; Alfred Crosby, *The Columbian Exchange: Biological and Cultural Consequences of 1492* (Westport, CT: Praeger, 2003 [1972]).

12. Brian Cowan, *The Social Life of Coffee* (New Haven, CT: Yale University Press, 2005), pp.55–77; John E. Willis, "European Consumption and Asian Production in the Seventeenth and Eighteenth Centuries," in *Consumption and the World of Goods*, ed. John Brewer and Roy Porter (London: Routledge, 1997), pp. 140–44; Kenneth Pomeranz, *The Great Divergence: China, Europe, and the Making of the Modern World Economy* (Princeton, NJ: Princeton University Press, 2000), pp. 14–165; Ebru Boyar and Kate Fleet, *A Social History of Ottoman Istanbul* (Cambridge: University of Cambridge Press, 2010), pp. 94–97, 249–70, quotation from p. 249.

13. Cowan, *The Social Life of Coffee*, pp. 79–132; Markman Ellis, *The Coffee House: A Cultural History* (London: Weidenfeld and Nicolson, 2004), pp. 25–41 and throughout. These two authors disagree on whether the first coffeehouse in England was in Oxford or London. Shorto, *Amsterdam*, pp. 15–16, 46; John L. Cramer-Byng and John E. Willis, "Trade and Diplomacy with Maritime Europe, 1644–c. 1800," in *China and Maritime Europe, 1500–1800: Trade, Settlement, Diplomacy, and Missions*, ed. John E. Willis, Jr. (Cambridge: Cambridge University Press, 2011), pp. 207–11; Willis, "European Consumption and Asian Production," pp. 140–44; Carole Shammas, *The Pre-industrial Consumer in England and America* (Oxford: Oxford University Press, 1990), pp. 121–56; Ron Chernow, *Washington: A Life* (New York: Penguin, 2010), p. 115.

14. Melinda Takeuchi, "City, Country, Travel, and Vision in Edo Cultural Landscapes," in *Edo: Art in Japan 1615–1868*, ed. Robert T. Singer (Washington, D.C.: National Gallery of Art, 1999), pp. 259–365; Janice Katz and Mami Hatayama, *Painting the Floating World: Ukiyo-e Masterpieces from the Weston Collection* (Chicago, IL: Art Institute of Chicago, 2018).

15. James L. McClain, "Edobashi: Power, Space, and Popular Culture in Edo," in *Edo and Paris: Urban Life and the State in the Early Modern Era*, ed. James L. McClain, John M. Merriman, and Ugawa Kaoru (Ithaca, NY: Cornell University Press, 1994), pp. 105–31; Nishiyama, *Edo Culture*, pp. 164–74, 212–50; Lillian M. Li, Allison Dray-Novey, and Haili Kong, *Beijing: From Imperial Capital to Olympic City* (Houndmills: Macmillan, 2007), pp. 80–81; Cowan, *The Social Life of Coffee*, pp. 79–132; Willis, "European Consumption and Asian Production," pp. 140–44; John Henley, "Through *gilets jaunes*, Strikes and Covid, Paris's 400-Year-Old Book Stalls Fight to Survive," *The Guardian* December 29, 2020, www.theguardian.com/world/2020/dec/29/gilets-jaunes-strikes-and-covid-paris-bouquinistes-book-stalls-fight-for-survival (accessed July 26, 2021).

16. Colin Jones, *Paris: Biography of a City* (New York: Viking, 2004), 188–89; Robert Darnton, *The Literary Underground of the Old Regime* (Cambridge, MA: Harvard University Press), 1985; Simon Schama, *Citizens: A Chronicle of the French Revolution* (New York: Vintage, 1989), pp. 134–36, 370–73.

17. Nishiyama, *Edo Culture*, pp. 41–91; Lauren Clay Jones, "The Bourgeoisie, Capitalism, and the Origins of the French Revolution," in *The Oxford Handbook of the French Revolution* (Oxford: Oxford University Press, 2015), 26–31; Andrew Gurr, *The Shakespearean Stage 1574–1642*, 4th ed. (Cambridge: Cambridge University Press, 2009); Louis Montrose, *The Purpose of Playing: Shakespeare and the Cultural Politics of the Elizabethan Theatre* (Chicago, IL: University of Chicago Press, 1996); John Astington, *Actors and Acting in Shakespeare's Time: The Art of Stage Playing* (Cambridge: Cambridge University Press, 2010); Virginia Crocheron Gildersleeve, *Government Regulation of the Elizabethan Drama* (New York: Columbia University Press, 1908).

18. Alan Hunt, *Governance of the Consuming Passions: A History of Sumptuary Law* (New York: St. Martin's Press, 1996).

19. Willis, "European Consumption and Asian Production," pp. 134–40; Boyar and Fleet, *A Social History of Ottoman Istanbul*, pp. 174–83; Nishiyama, *Edo Culture*, pp. 221–23.

20. Li et al., *Beijing*, pp., 77–80; Timothy Brook, *The Confusions of Pleasure: Commerce and Culture in Ming China* (Berkeley, CA: University of California Press, 1998), pp.114–16, 192–97; Sven Beckert, *Empire of Cotton: A Global History* (New York: Knopf, 2015), pp. 3–29, 35–36.

21. Quotation from Beckert, *Empire of Cotton*, p. 33.

22. Anne Goldgar, *Tulipmania: Money, Honor, and Knowledge in the Dutch Golden Age* (Chicago, IL: University of Chicago Press, 2008); Simon Schama, *An Embarrassment of Riches: An Interpretation of Dutch Culture in the Golden Age* (New York: Knopf, 1987), pp. 289–372.

23. Elizabeth Kowaleski-Wallace, *Consuming Subjects: Women, Shopping, and Business in the Eighteenth Century* (New York: Columbia University Press, 1997); Li et al., *Beijing*, pp. 77–80; Peter Burke, "Res et verba: Conspicuous Consumption in the Early Modern World," in *Consumption and the World of Goods*, ed. John Brewer and Roy Porter (London: Routledge, 1997), pp. 151–58; Cramer-Byng and Willis, "Trade and Diplomacy," pp. 211–22; Chernow, *Washington*, p. 617; Shammas, *The Pre-industrial Consumer in England and America*, pp. 157–94; Schama, *An Embarrassment of Riches*, pp. 305–6, 313–22, 375–480; Amanda Vickery, "Women and the World of Goods: A Lancashire Consumer and Her Possessions," in *Consumption and the World of Goods*, ed. John Brewer and Roy Porter (London: Routledge, 1997), pp. 274–303; Amy Stanley, "Maidservants' Tales: Narrating Domestic and Global History in Eurasia, 1600–1900," *American Historical Review*, 121 (2016): 437–460. On the relative lack of focus on house furniture in Istanbul, see Boyar and Fleet, *A Social History of Ottoman Istanbul*, pp. 173–74.

24. Mohammad Gharipour and Caitlin Declerq, eds., *Epidemic Urbanism: How Contagious Diseases Have Shaped Global Cities* (Bristol: Intellect, 2021).

25. Robert B. Marks, *China: Its Environment and History* (Plymouth: Rowman & Littlefield, 2012), pp. 203–22; Richards, *Unending Frontier*, pp. 89–147; Michael Williams, *Deforesting the Earth: From Prehistory to Global Crisis, An Abridgment* (Chicago, IL: University of Chicago Press, 2006), pp. 127–225.

26. For two different views of the impact of tea production, see Marks, *China*, pp. 216–17 and Williams, *Deforesting the Earth*, pp. 198–203. On sugar and cotton, see Richards, *Unending Frontier*, 165–67, 176–77, 327–29, 388–95, 412–62.

27. Richards, *Unending Frontier*, p. 110 (on deer herds in Taiwan) and pp. 463–546; Marc Ravina, *To Stand with the Nations of the World: Japan's Meiji Restoration in World History* (Oxford: Oxford University Press, 2017), p. 34.

28. Richards, *Unending Frontier*, pp. 547–73.

29. Richards, *Unending Frontier*, pp. 574–616; Callum Roberts, *The Unnatural History of the Sea* (Washington, D.C.: Island Press, 2007), pp. 130–62, 171–83, 199–214.

PART THREE CITIES OF HYDROCARBON

1. Quotation from Atish Patel, Caterina Monzani, Michael Safi, Jess Gormley and Chris Michael, "How Bad Is Delhi's Air? We Strapped a Monitor to a Rickshaw to Find Out," *The Guardian*, February 13, 2017, at www.theguardian.com/cities/video/2017/feb/13/how-bad-is-delhis-air-we-strapped-a-monitor-to-a-rick shaw-to-find-out (accessed August 20, 2021). *The Guardian* ran a series of articles on air pollution in Delhi in 2018. Figures on vehicles in Delhi are based on official counts of registered vehicles in the National Capital Territory, which appear to fluctuate in the case of auto-rickshaws according to the level of enforcement. The actual numbers are probably considerably higher. For official figures, see www .statista.com/statistics/665712/total-number-of-vehicles-registered-in-delhi-india/ and www.statista.co m/statistics/1073966/india-registered-number-of-three-seater-rickshaws-in-delhi/ (both accessed August 20, 2021).

10 CHIMNEYS TO SMOKESTACKS

1. My argument in this chapter is heavily built around spatial cues and economic data from Robert C. Allen, *The British Industrial Revolution in Global Perspective* (Cambridge: Cambridge University Press, 2009).

2. Xu Huimin and Huang Chun, "Bei Song shiqi Kaifeng de ranliao wenti" ["The Fuel Issue in Northern Song Kaifeng"], *Yunnan shehui kexue* [*Yunnan Social Science*] 1988.6 (1988): 79–89, 95. The author acknowledges help from Tim Wright and Kristin Stapleton in researching this matter. Shengkai Xu located this article and prepared a summary in English for me, for which I am deeply grateful. Also see Tim Wright, "An Economic Cycle in Imperial China? Revisiting Hartwell on Iron and Coal," *Journal of the Economic and Social History of the Orient* 50 (2007): 415–18; Qinghua Guo, "The Chinese Domestic Architectural Heating System [*Kang*]: Origins, Applications and Techniques," *Architectural History* 45 (2002): 32–48.

3. Quotation from Priya Satia, *Empire of Guns: The Violent Making of the Industrial Revolution* (New York: Penguin, 2018), p.167.

4. Allen, *The British Industrial Revolution*, pp. 21–22.

5. Allen, *The British Industrial Revolution*, pp. 80–105.

6. John Hatcher, *The History of the British Coal Industry, Volume 1. Before 1700: Toward the Age of Coal* (Oxford: Clarendon Press, 1993), pp.41–42. Allen, *The British Industrial Revolution*, pp. 84–90.

7. Quotation from Hatcher, *The History of the British Coal Industry*, p. 409.

8. Hatcher, *The History of the British Coal Industry, p.* 412.

9. John L. Brooke, *Climate Change and the Course of Global History: A Rough Journey* (Cambridge: Cambridge University Press, 2016), p. 461; Allen, *The British Industrial Revolution*, pp. 116–21.

10. Allen, *The British Industrial Revolution*, pp. 57–106.

11. Allen, *The British Industrial Revolution*, pp. 96–104

12. Allen, *The British Industrial Revolution*, pp. 25–57, 135–55.

13. Allen, *The British Industrial Revolution*, pp. 156–81.

14. Eric Preston, *Thomas Newcomen of Dartmouth and the Engine That Changed the World* (Dartmouth: Dartmouth and Kingswear Society and Dartmouth History Research Group, 2012). Note that the neighboring city of Wolverhampton also claims credit for the first Newcomen steam engine. Wolverhampton's claim is based on a document dating from the following year.

15. Allen *The British Industrial Revolution*, pp. 164–76.

16. Allen, *The British Industrial Revolution*, pp. 217–37; Anonymous, "How the Bottle Kiln Works: Notes on the History of Stoke on Trent" at www.thepotteries.org/bottle_kiln/bottle_kiln_two.htm (accessed July 27, 2021).

17. Nicholas Crafts and Anthony Venables, "Globalization in History: A Geographical Perspective," in *Globalization in Historical Perspective*, ed. Michael D. Bordo, Alan M. Taylor, and Jeffrey G. Williamson (Chicago, IL: University of Chicago Press, 2003), pp. 347–50.

18. Allen, *The British Industrial Revolution*, pp. 182–216; Joshua B. Freeman, *Behemoth: A History of the Factory and the Making of the Modern World* (New York: Norton, 2018), pp. 8–20.

19. Freeman, *Behemoth*, pp. 43–79.

20. Andrew Lees and Lynn Hollin Lees, *Cities and the Making of Modern Europe* (Cambridge: Cambridge University Press, 2007), pp. 41–69; Freeman, *Behemoth*, pp. 8–14; Allen, *The British Industrial Revolution*, pp. 238–71; Edmund Davies, Greater Manchester Clocks and Clockmakers (Ashbourne: Mayfield Press, 2007); Satiya, *Empire of Guns*, p. 172; A. E. Musson and E. Robinson, "The Early Growth of Steam Power," *Economic History Review* 11 (1952): 418–39.

21. Sven Beckert, *Empire of Cotton: A Global History* (New York: Knopf, 2014), pp. 29–135.

11 PLANET OF THE PEOPLE I: THE ATLANTIC CAULDRON

1. Walter Scheibel, *Escape from Rome: The Failure of Empire and the Road to Prosperity* (Princeton, NJ: Princeton University Press, 2019); Maartin Prak, *Citizens without Nations: Urban Citizenship in Europe and the World, c. 1000–1789* (Cambridge: Cambridge University Press, 2018); Mary Lindemann, *Merchant Republics: Amsterdam, Antwerp, and Hamburg, 1648–1790* (Cambridge: Cambridge University Press, 2015); Maarten F. Van Dijck, "Democracy and Civil Society in the Early Modern Period: The Rise of Three Types of Civil Societies in the Spanish Netherlands and the Dutch Republic," *Social Science History* 41 (2017): 59–81; Simon Gunn and Tom Hulme, eds., *New Approaches to Governance and Rule in Urban Europe since 1500* (London: Routledge, 2020).

2. Tonio Andrade, *The Gunpowder Age: China, Military Innovation, and the Rise of the West in World History* (Princeton, NJ: Princeton University Press, 2016), pp. 237–56. Quotation from Paul Cheney, *Cul de Sac: Patrimony, Capitalism, and Slavery in French Saint-Domingue* (Chicago, IL: University of Chicago Press, 2017), p.176.

3. Prak, *Citizens without Nations*, pp. 253–73; Keith Lindley, *Popular Politics and Religion in Civil War London* (Aldershot: Ashgate, 1997); Gary S. De Krey, "Political Radicalism in London after the Glorious Revolution," *Journal of Modern History* 55 (1983): 585–617.

4. De Krey, "Political Radicalism in London," 588.

5. De Krey, "Political Radicalism in London"; Robert B. Shoemaker, "The London 'Mob' in the Early Eighteenth Century," *Journal of British Studies* 26 (1987): 273–304; Tim Harris, *London Crowds in the Reign of Charles II: Politics and Propaganda from the Restoration to the Exclusion Crisis* (Cambridge: Cambridge University Press, 1987).

6. Julius S. Scott, *Common Wind: Afro-American Currents in the Age of the Haitian Revolution* (London: Verso, 2018); Peter Linebaugh and Marcus Rediker, *The Many-Headed Hydra: Sailors, Slaves, Commoners, and the Hidden History of the Revolutionary Atlantic* (Boston, MA: Beacon, 2000); Janet Polasky, *Revolutions without Borders: The Call to Liberty in the Atlantic World* (New Haven, CT: Yale University Press, 2015), pp. 17–137.

7. Scott, *Common Wind*, pp. 1–37; Ruma Chopra, *Almost Home: Maroons between Slavery and Freedom in Jamaica, Nova Scotia, and Sierra Leone* (New Haven, CT: Yale University Press, 2018).

8. Manisha Sinha, *The Slave's Cause: A History of Abolition* (New Haven, CT: Yale University Press, 2016), pp. 9–64; Adam Hochschild, *Bury the Chain: Prophets and Rebels in the Fight to Free an Empire's Slaves* (Boston, MA: Mariner Books, 2005), pp. 69–97, 106–42; Polasky, *Revolutions without Borders*, pp. 75–110, 138–71.

9. Gary B. Nash, *The Urban Crucible: The Northern Seaports and the Origins of the American Revolution*, abridged edn. (Cambridge, MA: Harvard University Press, 1986 [1979]), pp. 1–39, 70–74, 80–87, 101–28, 138–83.

10. Nash, *The Urban Crucible*, pp. 184–249.

11. Alan Taylor, 'Global Revolutions," in *The American Revolution: A World War*, ed. David K. Allison and Larrie D. Ferreiro (Washington, D.C.; Smithsonian Institution, 2018), pp. 16–33, and Andrew Lambert, "The British Grand Strategy," in *The American Revolution: A World War*, ed. David K. Allison and Larrie D. Ferreiro (Washington, D.C.; Smithsonian Institution, 2018), pp. 34–51.

12. Olivier Chaline and Jean-Marie Kowalski, "French Naval Operations," in *The American Revolution: A World War*, ed. David K. Allison and Larrie D. Ferreiro (Washington, D.C.; Smithsonian Institution, 2018), pp. 52–65; Richard Sambavasinam, "British Global Ambitions and Indian Identity," in *The American Revolution: A World War*, ed. David K. Allison and Larrie D. Ferreiro (Washington, D.C.; Smithsonian Institution, 2018), pp. 92–107.

13. Andrew Lees and Lynn Hollin Lees, *Cities and the Making of Modern Europe* (Cambridge: Cambridge University Press, 2007), pp. 70–99. Quotation from Daniel Roche, *The People of Paris: An Essay in Popular Culture in the 18th Century* (Berkeley, CA: University of California Press, 1987), p. 10. Danielle Chadych and Dominique Leborgne, *Atlas de Paris: Évolution d'un paysage urbain* (Paris: Parigramme, 1999), pp. 100–1; Simon Schama, *Citizens: A Chronicle of the French Revolution* (New York: Vintage, 1989), pp. 369–77.

14. Chadych and Leborgne, *Atlas de Paris*, pp. 90–109; Roche, *The People of Paris*.

15. Schama, *Citizens*, pp. 369–77; Jean-Charles Pierre and Robert Darnton, "The Memoirs of Lenoir, Lieutenant of Police, 1774–1785," *English Historical Review* 85 (1970): 532–59.

16. Schama, *Citizens*, pp. 369–77. Quotation from p. 369.

17. Jeremy Popkin, "Revolutions and Changing Ideas in France, 1787–89," in *The Oxford Handbook of the French Revolution*, ed. David Andress (Oxford: Oxford University Press, 2015), pp. 236–53; and Manuel Covo, "Race Slavery and Colonies in the French Revolution," in *The Oxford Handbook of the French Revolution*, ed. David Andress (Oxford: Oxford University Press, 2015), pp. 290–310.

18. D. M. G. Sutherland, "Urban Violence in 1789," in *The Oxford Handbook of the French Revolution*, ed. David Andress (Oxford: Oxford University Press, 2015), pp. 272–89; David Andress, "Politics and Insurrection: The *sans-culottes*, the 'Popular Movement,' and the People of Paris," in *The Oxford Handbook of the French Revolution*, ed. David Andress (Oxford: Oxford University Press, 2015), pp. 401–17.

19. Micah Alpaugh, "A Personal Revolution: National Assembly Delegates and the Politics of 1789," in *The Oxford Handbook of the French Revolution*, ed. David Andress (Oxford: Oxford University Press, 2015), pp. 180–200.

20. Schama, *Citizens*, pp. 369–441; Georges Lefebvre, *The Great Fear of 1789: Rural Panic in Revolutionary France* (Princeton, NJ: Princeton University Press, 1973 [1932]).

21. Schama, *Citizens*, pp. 456–71; Sutherland, "Urban Violence in 1789"; Andress, "Politics and Insurrection."

22. Chadych and Dominique Leborgne, *Atlas de Paris*, pp. 116–17.

23. Schama, *Citizens*, pp. 549–72.

24. Schama, *Citizens*, pp. 668–71

25. Paul R. Hanson, "From Faction to Revolt," in *The Oxford Handbook of the French Revolution*, ed. David Andress (Oxford: Oxford University Press, 2015), pp. 436–52; Dan Edelstein, "What Was the Terror?," in *The Oxford Handbook of the French Revolution*, ed. David Andress (Oxford: Oxford University Press, 2015), pp. 453–70.

26. Laura Mason, "Thermidor and the Myth of Rupture," in *The Oxford Handbook of the French Revolution*, ed. David Andress (Oxford: Oxford University Press, 2015), pp. 521–37.

27. Robert Asprey, *The Rise of Napoleon Bonaparte* (New York: Basic books, 2000), pp. 108–112.

28. Asprey, *Napoleon Bonaparte*, pp. 245–326.

29. Asprey, *Napoleon Bonaparte*, pp. 327–50, 489–99.

12 PLANET OF THE PEOPLE II: FEMINISTS, ABOLITIONISTS,

AND *LOS LIBERALES*

1. Joan Wallach Scott, *Only Paradoxes to Offer: French Feminists and the Rights of Man* (Cambridge, MA: Harvard University Press, 1999); Lisa L. Moore, Joanna Brooks, and Caroline Wigginton, eds., *Transatlantic Feminisms in the Age of Revolutions* (Oxford: Oxford University Press, 2012);

John Chasteen, *Américanos: Latin America's Struggle for Independence* (Oxford: Oxford University Press, 2018), pp. 50–54, 60–64, 97–98, 150–55.

2. Jacob Katz, *Out of the Ghetto: The Social Background of Jewish Emancipation, 1770–1870* (Cambridge, MA: Harvard University Press), pp. 191–222; John D. Klier and Shlomo Lambrozo, *Pogroms: Anti-Jewish Violence in Modern Russian History* (Cambridge: Cambridge University Press, 1992).

3. C. L. R James, *The Black Jacobins: Toussaint L'Ouverture and the San Domingo Revolution* (New York: Vintage, 1963); Adam Hochschild, *Bury the Chains: Prophets and Rebels in the Fight to Free an Empire's Slaves* (New York: Mariner, 2005); Ada Ferrer, *Freedom's Mirror: Cuba and Haiti in the Age of Revolution* (Cambridge: Cambridge University Press, 2014).

4. Hochschild, *Bury the Chains*, pp. 181–92.

5. Hochschild, *Bury the Chains*, pp. 256–79, quotation from p. 260.

6. Hochschild, *Bury the Chains*, p. 267

7. Hochschild, *Bury the Chains*, pp. 269–76, 292–94.

8. Hochschild, *Bury the Chains*, pp. 267–96.

9. Hochschild, *Bury the Chains*, pp. 299–308. For cities' subsequent role in abolition in the Atlantic, see Bronwen Everell, *Abolition and Empire in Sierra Leone and Liberia* (Basingstoke: Palgrave, 2013); Lorelle Semley, *To Be Free and French: Citizenship in France's Atlantic Empire* (Cambridge: Cambridge University Press, 2017); Jake Subryan Richards, "The Adjudication of Slave Ship Captures, Coercive Intervention, and Value Exchange in Comparative Atlantic Perspective, ca. 1839–1870," *Comparative Studies in Society and History* 62 (2020): 836–67.

10. John Tutino, *Mexico City, 1808: Power, Sovereignty, and Silver in an Age of War and Revolution* (Albuquerque, NM: University of New Mexico Press, 2018); Lyman L. Johnson, *Workshop of Revolution: Plebeian Buenos Aires in the Atlantic World, 1776–1810* (Durham, NC: Duke University Press, 2011), pp.17–50; Chasteen, *Américanos*, pp. 35–65.

11. Chasteen, *Américanos*, pp. 22–24.

12. Johnson, *Workshop of Revolution*, pp. 51–85, 149–78; Jeremy Adelman, *Sovereignty and Revolution in the Iberian Atlantic* (Princeton, NJ: Princeton University Press, 2006), pp. 56–100.

13. Chasteen, *Américanos*, pp. 35–122.

14. Chasteen, *Américanos*, pp. 35–122; Adelman, *Sovereignty and Revolution*, pp. 175–219.

15. Chasteen, *Américanos*, pp. 35–122; Tutino, *Mexico City*, pp. 205–48; Johnson, *Workshop of Revolution*, pp. 249–97; Adelman, *Sovereignty and Revolution*, pp. 175–257.

16. Chasteen, *Américanos*, pp. 122–48.

17. Chasteen, *Américanos*, pp. 149–58; Adelman, *Sovereignty and Revolution*, pp. 258–343.

18. Chasteen, *Américanos*, pp. 158–81; Adelman, *Sovereignty and Revolution*, pp. 344–93.

19. Chasteen, *Américanos*, pp. 182–88; Adelman, *Sovereignty and Revolution*, pp. 344–93; Pilar González Bernaldo de Quirós, *Civility and Politics in the Origins of the Argentine Nation: Sociabilities in Buenos Aires, 1829–1862*, trans. Daniel Philip Tunnard (Los Angeles, CA: UCLA Latin American Center Publication, 2006).

13 WEAPONS OF WORLD CONQUEST

1. John F. Richards, "Toward a Global System of Property Rights in Land," in *The Environment and World History*, ed. Edmund Burke III and Kenneth Pomeranz (Berkeley, CA: University of California Press, 2009), pp. 54–80; Alexia Yates, *Real Estate in Global Urban History* (Cambridge: Cambridge University Press, 2021), pp. 29–59.

2. George Fredrickson, *Racism: A Short History* (Princeton, NJ: Princeton University Press, 2002).

3. For two good examples of work on projects to dismantle city walls, see Anna Ross, "Down with the Walls! The Politics of Place in Spanish and German Urban Extension Planning, 1848–1914," *Journal of Modern History* 90 (2018): 292–322; and Guadalupe García, *Beyond the Walled City: Colonial Exclusion in Havana* (Berkeley, CA: University of California Press, 2016).

4. Priya Satiya, *Empire of Guns: The Violent Making of the Industrial Revolution* (New York: Penguin, 2018), pp. 116–54; Peter Shulman, *Coal and Empire: The Birth of Energy Security in Industrial America* (Baltimore, MD: Johns Hopkins University Press, 2015), pp.1–13, 125–63.

5. Satiya, *Empire of Guns*, pp. 308–37; Tonio Andrade, *The Gunpowder Age: China, Military Innovation, and the Rise of the West in World History* (Princeton, NJ: Princeton University Press, 2016), pp. 237–56; Marc Ravina, *To Stand with the Nations of the World: Japan's Meiji Restoration in World History* (Oxford: Oxford University Press, 2017), pp. 17, 25–27, 178; Stanford J. Shaw, "The Origins of Ottoman Military Reform: The Nizam-i-Cedid Army of Sultan Selim III," *Journal of Modern History* 37 (1965): 291–306.

6. Seve C. Topik and Allen Wells, *The Second Conquest of Latin America: Coffee, Henequen, and Oil during the Export Boom, 1850–1930* (Austin, TX: Univeristy of Texas Press, 1998); Victor Bulmer-Thomas, *The Economic History of Latin America since Independence*, 2nd ed. (Cambridge: Cambridge University Press, 2003); Rory Miller, *Britain and Latin America in the Nineteenth and Twentieth Centuries* (London: Longman 1993).

7. Carl H. Nightingale, *Segregation: A Global History of Divided Cities* (Chicago, IL: University of Chicago Press, 2012), pp. 79–83.

8. Nightingale, *Segregation*, pp. 75–112.

9. Veena Talwar Oldenburg, *The Making of Colonial Lucknow 1856–1877* (Princeton, NJ: Princeton University Press, 1985).

10. Nightingale, *Segregation*, pp. 113–29.

11. Nightingale, *Segregation*, pp. 118–32.

12. Valery M. Garrett, *Heaven Is High, the Emperor Far Away: Merchants and Mandarins in Old Canton* (Oxford: Oxford University Press), pp. 73–140; Stephen R. Platt, *Imperial Twilight: The Opium War and the End of China's Last Golden Age* (New York: Knopf, 2018), pp. xvii–xxii, 71–77; Toby Lincoln, *An Urban History of China* (Cambridge: Cambridge University Press, 2021), pp. 135–61.

13. Platt, *Imperial Twilight*, pp. 95, 396.

14. Platt, *Imperial Twilight*, pp. 187–216.

15. Platt, *Imperial Twilight*, pp. 217–71.

16. Platt, *Imperial Twilight*, pp. 272–389.

17. Platt, *Imperial Twilight*, pp. 390–419; Andrade, *The Gunpowder Age*, pp. 237–56.

18. Platt, *Imperial Twilight*, pp. 420–48; Lillian M. Li, Allison Dray-Novey, and Haili Kong, *Beijing: From Imperial Capital to Olympic City* (Houndmills: Macmillan, 2007), pp. 105–11; Isabella Jackson, *Shaping Modern Shanghai: Colonialism in China's Global City* (Cambridge: Cambridge University Press, 2017); Robert Bickers and Isabella Jackson, eds., *Treaty Ports in Modern China: Law, Land and Power* (London: Routledge, 2016).

19. Simon Parner *The Merchant's Tale: Yokohama and the Transformation of Japan* (New York: Columbia University Press, 2018); Ravina, *To Stand with the Nations of the World*, pp. 87–96; Edward Seidenstecker, *Low City, High City: Tokyo from Edo to the Earthquake* (New York: Knopf, 1983), pp. 36–42.

20. Ravina, *To Stand with the Nations of the World*, pp. 120–35; Stephen Platt, *Autumn in the Heavenly Kingdom: China, the West, and the Epic Story of the Taiping Civil War* (New York: Atlantic Books, 2012).

21. John C. Weaver, *The Great Land Rush and the Making of the Modern World* (Montreal: McGill-Queen's University Press, 2003), pp.46–87, 171–76; William Cronon, *Nature's Metropolis: Chicago and the Great West* (New York; Norton, 1991), pp. 31–54; Andro Linklater, *Measuring America: How the United States Was Shaped by the Greatest Land Sale in History* (New York: Plume 2002); John H. Reps, *Cities of the American West: A History of Frontier Urban Planning* (Princeton, NJ: Princeton University Press, 1978); Mary P. Ryan, *Taking the Land to Make the City: A Bicoastal History of North America* (Austin, TX: University of Texas Press, 2019), pp. 215–308; Carl E. Solberg, *The Prairies and the Pampas: Agrarian Policy in Canada and Argentina* (Stanford, CA: Stanford University Press, 1987), pp. 51–100; Kate Brown, "Why Kazakhstan and Montana Are Nearly the Same Place," *American Historical Review* 106 (2001): 17–48.

22. Peter Bernstein, *Wedding of the Waters: The Erie Canal and the Making of a Great Nation* (New York: Norton, 2005); Weaver, *The Great Land Rush*, pp. 3–132.

23. Weaver, *The Great Land Rush*, pp. 133–311.
24. Cronon, *Nature's Metropolis*, pp. 56–93; Ryan, *Taking the Land to Make the City*; Carl Abbott, *How Cities Won the West: Four Centuries of Urban Change in Western North America* (Albuquerque, NM: University of New Mexico Press, 2008), Chapters 1 and 2; Henry W. Berger, *St. Louis and Empire: 250 Years of Imperial Quest and Urban Crisis* (Carbondale, IL: Southern Illinois University Press, 2015); Yates, *Real Estate*, pp. 47–59.
25. Nightingale, *Segregation*, pp. 199–203.
26. J. B. Peires, "The British and the Cape, 1814–1834," in *The Shaping of South African Society, 1652–1820*, 2nd ed., ed. Richard Elphick and Hermann Giliomee (Middletown, CT: Wesleyan University Press, 1989), pp. 472–518.
27. Nightingale, *Segregation*, pp. 229–95.
28. Adam Hochschild, *King Leopold's Ghost: A Story of Greed, Terror and Heroism in Central Africa* (Boston, MA: Houghton Mifflin, 1998), pp. 21–184.
29. Thomas Pakenham, *The Scramble for Africa: White Man's Conquest of the Dark Continent from 1876 to 1912* (New York: Avon, 1991), pp. 141–246; Frederick Cooper, *Africa since 1940: The Past of the Present* (Cambridge: Cambridge University Press, 2002), pp.4–6; Nightingale, *Segregation*, pp. 172–85.
30. Zachary Karabell, *Parting the Desert: The Creation of the Suez Canal* (New York: Knopf, 2003); Lucia Carminati, "Port Said and Ismailia as Desert Marvels: Delusion and Frustration on the Isthmus of Suez, 1859–1869," *Journal of Urban History* 46 (2020): 622–47.
31. Pakenham, *The Scramble for Africa*, pp. 109–23, 257–357; Nightingale, *Segregation*, pp. 172–92.
32. Pakenham, *The Scramble for Africa*, pp. 358–71, 470–87, 525–56; Ayala Levin, "Haile Selassie's Imperial Modernity: Expatriate Architects and the Shaping of Addis Ababa," *Journal of the Society of Architectural Historians* 75 (2016): 447–68.
33. Population figures from John L. Brooke, *Climate Change and the Course of Global History: A Rough Journey* (Cambridge: Cambridge University Press, 2016), pp. 530–31.

14 CAPITALIST EXPLOSIONS

1. Sven Beckert, *Empire of Cotton: A Global History* (New York: Knopf, 2014), pp. 3–175.
2. Beckert, *Empire of Cotton*, pp. 83–135.
3. Beckert, *Empire of Cotton*, pp. 98–135; Edward E. Baptist *The Half Has Never Been Told: Slavery and the Making of American Capitalism* (New York: Basic Books, 2014).
4. Beckert, *Empire of Cotton*, pp. 136–74.
5. Quotation from Herman Melville, *Redburn, His First Voyage* (Project Gutenberg e-book, 2003 [1849]), Chapter 32.
6. Cyril Wood, *The Duke's Cut: The Bridgewater Canal* (Cheltenham: Tempus, 2002).
7. Katharina Pistor, *The Code of Capital: How the Law Creates Wealth and Inequality* (Princeton, NJ: Princeton University Press, 2019), pp.47–76; quotation from p. 19.
8. Frank Ferneyhough, *Liverpool & Manchester Railway, 1830–1980* (London: Robert Hale, 1980); Derek Hayes, *The First Railroads: Atlas of Early Railroads* (Buffalo, NY: Firefly, 2017).
9. Beckert, *Empire of Cotton*, pp. 190–241, 270–339.
10. Beckert, *Empire of Cotton*, pp. 190–241, 270–339.
11. Beckert, *Empire of Cotton*, pp. 240–73, 293–339.
12. Beckert, *Empire of Cotton*, pp. 242–340.
13. Beckert, *Empire of Cotton*, pp. 240–378.
14. Donald Wagner, *Science and Civilisation in China, Volume 5. Part 11: Ferrous Metallurgy* (Cambridge: Cambridge University Press, 2008), p. 361.
15. David Nasaw, *Andrew Carnegie* (New York: Penguin, 2006).
16. William Manchester, *The Arms of Krupp: 1587–1968* (Boston, MA: Little, Brown, 2003 [1968]).
17. Seiichiro Yonekura, *The Japanese Iron and Steel Industry, 1850–1990: Continuity and Discontinuity* (1994) (Houndmills: Palgrave MacMilllan, 1994); Chikayoshi Nomura, "Selling Steel in the 1920s: TISCO in

a Period of Transition," *Indian Economic & Social History Review* 48 (2011): 83–116; Shellen Xiao Wu, *Empires of Coal: Fueling China's Entry into the Modern World Order, 1860–1920* (Stanford, CA: Stanford University Press, 2016).

18. Martin W. Sandler, *Iron Rails, Iron Men, and the Race to Link the Nation: The Story of the Transcontinental Railroad* (Somerville, MA: Candlewick Press, 2015); Manu Karuka, *Empire's Tracks: Indigenous Nations, Chinese Workers, and the Transcontinental Railroad* (Berkeley, CA: University of California Press, 2019); Gordon H. Chang, *Ghosts of Gold Mountain: The Epic Story of the Chinese Who Built the Transcontinental Railroad* (Boston, MA: Houghton Mifflin Harcourt, 2019); David Burke, *Road through the Wilderness: The Story of the Transcontinental Railway, the First Great Work of Australia's Federation* (Sydney: New South Wales University Press, 1991); Steven G. Marks, *Road to Power: The Trans-Siberian Railroad and the Colonization of Asian Russia, 1850–1917* (Ithaca, NY: Cornell University Press, 1991).

19. William Cronon, *Nature's Metropolis: Chicago and the Great West* (New York; Norton, 1991), pp. 55–206.

20. Cronon, *Nature's Metropolis*, pp. 207–63; Robert Lewis, *Chicago Made: Factory Networks in the Industrial Metropolis* (Chicago: University of Chicago Press, 2008). See also Gergely Baics, *Feeding Gotham: The Political Economy and Geography of Food in New York, 1790–1860* (Princeton, NJ: Princeton University Press, 2016); Maria-Aparecida Lopes, "Struggles over an 'Old, Nasty, and Inconvenient Monopoly': Municipal Slaughterhouses and the Meat Industry in Rio de Janeiro, 1880–1920s," *Journal of Latin American Studies* 47 (2015): 349–76.

21. Kenneth Jackson, *Crabgrass Frontier: The Suburbanization of the United States* (New York: Oxford University Press, 1985), pp. 20–115; Robert Peschkes, *World Gazetteer of Tram, Trolleybus, and Rapid Transit Systems. Part One: Latin America* (Exeter: Quail Map Company, 1980); Robert Peschkes, *World Gazetteer of Tram, Trolleybus and Rapid Transit Systems. Part Two: Asia with USSR, Australasia, Africa* (London: Rapid Transit Publications, 1990); John P. McKay, *Tramways and Trolleys: The Rise of Urban Mass Transport in Europe* (Princeton, NJ: Princeton University Press, 1976); Allen Morrison, *Latin America by Streetcar: A Pictorial Survey of Urban Rail Transport South of the U.S.A.* (New York: Bonde Press, 1996); Martin Pabst, *Tram & Trolley in Africa* (Krefeld: Röhr Verlag, 1989); Liora Bigon, "Tracking Ethno-cultural Differences: The Lagos Steam Tramway, 1902–1933," *Journal of Historical Geography* 33 (2007): 596–618; Alexia Yates, *Real Estate and Global Urban History* (Cambridge: Cambridge University Press, 2021).

22. Matthieu Auzanneau, *Oil, Power, and War: A Dark History*, trans. John F. Reynolds (White River Junction, VT: Chelsea Green, 2018), pp. 9–64; Richard Rhodes, *Energy: A Human History* (New York: Simon and Schuster, 2018), pp. 225–26.

23. Rhodes, *Energy*, pp. 167–206; Graeme Gouday, *Domesticating Electricity: Technology, Uncertainty, and Gender, 1880–1914* (London: Pickering and Chatto, 2008); Thomas P. Hughes, *Networks of Power: Electrification in Western Society, 1880–1930* (Baltimore, MD: Johns Hopkins University Press, 1983).

24. Tom Standage, *The Victorian Internet: The Remarkable Story of the Telegraph and the Nineteenth-Century's Online Pioneers* (New York: Walker, 1998); Lynn Hollin Lees, *Planting Empire, Cultivating Subjects: British Malaya, 1786–1941* (Cambridge: Cambridge University Press, 2018), pp. 171–218; Adrián Lerner Patrón, *Jungle Cities: The Urbanization of Amazonia* (PhD Dissertation, Yale University, 2020).

25. Robert Rydell, ed., *World's Fairs: A Global History of Exhibitions* (London: Adam Matthew Digital, 2017); John McKean, *Crystal Palace: Joseph Paxton and Charles Fox* (London: Phaidon Press, 1994); Daniel T. Rodgers, *Atlantic Crossings: Social Politics in a Progressive Age* (Cambridge, MA: Harvard University Press, 1998), pp. 8–32.

26. On American financial centers, see David Scobey, *Empire City: The Making and Meaning of the New York Landscape* (Philadelphia, PA: Temple University Press, 2002); Thomas Kessler, *Capital City: New York City and the Men behind America's Rise to Dominance, 1860–1900* (New York: Simon and Schuster, 2003); Noam Magor, *Brahmin Capitalism: Frontiers of Wealth and Populism in America's First Gilded Age* (Cambridge, MA: Harvard University Press, 2017); Henry W. Berger, *St. Louis and Empire: 250 Years of Imperial Quest and Urban Crisis* (Carbondale, IL: Southern Illinois University Press, 2015); Peter Buitenhuis, "Aesthetics of the Skyscraper: The Views of Sullivan, James and Wright" *American Quarterly* 9 (1957): 316–24; quotation from p. 318. On factory elevators, see Joshua B. Freeman, *Behemoth: A History of the Factory and the Making of the Modern World* (New York: Norton, 2018), pp. 16–17.

27. Peter Thorsheim, *Inventing Pollution: Coal, Smoke, and Culture in Britain since 1800* (Athens, OH: Ohio University Press, 2006); Christine L. Corten, *London Fog: A Biography* (Cambridge, MA: Harvard University Press, 2015); Adam Rome, "Coming to Terms with Pollution: The Language of Environmental Reform, 1865–1915," *Environmental History* 1 (1996): 6–28; John L. Brooke, *Climate Change and the Course of Global History: A Rough Journey* (Cambridge: Cambridge University Press, 2016), p. 524.

28. Brooke, *Climate Change*, pp. 524–28.

29. Brooke, *Climate Change*, p. 526.

15 THE PHARAOHS OF FLOW

1. Andrew Lees and Lynn Hollin Lees, *Cities and the Making of Modern Europe* (Cambridge: Cambridge University Press, 2007), pp. 99–168; Françoise Choay, *The Modern City: Planning in the 19th Century* (New York: Braziller, 1969); Leonardo Benevolo, *The Origins of Modern Town Planning* (Cambridge, MA: MIT Press, 1963); John Duffy, *The Sanitarians: A History of American Public Health* (Champaign, IL: University of Illinois Press, 1900); Mark Harrison, *Public Health in British India: Anglo-Indian Preventative Medicine, 1859–1914* (Cambridge: Cambridge University Press, 1994); Mark Harrison, *Disease and the Modern World: 1500 to the Present Day* (Malden, MA: Polity, 2004), pp. 91–145; Carl H. Nightingale, *Segregation: A Global History of Divided Cities* (Chicago, IL: University of Chicago Press, 2012), pp. 88–94, 125–24, 159–228.

2. Nightingale, *Segregation*, pp. 88–95; Swati Chattopadhyay, *Representing Calcutta: Modernity, Nationalism, and the Colonial Uncanny* (London: Routledge, 2005); Partho Datta, *Planning the City: Urbanization and Reform in Calcutta, c. 1800–c. 1940* (New Delhi: Tulika, 2012).

3. Nightingale, *Segregation*, pp. 88–94, quotation from p. 121.

4. Nightingale, *Segregation*, pp. 88–94.

5. Datta, *Planning the City*, pp. 10–89; Chattopadhyay, *Representing Calcutta*, pp. 62–75.

6. Debjani Bhattacharyya, *Empire and Ecology in the Bengal Delta: The Making of Calcutta* (Cambridge: Cambridge University Press, 2018), pp. 45–110. For a history of New York that speaks to similar themes, see Ted Steinberg, *Gotham Unbound: The Ecological History of Greater New York* (New York: Simon and Schuster, 2014).

7. Harrison, *Public Health in British India*, pp. 99–116, 204–26; Datta, *Planning the City*, pp. 89–170.

8. Stephen Halliday, *The Great Stink of London: Sir Joseph Bazalgette and the Cleansing of the Victorian Capital* (Stroud: Sutton, 1999), pp. 17–57; Stephen Halliday, *An Underground Guide to Sewers or; Down, Through & Out in Paris, London, New York &c.* (Cambridge, MA: MIT Press, 2019), pp. 40–55.

9. Halliday, *The Great Stink of London*, pp. 124–43; Harrison, *Disease and the Modern World*, pp. 91–117.

10. Halliday, *The Great Stink of London*, pp. 58–76.

11. Halliday, *The Great Stink of London*, pp. 77–123.

12. Halliday, *The Great Stink of London*, pp. 144–63.

13. Nandy Kaberi, "Sanitation, Disease, and Death in Colonial Cities: A Case Study of Calcutta, 1860–1947" (Ph.D. Thesis, Jawaharlal University, Delhi, 2004), pp. 111–47.

14. David P. Jordan, *Transforming Paris: The Life and Labors of Baron Haussmann* (New York: Free Press, 1995); Howard Saalman, *Haussmann: Paris Transformed* (New York: Braziller, 1971); David Harvey, *Paris: Capital of Modernity* (London: Routledge, 2003).

15. James Sterling Young, *The Washington Community, 1800–1828* (New York: Columbia University Press, 1966), pp. 1–10; Patrick Barkham, "The Miracle of Kolkata's Wetlands – and One Man's Struggle to Save Them," *The Guardian*, March 9, 2016, at www.theguardian.com/cities/2016/mar/09/kolkata-wetlands-india-miracle-environmentalist-flood-defence (accessed August 6, 2021).

16. Jordan, *Transforming Paris*, pp. 185–210.

17. Jordan, *Transforming Paris*, pp. 185–210, 227–44.

18. Jordan, *Transforming Paris*, pp. 1–9.

19. Quotation from Jordan, *Transforming Paris*, p. 188.

20. Alexia M. Yates, *Selling Paris: Property and Commercial Culture in the Fin-de-Siècle Capital* (Cambridge, MA: Harvard University Press, 2015); Harvey, *Paris*, pp. 104–30.

21. Yates, *Selling Paris*; Robert Fishman, *Bourgeois Utopias: The Rise and Fall of Suburbia* (New York: Basic Books, 1987), pp. 103–33; Joseph Ben Prestel, *Emotional Cities: Debates on Urban Change in Berlin and Cairo* (Oxford: Oxford University Press, 2017), pp. 145–62.

22. Jordan, *Transforming Paris*, pp. 341–68.

23. Nightingale, *Segregation*, pp. 207–9; Samuel Grinsell, "Urbanism, Environment and the Building of the Anglo-Egyptian Nile Valley, 1880s–1920s" (Ph.D. Thesis, University of Edinburgh, 2020).

24. Nightingale, *Segregation*, pp. 206–7; Carl E. Schorske, *Fin-de-siècle Vienna: Politics and Culture* (New York: Vintage, 1981), pp. 24–115; Claus Bernet, "The Hobrecht Plan (1862)," *Urban History* 31 (2004): 400–19.

25. Nightingale, *Segregation*, pp. 206–18; Theresa Meade, *"Civilizing" Rio: Reform and Resistance in a Brazilian City, 1889–1930* (University Park, PA: Pennsylvania State University Press, 1997), pp. 75–101; Janet Abu-Lughod, *Cairo: 1001 Years of the City Victorious* (Princeton, NJ: Princeton University Press, 1971), pp. 99–117; Janet Abu-Lughod, *Rabat: Urban Apartheid in Morocco* (Princeton, NJ: Princeton University Press, 1980); Gwendolyn Wright, *The Politics of Design in French Colonial Urbanism* (Chicago, IL: University of Chicago Press, 1991); Michael G. Vann, "White City on the Red River: Race, Power, and Culture in French Colonial Hanoi, 1872–1954" (Ph.D. Thesis, University of California, Santa Cruz, 1999).

26. Nightingale, *Segregation*, pp. 159–92; Michael Vann, *The Great Hanoi Rat Hunt: Empire, Race, and Modernity in French Colonial Vietnam* (New York: Oxford University Press, 2018).

27. Stephen Legg, *Spaces of Colonialism: Delhi's Urban Governmentalities* (Malden, MA: Blackwell, 2007); Robert Grant Irving, *Indian Summer: Lutyens, Baker, and Imperial Delhi* (New Haven, CT: Yale University Press, 1981).

28. Nightingale, *Segregation*, pp. 218–28.

29. Nightingale, *Segregation*, pp. 218–28.

16 PLANET OF THE PEOPLE III: AN URBAN MAJORITY TAKES ITS SPACE

1. Dirk Hoerder, *Cultures in Contact: World Migrations in the Second Millennium* (Durham, NC: Duke University Press, 2002), pp. 275–442; Jürgen Osterhammel, *The Transformation of the World: A Global History of the Nineteenth Century*, trans. Patrick Camiller (Princeton, NJ: Princeton University Press, 2014), pp. 167–97; John L. Brooke, *Climate Change and the Course of Global History: A Rough Journey* (Cambridge: Cambridge University Press, 2016), pp. 513–18.

2. Nicholas F. R. Crafts, *British Economic Growth during the Industrial Revolution* (New York: Oxford University Press, 1985); Osterhammel, *The Transformation of the World*, pp. 216–26, 685–96, 706–9.

3. Osterhammel, *The Transformation of the World*, pp. 211–16; Toby Lincoln, *An Urban History of China* (Cambridge: Cambridge University Press, 2021), pp. 135–61; Eugen Weber, *Peasants into Frenchmen: The Modernization of Rural France, 1870–1914* (Stanford, CA: Stanford University Press, 1984).

4. Hoerder, *Cultures in Contact*, pp. 331–442; Osterhammel, *The Transformation of the World*, pp. 117–66.

5. Hoerder, *Cultures in Contact*, pp. 331–65.

6. Hoerder, *Cultures in Contact*, pp. 366–404.

7. Osterhammel, *The Transformation of the World*, pp. 690–91.

8. Hoerder, *Cultures in Contact*, pp. 393–404; Manu Karuka, *Empire's Tracks: Indigenous Nations, Chinese Workers, and the Transcontinental Railroad* (Berkeley, CA: University of California Press, 2019); Gordon H. Chang, *Ghosts of Gold Mountain: The Epic Story of the Chinese Who Built the Transcontinental Railroad* (Boston, MA: Houghton Mifflin Harcourt, 2019).

9. Adam McKeown, *Melancholy Order: Asian Migration and the Globalization of Borders* (New York: Columbia University Press, 2008), pp. 252–90.

10. McKeown, *Melancholy Order*; Paul A. Kramer, "Who Does She Stand For? As the Statue of Liberty Turned 100, Our Long Battle over Immigration Was Having Its Moment in Reagan's America," *Slate*, March 5, 2018, https://slate.com/news-and-politics/2018/03/reagans-statue-of-liberty-and-the-sanctuary-movement.html, (accessed August 2, 2021); Theresa Meade, *"Civilizing" Rio: Reform and Resistance in a Brazilian City, 1889–1930* (University Park, PA: Pennsylvania State University Press, 1997), pp. 29–32.

11. Nell Irvin Painter, *Exodusters: Black Migration to Kansas after Reconstruction* (New York: W. W. Norton & Company, 1976); Timothy Keegan, "The Dynamics of Rural Accumulation in South Africa: Comparative and Historical Perspectives," *Comparative Studies in Society and History* 28 (1986): 628–50.

12. Gareth Steadman Jones, *Outcast London: A Study in the Relationship between the Classes in London Society* (London: Verso, 1971), pp. 239–335, especially 307–14 on rack-renting.

13. Quotation from Friedrich Engels, *The Condition of the Working Class in England*, trans. W. O. Henderson and W. H. Chaloner (Stanford, CA; Stanford University Press, 1958 [1845]), pp. 61–62.

14. Quotation from Engels, *The Condition of the Working Class*, p. 75; Jones, *Outcast London*, pp. 320–33; Mike Davis, *Planet of Slums* (New York: Verso, 2006), pp. 20–22.

15. Quotation from David P. Jordan, *Transforming Paris: The Life and Labors of Baron Haussmann* (New York: Free Press, 1995), pp. 216–17. Yates, *Selling Paris*.

16. Meade, *"Civilizing" Rio*, pp. 69–74, quotation from p. 69; Prashant Kidambi, *The Making of an Indian Metropolis: Colonial Governance and Public Culture in Bombay, 1890–1920* (Aldershot: Ashgate, 2007), pp. 49–114, quotation from p. 54; Carl H. Nightingale, *Segregation: A Global History of Divided Cities* (Chicago, IL: University of Chicago Press, 2012), pp. 159–72.

17. Nightingale, *Segregation*, pp. 172–92, 254–60.

18. Catherine McNeur, *Taming Manhattan: Environmental Battles in the Antebellum City* (Cambridge, MA: Harvard University Press, 2014), pp.134–38, 183–88, 207–8; Lisa Goff, *Shantytown, USA: Forgotten Landscapes of the Working Poor* (Cambridge, MA: Harvard University Press, 2016); Jason Jindrich, "The Shantytowns of Central Park West: Fin de Siècle Squatting in American Cities," *Journal of Urban History* 36 (2010): 672–84; Kristin Poling, "Shantytowns and Pioneers beyond the City Wall: Berlin's Urban Frontier in the Nineteenth Century," *Central European History* 47 (2014): 245–74.

19. Nightingale, *Segregation*, pp. 309, 342–44; Martin Pawley, *Home Ownership* (London: Architectural Press, 1978), pp. 25–38, 65–69; Margaret Garb, *City of American Dreams: A History of Home Ownership and Housing Reform in Chicago, 1871–1919* (Chicago, IL: University of Chicago Press, 2005), pp. 46–48; Elaine Lewinnek, *The Working Man's Reward: Chicago's Early Suburbs and the Roots of American Sprawl* (Oxford: Oxford University Press, 2014); David Scobie, *Buenos Aires: Plaza to Suburb, 1870–1910* (New York: Oxford University Press, 1974).

20. Richard Belsky, *Localities at the Center: Native Place, Space, and Power in Late Imperial Beijing* (Cambridge, MA: Harvard University Asia Center, 2005), p. 3; Elizabeth J. Perry, *Shanghai on Strike: The Politics of Chinese Labor* (Stanford, CA: Stanford University Press, 1993), pp. 1–65; Blair A. Ruble, *Second Metropolis: Pragmatic Pluralism in Gilded Age Chicago, Silver Age Moscow, and Meiji Osaka* (Cambridge: Cambridge University Press, 2001).

21. Paige Glotzer, *How the Suburbs Were Segregated: Developers and the Business of Exclusionary Housing, 1890–1960* (New York: Columbia University Press, 2020); Ann Durkin Keating, *Building Chicago: Suburban Developers and the Creation of a Divided Metropolis* (Columbus, OH: Ohio State University Press, 1988); Robin L. Einhorn, *Property Rules: Political Economy in Chicago, 1833–1872* (Chicago, IL: University of Chicago Press, 2001). For more citations on this widely studied subject, see Nightingale, *Segregation*, pp. 147–58, 300–32.

22. Andrew Gordon, *Labor and Imperial Democracy in Imperial Japan* (Berkeley, CA: University of California Press, 1991), pp. 12–121.

23. Roger V. Gould, *Insurgent Identities: Class, Community, and Protest in Paris from 1848 to the Commune* (Chicago, IL: University of Chicago Press, 1995), pp.121–52.

24. Gould, *Insurgent Identities*, pp. 153–206. Quentin Deluermoz has written a pioneering global urban history of the Paris Commune entitled *Commune(s), 1870–1871: Une traversée des mondes au XIXᵉ siècle* (Paris: Seuil, 2020). He summarizes some of the arguments in this work in "The Paris Commune in

Global Urban History," trans. Cecilia Terrero Fernández, in the *Global Urban History* blog, at https:// globalurbanhistory.com/2016/07/28/the-paris-commune-in-global-urban-history/ (accessed August 2, 2021).

25. Anindita Ghosh, *Claiming the City: Protest, Crime, and Scandals in Colonial Calcutta, c. 1860–1920* (Oxford: Oxford University Press 2016), pp. 273–91; Kidambi, *The Making of an Indian Metropolis*, pp. 118–20; Meade, *"Civilizing" Rio*, pp. 1–4, 103–21.

26. Nightingale, *Segregation*, pp. 234–35.

27. Ophélie Siméon, *Robert Owen's Experiment at New Lanark: From Paternalism to Socialism* (London: Palgrave Macmillan, 2017); Andrew Lees and Lynn Hollin Lees, *Cities and the Making of Modern Europe* (Cambridge: Cambridge University Press, 2007), pp. 169–205; Daniel T. Rodgers, *Atlantic Crossings: Social Politics in a Progressive Age* (Cambridge, MA: Harvard University Press, 1998), pp. 130–59; Osterhammel, *The Transformation of the World*, p. 687.

28. Rodgers, *Atlantic Crossings*, pp. 181–208.

29. Sven Beckert, *Empire of Cotton: A Global History* (New York: Knopf, 2014), pp. 56–82; Joshua B. Freeman, *Behemoth: A History of the Factory and the Making of the Modern World* (New York: Norton, 2018), pp. 35–40; Osterhammel, *The Transformation of the World*, pp. 618–22. A few resources from among many others on urban police reforms from around the world include Clive Emsley, *The Great English Bobby: A History of Policing from the 18th Century to the Present* (London: Quercus, 2009); David M. Anderson and David Killingray, eds., *Policing the Empire: Government, Authority, and Control, 1830–1940* (Manchester: Manchester University Press, 1991); Thomas H. Holloway, *Policing Rio de Janeiro: Repression and Resistance in a 19th-Century City* (Stanford, CA: Stanford University Press, 1993); and Kristin Stapleton, *Civilizing Chengdu: Chinese Urban Reform, 1895–1937* (Cambridge, MA: Harvard University Asia Center, 2000), pp.77–110.

30. Mike Rapport, *1848: Year of Revolution* (New York: Basic Books, 2008); Osterhammel, *The Transformation of the World*, pp. 543–47.

31. Stanley Buder, *Pullman: An Experiment in Industrial Order and Community Planning, 1880–1930* (Oxford: Oxford University Press, 1970); Margaret Crawford, *Building the Workingman's Paradise: The Design of American Company Towns* (London & New York: Verso, 1995); Manchester, *The Arms of Krupp*, pp 207–9; Leif Jerram, *Streetlife: The Untold History of Europe's Twentieth Century* (Oxford: Oxford University Press, 2011), p.17.

32. Bruce Laurie, *Artisans into Workers: Labor in Nineteenth-Century America* (Champaign, IL: University of Illinois Press, 1989), pp. 1–14, 74–220.

33. Laurie, *Artisans into Workers*, pp. 141–46, 156–58, 201–10.

34. Laurie, *Artisans into Workers*, pp. 201–10.

35. Meade, *"Civilizing" Rio*, pp. 103–21; Melanie Yap and Dianne Leong Man, *Colour, Confusion and Concessions: The History of the Chinese in South Africa* (Hong Kong: Hong Kong University Press, 1996).

36. Perry, *Shanghai on Strike*, pp. 40, 261–64; Xiaowei Zheng, *The Politics of Rights and the 1911 Revolution in China* (Stanford, CA: Stanford University Press, 2018), pp.167–96; Lincoln, *An Urban History of China*, pp. 162–90.

37. Jerram, *Streetlife*, p. 1.

17 LAMPS OUT

1. Carl E. Schorske, *Fin-de-siècle Vienna: Politics and Culture* (New York: Vintage, 1981), pp. 24–116; in this chapter I do not seek to resurrect Schorske's claim that Vienna was "the birthplace of modernity," not on its own in any case, but merely see the city as a useful location from which to explore the global reach of *Belle Époque* sensibilities and their dangers. See Steven Beller, ed., *Rethinking Vienna 1900* (New York: Berghahn, 2001); Andrew Lees and Lynn Hollin Lees, *Cities and the Making of Modern Europe* (Cambridge: Cambridge University Press, 2007), pp. 206–43.

2. Schorske, *Fin-de-siècle Vienna*, pp. 181–366.

3. Schorske, *Fin-de-siècle Vienna*, pp. 208–78; Jerrold Siegel, *Bohemian Paris: Culture, Politics, and the Boundaries of Bourgeois Life, 1830–1930* (New York: Penguin, 1986), pp. 213–398.

4. Wolfgang Maderthaner and Lutz Musner, "Outcast Vienna 1900: The Politics of Transgression," *International Labor and Working-Class History* 64 (2003): 25–37.

5. Pieter M. Judson, *The Habsburg Empire: A New History* (Cambridge, MA: Harvard University Press, 2016), pp. 333–84.

6. Richard Basset, *For God and Kaiser: The Imperial Austrian Army, 1619–1918* (New Haven, CT: Yale University Press, 2016), pp. 365–457; Daniel Yergin, *The Prize: The Epic Quest for Oil, Money, and Power* (New York: Free Press, 1991), pp. i–v.

7. Schorske, *Fin-de-siècle Vienna*, pp. 116–80.

8. Judson, *The Habsburg Empire*, pp. 329–32, 341–50, 391–408; Hasan Kayalı, *Arabs and Young Turks: Ottomanism, Arabism, and Islamism in the Ottoman Empire, 1908–1918* (Berkeley, CA: University of California Press, 1997); Victor Roudometof, "From Rum Millet to Greek Nation: Enlightenment, Secularization, and National Identity in Ottoman Balkan Society, 1453–1821," *Journal of Modern Greek Studies* 16 (1998): 11–48; Richard G. Hovannisian, "The Armenian Question in the Ottoman Empire, 1876–1914," in *The Armenian People from Ancient to Modern Times, Volume 2. Foreign Dominion to Statehood: The Fifteenth Century to the Twentieth Century*, ed. Richard G. Hovannisian (New York: St. Martin's Press, 1997), pp. 203–38; Anindita Ghosh, *Claiming the City: Protest, Crime, and Scandals in Colonial Calcutta, c. 1860–1920* (Oxford: Oxford University Press 2016), pp. 248–91; Sumit Sarkar, *The Swadeshi Movement in Bengal, 1903–1908* (Ranikhett Cantonment: Permanent Black, 1973); Jim Masselos, *The City in Action: Bombay Struggles for Power* (Oxford: Oxford University Press, 2007), pp.15–152; David Silbey, *The Boxer Rebellion and the Great Game in China* (New York: Hill and Wang, 2012); Nancy Reynolds, *A City Consumed: Urban Commerce, the Cairo Fire, and the Politics of Decolonization in Egypt* (Stanford, CA: Stanford University Press, 2012).

9. Schorske, *Fin-de-siècle Vienna*, pp. 133–46; Volker Ullrich, *Hitler: Ascent 1889–1939*, trans. Jefferson Chase (New York: Knopf, 2016), pp. 30–49.

10. Andrew Gordon, *Labor and Imperial Democracy in Imperial Japan* (Berkeley, CA: University of California Press, 1991), pp.12–121; John W. Steinberg et al., eds., *The Russo-Japanese War in Global Perspective: World War Zero, Volume I* (Leiden: Brill, 2005); David Wolff et al., eds., *The Russo-Japanese War in Global Perspective: World War Zero, Volume II* (Leiden: Brill, 2005).

11. Abraham Ascher, *The Revolution of 1905: Russia in Disarray* (Stanford, CA: Stanford University Press, 1994); Matthieu Auzanneau, *Oil, Power, and War: A Dark History*, trans. John F. Reynolds (White River Junction, VT: Chelsea Green, 2018), pp. 61–64.

12. Christopher Read, *From Tsar to Soviets: The Russian People and Their Revolution, 1917–21* (New York: Oxford University Press, 2001), pp.16–24; Ascher, *The Revolution of 1905*; Robert C. Tucker, *Stalin as Revolutionary: A Study in History and Personality, 1879–1929* (New York: Norton, 1974), pp.152–54.

13. D. N. Collins, "The Franco-Russian Alliance and Russian Railways, 1891–1914," *The Historical Journal* 16 (1973): 777–88; Gordon Martel, *The Month That Changed the World: July 1914* (Oxford: Oxford University Press, 2014).

14. William Kelleher Storey, *The First World War: A Concise Global History* (Blue Ridge Summit, PA: Rowman & Littlefield Publishers, 2010); Robert Gerwarth and Erez Manela, eds., *Empires at War: 1911–1923* (Oxford: Oxford University Press, 2014); Ian F. W. Beckett, *The Great War: 1914–1918* (New York: Routledge, 2007), Chapters 3 and 6. For an excellent online cartographic rendering of developments on the Western Front, see "Cartographie 1914–1918: Le front ouest de la première guerre mondiale," at http://www.carto1418.fr/index.php (accessed August 3, 2021).

15. Beckett, *The Great War*, Chapters 11 and 12.

16. Mark Harrison, *Disease and the Modern World: 1500 to the Present Day* (Malden, MA: Polity, 2004), Chapter 7; David Killingray and Howard Phillips, eds., *The Spanish Flu Pandemic of 1918: New Perspectives* (London: Routledge, 2003); Kenneth C. Davis, *More Deadly Than War: The Hidden History of the Spanish Flu and the First World War* (New York: Henry Holt, 2018).

17. Read, *From Tsar to Soviets*, p. 25 for a good response to many Russian Revolution historians' exclusive focus on Petrograd as a way to glorify or disparage Lenin's personal role and ignore the revolution's many other crucial theaters and protagonists.

18. Read, *From Tsar to Soviets*, pp. 64–75.

19. Read, *From Tsar to Soviets*, pp. 11–24, 38–39, 92–120.

20. Despite historians' focus on events in Petrograd, a textured urban history of the Russian Revolution has yet to be written, though some good clues are given in Leif Jerram, *Streetlife: The Untold History of Europe's Twentieth Century* (Oxford: Oxford University Press, 2011), pp. 35–38, and most general accounts contain others. My own short sketch here is derived from these and evocative details in China Miéville's popular account, *October: The Story of the Russian Revolution* (London: Verso, 2017), pp. 5–65. His map, on unnumbered pages directly after the table of contents, is also very useful.

21. Jerram, *Streetlife*, pp. 35–38; Read, *From Tsar to Soviets*, pp. 32–38; Miéville, *October*, pp. 5–65.

22. Read, *From Tsar to Soviets*, pp. 33–48, 64–75, 121–42; Jerram, *Streetlife*, pp. 35–38; Miéville, *October*, pp. 39–65.

23. Read, *From Tsar to Soviets*, pp. 1, 33–48, 76–93; Jerram *Streetlife*, pp. 35–38; Miéville, *October*, pp. 66–126.

24. Read, *Tsar to Soviets*, pp. 76–93; Miéville, *October*, pp. 123–305.

25. Read, *Tsar to Soviets*, pp. 94–136; Mark Jones, *Founding Weimar: Violence and the German Revolution of 1918–1919* (Cambridge: Cambridge University Press, 2016).

26. John Lear, *Workers, Neighbors, Citizens: The Revolution in Mexico City* (Lincoln, NE: University of Nebraska Press, 2002); Ann Hagedorn, *Savage Peace: Hope and Fear in America, 1919* (New York: Simon & Schuster, 2007); Martin Kitchen, *Europe between the Wars* (Abingdon: Routledge, 2006 [1988]), pp.245–336; Michael Lewis, *Rioters and Citizens: Mass Protest in Imperial Japan* (Berkeley, CA: University of California Press, 1990), pp.82–134.

27. Charles Townshend, *Easter 1916: The Irish Rebellion* (Chicago, IL: Ivan R. Dee, 2006); Kitchen, *Europe between the Wars*, pp. 176–211; Cyrus Schayegh, *The Middle East and the Making of the Modern World* (Cambridge, MA: Harvard University Press, 2017), pp. 132–91.

28. David Fromkin, *A Peace to End All Peace: Creating the Modern Middle East* (New York: Henry Holt and Company, 1989).

29. Jim Masselos, *Indian Nationalism: A History* (New Delhi: Sterling, 2013), pp.156–59; Howard Spodek, *Ahmedabad: Shock City of Twentieth-Century India* (Bloomington, IN: Indiana University Press, 2011), pp. 37–94.

30. Abbas Khadim, *Reclaiming Iraq: The 1920 Revolution and the Founding of the Modern State* (Austin, TX: University of Texas Press, 2012); Adrian Vickers, *A History of Modern Indonesia* (Cambridge: Cambridge University Press, 2005), pp. 60–86; Frank Baldwin, *The March First Movement: Korean Challenge and Japanese Response* (New York: Columbia University Press, 1972); Peter Zarrow, "Politics and Culture in the May Fourth Movement," in *China in War and Revolution, 1895–1949*, ed. Peter Zarrow (New York: Routledge, 2005), pp. 149–69; Joseph T. Chen, *The May Fourth Movement in Shanghai* (Leiden: Brill, 1971), pp.111–78.

31. Carl H. Nightingale, *Segregation: A Global History of Divided Cities* (Chicago, IL: University of Chicago Press, 2012), pp. 307–17; Scott Ellsworth, *Death in a Promised Land: The Tulsa Race Riot of 1921* (Baton Rouge, LA: University of Louisiana Press, 1982); Hannibal B. Johnson, *Black Wall Street: From Riot to Renaissance in Tulsa's Historic Greenwood District* (Austin, TX: Eakin Press, 1998).

32. Nightingale, *Segregation*, pp. 317–18; Jeremy Krikler, *White Rising: The 1922 Insurrection and Racial Killing in South Africa* (Manchester: Manchester University Press, 2005), pp.130–50; W. A. Maguire, *Belfast: A History* (Lancaster: Carnegie, 2009), pp. 94–97, 135–43, 197–200.

33. Joshua Hammer, *Yokohama Burning: The Deadly 1923 Earthquake and Fire That Helped Forge the Path to World War II* (New York: Free Press, 2006), pp. 152–70; André Sorensen, *The Making of Urban Japan: Cities and Planning from Edo to the Twenty-First Century* (London: Routledge, 2002), pp. 85–150.

34. R. J. B. Bosworth, *Mussolini's Italy: Life under the Dictatorship 1915–1945* (London, Allen Lane, 2006); Aristotle Kallis, *The Third Rome, 1922–43: The Making of the Fascist Capital* (New York: Palgrave

MacMillan, 2014); Borden W. Painter, Jr., *Mussolini's Rome: Rebuilding the Eternal City* (New York: Palgrave MacMillan, 2005).
35. Ullrich, *Hitler*, pp. 73–130.
36. Ullrich, *Hitler*, pp. 131–64.
37. Ullrich, *Hitler*, pp. 165–85.

18 THE LABYRINTHS OF TERROR

1. Carolyn Daly and Melanie Nolan, eds., *Suffrage and Beyond: International Feminist Perspectives* (Auckland: Auckland University Press, 1994).
2. Kathy Peiss, *Cheap Amusements: Working Women and Leisure in Turn of the Century New York* (Philadelphia, PA: Temple University Press, 1986); Alys Eve Weinbaum et al., eds., *The Modern Girl around the World: Consumption, Modernity, and Globalization* (Durham, NC: Duke University Press, 2008); Abosede A. George, *Making Modern Girls: A History of Girlhood, Labor, and Social Development in Colonial Lagos* (Athens, OH: Ohio University Press, 2014); Su Lin Lewis, *Cities in Motion: Urban Life and Cosmopolitanism in Southeast Asia, 1920–1940* (Cambridge: Cambridge University Press, 2016), pp. 227–63; Cecilia Tossounian, "Figuring Modernity and National Identity: Representations of the Argentine Modern Girl (1918–1939)," in *Consuming Modernity: Changing Gendered Behaviours and Consumerism before the Baby Boom*, ed. Cheryl Krasnick Warsh and Dan Malleck (Vancouver: University of British Columbia Press, 2014), pp. 220–36; Simon Sleight, *Young People and the Shaping of Public Space in Melbourne, 1870–1914* (Abingdon and New York: Routledge, 2013); Leif Jerram, *Streetlife: The Untold History of Europe's Twentieth Century* (Oxford: Oxford University Press, 2011), pp. 101–72; Joseph Ben Prestel, *Emotional Cities: Debates on Urban Change in Berlin and Cairo, 1860–1910* (Oxford: Oxford University Press, 2017), pp. 75–135.
3. Theresa Runstedtler, *Jack Johnson, Rebel Sojourner: Boxing in the Shadow of the Global Color Line* (Berkeley, CA: University of California Press, 2012), Chapters 1 and 2; Prestel, *Emotional Cities*, pp. 136–88.
4. Lynn Abbott and Doug Seroff, *The Original Blues: The Emergence of the Blues in African-American Vaudeville, 1889–1926* (Jackson, MS: University Press of Mississippi, 2019); Charles Keil, *Urban Blues* (Chicago, IL: University of Chicago Press, 1991 [1966]); Paul Oliver, *The Story of the Blues* (Boston, MA: Northeastern University Press, 1998); James Lincoln Collier, *The Making of Jazz: A Comprehensive History* (New York: Dell, 1978); Al Rose, *Storyville, New Orleans: Being an Authentic, Illustrated Account of the Notorious Red-Light District* (Tuscaloosa, AL: University of Alabama Press, 1978).
5. Kevin Mumford, *Interzones: Black/White Sex Districts in Chicago and New York in the Early Twentieth Century* (New York: Columbia University Press, 1997); Tyler Stovall, *Paris Noir: African Americans in the City of Light* (Boston, MA: Houghton Mifflin, 1996); Marc Matera, *Black London: The Imperial Metropolis and Decolonization in the Twentieth Century* (Berkeley, CA: University of California Press, 2015), pp.145–236; Helmut Gruber, *Red Vienna: Experiment in Working-Class Culture, 1919–1934* (New York: Oxford University Press, 1991); Meng Yue, *Shanghai and the Edges of Empires* (Minneapolis, MN: University of Minnesota Press, 2006), pp.171–209; Edward Seidenstecker, *Tokyo Rising: The City since the Great Earthquake* (New York: Knopf, 1990), pp. 215–18, 291–95; Prestel, *Emotional Cities*; Nicholas Kenny, *The Feel of the City: Experiences of Urban Transformation* (Toronto: University of Toronto Press, 2014).
6. George Chauncey, *Gay New York: Gender, Urban Culture and the Making of the Gay Male World 1890–1940* (New York: Basic Books, 1994), quotation from p. 1; Matt Cook, *London and the Culture of Homosexuality, 1885–1914* (Cambridge: Cambridge University Press, 2003); Peter Ackroyd, *Queer City: Gay London from the Romans to the Present Day* (London: Penguin, 2017), pp.181–213; Dan Healy, *Homosexual Desire in Revolutionary Russia: The Regulation of Sexual and Gender Dissent* (Chicago, IL: University of Chicago Press, 2001), pp. 1–76, esp. 31–33; Jerram, *Streetlife*, pp. 247–316.
7. Weinbaum et al., eds., *The Modern Girl around the World*; Jerram, *Streetlife*; Chauncey, *Gay New York*.
8. Volker Ullrich, *Hitler: Ascent 1889–1939*, trans. Jefferson Chase (New York: Knopf, 2016), pp. 267–90, 380–412.
9. Ullrich, *Hitler*, pp. 185–266.

10. Ullrich, *Hitler*, pp. 290–379.
11. Ullrich, *Hitler*, pp. 412–76, 513–66, 657–81.
12. Ullrich, *Hitler*, pp. 682–758; Ian Campbell, *The Addis Ababa Massacre: Italy's National Shame* (London: Hurst, 2017).
13. Ullrich, *Hitler*, pp. 567–607.
14. Seidenstecker, *Tokyo Rising*, pp. 21–88; André Sorensen, *The Making of Urban Japan: Cities and Planning from Edo to the Twenty-First Century* (London: Routledge, 2002), pp. 85–150.
15. Andrew Gordon, *Labor and Imperial Democracy in Imperial Japan* (Berkeley, CA: University of California Press, 1991), pp. 237–301.
16. Gordon, *Labor in Imperial Japan*, pp. 302–30.
17. Marius Jansen, *The Making of Modern Japan* (Cambridge, MA: Harvard University Press, 2000), Chapter 17.
18. Jansen, *The Making of Modern Japan*, Chapter 17.
19. Karl Schlögel, *Moscow 1937*, trans. Rodney Livingston (Cambridge: Polity Press, 2013 [2008]), pp. 33–53.
20. Schlögel, *Moscow*, pp. 10–54.
21. Schlögel, *Moscow*, pp. 10–54.
22. Schlögel, *Moscow*, pp. 10–54.
23. Joshua B. Freeman, *Behemoth: A History of the Factory and the Making of the Modern World* (New York: Norton, 2018), pp. 169–96; Stephen Kotkin, *Magnetic Mountain: Stalinism as Civilization* (Berkeley, CA: University of California Press, 1995); Schlögel, *Moscow*, pp. 35–42, 236–37; Cynthia A. Ruder, *Building Stalinism: The Moscow Canal and the Creation of Soviet Space* (London: Tauris, 2018); Katherine Zubovich, *Moscow Monumental: Soviet Skyscrapers and Urban Life in Stalin's Capital* (Princeton, NJ: Princeton University Press, 2020).
24. Mark Harrison, ed., *Guns and Rubles: The Defense Industry in the Stalinist State* (New Haven, CT: Yale University Press, 2008).
25. Schlögel, *Moscow 1937*, pp. 54–80, 160–97, 413–32; Freeman, *Behemoth*, pp. 196–210.
26. Matthieu Auzanneau, *Oil, Power, and War: A Dark History*, trans. John F. Reynolds (White River Junction, VT: Chelsea Green, 2018), pp. 153–72; Daniel Yergin, *The Prize: The Epic Quest for Oil, Money, and Power* (New York: Free Press, 1991), pp. 288–371.
27. Quotation from James Dugan and Carroll Stewart, *Ploești: The Great Ground–Air Battle of 1 August 1943* (Washington, D.C.: Brassey's, 2003), p. 3. Yergin, *The Prize, pp. 311–32.*
28. Yergin, *The Prize*, pp. 289–310, 333–49.
29. Auzanneau, *Oil, Power, and War*, pp. 153–72; Yergin, *The Prize*, pp. 350–71.
30. Auzanneau, *Oil, Power, and War*, pp. 149–50, 163–67; Susan Freinkel, *Plastics: A Toxic Love Story* (New York: Henry Holt, 2011), p. 4.
31. Stefan Kühl, *The Nazi Connection: Eugenics, American Racism, and German National Socialism* (New York: Oxford University Press, 1994), pp.13–96; Gretchen Schafft, *From Racism to Genocide: Anthropology in the Third Reich* (Urbana, IL: University of Illinois Press, 2004).
32. John W. Dower, *War without Mercy: Race and Power in the Pacific War* (New York: Norton, 1986); *Greg Robinson, A Tragedy of Democracy: Japanese Confinement in North America* (New York: Columbia University Press, 2009).
33. Jeremy Sarkin, *Germany's Genocide of the Herero: Kaiser Wilhelm II, His General, His Settlers, His Soldiers* (Cape Town: University of Cape Town Press, 2011).
34. Ronald Grigor Suny, *"They Can Live in the Desert but Nowhere Else": A History of the Armenian Genocide* (Princeton, NJ: Princeton University Press, 2015).
35. Nikolaus Wachsmann, *KL: A History of the Nazi Concentration Camps* (New York: Farrar, Strauss and Giroux, 2015).
36. Christopher Browning, *The Origins of the Final Solution: The Evolution of Nazi Jewish Policy, September 1939–March 1942* (Lincoln, NE: University of Nebraska Press, 2004).
37. Raul Hilberg, *The Destruction of the European Jews* (New York: New Viewpoints, 1973 [1961]), pp. 561–72, 586–635.

38. Yuki Tanaka and Marilyn B. Young, "Introduction," in *Bombing Civilians: A Twentieth Century History*, ed.Yuki Tanaka and Marilyn B. Young (New York: New Press, 2010), pp. 1–7.

39. Tetsuo Maeda, "Strategic Bombing of Chongqing by Imperial Japanese Army and Naval Forces," in *Bombing Civilians: A Twentieth Century History*, ed.Yuki Tanaka and Marilyn B. Young (New York: New Press, 2010), pp. 135–53; Ronald Schaffer, "The Bombing Campaigns in World War II: The European Theater," in *Bombing Civilians: A Twentieth Century History*, ed.Yuki Tanaka and Marilyn B. Young (New York: New Press, 2010), pp. 30–45. For maps of London destruction see Laurence Ward, *Bomb Damage Maps 1939–45* (London: Thames and Hudson, 2015).

40. Yuki Tanaka, "British 'Humane Bombing' in Iraq during the Interwar Era," in *Bombing Civilians: A Twentieth Century History*, ed.Yuki Tanaka and Marilyn B. Young (New York: New Press, 2010), pp. 8–29.

41. Schaffer, "The Bombing Campaigns in World War II."

42. Schaffer, "The Bombing Campaigns in World War II."

43. Mark Selden, "A Forgotten Holocaust: U.S. Bombing Strategy in the Destruction of Japanese Cities and the American Way of War from the Pacific War to Iraq," in *Bombing Civilians: A Twentieth Century History*, ed.Yuki Tanaka and Marilyn B. Young (New York: New Press, 2010), pp. 77–96.

44. Selden, "A Forgotten Holocaust." Quotation from p. 83.

19 GATHERING VELOCITIES I: TAILPIPE TRACTS AND TOWER BLOCKS

1. "The Kitchen Debate: An Exploration into Cold War Ideologies and Propaganda," http://www3.sympatico.ca/robsab/debate.html (accessed August 6, 2021). The best history of American housing policy and the ideal of homeownership as a Cold War Priority is Nancy H. Kwak, *A World of Homeowners: American Power and the Politics of Housing Aid* (Chicago, IL: University of Chicago Press, 2015).

2. A graphic representation of escalating urbanization rates in the USSR can be found in "100 Years of Mass Housing in Russia," *ArchDaily*, July 23, 2018 at www.archdaily.com/898475/100-years-of-mass-housing-in-russia (accessed August 6, 2021).

3. These rankings are based on population figures on urban agglomerations collected by the United Nations since 1950. Several graphical representations, using this data, of the changing geography of urban acceleration as represented by the changing list of top ten and top-20 cities are available on line – in map form at "Luminocity," https://luminocity3d.org/WorldCity/#2/8.2/62.9 and in animated chart form at "Data Is Beautiful," www.youtube.com/watch?v=oOdmlaG9znI and at "Wamamu Stats," www.youtube.com/watch?v=5yjMSBbcXss (all accessed August 6, 2021).

4. Robert Fishman, *Urban Utopias in the Twentieth Century: Ebenezer Howard, Frank Lloyd Wright, Le Corbusier* (Cambridge, MA: MIT Press, 1982), pp. 3–90; Rosemary Wakeman, *Practicing Utopia: An Intellectual History of the New Towns Movement* (Chicago, IL: University of Chicago Press, 2016).

5. Fishman, *Urban Utopias*, pp. 91–162.

6. Fishman, *Urban Utopias*, pp. 163–279.

7. James Stevens Curl, *Making Dystopia: The Strange Rise and Survival of Architectural Barbarism* (Oxford: Oxford University Press, 2018).

8. Richard Harris and Charlotte Vorms, eds., *What's in a Name? Talking about Urban Peripheries* (Toronto: University of Toronto Press, 2017); André Sorensen, "Global Suburbanization in Planning History," in *Routledge Handbook of Planning History*, ed. Carola Hein (London: Routledge, 2018), pp. 35–45.

9. Joshua B. Freeman, *Behemoth: A History of the Factory and the Making of the Modern World* (New York: Norton, 2018), pp. 118–68; Daniel T. Rodgers, *Atlantic Crossings: Social Politics in a Progressive Age* (Cambridge, MA: Harvard University Press, 1998), pp. 367–91.

10. David Kennedy, *Freedom from Fear: The American People in Depression and War, 1929–1945* (New York: Oxford University Press, 1999), pp. 70–130.

11. Rodgers, *Atlantic Crossings*, pp. 409–85.

12. Carl H. Nightingale, *Segregation: A Global History of Divided Cities* (Chicago, IL: University of Chicago Press, 2012), pp. 341–58; David M. P. Freund, *Colored Property: State Policy and White Racial Politics in Suburban America* (Chicago, IL: University of Chicago Press, 2007).

13. Rodgers, *Atlantic Crossings*, pp. 391–408.

14. Arnold R. Hirsch, *Making the Second Ghetto: Race and Housing in Chicago, 1940–1960* (Cambridge: Cambridge University Press, 1983); Andrew Diamond, *Chicago on the Make: Race and Inequality in a Modern City* (Oakland, CA: University of California Press, 2017); Nightingale, *Segregation*, pp. 341–58.

15. Freeman, *Behemoth*, pp. 169–269; Gijs Mom, *Atlantic Automobilism: Emergence and Persistence of the Car, 1895–1940* (New York: Berghahn, 2015); Simon Gunn and Susan C. Townsend, *Automobility and the City in Twentieth-Century Britain and Japan* (London: Bloomsbury, 2019).

16. Peter D. Norton, *Fighting Traffic: The Dawn of the Motor Age in the American City* (Cambridge, MA: MIT Press, 2008), esp. pp. 65–101.

17. John H. Jakle and Keith A. Sculle, *Lots of Parking: Land Use in a Car Culture* (Charlottesville, VA: University of Virginia Press, 2004).

18. Norton, *Fighting Traffic*, pp. 103–71; Thomas L. Karnes, *Asphalt and Politics: A History of the American Highway System* (Jefferson, NC: McFarland, 2009); Kenneth Jackson, *Crabgrass Frontier: The Suburbanization of the United States* (New York: Oxford University Press, 1985), pp. 246–71.

19. Robert Caro, *Power Broker: Robert Moses and the Fall of New York* (New York: Knopf, 1974); Roberta Brandes Gratz, *The Battle for Gotham: New York in the Shadow of Robert Moses and Jane Jacobs* (New York: Nation Books, 2010); Christopher Klemek, *The Transatlantic Collapse of Urban Renewal: Postwar Urbanism from New York to Berlin* (Chicago, IL: University of Chicago Press, 2011).

20. Karnes, *Asphalt and Politics*; Jackson, *Crabgrass Frontier*, pp. 248–51; Llana Barber, *Latino City: Immigration and Urban Crisis in Lawrence, Massachusetts, 1945–2000* (Chapel Hill, NC: University of North Carolina Press, 2017).

21. Hirsch, *Making the Second Ghetto*; Caro, *Power Broker*; Martin Anderson, *The Federal Bulldozer* (Cambridge, MA: MIT Press, 1964).

22. Gail Radford, *Modern Housing for America: Policy Struggles in the New Deal Era* (Chicago, IL: University of Chicago Press, 1996), pp. 59–84; Rodgers, *Atlantic Crossings*, pp. 461–68; D. Bradford Hunt, *Blueprint for Disaster: The Unraveling of Chicago Public Housing* (Chicago, IL: University of Chicago Press, 2009).

23. Nightingale, *Segregation*, pp. 341–58.

24. Nightingale, *Segregation*, pp. 341–58; David M. P. Freund, *Colored Property: State Policy and White Racial Politics in Suburban America* (Chicago, IL: University of Chicago Press, 2007).

25. Freund, *Colored Property*.

26. Robert O. Self, *American Babylon: Race and the Struggle for Postwar Oakland* (Princeton, NJ: Princeton University Press, 2003), pp. 256–90; Matthew Lassiter, *The Silent Majority: Suburban Politics in the Sunbelt South* (Princeton, NJ: Princeton University Press, 2006), pp. 1–20, 69–93, 148–74; Kevin Kruse, *White Flight: Atlanta and the Making of Modern Conservatism* (Princeton, NJ: Princeton University Press, 2007), pp. 3–18, 78–104, 161–79.

27. Heather D. DeHaan, *Stalinist City Planning: Professionals, Performance, and Power* (Toronto: University of Toronto Press, 2013), pp. 40–63.

28. Philipp Meuser and Dimitrij Zadorin, *Toward a Typology of Soviet Mass Housing: Prefabrication in the USSR, 1959–1991* (Berlin: DOM, 2015); Katherine Zubovitch, *Moscow Monumental: Soviet Skyscrapers and Urban Life in Stalin's Capital* (Princeton, NJ: Princeton University Press, 2020).

29. First quotation from Nikita Khrushchev, "The Crimes of the Stalin Era: Special Report to the 20th Congress of the Communist Party of the Soviet Union, available at https://digitalarchive .wilsoncenter.org/document/115995.pdf?v=3c22b71b65bcbbe9fdfadead9419c995 (accessed August 6, 2021). Second quotation from Henry W. Morton, "Housing in the Soviet Union," *Proceedings of the Academy of Political Science* 35 (1984):72; Robert E. Philleo, "Building Materials and Components," essay delivered at the Conference on Soviet Construction and Urban Design, Washington, D.C., December 19, 1979, www.wilsoncenter.org/sites/default/files/media/docu ments/publication/op83_building_materials_components_philleo_1979.pdf (accessed August 6, 2021).

30. Robert E. Philleo, "Building Materials and Components"; Morton, "Housing in the Soviet Union"; Meuser and Zadorin, *Toward a Typology of Soviet Mass Housing.*

31. Quote from Ilya Uthekhin et al., "*Komunalka*: Communal Living on the Soviet Union," an "online ethnographic museum" at http://kommunalka.colgate.edu/cfm/about.cfm; quotation from essay on "Outer City Housing Complexes (Novostroiki) at http://kommunalka.colgate.edu/cfm/essays .cfm?ClipID=534&TourID=900 (accessed August 6, 2021); Steven E. Harris, *Communism on Tomorrow Street: Mass Housing and Everyday Life after Stalin* (Baltimore, MD: Johns Hopkins University Press, 2013).

32. Uthekhin et al., "*Komunalka*: Communal Living," see essays and videos on daily life in the Komunalki.

33. Annemarie Sammartino, "Mass Housing, Late Modernism and the Forging of Community in New York City and East Berlin, 1965–1989," *American Historical Review* 122 (2016): 492–521; Hervé Vieillard-Baron, *Les banlieues françaises, ou le ghetto impossible* (Paris: Éditions de l'Aube, 1994); Christian Bachmann and Nicole Le Guennec, *Violences Urbaines: Ascension et chute des classes moyennes à travers cinquante ans de politique de la ville* (Paris: Albin Michel, 1996); Sako Musterd and Wim Ostendorf, eds., *Urban Segregation and the Welfare State: Inequality and Exclusion in Western Cities* (London: Routledge, 1998); Enzo Mingione, ed., *Urban Poverty and the Underclass: A Reader* (London: Blackwell, 1996).

34. Rosemary Wakeman, *The Heroic City: Paris, 1945–58* (Chicago, IL: University of Chicago Press, 2009), pp. 42–50, 145–61, 312–27; Hervé Vieillard-Baron, *Les Banlieues: Des singularités françaises aux réalités mondiales* (Paris: Hachette, 2001), pp. 129–41.

35. Françoise Jarrige, Emmanuel Négrier, and Marc Smyrl, "Urban Governance, Land Use, and Housing Affordablity: A Transatlantic Comparison," in *The Suburban Land Question: A Global Survey*, ed. Richard Harris and Ute Lehrer (Toronto: University of Toronto Press, 2018), pp. 240–57.

36. Richard Harris, *Unplanned Suburbs: Toronto's American Tragedy, 1900–1950* (Baltimore, MD: Johns Hopkins University Press, 1996); Seamus O'Hanlan, "'A Victorian Community Overseas' Transformed: Demographic and Morphological Change in Suburban Melbourne, Australia, 1947–1981," *Urban History* 42 (2015): 463–82; Nightingale, *Segregation*, pp. 358–82.

37. Sonia Hirt, "Alternative Peripheries: Socialist Mass Housing Compared with Modern Suburbia," in *The Suburban Land Question: A Global Survey*, ed. Richard Harris and Ute Lehrer (Toronto: University of Toronto Press, 2018), pp. 43–61; Kimberly Zarecor, *Manufacturing a Socialist Modernity: Housing in Czechoslovakia, 1945–1960* (Pittsburgh, PA: University of Pittsburgh Press, 2011); Annemarie Sammartino, "The New Socialist Man in the *Plattenbau*: The East German Housing Program and the Development of the Socialist Way of Life," *Journal of Urban History* 44 (2017): 79–94.

38. Tony Judt, *Postwar: A History of Europe since 1945* (New York: Penguin, 2005), pp.250–54; Ann Tusa, *The Last Division: A History of Berlin, 1945–1989* (Boston, MA: Addison Wesley, 1997); Alexandra Richie, *Faust's Metropolis: A History of Berlin* (New York: Harper Collins, 1998).

39. Tusa, *The Last Division*, pp. 39–40, 192–95, 252–60.

40. Tusa, *The Last Division*, pp. 247–48, 270–71, 331–32.

41. Tusa, *The Last Division*, pp. 376–80.

20 GATHERING VELOCITIES II: LIBERATION AND "DEVELOPMENT"

1. Jim Masselos, *Indian Nationalism: A History* (New Delhi: Sterling, 2013), pp. 214–19, 233–35.

2. Stanley Wolpert, *Gandhi's Passion: The Life and Legacy of Mahatma Gandhi* (Oxford University Press, 2002), pp. 13–19; Frank Moraes, *Jawaharlal Nehru* (Mumbai: Jaico Publishing House, 2007), pp.17–31. For a history of another urban community who negotiated colonial subservience with opportunities within the British empire, see Bernard Z. Keo, "Between Empire and Nation(s): The Peranakan Chinese of the Straits Settlements, 1890–1948," in *Amidst Empires: Colonialism, China and the Chinese, 1839–1997*, ed. Peter Monteath and Matthew Fitzpatrick (Abingdon: Routledge, 2020).

3. Nicholas Owen, "The Soft Heart of the British Empire: Indian Radicals in Edwardian London," *Past & Present* 220 (2013): 143–84; Wolpert, *Gandhi's Passion*, pp. 20–28.
4. Moraes, *Jawaharlal Nehru*, pp. 3–47.
5. Marc Matera, *Black London: The Imperial Metropolis and Decolonization in the Twentieth Century* (Berkeley, CA: University of California Press, 2015), pp. 22–61; also see Lara Putnam, *Radical Moves: Caribbean Migrants and the Politics of Race in the Jazz Age* (Chapel Hill, NC: University of North Carolina Press, 2013).
6. Michael Goebel, "Forging a Proto-Third World? Latin America and the League Against Imperialism," in *The League Against Imperialism: Lives and Afterlives*, ed. Michele Louro, Carolien Stolte, Heather Streets-Salter, and Sana Tannoury-Karam (Leiden: Leiden University Press, 2020), pp. 53–78. An earlier use of this term is Mike Davis, *Late Victorian Holocausts: El Niño Famines and the Making of the Third World* (London: Verso, 2001), p. 289. Also see Michael Goebel, *Anti-imperial Metropolis: Interwar Paris and the Seeds of Third World Nationalism* (Cambridge: Cambridge University Press, 2015), pp. 1–175; Matera, *Black London*, pp. 62–144; Thomas Lindner, "Transnational Networks of Anti-imperialism: Mexico City in the 1920s" (Ph.D. Thesis, Technische Universität Berlin, 2016); William E. Nelson Jr., *Black Atlantic Politics: Dilemmas of Political Power in Boston and Liverpool* (Albany, NY: State University of New York Press, 2000); Putnam, *Radical Moves*; David Motadel, "The Global Authoritarian Moment and the Revolt against Empire," *American Historical Review* 124 (2019): 843–77.
7. Wolpert, *Gandhi's Passion*, pp. 219–20; on colonial cities as sites of resistance see Steven Legg, *The City as Site of Movements*, at http://egyankosh.ac.in/handle/123456789/44506 (accessed August 7, 2021); Howard Spodek, *Ahmedabad: Shock City of Twentieth-Century India* (Bloomington, IN: Indiana University Press, 2011); Su Lin Lewis, *Cities in Motion: Urban Life and Cosmopolitanism in Southeast Asia, 1920–1940* (Cambridge: Cambridge University Press, 2016), pp. 181–26.
8. Sumit Sarkar, *The Swadeshi Movement in Bengal, 1903–1908* (Ranikhett Cantonment: Permanent Black, 1973); Wolpert, *Gandhi's Passion*, pp. 99–114.
9. Prashant Kidambi, "Nationalism and the City in Colonial India: Bombay, c. 1890–1940," *Journal of Urban History* 38 (2012): 950–67; Richard I. Cashman, *The Myth of the Lokamanya: Tilak and Mass Politics in Maharashtra* (Berkeley, CA: University of California Press, 1975); Suranjan Das, *Communal Riots in Bengal 1905–1947* (Delhi: Oxford University Press, 1991); Jim Masselos, *The City in Action: Bombay Struggles for Power* (Oxford: Oxford University Press, 2007), pp. 15–45, 105–24; Nandini Gooptu, *The Politics of the Urban Poor in Early Twentieth-Century India* (Cambridge: Cambridge University Press, 2001).
10. Wolpert, *Gandhi's Passion*, pp. 135–52; Masselos, *The City in Action*, pp. 153–384.
11. Kidambi, "Nationalism and the City"; Masselos, *The City in Action;* Wolpert, *Gandhi's Passion*, pp. 153–81.
12. Wolpert, *Gandhi's Passion*, pp. 182–243.
13. Wolpert, *Gandhi's Passion*, pp. 244–68.
14. Toby Lincoln, "The Rural and Urban at War: Invasion and Reconstruction in China during the Anti-Japanese War of Resistance," *Journal of Urban History* 38 (2012): 114–32; Toby Lincoln, *Urbanizing China in War and Peace: The Case of Wuxi County* (Honolulu, HI: University of Hawai'i Press, 2015); Lyman P. Van Slyke, "The Chinese Communist Movement during the Sino-Japanese War, 1937–1945," in *The Cambridge History of China, Volume 13. Republican China, 1912–1949: Part 2*, ed. J. K. Fairbank and A. Feuerwerker (Cambridge: Cambridge University Press, 1986.), pp. 609–72, quotation from p. 631; Jonathan D. Spence, *The Search for Modern China* (New York: W. W. Norton, 2001), pp. 419–88.
15. Quotation from Spence, *The Search for Modern China*, p. 484.
16. Adrian Vickers, *A History of Modern Indonesia* (Cambridge: Cambridge University Press, 2005), pp. 87–116.
17. Marilyn Young, *Vietnam Wars, 1945–1990* (New York: Harper Collins, 1991), pp. 1–123.
18. Young, *Vietnam Wars*, pp. 124–299; Alberto Manuel Bautista, *The Hukbalahap Movement in the Philippines, 1942–1952* (Berkeley, CA: University of California Press, 1952); Richard Stubbs,

Hearts and Minds in Guerilla Warfare: The Malayan Emergency 1948–1960 (Singapore: Eastern University Press, 2004).

19. Frederick Cooper, *Africa since 1940: The Past of the Present* (Cambridge: Cambridge University Press, 2002), pp. 20–37; Frederick Cooper, *Decolonization and African Society: The Labor Question in French and British Africa* (Cambridge: Cambridge University Press, 1996); Frederick Cooper, ed., *Struggle for the City: Migrant Labor, Capital, and the State in Urban Africa* (Beverly Hills, CA: Sage, 1983); Emily Callaci, *Street Archives and City Life: Popular Intellectuals in Postcolonial Tanzania* (Durham, NC: Duke University Press, 2017); George Robert, *Revolutionary State-Making in Dar es Salaam: African Liberation and the Global Cold War, 1961–1974* (Cambridge: Cambridge University Press, 2021).

20. Quotation from Cooper, *Africa since 1940*, p. 33.

21. Cooper, *Africa since 1940*, pp. 38–84.

22. Jeffrey James Byrne, *Mecca of Revolution: Algeria, Decolonization, and the Third World Order* (Oxford: Oxford University Press, 2016); Elaine Mokhtefi, *Algiers, Third World Capital: Freedom Fighters, Revolutionaries, Black Panthers* (London: Verso, 2018).

23. Mokhtefi, *Algiers, Third World Capital*; Zohra Drif, *Inside the Battle of Algiers: Memoir of a Woman Freedom Fighter*, trans. Andrew Farrand (Charlottesville, VA: Just World Books, 2017); Todd Shepherd, *The Invention of Decolonization: The Algerian War and the Remaking of France* (Ithaca, NY: Cornell University Press, 2006), pp. 229–42.

24. Sharon Rotbard, *White City, Black City: Architecture and War in Tel Aviv and Jaffa* (Cambridge, MA; MIT Press, 2015); Walid Khalidi, *From Haven to Conquest: Readings in Zionism and the Palestinian Problem until 1948* (Washington, D.C.: Institute of Palestinian Studies, 1967); Yael Allweil, *Homeland: Zionism as Housing Regime, 1860–2011* (London: Routledge, 2017); Ayala Levin, "South African 'Know-How' and Israeli 'Facts of Life': The Planning of Afridar, Ashkelon, 1949–56," *Planning Perspectives* 34 (2019): 285–309.

25. Ilan Pappé, *The Ethnic Cleansing of Palestine* (Oxford: Oneworld, 2006); Benny Morris, *The Birth of the Palestinian Refugee Problem Revisited* (Cambridge: Cambridge University Press, 2004); Rotbard, *White City, Black City*; Carl H. Nightingale, *Segregation: A Global History of Divided Cities* (Chicago, IL: University of Chicago Press, 2012), pp. 411–21.

26. Nightingale, *Segregation*, pp. 358–82, 411–21.

27. T. R. H. Davenport and Christopher Saunders, *South Africa: A Modern History* (London: Macmillan, 2000), pp. 406–25, 449–54, 466–71; Tom Lodge, *Sharpeville: An Apartheid Massacre and Its Consequences* (Oxford: Oxford University Press, 2011); Philip Bonner and Lauren Segal, *Soweto: A History* (Cape Town: Maskew, Miller, Longman, 1998), pp. 78–82; Sifiso Mxolisi Ndlovu, *The Soweto Uprisings: Counter-memories of 1976* (Johannesburg: Ravan, 1998); George Roberts, "Politics, Decolonisation, and the Cold War in Dar es Salaam c. 1965–72" (Ph.D. Thesis, University of Warwick, 2016).

28. Seve C. Topik and Allen Wells, *The Second Conquest of Latin America: Coffee, Henequen, and Oil during the Export Boom, 1850–1930* (Austin, TX: University of Texas Press, 1998); William Roseberry, Lowell Gudmundsom, and Mario Samper Kutschbach, eds., *Coffee, Society, and Power in Latin America* (Baltimore, MD: Johns Hopkins Press, 1995); Sven Beckert, *Empire of Cotton: A Global History* (New York: Knopf, 2014), pp. 93–94, 256–57, 399–401.

29. William Blum, *Killing Hope: U.S. Military and CIA Interventionism since World War II* (Monroe, ME: Common Courage Press, 1995); Thomas C. Wright, *Latin America in the Era of the Cuban Revolution* (New York: Praeger, 2000); Stephen Schlesinger and Stephen Kinzer, *Bitter Fruit: The Story of the American Coup in Guatemala* (Cambridge: Harvard University Press, 2005 [1982]); Julia E. Sweig, *Inside the Cuban Revolution: Fidel Castro and the Urban Underground* (Cambridge, MA: Harvard University Press, 2004); Antonio Rafael de la Cova, *The Moncada Attack: Birth of the Cuban Revolution* (Columbia, SC: University of South Carolina Press, 2007).

30. Arturo Almandoz, *Modernization, Urbanization, and Development in Latin America 1900–2000* (Abingdon: Routledge, 2015); Michael L. Conniff, *Urban Politics in Brazil: The Rise of Populism, 1920–1945* (Pittsburgh, PA: Pittsburgh University Press, 1981); Alejandro Groppo, *The Two Princes: Juan D. Perón and Getúlio Vargas: A Comparative Study of Latin American Populism* (Villa María, Córdoba: Editorial Universitaria Villa María, 2009); Neil Lochery, *Brazil: The Fortunes of War: World War II and*

the Making of Modern Brazil (New York: Basic Books, 2014); Warren Dean, *The Industrialization of São Paulo* (Austin, TX: University of Texas Press, 1969).

31. Sankar Ghose, *Jawaharlal Nehru: A Biography* (Delhi: Allied Publishers, 1993), p. 550; Felix Wemheuer, *A Social History of Maoist China: Conflict and Change, 1949–1976* (Cambridge: Cambridge University Press, 2019), pp. 131–34; Toby Lincoln, *An Urban History of China* (Cambridge: Cambridge University Press, 2021), pp. 191–222; Cooper *Africa since 1945*, pp. 99–103; Norma Evenson, *Two Brazilian Capitals: Architecture and Urbanism in Rio de Janeiro and Brasília* (New Haven, CT: Yale University Press, 1973). Population figures for Brasília from www.macrotrends.net/cities/20187/brasilia/population (accessed August 7, 2021).

32. For the role of the Lagos Town Council in the Nigerian independence movement, see Titlola Halimat Somotan, "'In the Wider Interests of Nigeria as a Whole': Lagos and the Making of Federal Nigeria, 1941–76" (Ph.D. Thesis, Columbia University, 2020).

21 GREATEST ACCELERATIONS I: NEW EMPIRES, NEW MULTITUDES

1. Government of Delhi National Capital Territory, Planning Department, *Economic Survey of Delhi 2018–19*, pp. 23–41, available at http://delhiplanning.nic.in/content/economic-survey-delhi-2019-20 (accessed August, 8, 2021); United Nations (UN), *The World's Cities in 2018*, p. 4, available at www.un.org/en/events/citiesday/assets/pdf/the_worlds_cities_in_2018_data_booklet.pdf (accessed August 8, 2021).

2. Government of India, Ministry of Housing and Urban Affairs, National Capital Region Planning Board, *Annual Report 2017–18*, p. 3, available at http://ncrpb.nic.in/annualreports.html (accessed August 8, 2021); Mike Davis, *Planet of Slums* (London: Verso, 2006), pp10–11.

3. UN, *The World's Cities in 2018*, p. 6. A fantastic tool to compare these especially large and dense urban–rural built environments is the Earth Observation Center's "Basemaps of the Global Urban Footprint." Zoom in on each of the regions mentioned in this paragraph and compare them, for example, with Britain, the Lower Rhine, the Kanto and Kansai regions of Japan, or the East Coast of the USA, at https://geoservice.dlr.de/web/maps/eoc:guf:3857 (accessed August 8, 2021); Christopher Silver, *Planning the Megacity: Jakarta in the Twentieth Century* (London: Routledge, 2008).

4. Paul Kramer, "Power and Connection: Imperial Histories of the United States in the World," *American Historical Review* 116 (2011): 1348–91, quotations from p. 1366.

5. Joshua Freeman, *American Empire: The Rise of a Global Power, the Democratic Revolution at Home, 1945–2000* (New York: Viking, 2012), pp. 12–24, 85–90; Bruce Cumings, *Dominion from Sea to Sea: Pacific Ascendancy and American Power* (New Haven, CT: Yale University Press, 2009); Roger W. Lotchin, *Fortress California, 1910–1961: From Warfare to Welfare* (Champaign, IL: University of Illinois Press, 2002); Ann Markusen, Peter Hall, Scott Campbell, and Sabina Deitrick, eds., *The Rise of the Gunbelt: The Military Remapping of Industrial America* (New York: Oxford University Press, 1991); Kate Brown, *Plutopia: Nuclear Families, Atomic Cities, and the Great Soviet and American Plutonium Disasters* (Oxford: Oxford University Press, 2013); Kate Brown, *Manual for Survival: A Chernobyl Guide to the Future* (New York: Norton, 2019). Also, Maureen Mahoney et al., "Imperial Cityscapes: Urban History and Empire in the United States," *Neoamericanist* 5 (2010), no longer available online. A useful global "Almanac" of nuclear testing, stockpiling, launch, power generating, and disaster sites can be found at www.atomicarchive.com/almanac/index.html (accessed August 8, 2021).

6. Quotation from David Vine, "The Pentagon's New Generation of Secret Military Bases," *Mother Jones* (July 16, 2012). Daniel Immerwahr, *How to Hide an Empire: A History of the Greater United States* (New York: Farrar, Strauss and Giroux, 2019), pp. 355–71; map of "Soviet Naval Bases and Anchor Rights Abroad in 1984," at https://commons.wikimedia.org/wiki/File:Soviet_Navy_Bases_1984.png (accessed August 8, 2021).

7. Numerous maps, news clippings, audio files, and other artifacts from life on Clark Air Base can be found at www.clarkab.org/ (accessed August 8, 2021); Roshni Kapur, "After Murder, Mass Protests in Okinawa against US Bases: Tens of Thousands of Demonstrators Attended the Anti-U.S. Military Rally

in Okinawa," *The Diplomat*, June 22, 2016 at https://thediplomat.com/2016/06/after-murder-mass-protests-in-okinawa-against-us-bases/ (accessed August 8, 2021).

8. Michael M. R. Izady, "Urban Unplanning: How Violence, Walls, and Segregation Destroyed the Urban Fabric of Baghdad," *Planning Perspectives* 19 (2020): 52–68; Ron Robin, *Enclaves of America: The Rhetoric of American Political Architecture Abroad, 1900–1965* (Princeton, NJ: Princeton University Press, 1992); Jane C. Loeffler, *The Architecture of Diplomacy: Building America's Embassies* (Princeton, NJ: Princeton Architectural Press, 2011); Rajiv Chandrasekeran, *Imperial Life in the Emerald City: Inside Iraq's Green Zone* (New York; Knopf, 2006); Trevor Paglen, *Blank Spots on the Map: The Dark Geography of the Pentagon's Secret World* (New York: Duton, 2010); Philip Kennicott, Susannah George, and Lorenzo Tugnoli, "How 20 Years of Conflict Have Reshaped Afghanistan's Capital and Life in It," *Washington Post*, March 25, 2021, at https://www.washingtonpost.com/world/interactive/2021/kabul-architecture-war-us-afghanistan/?no_nav=true&tid=a_classic-iphone (accessed March 25, 2021).

9. Raymond Pearson, *The Rise and Fall of the Soviet Empire* (Houndsmill: Palgrave, 2002); David Zucchino and Kiana Hayeri, "In the Shabby Chic Towers in Kabul's Heart, History Lives," *New York Times*, April 10, 2020, at https://nyti.ms/2JXDSnb (accessed August 8, 2021).

10. Andrew Friedmann, *Covert Capital: Landscapes of Denial and the Making of U.S. Empire in the Suburbs of Northern Virginia* (Berkeley, CA: University of California Press, 2013); John L. H. Keep, *Last of the Empires: A History of the Soviet Union 1945–1991* (Oxford: Oxford University Press, 1995), pp. 183–202; William Blum, *Killing Hope: US Military and CIA Interventions since World War II* (London: Zed Books, 2003); Stephen Kinzer, *Overthrow: America's Century of Regime Change from Hawaii to Iraq* (New York: Times Books, 2006); Noel Maurer, *The Empire Trap: The Rise and Fall of U.S. Intervention to Protect American Property Overseas, 1893–2013* (Princeton, NJ: Princeton University Press, 2013); Kyle Keith, *Suez: The End of Britain's Empire in the Middle East* (London: Tauris, 2003); Camilo Trumper, *Ephemeral Histories: Public Art, Politics, and the Struggle for the Streets in Chile* (Berkeley, CA: University of California Press, 2016).

11. Saskia Sassen, *The Global City: New York, London, Tokyo* (Princeton, NJ: Princeton University Press, 2002); André Sorensen, "Building World City Tokyo: Globalization and Conflict over Urban Space," *Annals of Regional Science* 37 (2002): 519–31. For more on growing downtown business districts from the 1970s, see Tracy Neumann, *Remaking the Rustbelt: Postindustrial Transformation of North America* (Philadelphia, PA: University of Pennsylvania Press, 2016), pp. 107–36; Gary McDonagh and Marina Peterson, eds., *Global Downtowns* (Philadelphia, PA: University of Pennsylvania Press, 2012); Seamus O'Hanlon, *Melbourne Remade: The Inner City since the Seventies* (Melbourne: Arcade, 2010).

12. Katharina Pistor, *The Code of Capital: How the Law Creates Wealth and Inequality* (Princeton, NJ: Princeton University Press, 2019), pp. 132–235; Sassen, *The Global City*.

13. John L. Brooke, *Climate Change and the Course of Global History: A Rough Journey* (Cambridge: Cambridge University Press, 2016), pp. 530–32; John R. McNeill, *Something New under the Sun: An Environmental History of the Twentieth-Century World* (New York: W. W. Norton, 2000), pp. 269–95; United Nations Dept of Economic and Social Affairs, *World Population Prospects 2019* (New York: United Nations, 2019).

14. McNeill, *Something New under the Sun*, pp. 192–227.

15. McNeill, *Something New under the Sun*, pp. 192–227; Steven Johnson, *Extra Life: A Short History of Living Longer* (New York: Riverhead, 2021), pp. xi–34; Tasha Rijke-Epstein, "The Politics of Filth: Sanitation and Competing Moralities in Urban Madagascar 1890s–1972," *Journal of African History* 60 (2019): 229–56; Celia Miralles Buil, "La tuberculose et la surpopulation urbaine en Espagne au début du XXe siècle," *Histoire, Economie, Société* 1 (2017): 57–75.

16. Mark Harrison, *Disease and the Modern World: 1500 to the Present Day* (Malden, MA: Polity, 2004), Chapters 5 and 6.

17. Harrison, *Disease and the Modern World*, Chapters 6 and 7.

18. Susan George, *A Fate Worse Than Debt: The World Financial Crisis and the Poor* (London: Penguin, 1988).

19. Quinn Slobodian, *Globalists: The End of Empire and the Birth of Neoliberalism* (Cambridge, MA: Harvard University Press, 2018); Harrison, *Disease and the Modern World*, Chapter 8.

20. McNeill, *Something New under the Sun*, pp. 192–227; Harrison, *Disease and the Modern World*, Chapter 8; Lawrence Wright, *The Plague Year: America in the Time of Covid* (New York: Knopf, 2021), pp. 194–203.

21. UNICEF and the World Health Organization (WHO), *Progress on Household Drinking Water, Sanitation, and Wastewater, 2000–2017: A Focus on Inequalities* (New York: UNICEF/WHO, 2019).

22. Athar Hussein and Saif Said, "Pollution Mapping of Yamuna River Segment Passing through Delhi Using High-Resolution GeoEye-2 Imagery," *Applied River Science* 9 (2019): article 46, at https://doi .org/10.1007/s13201-019-0923-y (accessed August 8, 2021); Water Privatisation and Commercialization Resistance Committee, "Privatisation of Water Services in New Delhi: Myth and Reality," booklet, 2012, at www.indiawaterportal.org/articles/privatisation-water-services-new-delhi-myth-and-reality-report-water-privatisation (accessed August 8, 2021).

23. Delhi-specific data are available in Government of the National Capital Territory, *Delhi Human Development Report 2013* (New Delhi: Academic Foundation, 2014), pp. 122–61. Ramanan Laxminarayan and Nirmal Kumar Ganguly, "India's Vaccine Deficit: Why More Than Half of Indian Children Are Not Fully Immunized, and What Can – and Should – Be Done," *Health Affairs*, June 2011 at www.healthaffairs.org/doi/full/10.1377/hlthaff.2011.0405 (accessed August 8, 2021).

24. Nick Cullather, *Hungry World: America's Cold War Battle against Poverty in Asia* (Cambridge, MA: Harvard University Press, 2010), Introduction and Chapter 1.

25. Cullather, *Hungry World*, Chapters 2, 6, and throughout.

26. Cullather, *Hungry World*. Quotations from Nehru and Nasser in McNeill, *Something New under the Sun*, pp. 161, 168–69.

27. Felix Wemheuer, *A Social History of Maoist China: Conflict and Change, 1949–1976* (Cambridge: Cambridge University Press, 2019), pp. 120–160; Toby Lincoln, *An Urban History of China* (Cambridge: Cambridge University Press, 2021), pp. 191–222.

28. Joshua Eisenmann, *Red China's Green Revolution: Technological Innovation, Institutional Change, and Economic Development under the Commune* (New York: Columbia University Press, 2018), pp. 1–25 and Figure 1.4, p. 23. Wemheuer, *A Social History of Maoist China*, pp. 100–6, 120–52; Joshua B. Freeman, *Behemoth: A History of the Factory and the Making of the Modern World* (New York: Norton, 2018), p. 275–79.

29. Cullather, *Hungry World*, Introduction.

30. R. S Deshpande and Saroj Arora, *Agrarian Crisis and Farmer Suicides: Land Reforms in India, Volume 12* (New Delhi: Sage, 2010); Vandan Shiva, *The Violence of the Green Revolution* (Lexington, KY: University Press of Kentucky, 2016); Puneet Kumar Sharma, "Farmers from UP March towards Delhi to Protest over Agri Crisis, Heavy Security Deployed," *India Today*, September 21, 2019, at www.indiatoday.in/ india/story/farmers-from-up-march-towards-delhi-protest-over-agri-crisis-heavy-security-deployed-160 1557-2019-09-21 (accessed August 8, 2021); Jeffrey Gettleman, Suhasini Raj, and Sameer Yasir, "New Delhi Streets Turn into Battleground Hindus vs Muslims," *New York Times*, February 25, 2020 at www .nytimes.com/2020/02/25/world/asia/new-delhi-hindu-muslim-violence.html (accessed August 8, 2021).

31. Quotation from Julia Adeney Thomas, Mark Williams, and Jan Zalasiewicz, *Anthropocene: A Multidisciplinary Approach* (Cambridge, UK: Polity Press, 2020), p. 27; also see Johan Rockström et al., "Planetary Boundaries: Exploring the Safe Operating Space for Humanity," *Ecology and Society* 14, no. 2 (2009): online at https://www.ecologyandsociety.org/vol14/iss2/art32/.

32. Deshpande and Arora, *Agrarian Crisis and Farmer Suicides*.

33. Cullather, *Hungry World*, Chapters 8–10; Bogumil Terminski, *Development-Induced Displacement and Resettlement: Causes, Consequences, and Socio-legal Context* (Stuttgart: Ibidem Press, 2015). On Slavery, UN Migration, "Migration Trends," at www.iom.int/global-migration-trends (accessed August 8, 2021).

34. United Nations International Organization for Migration (IOM), *World Migration Report 2015 – Migration and Cities: New Partnerships to Manage Mobility* (Geneva: IOM, 2015); IOM, *International Migration Report 2020* (Geneva: IOM, 2020).

22 GREATEST ACCELERATIONS II: SHACKS AND CITADELS

1. United Nations Human Settlements Program (UN HABITAT), *The Challenge of Slums: Global Report on Human Settlements, 2003* (London: UN HABITAT, 2006).

2. Ananya Roy, "What Is Urban about Critical Urban Theory?," *Urban Geography* (2015): 1–14; Ananya Roy, "Urbanisms, Worlding Practices and the Theory of Planning," *Planning Theory* 10 (2011): 6–15; Gautam Bhan, *In the Public's Interest: Evictions, Citizenship and Inequality in Contemporary Delhi* (Athens, GA: University of Georgia Press, 2016), pp. 11–12; Alan Mayne, *Slums: The History of a Global Injustice* (London: Reaktion Books, 2017), pp. 7–18, 157–288.

3. Mike Davis, *Planet of Slums* (London: Verso, 2006), pp. 50–69; Brodwyn Fischer, *A Poverty of Rights: Citizenship and Inequality in Twentieth-Century Rio de Janeiro* (Stanford, CA: Stanford University Press, 2008), pp. 89–150; Emilio de Antuñano, "Planning a 'Mass City': The Politics of Planning in Mexico City, 1930–1960" (Ph.D. Thesis, University of Chicago, 2017); AbdouMaliq Simone, *For the City Yet to Come: Changing African Life in Four Cities* (Durham, NC: Duke University Press, 2004), pp. 164–78; Akin L. Mabogunje, "Urban Planning and the Post-colonial State in Africa: A Research Overview," *African Studies Review* 33 (1990): 121–203; Godwin Arku and Richard Harris, "Housing as a Tool of Economic Development since 1929," *International Journal of Urban and Regional Research* 29 (2005): 895–915; Richard Harris, "Development and Hybridity Made Concrete in the Colonies," *Environment and Planning A* 40 (2008): 15–36.

4. Nancy H. Kwak, *A World of Homeowners: American Power and the Politics of Housing Aid* (Chicago, IL: University of Chicago Press, 2015), pp. 46–165, 207–36, quotation on p. 156; Amy Offner, *Sorting Out the Mixed Economy: The Rise and Fall of Welfare States and Developmental States in the Americas* (Princeton, NJ: Princeton University Press, 2019), pp. 79–114; Richard Harris, "Slipping through the Cracks: The Origins of Aided Self-Help Housing 1918–1953," *Housing Studies* 14 (1999): 281–309; Leandro Benmergui, "The Alliance for Progress and Housing Policy in Rio de Janeiro and Buenos Aires in the 1960s," *Urban History* 36 (2009): 303–26; Alexandra Biehler, Armelle Choplin, and Marie Morelle, "Social Housing in Africa: A Model to be (Re)Invented?," trans. Oliver Waine, PDF from *Metropolitiques.eu* at https://metropolitiques.eu/Social-housing-in-Africa-a-model.html (accessed August 10, 2021).

5. Xing Quan Zhang, "Chinese Housing Policy, 1949–76: The Development of a Welfare System," *Planning Perspectives* 12 (1997): 433–55; Felix Wemheuer, *A Social History of Maoist China: Conflict and Change, 1949–1976* (Cambridge: Cambridge University Press, 2019), pp. 87–96, 131–34; Toby Lincoln, *An Urban History of China* (Cambridge: Cambridge University Press, 2021), pp. 191–222; Zhu Qian, "Shanghai's Socialist Suburbanization 1953–1962," *Planning Perspectives* 17 (2018): 226–47.

6. Quotation from Wemheuer, *A Social History of Maoist China*, p. 68, also see pp. 96–98, 164–70.

7. Dirk Hoerder, *Cultures in Contact: World Migrations in the Second Millennium* (Durham, NC: Duke University Press, 2002), pp. 564–82.

8. Davis, *Planet of Slums*, pp. 51–61; Deborah Cohen, *Braceros: Migrant Citizens and Transnational Subjects in Postwar United States and Mexico* (Chapel Hill, NC: University of North Carolina Press, 2011); Mae Ngai, *Impossible Subjects: Illegal Aliens and the Making of Modern America* (Princeton, NJ: Princeton University Press, 2004), pp. 127–66.

9. Susan K. Brown and Frank D. Bean, "International Migration," in *Handbook of Population*, ed. Dudley L. Poston and Michael Micklin (Boston, MA: Springer, 2005), pp. 347–82.

10. Elizabeth Vallet, ed., *Borders, Fences, and Walls: State of Insecurity?* (Farnham: Ashgate, 2014); Sasha D Pack, *The Deepest Border: The Strait of Gibraltar and the Making of the Modern Hispano-African Borderland* (Stanford, CA: Stanford University Press, 2019); Sarah Lopez, *The Remittance Landscape: Spaces of Migration in Rural Mexico and Urban USA* (Chicago, IL: University of Chicago Press, 2015); C. J. Alvarez, *Border Land, Border Water: A History of the Construction of the US–Mexico Divide* (Austin, TX: University of Texas Press, 2019).

11. The best resource on contemporary detention centers and policies is the website of the Global Detention Project at www.globaldetentionproject.org (accessed August 10, 2021). Also, UNHCR,

"Global Trends: Forced Displacement 2018," at www.unhcr.org/figures-at-a-glance.html; Warsaw Institute, "US and European Immigration Policies," at https://warsawinstitute.org/us-eu-immigration-policies (both accessed August 10, 2021). For an article on a Madrid shantytown during the Covid-19 epidemic, see Leah Pattem, "Spanish Shantytown Residents Face Third Month without Power as Snow Forecast," *The Guardian*, December 7, 2020 at www.theguardian.com/world/2020/d ec/07/spain-shantytown-residents-facing-third-month-without-power-as-snow-forecast-canada-real (accessed August 10, 2021).

12. A useful list of refugee camps is contained in the Wikipedia article "Refugee Camp," at https://en .wikipedia.org/wiki/Refugee_camp (accessed August 10, 2021). For city-like camps, see "Inside the World's Largest Refugee Camps," at www.arcgis.com/apps/MapJournal/index.html?appid=8ff1 d1534e8c41adb5c04ab435b7974b (accessed August 10, 2021).

13. Joshua Freeman, *Working Class New York: Life and Labor since World War II* (New York: New Press, 2000); Kim Phillips-Fein, *Fear City: New York's Fiscal Crisis and the Rise of Austerity Politics* (New York: Holt, 2017).

14. Phillips-Fein, *Fear City*.

15. Howard Wachtel, *Money Mandarins: The Making of a Supranational Monetary Order* (Armonk, NY: M. E. Sharpe, 1990); Adam Tooze, *Crashed: How a Decade of Financial Crises Changed the World* (New York: Penguin, 2019).

16. Saskia Sassen, *The Global City: New York, London, Tokyo* (Princeton, NJ: Princeton University Press, 2002); Sharon Zukin, *Loft Living: Culture and Capital in Urban Change* (New Brunswick, NJ: Rutgers University Press, 1989); Aaron Shkuda, *The Lofts of Soho: Gentrification, Art, and Industry in New York, 1950–1980* (Chicago, IL: University of Chicago Press, 2016). Quotation from "Frances Goldman, 95, Firebrand Who Fought for the Lower East Side for Decades," *New York Times*, May 19, 2020.

17. Robert Fitch, *The Assassination of New York* (New York: Verso, 1993); Jonathan Sofer, *Ed Koch and the Rebuilding of New York City* (New York: Columbia University Press, 2010).

18. Americas Society (AS)/Council of the Americas (COA), *Immigration to New York City: The Contributions of Immigrants to the Revival of New York's Renaissance 1975–2013* (New York: AS/COA, 2014); Sassen, *The Global City*.

19. Neil Smith, *The New Frontier: Gentrification and the Revanchist City* (London: Routledge, 1997); Neil Smith, *Uneven Development: Nature, Capital, and the Production of Space* (Athens, GA: University of Georgia Press, 2008 [1984]); Saul Stein, *Capital City: Gentrification and the Real Estate State* (London: Verso, 2019); Peter Moskowitz, *How to Kill a City: Gentrification, Inequality, and the Fight for the Neighborhood* (New York: Nation Books, 2018); Judith De Sena and Timothy Shortell, eds., *The World in Brooklyn: Gentrification, Immigration, and Ethnic Politics in a Global City* (Lanham, MD; Lexington, 2011); Susan S. Fainstein, *The City Builders: Property, Politics, and Planning in London and New York* (Oxford: Blackwell, 1994); Loretta Lees, *Planetary Gentrification* (Cambridge: Polity Press, 2016); Alexia Yates, *Real Estate in Global Urban History* (Cambridge: Cambridge University Press, 2021).

20. If "outstanding derivatives" are not included in the measure of the value of financial assets, real estate wealth is larger than wealth in financial instruments, at least as measured in these two reports: Yolanda Barnes, "8 Things to Know about Global Real Estate Value," in Savills, *Impacts: The Future of Global Real Estate*, July 2018 at www.savills.com/impacts/market-trends/8-things-you-need-to-know-about-the-value-of-global-real-estate.html (accessed August 10, 2021); Saskia Sassen, "Investment in Urban Land is on the Rise: We Need to Know Who Owns Our Cities," *The Conversation*, August 6, 2016 at https://theconversation.com/investment-in-urban-land-is-on-the-rise-we-need-to-know-who-owns-our-cities-63485 (accessed August 10, 2021). For historical contexts of this land war, see Yates, *Real Estate*; André Sorensen, "Institutions in Urban Space: Land, Infrastructure and Governance in the Production of Urban Property," *Planning Theory and Practice* 19 (2018): 21–38; Fainstein, *The City Builders*, pp. 170–217; Teresa P. R. Caldeira, *City of Walls: Crime Segregation, and Citizenship in São Paulo* (Berkeley, CA: University of California Press, 2000).

21. Tooze, *Crashed*; Christopher K. Odinet, *Foreclosed: Mortgage Servicing and the Hidden Architecture of Homeownership in America* (Cambridge: Cambridge University Press, 2019).

22. Heiko Schmid: *Economy of Fascination: Dubai and Chicago as Themed Urban Landscapes* (Berlin: Bornträger, 2009); Oliver Bullough, *Moneyland: The Inside Story of the Crooks and Kleptocrats Who Rule the World* (New York: St. Martin's Press, 2018).

23. Quotation from Real Insights, "Savills Report: How Much Is the World Worth? India Is Set for Rapid Gains in the World's Most Valuable Asset," in *Smartowner* (Bangalore) January 17, 2019 at www .smartowner.com/blog/author/smartowner-insights/ (accessed August 10, 2021).

24. D. Asher Ghertner, *Rule by Aesthetics: World-Class City-Making in Delhi* (Oxford: Oxford University Press, 2015). An engaging literary expose of life among Delhi's elite is Rana Das Gupta, *Capital: The Eruption of Delhi* (New York: Penguin, 2014); "Savill's Report." For similar dynamics in Brazil, see Caldeira, *City of Walls*.

25. Erhard Berner, "Learning from Informal Markets: Innovative Approaches to Land and Housing Provision," *Development in Practice* 11 (2001): 292–307, first quotation from p. 295. Second quotation from Nandini Gooptu, *The Politics of the Urban Poor in Early Twentieth-Century India* (Cambridge: Cambridge University Press, 2001), p. 84; Anahí Ballent, *Las huellas de la política: Vivienda, ciudad, peronismo en Buenos Aires, 1943–1955* (Bernal: Editorial Universidad Nacional de Quilmes, 2009); Leandro Benmergui, "The Alliance for Progress and Housing Policy in Rio de Janeiro and Buenos Aires in the 1960s," *Urban History* 36 (2009): 303–26.

26. Davis, *Planet of Slums*, pp. 95–120; Ananya Roy, "The Gentleman's City: Urban Informality in the Calcutta of New Communism," in *Urban Informality: Transnational Perspectives from the Middle East, Latin American, and South Asia*, ed. Ananya Roy and Nezar AlSayyad (Lanham, MD: Lexington Books, 2004), pp. 147–70; Sheetal Chhabria, *Making the Modern Slum: The Power of Capital in Colonial Bombay* (Seattle, WA: University of Washington Press, 2019); Constanza Castro Benavides, "El mercado global y la ciudad de los pobres: La política de la vivienda social en Colombia 2010–2018" (Ph.D. Thesis, Universidad De Los Andes, 2018); Michael Sugarmann, "Reclaiming Rangoon: (Post-) Imperial Urbanism and Poverty, 1920–1962," *Modern Asian Studies* 52 (2018): 1856–87; Janice E. Perlman, *The Myth of Marginality: Urban Poverty and Politics in Rio de Janeiro* (Berkeley, CA: University of California Press, 1976), pp. 195–241; Fischer, *A Poverty of Rights*, pp. 50–89, 213–301. Quotation from René Collignon, "La lutte des pouvoirs publics contre les 'encombrements humains' à Dakar," *Canadian Journal of African Studies* 18 (1984): 573–82.

27. Qin Shao, *Shanghai Gone: Domicide and Defiance in a Chinese Megacity* (Lanham, MD: Rowman & Littlefield, 2013); Harriet Evans, *Beijing from Below: Stories of Marginal Lives in the Capital's Center* (Durham, NC: Duke University Press, 2020); Dorothy J. Solinger, *Contesting Citizenship in Urban China: Peasant Migrants, the State, and the Logic of the Market* (Berkeley, CA: University of California Press, 1999); You-tien Hsing, *The Great Urban Transformation: Politics of Land and Property in China* (Oxford: Oxford University Press, 2010), pp. 1–59; Yan Zhang and Ke Fang, "Is History Repeating Itself? From Urban Renewal in the United States to Inner-City Redevelopment in China," *Journal of Planning Education and Research* 23 (2004): 286–98; Lincoln, *An Urban History of China*, pp. 223–53; Jo Blason, "China's Nail Houses: The Homeowoners Who Refuse to Make Way," *Guardian*, April 15, 2014, at www .theguardian.com/cities/gallery/2014/apr/15/china-nail-houses-in-pictures-property-development (accessed August 10, 2021). For a fantastic photographic journey into Shanghai's quickly disappearing Old Town, see Katya Knyazeva and Adam Sinykin, *Shanghai Old Town, Volume 1. Topography of a Phantom City* and *Shanghai Old Town, Volume 2. The Walled City* (unknown location: Suzhou Creek Press, 2018).

28. Davis, *Planet of Slums*, pp. 121–50. Quotation from Geddes in Lewis Mumford, *The City in History: Its Origins, Its Transformation, and Its Prospects* (New York: Harcourt Brace and World, 1961), p. 433.

29. Berner, "Learning from Informal Markets"; James Holston, *Insurgent Citizenship: Disjunctions of Modernity and Democracy in Modern Brazil* (Princeton, NJ: Princeton University Press, 2007); Janice E. Perlman, *Favela: Four Decades of Living on the Edge in Rio de Janeiro* (New York: Oxford University Press, 2009); Fischer, *A Poverty of Rights*, pp. 213–318; Okwui Enweazor et al., eds., *Under Siege: Four African Cities, Freetown, Johannesburg, Kinshasa, Lagos* (Ostfildern-Ruit: Hatje Cantz, 2002); J. Abiodun, "Urban Growth and Problems in Metropolitan Lagos," *Urban Studies*, 11 (1974), 341–47; Margaret Peil,

"African Squatter Settlements: A Comparative Study," *Urban Studies* 13 (1976): 155–76; Olusegun Ade Olayemi, "Sub-standard Housing and Slum Clearance in Developing Countries: A Case Study of Nigeria," *Habitat International* 4 (1979): 345–54; Andrew Hake, *African Metropolis: Nairobi's Self-Help City* (New York: St. Martin's Press, 1977); Katherine Boo, *Behind the Beautiful Forevers: Life, Death, and Hope in a Mumbai Undercity* (New York: Random House, 2012); Bhan, *In the Public's Interest.*

30. Davis, *Planet of Slums*, pp. 20–49, esp. p. 33; Aurora Almendral, "In Slum at Epicenter of Duterte's Drug Crackdown, Fear and Love Coexist," *New York Times*, April 2, 2020, at www .nytimes.com/2020/04/02/world/asia/philippines-manila-duterte-market-three.html (accessed August 10, 2021).

31. Quotation from Davis, *Planet of Slums*, p. 93.

32. Davis, *Planet of Slums*, pp. 121–50.

33. Berner, "Learning from Informal Markets"; George Vernez, "Pirate Settlements: Housing Construction by Incremental Development and Low-Income Housing Policies," RAND Paper (Washington, D.C.: Rand Corporation, 1973); Davis, *Planet of Slums*, pp. 37–42.

34. Kwak, *A World of Homeowners*, pp. 207–32.

35. Bhan, *In the Public's Interest*, pp. 218–20; Juliana Bosslet, "The Making of Imperial Peripheries: The *musseques* in Late-Colonial Luanda," *Global Urban History* blog, October 30, 2017, at https://globalurban history.com/2017/10/31/the-making-of-imperial-peripheries-the-musseques-in-late-colonial-luanda/ (accessed August 10, 2021).

36. Quotation from Holston, *Insurgent Citizenship*, p. 21. Fischer, *Poverty of Rights*, pp. 219–52; Bhan, *In the Public's Interest*, pp. 1–43, 146–87; Arne Tostensten, Inge Tvedten, and Mariken Vaa, eds., *Associational Life in African Cities: Popular Responses to the Urban Crisis* (Uppsala: Nordiska Afrikainstitutet, 2001).

37. Bhan, *In the Public's Interest*, pp. 44–94.

38. Gautam Bhan, "'This Is No Longer the City I Once Knew': Evictions, the Urban Poor and the Right to the City in Millennial Delhi," *Environment and Urbanization* 21 (2009): 127–42.

39. Bhan, *In the Public's Interest*; Bhan, "'This Is No Longer the City I Once Knew.'"

40. Delhi Planning Department (DPD), *Economic Survey of Delhi 2018–19* (New Delhi: DPD, 2020), pp. 238–67, quotations from p. 244.

23 GREATEST ACCELERATIONS III: PLEASURE PALACES AND SWEATSHOPS

1. Mark Tungate, *Adland: A Global History of Advertising* (London: Kogan Page, 2007). Advertising history quote from New York at https://dashtwo.com/blog/the-history-of-billboards/ (accessed August 12, 2021). Stuart Ewen and Elizabeth Ewen, *Channels of Desire: Mass Images and the Shaping of American Consciousness* (New York: McGraw-Hill, 1982); Frank Rowsome and Carl Rose, *The Verse by the Side of the Road: The Story of the Burma-Shave Signs and Jingles* (Brattleboro, VT: Stephen Greene Press, 1965).

2. Tungate, *Adland.*

3. Johnny Ryan, *A History of the Internet and the Digital Future* (London: Reaktion Books, 2010); Alec MacGillis, *Fulfillment: Winning and Losing in One-Click America* (New York: Farrar, Straus and Giroux, 2021).

4. For example, see the website for Delhi's outdoor advertising firm MediaAnt at www.themediaant.com /outdoor?location=Delhi NCR (accessed August 12, 2021).

5. Vicki Howard, *From Main Street to Mall: The Rise and Fall of the American Department Store* (Philadelphia, PA: University of Pennsylvania Press, 2015); also see Pamela Klaffke, *Spree: A Cultural History of Shopping* (Vancouver: Arsenal Pulp Press, 2003). Thus far, speaking of the power of the internet, Wikipedia has outpaced scholarly work on the global spread of malls. For a long list of the largest malls in the world, complete with pictures, see "Shopping Mall" at https://en.wikipedia.org/wiki/Shopping_mall (accessed August 12, 2021).

6. Paul Stoller, *Money Has No Smell: The Africanization of New York City* (Chicago, IL: University of Chicago Press, 2002). For a fantastic visual tour of small shop fronts in New York City, see James T. Murray and

Karla L. Murray, *Store Front: The Disappearing Face of New York* (Berkeley, CA: Gingko Press, 2008) and James T. Murray and Karla L. Murray, *Store Front II* (Berkeley, CA: Gingko Press, 2015).

7. Ryan, *A History of the Internet*, pp. 120–37.

8. Rosemary H. Sweet, *Cities and the Grand Tour: The British in Italy, c. 1690–1820* (Cambridge: Cambridge University Press, 2012).

9. Figures from Will Steffen, Wendy Broadgate, Lisa Deutsch, Owen Gaffney, and Cornelia Ludwig, "The Trajectory of the Anthropocene: The Great Acceleration," *The Anthropocene Review* 2 (2015): 81–98; Jean-Christophe Lefevre, *Histoire de l'hôtelerie: Une approche économique* (Paris: Publibook, 2011), pp. 263–362; A. K. Sandoval-Strausz, *Hotel: An American History* (New Haven, CT: Yale University Press, 2007), pp. 75–13; Annabel Jane Wharton, *Building the Cold War: Hilton International Hotels and Modern Architecture* (Chicago, IL: University of Chicago Press, 2001); Mark Salter *Politics at the Airport* (Minneapolis, MN: University of Minnesota Press, 2008); Nigel Halpern and Anne Graham, *Airport Marketing* (New York: Routledge, 2013); Norman J. Ashford, Saleh Mumayiz, and Paul H. Wright, *Airport Engineering: Planning, Design, and Development of 21st Century Airports*, 4th ed. (Hoboken, NJ: John Wiley & Sons, 2011).

10. Aaron Shkuda, *The Lofts of Soho: Gentrification, Art, and Industry in New York, 1950–1980* (Chicago, IL: University of Chicago Press, 2016); Peter Moskowitz, *How to Kill a City: Gentrification, Inequality, and the Fight for the Neighborhood* (New York: Nation Books, 2018), pp. 31–44.

11. George Ritzer, *The McDonaldization of Society* (Thousand Oaks, CA: Sage, 2013 [1983]); Reinhold Wagenleitner, *Coca-Colonization and the Cold War* (Chapel Hill, NC: University of North Carolina Press, 1994); Steven Flusty, *De-Coca-Colonization* (New York: Routledge, 2004); Marc Pendergrast, *Uncommon Grounds: The History of Coffee and How It Transformed Our World* (New York: Basic Books, 2010).

12. Paul Hopper, *Understanding Cultural Globalization* (Cambridge: Polity Press, 2007).

13. Richard Kieckhefer, *Theology in Stone: Church Architecture from Byzantium to Berkeley* (New York: Oxford University Press, 2004). Anne C. Lovel and and Otis B. Wheeler, *From Meetinghouse to Megachurch: A Material and Cultural History* (Columbia, MO: University of Missouri Press: 2003); Charles S. Prebish and Martin Baumann, eds., *Westward Dharma: Buddhism beyond Asia* (Berkeley, CA: University of California Press, 2002); Christopher John Fuller, *The Camphor Flame: Popular Hinduism and Society in India* (Princeton, NJ: Princeton University Press, 2004); Robert R. Bianchi, *Guests of God: Pilgrimage and Politics in Islamic World* (Oxford: Oxford University Press, 2004).

14. United Nations (UN) Development Programme, *Human Development Report 2019: Beyond Income, Beyond Averages, Beyond Today: Inequalities in Human Development in the 21st Century* (New York: UN Development Programme); Jürgen Kocka, *Capitalism: A Short History*, trans. Jeremiah Riemer (Princeton, NJ: Princeton University Press, 2016), pp. 124–44; Saskia Sassen, *The Global City: New York, London, Tokyo* (Princeton, NJ: Princeton University Press, 2002).

15. Rachel Heiman, Carly Freeman, and Mark Liechty, *The Global Middle Classes: Theorizing through Ethnography* (Santa Fe, NM: School for Advanced Research Press, 2012); A. Ricardo López and Barbara Weinstein, eds., *The Making of the Middle Class: Toward a Transnational History* (Durham, NC: Duke University Press, 2012); Gabriel Winant, *The Next Shift: The Fall of Industry and the Rise of Health Care in Rust Belt America* (Cambridge, MA: Harvard University Press: 2021).

16. Rachel Heiman, Carly Freeman, and Mark Liechty, "Introduction," in *The Global Middle Classes: Theorizing through Ethnography*, ed. Rachel Heiman, Carly Freeman, and Mark Liechty (Santa Fe, NM: School for Advanced Research Press, 2012), pp. 3–30.

17. Heiman, Freeman, and Liechty, "Introduction"; Toby Lincoln, *An Urban History of China* (Cambridge: Cambridge University Press, 2021), pp. 223–53.

18. López and Weinstein, *The Making of the Middle Class*.

19. Margaret O'Mara, *The Code: Silicon Valley and the Remaking of America* (New York: Penguin, 2019); William R. Kerr and Frederic Robert-Nicoud, "Tech Clusters," *Journal of Economic Perspectives* 34 (2020): 50–76. A convenient list of tech centers worldwide can be found at "Technology Centers," https://en.wikipedia.org/wiki/List_of_technology_centers (accessed August 12, 2021).

20. Joshua B. Freeman, *Behemoth: A History of the Factory and the Making of the Modern World* (New York: Norton, 2018), pp. 270–313; Lincoln, *An Urban History of China*, pp. 223–53; Jieheerah Yun, *Globalizing Seoul: The City's Cultural and Urban Change*, (London: Routledge, 2017).

21. Freeman, *Behemoth*, pp. 270–313.

22. Thomas Farole and Gokhan Akinci, eds., *Special Economic Zones: Progress, Emerging Challenges, and Future Directions* (Washington, D.C.: World Bank, 2011); Marion Werner, *Global Displacements: The Making of Uneven Development in the Caribbean* (Hoboken, NJ: Wiley-Blackwell, 2015).

23. Laura Hapke, *Sweatshop: The History of an American Idea* (New Brunswick, NJ: Rutgers University Press, 2004); Andrew Ross, ed., *No Sweat: Fashion, Free Trade and the Rights of Garment Workers* (London: Verso, 1997); Christie Watkins, *Child Labor and Sweatshops* (New York: Greenhaven, 2010); Benjamin Powell, *Out of Poverty: Sweatshops in the Global Economy* (Cambridge: Cambridge University Press, 2014); Freeman, *Behemoth*, pp. 270–313.

24. Ross, *No Sweat*; Watkins, *Child Labor and Sweatshops*.

25. Kalima Rose, *Where Women Are Leaders: The SEWA Movement in India* (London: Zed Books, 1992); Ananya Roy, *City Requiem, Calcutta: Gender and the Politics of Poverty* (Minneapolis: University of Minnesota Press, 2003); Martha Chen and Françoise Carré, eds., with Women in Informal Employment Globalizing and Organizing (WIEGO), *The Informal Economy Revisited: Examining the Past, Envisioning the Future* (Abingdon: Routledge, 2020); WIEGO, "Informal Economy," at www.wiego.org/informal-economy (accessed August 12, 2021); Self-Employed Workers Association Delhi (SEWA Delhi), "Informal Economy," at http://sewadelhi.org/abo ut-us/informal-economy/ (accessed August 12, 2021); United Nations Human Settlements Programme (UN HABITAT), *The Challenge of Slums: Global Report on Human Settlements, 2003* (London: UN HABITAT, 2006), pp. 34–61, 96–103; Mike Davis, *Planet of Slums* (New York: Verso, 2006), pp. 151–98.

26. International Labor Office, *Care Work and Care Jobs: For the Future of Decent Work* (Geneva: International Labor Office, 2019); Chen and Carré, eds., *The Informal Economy Revisited*; Watkins, *Child Labor and Sweatshops*; Davis, *Planet of Slums*, pp. 159–63.

27. Chen and Carré, eds., *The Informal Economy Revisited*; Domestic work drivers garners laundry work; SEWA Delhi, "Domestic Workers," at http://sewadelhi.org/advocacy-campaigns/domestic-workers/ (accessed August 12, 2021).

28. Chen and Carré, eds., *The Informal Economy Revisited*; SEWA Delhi, "Street Vendors," at http://sew adelhi.org/advocacy-campaigns/street-vendors/ (accessed August 12, 2021).

29. Chen and Carré, eds., *The Informal Economy Revisited*. Informal enterprise commerce crafts bootstraps microlending SEWA Delhi, "Community Microfinance," at http://sewadelhi.org/programs/com munity-microfinance/ (accessed August 12, 2021).

30. Chen and Carré, eds., *The Informal Economy Revisited*; SEWA Delhi, http://sewadelhi.org/advocacy-campaigns/construction-workers/ (accessed August 12, 2021).

31. For the early history of French consultation on subway systems, see Andra Chastain, "Vehicle of Progress: The Santiago Metro, Technopolitics, and State Formation in Chile, 1965–1989" (Ph.D. Thesis, Yale University, 2018).

32. M. Khosa, "Routes, Ranks and Rebels: Feuding in the Taxi Revolution," *Journal of Southern African Studies* 18 (1991): 232–51; Karabo Keepile, "My City, My World Cup: Taxi Drivers," *Mail and Guardian*, June 11, 2010, at https://mg.co.za/article/2010-06-11-my-city-world-cup-taxi-drivers/ (accessed August 12, 2021); Daniel E. Agbiboa, *Transport, Transgression and Politics in African Cities: The Rhythm of Chaos* (London: Routledge, 2020).

33. Quotation from Ed Sobey, *A Field Guide to Automotive Technology* (Chicago, IL: Chicago Review Press, 2009), p. 172; James Francis Warren, *Rickshaw Coolie: A People's History of Singapore, 1880–1940* (Singapore: National University of Singapore Press, 2003); Fung Chi Ming, *Reluctant Heroes: Rickshaw Pullers in Hong Kong and Canton, 1874–1954* (Hong Kong: Hong Kong University Press, 2005).

34. Subir Bandyopadhyay, *Calcutta Cycle-Rickshaw Pullers: A Sociological Study* (Delhi: Minerva Associates Publications, 1990); Luis David Berrones-Sanz, "The Working Conditions of Motorcycle Taxi Drivers in Tláhuac, Mexico City," *Journal of Transport & Health* 8 (2012): 73–80.

35. Yamuna River Project, "Mapping Delhi's Landfills," at https://yamunariverproject.wp.tulane.edu/2016/11/28/mapping-delhi-landfills/ (accessed August 13, 2021).

36. Chen and Carré, eds., *The Informal Economy Revisited;* Ellen Gunsilius, Bharati Chaturvedi, and Anne Scheinberg, "The Economics of the Informal Sector in Solid Waste Management," at www.wiego.org/publications/economics-informal-sector-solid-waste-management (accessed August 12, 2021); WIEGO, "Waste Pickers," at https://www.wiego.org/informal-economy/occupational-groups/waste-pickers (accessed August 12, 2021).

37. Chen and Carré, eds., *The Informal Economy Revisited;* Gunsilius et al., "The Economics of the Informal Sector"; Amita Bhaduri, "Down in the Dumps: The Tale of Delhi's Waste Pickers," *The Wire,* April 17, 2018, at https://thewire.in/health/down-in-the-dumps-the-tale-of-delhis-waste-pickers (accessed August 12, 2021); Shivani Singh, "Metro Matters: How Waste-Pickers Are Delhi's Greatest Warriors against Trash Mountains," *Hindustani Times,* March 12, 2018, at www.hindustantimes.com/delhi-news/how-ragpickers-are-delhi-s-greatest-warriors-against-mountains-of-waste/story-oDiaQhIV3xLrdVfDAwsYNL.html (accessed August 12, 2021).

24 GREAT ACCELERATIONS IV: MAXIMAL HYDROCARBON, MAXIMAL WASTE

1. Emily Elhacham, Liad Ben-Uri, Jonathan Grozovski, Yinon M. Bar-On, and Ron Milo, "Global Human Mass Exceeds All Living Biomass," *Nature* 588 (2020): 442–45.

2. Hannah Ritchie and Max Roser, "Land Use," Our World in Data, at https://ourworldindata.org/land-use (accessed August 16, 2021).

3. Hannah Ritchie and Max Roser, "Forests and Deforestation," Our World in Data, at https://ourworldindata.org/forests (accessed August 16, 2021). Quotations from Michael Williams, *Deforesting the Earth: From Prehistory to Global Crisis, An Abridgment* (Chicago, IL: University of Chicago Press, 2006), pp. 395–96.

4. Kees Klein Goldewijk, Arthur Beusen, Gerard van Drecht, and Martine de Vos, "The HYDE 3.1 Spatially Explicit Database of Human-Induced Global Land-Use Change over the Past 12,000 Years," *Global Ecology and Biogeography* 20 (2011): 73–86; UN Food and Agriculture Organization (FAO), data tabulated by the World Bank, "Agricultural Machinery, Tractors," at https://data.worldbank.org/indicator/AG.AGR.TRAC.NO (accessed August 16, 2021); Kees Klein Goldewijk, Arthur Beusen, and Peter Janssen, "Long-Term Dynamic Modeling of Global Population and Built-Up Area in a Spatially Explicit Way: HYDE 3 .1," *The Holocene* 20 (2010): 565–573; Will Steffen, Wendy Broadgate, Lisa Deutsch, Owen Gaffney, and Cornelia Ludwig, "The Trajectory of the Anthropocene: The Great Acceleration," *The Anthropocene Review* 2 (2015): 81–98.

5. Ritchie and Roser, "Land Use." Also see Shlomo Angel, Jason Parent, Daniel L. Civco, and Alejandro M. Blei, *The Persistent Decline in Urban Densities: Global and Historical Evidence of Sprawl* (Cambridge, MA: Lincoln Institute of Land Policy Press, 2009); Shlomo Angel et al., *Atlas of Urban Expansion, Volume 1. Areas and Densities* (New York: NYU Urban Expansion Program at New York University, UN-Habitat, and the Lincoln Institute of Land Policy, 2016); and urban coverage and density figures maps and data at the National Aeronautic and Space Administration (NASA), "Global Rural–Urban Mapping Project (GRUMP)," at https://sedac.ciesin.columbia.edu/data/collection/grump-v1/ (accessed August 16, 2021).

6. Figures from Central Intelligence Agency (CIA), *World Factbook,* at www.cia.gov/the-world-factbook/countries/world/ (accessed August 19, 2021) under the headings "Energy," Transportation," and "Communications." Some of these tables have been republished and supplemented in more user-friendly form in various Wikipedia articles such as https://en.wikipedia.org/wiki/List_of_countries_by_road_network_size (accessed August 16, 2021), https://en.wikipedia.org/wiki/List_of_countries_by_rail_transport_network_size (accessed August 16, 2021), and https://en.wikipedia.org/wiki/List_of_international_airports_by_country (accessed August 19, 2021). On electric grid size see Modern Power Systems, "The Key to Transmission: Worldwide Trends," Modern Power Systems, at www.growthmarkets-power.com/features/featurethe-key-to-transmission-worldwide-trends-4622437/

(accessed August 16, 2021). On satellites, see Union of Concerned Scientists (UCS), "UCS Satellite Database," at www.ucsusa.org/resources/satellite-database (accessed August 16, 2021). For striking visualizations of this global infrastructure and its inequalities see the maps at https://globaia.org (accessed August 16, 2021).

7. Statistics from the US Geological Survey, cited in "A History of Concrete," by the trade organization The Concrete Protector. See https://theconcreteprotector.com/history-of-concrete/ (accessed August 16, 2021). Eisenhower quotation from Matthieu Auzanneau, *Oil, Power, and War: A Dark History*, trans. John F. Reynolds (White River Junction, VT: Chelsea Green, 2018), p. 305.

8. Steve Mohr, Damien Giurco, Mohan Yellishetty, James Ward, and Gavin Mudd, "Projection of Iron Ore Production," *Natural Resources Research* 24 (2014): 317–27; C. Reichl and M. Schatz, *World Mining Data 2020* (Vienna: International Committee for the World Mining Congresses and Austrian Federal Ministry of Agriculture, Regions, and Tourism, 2020), pp. 4–5. Also statistics from Mining Technology, at www.mining-technology.com/features/featurethe-worlds-11-biggest-iron-ore-mines-4180663/ and www.mining-technology.com/features/featureferro-giants-the-worlds-biggest-iron-ore-producers-4280601, and World Nuclear.org, at www.world-nuclear.org/information-library/nuclear-fuel-cycle/mining-of-uranium/uranium-mining-overview.aspx (all accessed August 16, 2021).

9. "Global Coal Power," Carbon Brief, at www.carbonbrief.org/mapped-worlds-coal-power-plants (accessed August 16, 2021).

10. Carola Hein, "Oil Spaces: The Global Petroleumscape in the Rotterdam/The Hague Area," *Journal of Urban History* 44 (2018): 887–929; Carola Hein and Mohamad Sedighi, "Iran's Global Petroleumscape: The Role of Oil in Shaping Khuzestan and Tehran," *Architectural Theory Review* 21 (2016): 349–74; Neeraj Bhatia and Maria Casper, eds., *The Petropolis of Tomorrow* (Houston, TX: Actar, 2013).

11. Daniel Yergin, *The Prize: The Epic Quest for Oil, Money, and Power* (New York: Free Press, 1991), pp. 263–87; Auzanneau, *Oil, Power, and War*, pp. 175–91.

12. Craig Unger, *House of Bush, House of Saud: The Secret Relationship between the World's Two Most Powerful Dynasties* (New York: Scribner, 2004), Chapters 2 and 3.

13. On the early work of the bin Ladens for the Saudi dynasty, see Unger, *House of Bush, House of Saud*, Chapter 2; and Abdulaziz Al Shahib and Sam Ridgeway, "Oil + Architecture," *Fabrications* 20 (2019): 131–53. For recent memoirs about life in Dhahran, see Ayesha Malik, *Aramco above the Oil Fields* (Durham, NC: Daylight, 2020); and Keija Parsinnen "The US–Saudi Story, through the Eyes of an Aramco 'Brat,'" *New York Review of Books*, January 31, 2020, at www.nybooks.com/daily/2020/01/31/the-us-saudi-story-through-the-eyes-of-an-aramco-brat/ (accessed August 16, 2021).

14. Yergin, *The Prize*, pp. 372–500; Auzanneau, *Oil, Power, and War*, pp. 175–251; Hou Li, *Building for Oil: Daqing and the Formation of the Chinese Socialist State* (Cambridge, MA: Harvard University Asia Center, 2018).

15. Hein, "Oil Spaces." A magnificent interactive map of the growth of Rotterdam's oil facilities can be found in Carola Hein, "Analyzing the Palimpsestic Petroleumscape of Rotterdam," Global Urban History blog, September 28, 2016, at https://globalurbanhistory.com/2016/09/28/analyzing-the-palimpsestic-petroleumscape-of-rotterdam/ (accessed August 16, 2021). See also United States Bureau of Transportation Statistics (BTS), "World Motor Vehicle Production, Selected Countries," at www.bts.gov/content/world-motor-vehicle-production-selected-countries (accessed August 16, 2021); Simon Pirani, *Burning Up: A Global History of Fossil Fuel Consumption* (London: Pluto, 2018), pp. 79–92; Susan Freinkel, *Plastic: A Toxic Love Story* (New York: Henry Holt, 2011); and Science History Institute, at www.sciencehistory.org/the-history-and-future-of-plastics (accessed August 16, 2021).

16. Yergin, *The Prize*, pp. 615–96; Auzanneau, *Oil, Power, and War*, pp. 319–76; Pirani, *Burning Up*, pp. 93–106; BTS, "World Motor Vehicle Production."

17. Yergin, *The Prize*, pp. 697–749; Auzanneau, *Oil, Power, and War*, pp. 389–411; Pirani, *Burning Up*, pp. 122–37.

18. Auzanneau, *Oil, Power, and War*, pp. 412–28; Pirani, *Burning Up*, pp. 138–52.

19. Auzanneau, *Oil, Power, and War*, pp. 412–44.
20. Auzanneau, *Oil, Power, and War*, pp. 467–95; Ahmed Rashid, *Taliban: Militant Islam, Oil, and Fundamentalism in Central Asia* (New Haven, CT: Yale University Press, 2000); Lawrence Wright, *The Looming Tower: Al-Qaeda and the Road to 9/11* (New York: Vintage, 2006).
21. Auzanneau, *Oil, Power, and War*, pp. 480–552.
22. Auzanneau, *Oil, Power, and War*, pp. 516–52; Pirani, *Burning Up*, pp. 153–72.
23. Statista.com, "Global Gas and Oil Rig Numbers by Region," at www.statista.com/statistics/326727/global-gas-and-oil-rig-numbers-by-region/ (accessed August 16, 2021); United States Energy Information Administration (EIA), "Hydraulically Fractured Horizontal Wells Account for Most New Oil and Natural Gas Wells," at www.eia.gov/todayinenergy/detail.php?id=34732 (accessed August 16, 2021). For a closely researched fictionalized account of the ebb and flow of the built environment of the Bakken oilfield, see John Sayles, *Yellow Earth* (Boston, MA: Haymarket Press, 2020). Figures from *Oil and Gas Journal* from https://en.wikipedia.org/wiki/List_of_oil_refineries (accessed August 16, 2021). Information on tankers from Jean-Paul Rodrigue, *The Geography of Transport Systems* (New York: Routledge, 2020), available at https://transportgeography.org/contents/applications/petroleum-transportation-resource/ (accessed August 16, 2021).
24. Auzanneau, *Oil, Power, and War*, p. 557; BTS, "World Motor Vehicle Production"; Statista.com, "Global Plastic Production," at www.statista.com/statistics/282732/global-production-of-plastics-since-1950/ (accessed August 16, 2021).
25. Jillian Ambrose, "Oil Prices Slump as Market Faces Lowest Demand in 25 years," *The Guardian*, April 15, 2020 at www.theguardian.com/business/2020/apr/15/oil-prices-slump-as-market-faces-lowest-demand-in-25-years-covid-19 (accessed August 16, 2021).
26. Maninder Dabas, "By 2020, Ghazipur Garbage Mountain in Delhi Will Be Taller Than the Taj Mahal and It's Not a Good Thing," *India Times*, June 5, 2019, at www.indiatimes.com/news/india/by-2020-ghazipur-garbage-mountain-in-delhi-will-be-taller-than-the-taj-mahal-and-it-s-not-a-good-thing-368604.html (accessed August 16, 2021); Assa Doron and Robin Jeffrey, *Waste of a Nation: Garbage and Growth in India* (Cambridge, MA: Harvard University Press, 2018).
27. Françoise Jarrige and Thomas Le Roux, *The Contamination of the Earth: A History of Pollutions in the Industrial Age*, trans. Janice Egan and Michael Egan (Cambridge, MA: MIT Press, 2020), pp. 406–16.
28. Elizabeth Royte, *Garbage Land* (New York: Little Brown, 2005); World Health Organization, "Household Air Pollution and Health," at www.who.int/news-room/fact-sheets/detail/household-air-pollution-and-health (accessed August 16, 2021).
29. Mukhesh Sharma and Onkar Dikshit, *Comprehensive Study on Air Pollution and Greenhouse Gases in Delhi: Final Report, Air Pollution Component* (Kanpur: Kanpur Institute of Technology, 2016), pp. i–xx; UN FAO, "Wood Energy," at www.fao.org/forestry/energy/en/ (accessed August 16, 2021).
30. Jarrige and Le Roux, *The Contamination of the Earth*, pp. 231–405.
31. Lorraine Boissoneault, "The Cuyahoga River Caught Fire at Least a Dozen Times but No One Cared until 1969," *Smithsonian Magazine*, June 19, 2019, at www.smithsonianmag.com/history/cuyahoga-river-caught-fire-least-dozen-times-no-one-cared-until-1969-180972444/ (accessed August 16, 2021). For a useful map of the world's dead zones, see Robert Simon and Jesse Allen's map from the NASA Earth Observatory, at https://commons.wikimedia.org/wiki/File:Aquatic_Dead_Zones.jpg (accessed August 16, 2021).
32. Jarrige and Le Roux, *The Contamination of the Earth*, pp. 231–59.
33. Johan Bentinck and Shilpa Chikara, "Illegal Factories in Delhi: The Controversy, the Causes, and the Expected Future," Working Paper presented at the International Workshop on "Coping with Informality and Illegality in Human Settlements in Developing Cities," May 23–26, 2001, at www.ucl.ac.uk/dpu-projects/drivers_urb_change/urb_economy/pdf_infor_econo/ESFN_AERUS_Bentinck_Illegal factor.pdf (accessed August 17, 2021). On the Chhat Puja incident, see "Delhi Pollution: Devotees Stand Knee-Deep in Toxic Foam in Yamuna for Chhath Puja," *Economic Times*, November 4, 2019, at https://economictimes.indiatimes.com/news/politics-and-nation/delhi-pollution-devotees-stand-knee-deep-in-toxic-foam-in-yamuna-for-chhath-puja/toxic-yamuna-water/slideshow/71888429.cms (accessed August 17, 2021).

NOTES TO PAGES 640–48

34. For excellent photographs and descriptions of e-waste sites, see Valentino Bellini, Giorgio Grizzioti, and Gianluca Gianelli, "The Bit Rot Project: The Wired World of E-Waste," at www.bitrotproject.com (accessed August 17, 2021); and Adam Minter, "The Burning Truth behind an E-Waste Dump in Africa," *Smithsonian Magazine*, January 26, 2016, www.smithsonianmag.com/science-nature/burning-truth-behind-e-waste-dump-africa-180957597/ (accessed August 17, 2021). Also Adam Minter, *Junkyard Planet: Travels in the Billion Dollar Trash Trade* (New York: Bloomsbury, 2013).

35. Caleb Finch, *The Role of Global Air Pollution in Aging and Disease: Reading Smoke Signals* (Amsterdam: Elsevier, 2018). For a devastating multimedia report on the effects of air pollution on children in Delhi, see Jin Wu et al., "Who Gets to Breathe Clean Air in New Delhi?," *New York Times*, December 12, 2020, at www.nytimes.com/interactive/2020/12/17/world/asia/india-pollution-inequality.html?utm_source=pocket-newtab (accessed August 17, 2021).

36. Antonia Juhasz, *Black Tide: The Devastating Impact of the Gulf Oil Spill* (Hoboken, NJ: John Wiley, 2011); Benjamin Storrow, "Methane Leaks Erase Some of the Climate Benefits of Natural Gas," *Scientific American*, May 5, 2020, at www.scientificamerican.com/article/methane-leaks-erase-some-of-the-climate-benefits-of-natural-gas/ (accessed August 17, 2021).

37. Freinkel, *Plastic*, pp. 115–38; Charles G. Moore and Cassandra Phillips, *Plastic Ocean* (New York: Penguin, 2011).

38. John L. Brooke, *Climate Change and the Course of Global History: A Rough Journey* (Cambridge: Cambridge University Press, 2014), pp. 543–58; US Environmental Protection Agency (EPA) "Global Greenhouse Emissions Data," at www.epa.gov/ghgemissions/global-greenhouse-gas-emissions-data (accessed August 17, 2021); Center for Climate and Energy Solutions, "International Emissions," at www.c2es.org/content/international-emissions/ (accessed August 17, 2021); Union of Concerned Scientists, "The Planet's Temperature is Rising," at www.ucsusa.org/resources/planets-temperature-rising (accessed August 17, 2021).

39. Julia Adeney Thomas, Mark Williams, and Jan Zalasiewicz, *The Anthropocene: A Multidisciplinary Approach* (Cambridge, UK: Polity Press, 2020), pp. 52–67.

25 2020 HINDSIGHT . . . AND FORESIGHT?

1. Jeffrey Gettleman, Karan Deep Singh, and Hari Kumar, "Thousands Block Roads to India's Capital in a Protest of Farm Policies," *New York Times*, November 30, 2020, at https://nyti.ms/3lmvApi;Vijay (accessed August 30, 2021); Veena Dubal and Navyug Gill, "'Long Live Farmer–Laborer Unity!' Contextualizing the Massive Resistance Going On in India," Law and Political Economy Project, December 28, 2020, at https://lpeproject.org/blog/long-live-farmer-laborer-unity-contextualizing-the-massive-resistance-going-on-in-india/ (accessed August 30, 2021); "The Farmers' Revolt in India," *Tricontinental* 41 (June 14, 2021), at https://thetricontinental.org/dossier-41-india-agriculture/ (accessed September 1, 2021).

2. Tianhao Le et al., "Unexpected Air Pollution with Marked Emission Reductions during the COVID-19 Outbreak in China," *Science* 369 (August 7, 2020): 702–6; Jillian Ambrose, "Oil Prices Dip Below Zero as Producers Forced to Pay to Dispose of Excess," *Guardian*, April 20, 2020, at www.theguardian.com/world/2020/apr/20/oil-prices-sink-to-20-year-low-as-un-sounds-alarm-on-to-covid-19-relief-fund (accessed August 30, 2021).

3. Daniel Hoornweg and Kevin Pope, "Population Predictions for the World's Largest Cities in the 21st Century," *Environment and Urbanization* 29 (2017): 195–216.

4. International Trade Union Confederation, "Climate Frontlines Briefing – No Jobs on a Dead Planet," March 2015 at https://www.ituc-csi.org/ituc-frontlines-briefing-climate (accessed November 10, 2021); United Nations Framework Convention of Climate Change "Paris Agreement," p. 2. At https://unfccc.int/process-and-meetings/the-paris-agreement/the-paris-agreement (accessed November 10, 2021). For a useful set of materials on the concept of Just Transition see Climate Justice Alliance, "Just Transition" at https://climatejusticealliance.org/just-transition/ (accessed November 10, 2021).

5. See, for example, James Cheberti and Oliver Uberti, *Atlas of the Invisible: Maps and Graphics That Will Change the Way You See the World* (London: Penguin, 2021); the maps and graphics available on the Globaïa website at https://globaia.org/ (accessed September 6, 2021); and EOC Geoservices's "The Global Urban Footprint," at https://geoservice.dlr.de/web/maps/eoc:gu f:3857 (accessed September 6, 2021).

6. UNESCO, *Reading the Past, Writing the Future: Fifty Years of Promoting Literacy* (Paris: UNESCO, 2017), pp. 19–36.

7. On universities: www.statista.com/statistics/918403/number-of-universities-worldwide-by-country/ (accessed August 30, 2021). On museums: https://en.unesco.org/themes/museums (accessed August 30, 2021). On hospitals: http://hospitals.webometrics.info and www.statista.com/statistics/ 1107086/total-hospital-number-select-countries-worldwide/ (both accessed August 30, 2021). On research parks: Michael I. Luger, and Harvey A. Goldstein, *Technology in the Garden: Research Parks and Regional Economic Development*(Chapel Hill, NC: University of North Carolina Press, 1991); Rachelle L. Levitt, ed., *Research Parks and Other Ventures: The University/Real Estate Connection* (Washington, D.C.: Urban Land Institute, 1987); and "List of Research Parks," at https://en .wikipedia.org/wiki/List_of_research_parks (accessed August 30, 2021).

8. George Lipsitz, *Dangerous Crossroads: Popular Music, Postmodernism and the Poetics of Place* (London: Verso, 1994); Tricia Rose, *Black Noise: Rap Music and Contemporary Culture in the United States* (Middletown, CT: Wesleyan University Press, 1994); Robin Kelley, *Race Rebels: Culture, Politics, and the Black Working Class* (New York: Free Press, 1994).

9. Quotation from Ramachandra Guha, *Environmentalism: A Global History* (New York: Longman, 2000), p. 20.

10. Robert Fishman, *Urban Utopias in the Twentieth Century: Ebenezer Howard, Frank Lloyd Wright, Le Corbusier* (Cambridge, MA: MIT Press, 1982); Guha, *Environmentalism*, pp. 59–68, 76–77; Lewis Mumford, "The Sky Line: Mother Jacobs's Home Remedies," *New Yorker*, December 1, 1961, pp. 144–79. Quotation from p. 178.

11. Ruth M. Alexander, "In Defense of Nature: Jane Jacobs, Rachel Carson, and Betty Friedan," *Journal of Women's History* 31 (2019): 78–101; Jane Jacobs, *The Death and Life of Great American Cities* (New York: Vintage, 1961); Christopher Klemek, *The Transatlantic Collapse of Urban Renewal: Postwar Urbanism from New York to Berlin* (Chicago, IL: University of Chicago Press, 2011); Roberta Brandes Gratz, *The Battle for Gotham: New York in the Shadow of Robert Moses and Jane Jacobs* (New York: Nation Books, 2010).

12. Betty Friedan, *The Feminine Mystique* (New York: Norton, 1963).

13. Mark Kurlansky, *1968: The Year That Rocked the World* (New York: Ballantine, 2004); David Carter, *Stonewall: The Riots That Sparked the Gay Revolution* (New York: St. Martin's Press, 2004).

14. Edouard Morena, Dunja Krause, and Dimitris Stevis, *Just Transitions: Social Justice in the Shift towards a Low-Carbon World* (London: Pluto Press, 2019); Mark Swilling and Eva Annecke, *Just Transitions: Explorations of Sustainability in an Unfair World* (Claremont: University of Cape Town Press, 2012); Paul Hawken, *Blessed Unrest: How the Largest Movement in the World Came Into Being and Why No One Saw It Coming* (New York: Penguin, 2007).

15. Bert Bollin, *A History of the Science and Politics of Climate Change* (Cambridge: Cambridge University Press, 2007); Hariett Bulkely, *Cities and Climate Change* (Abingdon: Routledge, 2013). Johan Rockström et al., "Planetary Boundaries: Exploring the Safe Operating Space for Humanity," *Ecology and Society* 14, no. 2 (2009), online at https://www.ecologyandsociety.org/vol14/iss2/ar t32/ (accessed November 10, 2021). Also see the website for the C40 Cities at www.c40.org (accessed August 30, 2021).

16. International Renewable Energy Agency (IRENA), *Renewable Capacity Statistics 2021* (Abu Dhabi: IRENA, 2021), pp. 13–27, available at www.irena.org/publications/2021/March/Renewable-Capacity-Statistics-2021 (accessed September 1, 2021).

17. Paul Hawken, ed., *Drawdown: The Most Comprehensive Plan Ever Proposed to Reverse Global Warming* (New York: Penguin, 2017), pp. 2–37. On the history of New Town planning principles that have followed from Howard's work see Rosemary Wakeman, *Practicing Utopia: An Intellectual History of the*

New Towns Movement (Chicago, IL: University of Chicago Press, 2016). Richard Sennett, *Building and Dwelling: Ethics for the City* (New York: Farrar, Straus, and Giroux, 2018).

18. Hawken, ed., *Drawdown*, pp. 2–37, 76–107; Shalonda Baker, *Revolutionary Power: An Activist's Guide to the Energy Transition* (Washington, D.C.: Island Press, 2021), pp. 89–160.

19. Hawken, ed., *Drawdown*, pp. 188–89, 196–99, 210–11.

20. Hawken, *Drawdown*, pp. 84–107; Peter Newman and Isabella Jennings, *Cities as Sustainable Ecosystems: Principles and Practices* (Washngton D.C.: Island Press, 2008); Colin McFarlane, "Repopulating Density: COVID-19 and the Politics of Urban Value," *Urban Studies* (June, 2021), at https://journals.sagepub.com /doi/full/10.1177/00420980211014810 (accessed September 1, 2021); Jacques Teller, "Urban Density and Covid-19: Towards an Adaptive Approach," *Buildings and Cities*, 2 (2021): 150–165, at http://doi.org /10.5334/bc.89 (accessed September 1, 2021); Helen V. S. Cole et al., "The COVID-19 Pandemic: Power and Privilege, Gentrification, and Urban Environmental Justice in the Global North," *Cities and Health* (July 28, 2020), at www.tandfonline.com/doi/full/10.1080/23748834.2020.1785176 (accessed September 1, 2021).

21. Hawken, ed., *Drawdown*, pp. 28–29, 38–75, 108–35, 158–71; Eric Toensmeier, *The Carbon Farming Solution: A Global Toolkit of Perennial Crops and Regenerative Agriculture Practices for Climate Change Mitigation and Food Security* (White River Junction, VT: Chelsea Green, 2016).

22. Judith Blau, *The Paris Climate Agreement: Climate Change, Solidarity, and Human Rights* (London: Palgrave Macmillan, 2017); Jordan Johnson, *From Kyoto to Paris: Global Climate Accords* (New York: Cavendish, 2018); Max Roser, "Democracy," at https://ourworldindata.org/democracy#number-of-democracies (accessed August 31, 2021); Global State of Democracy Initiative, "Global State of Democracy Indices," at www.idea.int/data-tools/tools/global-state-democracy-indices (accessed August 31, 2021).

23. Roser, "Democracy."

24. Marius Korsnes, *Wind and Solar Energy Transition in China* (Abingdon: Routledge, 2020).

25. Somini Senguta, "China, in Pointed Message to U.S., Tightens Its Climate Targets," *New York Times*, September 22, 2020; Li Xing, ed., *Mapping China's "One Belt One Road" Initiative* (London: Palgrave Macmillan, 2019); Julien Chaisse and Jędrzej Górski, eds., *The Belt and Road Initiative: Law, Economics, and Politics* (Leiden: Brill, 2018); Bruno Maçães, *Belt and Road: A Chinese World Order* (Oxford: Oxford University Press, 2018); Toby Lincoln, *An Urban History of China* (Cambridge: Cambridge University Press, 2021), pp. 223–53.

26. Maçães, *Belt and Road*; Sean Roberts, *The War on the Uyghurs: China's Internal Campaign against a Muslim Minority* (Princeton, NJ: Princeton University Press, 2020); Derek Watkins, "What China Has Been Building in the South China Sea," *New York Times*, October 27, 2015, at www.nytimes.com/interactive/ 2015/07/30/world/asia/what-china-has-been-building-in-the-south-china-sea.html?action=click&mo dule=RelatedLinks&pgtype=Article (accessed August 30, 2021); Steven Lee Myers, "Beijing Takes Its South China Seas Strategy to the Himalayas," *New York Times*, November 29, 2020, at www.nytimes.com /2020/11/27/world/asia/china-bhutan-india-border.html (accessed August 30, 2021); Jeffrey Wasserstrom, *Vigil: Hong Kong on the Brink* (New York: Columbia Global Reports, 2020); Antony Dapiran, *City on Fire: The Fight for Hong Kong* (Brunswick, Australia: Scribe, 2020).

27. Hayden Washington and John Cook, *Climate Change Denial: Heads in the Sand* (Abingdon: Routledge/ Earthscan, 2011); James Hoggan, *Climate Cover-up: The Crusade to Deny Global Warming* (Vancouver: Greystone, 2009).

28. Timothy Snyder, *The Road to Unfreedom: Russia, Europe, America* (New York: Tim Duggan, 2018); Soner Cagaptay, *The New Sultan: Erdoğan and the Crisis of Modern Turkey* (London: Tauris, 2017); Richard Lapper, *Beef, Bible, and Bullets: Brazil in the Age of Bolsonaro* (Manchester: Manchester University Press, 2021); Dexter Filkins, "Blood and Soil in India," *The New Yorker*, December 9, 2019 (online edition).

29. Lisa Friedmann, "U.S. Quits Paris Climate Agreement: Questions and Answers," *New York Times*, November 4, 2020, at www.nytimes.com/2020/11/04/climate/paris-climate-agreement-trump.html (accessed August 30, 2021).

30. The idea that the "public sphere" contains "capillaries" comes from Carolyn Hamilton and Lesley Cowling, eds., *Babel Unbound: Rage, Reason, and Rethinking Public Life* (Johannesburg: Wits University Press, 2020), p. 6.

31. Hawken, *Blessed Unrest*. The most exhaustive list of non-violent protest techniques is Gene Sharp, *The Politics of Nonviolent Action* (Boston, MA: Porter Sargent, 1973). Comparisons of the effectiveness of non-violent with violent popular action include Maria J. Stephan and Erica Chenoweth, "Why Civil Resistance Works: The Strategic Logic of Nonviolent Conflict," *International Security* 33 (2008): 7–44.

32. Martin Luther King, *Strides toward Justice: The Montgomery Story* (Boston, MA: Beacon Press, 1958), pp. 77–96.

33. Martin Luther King, "Letter from the Birmingham City Jail," in *Testament of Hope: The Essential Writings and Speeches of Martin Luther King, Jr.*, ed. James Melvin Washington (New York: Harper San Francisco, 1986), pp. 289–302.

34. Stephanie Luce, *Labor Movements: Global Perspectives* (Cambridge, MA: Polity Press, 2014); James K. McCallum, *Global Unions, Local Power: The New Spirit of Transnational Labor Organizing* (Ithaca, NY: Cornell University Press, 2013).

35. See essays in Alex Lichtenstein, ed., "AHR Reflections: 1968," *American Historical Review* 123 (2018): 706–78; Tamara Chaplin and Jadwiga E. Pieper Mooney, eds., *The Global 1960s: Convention, Contest, and Counterculture* (Abingdon: Routledge, 2018); Mark Kurlansky, *1968: The Year That Rocked the World* (New York: Ballantine, 2004); Erica Chenoweth and Maria J. Stephan, *Why Civil Resistance Works: The Strategic Logic of Nonviolent Conflict* (New York: Columbia University Press, 2011); Erica Chenoweth, *Civil Resistance: What Everyone Needs to Know* (Oxford: Oxford University Press, 2021).

36. Anna Konieczna and Rob Skinner, eds., *A Global History of Anti-Apartheid* (Cham: Palgrave Macmillan, 2019); Adam Roberts and Timothy Garton Ash, eds., *Civil Resistance and Power Politics: The Experience of Non-violent Action from Gandhi to the Present* (Oxford: Oxford University Press, 2009); Victor Sebestyn, *Revolution 1989: The Fall of the Soviet Empire* (New York: Vintage, 2009).

37. Roberts and Garton Ash, eds., *Civil Resistance*; Chenoweth and Stephan, *Why Civil Resistance Works*; L. A. Kauffmann, *How to Read a Protest* (Berkeley, CA: University of California Press, 2018); Pierre Hammel, Henri Lustiger-Thaler, and Margit Mayer, *Urban Movements in a Globalising World* (London: Routledge, 2000); Carnegie Endowment for International Peace, "Global Protest Tracker," at https://carnegieendowment.org/publications/interactive/protest-tracker (accessed September 1, 2021). To get a sense of the sheer number of protests in the twenty-first century alone and read short descriptions, see Wikipedia, "List of Protests in the 21st Century," at https://en.wikipedia.org/wiki/List_of_protests_in_the_21st_century (accessed September 1, 2021).

38. Chenoweth and Stephan, *Why Civil Resistance Works*, Chapter 1.

39. Michael Méndez, *Climate Change from the Streets: How Conflict and Collaboration Strengthen the Environmental Justice Movement* (New Haven, CT: Yale University Press, 2020); Editors of World Politics Review, "The Era of Global Protest," June 2021, at https://www.worldpoliticsreview.com/insights/29146/blm-protests-and-the-age-of-global-protest (accessed September 6, 2021).

Index

Page numbers in *italics* refer to content in figures and maps.

INDEX

Egypt (cont.)
trade routes, 112
urban planning, 382
"urban regions," 523
urban worlds, 63
Eiffel Tower (Paris), 283, 358
Eighty Years' War, 215, 272, *see also* Holland
Einsatztruppen, 463
Einstein, Albert, 415
Eisenhower, Dwight D., 619
elections, 56, 496
electric vehicles, 659, *see also* cars
electric wires, 355, *356*, 617, 621
electricity, 355, *576*, 620, 658–62
elephants, 149
elevators, 358
Elizabeth I, Queen of England, 256
Ellis Island, 393, 436, *see also* migration
Elmina Castle, 176, 187, 195
emancipation proclamation (French), 298
embassies, 527–28
emperors
Confucius on, 122
consumer culture, 229
etymology of, 68
families, 69
power, 269
propaganda, 120, 121
roads, 73
slavery, 90
texts, 121
wealth, 83
empires, *see also* imperialism
boundaries, 78
capitalism, 341
cities and, 61–63, 280, 309–14
etymology of, 68
gender roles, 69
empresses, 70
"enclosure movement," 259, 391
encomienda system, 202
encyclopedic works, 227, 235
Encyclopédie (Diderot and d'Alembert), 235
"Endless Palace" (Weiyang), 67
endogenous forces (of climate change),
137, 139
"energized crowding"
armies, 51, 76
capitalism, 85
cities, 24–25, 117
proximity power, 44
revolutions, 54

shops, 95–97
energy, *see also* coal; fossil fuels
electricity, 355, *576*, 620, 658–62
future of Earthopolis, 658–62
geo-solar, 38, 41, 139, 146
renewable, 661, 663, 664
solar, 620, *657*, 658–62, 664
urban planning, 658–59
water, 621
wind energy, 99, 621, *657*, 658, 664
Enfield, 263
Engels, Friedrich, 396–97
England, *see* Great Britain
English Channel, 356
English language, 56, 68, 104, 594
Enki (Mesopotamian god), 29–30, 40
Enlightenment, 222, 226–29, 236, 414
enlightenment (Buddhist), 136
enterprises, 258, 607
entertainment, 222, 229, 442, *see also* leisure
environmentalism
early modern, 235, 245
knowledge, 655–56
London, 235, 245
waste, 635, 637
Epic of Gilgamesh (poem), 97
epidemics, 141, 371, 536, 660, *see also*
diseases
Equiano, Olaudah, 278
Erdoğan, Recep Tayyip, 667
Eridu, 29, 40
Erie Canal, 313, 328
Erlitou, 48
Escravos, Casa da (Lisbon), 215
Eshu (Nigerian god), 136
Essen, 316, 349, 350, 409, 425
Estado da India, 178, 181, 211, 216
estates, 202
Estates General (France), 286
Estonia, 526
ethnic associations, 401, *406*, *see also*
migration
eugenics, 461, 463
eunuchs, 69
Euphrates River, 10, 29, *34*, 39, 78, 463, *see*
also Mesopotamia
Euripides (dramatist), 128
Europe, *see also specific nations*
arms races, 162–63, 424–27
cities, 164
coffee, 233
colonialism, 192–94, 334–35

INDEX

Prudhoe Bay, 630
Pruitt-Igoe (St. Louis), 486
"pseudo-democracies," 663
psychiatric patients, 462, 463
Pu Yi, 453
public health, *see also* sanitation
  austerity, 539–42
  China, 539, 545
  Cold War, 537–42
  development aid, 535–42
  India, 542
  measures, 142, 363, 399, 404
  Paris, 377
  racism, 399
  sewage, 143
  smells, 143
  vaccines, *538*
  World Bank, 540
public housing, *see* housing
public spaces
  Enlightenment, 236
  leisure, 442–45, 446
  revolutions, 301–4, *303*
  subversive ideas, 403
public transit, *356*, 492, 659, *see also*
  rickshaws
pucca houses, 574
Pudong New Area (Shanghai), 602
Puebla, 346
Pueblo builders, 23
Puerto Rico, 306, 485, 517
Pullman (IL), 409, 410
pulperías, 301, *303*
pumps, 261
Pune, 318, 504
Punic Wars, 72
Punjab region, 435, *549*
Punto Guajiro music, 444
Puritans, 225, 275
purity, ritual, 124
"Purple Forbidden City" (Beijing), 166
Putilov weapons works (St. Petersburg),
  316, 429, *430*
Putin, Vladimir, 663
putsches, 439, *see also* coups d'état
Puuc region, 41
pyramids, 41, 48, 119

Qapu Palace, al- (Isfahan), 165
Qatar, 663
Qianlong Emperor, of Qing, 168

Qing dynasty
  Beijing, 166, 226, 325, 326
  Buddhism, 223
  coal, 253
  conquest, 167, 182
  fur, 243
  merchants, 322
  segregation, 322
  taxes, 391
  weapons, 315
  Xinhai Revolution, 389, 411
Quakers, 189, 225, 275, 278
quality of living, 387–90
quarantine, 143, 393
Quebec, 189, 243, 279, 675
Quechua (Indigenous people), 301
queens, *see also specific queens*, 70
queer people, *see* gay people
Quetta, 629
quilombo, 277
Quit India Movement, 503
Quran, 131

Ra (Greek god), 47
Rabat, 383
race riots, 436
racism, *see also* segregation, racial
  barbarism, 117
  colonialism, 328
  diseases, 368, 399
  emergence of concept, 201
  gold mining camps, 393
  imperialism, 311
  Japan, 452
  lynch mobs, 395, 402
  Mexico City, 203
  migration, 394
  propaganda, 461
  revolutions, 436–37
  "science" of race, 222, 417–20
  slavery, 208
  slum vocabulary, 579
  sports, 443
  USA, 401, 402
  World War II, 461–65
radiation, 415, 526
radio, 442, 461, 588
railroads
  amount of, 617
  Canadian Pacific Railway, 352
  Chinese migrants, 393
  companies, 351–52